BAROQUE AND ROCOCO

Opposite: 'Swashbuckler' plate from Montelupo.

Overleaf: Trasparente by Narciso Tomé in Toledo Cathedral.

BAROQUE
AND
ROCOCO

SACHEVERELL SITWELL

G.P.PUTNAM'S SONS
200 MADISON AVENUE NEW YORK

TO OSBERT

in 1967 as in 1921

Contents

List of Illustrations

Forum at Jerash, Jordan (*A. F. Kersting*)
Sant' Ivo alla Sapienza, Rome (*Leonard von Matt*)
Sant' Andrea al Quirinale, Rome (*Leonard von Matt*)
Syracuse Cathedral (*A. F. Kersting*)
Pannini, *Carlos III Visiting Pope Benedict XIV in the Quirinal Coffee House*. Naples, Museo di Capodimonte (*Gabinetto Fotografico Nazionale*)
Santa Maria della Pace, Rome (*Leonard von Matt*)
Khazné Faraóun, Petra (*A. F. Kersting*)
Engraving after Hawksmoor of the great Temple at Baalbek; from Henry Maundrell, *A Journey from Aleppo to Jerusalem*, 1721. British Museum
South façade of Valencia Cathedral (*Ampliaciones y Reproducciones Mas*)
Porch of Palacio de Dos Aguas, Valencia (*Viollet*)
Two *gopurams* at Madurai (*Ian Graham*)
Ivan of Great Mosque at Isfahan (*Wim Swaan*)
Detail of mosaics in the Ommayad Mosque, Damascus (*Viollet*)
Murcia Cathedral (*ND – Viollet*)

'ALLA VENEZIANA'   78
The Venetian lagoon from San Giorgio Maggiore (*Marianne Adelmann*)
Domenico Tiepolo, *La Partenza della Gondola*. Wrightsman Collection, New York
Wall-painting of a harbour, from Stabiae (*André Held*)
Interior of *Ridotto Venier*, Venice (*Alinari*)
Palladian Bridge at Stowe (*Penelope Reed*)
Staircase ceiling of 20, Lower Dominick Street, Dublin (*Irish Georgian Society*)
G. B. Tiepolo, *The Banquet of Antony and Cleopatra*. Melbourne, National Gallery of Victoria (*Royal Academy of Arts*)

BORROMINI, GUARINI, JUVARRA, VITTONE   99
Centre of lantern above Chapel of the Holy Shroud, Turin (*Marianne Adelmann*)
Statue of San Carlo Borromeo on façade of San Carlino, Rome (*Marianne Adelmann*)
Tower of Sant' Andrea delle Fratte, Rome (*Leonard von Matt*)
Cortile of San Carlino (*Leonard von Matt*)
Interior of dome of San Carlino (*Leonard von Matt*)
Lantern of Sant' Ivo alla Sapienza, Rome (*Marianne Adelmann*)
Interior of dome of Sant' Ivo (*Leonard von Matt*)
Lantern above the Chapel of the Holy Shroud, Turin (*Marianne Adelmann*)
Interior of dome of Chapel of the Holy Shroud (*Edwin Smith*)
Detail of brickwork on Palazzo Carignano, Turin (*Marianne Adelmann*)
Elevations by Guarini of the Santuario d'Oropa, the Chapel of the Holy Shroud, Turin, and Santa Maria della Divina Providenza, Lisbon; from his *Architettura Civile*, 1737. British Museum
Santuario at Vallinotto (*Marianne Adelmann*)
Interior of dome of the Assunta, Riva (*Marianne Adelmann*)
Balcony and ceiling of the Consolata, Turin (*Marianne Adelmann*)
Interior of dome of San Bernardino, Chieri (*Marianne Adelmann*)

COLOUR ILLUSTRATIONS

Endpaper: Azulejos in the chapter house of São Vicente, Lisbon (*Erika Groth-Schmachtenberger*)

Jacket illustrations: (*front*) Altar of the Pilar church, Ouro Preto (*Timothy Benton*); (*back*) Elevation of the Santuario d'Oropa; from Guarini's *Architettura Civile*, 1737. British Museum

Design of book by John Wallis

ACKNOWLEDGMENTS

The author and publishers wish to thank the museums, collectors and photographers mentioned above, for kind permission to use their photographs.

The author wishes to thank Miss Marianne Adelmann for undertaking special journeys to Italy and Spain to take photographs for this book; and Mr Michael Raeburn for his great help in illustrating the book and in correcting the proofs.

To happy convents, bosom'd deep in vines,
Where slumber abbots, purple as their wines:
To isles of fragrance, lily-silver'd vales,
Diffusing langour in the panting gales:
To lands of singing or of dancing slaves,
Love-whispering woods, and lute-resounding waves.
But chief her shrine where naked Venus keeps,
And Cupids ride the lion of the deeps;
Where eased of fleets the Adriatic main
Wafts the smooth eunuch and enamour'd swain.

The Dunciad. Book IV: Alexander Pope

I

Preludio

It is an odd experience, and one which does not fall to the lot of every author, to be writing finally and for the last time upon a subject which first interested him more than forty years ago. But my book *Southern Baroque Art* appeared in the spring of 1924, and in the introduction to its first edition, dated July 1923, I mention that I had been engaged for the previous two and a half years upon its pages which takes us back to December 1920, all of forty-five and on the way to fifty years ago. It is a frightening thought, no less so if I may be allowed to detail in a moment the circumstances in which that book was begun. Nothing indeed seemed particularly propitious about it. My brother had been hawking round the MS month after month to nearly every London publisher, and in the end I had to pay fifty pounds, a big sum in those days out of a small allowance, to get it printed, having made my début some time before this in June 1918 with a first book of poems.

But now for the story of how the book was started, and if I am to give details of this I would ask that their strange nature be accepted for the truth. I was taken ill immediately after my return to England in December 1920 from an expedition to see D'Annunzio in Fiume, undertaken not out of political motives but because I admired the author of *Il Fuoco* and *La Città Morta* as the greatest living poet of the day, and wanted him to agree to write the introduction to an edition of Rabelais in French and English (Sir Thomas Urquhart's translation), a project for which I had already asked Picasso to make the drawings. My brother and I had before this been in negotiation with Picasso to paint frescoes in one of the rooms in my father's house in Tuscany. Not, then, forty years old and at the height of his genius, only a year after he had designed the dresses and scenery and painted the curtain for Falla's Andalusian ballet, it is a pity on all accounts that this scheme came to nothing because of the sum of money asked by the painter, an amount which would not buy the smallest of his drawings or a couple of his lithographs at the price they fetch today. I think it was these excitements and their attendant frustrations that in some curious way curdled my blood and made me ill. On reaching Paris on the way home from Fiume I had the

I

presentiment of illness, and remember wishing to be in pain in order not to feel this terrible anxiety and to know at least that I had some definite thing wrong with me.

I have no memory of the intervening few nights I must have spent in London at our house in Chelsea. But arrived at Scarborough after the last journey I was ever to make thither from King's Cross, the station familiar to me from childhood and during all my school days, I had written no more than the first five or six pages of *Southern Baroque Art* when I was taken ill, and nearly died. I can still mark the sentence where I stopped writing on that evening. The immediate cause of it came from walking on the rocks at low tide, when I jumped from one rock-pool to another, sprained myself, and started blood-poisoning in the groin. I have never thought this was sufficient reason for what followed. But I woke in the middle of the night, and had to go along to my brother's room and spend the rest of the night there, feeling certain in my mind that I was dying.

I was in bed for nearly three months, all through January, February and March 1921, and while lying in bed was measured by the tailor for some new suits. When I got out of bed and was well enough to try them on I remember my mother screaming when I came into the room, for during the illness I had grown to six foot six inches tall. But in less than two weeks I had shrunk three inches to my normal height, and was left with new suits that came down over my wrists to my knuckles. It appears that it is possible to have this abnormal growth during and after an illness until one is twenty-three years old, and my twenty-third birthday had been a month before I went to Fiume.

When the abcess on the groin had burst, I was left with some form of nervous prostration which continued in the shape of sleeplessness for many months. At its worst, during those weeks I was ill in bed, I felt acutely ill and almost fainting at the thought of any form of personal responsibility. The notion of the Prime Minister who had to make grave decisions of policy made me ill, and I remember that the mere thought of the duties of an engine-driver caused me to feel I must lie back and gasp for breath.

So I nearly died where I was born, at Scarborough. Nearly died after, and one could almost add, because of writing my first page or two of prose. For that was certainly the effect of it, as if it was some kind of ritual sacrifice, or delayed ceremony of puberty; and I have no doubt that other young persons of a like disposition or quality have perished in it. Dying, as I say, in Scarborough where I was born. Forgotten by the world next morning, or by the evening edition of the local newspaper; and only alive so many years later in my brother's and sister's memory if they happened to think of me which for all their affection would not be often now. It was quite obviously some form of psychic illness, nearly impossible to diagnose. An illness of the soul or psyche which has no lodgement and therefore eludes treatment. But during, and before that, I like to think the magic touchstone had been for a few moments in my keeping.

In this manner.

In a long work of which only the first part has so far been published I have written of *The Kingdom of Green Fingers*, taking for this purpose the Green Boy and Girl out of a mediaeval legend or folk tale. They come up in mystery into the world, 'finding themselves all at once among the reapers in the harvest field', and are in symbol for what is instinct in the arts and is not born of learning and acquired knowledge. It is the discussion of a golden age when the hand of man cannot go wrong. Perhaps in results it is the antithesis to the sterile delvings of the art-historian. It infers the lightning rapidity of the imagination in contrast to the futile explaining of what should not, and cannot be explained. I think that for a little time, for a year and a day, meaning for an indefinite period, I was one of the Green Children, but it was chiefly in 1917 during the War, while I was in the army and had begun writing poetry, and I would say it had left me by the following year. Or did it indeed stay for a little longer than that? For I remember to have felt it at certain times.

It cannot come back again now. For that would be impossible. But I learned to work. And that was better for the other course leads to misery and to the burnt out wreck or shell, of which there are instances in each generation. That is always the danger. If I was one of them, ever, or at all, of which I am certain, the transition back again took place during those weeks after my illness in the winter of 1920-1.

But now we come to the point of these preliminaries. For I must further explain that I had passed the autumn months before I was ill at Naples where I had come into contact for the first time in my life with the painting and architecture of the South about which I was to write. In the early autumn before all this my brother and I had been marooned with my parents in a hotel at Baveno on Lake Maggiore, always my father's first halting-place in Italy. It was September, but it never stopped raining night or day even for a moment. I still remember the ceaseless jangle of rain on the lake water as we made a despairing trip to Isola Bella for we had reached the point of desperation and longed to get away. Armida's galleon looked decidedly at its worst that afternoon with the rain 'siling'* down upon its decks and terraces, with the white peacocks driven indoors into the potting-sheds and the water dripping off the leaves of the lemon-trees in their wet and rain-darkened terracotta pots. It was next morning that my father tried to detain us with the offer of books from his travelling library, with the titles of which my brother made amusing play in a volume of his autobiography. But to get away we

* A Hallamshire descriptive word for pouring rain.

3

were determined, and our goal was not even Rome, but Naples; at a time when I had never been further south than Florence. Our escape had every element of excitement, for it may scarcely be believed, but by then the floods were out and had risen above the front steps of the hotel. We had to leave by boat from beside the concierge's desk. An embarkation it certainly was in more senses than one, for my career as a writer, such as it has been, dates from that flight, though my parents were soon to join us after the waters had subsided in what my instinct told me, all shortcomings forgotten, was yet the warm and glittering South.

All of October and November we were in Naples, and I can never forget the excitement of discovering for myself the two long narrow streets that traverse the old town with all their palaces and churches; and the huge and wonderful old convent-church of Santa Chiara with its majolica cloister, the ball-room of a church (as I remember it) with Sebastiano Conca's ceiling painting of *David dancing and playing the harp before the Ark*, the opera-boxes in its grand tier where the nuns looked down through gilded lattices to join in the Mass, its air in general of an autocracy of noble nuns; or the Certosa di San Martino above the town, all flashing whiteness, white stucco, white marbles, even the one or two white-robed monks, with belvedere or balcony looking over the roofs of Naples across the bay to the smoking volcano and down again to the tenor voices, the carnations and mandolines of the modern town. There were the score or more of other old churches, San Gregorio Armeno among them; but in those days one could only find the church open at haphazard and unlikely hours with no more than the sight of a nun, if one was lucky, in her scarlet and black habit, and there was no intimation of the cloister garden, or of the many and fascinating treasures in the long corridor upstairs that runs along parallel to, and looking down into, the church; not least, there were the open double-geometrical staircases by Ferdinando Sanfelice, an architectural feature unique to Naples to add a fugal or contrapuntal finish to the fanfares and flourishes of the exuberant, the vociferous South.

Here, then, in the Parthenopaean city that alone among Mediterranean towns had come down with a large and teeming population from the Classical past, though with its old dwellings, palace and slums alike, built as though on purpose with their backs turned so as not to look out upon the Siren Bay, there had been, to quote from my introduction, 'many excellent architects and painters upon whom a strong light had not yet been flashed . . . and who were not yet tarnished with a too extravagant admiration,' and I had found the theme or subject I was looking for.

But to the identity of their contents there was no key, and little more than the mere name of church or palace, until some months later Octavian Blewitt's *Guide to Naples.* 1853, fell into my hands, or, more literally, was

4

found by me on a bookshelf in my old home, a stroke of fortune only paralleled by the finding of Flaubert's *Salammbô* in English translation (the Lotus Library) in the post office at Eckington when I was fourteen years old. It will be understood that after the fall of the Bourbon dynasty in 1861 and the unification of Italy all interest was lost in Naples as capital of a kingdom of its own, and it is even curious that as late as the middle of the last century so many details should be given concerning the painters and architects of the preceding period of utter decadence, universally condemned as such. That it had not always been so was proved to me by another personal discovery, for that was what it amounted to, the finding in the Reading Room of the British Museum of the Abbé de Saint-Non's *Voyage Pittoresque au Royaume des Deux Siciles*, 1786, with its engravings after paintings by Solimena from no less a hand than that of Fragonard. But it was not a question of Naples only, there was for those days the very personal discovery of the Palace of Caserta, the 'Versailles' of the Kingdom of Naples; but Versailles can never have been even for a single day as deserted as was Caserta when I first saw it, not knowing then that it was the last work of slave labour*– both palace and gardens of Caserta were largely built by Turkish galley slaves – but struck with amazement at the theatrical, if Neronic splendour of the marbled atrium or vestibule above the grand stair, a 'realisation' in precious marbles, the spoils of the ancient world, of a stage design of the Bibiena school, giving Roman permanence to what was essentially but painted wood and canvas.

Nor was this all. There were other discoveries such as the octagonal Loreto or Palazzo Badiale below the shrine of Monte Vergine where the older monks lived to escape the mountain cold, with its pharmacy of the eighteenth century and apartments for the Bourbon Kings kept in such a condition of sleepy preparedness that they could be arriving tonight or moving in tomorrow. And there was the Certosa di Padula, far away out in the earthquake country of the Basilicata, with its three vast courts, the equivalent of an Escorial or even an Angkor in the imagination for it was at long distance, the roads were bad and motor-cars were expensive to hire, though at last a year or two later conquered, which is to say, attained and seen.

All this had been in the autumn of 1920, but my first ambition on recovering from that long illness in the early months of the following year was to go to Lecce. That phrase of Gregorovius, 'the Florence of Rococo Art', describing Lecce, had been familiar to me since a schoolboy at Eton, and Martin Shaw Briggs' book *In the Heel of Italy*, 1910, I had certainly read before the 1914 war. My father owned a copy of it. But, also, he had been there himself even earlier than that. He must have been travelling in the

---

* Unless we count the railway tunnels through the Apennines between Florence and Bologna, and along the Italian Riviera all the way from Ventimiglia nearly to Spezia, which were hewn by convicts.

South of Italy in 1906 or 1907, enduring on one occasion eighty flea-bites on an arm between wrist and elbow as souvenir of a night spent at Manfredonia on the Gargano peninsula, not far from where Padre Pio now holds court and performs near miracles. It was to my father, then, that I owed pre-information of the beautiful buildings to be found in Lecce; and I was hardly well again before arriving there after a twelve-hour train journey from Salerno to Brindisi in April or May of 1921. I will not narrate again how the notables of the town would not allow us to pay for our meals in Lecce, a habit of hospitality which I would say must have been some two hundred years old at the time we experienced it; and can only stress how, here, and in the surrounding country towns of this part of Apulia, there is even now the sensation that it is another country from Naples or from Rome, as different in fact, as I said all those years ago, as Portugal is from Spain.

Our arrival in Lecce had been late at night and I can never forget coming out of the hotel next morning into the square in front of the church and convent of the Celestini in the strong light of an Apulian April morning. The latter is now the Prefettura. But why call it by a name so shorn of interest and romance? The two buildings are the convent of the Celestini and the church of Santa Croce; adjoining buildings in such harmony with each other that in the first shock of surprise on beholding them it would seem they are of the same date and style. Both are built in the local stone which lends itself so easily to exuberance for it hardens and sets after being carved. But the façade of Santa Croce, which from the row of animal caryatids under its balcony and its rose-window seems to be in some kind of delayed and fantasy-Romanesque, really dates from late in the sixteenth century – and one asks oneself, looking at it again, where is this? Is it in Provence, or Spain? Or, even, some unknown part of Greece where the architecture is Latin, and not late Byzantine? But the church of Santa Croce was begun in about 1580 and finished in about 1640; and only twenty years after that Giuseppe Zimbalo, the Leccese architect of euphonious name, started on the façade of the convent next door, finishing in about 1695, which is exactly what one would guess from the window-frames that now reveal themselves as the counterpart of picture or mirror-frames anywhere else – late Louis XIV in France, or William III in England – and not even so very different from the more ornate of Wren's window-frames to the river front of Hampton Court.

Yet, after another look at them, how Spanish they are in feeling; more subtly differenced on the lower than on the upper floor, where their cornices and surrounding swags are much the same. They are not gilded, of course, like real mirror-frames, but they have the richness of gilding in the colour of the stone and in the sharpness of its cutting. The Celestini and Santa Croce would be fine buildings in any country; lovely, too, by moonlight as I have seen them more than once, and now flood-lit at night, if that is an improvement. Something comparatively modest in their scale, and opposed to the megalomaniac, as though the building craze of which they were part was not going to lose its head and ruin itself in senseless expenditure, gives strength to the impression that this was a considered, almost a separatist movement of its own, on a provincial scale. At Lecce it would seem that it was beauty more than extravagance they were after. Down there right in the heel of Italy they knew they were in a Spanish and, I think, also a Greek influenced world of their own remote from anywhere, and of a certainty very far from Rome.

Lecce is one of the most beautiful of cities to walk in, with – if no more than that – a lovely balcony at every turn. An extraordinary and blinding whiteness is its peculiar note; and after two or three more of the balconies, another, and yet another façade of church or palace comes into view. I remember in 1920, seeing figures of Pulcinella drawn on the white house walls; and would like to repeat again that this was the land of Pulcinella, and that up till 1860 the Apulian brigands went about their work masked and in this disguise, which must in its origin have been the dress, the white loose shirt and trousers of the Apulian peasant. Coming on this occasion from Lecce straight back to Paris, I attended the first performance at the Opéra (15 May 1920) of Stravinsky's *Pulcinella*, which had Neapolitan dresses and scenery by Picasso, and remember telling the artist during an interval that I had just come from a town in the south of Italy where there were drawings of Pulcinella on the white walls of the houses.

The hand of Zimbalo is to be seen in several other buildings beside the Celestini. He can be admired, too, in the second or lesser façade of the Duomo which, again, is puzzling in date (1659–82) for it is reminiscent in detail of the earlier Santa Croce in which he had no hand. It has fluted composite columns and pilasters, a balcony like that of Santa Croce, but without the caryatids; and above that a huge free-standing frontispiece framing a statue of Sant'Oronzo; and of course as in all the churches of Lecce there are columns wreathed with cupids when you walk inside. The interiors, generally, are pointlessly exuberant. It is a city of balconies and façades. Bishop Berkeley, the philosopher, who visited Lecce just at this time while the new buildings were going up, was scarcely exaggerating when he writes; 'the most beautiful city in Italy lies in the heel. Lecce, the ancient Aletium, is the most luxurious in all ornaments of architecture of any town that I have ever seen. I have not in all Italy seen such fine convents . . . Surely there is not a like rich architecture in the world.'[*] He must have seen and admired Santa Croce and the Celestini, while the façade of the Chiesa del Rosario which is outstandingly beautiful cannot have been more than three-quarters built when Bishop Berkeley visited the city. Little enough is still known about

---

[*] *Bishop Berkeley: His Life, Writings and Philosophy*, by J. M. Hare and M. M. Rossi, London, 1931, pp. 103, 105, 106. Bishop Berkeley was at Lecce in 1719.

Giuseppe Zimbalo; and in particular little is known about his travels.

Another of the architectural glories of Lecce, which may have had no more than ten or fifteen thousand inhabitants in its prime, is the Seminario which stands in a splendid square opposite the Duomo. It is by Zimbalo's pupil, Giuseppe Cino, and was begun just about the time (1695) when the Celestini was finished. The Seminario has many points of resemblance to the latter; in being built for instance of the same brick-like units of the soft local stone. Its front being broken, too, by the same pilasters of masonry among the stone 'bricks'; and having window-frames of nearly identical picture or mirror-frame invention. But their shapes are not so imaginative; the same idea, second time done, is less dramatic of impact despite the beautiful square in which it stands. It would seem that in the Seminario Cino was in purposeful rivalry with Zimbalo his master; if perhaps a certain hesitance or reluctance in its detail might show that he was impelled to it, that it was demanded of him, and he had not his heart in it.★

In any event the other buildings by Cino show a different and imaginative hand. The monastery church of SS. Nicola e Cataldo, just outside the town, incorporates a round-headed Romanesque doorway, and despite a leading authority's remark that Cino 'shows a spirit closer to the international Baroque'†, it is curiously antiquarian and sixteenth-century in appearance. It would be difficult indeed to guess that it dates from 1716. Its two storeys of fluted pilasters which have the responsibility of framing in a circular Romanesque window are curiously subdued, as though obedient to some stipulation. Indeed it is about the only façade in all Lecce which is just a front and has none of the eloquence of a façade. The only licence is in its sculptures, though even these are heavy and muddled as they crowd the skyline. But, then, at SS. Nicola e Cataldo it is restful to be outside the town, and almost anything in this golden stone is beautiful against the blue Apulian or Adriatic sky. And it is not without a contributory importance that from the roof there is a view 'extending to the coast of Epirus' which is not more than forty miles away.

Other churches by Giuseppe Cino in Lecce are Santa Chiara, Sant' Irena, and the Carmine, all of which have the façades to be expected of them in this city of easy eloquence and grace. It must, too, have had beautiful music in its time. Dr Burney in his *Musical Tour* mentions the Leccese folk songs that he heard sung at Naples, and remarks that many of the great *castrati* were obtained from Apulia, chiefly because there were many good singers there, but also because the manufacture of these *virtuosi* – a practice strictly forbidden by law – was carried out more easily so far away from Naples. The tradition

★ The incongruous and dull upper storey to the Seminario, which much spoils its effect, is of course a later addition.

† Rudolf Wittkower, *Art and Architecture in Italy*, Harmondsworth, 1958, p. 264.

of good voices still continues; and no one who heard Tito Schipa, only lately dead, accompanying himself on the guitar while singing the serenade from *Il Barbiere* would find it surprising that the tenor came from this city of façades and midnight strollings. Santa Chiara and the Carmine, as has just been said, are both by Cino and are musical in the extreme, if this can be said of anything in architecture, waiting alike in sun and moonlight, for the singing of Lindoro from below the nearest balcony; while the church of Rosario is also by Giuseppe Cino, and has on its façade huge stone bowls of flowers and fruit at which stone birds are pecking, a beautiful and poetic concept. The cloister at the back has a stone well-house with twisted columns that carry a beautiful carved frieze and stone-tiled roof, a model of its kind. It was the pillars, not of this well-head but of the cloister, that my father wanted to copy for his lake pavilion at Renishaw. Its sixteen pillars were to have capitals 'with water lilies at the corners, as with the quadrangle at Lecce'.

There is no end to façade viewing in this Apulian town. The Gesù, and San Agostino (by Zimbalo) are other churches. All, or all but one, are beautiful, and the exception which is San Matteo is at least interesting from the conceit of having its upper storey with a three-windowed balcony concave, while the lower storey behaves in opposite fashion and is convex, a not very successful experiment. Its façade is covered with stone scales as though the architect Carducci, tired of the 'bricks' of Leccese stone, was trying for something new, but it is reminiscent of the shingle roofs of 'habitant' Canada and faultlessly Catholic as that may be, is not suited to the Adriatic air and the proximity of Albanians, the nearest foreigners, as well as Greeks and Turks.

But one of the delights of this terminus of all Latinity, the true *finisterra* of the Latins – has not Brindisi only some twenty miles off a Roman column that marks the ending of the Appian Way? – is in the villages and small towns near Lecce. A pair of these, Galatina and Galatone, but a mile or two apart, have beautiful buildings of our period; the door jambs of a church in the latter of these villages being carved with arabesque ornament of a jewel-like finish more easy to associate with the Tempio Malatestiano at Rimini or the Ducal Palace at Urbino than with this remote place at the end of nowhere. The frieze above the doorway is a Roman triumph copied from some antique bas-relief on a sarcophagus, and until this local architecture receives proper, scientific investigation it would be hazardous in the extreme to guess its date. But the higher storey of the façade with its niches and great window-frame in the centre is an easier problem and is clearly mid or late seventeenth-century though, unlike the Leccese buildings, this façade at Galatone is not eloquent and has nothing about it of the theatre. It comes, as it were, from a time before façades were thought of.

Nardo, a larger town, is yet more interesting. This has a piazza complete with the local variant of the *guglie* or lily-monuments of Naples; and churches, as well, with most curious grotesque caryatids, in some cases standing on each other's heads; bearded heads, garlanded and ending in stone flourishes like a garden term, and on top of brackets held up on their heads, seated figures, or bearded dwarfs usurping the place of a column and supporting the capitals on their own heads. Again, as at Galatina and Galatone, these are without the sophistications of the Leccese buildings, and indeed more resembling Mexican country churches, or those on the Altiplano of Peru; in fact, entirely disorientated, difficult to date, and from drawings or photographs impossible to place geographically, least of all, perhaps, to any part of Italy.

Gallipoli, Copertino, Sternatia, Maglie, are other little towns of dazzling white walls with shrill green spring vegetables in the fields around them, a spring which comes three times over for they have three crops a year with, it seems, little to choose between one *prima vera* and the next. Also, there is variety in their architecture; the buildings in one village can be very different from the next. But it is to be noted how it is possible to come across an architectural detail, the capital of a wreathed column with an eagle of outstretched wing usurping the place of palmetto fronds or the acanthus, and on the architrave above that a pair of birds pecking at stone flowers below the light and shadow of the cornice, and how this almost associates itself out of Italy to the other coast of the Adriatic. This can be true, I think, of ten or fifteen small towns or villages within a near radius of Lecce. A town I have not seen, Martina Franca, further away north of Otranto, in the country of the *trulli* (stone beehive villages), is described as 'having the finest Baroque in Apulia', but it is a Baroque of a more ordinary and accustomed kind to judge from photographs.* The Valle d'Istria, 'dotted with *trulli* and cultivated with vineyards', must give a landscape of another character from the white cube, Pulcinella-haunted houses of the *terra di Lecce*, and without that subtle, classicising influence, from across the Adriatic. It is true that villages between Lecce and Gallipoli, and less than a dozen miles from the former, are described as having 'traces of Greek influence still abundant in their local dialect', though this has little to do with the Greek settlements of Magna Graecia and is a survival from Byzantine rule of a thousand years ago. Yet, all the same, there are the affinities of historical repetition; of identical conditions offering themselves, or having lain latent, for twenty centuries or more. What did the Leccese architects imagine that they were doing? It was not necessary for them even to think across the Adriatic to the mainland of Greece. Their local antiquities were of Greek origin from Magna Graecia.

---

* Martina Franca has the Ducal Palace of the Caracciolo family, 'designed by Bernini, this great artist's only work in Southern Italy', and according to the local guide, 'frescoes by Carella, with portraits, in two Arcadian scenes of the court of the Duke Francesco III Caracciolo'. Is this an Arcadian overstatement?

Rome was hundreds of miles away. Greek antiquity lay at hand and all around. So it could be suggested that the art movement of which these buildings are the evidence was less Italian than Greek of aspiration, and that this explains its lightness and gracefulness of hand. Perhaps, too, it is a clue to the Sicilian buildings we are now nearing, where to some little extent the same conditions reproduced themselves that had made it possible two thousand five hundred years before.

The trend of these preliminary remarks, as the reader may remember, takes us to where it leaves us in April or May of 1921.

Thenceforward, for some considerable part of my working life though by no means for all of it I have been concerned with the Baroque and Rococo and their affinities in every country where they could be found. These experiences however are so bound up with my early life of apprehension that I have thought it better to deal with those here and now in this preliminary chapter so that they do not obtrude themselves into the body of the book once it has properly begun. It was in this sense that as long ago as that same year of 1921 I was able to see Würzburg, Vierzehnheiligen, and other places, including the Amalienburg; and the year after that with the first Salzburg Festival as an excuse had my first sight of Melk and St Florian, which meant the dawning of new names of architects, Fischer von Erlach, Lukas von Hildebrandt, the splendidly sonorous Kilian Ignaz Dientzenhofer, and soon after that, the Asam brothers, J. M. Fischer, Johann Balthasar Neumann. It was first intimation of the monasteries along the Danube, of little towns like Dürnstein, and the palace stairways of Vienna; and following on that the whole glittering and brightly coloured world of the German eighteenth century from the interiors of Potsdam in their different tones of gold to the enchantments of the Court dwarf Count Cuvilliés at the Residenz Theatre and elsewhere, and from the churches of the brothers Zimmermann to the Court of the Grand Mogul Aurungzeb and other fantasies of the goldsmith J. M. Dinglinger in the 'Green Vaults' at Dresden. My first work on these subjects, imperfect as it may have been, came out as long ago as 1926 and was at least the earliest book on this theme to be printed in the English language, to be followed by books of other authors at long interval in 1958 and 1959. It alone could be the study, or more appropriately the recreation of a lifetime with, palaces apart, some fifteen to eighteen churches of the first order of imagination and exuberant feeling in Austria and Bavaria to be kept in mind.

But there is Spain, as well. A first visit there in April 1919 was confined to the Escorial – how could one forget that first sighting of Greco's *St Maurice and the Theban Legion*! – to the Prado, and to the paintings by El Greco in the churches of Toledo. And then in the spring of 1925 I was able to see Seville and Granada, and where this subject in particular is concerned, the Cartuja of Granada. But the opportunity for study came much later when for a few weeks each spring from 1947 to 1949 I was enabled to go from end to end of Spain. It was, then, I saw Salamanca and Santiago de Compostela, this latter then, already, for the third time. Since then the Baroque of Córdoba and Granada has been further explored to reveal the beautiful churches at Priego de Córdoba by F. X. Pedraxas, news of which came to me at so late an hour that it could only be put into a footnote in the book I published on Spain in 1950.

The abbeys in Portugal, Belém, Alcobaça, Batalha, Tomar, first seen in 1925, led to further explorations from the Royal Palace of Queluz, so little known or thought of forty years ago, to the realisation of such wonders in their kind as the Convent of Jesus at Aveiro and the *coro alto* of the nunnery of Santa Clara at Oporto. Later visits, and in especial one journey round Northern Portugal, to Tras-os-Montes, to Bragança, and the Minho in the summer of 1953, led to the knowledge that there were some eight or ten monasteries or nunneries thereabouts deserving at least as much admiration in their different ways as Melk or St Florian, as Ottobeuren or Zwiefalten; among them, just to recall the first that come to mind, Arouca with its golden organ-case, and the more than life-size granite statues of Cistercian nuns with painted faces in the choir; Lorvão with its choir-stalls, two dozen of them, set antiphonally, to either side; Travanca with chests of drawers for vestments in the sacristy painted with chinoiseries and *scènes champêtres* in green and gold; Santo Tirso, Tibães, Bouro, are three more of them. The elements of decoration are of course different from Austria and Bavaria. In Portugal it is a matter of gilded organ-cases upheld by figures of satyrs and mermen, and tile-pictures of blue and white *azulejos*. But, as well, the Portuguese carpenters were unexcelled whether working on benches and cupboards in the native chestnut, or the jacaranda from Brazil; the gilded pelmets are a world of fantasy to themselves; and the stepped-back high altars that are like tiers of gold boxes ascending and diminishing in size are unique to Portugal.

The natural concomitant to any experience of Spain and Portugal is the wish to see Latin America, an ambition that was delayed and held fire, as I have explained elsewhere in this book, for nearly thirty years until 1952. It is now at last fulfilled in the pair of chapters I have written here on Mexico and on Brazil. I am lucky enough to have seen Peru as well as Mexico which is not often the case with writers who come from Europe, but Cuzco, from the Spanish point of view, architecturally, is of an earlier dispensation, its buildings being in delayed High Renaissance, as it might be a provincial cathedral city in Spain. Quito, in Ecuador, is more interesting with its church of San Francisco and the Jesuit church of La Compañía, of legendary scarlet-lacquered interior, if the report of it is more than a little exaggerated.* I have at least visited and seen most of the Colonial cities of the Latins, excepting Goa and Manila, and it is all to some degree time wasted, apart from Mexico. For there is '*le style mexicain*', of that there is no question. But Mexico excepted, there is little more to say. The late architecture of the Latins flowered best at its own fountain-heads and on its own roots, which are in Europe, whether in Italy or Spain.

But there are others beside the Latins. I have suggested that the most beautiful city in Europe after Rome and Venice, architecturally, is Prague, both from the mediaeval and the later point of view. It is true that the phrase 'the most beautiful' is in itself nonsensical. Does not a chapter in this present book open with the words that 'the three most beautiful cities of Europe, perhaps of the world, are on the water. They are Venice, Lisbon and Istanbul'. What, then, of Leningrad; or call it, rather, St Petersburg? For it is supreme even in photographs. And how much of this is due to Rastrelli, architect of the Winter Palace, of the Smolny Convent, and of a large part of Tsarskoe Selo – of the church, too, of St Andrew at Kiev, on its terrace above the river Dnieper – for Rastrelli cannot be denied his place as one of the great architects of the Baroque age, or that, at least, in scale; for in detail, in his doorways for instance at Tsarskoe Selo, in the pink and gold iconostasis in the church at Kiev, he is Rococo, as also in the gaily painted exteriors of his buildings. Very decidedly Italian in feature, to judge from his portrait by Rotari, he was born in Russia, of Italian name and origin. And the other Italians, Rainaldi, Quarenghi, who worked in Russia? They were Italians working in Russia. They had not the Russian touch in them.

Perhaps the only unknown region still left to investigate is a part of Poland, always allowing for destruction in so many wars with Swedes and Tartars, Turks and Russians, and for redoubled devastation by both Russians and Germans, too, in both world wars. It is difficult indeed to find out how much is left, whether even one stone is left standing on another after the holocaust of the last world war. Not in the region so much of Warsaw, of Cracow, or in and around Lwow, where there were good buildings of the period, in particular the Greek-Catholic or Ruthenian Cathedral of St George by Bernardo Merettini, become Bernard Meretyn, even if it is only a little more interesting than the Warsaw churches. In that direction, but down towards Rumania, towards the Bucovina and Bessarabia, the Rococo town hall of Buczacz, built by one of the Potocki family, with its high and floreated frontispiece and tower of elaborate shaping, appears graceful and unusual of outline even in the photograph. But the region to study, and where few have been, is Vilna; and of the region beyond Vilna to the north-east nothing has

* There are two chapters on Cuzco and a chapter on Quito in my *Golden Wall and Mirador*, 1961. It contains a chapter, also, on Havana.

been heard for a quarter of a century, and it should be worth visiting. It would include between two lakes the domed and four-towered church of Głebokie; the dash through the letter 'l', signifying it should be pronounced more like the letter 'w', alone, accenting its distance and inaccessibility; with at the far end of a lake a mile or two away, the Basilian monastery at Berezwecz, two-towered with richly articulated white façade shown in the photograph reflected in the lake water. A Rococo synagogue in brick in a nearby town, and the local railway junction named Królewszczyzna are in multiplication of the loneliness; and perhaps that long name bears witness to the theory that the Poles of themselves in natural instinct unconsciously added to and increased the difficulties of their own language in order to make their tongue unintelligible to their invaders. As to what lies beyond that through the lakes and firwoods, beyond the marshes, into what was Lithuania, little is known and for more than a quarter of a century nothing has been written. But the population was Catholic and there were monasteries and convents. If Vilna has fine buildings in its own local style, there should be good buildings, too, in Kaunas (Kovno). It is thither, to this far north-eastern corner of Poland, if not to Russian-occupied Lithuania which must present special difficulties of access of its own, that someone young and adventurous should go to discover what is left from the old Poland of *Pan Tadeusz*, to look for the white shadows of churches and for the wooden manor-houses that Mickiewicz wrote of among the sad-looking lakes and near the mushroom-woods that he describes with such loving care.

The thought of which has led us far indeed from the classical, or sub-classical South of warmth and eloquence which was my opening theme, and to which I now return as from the sensation of growing old to being young again. It is true, thinking back to it, that no subsequent visit has ever effaced that first impression of descending to the South out of the rain of the Italian lakes, and it may be inevitable that I should remember it with something of the shock and delight of first seeing Venice. But having spent some considerable part of my childhood in Florence that was the subject that would have come easiest to hand though there was little or nothing new to discover there, dull feats of primitive recognition apart, and it was still too tainted with Anglo-Saxon enthusiasms of the eighteen-eighties and by the attitudes and acerbities of the English colony. It was a voyage of exploration I was in search of, and that it inspired a poetic or an instinctive more than a factual narrative of experience has been the point of argument of these few preliminary pages. Having said which, we must now look at Naples with a more serious if not more jaded eye.

2

The Kingdom of the Three Sicilies

One of the characteristic enlivenments of the street scenes of Naples is with the *guglie* or lily-monuments – what else are we to call them? – in front of the churches of San Domenico and of the Gesù Nuovo, obelisks of grey and white marble covered with sculptures and with a statue on top, serving no practical purpose whatever and with the aim only of gaiety and exuberance. Bernini was a Neapolitan, but there is nothing of Bernini's fountains in them, and in any case their play is not halted with water. They are there only for ornament and high spirits, with the air of some processional contrivance halted and made permanent, of some 'juggernaut' of Hindu festivals anywhere from Madura to Katmandu. But their true analogy of relationship is to the wooden towers or *guglie* crowded with living statues in the shape of children with gauze wings dressed as angels, and so forth, that are carried through the streets of Nola, a town in the Campagna Felice, for the festival of St Paulinus.★ Then, again, there is the Trinity Column in the Graben at Vienna, which is by the Italian theatrical painter Burnacini, and there are similar columns or monuments in Linz and other Austrian towns; all of them of the nature of the Neapolitan *guglie* or lily-towers, but with a difference which is a matter of climate and of the southern population.

At the foot of the Guglia del Gesù we are in the heart of old Naples, and if we but come through the door of the Gesù we will see one of the pyrotechnical feats of its native school of painters. Inside the church, on its entrance wall with layers of dust lying thick upon it, is the huge fresco painting by Solimena of *The Expulsion of Heliodorus from the Temple*; and Dr Lemprière of Pembroke College, Oxford, writing as long ago as November 1788 only remarks of Heliodorus in his *Classical Dictionary* that he was 'one of the favourites of Seleucus Philopater, King of Syria, who attempted to plunder the temple of the Jews about 176 years before Christ,

★ The procession of these dancing towers through the streets of Nola – there are nine of them belonging to the different guilds of the town – and the possible descent of this pagan festival from the rites of Adonis, which were nearly identical with those of the Egyptian Osiris, are described in my *Primitive Scenes and Festivals*, 1942, pp. 261–78.

by order of his master.' In other words it was such a competition subject as was set to academy students all over the civilised world (as it then was) and not one upon which Solimena can have harboured any deep feelings. It was just an excuse for a huge composition built up along accepted lines, or, indeed, properly composed, and the fresco is in fact an extraordinary achievement for a student only eighteen years old. But it does, also, as has been remarked before, carry a more than remarkable resemblance to the 'grands sujets' or 'grandes machines' of Delacroix, which was disconcerting at a time when Solimena was thought of as less than nothing while the French master was extolled as second only to Rubens in the hierarchy of great painters.

But it would seem that the reason for the infliction of this recondite choice of subject upon Solimena was that in another Neapolitan church, that of San Filippo Neri only a short walk away, there is a huge fresco of *Christ Driving the Moneylenders from the Temple* by Luca Giordano, likewise over the principal entrance, placing Solimena therefore in direct confrontation or competition with his predecessor, the leading painter of the previous generation, for Solimena (1657–1747) was some twenty-five years younger than Luca Giordano (1632–1705). Another place where these two painters could be seen competing with each other was at Monte Cassino where Luca Giordano, 'Fa Presto' as he was called, painted the ceiling of the nave, and four huge paintings by Solimena, probably his best work, hung in the choir. But the Battle of Monte Cassino obliterated the trials of skill of both painters.

'Fa Presto' who was a remarkable '*pasticheur*' and could paint in the style of Ribera or of his master Pietro da Cortona – he has even been mistaken for a not too distant follower of Velázquez – is to be seen in places as unlikely as they are distant from each other. In the Palazzo Riccardi at Florence – under the same roof as the chapel fresco'd by Benozzo Gozzoli – where his ceiling painting of the *Medici as Gods of Light among the Deities of Olympus* is among the three or four great painted rooms of post-Raphaelite Italy;* but, also, on the ceilings of the Biblioteca Riccardiana, and on the dome of the Corsini chapel in the church of Santo Spirito in that same city. 'Fa Presto' spent the years 1682–3 in Florence and went to Spain ten years later, in 1702, where, after improvising in the presence of the semi-imbecile Carlos II and his court a picture in the style of Bassano, a curious spectacle in itself, he painted ten vaults in the roof of the church at the Escorial and the running frieze of the great stair, his themes being the *Capture of the Connétable de Montmorency at*

---

* The others are the ceiling by Pietro da Cortona (1596–1669) in the Palazzo Barberini, and his frescoes from *The Aeneid* in the Palazzo Pamphilj, both in Rome; Tiepolo's *Banquet of Anthony and Cleopatra* in the Palazzo Labia, at Venice, and his less known, but equally beautiful ceiling painting of *The Course of the Sun*, in the Palazzo Clerici at Milan. Tiepolo's great masterpiece, the painted ceiling of the staircase at Würzburg, having the dimensions of a station or airport hall, qualifies for more than its mere mention as a painted room.

St Quentin and *Philip II with the Architects of the Escorial*. And, as well, Giordano painted a hall at the palace of Buen Retiro in Madrid with the *Founding of the Order of the Golden Fleece*; nine large canvases for the *camarín* at the far off monastery of Guadalupe in the wilds of Estremadura; while his other masterwork beside the Palazzo Riccardi in Florence is his fresco'd ceiling to the *sacristía* of Toledo Cathedral. Its subject is *The Miracle of San Ildefonso*; and if you see his fresco by morning light, a ray emanating from the figure of God the Father crosses the painted ceiling; all this above and over the great *Expolio* of El Greco, of whom it would be interesting to have had 'Fa Presto's' expressed opinion.

And after it all he obtained leave from the King of Spain and came home to Naples, where in the Certosa di San Martino above the town he painted a roof and a cupola in the Treasury, while the Sacrament was kept exposed, non-stop, in forty-eight hours – and died in the following year. These frescoes are extremely pretty, with his use of green as setting and background for the figures high above the inlaid presses made by one of the Carthusian monks, showing still lives as formal and complicated as those of the early Cubist painters, piles of books and vases of flowers, with here and there a guitar lying among them that Picasso might have left behind in that phase of his Protean career. Here, and at the Palazzo Riccardi in Florence, you may see Luca Giordano at his best.

Solimena's travels were tame in scope compared to those undertaken by his predecessor, though they took him to Genoa where he made paintings for the Palazzo Ducale or Doges' Palace; and of all improbable places to Assisi where he painted a *Last Supper*, never in request now from the tourists, in the friars' refectory.★ But perhaps Solimena is to be admired at his best in his wall frescoes of the *Conversion of St Paul* and the *Fall of Simon Magus*, in the sacristy of San Paolo Maggiore in Naples, a room that, as I first remember it, had high gilt mirrors and tall-backed chairs, there were priests sitting there taking snuff, and in fact it was little changed since Fragonard as a young man visited it and took his sketch of one of the frescoes for the Abbé de Saint-Non's huge work, when these paintings were esteemed the 'triumph' of Solimena, and worth the consideration of all visiting artists and dilettanti – this in the church which still has for portico two of the Corinthian columns and a part of the architrave of the temple of Castor and Pollux where, better still, the cloister is on the site of the theatre where Nero played and sang. The white horses of Solimena are conspicuous in these forgotten paintings, and again they have something of the touch and hand of Delacroix.

How well I remember from forty years ago the afternoon spent in trying

★ There is a family group by Solimena of the Horner-Strangways family, to be admired in the bucolic setting of the deer park at Melbury in Dorset, painted when that family were on the Grand Tour. And the masterpiece of Conca is his fresco of *The Pool of Bethesda* in the Ospedale at Siena!

to find the summer villa of 'l'Abbate Ciccio', as Solimena was nicknamed, somewhere near Portici, on the slopes between Vesuvius and the sea along those roads noisy with open carriages or *corricolos*. Nor will I forget a long, it seemed an eternal hot afternoon when with my father in one of his moods 'in character', longing for my brother or myself to play Bouvard to his Pécuchet, we had to spend a whole afternoon scrambling over the ruins of the old castle at Nocera de' Pagani because Helena, widow of King Manfred, had been held prisoner there after the battle of Benevento in 1266. Much time, more than a day or two, was wasted in the hotel at La Cava where the visitors' books on view in the *salone* still held the signature of English travellers back to the eighteen-thirties. But our real reason for coming here was in order to see whether there were paintings by Solimena in the churches of Nocera de' Pagani, which town was his birthplace. Yet another unforgettable morning was that in which we tried to find the room fresco'd by Solimena in the Palazzo Sanfelice in Naples itself, built by that architect for his own use; a huge palace full of apartments and with no less than two of the double geometrical staircases for which Sanfelice was famous. But the house itself had become a howling slum and we never found the painted room. There are, or were, at least two more of these open staircases by Sanfelice in the Palazzo Spagnuolo in the Strada de Vergine, and at the Palazzo Majo. But the finest stair of all, though not of this character because it is an enclosed or courtyard stair, is at the Palazzo Serra Cassano in that high-lying part of the town just above the Royal Palace, called the Pizzofalcone. This palace which is still inhabited by its family, and is also by the hand of Sanfelice, is on a scale of splendour that equates it to the grandest private palaces of Rome or Vienna.

In general, then, what are we to think of the Neapolitan school of painting, which should include Ruoppolo of the flowers and halved watermelons with their black seeds, and Recco of the gleaming, grimacing fishes, two still-life painters of the seventeenth century, as noisy and boisterous of technique as the fruit and fish-stalls of the market? The canvases are Snyders-like in dimension and as large as Hondecoeters. They look in general as though they were painted one day to be thrown away the next. With Luca Giordano or Solimena we are upon another scale for they were approved masters of the European gambit, very different in achievement from such a minor and negligible painter as Verrio who was able to impose himself upon the English scene. They had undergone the proper schooling. Luca Giordano had studied under Pietro da Cortona who was one of the great masters in his line. If both Giordano and Solimena made both themselves and each other more than a little absurd by their facility of execution they are far from deserving to be neglected and ignored. Just as, indeed, any opera by Rossini or Donizetti is sure to contain good things and the music lover is to be pitied

Naples

The Guglia
del Gesù.

Carvings over the porch on the diamond-studded façade of the Gesù.

Right: Interior court of the Certosa di San Martino by Cosimo Fansaga.
Below right: Staircase to San Paolo Maggiore, with the columns from the Temple of Castor and Pollux.
Below: Ferdinando Sanfelice's staircase in the Palazzo Sanfelice.

Top: Luca Giordano, *Commerce and Navigation*; detail from the fresco'd ceiling
in celebration of The Medici, in The Palazzo Riccardi, Florence.
Bottom: Fragonard's engraving of Solimena's fresco in the Gesù Nuovo, Naples:
The Expulsion of Heliodorus from the Temple.
Opposite: Luca Giordano, *The Miracle of St Ildefonso*; fresco in the *sacristía* of Toledo
Cathedral with a ray of light emanating from God the Father to illumine the vision
of the saint.

Above: Giuseppe Bonito (formerly attributed to Francesco de Mura), *The Construction of the Temple*; fresco in Santa Chiara, Naples.
Opposite: Sebastiano Conca, *David Dancing before the Ark of the Covenant*; fresco in Santa Chiara.

who would forego the chance of hearing such a rarity in performance, as, shall we say, *La Donna del Lago* of the one composer, or *Roberto Devereux* or *Parisina* of the other, so there are unexpected features of strength and lyrical passages that may come without warning in any painting, above all in any fresco by either of these two painters. Like the two musicians just named they knew, and were masters of their métier, even if they were hurried or prone to exercise it at every turn. Nor can a great proportion of talent be denied to the last painter of the school, Francesco de Mura (1696–1782), whose large painting of the rebuilding of the church used to hang over the organ in Santa Chiara.★ His best ceiling paintings were in the church of Santa Maria dell'Annunziata, where, also, he painted the pictures of the high altar and the transept.† On the death of de Mura a number of his pictures were removed to a charitable institution called the Pio Monte della Misericordia, where many of them were still hanging not so many years ago. Perhaps, too, this is the place for mentioning the beautiful eighteenth-century *farmacia* of the Ospizio degli Incurabili, consisting of three halls; one with blue majolica pots on shelves and a blue ceiling, with a blue curtain of painted stucco at one end; a second room with cupboards of walnut wood, holding majolica pots, chiefly yellow in colour and with elaborately carved and gilded centre pieces in the middle of each wall; while the third hall has tall armchairs with green silk backs grouped round a table, as though indeed this was the consulting or committee room presiding over the Ospizio. When last seen this was among the most beautiful of old pharmacies, if only medicinal in interest and without the potions and preparations of the monks and nuns.

So much for Naples, which is only one of the Two Sicilies – and there is the other – if indeed there should not in fact be three of them, the third being Apulia, which is perfectly and absolutely distinct from the other two. Where the island of Sicily alone is concerned, being a lover of lost causes I found myself more interested in Messina, of which the past was nearly entirely obliterated by an earthquake in 1908, than in Palermo where the present is only too obvious in its poverty and hopelessness, the climate and even the painted carts notwithstanding. But in this city of Arabian-Norman antecedent, where alleviation is to be sought in the wall mosaics and Saracenic ceiling of the Cappella Palatina, or at the five red domes of the mosque-like San Giovanni degli Eremiti, there are also the little chapels or Oratorios of Serpotta. There are three of these in Palermo,‡ Giacomo Serpotta being one

---

★ Now attributed to another painter of the school, Giuseppe Bonito (1707–89), and described as *The Construction of the Temple*.

† And where, in a hall at the back, called *l'Udienza del Governo*, the ceiling was fresco'd by Solimena, but I was never successful in seeing this.

‡ Oratorios della Compagnia del Rosario, di Santa Zita, and di San Lorenzo. Serpotta can also be seen in the hospital chapel, in the Archbishop's palace; and outside Palermo, in Santa Chiara, and in the octagonal Badia Nuova at Alcamo, some fifty miles along the coast towards the west.

Opposite top: Engraving of the palace of Caserta, from Vanvitelli's book of engravings of the palace, with Vesuvius in the distance.
Opposite bottom: Terrace at Caserta above the cascade of Aeolus.

of those sculptors who lifted a minor art quite out of itself into an eminence of its own where it can exist apart from architecture, and indeed for no other reason. His facility is astonishing; flowers and fruits of stucco grow and burgeon from his hand, and there are full length female figures by him that are as tall and graceful as women's portraits by Thomas Gainsborough. The different Oratorios are difficult to tell apart in memory; that of the Rosario di San Domenico, with an altar piece by Van Dyck, being the most imposing of them. It has great framed medallions of stucco scenes by Serpotta and his pupils, and full-length statues, one or two of them of extreme beauty, underneath those. But the Oratorio di Santa Zita is more strange than beautiful. The little bas-reliefs below the windows have life-size figures perched on top of them as though sitting on a wall, while the huge *pièces montées* of naval scenes in stucco at the ends of the room, flanked by whole troops of cupids folding and pulling back a stucco curtain with the Madonna in transformation cloud-scene in the centre, have carried mere illusionism too far. The galleys with their long oars could as well be toy-ships, and the whole effect is as incongruous as the motor-car or model aeroplane upon a wedding-cake. One would like to have a count of the cupids in the little Oratorios of Palermo, a total which must run into some hundreds, but this is not said to detract from Serpotta who at his best made something unique of these little chapels.

The villas at Bagheria, outside Palermo, are now almost too dilapidated to repay the trouble of seeing them, especially to one who can recall them, and the Villa Palagonia in particular, when that appeared nearly pristine, if in battered, fairground condition. I can never forget the statues of a Chinaman and of the vegetable-pierrot on their pedestals beside the gate-pillars. In its state of ruin let us remember it for the ball-room with its ceiling of slabs of mica; for the coat-of-arms of Prince Palagonia which was a satyr looking in a mirror; and for the description by Goethe in his *Italian Journey*, of Prince Palagonia, 'a tall, thin old gentleman, dressed in the height of fashion, preceded by a lacquey with a silver salver', collecting ransom in the main street of Palermo for the slaves taken captive by the Barbary pirates.* It was this prince who crowded out his father's villa with eccentric statues.

And now for Messina. When I was spending the winter at Amalfi, trying to learn how to write, at about the time of these first impressions, an amateur watercolour painter, who had circled, I surmise, on the outer fringe of the notorieties of the eighteen-nineties, put in an appearance, and he could

---

* The architect of the Villa Palagonia was a priest, T. M. Napoli (1655–1725) author, also, of some of the open stairways in houses in Palermo. The Principe Palagonia, observed by Goethe, was the builder's son. Probably the family had two generations of 'eccentrics'; the problem might perhaps repay study. T. M. Napoli went twice to Vienna, but there is little sign of Viennese influence in the Villa Palagonia, or in the Villa Valguarnera which is also by him.

remember Messina before it was destroyed. That can have been no more than some fifteen years before this, but seemed, I recall, like talking to someone who remembered the Indian Mutiny or Crimean War. In any event he could describe nothing of interest; only 'the masses of masonry', this when the churches and palaces were still standing, and there was the famous view over the Straits from the terrace above the town. I have never met anyone else who remembered Messina, and there is a paucity of drawings or information about it. Perhaps the best, if critical account of its lost buildings is Augustus Hare's reference to 'the succession of staircases leading to the fantastic conventual church of San Gregorio . . . from ridiculous designs by Andrea Calamech'; in detail, a tower like a spiral lighthouse and an interior on the plan of a Greek cross, all worked in *pietre dure* or inlaid marble. This same Andrea Calamech being sculptor of the still surviving bronze statue of Don John of Austria (1572); and what a personage of romance to discover even in counterfeit, whether with face or back turned to the blue Strait and the orange groves, the palms and pomegranates of Calabria as that comes down to the sea! So Messina, or nearly all of it is gone, taking with it the works of its local school of painting, as named in a book published in the city in 1821, where we read that the gallery in the palace of Prince Brunaccini had paintings by Monosilio, Comandé, Rodriguez, Onofrio Gabriello, Fulco, Maroli, Suppa, Scilla, the two Catalanis, Giannotto, Menniti, Filocami, Tuccari, the two Cardillos, Tancredi, Quagliata, Bova, Paladino, Polidoro, and Barbalungo. The same author details their paintings in the different churches. They may on the other hand have been no more interesting than the local painters of Palermo. But, now, in any case it is too late to know.

It must have been in the winter of 1922–3 that I went to Noto, drawn there by the statement I had read somewhere that it had been rebuilt after an earthquake in 1693. Its beautiful buildings were even more of a revelation than those of Lecce, and I really believe that my brother and myself were the first persons of any nationality to take notice of them since they were built. Perhaps there was some premonition of what to expect of Sicily at its best in the little Oratorios of Palermo with their stucco sculptures by Serpotta, or in the graceful Rococo façade of the Duomo in the square at Syracuse. Even perhaps in the fanciful staircase of the Palazzo Biscari at Catania. Attempts to make of Catania, at the hands of its architect Vaccarini, 'one of the most fascinating eighteenth-century cities in Europe', must fail because of the ugliness of the building material which was dark volcanic tufa from Mount Etna, and can only have been remarked by someone who has not seen Noto, still less Modica and Ragusa.

But Noto, a provincial town about twenty miles from Syracuse, is a city of buildings that compete in the urban graces with Bath, or Potsdam, or with the Place Stanislas at Nancy, without the upper middle class or aldermanic solidity

of the one, the military accents of the second, or the Louis ... Louis ...
'Quatorze the Fifteenth' chicness and vapidity of the last named, to rate that at
its lowest denomination, apt and beautiful though the wrought-iron gates and
balconies of Lamour may be.

But the drawback or defect of Noto is that it is all façade. Those palaces
with superb and fanciful balconies, all with five brackets or supports to them,
and each of these a galloping, winged horse in packs of five, or, at another
palace, as many Chinamen, pierrots, or sea-monsters, are palaces with
nothing worth looking at inside them. Homes of the local noblesse, some
few of whom of Norman-Aragonese descent are given in the *Almanach de
Gotha* as resident in Noto; of as dull lives as their confrères of Catania whom
we met in the hotel at Syracuse, who had never been up the coast as far as
Taormina, fifty miles away. It was the carriages of these families, each with a
coachman sitting on the box, that were drawn up in a line outside one of the
palaces at ten o'clock in the morning the day we got to Noto. It was a
fashionable wedding, and at six in the evening the carriages were still there.
Noto seemed lost like a fly in amber in its own past. Nothing seemed to have
happened there for a hundred years. Perhaps the giving of the title of Count
of Noto to one of the younger Bourbon princes had been the last event in its
history,★ and how much or how little effect can that have had upon the
inhabitants! And so the vacuum continued for all of a hundred years until the
ultra-sophisticated architecture of this Sicilian country town was used in the
film *Divorce – Italian Style* as background for dull lives of comparable kind
and the fine cynicism of Marcello Mastroianni's acting.

A 'perambulation' with Dr Pevsner through the streets of Noto, a town
which even now with the post-war swarming of the population has fewer
than thirty thousand inhabitants, would be productive of more surprises than
his promenades through Bath or Cheltenham. The approach to it through
the surrounding orange-groves – they are the best oranges in Sicily – is of
hallucinatory nature for you find yourself in a long street or promenade that
opens into no fewer than three fine squares, with Baroque stairways of bold
design connecting with the terraces on which the city stands. You are always,
therefore, looking up a flight of steps at a façade, or with one of the balconies
of Noto at a slant above you. After what we are expecting, and have been led
to believe will be here, the Cathedral up two flights of steps by a neo-
classicist architect of the eponymous name Sinatra, may be a little disappointing in its rigid correctness and deliberate shunning of sentiment and feeling.†
But, nearby, are the balconies with the five winged horses, with the China-

---

★ Other sons of Francis I (1777–1830) and of Ferdinand II, 'King Bomba' (1810–59), were Counts of
Caserta, Trani, Girgenti, Bari, Capua, Syracuse, Aquila and Trapani.

† Paolo Labisi and Rosario Gagliardi were other architects but, as yet, little is known about them and
they have not been studied.

men and the mermen, if that is what they are, for they resemble also the 'wild men' of the middle ages who were intended for satyrs. And if our perambulation now takes us up the steps and into the upper town we will see façades in plenty and more balconies. The whole effect is of unrivalled scenic splendour and imagination, as much perhaps as any town in Europe. What manner of persons can they have been who lived here? It is inconceivable that there were not brilliant conversationalists in Noto. It is not possible that it was as dull then as it is today. We find ourselves looking, half-unconsciously, for posters of the opera season, for a splendid looking café, or a restaurant. And there are none. They cannot have finished building the town just in order to have no more to do and shut themselves away. And for once it is not all churches. As well as palaces, there should be clubs as splendid as in Pall Mall or St James's Street, fine shops, even casinos with as much of gilding, of female statuary, and chandeliers as at Monte Carlo or Baden-Baden. But there is nothing. Only the architecture and that is all. And the perambulation continues and ends with that hallucinatory feeling.

At the time of writing *Southern Baroque Art* I had not been to Modica and Ragusa, a pair of towns further inland, cities of larger and richer population than Noto and where the buildings were proportionately bigger, and the churches, if anything, more splendid still. So I only mentioned them in a footnote to that book and visited them two years *after* the book was published, and in curious if congenial circumstances in January or February 1926, a month or two after I was married. My wife and I went there from Syracuse where we had been staying with my parents; and the expedition was organised by my father who 'mounted it', to use the military expression, in his own inimitable fashion. We were to go one way by road and return by rail in order to confuse the brigands who were an obsession with him, and one which added greatly to his enjoyment of such a jaunt, though recent acts of the Mafia down to the present time, whether on their home ground, or in export to New York, to Chicago, and even to Australia, do not allow any underestimate of his apprehensions. And so we set off in a car with my father and with Henry Moat, who had been by then for nearly forty years his manservant and bodyguard; and I recall after some half-hour on the road the expression of horror on my father's face when he discovered that my wife, a girl of twenty, had brought some jewellery with her, an act of folly that as good as sealed our fate. As a result, on reaching Noto which was on our way, we were allowed no more than a couple of minutes in any of the churches, leaving Henry outside to watch over the car and keep an eye on the driver, and emerging if possible by another door from that by which we entered in order to take any waiting bystanders by surprise and note if anything untoward was happening. Noto, we saw, therefore, under somewhat stringent circumstances, having only been permitted a quick drive round its streets with the injunction to do nothing whatever to attract attention to ourselves.

On arrival at Ragusa we went straight to the hotel, which did in fact have for proprietor a 'baron' reputed to be the local brigand-chief and to hold high rank in the hierarchy of the Mafia. We no more than caught sight of him, a fat man in a brown suit, chewing, I noticed, a handful of aspirin at a time. But this seemed to be the habit of all the better dressed persons in Modica and Ragusa; and I have since thought it may have been something more potent than simple aspirin. Or were they quinine tablets taken as an antidote against malaria? During one of our days in Modica and Ragusa, a trembling, rather horrible elderly man with a high squeaking voice got into the cab in which we were driving – this, too, not the car, in order to distract attention – with the offer of taking us to see a collection of Greek coins; and it was only when we had got rid of him that we learned he was a survivor of the massacre of the Italian army by the Abyssinians at Adowa in 1896.

Dinner was farcical indeed. It was Lent and we had fish ('un pesce di famiglia' as the Italians call it) drinking, meantime, the boiled water my father had brought with him in a flask from Syracuse; and all the time we could see Henry behind a curtain dining by himself and drinking a fiasco of red wine. As soon as my father had gone to bed, early as usual, we sat talking with Henry and drinking another bottle till it was time to go upstairs. The window of our bedroom gave directly onto a church, near the belfry, which seemed of no particular moment for almost immediately there were voices and a loud disturbance in the passage, and looking through the bedroom door we saw Henry in blue and white striped pyjamas at the head of the stair using his immense strength in wrestling with and hurling down a party of four or five late revellers, drunks, bona fide travellers, partisans of the 'baron', or whatnot, we were never able to discover, but Henry certainly had routed them, and my father could feel justified in his precautions. Sleep for the rest of the night was difficult in case there was a further alarm, and it was no longer even a surprise when dawn came, and soon afterwards the bell for early Mass came swinging in and out of our bedroom through that glass-less window.

Two incidents, much in keeping with the strange character of this pair of towns, unfolded themselves upon the following morning. It was Lent, as I say, and the high altar in the Duomo of Ragusa Superiore at the head of its processional, stone flight of stairs was veiled with huge canvas hangings, some forty or fifty feet tall, painted with architectural ruin scenes in the Roman *veduta* style of G. P. Pannini (1692–1765), which paintings, we were told, were the work of a pair of brothers, local painters, working as lately as the eighteen-sixties. There were these painted hangings in several of the churches in both Modica and Ragusa. The other curious happening was when we were looking at an altar painting in another of the huge churches★ – a painting which showed a child ill in bed and an angel coming down and touching her to heal her with a golden spear, a painting in the direct tradition of Bernini's *Ecstasy of St Theresa*, but painted as by the hand of a follower of G. B. Tiepolo – when the sacristan advanced on us to enquire whether we would care to be taken to see the child, now an old woman and still living in the town. So this painting which had the air of a picture painted not later than, say, 1770, must have dated from not earlier than 1840. What a pity we never went to call upon that survivor of a miracle!

Ragusa and Modica are not for palace architecture, but it would be difficult to exaggerate the splendour of their churches, which we can now examine in some detail as a result of the series of photographs taken in the summer of 1965 by Timothy Benton, and I think it can be said of them that they fulfil the expectation held of them more than forty years ago.† Modica is the first of the two towns you arrive at coming from Syracuse, via Noto. What can be the explanation of its huge churches and of their sophistications? Here indeed it would seem that the architect or architects must have had outside experience from further away than Rome or Naples. And from whatever direction, which is perhaps no more than natural, ignoring Noto which is the city nearest to them. Modica is not a town of promenades and palaces. It is a climbing town of churches on terraces at the top of staircases. It has not the feeling of absent clubs, casinos, theatres, restaurants, that is so strongly in the air at Noto. There are old Catalan-Gothic doorways in both towns, and the steep streets are still of mediaeval appearance. But surprises are coming; and the great church of Modica seen from afar as we approach the town, now appears in majesty above its stair, with its three-storeyed frontispiece that – more imposing than any façade in Austria, more of an architectural invention than the double towered front of Melk on its cliff above the Danube – does for all its being Sicilian, and in remote Sicily at that, suggest Austrian influence and that of Lukas von Hildebrandt in particular. It is of Hildebrandt, or of Kilian Ignaz Dientzenhofer, architect of St Nikolaus-Kleinseite in Prague, that one is reminded. The belfries to some of the Modican and Ragusan church towers are surely of this parentage and it is difficult to compare them with anything that is Italian.

The three-storeyed frontispiece in question rises from a pair of wings of

---

★ There are, as I remember, three churches – San Giorgio Grande, San Giovanni, and San Pietro – in Modica; Ragusa Superiore has the Duomo of San Giovanni on a terrace above the town; and Ragusa Inferiore the church of San Giorgio, five of them in all, and all, I believe I am correct in saying, at the top of stone staircases.

† There is mention of the churches in a book on Sicily, by Douglas Sladen, 1905, but no other notice that I know of; and as late as the 1930 edition of Baedeker's *Southern Italy* there is no hint that these towns contain anything of architectural interest. Nor is attention drawn to them in the *Guide Michelin, Italia*, 1963.

which the classical elegance is best appreciated if you can catch sight of one of them coming down to it from a side street, when you see the two side doors between their columns, the inner door and the window over it which is oblong, being slightly larger than the outer door with circular windows above it, all of which rises like a stone screen next to a house with scenic balconies giving upon the flights of steps. Between these screens or wings rises the ovoid tower faced with double columns on all three floors, to end in fluttering cornices and broken pediments below the stone cupola; the whole, I venture to suggest, like a rendering of Hildebrandt or Dientzenhofer with the actor's sense of the native Sicilians superadded. Another Modican church is of more rounded central body, of which the sense almost loses itself in the array of jutting and self-asserting cornices. It is of a complexity, all in golden stone, not far removed from Garnier's Opéra in Paris. Perhaps only the sunlight saves it from this comparison; but, all in all, what with the huge stone vases that share the ornament this is a strange structure for a small Sicilian town.

Ragusa, only five or six miles away, consists really of three distinct and separate towns with deep ravines between them, Ibla and Vittoria, with Ragusa in the middle. The churches here, probably blackened by now from the oil-wells, are surely by the same architect. They, too, have the façades or frontispieces in three storeys. Even one of the lesser of them, not big and large enough to afford wings, rises with but little in the way of sculpture, with slightly convex or bombé front and a light, open screen for its third storey, and presides over its little piazza with elegance and dignity. The Ibla quarter has its church of San Giorgio, and Ragusa proper its Chiesa Madre on a great terrace. San Giorgio with its high dome behind it, triple-tiered again as to its façade, and with triple columns to each side of its main body, is in its way a stupendous creation for so small a city on the southern corner of Sicily, and facing Africa. How many domed churches are there in London? St Paul's Cathedral and Brompton Oratory is the answer.

Here in Ragusa the dome of San Giorgio is manipulated with expert hand, but it is little in comparison to the invention lavished on the façade which is beautiful indeed by any standard, to be admired from below at the foot of the steps between the palm trees, where it upholds its golden front of fine columns and the stone flourishes at its sides that make a pedestal for statues, and above that up to the smaller, but similar whorls or flourishes below the cupola which surely yields a clue to origins. We may think that San Giorgio is as fine a piece of urban architecture as any Baroque church in Prague, which is a city of fine churches. The explanation, not yet forthcoming, may be no more of a mystery than the spires and towers and clerestories of villages in East Anglia or Somerset, but it is one of the latest in history of such architectural fevers, and it is of interest if only for the reason that these may

The Other
Sicilies

Detail of
fountain in
the courtyard
of the
Seminario,
Lecce.

Opposite: Well-head in the courtyard of SS. Nicola e Cataldo, Lecce.
Right: Balcony supported by lions at Noto, Sicily.
Below right: Detail of the façade of Santa Chiara, Lecce.

Above: 'The fantastic conventual church of San Gregorio . . . from ridiculous designs by Andrea Calamech' at Messina; destroyed in the earthquake of 1908. *Opposite:* Church of San Giorgio, Modica.

Opposite: San Giorgio at Ragusa. *Right:* Detail of columns on the façade of San Giorgio, Ragusa.

FORTITVDO

not come again. An earthquake of our day with aid from every form of international relief has never led to such rebuilding.

As should already have been established, there is great variety of style in Sicilian seventeenth and eighteenth-century architecture. Palermo, Catania, Messina, were all centres of activity; the latter city so irretrievably damaged by the earthquake of 1908 that it is difficult to form a coherent opinion of its local style. There can be curious encounters in this architecture. The grotesque masks that maladorn a building at Acireale near Catania within sound of Etna, have near resemblance to the keystone masks on the Assize Court at Northampton, which has been ascribed to Talman. Other Sicilian cities, Agrigento (Girgenti), Trapani, have their architecture of this time, which does not amount to much. The great interest is in Modica and Ragusa, and in Noto. The latter stands by itself, as though its own rebuilding after the earthquake in 1693 took up all its energy leaving none to spare. But from Ragusa and Modica it flowed over to the neighbouring towns. Caltagirone, a provincial capital also rebuilt after earthquake, with at least four churches of the time, and another town, Piazza Armerina, are far away enough to qualify for a local sub-style of their own. Other small towns in that vicinity, like Buscemi, must doubtless have fine buildings, but particular attention should be drawn to Grammichele, post-earthquake built and laid out with radiating streets on the pattern of a spider's web, but a spider's web constructed into a hexagonal design. The mere ground plan of Grammichele is an intriguing delight to look at. One of its churches, of date 1770 put obligingly beneath its cornice, has a trophy over that of the crossed keys flanked by cornucopias that are spilling out what can be nothing other than ripe oranges. Or are they lemons? It matters little in this Arcadian setting with poverty and misery on every doorstep.

But the towns under influence from Modica and Ragusa are Vittoria and Comiso. One of the only authors even to mention them writes that 'few architectural visions could be more delightful than the main square of Vittoria, or the towers and domes of Comiso.'* Both towns are within twenty or thirty miles of Ragusa. It is curious indeed that they should have remained unobserved so long. No one now ever draws or sketches buildings. The camera is so much quicker; and it is true that these southern towns are peculiarly suited to photography. They may be indeed among the most photogenic of all buildings. But the churches only of the mother towns Modica and Ragusa form a subject in themselves; scenographically, no less so, it could be said, than Whistler's Venice; an etcher who in any case sought out his own effects, and by and large left the architecture alone. It could be said with safety that anyone who made a collection of studied drawings of these Sicilian buildings, and put them on exhibition without saying what or where

* *The Land of Italy*, by Jasper More, London, 1949, pp. 249–50.

Opposite: *Fortitude*, stucco by Serpotta in the Oratorio del Rosario, Palermo.

they were, would be the cause of a minor sensation. It would be impossible on such evidence to credit the churches and palaces of Noto – perhaps the tell-tale balconies excepted – or the majestic, terraced basilicas of Ragusa and Modica to remote towns in Sicily. Still less, because unknown even by name, Grammichele of the spider-web plan, or Vittoria and Comiso. But such towns have doubled, or even trebled their inhabitants in the ominous swarming of the population. May this not be as much of a danger to their future as another earthquake!

3

The Art of Façade

In order to show that the Baroque and Rococo are recurring phases in aesthetics, that they have been before and one day, when the tumult and conflict of styles dies down, are bound to come again, it is only necessary to look at one or two of the wall-paintings from Pompeii now in the Museum of Naples. There is more than one room of these faded paintings; some, theatrical in effect and tendency as by a precursor of the Bibiena family of scene-painters, if a little sated and wearying of the Neronian splendour; others, freer in handling as though from the brush of a spiritual ancestor of Francesco Guardi. They include paintings of villas with porticos on two floors opening to the Parthenopaean shore and siren bay; an architectural frontispiece like a theatre curtain or drop scene but only reaching to half the height of the proscenium arch, and over the top of that we see an endless perspective of column and cornice receding backstage into the distance; and one wall-painting in particular that comes from a villa at Stabiae on the Bay of Naples and shows a harbour scene that in its rapid and sketchy realism is rather more than astonishing.

The entrance to the harbour lies between an arch of rock on which beetle or ant-like fishermen mysteriously disport themselves, and a double row of open porticos like Customs sheds leading to a pier which stands out in the middle foreground of water. Round the corner of this is the inner harbour pool where boats with furled sails are lying that could be the *trabaccoli* of Venice, coastal trading vessels sailing to Trieste and Istria, or *topi* and *bragozzi* of Chioggia, the fishing town at the far end of the lagoon, this, as in a Venetian view by Guardi, seventeen centuries earlier in time and at the foot of four enormous statue-bearing columns that would dwarf the pair of granite columns of the Piazzetta, with the pillared buildings of the city crowding the distance in every direction behind them. It is an extraordinary evocation of a harbour in the heyday of the Roman Caesars, but empty of human forms except for the statues on their columns and those few beetle or frog-like creatures of uncertain import. Something equivocal in their attitudes, and the scrawling of signatures all over the plaster since this wall-painting was

45

recovered from the past, give a nightmare, cloacal quality to this harbour scene as though it consisted of graffiti from the latrines of some Plutonian underworld or Hades.

But Pompeii was destroyed by earthquake and eruption in AD 79, and for a full picture of the Baroque and Rococo of the ancient world we have to think less of Rome itself than of Greco-Oriental towns like Alexandria and Ephesus or Antioch, with classical buildings more than a thousand years later than the Parthenon, when architecture had gone through phases which are paralelled in Vanbrugh, in Bernini, and in Borromini. Antioch, to take but one of these, had streets of columns with double colonnades, one of them four miles long and crossing the city from end to end like the Diagonal of Barcelona; Diocletian built a huge palace on an island in the Orontes in the middle of the city, which island later given over entirely to theatres and pleasure haunts was joined to the town by no fewer than five bridges; and the Chinese had trading relations with Antioch, which they thought to be the capital of the Roman world. All this before Constantine founded the second or new Rome on the shores of Europe and of Asia.

There were these colonnaded streets throughout the Oriental provinces of the Roman world. It has been said that T.E.Lawrence 'had personally discovered traces of over a hundred and twenty colonnaded towns within a twenty-mile radius of Aleppo.'* There is a colonnaded street running straight through Palmyra for some two-thirds of a mile, with a hundred and fifty, or nearly half of its columns, each fifty feet high, still standing, a corbel or bracket projecting a little more than half-way up each one of them to support a statue. Half-way down this street is a quadruple arch or tetrapylon of ingenious design for it conceals a shifting or changing of the axis in the street to either side, an architectural deceit that shows the working of a masterhand.

At Jerash, too, there is a colonnade or street of columns half a mile long with a triple gate at its main crossing; but the beauty of Jerash is its elliptical or horseshoe-shaped Ionic forum with the pillared street leading out from the back of it like, as I have written elsewhere, 'the long handle of a spoon'; adding that 'it is among the most graceful of all classical remains', and that 'our parallel age of architecture from Mansart and Wren down to Wood of Bath and Gabriel can offer nothing better, not the Peyrou of Montpellier, nor the ovoid colonnade leading from the Pepinière at Nancy'. This was not Roman, but Greek classical architecture in its decadence, and it would have, thereby, a lighter hand and be more imaginative than the Roman. It was Greek, and of Asiatic or Ionian Greece at that, portending the genius of the race that built the Temple of Poseidon on Cape Sounion, further tempered and softened by the Lydian air, arriving at something which is very different from the Roman of the triumphal arch, the circus and the military road. A

* *From an Antique Land*, by Sir Julian Huxley, London, 1954, p. 146.

46

cosmopolitan world where, 'in considering the vast expanse of Roman influence, amidst the woods and fields of Gloucestershire, Herefordshire or Essex, can be dug up Italic wares identical in kind and origin with those which have been found six thousand miles away on the Coromandel coast.'★ A world where by now even the Caesars were often not of Roman origin; where Septimius Severus, of African descent, who was born at Leptis and called in the foremost architects of the day to adorn his birthplace, who had mulatto features 'and spoke Latin with an African accent', spent the last three years of his life in Britain and died at York. The fearful Caracalla was his son, and the effeminate and insupportable Heliogabalus his grandson; both of whom were builders of Baalbek where, the gigantic Temple of Bacchus apart, which spiritually, or just for the lack of that, it is not altogether unfair to compare to Selfridge's in ruins, there is the Temple of Venus. This is a circular building or *cella*, not much bigger than a municipal bandstand, with a surround of unfluted Corinthian columns and a concave, not convex, external frieze and entablature running in deep loops or segments, allowing for five semi-circular bays; in fact a circle indented on the outside into a decagon in ground plan, which with its cupola roof, now fallen, its shell niches and swagged or garlanded pilasters is less suited, I have suggested, for the purposes of a temple than to be the supper room for Louis XV and Mme du Barry in her pavilion at Louveciennes. This circular shrine or Temple of Venus, so called, appears again – or is it mere coincidence? – as the lantern of Borromini's Roman Church of Sant' Ivo alla Sapienza where the architect has superimposed upon it a spiral tower that one writer compares to 'the horn of a Sicilian goat'† though it might be truer to describe it as hybrid of a beehive and a lighthouse, there being some authority for at least the first half of this parentage when it is known that Borromini built the interior of Sant' Ivo in the shape of a bee with folded wings in honour of the Barberini Pope Urban VIII, whose family device or crest was a bee.

It could even be argued that Borromini in his architectural probings after originality was possessed of some form of extrasensory perception, in this instance with the façade of San Carlo alle Quattro Fontane, or San Carlino, where the little tambour-shaped pavilion over the door nearly reproduces that on the façade of the Khazné Faraóun at Petra. This is the temple which confronts one with such dramatic and extraordinary effect when riding down the long rocky defile at Petra, coming out from the dark shadow into the glare of sun. But San Carlino dates from 1634 and Petra of the Nabataean Kings was only rediscovered by Burckhardt in 1811; the coincidence being thus a phantom by circumstance, or if we prefer it, by historical recurrence. But a façade it is, that of the Khazné Faraóun, and in most decided manner;

★ *Roman Art and Architecture*, by Sir Mortimer Wheeler, London, 1964, p. 222.
† *Baroque in Italy*, by James Lees-Milne, London, 1959, p. 155.

as much so as with any of the churches of Bernini's Rome, and of their date, though some fifteen centuries earlier in time; of their date, and that of the churches in the Strand, as though in proof of our opening sentence that the Baroque and Rococo are recurring phases that have been before and are sure to come again.

And we take leave of the Classical world of the ancients beneath the great panels of mosaic in the Mosque of the Ommayads at Damascus, work of Greek craftsmen at the beginning of the eighth century working to the Caliph El Wêlid's orders, and in consequence without human figures. Instead, the mosaics are an architectural fantasy of bridges and kiosques and pavilions, with villages or individual houses built on rocks or crags, house piled on house as in the valleys of Lebanon, all in an umbrageous valley of plane trees and date palms which may portray the surrounding plain or Ghûta of Damascus. A river flows all through the great panel of mosaic, which is more than a hundred feet long, and a certain bridge in the mosaic has been taken for that over the river Barada, meaning 'cold', the Abana of the Old Testament, and the 'golden stream' or Chrysorrhoas of the Greeks, a bridge with shops and houses on it like old London Bridge, or the Ponte Vecchio at Florence.

According to the Arab geographer Muqaddasi, who wrote at the end of the tenth century, the mosaics were the gift of the Byzantine Emperor and every city of the known world was figured on the walls. If this is so, they have been reduced to the most simple expression of their forms, so that a town consists of no more than its most conspicuous or famous building.

If it is indeed Damascus in the mosaic, then it is probable that we may find a reminiscence, if no more than that, of other wonders of the Classical past that survived into the Dark Ages. We would look for something of Aleppo, of Alexandria, or of Antioch, which was rebuilt by Justinian after the catastrophe of an earthquake in which half-a-million persons perished. But, as well, there may be representations of more distant places. Other towns and buildings might be recognised, all standing on the banks of the stream which flows like the river of paradise through the scene. Córdoba, under the same Ommayad dynasty as Damascus, may be depicted, at a time when the Arab conquerors, Arabs and not Moors, still spoke the pure Yemeni of Arabia. More likely it is but a fanciful view of the Classical world at the end of its immense architectural trajectory, which had lasted by then for more than twelve hundred years since the age of Pericles, had in fact already been overcome by the Oriental and was no longer Roman or even Greek but Byzantine, with Armenian and even Persian influence brought to bear upon it.*

* A longer account of the great mosaic in the Mosque at Damascus is attempted in my *The Hunters and the Hunted*, 1947, pp. 11–16.

Most intriguing are the pair of octagonal pavilions with conical roofs, apparently gleaming with gold and immensely high. Are they, then, authentic buildings in the mosaic; perhaps famed twin pavilions of the Dark Ages, known to all travellers, and recognised? The twin pavilions are a pair of *tholoi*. They are circular temples of the Greeks come down after many changes to their present and last form. The temple of the Sibyl at Tivoli with its eighteen Corinthian columns in an open colonnade is a *tholos*, though but a Roman copy of a Greek original, for the circular temple was one of the most beautiful inventions of Hellenic architecture. There were two *tholoi* in particular. One was at Delphi, in the valley nearly below the Castalian fountain; and the other, much admired by Pausanias, was at Epidaurus. Are the twin buildings real and substantial? Or are we to see in them kiosques and pavilions like those of the Ptolemies, made of wood and painted canvas and boughs and fronds of trees for their entertainments at court, as described by Callisthenes? It is just such buildings that appear in the wall-paintings of Pompeii and Boscoreale and that were discussed a page or two back in the opening paragraph. There were among those, we said, paintings that nearly resemble theatre curtains and theatre scenery; fanciful buildings that are not real indeed but façade, a word which the dictionary defines as the front of a building, not the interior, giving us thereby the cue or password for what is to follow.

But it has its equivalent in other architectures; in the *gopurams* or gate-towers of the Hindu and Dravidian temples. In the four giant *gopurams* of Madurai, a hundred and fifty feet high, and its seven lesser ones, eleven in all, as crowded with gods and animalistic deities as the benches at bull fight or football match above the temple courts and the bathing-tank or 'Pool of the Golden Lilies', so called;* or in any of a dozen other temples in Southern India. And not only in the shrines of the Hindus, for it has another parallel in the *ivans* or porches of the mosques in Iran. The *ivans* give the peculiar character to the Persian mosques. I have described them as like so many giant scaffolds or hoardings or stage sets. Or as when a child playing at card houses has to put up a bigger building of cards in the middle of each side of the house in order to prevent it falling down. In accordance with which there is an *ivan* always in the middle of the wall of a court, never in the corner, or at one side. And indeed, once evolved, this curious invention had become a kind of clothesline or towel-horse on which the Persians hung their tile-panels. They were display screens with no other purpose. At the Mosque and Shrine of the Imam Reza in the holy city of Meshed there are three tiled courts and should

---

* The temple of Sriringam, not far from Madurai, has twenty-five *gopurams* in descending order of magnitude from the outside inwards. The outermost, which was never finished, would have been three hundred feet high. cf. *Splendours of the East*, edited by Sir Mortimer Wheeler, London, 1965, p. 126.

be twelve of these porches or *ivans*, but I seem to remember counting fourteen or sixteen. Looking down from the minaret there seemed to be one of the *ivans* in every direction you looked, like some part of a huge film-set, particularly when they have no back. But some are, so to speak, double *ivans* with two faces of tilework, in and out.

We see from this that the art of façade is not confined entirely to the Mediterranean region but that it has its counterpart, or something not far removed from that, in other lands. And certainly it was not a phase of either Baroque or Rococo that the Iranians were undergoing. Much to the contrary, the twelve or fourteen or more unnecessary porches or *ivans* at the Mosque and Shrine of Meshed were the work of Gauhar Shad Begum, wife of Shah Rokh, and daughter-in-law of Tamerlane, one of the few women other than Fatima in Moslem history. Together with their sister shrines in Samarcand, the work of Tamerlane himself, they are the finest buildings of the Moslem world and certainly the hint of decadence does not apply to them.*

All in all there could be no more fitting overture to a book on the Baroque and Rococo than a collection of façades, and it is both curious and significant that it has not been attempted before. For it is among the basic and prime expressions of the age, and in relation to that to be compared to the gestures Latins make when talking, with their hands. A form of eloquence in architecture and compound of both explanation and evasion. An attempt to make and leave a good impression, as of putting on the best suit of clothes for the first meeting, with the working clothes not in evidence and hidden away. An extension even of one of the only lessons we learn at school which is never to leave the room first because one will be discussed as soon as one's back is turned. Always, therefore, to face the conversation and keep it going. A readiness to be interrogated at any hour of the day or night and in all weathers; in the glare of mid-day, by moonlight, and even to attract a glance in pouring rain. Of predilection for the warm south if only in a theatrical sense for its better lighting but, also, for congenital reasons in view of language and place of origin. But, also, a certain frugality despite richness of apparel, as of an inborn and underlying necessity for economy. An outward extravagance which is all it can afford beside eloquence of gesture. But of its very nature a contribution towards gaiety and politeness of manner. A determination to be both contemporary and civilised and to be in harmony; and to surprise when in a remote place by its centrifugal aplomb or self-possession and its urbanity.

Thus the art of façade, a play of eloquence among the Latins, and the exercise of some of their best minds. Embarked upon, not in the mood of a

* A fuller account of the mosques of Isfahan and Meshed is given in my *Arabesque and Honeycomb*, 1957, from which a few sentences are quoted here.

Opposite: El Obradoiro, the west façade of the Cathedral of Santiago de Compostela.

huckster crying his wares, but persuasive in tone and while keeping its old *clientèle* inviting the passer-by as well. That it is a theatrical art in spirit and essence should not detract from its appeal unless we are to deny all forms of rhetorical entertainment. With but a little tasting of its sweets which are the sparkling wine of architecture one comes to associate it with the air and climate of the Mediterranean, being principally the invention of Bernini's Rome. An indigenous development more than a discovery, and in the case of its chief practitioners their inner self or second nature. That it has nothing behind it is the complaint of those who are unused to it, or are temperamentally untuned to its musical progressions. Often and again in some town in Italy we are confronted with the façade of a church which is a mere frontispiece; and walking but a pace or two to the rear of it we can see it is but stone-thick, and the top part of its upper storey but the outer dressing for something which is not there at all; all for effect and for no other purpose.

It should perhaps be conceded that the ideal city of a Baroque architect would be one in which façades or fronts of churches, palaces and monasteries, rise in every direction and statues crowd the skyline, an ideal which only approaches realisation in Prague and in Santiago de Compostela. But Prague, however admirable the disposition of its buildings upon hills at different levels, and with an added advantage of the Moldau flowing through it with its excuse for bridges, is noted more for its Baroque domes and towers; while Santiago, beautiful indeed, 'but with the rainiest climate in all Spain', is lacking in one of the prerequisites of façade viewing. In Rome which is the city where the greatest number of façades or architectural frontispieces, as we now understand them, present themselves for inspection, the ancient monuments compete with the Baroque and Rococo for attention; while in Venice, however splendid the theme of buildings rising from the water, and however marvellous of accomplishment with Palladio's San Giorgio Maggiore at its mooring-post of white stone, or Longhena's Santa Maria della Salute or his Cà Rezzonico, there is nothing higher to rise from than the water level, and this is the only thing to detract from the most beautiful city in the world.

But in Rome, city of façades, where the rival architects of the *Seicento* shuffled their cards and performed their card tricks in endless ingenuity in use of the same constituents, there are architectural feats that make an unforgettable impression. Among the fifty to sixty such frontispieces to Roman churches, for all told they must amount to about that number, Bernini's façade to Sant' Andrea al Quirinale is a masterpiece, and that by the greatest of the Roman masters who builds here in utmost force, but simplicity, of the native travertine, in about the years (1658–70) when he was building the Doric colonnades to St Peter's, when his exuberant spirits had settled into deeper and more serious conviction, with the result that those colonnades of plain Doric columns are sculptures in the travertine almost more than

51

Opposite: Shrimp-coloured façade of the
Santuario de Ocotlán, near Tlaxacala, Mexico.

architecture. Sant' Andrea is a small oval or elliptical building, not much bigger than a chapel, opposite the Quirinal gardens, with marbles of great beauty and rarity in its interior, the spoils of the ancient world, and with this marvellous exterior which again is less architecture than sculpture.

It is framed by tall Corinthian pilasters; and the hemicycle of stone steps leading to the door is like rings of water that seem to enlarge themselves while we look at them, as though going back in obeisance before the portico, which is semi-circular, and has a pair of Ionic columns, over which the Pamphilj coat-of-arms is held up in perpetual exhibition or demonstration. But in fact this portico with the semi-circular arch above and behind it is like a mouth, like the orifice or opening of some insectivorous flower, of implication that, once inside, you will stay there and not get out again; the unconscious expression, it may be, of Bernini's own increasing involvement with religious feelings as he grew older and knew he was caught himself, as indeed it would be his hope and wish to be. The paradisal splendour of the marbles within, and the deceptively austere way of entrance into this Elysium all go to affirm this meaning. It was, too, the son tells us in his memoir, Bernini's favourite among his own buildings, to which he often came alone in contentment, never satisfied with his other works.

A façade, if true to its principles, has in most cases to be studied in itself and without regard to its neighbour buildings. Many good examples are to be found in the crowded Roman streets where, while providing a focus of stillness, they add further animation to the scene. One of them, whose expressed purpose is but to interest and please, is Martino Longhi's façade to SS. Vincenzo ed Anastasio, in the piazza of the Fontana di Trevi, a church front that many tens of thousands of persons must have looked at even if they did not particularly notice it since that most sensational of Roman fountains was finished around 1760. To be noted, first of all, how much the façade gains from having been left at an angle and not set four-square to the fountain and to the public looking and listening to the waters. It is raised up on a platform of seven steps shaped like the three near angles of an octagonal stage; a frontispiece of two storeys, the main feature in both being a trio of free-standing columns to each side of its doorway, which triad of columns are repeated again above this, to each side of the window of the upper storey. Here, the triple cornices and even the columns jut forward in front of one another to frame in the *stemma* or coat-of-arms which is like a glorious hat-badge set in place over the window, held up by winged angels, and complete with cardinal's hat, its tassels, and a pair of cupids whose long trumpets cone up above the pediment and pierce the skyline. Making in all twelve columns in two triads, and again two triads; which array of columns reminds one writer of 'a range of powerful organ pipes'; while another, with more imagination, and perhaps more in the spirit of Baroque Rome, sees their smooth white shapes as 'a row of Caravaggesque nudes',★ a project never attempted by Caravaggio, but which would have moved him a place nearer to El Greco. Though after all they are but columns; and their very pallor against the dark surface of wall invites the traveller in for a rest from sightseeing, from the noise of the traffic, and the confusion and indigestion of the Roman ruins.

Another example of the façade is that of Santa Maria della Pace by the painter-architect Pietro da Cortona, whose genius is only overshadowed by Bernini, and by the fact that Cortona did not spend all his working life in Rome, but worked as well for the Medici Grand Dukes in Florence. The church has a portico in the form of a drum or apron of Doric columns, the upper storey of the façade being backed and supported, at the sides, by the advancing wings of an architectural, or, much more, a stage screen. It has been observed by Professor Wittkower and others that Cortona 'has applied the experience of the theatre' to the piazza in which the church stands. This is indeed fairly obvious to the spectator, but not nearly so much so as in the piazza in front of Sant' Ignazio, where the architect Raguzzini has really set out the blocks of dwelling houses like the wings of a stage in front of the church, which as in the similar case of SS. Vincenzo ed Anastasio and the Fontana di Trevi was already standing there when he set to work. In the Piazza Sant' Ignazio the theatrical flavour is as pronounced as in almost any etching by the 'stage-struck' Stefano della Bella, who is typically Florentine although he lived so long (ten years) in Paris.

Such was Rome of the façades, and of the colonnades and fountains; a city and capital of ecclesiastics, but no more of an anachronism to its inhabitants than Lhasa to the Tibetan lamas, or the Holy Mountain to the monks and hermits of Mount Athos. But we have in our minds to nearly empty its streets, and mute or emasculate the roar of motor-traffic in order to see it as it was meant and intended to be seen. Thus it is in the Roman *vedute* of Pannini and other painters; but with the piazzas, if half-empty, enlivened by the different ecclesiastical costumes and by gilded coaches and their running footmen. As to the Roman fountains, those, apart, of the Piazza Navona which are by Bernini and his pupils and the Fontana di Trevi which may be from his designs, it could be felt that they are the jokes or *feux d'artifice* of the master compared to what might be expected of him. The Fontana del Tritone in the Piazza Barberini – yes! that is beautiful, with the triton standing on his forked tail in a huge bivalve, lifting high both arms and drinking from a conch shell; with the Papal tiara of Urban VIII, and the Barberini bees on the base of it, all upheld by dolphins with their snouts in water. But the Barcaccia

★ Victor L. Tapié, *Baroque et Classicisme*, Paris, 1957, and James Lees-Milne, *op. cit.* p. 109. Martino Longhi, the younger, built SS. Vincenzo ed Anastasio for Cardinal Mazarin in 1646–50. Thus the church stood there a hundred years before the fountain.

or leaking boat, for that is the point of it, in the Piazza di Spagna, Papal tiara again on the prow, and more Barberini bees; and the Fontana delle Api of the Piazza Barberini, three more of the family bees spouting water, improbably, at the base of a half-shell, the oyster-less, 'on the shell' of transatlantic menus; they, all of them, are not worthy of the Roman aqueducts that brought water into the metropolis of the ancient world from miles away and that even in their broken order must have been the wonder of the Dark Ages and the Middle Ages, too. The Roman Carnival, though not a water-spectacle as that of Venice or masked to that degree of concealment with the bird-beak or *bautta* and the *volta*, but as celebrated down to the day of Berlioz for its wine-drinking and pasta-eating and the dancing of the saltarella, is to be enjoyed in the coloured drawings to *Un An a Rome* by J. B. Thomas, a pupil of David. But in thinking of it, and almost hearing it, I only wish I could rid my memory of the account I read somewhere, I think in the *Roman Journal* of Gregorovius, of the execution of criminals, probably robbers or brigands, on a scaffold in the Piazza del Popolo. They were killed by being hit on the head with mallets, by the hangman dressed up for the occasion as a harlequin. The Roman façades have seen more things, then, than religious processions and gaping foreigners.

But now for Sicily and the façade of the Duomo at Syracuse that masks the Doric, not Norman columns of the Greek temple that lies within; of uncertain provenance whether by an architect from Syracuse or Palermo, of Roman derivation from the façade of Santa Maria in Campitelli, it may well be, because all things have their origin; but the art historian can only document and cannot explain how the miracle is brought about and this façade is able both to interpret and celebrate the light and sparkle of the South. In a beautiful piazza, it is certain, with the Palazzo Bosco in front of it of romantically secret impact for during half a lifetime it has defied all attempts at entry; with the window grilles of a convent of secret harem implication fully in view to complete the setting. A façade of Corinthian columns and pilasters with bold, shadow-throwing cornice to complement them; a window above that framed in an advancing quartet of more columns, each of a pair behind its other; and to each side a huge and beautiful vegetable scroll of the golden stone of Syracuse leading down to the mitred statue of a bishop, crozier in hand, on the Corinthian-borne pilaster at its flank, with perspective view of the Doric columns of the Greek temple of Athena backing down the distance into the side street. Such is a sample of the Sicilian architecture that given its opportunity after a destructive earthquake, produced the façades and balconies of Noto and the churches of Modica and Ragusa at the top of their panoramic terraces and flights of steps.

It would be obvious that the façades and frontispieces would not stop short of Italy but would have their appeal in Spain, but not to all parts of Spain for it is nearly a question of regional temperament. Thus, it is of small consequence to the Catalans but has already become of interest in Valencia, as witness the south front of the Cathedral and the iridescent, *art nouveau* anomaly of the Palacio de Dos Aguas.★ This is because of the warmer temperament of the Levante and a tendency to excitement that anyone would agree to who has experienced the floats, the fireworks and the mini-artillery explosions of their yearly *Fallas de San José*. Further south still, the mood alters again and it is not to be expected of the Córdobans and their mingling of a dour Arab and a stern Roman strain. It alters once more at Granada with the Granadines, though here it is interior glitter and richness, as of influence from the red exterior walls of the Alhambra and the contrasting stalactitic intricacy of the Moorish courts within, for proof of which are the fretted pilasters and the mirror-inlay of the interior walls of San Juan de Dios, more sophisticated parent to the altars of looking-glass in the *mestizo* convent of Santa Clara in its para-Tibetan setting at Cuzco so many thousands of miles away.

In Seville, too, it is an interior extravagance with the twisting Salomonic columns, the altar with blue glass inlay and the gilded, nuns' opera-boxes of San Luis. The whitewashed alleys of Seville are no place for façade-viewing; despite their brilliance and sparkle they are too near in kinship to the rat-runs of Fez and the whitened house-lanes of Sallee. It is a commonplace that the differing temperaments of the Sevillans and Córdobans have a counterpart in their respective schools of bull-fighting; the one tinged with the *gitano* and all fire and gesture, the other chilly and classical with more dignity. So it is said, and believed; but you do not have to be more than a few days in Seville and Córdoba to become convinced that there are these differences in the populace of both cities of the Andaluz, and that such differences affect their manners and the buildings that they live in.

But there is another city, not Seville, not Córdoba, nor Granada, but Murcia, a city not of Andalucia but of the Levante, and it is no exaggeration to say that a mere glance at its coloured domes would warn us to be on the look out for façades and for religious processions. Differing, again, as to these latter, from those of Seville for the *pasos* of Murcia are by Francesco Zarcillo (1707–83), a sculptor of origin from Naples, while as to the façade of the Cathedral which is as the magnet drawing us to Murcia, it could be said of it at once that just the concavity of its front appears to be drawn into itself as though to facilitate the exit of floats and processions through its three main portals. It seems even to take in its breath the better to blow them from its

★ Can the 'shimmering, rose-and-green, sunset-after-rain colouring of the delicate and fanciful Dos Aguas', as I have described it elsewhere, which is comparable in effect to watered silk, be due to the fact that half of the population of Valencia in the eighteenth century was employed in the silk industry?

doors. The architect was Jaime Bort, of whom little is known; and learned opinion always digging for origins, and losing touch while doing so with the truth that nothing being wholly original it is not the derivation but the evolution which is the mystery, has credited Jaime Bort with an assistant or 'principal craftsman who was a Fleming and had worked at Versailles'. Both assertions of fact seem far removed from the façade of Murcia, though it does have some little caricatural analogy to the back of a Louis Quinze chair, if only to that degree of overall, abstract resemblance which inspired Daumier to draw Louis-Philippe as a pear. Murcia, then, is a recessed or concave façade – and if it is far indeed from Versailles, how much further yet from 'the recessed arches (81 ft high), gables, parvise, and sculptures' of Peterborough which, yet, being recessed, as if Aryan, too, is undeniably of its kind. The recessed or concave fronts of churches are few in number, and this has other odd features to it such as its articulation as though into separate pieces that take apart and can be put together again. The fluted Corinthian pillars of the lower order, for instance! Could they not be taken out separately and put in a special box where there are places for them? And the same with the Composite pillars of the upper order; and the hood above those of red-golden stone in the strong sunlight, which almost has a grip for the fingers to lift it off! It is an open-air theatre scene with graceful and lovely side wings. And the wide spread of those side wings as though to give it foothold; and the way they are pegged down in the far corners by buttresses that are like rounded sentry boxes, and that even have an open niche with a statue in each. And other statues for full measure on their rounded tops, which statues all work in together with the statues at every elevation and on all vantage points, as many statues nearly as on the *gopuram* or gate tower of a Hindu temple, but these are more elegantly disposed and show a theatre sense which is lacking in the Hindus or Dravidians! It is not solid and static, but has movement and could itself progress like a crowded float or processional car; could move forward a few steps down the square across the sunlight, even, one imagines, in 'the parching dust of the *leveche*', which is the blight of Murcia in the dog-days and dog-nights of high summer.

It has become the convention to couple this façade of the Cathedral at Murcia with El Obradoiro, 'the work of gold' or west façade of Santiago de Compostela except that far from lighthearted as its Southern companion, it is also open to criticism as a work of architecture. Even in a photograph it can be seen that the six large window surfaces are awkward and ungainly in themselves, as well as playing no part in the architectural scheme.* Above these it is a flat gabled front like the top of a seventeenth-century mirror-

---

* But the purpose of the window surfaces was to protect and leave visible the Romanesque Portico de la Gloria for which they act as screen. The architect was faced with this problem and had no choice in the matter.

frame, with first a pair of niches, and then one huge niche, holding statues, that increase in size, of St James. And then it spreads itself with two lesser gables across the base of the two towers, which indeed are the feature of El Obradoiro and its beauty. They are immensely high towers; their first storey being on a level with the topmost and largest statue of St James; and then they climb for two more storeys, ending in a tall cupola and balustrade of obelisks. It is the towers and the double stair at the foot of El Obradoiro that make the fame of the local Gallego architect, Fernando de Casas y Novoa; those, and the snapdragons growing from the towers. But those are not the work of the architect. They are the effects of time; and how, were they left so long standing, would time work on the Radio City, or Rockefeller Center, and the Seagram Tower?

If the splendour of El Obradoiro is its towering height above the plaza in which it stands, good examples for contrast of what can be achieved in narrow streets are a pair of the rare, recessed façades; the one, the south front of Valencia Cathedral; the other, the little street church of Santa María, in San Sebastián, of all unlikely towns. But the first of these is improbable, too, and would never be anticipated of Valencia Cathedral, the exterior of which is of a Gothic that would not inspire strong emotions. But this south façade that faces down a narrow street has been consistently abused by most shades of opinion, from Richard Ford who calls it 'a confused, unsightly jumble of the Corinthian order, with bad statues of the local saints' to the 'heavy' and 'unsuccessful' that are still thrown at it today. But it is in fact pretty and graceful; a concave front like a three-leaved screen in golden stone. It appears to have been begun in 1713 by Konrad Rudolf, an itinerant Austrian who had studied under Bernini, and was then completed by one of the local Vergara family of architects and sculptors. Where, then, is the 'jumble'? For the Corinthian order is not over-emphasised and there is no confusion about it. This stone 'screen' has not even Corinthian columns in pairs; singly, and alone they are enough to mark the divisions or leaves of the screen; while, as for the 'bad statues of the local saints', the panels of bas-relief are beautifully placed, and the individual statues are eloquent and graceful. In fact, whether standing within its railed forecourt looking up at the golden stone, or from across the street, this is a part, and an integral part of the Valencian domestic scene, in the sense that it is street architecture, and all prejudice forgotten, no unsuitable adornment for the fiestas and flower festivals or floral games of the Levante.

The other street façade, that of Santa María in San Sebastián,★ is the solution of problems that are not dissimilar except that the street is even narrower and there can have been less money to spend in what was, then, a small Basque country town. There is no railed forecourt, only a flight of five

★ Built between 1743–64. Architects: Pedro Ignacio de Lizardi and Miguel de Salazar.

steps, and not much more space than the overhang of the recessed porch which is shell-shaped with sculptures in niches, the whole framed in by pilasters that, inadvertently, or not, just fit in with the width of the street in front. Over this, the cornice acts as pediment to a statue in a deep, sculptured frame and the façade finishes just above the level of the houses facing it. As a whole, it is unsensational but original, and an example of the sort of thing that is a commonplace in Italian towns from Piedmont down to Sicily and the heel of Italy, but rare in Spain, rarer still on the Bay of Biscay and at the foot of the Pyrenees. For which reason it is quick to show its effectiveness, its elegance and light spirits even in the greyer stone of the North, and its promise of warmer and better things to come.

So much, then, for this octuor of façades, an art of Italian invention and the by-product of their gesture and eloquence. Traits of national character that are vanishing quickly under the influence of radio and the cinema, so that it is already a long time ago since an English child would be taken to the Galleria in Milan or in Naples to watch the Italians gesturing and talking. How well I remember the Galleria in Milan with the Duomo down one arm of it, and the roar of all those voices outside the cafés, in the four aisles of the arcade and under the glass roof of the octagon in the middle! Or the Galleria in Naples just opposite to the San Carlo Opera and the Royal Palace! Glass arcades built on purpose for the sound and joy of talking. But that was still the Italy of coming out from the railway tunnel into the sunlight, of the customs house officers in the shiny black bowlers, of the frontier Alpini with feathers in their caps, and the blowing of a horn before the train started slowly downhill out of the north down to the Italian Lakes. The Italy of the bicycle bands of the Bersaglieri blowing their bugles as they rushed past; and of the boxes of wax-matches with the heads of dark-browed Italian beauties among roses and carnations on their elastic-guarded lids. The old Italy, now altering fast, so that even opera is dying as an Italian art form, and the provincial opera houses are closing one by one, killed by television, football, and similar forms of entertainment. The Italians, the foremost actors of the world, have not produced many great cinema stars, male or female. Perhaps the film is too dead for them and they need something living that changes from day to day, from performance to performance and that allows them to improvise.

And now after studying, however superficially, that very Italian architectural invention and speciality which is the act of designing and building a façade, something of which there would be few if any examples were it not for Italy in general and in particular the Rome of Bernini and his contemporaries, we leave the façade for what is behind it which in a sense is not there at all. For it is mere pretence. The Italians were the first actors of the modern world as it emerged from the mediaeval into the Renaissance. The first theatres were Italian and the first operas. The technical language of music is Italian with its own vocabulary. Even the din of voices and the shouting in the Galleria Vittorio Emanuele (213 yards in length, 16 yards in breadth, and 85 feet in height,) in the form of a Latin cross, with an octagon in the centre, crowned at the height of 157 feet with a glass cupola, 'the most imposing structure of the kind in Europe' – or the Galleria Umberto Primo of Naples with the opera house at one end of it which, typically, connects directly with the Royal Palace – where could they be but in Italy, where the Italians are, or were natural actors, and singers, too, as you hear them in the street below coming home late at night.

It is not a question of raising the curtain. Neither is there scenery. If shortsighted you can look through the lens formed by putting thumb and forefinger together into a circle which you can widen or narrow in order to alter the focus, thinking as you do so, if you are the sort of person I am, of the Emperor Nero who watched the Roman games through the cut facets of an emerald. Thus, and in the light of that, did he behold the *retiarii* or net-throwers, and their opponents the *secutores* who were armed with a sword and a round shield or buckler. The *retiarii* who held a trident in their left hand had a net to throw over the head of their antagonist in order to entangle him and prevent him from striking back. If he failed in this he had to take to flight. This running away of the *retiarii* will have been one of the recognised conventions of the Roman circus. It must have had innumerable tricks and turns, some of them special to a particular performer, if indeed the fighting life of any gladiator lasted long enough for him to display form or style. So, it is said, did Nero see Christian or other malefactors being devoured by wild animals, and by the light of living torches of his own devising he watched the swelling, darkening bloodstains on the sands.

What we see, if relatively the same in scale, small enough that is to say to be seen between thumb and forefinger, is very different in every other way. It is two little figures, no more than a few inches high; and what are peculiar to them are the feathers in their caps and the gesticulations of their hands. They are in breeches and doublets, dressed nearly alike except that the shirt of one of them has come out above his breeches, and that this one of the pair of them wears a black mask. The two feathers each wears in his cap or bonnet are identical and are like fern-fronds, or even antlers formed of some stalk-like, or other vegetable substance that would snap and break easily if touched. At their feet – and even their shoes are alike and of the same shape – a glass of wine stands upon a three-legg'd stool; and one hand of each of them gesticulating over and above it suggests somehow that this is the prize or reward for whoever wins. The other hand gestures to empty air. It must be a wager, or some form of betting game.

It is the game of *morra*, which is still played by Italian children and consists in guessing the number of fingers held out by your opponent, a simple, even a rudimentary game but one peculiarly apt and suited to the eloquent fingers and the gesticulations of the warm South. As it is a game which depends upon outwitting your opponent, the players of *morra* are always watching each other closely, staring each other in the eye, as much as ever the *retiarii* were running, net in hand, looking back over their shoulder in the Roman games. But this does not explain what is wholly and entirely fantastic about this pair of gamblers. Who, and what can they be? One can almost hear their voices. Are they actors of the Commedia dell'Arte, or masqued gondoliers?

They are in fact Venetian glass figures of mid-seventeenth century date from a set of fantastic masqued figures, all playing *morra*, the work of some highly stylised and unknown master, now, and for some two centuries and more in that red brick treasure house of objects of virtù and curiosities of all kinds which is Rosenborg Castle, in the very midst of Copenhagen. There they are, forgotten almost among the ships' models of ivory with bellying sails, the badges of the Armed Hand or mailed arm in green enamel with diamonds, the jewelled badges of the Order of the Elephant, the 'polonaise' carpets woven with silver in shades of pale green and almond and pistachio, the three silver lions, and the throne of narwhal tusks from Greenland. None, or any of which has relation or bearing on the street game that they are playing.

But whence comes that warm wind which inspires their gestures and seems even to inflate their ragged clothing? This is not so difficult to determine. It blows straight from the woodcuts and etchings of Jacques Callot, a draughtsman whose best work once seen is never forgotten owing to the individuality and the nervous vitality of his line, though very little is known about him as a person. Born at Nancy, in Lorraine, in 1592–3 there is no reason to doubt the legend that he ran away from home in order to go to Italy. Before he was twenty he was in Florence and in Rome, in just the years when there was a tradition of vagabondage among young painters from the north who were studying in Italy. Hikers, hobos, wandervogels, then, as now, were on the road to Rome, not a few of whom, dropping all pretension to paint brush or charcoal, would have taken up the camera instead and been among the *papparazzi* who throng the pavement and cafés of the Via Veneto in pursuit of celebrities whom they follow to restaurant or night club and photograph against their will. For all the would-be painters who went to Rome and were heard of again, there were dozens or even scores who failed and left no mark at all behind them.

Caravaggio, prime exemplar of the artist as reprobate painter in the footsteps of Cellini, was just about to die, or dead, and a number of northern painters, Honthorst and Terbruggen among them, both from Utrecht, were in Rome at this time painting religious subjects but, also, brothel scenes in his manner or that of Manfredi his imitator, and eventually founding the Bent, a name derived from Bentvueghels, 'birds of a flock', a group of northern artists working in Rome and banded together against their Italian colleagues and against the law.★

But there is reason to think that the roistering and Bohemianism of Callot were of another sort. If, that is to say, internal evidence derived from a study of his woodcuts counts for anything. He was spectator, not participant, and as such ideally suited to be portrayer and limner of performances in which he never took a part, which is the reason why his frontispieces to masques and plays are as the involvement of a one-man audience at a rehearsal in an empty theatre. To this draughtsman more than painter – there are no authenticated paintings by his hand – born in the very middle of Shakespeare's lifetime, the theatre was as much his discovery as if it were his own invention, and where else could he have gone for this except to Italy? It holds true of all his career down to *Les Misères et Mal-Heurs de la Guerre* of 1633, but a year or two before his death, at the Grand Guignol horrors of which, as we would expect, he is spectator and commentator but without the physical and personal involvement of Goya in his *Desastros de la Guerra*. He looks on, horrified; or, in his other themes, entranced, but always and ever detached so that he is the complete and perfect audience. He is not of the same dimension as his subject owing to the theatre which was the new and marvellous discovery of his generation. Tempting as it may be, we are not to imagine him at the Globe Theatre in Southwark, on the south bank of the river, where the words would be lost upon him and he would not have realised the immortality that he was witnessing. Yet, all in due scale, as much as Shakespeare (d.1614), or Monteverdi (d.1643), who were his contemporaries, he is of the theatre; and just as no one has made explorations since Columbus discovered America, has played the violin as did Paganini, or printed books as Caxton, so this first of theatrical artists and draughtsmen remains without a rival, not designer, but prime delineator of the actors and the scene. The first impact in all such instances is the one that counts and lasts.

It was Florence, more particularly, that left its mark upon him, that is, unless we prefer to think it was the reverse process, and that we see Florence of the early seventeenth century when its golden age was over and the *bruto seicento* had set in mainly, if not entirely, through his eyes. And this, it is remarkable to think, on the strength of a handful of prints and frontispieces. But those, and their supporting or satellite prints by his self-evident disciple and follower Stefano della Bella are in harmony with the bat-wing volutes of

★ 'As more Northerners flocked to Rome the Bentvueghels got more rowdy and held huge drinking parties ending in Santa Costanza, where scores of their names are still scratched on the walls. Their riotousness and mock baptisms caused the Pope to suppress them [a hundred years later] in 1720.' Quoted from *A Dictionary of Art and Artists*, by Peter and Linda Murray, Harmondsworth, 1959.

the Florentine buildings, and their spirit could be said to inhabit the busts and statues of the later Medici Grand Dukes and their relations. I think that anyone who lived in Florence as a child, as I did, would remember in these terms the bust of Cardinal Leopoldo de' Medici with his long thin face and Habsburg jaw at the top of the atairs in the Uffizi, the Cappella dei Principi with its huge sarcophagi of the Medici Grand Dukes and its funeral marbles, the treasure vaults in the Palazzo Pitti and their eccentric treasures, or the cypresses, the fountains and the grottoes of the Boboli Garden. Even the oft-seen *stemma* or coat-of-arms of the Medici above a doorway or a building is redolent of Callot and of della Bella.

The story that Callot made his way through Italy with a band of Gypsies may, or may not be true, but, certainly, had he met them, he would have studied them. He seems to have left his native Lorraine in 1608 when no more than fifteen or sixteen years old having already, it may be, been shown engravings by Hieronymus Bosch or Pieter Bruegel, Lorraine being near to Flanders, and having had his flair for the pictures and the eccentric already aroused and set in motion. His taste was for extremes; for plays and masques put on by princes, the theatre itself being both a mirror and a deception, and for vagabonds and beggars. And before he encountered the first mentioned and they afforded him his subject, he had fallen in with and perhaps gone along with the second, and if so when he was probably young indeed, and not yet twenty years old. His vagabondage was of more fruitful sort than the drinking and whoring of the German and Dutch students, and we may think we see evidence in him of a solitary and introspective nature.

What we are about to see, let me recall once more, was playing within the lifetime of Shakespeare. This it is that makes it curious indeed to hold the little book of woodcuts in one's hand. And woodcuts they certainly are; as much so as if Callot had cut them on the spot using the point of his knife upon anything that came to hand, a wooden bench, the corners of a trestle stage, or kitchen table. They are the *graffiti* of a genius, miraculously preserved; no less so if it be the fact that he took his drawings home with him and the actual woodcuts were done at Nancy. For the thickening and widening of his line are as true as though he were sitting there in front of us, clasp-knife in hand. How can it be his sketches were not made more elaborate and spoilt? There had never been anything like them before in history.

What we are witnessing are the *Balli di Sfessania* or *Neapolitan Dances* of Callot. There are twenty-three of the little woodcuts with a frontispiece showing three masqued figures before a curtain, one of them holding a wooden box or tray which is in fact their collecting-box. There are childrens' heads peeping round or below the curtain to show that it is impermanent and but a trestle stage, like indeed the pierrots' booths I remember as a child upon the tidal sands. But there all, or nearly all resemblance ends. For certainly, though it differed every time, this was not a performance that would have been allowed upon the foreshore.

But it would seem that Callot went further south than Florence or Rome. Had he perhaps been following the actors to some small town in the Campagna Felice or plain round Naples, one of the most fertile and densely populated regions of the world, which yields in addition to the vines and fruit trees, two crops of grain and one of fodder in the same season? It is only curious that in not one of the little woodcuts is there even the outline or shadow of Mount Vesuvius. A shape so often to be seen by the white cube of a house; or where the vines are wreathed from tree to tree. But all his interest was on the actors and the stage. Are we ten or twelve miles, no more than that, from the Parthenopaean city? Is it Capua, where once there were schools for the training of gladiators? Or even nearer than that to the city?

It is Aversa, the ancient Fescennia, and Callot called his woodcuts *Balli di Sfessania* from the town where the Fescennine verses were invented, which were 'a kind of rustic dialogue spoken extempore'; and if proscribed in the time of Augustus, they were reborn in the Commedia dell' Arte of which this is the near-immortal record; or they were, we must suppose, endemic in the soil and never really dead.

But in fact it is only Aversa or Fescennia in Callot's imagination and for the sake of the title. It is this absence of views of Vesuvius in the background of the woodcuts that settles the question once and for all. Only a glance at them will show that it is Tuscany all the time, perhaps in some small town like Empoli, or Montelupo, or in Callot's favourite Impruneta.

The first of the woodcuts coming after the frontispiece is little but a foretaste of what is to follow, and the series really starts with the second of the set which show Capitan Cerimonia, a masqued gallant of eccentric aspect holding his plumed hat, with plumes reversed feathers down, right under his own nose, in order to do honour to a lady, Signora Lavinia. On his back a piece of his cloak – or is it his other sleeve – pokes up like a cloth held up on a stick or umbrella and gives him the look of some kind of one-winged bird. Capitan Cerimonia seems only to wish to greet Signora Lavinia; or will he begin strutting around her like that same strange kind of bird? In the background are small figures of a pair of dancers, some onlookers, and a man playing a guitar with an exaggeratedly long stalk to it; pulled out in fact like the Chianti flasks that have the elongated necks.

These are but the preliminaries. In the next, or fourth woodcut we are in the very midst of the *Balli di Sfessania*, an itinerant fairground theatre playing in a village or on the outskirts of a town, in Tuscany, to be sure, though we do not see the cypresses or stone pines. Nor do we follow the woodcut pages inch by inch for the rapidity of action is quite impossible to put into words. But we may imagine for ourselves, if we cannot hear it, the staccato, falsetto shouting, if the clyster, scratch-dog humour needs no explaining. Where voices are concerned, it is not so much that beings from another planet have arrived as that a race of talking-birds have come down from the trees; this, too, from the quick movement of their heads and necks. They have that quick convulsive jerking and twitching, though flightless without wings. But, also, they are dog-like; dog-like in the lurid postures of their couplings and amours. Francatrippa, Cucurucu, whom we get to know by name, have worked themselves into a Fescennine frenzy of twitching and scratching, dog-like again of step. Capitan Cocodrillo, or Capitan Zerbino, in long nosed mask and spectacles, with immense goose-quills in his cap, bargains with Scapino. Two more of the Captains of comedy or 'Spanish' bravos, Capitan Bonbardon and Capitan Grillo are in a weird and extraordinary state of animal activity; both masked, but Bonbardon dances like a frenzied dog and Grillo in receptive canine posture, his wrists turned out and legs askew, looks ready to yelp and run away. We are near the climax of their nightmare courtship-dance. Nothing much more can happen.

The actors seem to have got down from the trestles and be performing in the half-empty street. In no one of the woodcuts do we see them on the stage; though there is the stage far away at the back in one of the woodcuts, but, then, Razullo and Cucurucu are playing the lute and dancing in the foreground. In other of the woodcuts there are tumblers turning cartwheels, and pairs of actors walking upon stilts, all in the distance. Why did Callot take them off the stage into the street? Because there was more room for them? Because it was more exciting to see them down among the audience, and made their antics the wilder and more peculiar still? In no one of the plates is there an audience, or even a single spectator in front of the actors; that is to say between Scapino or Cucurucu and ourselves, which gives the feeling that with a 'half-empty house', to judge from the few persons in the background, the performance is chiefly for ourselves. It takes place so clearly in some dusty Tuscan village or small town. Those will have been dusty long before the motors came. Despite their name *Balli di Sfessania*, anglicised as *Neapolitan Dances*, there is not the least hint of Naples except in the loucheness of certain of the dances. Some learned Latinist and friend of Callot, perhaps a priest, must have thought of this name which has a built-in excuse in it for the set of woodcuts. The title, of Latin derivation and history, turned into Italian, took the opprobrium away and laid the blame on Naples.

Do they portray one band of actors? It would seem not; were it so, there would be more reminiscence of background and of incident. The young ladies of the company, Fracischina, Riciulina, dance and play the tambourine; otherwise they are not interesting. These are certain acts and dances of the comedians noted down whenever he passed a fairground, and of course improved in his imagination, for we are not to think that they or any of them were a first-rate company. But one or two of the dancers must and will have been known actors. It is inconceivable that Callot can have invented them out of his brain. There will have been not more than four or five men and probably two or three women in any troupe. Were all his 'Capitanos', Cocodrillo, Spezzafer, Zerbino, the same actor; even when two 'Capitanos', Grillo and Bonbardon, appear together in the same woodcut?

There is one possible clue to the *Balli di Sfessania* which I have never seen mentioned. This is the 'swashbuckler' plates of Montelupo from the town of that name. They are of course pottery, nearly always on a yellow ground, as of dawn or sunset under a thunder cloud, and depict bravos or swashbucklers in slashed doublets and breeches, sometimes musket on shoulder, more often armed with a rapier, and occasionally with sword and dagger in each hand. They must be exactly contemporary to the dancers of Sfessania and to Callot's 'Capitanos'. To judge from those still in existence, large numbers of the 'swashbuckler' plates must have been produced and Callot will certainly have seen them. Why there should have been this industry in Montelupo is not known, but these Spaniards or mercenaries, whoever they may have been, were a popular folk subject. No one who was brought up with the Montelupo plates under his eyes, as I was, could forget these bravos walking out, looking for trouble; and as I write this I can recall some five or six of them in great detail from my old home. They are not less fantastic and far fetched in their slashed clothes under their yellow skies than Callot's 'Capitanos'. In the *Musée Imaginaire*, where all things can happen and no coincidental meetings are too improbable, one would like to think of stalls of the Montelupo plates at country fairs where strolling players were performing; just as one could wish that Callot had seen and drawn 'Valentin le désossé' dancing at the Moulin Rouge; and again that Sharaku, the master of masters of the Japanese actor print, had seen the dancers of Sfessania. But in fact the swashbucklers and the 'Capitanos' are of long descent, as witness the alarming, even terrifying drawings of the roystering Swiss landsknechts by Urs Graf of Basle (1485–*c.* 1528), who was a 'vile' and fearsome ruffian, himself. The Italians had mercenary soldiers of all races rampaging up and down the land for a century and more before the 'Capitanos' of Sfessania.

4

'alla Veneziana'

*Shall call the winds thro' long arcades to roar
Proud to catch cold at a Venetian door'*

ALEXANDER POPE

The three most beautiful cities of Europe, perhaps of the world, are on the water. They are Venice, Lisbon, and Istanbul. The second of these triumphs by virtue of its situation alone for it is not famous for its buildings, or works of art. But in the other two the architecture almost prevails upon the water-setting. Istanbul is the only great city of the Orient that is on the water, there is no other. And no one who has ever arrived there by sea, even if on a wet, grey day, can forget that moment when the outline of her mosques and minarets shows up against the skyline. First, the Mosque of Soltan Achmet with its half-dozen minarets, only mosque in the world beside the Ka'aba of Mecca to have this number; and the building with four minarets a little below it is Santa Sophia. The continent of Asia is so near you could almost touch it with your hand. And now the Golden Horn opens before us: and one after another we see the Imperial Mosques of Istanbul upon or below the skyline; the Suleimaniye, or Mosque of Suleyman the Magnificent, standing upon the third hill; the Mosque of Bayazit on the same hill below it; or of Mohammad the Conqueror or the Fetiye upon the fourth hill; of Soltan Selim upon the fifth hill; of the Shehzade perhaps most beautiful of all; and down below coming up out of the smoke of the town, the Mosque of Yeni Cami. Mosques that look to be, and are in the main, the work of one man, the Turkish architect, Sinan; mosques with something menacing and martial in their air, that stand on the skyline like huge kettledrums.

Lisbon has nothing that can compare with this. There is but the abbey of Belém, with its fretted pillars echoing, one might think, mariner's tales of the temples of Golconda; and after that, and the blue and white, china-tiled churches, we might wish to see a procession of the golden coaches from Belém drawn by piebald horses, as the traveller Baretti saw them, with plaited manes and tails, trained to move forward at 'so short a gallop' that they could keep pace with the footmen walking beside them. How did the

The Art of Façade

Façade of the Roman church of Santissima Trinità de' Monti, lit by fireworks in celebration of Louis XIV's recovery from illness. Engraving by Sanfelice.

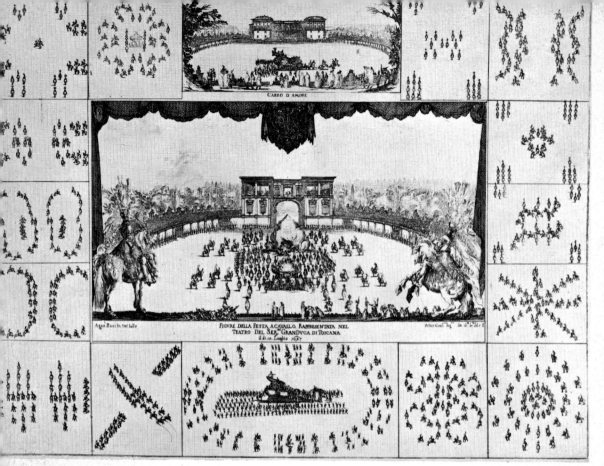

Top: Frontispiece by Stefano della Bella for an equestrian ballet at the court of the Grand Duke of Tuscany in Florence.
Bottom: The elliptical forum at Jerash, in Jordan.
Opposite: Façade of Borromini's Sant' Ivo alla Sapienza in Rome, from the courtyard.

Opposite: Façade of
Bernini's favourite
church of Sant'Andrea
al Quirinale, Rome.
Right: Façade of
Syracuse Cathedral.
Right below: Rome:
Pannini's painting of
Carlos III of Spain
received by Pope
Benedict XIV at the
Quirinal Palace.

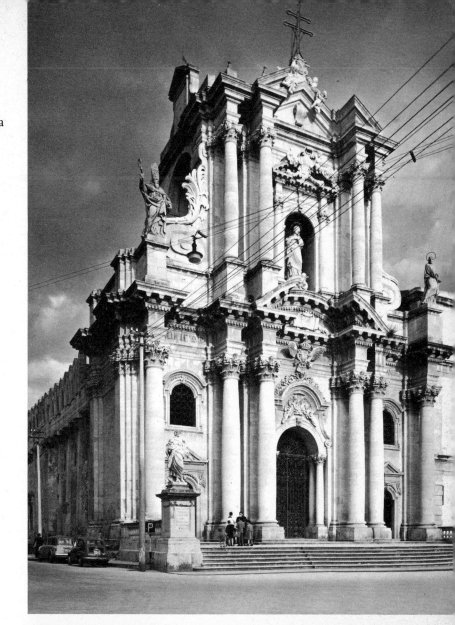

Opposite: Santa Maria della Pace, Rome, by Pietro da Cortona.
Right: Façade of the Khazné Faraóun at Petra, in Jordan.
Right below: Engraving of the great temple at Baalbek, after a drawing by Nicholas Hawksmoor.

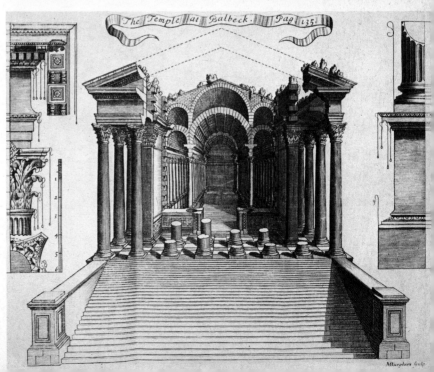

Opposite: South façade of the cathedral of Valencia by Konrad Rudolf.
Right: Porch of the Palacio de Dos Aguas, Valencia.
Right below: Two *gopurams* or gateways to the great temple of Madura, in southern India.

Left: Ivan of the Great Mosque at Isfahan.
Left below: Mosaics in the Ommayad Mosque at Damascus, showing famous buildings of the ancient world.
Opposite: Façade of the Cathedral of Murcia.

'alla Veneziana'

The lagoon from Palladio's San Giorgio Maggiore.

Below: Domenico Tiepolo, *La Partenza della Gondola.*
Bottom: Pompeian harbour; wall-painting from a villa at Stabiae.

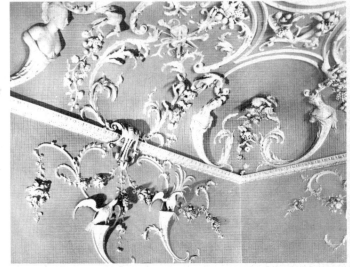

Above: Palladian Bridge,
of Venetian inspiration, in
the gardens at Stowe.
Right: Stucco by
Benjamin West in no. 20,
Lower Dominick Street,
Dublin.
Opposite: Stucco'd interior
of the *Ridotto Venier*, in
Venice.

G. B. Tiepolo, *The Banquet of Antony and Cleopatra.*

lumbering coaches, we may wonder, achieve the steep hills of Lisbon? At least in Venice there are no hills; and only the four bronze horses from the Golden House of Nero that stand above the doorway of St Mark's. Those, and the charger ridden by Colleoni, the *condottiere* – an archetypal figure from Italian history – in Verroċchio's statue. And we find ourselves not for the first time making up the Grand Canal, whether by gondola or vaporetto, and conjecturing to what extent the water-setting of Venice influenced its architecture and its painting. For Istanbul and Lisbon are built on and above the water. Venice is built in the water; and its inhabitants are bound to hear the lapping of waves and be conscious of it nearly as much as if they lived on board ship. The builders of the early palaces, those of the *duecento* and *trecento*, with *bifora* windows and inlay of verde antique and porphyry on their external walls certainly knew this, and exulted and took pleasure in it. In such a building as the Palazzo Grimani, 'the masterpiece of Sanmichele', there is less sign of it. This palace could stand on a street in Padua or Verona. It has no water-consciousness. But although I do not admire them, being no lover of Italian Gothic, I think this is present in the reddish Palazzo Foscari, of Ruskinian fame, and in the two Palazzi Giustiniani that stand next to it, on the bend of the Grand Canal. No active mind of the fifteenth century would have thrown away the opportunity of building in the water.

But I would say that along the whole length of the Grand Canal the most water-conscious or really marine or aquatic buildings are the Pesaro and Rezzonico palaces and the church of the Salute, all three of them by the same architect, Baldassare Longhena (1598–1682). With the Palazzo Rezzonico it is the bold rustication of the ground floor that though above water-level seems designed for the growth of green weeds and for small sea-shells to cling to it, while the two upper storeys with their open colonnades are for the breezes off the lagoon to play through, and in order to steal and keep the lights and reflections from off the water. How splendid, too, the helmeted and plumed masks and the curving flank of the Pesaro, the utility of which is not obvious so that it must have been for marine luxury and theatricality of effect! While, as to the Salute, it has been said before that shell-like of structure with the inner and outer vaults of its dome giving credence to the comparison, and with its whorled buttresses resembling again the curves of sea-shells and crustaceans, it stands 'like a huge shell upon its own steps or platform that could be self-formed of pale madrepores or blanched coral'.

By which time we may well be going past the Accademia which it is not possible for a lover of painting to do without being reminded of Carpaccio's paintings of *The Legend of St Ursula*, and conjecturing to what extent as a Venetian it could be said of him that the water-setting of Venice affected him and made its appearance in his pictures. This it does in four at least of the nine paintings; these being, typically, neither landscapes, nor interiors, but

E

quay-side scenes, no more, nor less. And it is in the painting of a double subject, the finest and largest of the series, that Carpaccio shows most clearly his absorbing passion for quays and shipping. The figures in the painting are all grouped along a temporary wooden bridge or platform with water reaching out beyond it and a beached vessel, a wonderful subject in itself, lying on its side with its mast aslant and almost touching on the Sforzesco-looking castle in the foreground.

But the theme of the painting is in fact divided into two subjects by a flagstaff with its streamers rising from the middle of the wooden bridge; a wooden flag pole resembling those three in the Piazza of St Mark's which of old flew the banners of Cyprus, Crete, and the Morea; to either side of which wooden pole, and some half-way up its height, signifying that they are in the middle distance, there is a multitude of shipping. A galleon with bellying sail that has caught the wind is starting to move, while another furls its sail and is about to enter port; while to the right of the flagstaff there are three large vessels, two of them lying at anchor, and a third tied up to the quay. All their masts have the little crow's nests near their summits that appear on the 'golden angels' of our Plantagenet Kings, and yet two more tall masts of which we can only see the tops and the crow's nests show from behind a building.

In three of the other pictures it is no different. They are quay-side scenes. Of course in Carpaccio's masterpiece, *The Miracle of the Holy Cross* – also in the Accademia – a painting which has the old wooden bridge of the Rialto for background, there is no excuse for his not bringing in all the gondolas he wants as the scene is on the Grand Canal. No fewer than ten or twelve of them are manoeuvring and jostling against each other in the pool of water in the foreground; the gondoliers, popinjays all of them, in striped hose, one of them, a negro gondolier, being nearest to the spectator. But we are long past the Accademia by now, and alongside the Dogana di Mare, a little building, contemporary with Longhena, familiar to many tens of thousands of persons during the three centuries it has stood there at the mouth of the Grand Canal, in one of the greatest of cues or entrances in all architecture, and that keeps its importance as part of the composition of the Salute on its raft or quay of Istrian limestone. A little ahead of us to the left we see the Doges' Palace which it is impossible to believe was not built with the open Adriatic and the Bacino di San Marco in mind, and now the domes and howdahs of St Mark's are just coming into view. Opposite to us on our right hand side there is San Giorgio Maggiore on its own island, but although this completes and in a sense fulfils the whole Venetian composition it could be said of it that Palladio's façade to the church is a disappointment, correct and adequate to the point of dullness, as, too, the yet more unimaginative front of the Redentore, half-a-mile across the water and facing us on the Giudecca. What was the matter with Palladio when he worked in Venice? Was it simply that he preferred the trees and hills and vineyards of Vicenza and the *terra firma*?

But our theme which has drawn us in imagination from one end of Venice to the other does not really begin before the lifetime of Longhena, and it has to be said that apart from him the seventeenth century was a dull time in Venice. So, too, were the first thirty years of the following century until the coming of Tiepolo. This great genius in the art of decorative painting belonged to the generation of Bach and Handel and Domenico Scarlatti. Seldom have there been more fruitful decades than those closing years of the seventeenth century when their great talents saw the light. But time moved more slowly, then, than now. Bernini, who has been called with justice 'the last great universal genius of the Italian Renaissance', was born a hundred years before their time.* It is difficult to believe they were separated from him by as many as four generations of human beings. Constant, nervous changes of style as with Stravinsky and Picasso, the geniuses of our day, were no necessity to them. It is even salutary to remember that Bach never met or set eyes upon Handel, and it is almost certain had never even heard mention of Scarlatti, who, incidentally, had only one twentieth of his compositions printed in his lifetime. It is a symptom, also, that Handel who of the three musicians in question has the most worldly and public of careers should have been the one of them to suffer from nervous strains and breakdowns. Such were no problem with Bernini; neither does it seem to have troubled Giambattista Tiepolo, except when he complains to his impresario, Count Algarotti, when painting frescoes for the Villa Cordellina, near Vicenza. 'Here I am, and I can do nothing because there are too many visitors.'† This was in the autumn of 1743.

Tiepolo was then between forty and fifty years old, having been born a Venetian in its strict sense, the son of a sea-captain who was part-owner of a merchant vessel. 'La Serenissima', the great Venetian Republic, had been by now for a century and more in much the condition of decay and lost splendour that obtained in Spain during the youth of Goya, with the difference that Venice itself had become the pleasure centre of Europe. We shall see that the minor arts still had some little life in them; but it was an unlikely moment for a *peintre noble* to appear who was to unite in his person the splendours of Venetian painting that died with Paolo Veronese in 1588 with the experience of a century and more of Italian fresco-painters and perspectivists from Pietro da Cortona to Luca Giordano, and from Fratel Pozzo and Baciccia to the Bibienas and other dynasties of theatrical designers. Yet that was his achievement, and behind his fluency and ease of execution it is easy to lose sight of its long pedigree and complicated evolution.

* Bernini b. 1598; Bach, Handel and Domenico Scarlatti, b. 1685; Tiepolo b. 1696.
† Antonio Morassi, *G. B. Tiepolo: his life and work*, London, 1954, p. 21.

All this is to be studied in the side wings and set scenes or tableaux of his *History of Antony and Cleopatra* at the Palazzo Labia in Venice. This, perhaps the most famous painted room in Europe – for it is true that Pietro da Cortona's frescoes in the Barberini and Pamphilj palaces in Rome are almost forgotten – could have advanced against it that the painted architecture by Mengozzi-Colonna, Tiepolo's *quadraturista* or perspectivist assistant, is both too illusionist and too heavy and insistent. In many respects it could be said almost to spoil this most beautiful of fresco'd rooms by its cleverness. There is such a coupling of Corinthian pilasters, such an array of painted architraves and jutting cornices that there comes a longing for more space to look at the paintings. Many, many viewings of the Palazzo Labia since childhood have only continued and strengthened this impression. If only there were less simulated architecture the fresco paintings could be better seen. There is confusion between the real and false windows in the second storey of this painted hall. And again the ceiling is almost empty and meaningless above the historiated scenes. Perhaps it should not have been left flat but have been lifted into a vault, as in Luca Giordano's vaulted ceiling with the *Medici as Gods of Light among the Deities of Olympus*, which grandiloquent theme in the Palazzo Riccardi in Florence is among the masterpieces of the art of fresco painting.

The theme of *Antony and Cleopatra* seems to have been a favourite one, amounting almost to an obsession with the painter, perhaps because in its very protagonists it personified youth and physical beauty, and then again it had the authority of antiquity behind it. But, also, it could be called Mediterranean in subject for this was no Northern legend, and perhaps in its commerce with classical towns like Alexandria the painter identified it with the golden age of his native Venice which decidedly was fixed in his imagination in the time of Veronese. It was Ancient Egypt; and, no archaeologist, Tiepolo could bring in negro pages and his favourite Orientals. Had he read Shakespeare's play? This would seem unlikely; and yet he treats his two scenes or tableaux of the *Meeting or Disembarkation* and *The Banquet of Antony and Cleopatra* as though they were moments or situations from a masque or play. The pair of painted flats or wings to each side of the set scene heighten the theatrical illusion in marvellous fashion and work up the excitement. To the left of the meeting of hero and heroine it is a pair of beautiful young women coming away from the galleon and the head, just the head, of one of Tiepolo's white stallions, with only the right leg and spurred boot of its rider, and high in the air the standard he holds; while to the right, it is a ship's captain, it can be no other, who looks on and superintends the disembarking. In the other pairs of painted wings, the silver dishes and flagons are piled high as upon tall buffets, which is a feature taken whole from the banquet scenes painted for the Venetian refectories by Veronese; in the left-hand painting, two attendants seem to be checking a list with the silver lined up high above them; and in the panel to balance that, a negro page with his back to us, who is looking at the banquet, waits for a glass to be filled by one of Tiepolo's red-haired and aquiline Orientals, who were intended for Turks but were more probably Albanians.

They are but the subsidiary or supporting scenes. But to the two *grands sujets*, the *Banquet* and the *Meeting*, the painter returned again and again, outside and apart from the Palazzo Labia, making in all nine or more differing versions of this double theme, and playing about with it as though he could not be satisfied with it and get it right. In the version of the *Meeting* now in the National Gallery of Scotland, to take one example, the flat line of heads of the spectators standing just beside the figure of Cleopatra, as in the fresco of this same subject, is in fact clumsily handled and detracts from the whole effect. But in both frescoes there were innumerable difficulties that he had to face were he to meet Veronese on his own ground and vanquish him. It may be thought that not even the frescoes in the Labia are an unqualified success. But Tiepolo's undoubted masterpiece is his *Banquet of Antony and Cleopatra* which was in The Hermitage, was bought by the National Gallery in Melbourne, was exhibited in London on its way to Australia, and made an appearance again in London a few years ago when it was cleaned and put on show. There can be little question that this is the most beautiful European painting of the whole eighteenth century;* in the grand manner of its predecessors of two hundred years before, but even more in this instance a kind of painting of which it is the climax, and a culmination that can never come again. For at the back of Veronese there may have been assistants, but they were not trained in the technique of the theatrical painters and perspectivists. The Italian theatre was newborn in the day of Veronese, but it was seven or eight human generations old by the time the Labia frescoes were painted, and this is self-evident in this picture in both the conception and the handling. When on view in the National Gallery in London it was indeed a wonderful experience worth going to enjoy time after time.

In this he has solved the problem of the composition once and for all. Again the ugly line of heads of spectators in the fresco is missing; and if that is a gain to the oil-painting, there are perhaps two things in the fresco of which we feel the loss in this final version of the subject. They are the turban'd Oriental behind Cleopatra, another of the aquiline red-haired type, and the flashing white obelisk or needle-like pyramid in the background of the fresco in token that this is Egypt. Instead, an Oriental of a different type is seated at the banquet table, and the old nanny-goat Turk who occurs in Tiepolo's drawings stands watching the Banquet beside Antony's chair. What is surpassingly beautiful is the figure of Cleopatra herself, to whom this epithet

* *Le Grand Gilles* of Watteau, in the Louvre, is its only rival but this in its expressed essence belongs almost more to the theatre and to poetry than to painting.

must be denied in the Labia fresco where she is too close to the physical type in Veronese's paintings, of heavy build as are the women in both Titian and Rubens, a Renaissance type of looks that had become gross indeed compared to the young androgynous girls of Botticelli and Filippino Lippi. Furthermore, there is a monotony in the brocaded dresses of Cleopatra in the frescoes of both the *Banquet* and the *Embarkation*, though it is perhaps that the patina of the paint has worn thin so that the patterns look as though stencilled upon the plaster.

What is beautiful and unforgettable in the fresco version is the golden prow of the galley, the white horse's head held by its kneeling, turban'd attendant, and the wooden landing-stage which has the effect of a stage staircase down the boards of which treads the fair-haired page *en travesti* carrying the crown of Egypt on a silken cushion. This time in the painting we see the dwarf facing us, climbing the steps towards Cleopatra in his patched clothes, but at the back of the picture talking to a negro attendant, and he is the identical dwarf of the frescoes of the Palazzo Clerici in Milan; the same dwarf seen from the back again, climbing the steps and pulling the carpet straight in the fresco of the *Marriage of Barbarossa*, in the Residenz at Würzburg.★ In the painting from Melbourne the figures are reversed, that is to say, Cleopatra is on the left of the picture, Antony on the right, compared to their positions in the fresco at the Labia; and it is the painting of the silk stuffs in particular that is such a pleasure to the eye. But the wonderful beauty of Cleopatra apart – and merely the rendering of her fair hair is a most ravishing passage of painting – there is the mysterious cloaked figure in the left foreground; but in fact though his purpose and the reason for his being there at all are not obvious he is after Cleopatra the most important figure in the painting. His yellow silk robe, and the piece of striped material drooping from his left sleeve are of miraculous and ecstatic texture; he is carrying a dish, balancing it with his left hand and shoulder, but his whole stance is in a sense unreasonable and purposeless. Yet he gives balance to the composition, and is so typical a piece of Tiepolo's handling that we could recognise and know him for such if only from his shoes or sandals, as is the case, too, with the identical objects of recognition in each and all of Tiepolo's paintings of *Rinaldo and Armida*.

Although it is less well known than the Labia, the genius of the painter is better appreciated at the Palazzo Clerici in Milan, but then Milan is not Venice, and hence the reason that this painted room is so little seen. It was begun by Tiepolo in 1740, some five years before the Labia, for a General in the Austrian forces of Maria-Theresa. The subject was *The Course of the Sun* – the chariot of the sun driven by Mercury crossing the continents of the world – the land masses with their appropriate inhabitants, human and animal, being kept to the edges of the ceiling leaving its centre down the length of the

★ This 'studio dwarf' appears, also, in *The Finding of Moses*, now in the National Gallery of Scotland.

room free for the clouds and the passing of the quadriga of white horses. It is
indeed most startlingly and breathtakingly beautiful where this marvellous
white horsedrawn chariot comes up like the dawn out of a bank of clouds
over Africa, where the negroes in striped clothes, but slaves none the less,
and the trumpeting elephants are already awake. Whereas in the Luca
Giordano fresco of the deities of Olympus, just mentioned, his invention is
taken for granted, and however much you may admire the ceiling you
hardly notice it in detail, here the eye is continually discovering new feats of
imagination on Tiepolo's part, as for instance the nereids with sprigs of coral
in their hair, there being many nereids down the length of all four sides of
Giordano's ceiling but none of them of this poetic fancy. But perhaps the
theme of the white horses reaches to its apotheosis on the ceiling of the
Kaisersaal at Würzburg, where Apollo leads the bride to Barbarossa who
awaits her on top of a stepped pyramid. The chariot of Apollo with its white
coursers is losing height, banking down, coming into low cloud which it will
soon emerge from; no one visible has the reins in hand, the bride with arm
outstretched as though to music is preparing for the arrival, and the spectator
lost in wonder, even with some little amateur experience of air-borne
journeyings, tries to conjecture where and how the white coursers and their
convoy will touch down and effect their landing.

Alas! that there is not space here for looking in detail at his huge ceiling of
Olympus and the Four Continents in the Residenz at Würzburg. At the
Amazonian Queen in her plumes throned on an alligator; at the cranes and
pagoda hats of Asia – how much one could wish that the painter had seen
with his own eyes only the Korean old gentlemen and the literati, wisp-
bearded sages in their white Ming court robes and tall, black lacquered hats of
gauze, if nothing more than that! – at the singers and the band of musicians
playing stringed instruments by whom he portrayed Europe, with in the
foreground on the very cornice seated on a cannon, near a splendid greyhound, in his uniform as military engineer a portrait of the great German
architect of the Baroque, Balthasar Neumann, the genius of Vierzehnheiligen
and of the Residenz; or at the panorama of Africa along one side of the ceiling
with its marvellous array of negroes and negresses and turban'd Orientals.
One would have liked, too, to look once more over the Villa Valmarana at
Vicenza, if only to admire *The Sacrifice of Iphigenia*, a tableau taking place
within a portico of four painted pillars, but the painter with incredible daring
has exploded a cloud between ourselves and two of the pillars as though a
cracker or petard has been thrown against them, just in proof of his technical
virtuosity as a cloud master and sky painter. Or we could have looked at his
last great fresco painting in the Throne Room of the Royal Palace at Madrid,
but it is in fact difficult to advance along the floor near enough to see it, where
near a great porcelain vase from China, in confusion of geography, a glorious

turban'd Oriental smoking a long pipe sits with his back turned right against the cornice; and there are figures depicting the different Spanish provinces; or we see the booty of Columbus and the Conquistadores carried ashore in great corded bales and boxes, behind this a huge sail is being furled, and the empyrean, empty of figures and nearly cloudless, is in symbol of the painter's frustration with the flow of opinion turning against him, and perhaps in sign, too, of his failing powers.

With the death of G. B. Tiepolo in Madrid in 1770 the sky-trips of the fresco painters were over and done with for ever. Goya's paintings in the dome of the little Ermita di San Antonio de la Florida in Madrid, begun in 1792, are in fact the last good frescoes ever painted and they, too, show the influence of Tiepolo, if not of Giambattista, of his son Domenico, and of that son when he was a genre painter and not assistant to his father. And so the melancholy decline of La Serenissima continued, if relieved by the *vedute* paintings of Canaletto and G. B. Tiepolo's brother-in-law, Francesco Guardi. There were also the little pictures of interiors by Pietro Longhi, a painter of the stature of Arthur Devis, but improved in value by their Venetian setting. In the person of Tiepolo the last lion of Venice was gone and he had outlived the sculptors and the architects. Huge country houses, the Villa Pisani at Strà, and the Villa Manin at Passariano, near Udine, were built earlier in the century but the spirit had fled. It would not be an exaggeration to say that the most beautiful interior of the eighteenth century in Venice is that of the Fenice Opera House begun in 1791, with its rows of boxes contrived or carried out in green lacquer. And that apart, and the one or two flats or apartment floors with fine stucco decorations in older palaces, it is typical of the Venetian decadence that there should be superlative workmanship in the *stucchi* and the intricate floor patterns of the Ridotto Venier, a nest of little rooms formerly a gambling-hall in the first house across one of the bridges along the Merceria.

But the influence of Venice did not die there in its own dust and debris. It spread far and wide through two channels, one of them serious and the other frivolous, these being the Palladian cult and the Comédie Vénitienne. So it came about that behind Palladian façades in England and in Ireland, too, there are finer 'Venetian' interiors than you can find in Venice herself or on her *terra firma*. But they are a century and a half to two centuries later than Palladio. And to what extent are they really Venetian? For they have altered because of their surroundings even when they are exact copies; and to descend to detail, when the stuccoists were called 'Venetian' it does not follow that they were from Venice. In fact they were most likely but another invasion of the stuccoists who went to most countries in Europe from the Swiss canton of Ticino. It seems unlikely that so much importance should attach to a mere worker in stucco, but it is a medium of the Italians and not to

90

Opposite: Vittorio Carpaccio, *The Miracle of the Holy Cross.*
Overleaf: Giambattista Tiepolo, *Sacrifice of Iphigenia*;
fresco in Villa Valmarana, Vicenza.

be despised any more than fresco painting just because that needs to be done by workmen up a ladder. Does not James Gibbs, architect of our St Martin's-in-the-Fields, refer to Artari, 'of' the ubiquitous Artari and Bagutti – ubiquitous because at one time more work was attributed to them than they could possibly have accomplished – as 'gentleman' plasterer?★

It is only necessary to visit the Villa Pisani at Strà to feel the difference between the Palladian ideal on its native *terra firma* and when transferred to England. There was a second wave of native Palladians, little studied as yet, and the Villa Pisani is the work of one of them, Frigimelica, most suitably named.† It was begun in about 1740 for the Doge Alvise Pisani, in utmost frigid splendour and cold emptiness. Even Tiepolo's ceiling in the ballroom of the *Apotheosis of the Pisani Family* cannot raise the temperature for it is in fact too silly and impossible a theme; and one wonders what their contemporaries can have thought of the Pisani free of the laws of gravity and floating up there among the clouds. Only at one end of the oval painting is there some sense, where in the shade of his favourite Friulian pine trees – or were they the result of his three years in Franconia? – a young man with his leg over the parapet into reality plays a long-necked lute, a young girl near to him sings to it, and what appears to be nothing else than a picnic table is laid out almost touching them underneath the trees. In the annals of exiled Royal personages can there have been any experience more unwelcoming than the arrival here of Carlos IV and Maria-Luisa, the 'Goya' King and Queen of Spain? Even the stables are large and pompous; and the statuettes of *haute école* horses on the pillars between the boxes are different indeed in spirit from what would be the hunters or race horses of an English stable.

Though this seems an appropriate moment in which to mention it, the Villa Pisani is in fact not the place in which to study the Venetian painted or lacquered furniture. This is better seen in the Palazzo Donà dalle Rose; and the Villa Pisani also excuses more than reference to G. B. Brustolon, the carver of tortuously intricate chairs, figures of blackamoors, and so on. But the painted Venetian furniture, again, is in complete antithesis to what is intended in England by 'Venetian' furniture, a term which is in fact much more suited to its purposes and setting. The work of the Venetian craftsmen is of capricious form, with never a straight line, and for the most part painted with a profusion or *potpourri* of little flowers. The lacquering process is rudimentary, the wood itself seldom of fine quality, and the furniture in consequence hardly ever in good condition. In addition to which it is of all styles of furniture perhaps the easiest to copy, so that the good and genuine is not often seen.

★ Either of them, or both together, made chimney-pieces, stucco'd walls and ceilings for Houghton, Mereworth, Sutton Scarsdale, and Moor Park, among other houses.

† Recently assigned to F. M. Preti. cf. Wittower, *op. cit.*, p. 372, footnote 50.

Opposite: Two Gentlemen in Venice; page of a sketchbook by Luca Carlevaris (1665–1731).

As to the 'Venetian' furniture in England, the problem of its correct attribution and the mystery of who made it will never be settled until a properly documented William Kent exhibition has been organised and held, when as many questions may be answered by absence as by presence. Were they in fact Italian carpenters and craftsmen? It is probably only because of the known 'Englishness' of Grinling Gibbons and his school – woodcarvers such as Samuel Watson, and others, who worked at Chatsworth – that their nationality has ever been disputed. If it is true that on the one hand Kent employed the Italian sculptor Guelfi, presumably on some of the side-tables at Houghton, it is equally the case that the bed in the green velvet state-room there was 'carried out' by the firm of Turner, Hill and Pitter in the Strand. Perhaps a number at least of the typical gilt Kent tables with their dolphin or lion supports and their use of masks and shells must have been made in London by Italian workmen, which are in fact a staider, more Palladian version of furniture that Kent must have seen during his formative years in Italy (1710–16). They are, as one would expect, typical of the Italian *seicento* in style, retarded about fifty to a hundred years from their Italian equivalents, and with a Northern, restraining hand upon them despite their heaviness. But certain pieces in mahogany, library tables and hall settees, formerly at Devonshire House, cannot surely be of anything but English workmanship. No qualification but that of 'Palladian' could apply to the Royal Barge designed by Kent for Frederick, Prince of Wales, and now in the National Maritime Museum, where the carving was executed by James Richards and the gilding by Paul Pettit, in proof that by then (1732) Italians were no longer indispensable and English craftsmen were employed.★

It is a curious thought that while Lord Burlington and his satellite Palladians, William Kent chief luminary among them, were recreating their Arcadia from Palladio's plans and drawings, Giambattista Tiepolo was reviving and emulating the golden age of Paolo Veronese. For in the result, their endeavours could hardly be more different although Veronese and Palladio were contemporaries and had worked together, in particular at Villa Maser. Nor was this the only inherent and built-in contradiction. The stucco of the colonnades from villas on the Venetian *terra firma* was transmuted to stone in England, poverty turned to riches, and what was intended for coolness carried from the sun of Italy to the predominantly cold and wet English countryside. It was of this Venetian mania that Alexander Pope wrote – and those he criticised were his friends:

> 'Shall call the winds thro' long arcades to roar,
> Proud to catch cold at a Venetian door,'

a solecism not likely to lose its force on any of Pope's contemporaries who had stood on a wet day under the porticos of Chiswick or Mereworth, or

★ cf. *The Work of William Kent*, by Margaret Jourdain, London, 1948, p. 82, footnote 5.

shivered in the cold passages and colder bedrooms of Holkham or Houghton. As an importation from abroad it was inappropriate and an anachronism, as much so as are the Mid-Victorian monuments and embellishments of Bombay. But it suited the cold reserve of the typical Englishman of the upper classes, and as such whatever the expense and inconvenience it had to stand. It was indeed no more unlikely than the conversion of those sporting circles to the tea-ceremony of Japan. But, once done, it was irremoveable except by bulldozer and the demolition squad, and is now an accepted part of the art and landscape of the land.

Yet behind the English Palladians there is delight in the exterior and a latent pleasure which was to become a hobby with amateurs in the designing of façades. Lord Scarsdale, who is the rake in *The Rake's Progress* and is shown looking at the plan of a building in Hogarth's painting, designed the façade of Sutton Scarsdale, in Derbyshire, with the help of Smith of Warwick; while the Palladian bridge in the pleasure grounds at Wilton was designed by Lord Pembroke and his architect Roger Morris. The amateur had broken into architecture; and the Palladian bridge, one of the beauties of England, bears out the argument that works of art can alter because of their environment even when they are exact copies. For there is another Palladian bridge at Stowe, and yet another at Prior Park, outside Bath, the latter being slightly different in scale; but the poetry is altogether different, and it is the difference between a superlative and an only moderate performance of the same piece of music.

William Kent, who was one of the 'universal providers' in architecture – and the first Englishman to fill the rôle – cuts of course a somewhat provincial figure beside Bernini, first inventor and practitioner of the genre, whom one hesitates between calling architect or sculptor, and for whom new terms could be coined in description of his activities as artificer of the Cathedra Petri and baldacchino of St Peter's, and as designer or water-architect of the Roman fountains. Kent, with his limited if strong talents in particular directions, did well to confine himself to the rigid grammatical rules of the Palladian strait-jacket. Had he broken out of that in exuberance his weaknesses would soon have shown themselves. He stayed in Rome long enough to leave a fresco'd memorial behind him in the vault of San Giuliano dei Fiamminghi, an obligatory gesture like that of having your name carved on leaving school. His masterpiece, undoubtedly, is the great hall at Holkham with its fluted pillars of Derbyshire alabaster, its glorious frieze and coffered ceiling; its plan that of a basilica, 'in origin a design of Vitruvius to which Palladio draws attention,' the magic name and recommendation acting, as always on Kent and his circle, with somewhat of the benign, if incontrovertible authority of Chairman Mao. No less magnificent are the two-storeyed chimneypieces at Holkham by the sculptor Rysbrack for which Kent designed the architectural setting, and the ceilings, doorways, and the gilt chairs and tables; as, too, at Houghton, near by, showing this considerable designer in his Venetian manner at its best, furniture which you may look for in vain in the Venetian villas of the *terra firma* for it never had existence and was never made.

Most Venetian of all, it need scarcely be said, is the villa at Chiswick in variation upon Palladio's Villa Rotonda at Vicenza, built for Kent's patron, Lord Burlington; but it was a feat in which he had been anticipated by Colin Campbell who had already produced his version of it at Mereworth Castle, a house which is beautiful indeed but according to weather, and not even the amenities of electric light, central heating, telephone, or stereophonic music, can make it suited to the climate or banish the thought of how cold and uncomfortable it must have been to earlier generations of its inhabitants. There were even another couple of versions of the Villa Rotonda; at Foots Cray in Kent, and Nuttall Temple near Nottingham, the latter, with its delightful, octagonal domed hall, long ago torn down as though it were a plague spot by the local corporation. Further than these four prime exemplars of the Palladian fever it would be unwise to proceed, or these pages could be distorted into a history of architecture in England during the eighteenth century.

The same strictures apply to the study of the stuccoists though this was in essence an Italian art, and it is stretching a point in any case to say it was Venetian. Who, then, were the brothers Franchini who worked at 15, Queen's Square, Bath, where they contrived a framed panel of St Cecilia under an archway, seated at the organ; who worked, as well, at Carton in Ireland for the Duke of Leinster; at the Rotunda Chapel in Dublin; and it is conjectured at Riverstown House, Co. Cork, lately rescued by the Irish Georgian group. And Bagutti and Artari, once again. Who were they? The authority is surely correct who traces them to one of 'the successive waves of stuccadors . . . from fertile hives in the valleys to either side of the Swiss Alps'.★ But it was work which varied much in quality, to return for a moment to the international scene. In the old houses at The Hague ascribed to Daniel Marot, the *stucchi* are incomparable in their delayed Louis XIV or even Régence manner; at Clausholm, in far off Jutland, the brothers Carbonetti and Francesco Quadri, just as those others from the Canton of Ticino, did stucco work of prodigious beauty making of it, as I have written elsewhere, 'the veritable castle of the Sleeping Princess'. The Swiss Italian stuccadors even worked in the monasteries round Moscow. I would not say that the work of the Franchini brothers is pre-eminent in comparison with these. The inevitable Bagutti and Artari, to reverse their order for once, were the better craftsmen.

★ C.P. Curran, in *Irish Georgian Society Bulletin*, January–March 1966, p. 19.

It was the second generation of stuccoists, who were native and not Italian, who gave the individuality to Dublin houses; Dublin, said advisedly, because Richard West and Stapleton, foremost of them, seem not to have journeyed like the Italians to the far ends of Ireland. Both men attained to civic importance in Dublin as heads of their guilds, and were citizens of wealth and substance. The place above all others in which to admire West's prowess with the trowel and scalpel is 20, Lower Dominick Street, now a house of the Jesuits. The stair is decorated with gilt *stucchi* in which birds play a large part, being indeed the signature and almost the special forte of this stuccoist. Here they are to be seen in quantity, to the number perhaps of fifty or sixty in all in a decoration of gold leaves and flowers; a scheme handled with delicacy and imagination even if it reminded one admirer of the wooden swallows stuck all over the walls and ceiling of the barber's shop in King's Road, Chelsea, a relic of the Dr Phené who built the 'freak' house in Beaufort Street, round the corner, with a condition of the tenancy that the swallows be left there in perpetuity.* But that is to be reminded of good music by a tune upon a barrel-organ, because the *stucchi* at the house in Lower Dominick Street are of the highest beauty, in reminder of the time when Dublin was the third city in Europe after London and Paris and a centre of wit and gaiety.

* Both Dr Phené's house and the hairdresser's with swallow decoration, inspired perhaps by visits to a Swiss châlet, have long since been demolished.

5

Four Men in Black:
Borromini, Guarini, Juvarra, Vittone

In all the human arts great geniuses appear from time to time in whose hands everything changes and after whose death nothing is ever the same again. Of such was Gianlorenzo Bernini, so often and justly described as the last universal genius of the Italian Renaissance, but someone who was enabled so fully to express and put into being his own potentialities that he left behind him more of finished fact than influence, or paths for others after him to follow and pick up. So successful was Bernini in his career that reaction against him was bound to set in, and in all probability within his own lifetime. It would be interesting in this context to have heard the talk about him in the Roman studios which were to the seventeenth century what the studios of Paris have been to the last century or so. Those eager to take and explore new direction from Bernini would have found themselves opposed by a finality as complete and fruitless of progeny as Wagner's music dramas or Beethoven's Symphonies. Like those other two geniuses he had a stultifying and deadening effect on all who tried to follow him. All such had to look elsewhere than *The Ring of the Nibelungs*, the *Choral Symphony*, or the colonnades and baldacchino of St Peter's.

The fructifying force for the future was not Bernini but Borromini who was born in 1599 on Lake Lugano, in the Italian-speaking canton of Ticino, in a district which produced sculptors and stucco-carvers for many generations. But Borromini was primarily a stone-carver, and it was in this capacity that he went at an early age to Rome where he worked till thirty years old on the decorative details of St Peter's. Here, he was perhaps forwarded in his career by Carlo Maderno the Papal architect, who was his cousin, and who certainly made use of him as architectural draughtsman. With Bernini while he was working on St Peter's his relations were difficult, and taking Michelangelo for his ideal he had become critical of Bernini's ease and fluency. From Bernini he was set apart by instinct, being cerebral more than sensual, silent by nature, celibate, deeply religious, and difficult to know. He frightened people, was dressed in funeral black like a Spaniard, and only sported red garters and rosettes on his shoes – all this from G.B.Passeri his contemporary, who made every enquiry concerning him.* His first chance came in 1634 with the little church of San Carlo alle Quattro Fontane, or San Carlino, in which he produced novel and sensational effects with his array of sixteen Corinthian columns in winding procession to the high altar; effects won indeed not through simplicity but by ingeniously complicated means, the originality of which is most quickly evident in the extraordinarily shaped coffers of the dome. They are hexagons and octagons, intermixed with crosses diminishing in size as they near the lantern, and which get their effect from geometry and mathematical skill in a style that is entirely alien to the sweep and flow of Bernini.

This small church on its corner site was much talked of and admired, if perhaps discussed more than praised; so much so that it was hardly finished before the much bigger commission was given to him to build the church of Sant' Ivo alla Sapienza, which is his extremely original and curious master-piece. It would seem to be true that Borromini planned it in the shape of a bee with folded wings in tribute to Pope Urban VIII who was of the Barberini family, and certainly it looks like that in plan.† But it resembles in outline and in striation some involved geranium or pelargonium petal for which there could be no altruistic or ulterior meaning and this was long before geraniums were grown in greenhouse or in garden. In fact it is a concealed or elaborated star-hexagon, approached through an elongated arcaded court, and arousing immediate interest because of the extraordinary nature of its dome and cupola. And as though to emphasise that this is no cathedral or basilica but yet something that is more than a little secret and important, Borromini gives it no façade of its own but the simple curve of the curtain of the original and earlier courtyard, with the star of the Chigi to fill the blank openings or windows in its parapet – and over those, at the corners, little turrets to each side formed of the star-surmounted hills or sugar-loafs which are the emblem of the same family – behind and above which climbs the drum of his, to this point, interesting but unspectacular new building, but with the drum of course going in inverse direction to the curve of the wall below it which serves as its façade. Above this drum the dome rises in pyramid shape surmounted by the hexagonal lantern with its double columns and entablature in deep concave curves – of derivation from the not long discovered Temple of Venus at Baalbek, it is fairly certain. And on top of

* *Vita de pittori, scultori ed architetti . . . in Roma dal 1641 fino al 1673*, republished 1772 and 1934 (in Vienna).

† The *Poemata*, or Latin poems, of Urban VIII (1631), has an allegorical design, full page, of a bee ploughing a field, and scattered up and down its pages are woodcut bees, some in black and some in red, which are by Bernini, who, also, designed the beautiful frontispiece of David wrestling with the lion.

that is the twisting spire which has been said to resemble 'the horn of a Sicilian goat' and is the grand and final curiosity of Sant' Ivo alla Sapienza.

The interior of Sant' Ivo, of fascinating but, it must be admitted, tortured shape, is both less satisfying and less surprising. It has been forced reluctantly, even painfully into shape; to be compared with one of those organ fugues of J. S. Bach which are perfect, as it were, in spite of themselves, have every weight of symbolic meaning in his secret language or cipher, and yet of their very mathematical perfection lose human warmth and understanding. The interior of the dome of Sant' Ivo is obviously an engineering and geometrical masterpiece with, again, its bee-shaped or pelargonium-petal outline; but the segments leading up to that are too pinched and narrow to be pleasurable and the, doubtless, symbolical rows of stars, both up those segments of the wall and in the spandrels of the dome, are a little obvious in their higher geometrical or mathematical setting. It is the shape of the interior of Sant' Ivo and its entirely original exterior – if it be that to borrow an idea for it from ancient Baalbek of the Classical decadence? – that together form the masterpiece of Borromini.

His other, most sensational work is the tower to Sant' Andrea delle Fratte which, it could be said in truth, resembles nothing built before or since. Borromini was in this instance finishing, not building a whole church, and at his death he left it uncompleted. The tower is in three tiers or units designed like Wren's spire on Ludgate Hill to be seen from opposite as one comes down towards it, though not in this case with the huge and beautiful dome of St Paul's behind it. But it was meant to arrest and draw attention, towards which end it begins simply enough from a square foundation tier; with the one above that circular and of another rhythm altogether; a strongly marked or accented balustrade to top that; on the curve of which rests the feet of the pairs of herms above that. They are herms with angels' not satyrs' faces, and folded wings; naturalistic wings as though studied on the spot in cage or aviary. The tower of Sant' Andrea at this point is already sculpture, or, at the least, the very finest stone-masonry, more than architecture, and it now climbs again from another 'Temple of Venus' recessed cornice of entablature in the form of eight stone ornaments in pairs and raising their heads as ornaments or flambeaux (as they look from the street below); over which, once more, four stone scrolls of bold, even flaunting design uphold a crown with spikes or flanges of special, even personal cut and sharpness as though, which must be true, particular care and trouble had been taken with them. The tower of Sant' Andrea, an unimportant Roman church, is conceived as a piece of sculpture to hold the attention but it could also be a table ornament, or a pyx or other sacred vessel in a sacristy or treasury.

Such in barest outline are the most sensational of Borromini's buildings, and the myriad details of his invention must go unnoticed. Even, for instance,

Borromini, Guarini, Juvarra, Vittone

Centre of lantern in Guarini's dome above the Chapel of the Holy Shroud, Turin.

Right: Tower of Sant' Andrea delle Fratte by Borromini.
Below: Statue of San Carlo Borromeo on the façade of Borromini's church of San Carlino, Rome.

Borromini's
graceful *cortile* of
San Carlino.

View into interior
of coffered dome
of San Carlino.

Opposite: Interior of the dome of Sant' Ivo alla Sapienza by Borromini.
Below: Lantern of Sant' Ivo, with drum of derivation from the Temple of Venus at Baalbek, surmounted by a twisting spire.

Left: Lantern above Guarini's dome over the Chapel of the Holy Shroud, Turin.
Opposite: Interior the dome of the Chapel of the Holy Shroud.

Detail of the brickwork of Palazzo Carignano, Turin,
with the typical star motif of Guarini.

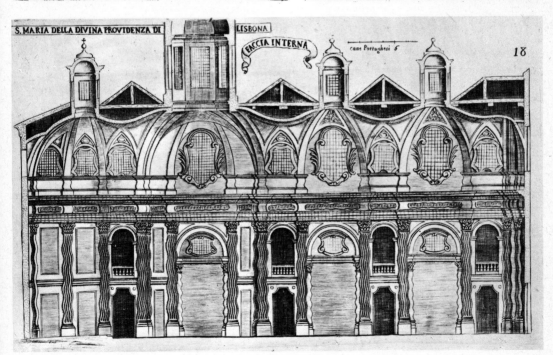

Engravings from Guarini's *Architettura Civile*, which show (*top left*) the Santuario d'Oropa; (*top right*) the construction of the dome of the Santo Sudario; and (*bottom*) Santa Maria della Providenza, Lisbon, destroyed in the earthquake of 1755.

Left: Three-storeyed sanctuary by Bernardo Vittone at Vallinotto.

Opposite: Dome of San Bernardino, Chieri, by Vittone.

Left: Interior of Vittone's dome in the church of the Assunta, Riva.

Opposite: Balcony and gilt ceiling in the Consolata, Turin, built by Guarini and altered by Juvarra.

Opposite: Exterior detail of the Consolata.
Right: One of the campaniles of Juvarra's basilica of La Superga outside Turin.

VEDUTA DI STUPINIGI

Left: Departure for the hunt from Stupinigi, Juvarra's *Palazzina di Caccia* built for the Dukes of Savoy.
Below: Interior of the ball-room of Stupinigi, decorated with wall-sconces incorporating stags' heads, designed by the architect.
Opposite: Inlaid altar by Pietro Piffetti in a chapel in the Royal Palace, Turin.

wonders such as the extraordinary fantasy of his pair of terms to each side of the statue of San Carlo Borromeo above the doorway to San Carlino. These are angel faces of great beauty, one wing folded and at rest down the term which has no semblance of the angel body, and the other wing outspread to touch the opposing angel wing, their pinions just meeting above the niche in which the statue stands.

But the importance of his peculiar genius, and of his strange temperament which led him in the end to kill himself, was that as a celibate and a recluse from society Borromini brought into the High Baroque of seventeenth-century Rome a sensibility deeper and no less eloquent than that of the master of all arts, Bernini – eloquent but, as it were, speechless or making sense by signs. In his hands the ease and fluency of Baroque are gone; and the results only come from intensity and pain of thinking, in a private language or cipher as full of symbols, as fiery of feeling as in El Greco, but with abstruse geometry and mathematics as machinery and background in the place of Byzantium and Venice. It is a cerebral Baroque only possible of accomplishment in experienced hands and different indeed from the worldly urbanity of Bernini. If it be true that the physique of an artist enters into the works of his hands – then, the mere portrait in words of Borromini, his black clothes, his taciturnity, and in the end his suicide, will give us all the difference we need between him as person and architect and Bernini. His is the type that one would think solitary and unique, and unlikely to be historically repeated. Yet the very opposite happened. Not only did his fame not die with him, but it was continued in other hands.

This was indeed a very unexpected thing to happen. Borromini died in 1667, fifteen years before Bernini, with the shadow of insanity upon his fame, and it was never to be thought that his tortuous ingenuity finding expression for its secret symbols in architecture by way of mathematical and geometric drawing would find posthumous fruition. It is in antithesis to the free flowering of the art in Southern Italy or Spain, but it is to be kept in mind that there is ever a Don Basilio, as well as a Figaro and a Count Almaviva upon the southern scene. Or, nearer home, 'a man in black' to appear out of nowhere, argue with George Borrow and ignore Isobel Berners in the firelit dell. It is the extreme pietistic spirit of the Counter-Reformation and its insistence on celibacy, with what that loses and what it gains in intellectual fibre, trailing off in the spiritual descendants of Borromini into a show of pyrotechnics against a colder sky. That it found realisation in Piedmont, 'the mountain-foot', the most northerly or at any rate most sub-Alpine division of Italy, is tribute both to its remoteness which would attract the least renowned of architects trained in the schools of Rome, and to the extreme pietistic tendencies of the Dukes of Savoy. But in this instance, not for the first time – as of drawing-master or music-teacher not of significant importance – the

Opposite: Façade of Juvarra's church of Santa Cristina, Turin.

wandering artist who had to put up with every humiliation and disappointment turned out to be the architectural genius of his day. That he was given
opportunity, we will see, is not to be gainsaid, and his difficulty of character
may have spoiled his chances. But, also, he made extreme demands upon his
patrons, all, or much of which is to be seen in his engraved portrait, poor
likeness though that may be.

It is the head and shoulders of a bearded man, dressed in clerical black, with
some quarter-inch or less of his white undershirt showing at the neck, and
unrelieved darkness for his background, which is in fact nothing exceptional
for an engraved frontispiece of the time, but yet it suggests and explains the
man of whom little more could be said by way of identification than that he
was a priest, a bearded man with prominent aquiline nose, and with no more
than that for his 'identikit'. Guarino Guarini was born at Modena in 1624, and
it is of significance that he entered the Theatine Order when only fifteen years
old, was fully ordained when twenty-three, and that all five of his brothers
joined the same Order.★ He stayed in Rome four years studying for the
priesthood, where the churches of Borromini must have fascinated him, and
in fact the interior of San Carlino was then being built. Soon he was back at
Modena lecturing on philosophy, and involved in a dispute with the Duke
over the Theatine church on which he had been consulted. This gives him
undue prominence so quickly after his return home, but Modena was one of
the smallest of the Italian Duchies. He lived there, in all, for eight years; and
five years after that, in 1660, he was in Messina as teacher of philosophy and
mathematics. Writing, also, a tragi-comedy of morality, *La Pietà Trionfante*,
and drawing plans for the building of two churches; one of which never got
further than the drawing-board, while the other was entirely destroyed in the
Messina earthquake of 1908 before it was properly photographed or studied.†
This was typical of the misfortunes that befell Guarini. 'Il segreto delle
ordinarie mie sfortune mi parla al cuore e mi fa tremare di sinistra risposta' –
'the secret of my continual misfortunes appeals to the heart and makes me
tremble at thought of an unfavourable reply', as Guarini, himself, writes many
years later to the Duke of Modena, asking permission to return home after
long absence. At that date (1673) he had already been working for some
years on the chapel of the Santo Sudario, his masterpiece, and might be

★ 'Strange destiny that a family should thus determine its own end', translated from *Guarino
Guarini*, by Paolo Portoghesi, Milan, 1956, a most excellent monograph and the only work so far
devoted to Guarini.

† The church of the SS. Annunziata and the Theatine monastery next to it at Messina were destroyed
and the hexagonal church of the Padri Somaschi was never built. An engraving of the former, reproduced in Paolo Portoghesi, *op. cit.*, pl. 7., shows the long façade of the Teatini monastery with awkward
fenestration on all four ground floors, and a church rather resembling that of San Matteo at Lecce, with
a façade, that is to say, convex in its lower storey, concave in the upper, and a storey above that like a
'blind' triumphal arch. Neither church nor monastery look very interesting, but Guarini had not yet
fully attained his style.

thought to have outlived the disappointments of his younger days. But those were in fact profound and genuine. When the Duke of Modena had exiled him in 1655, Borromini spent some time in Parma and in Guastalla before settling in Messina, and it was at this latter that he first was able to experiment in a stucco chapel with his 'undulating line', a device of which he makes great play in his *Architettura Civile* and an invention that was to spread not only to Bavaria but even to country districts in Portugal and in Brazil where the chapels with undulating outline and of oval or octagonal shape owe their being to Guarino Guarini by way of his forerunner Borromini.

The next disappointment of his career was in Paris where he built the church of the Theatines, Sainte-Anne-La-Royale – all his travels to this point being to different houses of his Order. But Guarini was one of those to whom misfortune comes not only in their lifetime but posthumously as well. The church was never finished in his lifetime, and was demolished entirely in 1823. It had a waving or undulating façade, an exterior resembling a pagoda in five tiers – but like no pagoda in Nepal or China or Japan – and its dome had 'windows reminiscent of the bellies of violins'.★ While in Paris this extra-ordinary man taught theology and published his *Placita Philosophica* which of all his writings, being without his intensely characteristic and personal drawings even when these are in geometrical form, is about the most difficult to concentrate upon and understand.† During these years he must have been perfecting his mathematical studies though the full flood of his learned publications was to come later (five books on fortification, on geometry and on astronomy between 1674 and 1678). During these earlier years Guarini may, or may not have been to Spain and Portugal. There is no direct evidence of his visit, but plenty of ground for assuming he went there. He must surely have been to Córdoba and studied the Arab cupolas in the Mezquita; and as surely he had seen and studied the vaults of mediaeval cathedrals on his way through France to Spain. It could be said that his finished style when it appears is compounded of mediaeval and even Moorish influences, and of his acknowledged master Borromini.

But in the meantime there were his other failures, and it is perhaps better to group them together however apart in geography and in time in order to deal at last with his successes. There was the church of Santa Maria della Divina Providenza which he built in Lisbon, or which was carried out to his design. It seems unlikely if he went to Spain that he should not have not gone a little further to Portugal where his church was being built. Destruction came to it in the terrible earthquake of 1755, but its plan is preserved in the

★ Rudolf Wittkower, *op. cit.* p. 269.

† There are eight hundred pages of this book in Latin. Perhaps, for sheer impenetrability, the only work to surpass it is the *Causes intérieures de la faiblesse extérieure de l'Eglise*, by Liszt's friend, Princess Sayn-Wittgenstein. It is in twenty-four thick volumes.

Architettura Civile; a bow-shaped façade, undulating body with a pair of chapels to each side, octagonal chapels in the transepts, and rounded chapel for the high altar. It is probable that this church with its capricious outline had a strong influence upon local architects and may be an explanation for the beautiful and originally planned churches of Northern Portugal. Of Lisbon, itself, it is difficult to judge; so much was lost in the earthquake, and no paintings or drawings are left. The church of St Mary of Altötting, at Prague, was yet another posthumous disaster for it still stands, but altered beyond recognition. From the engravings in the *Architettura Civile* it had domed chapels and his accustomed undulating outline. It is a late work, planned in his last years; and here again it much influenced the local architects all over Central Europe. One may guess as to what extent it was studied by the brothers, Egid Quirin and Cosmas Damian Asam. The *Architettura Civile* of Guarini was not published until 1737, as we will see, but the engravings for it were in circulation as early as 1686 and must have been known to architects both in Central Europe and in Portugal.

So many living failures and posthumous disappointments but, at last, the tide of fortune was to turn when Guarini found himself moved by his Order in 1666 to the Theatine monastery in Turin. In this sub-Alpine capital there was already considerable building activity under Duke Carlo Emanuele II by the Castellamontes, father and son, who began laying out the capital on a regular plan. The elder Castellamonte built the Castello del Valentino in a park along the banks of the river Po, with four corner pavilions completely in the French style, and indeed its inhabitant was to be the Duchess Christina who was a daughter of Henri Quatre. The Dukes of Savoy, boundless of ambition, and pietistic to near madness, gave up all surplus energy to the chase, as witness their hunting palaces, Stupinigi, Racconigi, and the rest.★ But, now, fortuitous chance, which led Guarini to build the church of San Lorenzo, resulted in the capital of the late Italian architects being removed from Rome to Turin where the last great masters Guarini and Juvarra had their day.

The Theatine church of San Lorenzo is one of the two masterworks of Guarini in which his mathematical, geometrical genius found full play. The porch apart, the nave or body of it appears to be square-shaped from outside. But, within, it is a concave octagon which lifts itself into a Greek cross in its upper storey, while the entire vessel or body of the church consists of three domed spaces; or, rather, the Cappella Maggiore is circular with its own dome within the outer dome of the octagon around it, while there is, as well,

★ Also, their hunting books, of which *La Venaria Reale* of 1672, with its frontispiece, *à la chasse d'Henri Quatre*, is a beautiful example. A little further on comes a full page 'flourish' of calligraphy reminiscent of Picasso's 'without taking the pen off the paper' drawings to Jean Cocteau's *Le Coq et l'Harlequin*.

the domed high altar. The interior effect is of lightness, too light, even, for the complication of its planning. With the interior of San Lorenzo we are dealing with a structure, as complicated, but of as seemingly simple a surface, as J. S. Bach's *Canonic Variations* for organ on the Chorale *Vom Himmel hoch* behind which the most extreme and hair-raising feats of virtuosity are in progress without our being aware of them. All that we see in San Lorenzo is an octagon marked out with pillars. We become aware of something different, though, when we look up into the dome which is the end to which Guarini has lent all his ingenuity and which is his visual, as against his concealed or hidden, showpiece.*

It is, this is true, not quite as strangely improbable as the inside of the cupola of the chapel of the Sudario but, again, as there, it is that moment while an organ is being played in some cathedral in Spain and we look up in the semi-dark and see the organ, perhaps a double-organ, levelling its broadsides and artillery of pipes at us. The entrance into the lantern, beyond and higher than the dome, appears to be resting on a criss-cross series of slightly curving slats or straps which closely resemble, to the extent of almost copying, those of the ninth-century Capillo Villaviciosa in the Mezquita of Córdoba. In fact, the rosette-shaped cupola appears to be slung on a kind of cats' cradle though it is far above it, and derived from the 'op-architectural' tricks or inventions of Borromini, this being a speciality which will be carried still further in the next generation by Bernardo Vittone.

A year or two after he had begun work at San Lorenzo the commission came to Guarini from Duke Carlo Emanuele II to build a chapel leading from the Cathedral to house the Holy Shroud, a mysteriously beautiful and inexplicable sacred object, even if it is not what it purports to be but the shadow or negative of a crucified man imprinted by some freak of nature on a winding-sheet, and a being whoever he may have been with features as though drawn by Leonardo. It is very doubtful if Guarini could have seen this holy object, it is so seldom shown, but it was something which would have a strong appeal to him because of its reticence and mystery. In building this no less than marvellous chapel which is circular in shape and constructed of dark brown, black and grey marbles, he must have had in mind the octagonal Cappella dei Principi at Florence with its sarcophagi of the Medici Grand Dukes and the octagonal Panteón de los Reyes at the Escorial, both of them funeral chapels. But, as well, the Chapel of the Sudario has a solemn theatrical air, as though intended for funeral pageants and processions, this, because of its three entrances in true theatrical tradition. A pair of these entrances lead up flights of steps from either side of the high altar of the Cathedral, while the other for the Duke and his Court descends from

---

* Guarini lived to celebrate the first Mass in San Lorenzo, though the church was not completed. It may have been his spiritual reward for many failures and disappointments.

immediately opposite across the chapel and leading directly from the Royal Palace, these flights of steps being of obvious suggestion from the staircase at the Laurenziana by Michelangelo, who was Guarini's idol. But it is the interior of the dome which is the transcendental feature of the Cappella del Sudario, and towards which the eye is led up by the coffers of different shapes that decorate the spandrels, as far as the grand circle and opening of his pyrotechnics. These begin with six windows framed with pilasters and niches between them in strict Palladian canon, above which the criss-cross of ribs or arches rise in regular, stepped order to the rosette and the star within it which is the climax of the adventure.* Looking into this extraordinary cupola is like being let into a secret; but one is not told what it is all about. Professor Rudolf Wittkower† suggests that the whole chapel is a Trinitarian conception, and finds triads and multiples of three in every detail and in all directions, even in the three-storeyed 'pagoda' above the chapel, a feature which with differences of detail is decidedly of the blood of Borromini's Sant' Ivo alla Sapienza, in fact it would not be difficult to confuse both 'pagodas' in one's mind. The drum of the Sudario has high windows and the continual lift and fall of an 'eyebrow' cornice above those, to compare with the one window visible in the drum of Sant' Ivo as one walks towards that through the courtyard. But the stepped or ringed motif in the roof of Sant' Ivo has been immensely elaborated and made into a feature at the chapel of the Sudario. It has the look almost of zigzag, criss-cross or 'monkey walk' tracks leading – somewhere? And they lead upwards to what is nothing more nor less than a three-tiered *stupa* in miniature, plain and unadorned, but in distant relation to Borobudur and to every other Buddhist *stupa* from Kelaniya in Ceylon to the *stupas* in India, Further India and Japan. But it is only the hint of this at the chapel of the Sudario, and then the cupola rises again with triple tiers, six lighthouse windows in each diminishing in size to end in nothing. Had Guarini seen the engravings to Romeyn de Hoogh's *Les Indes Orientales et Occidentales* (1680)? It is more than probable.

The suggestion of a *stupa*, and of the steps or paths leading up to it, in the roof of the chapel of the Sudario is too marked to be passed by and ignored. That he had admired and studied the mediaeval cathedrals is stated with emphasis in his own writings, a thing which alone and by itself makes him unique among his contemporaries. That he had, also, seen and studied the Moorish vaulting in the Mezquita at Córdoba would seem evident, and that he had given his attention to engravings of mosques and heathen temples is not at all improbable in virtue of his enquiring mind. The terms at the

---

* Mr James Lees-Milne, *Baroque in Italy*, 1959, p. 77, writes of the interior of the cupola as 'a receding tunnel of stepped and curved arches . . . the impeccable precision of the work suggests the carefully laid twigs of a bird's nest.' His description could not be bettered and is inevitable of quotation.

† *op. cit.*, p. 272.

entrance to the chapel of the Sudario are abstractions of the human form, but it is true that they suggest a black body, a female body in the little skirt of a savage woman or Nubian slave. What, then, is the significance, the esoteric meaning of the extraordinary interior of the cupola of the Sudario? For it must have its spiritual and symbolic meaning. That zigzag 'monkey walk' of crossbeams was after all unnecessary and could have been concealed by a false dome the intricacies of which would have come easy to him. But far from their being concealed, they are made into the *raison d'être* and the feature, inside and out, of the Sudario. The suggestion they imply is of a struggle, an endless ascent into some scaffolding or rigging with, at its summit, the aim attained with the rays of light coming forth and the promise and affirmation of redemption. The Palladian windows and niches below the start of this puzzle or mesh of intersecting lines appear like the sanity of ordinary life before the spiritual torments of dying, and those cannot be far absent from any reminder of the beautiful, but terrible countenance impressed upon the winding-sheet of the Sudario.

Guarini's church of San Filippo at Turin was later so much remodelled by Juvarra that it is no fair criterion of his undoubted genius. In the plates of his *Architettura Civile* it advances in three equal bodies flanked by as many side chapels to the altar, but the façade has four clusters of three pillars each on its second storey to frame a window of bizarre shape the form of which suggested the windows in the clerestory and along the nave. It would be a solace to our curiosity to think that San Filippo may not have been among the most original of Guarini's buildings. But the Santuario della Consolata, also in Turin, is another matter, although worked over subsequently by Juvarra and later 'modernised'. It is in fact, not one, but two churches built into each other; first, an oval church and then the hexagonal Santuario with its circular side chapels all built apparently on an airy and inconsequential plan. But it serves to give some idea of his unrealised, or destroyed buildings; the hexagonal church of the Padri Somaschi at Messina, with a square storey superimposed on its six sides, and then another hexagon to support its dome; San Filippo at Casale Monferrato (in Piedmont) which looks so extraordinary and beautiful in plan with two domed circular chapels flanking the larger circle of the main building, smaller and bigger oval chapels, it seems to be, in every direction, opening further into three circular domed chapels which would have given with their five domes together a distinct impression of a Kremlin, which is indeed not dissimilar to that imparted by the exterior of La Consolata.★

Another plan for a church in Turin from the *Architettura Civile* shows an

---

★ It is at Casale Monferrato, between Vercelli and Alessandria, that Guarini must have seen the peculiar, ribbed vaulting in the twelfth-century Duomo, Mozarabic of appearance, and which is cited for its influence upon him by those dubious of his having seen the Mezquita at Córdoba.

unsymmetrical or lop-sided front for which the terrain must be accountable, and then the chapels along both aisles proceed in the 'nickel and dime' formula of Mr Philip Johnson's masterpiece of our day, the pre-Columbian Library at Dumbarton Oaks – of larger and smaller circular chapels leading into one another, but the right aisle shorter of limb, a couple of chapels short from its lop-sided start, until both aisles and the three units of the nave merge into the transept, where again Guarini has had to trick the planning in order to achieve symmetry within the undulating line of his exterior, this being perhaps the extreme instance of that in all his ground plans. This part of Italy, near to the Alps, is rich in *Santuarios* and *Sacro Montes*,★ among them the Santuario d'Oropa for which the plan appears in *Architettura Civile*; a wide flight of steps leading to an octagonal building which is only just not circular, with three oblong chapels to each side, a huge central chamber for the crowd of pilgrims, and a chapel beyond that and opening from it which fills three-quarters of a circle. But like how many more of his schemes little is left at Oropa that betrays his hand.

In all Guarini spent seventeen years of his life at Turin, and during this time was no less active in designing town palaces and country villas. Of these the Palazzo Carignano with its winding or serpentine brick façade is the most remarkable, and its undulating front was not without effect upon the palace builders of Vienna. Wren's Hampton Court apart, the Palazzo Carignano was unique in being built of brick. Guarini, who of his nature was original in everything, determined on a palace unlike to any other, and contrived to draw effects from brick which are without parallel before or since. He has different treatments of his brick pilasters, sometimes incising them with a flattened skull and crossbones motif, or cutting or moulding them in star shapes reminiscent of the brass stars inlaid into the grey marble pavement of the Cappella del Sudario. In the interior court of the Palazzo Carignano between double bands or ascents of his brick stars he has contrived windows of novel shape adapted with slight deviation from those of his Theatine monastery at Messina, next door to the Annunziata; with windows of grander outline on the outer façade, of true mirror or picture-frame sort, distinguished by his undulating line and indicative had they been in England of their Carolean date, one of the few instances in which a clear signature of time lies upon any of his details. Within the hall or pillared atrium Guarini takes decisive command and rules with a firm hand. The oval hall is in stern classical idiom of military severity, if turned luxurious by its coupled columns and the walkabout which is made possible round and among the pillars, all of which leads to right and left hand to the double stair, the very

★ Varallo, Varese, Orta have each their *Sacro Monte*, and there is another at Crea, near Casale Monferrato. *Santuarios* are more numerous still but less interesting for their works of art than the 'sacred mountains'.

steps themselves turning their direction at the first platform stop or landing, and the ascent made livelier and more interesting by the oval openings or window frames within the staircase wall.

The Palazzo Carignano (1679) is a late work by Guarini,* and so is the Collegio dei Nobili which was built for the Jesuits, and in which Guarini seems to be emulating the Venetian architects, and in particular, Longhena. Despite the difference in material, being built of brick, it is of the Palazzo Rezzonico or the Palazzo Pesaro that the Collegio dei Nobili is reminiscent, and one misses the lap of the waters and the green scum where one's hand can touch upon its lower walls. It rises in three main storeys, the ground floor lost a little in confusion, but the windows of the two upper floors showing his favourite device since his monastery for the Theatines at Messina, of lifting the arms of the broken pediments above his windows in order to hold and excuse the *oeil-de-boeuf* openings in the mezzanine floor above them.

In the last two years of his life Guarini was allowed or invited back to his native Modena, where he worked a little on the Ducal Palace, and died shortly afterwards (1683) on a visit to Milan. There are but the traces of his hand, and no more than that, alike at Modena and at the Villa Reale at Racconigi, another of the palaces outside Turin, where an oval or elliptical garden pavilion or temple was designed by him, long since destroyed.† But the geometrical figures in the margin of the plate of this temple in his *Architettura Civile* are as fascinating as the design of the temple itself. Perhaps Guarini may have been, as well as architect, the most consummate mathematical or geometrical draughtsman there has ever been. And one could be inclined to think that it was owing to his exact drawings that so complicated a structure as the cupola of the Sudario could be carried to completion, till one remembers the equally extraordinary, but early fourteenth-century Octagon at Ely, a feat at which we may feel certain that Guarini would have been lost in admiration. Nevertheless, his drawings and inventions alone, as displayed in his many learned and theoretical works, are in a class to themselves and have an aesthetic life and a value of their own. Some are nearly, if not quite impossible for anyone but an advanced mathematician to follow, but they are works of art in themselves without extraneous purpose. He must have been in the mathematics of architecture an equivalent in music to a past-master of contrapuntal theory, which is the reason why such a structure as the Cappella del Sudario with its symbolic undertones and eventual meanings calls to mind the fugues and counterpoint of the Northern masters, and in particular the *Art of Fugue* and the organ fugues of J. S. Bach. Guarini was

* Built for Emanuele Filiberto of the Savoie-Carignan branch of the Royal family from whom Vittorio Emanuele II was descended.

† Paolo Portoghesi describes it as an enriched and personal variant on Bramante's *tempietto* in the court of San Pietro in Montorio. Or, it could be added, in wingless variation upon the temple in Raphael's *Sposalizio* in the Brera at Milan.

born to the south of the Alps, but he had tasted the Northern Gothic during his years in France, had studied the cupolas of the Moors at Córdoba, so it must be assumed, lived in the fermenting Rome of Bernini and Borromini where Michelangelo had been his demigod and titan, and savoured the airs of the South in Messina. And just as, having heard and written of the organ of Buxtehude in the old church at Lübeck, I know now that the ideal setting in which to hear the organ fugues of Bach is in a Spanish cathedral like that of Seville or Córdoba, so the funeral masterpiece of this priest and celibate and 'man in black' is the more moving and impressive for his eclecticism because he had tasted and studied things which were left untouched by his contemporaries. It is a superfetation, something added to the ordinary and normal, like the experience of seeing sun and moon shining together at different ends of the sky, or seeing blossoming fruit trees in the snow, an experience which adds up to the supranormal or transcendental. Of such, whether one likes it or not, is the Cappella del Sudario.

But even with the death of Guarini the age of architecture in Turin was not over, although it progressed by slow succession. That is to say, Guarini died in 1683, as we have seen, when the next great architect to work in Turin was but five years old and born, which is curious, in Messina where he must have had Guarini's church of the Annunziata and the house of the Theatines adjoining continually before his eyes. At twenty years old Filippo Juvarra★ went to Rome to study architecture under Carlo Fontana, born near Como, but one of the last of the Roman masters. Juvarra was always intended for the Church and took minor orders, being, therefore, a celibate just as Borromini and Guarini before him, but he was a very different character both in his person and his buildings, being an obvious extrovert, untroubled spiritually, and blessed with a marvellous genius for creation on a large scale or small. At Rome he entered the service of Cardinal Ottoboni for whose private theatre he made innumerable drawings. There he met singers and musicians – Handel and Domenico Scarlatti in all probability among their number – and developed into a theatrical designer with all the ability and perhaps more of taste than the Bibiena family. A drawing of him during his Roman period by the caricaturist Pierleone Ghezzi shows him very much as we might imagine him to be, not too priest-like of garb, but short and stout with the prominent nose of someone who organises and gets things done. In 1714 when he was thirty-six years old Vittorio Amedeo II of Savoy, son of the patron of Guarini, who was at that time (1713–18) King of Sicily and was later to become King of Sardinia, engaged him from Messina to become his Court architect, and he removed to Turin where he embarked on a career of ceaseless activity, not confined to that capital alone for he had an international reputation. Even so, many of his designs were never carried out; among them

★ Juvarra would seem to be the Sicilian form of the surname Guevara, well known in Spain.

for Rome alone, schemes for the stairs in the Piazza di Spagna, for a new façade for the Lateran, and a sacristy for St Peter's. His fecundity is good to read about and as cordial as a tonic, until in this context we remember the longer career and even greater list of works of the grand iconoclast, Sir Gilbert Scott. What greater contrast, though, than between the hunting-castle of Stupinigi and St Pancras Station Hotel! Yet, a masterwork, none the less!

Had Juvarra lived to a greater age he might have attained the international fame of Bernini. He spent most of the year 1720 in Portugal, partly it may be on diplomatic business, but also making plans for the palace at Mafra, building the church and palace of the Patriarch, and designing the lighthouse in the harbour. In the same year he visited London where he dedicated a book of drawings to Lord Burlington, a compliment which he paid later to Augustus the Strong of Saxony – scattered designs for façades with the ease of autographs, and eventually repaired to Spain at the invitation of Philip v – the patron of Farinelli – to make suggestions for the country palaces of La Granja and Aranjuez and to design the Royal Palace at Madrid. And in Madrid he caught influenza and died, aged fifty-eight, in 1736.

During his twenty and more years in the service of Vittorio Amedeo his activity had been prodigious, building four Royal palaces and five churches in Turin alone, besides works of various sorts in at least a dozen other Italian towns. Among his achievements on a superb scale in Turin is his great stairway in the Palazzo Madama. The statue and urn-crowned façade of this palace invites entry with the hint of magnificence within from its Corinthian pillared frontispiece in the belated Baroque fullness of seventeenth-century Rome. It is a double stairway, taking up all but a couple of bays of the front, and rising in splendour out of the pillared hall to the turn at its half-landing, whence the huge windows that light the great landing and the bridge that leads from that across and above the atrium into the palace are to be admired. After Michelangelo's stairway in the Laurenziana which is almost too heroic and masculine in its aggressiveness and violence this may well be the finest of all Italian grand stairways, much to be preferred even to the stairway of Longhena at San Giorgio Maggiore in Venice, fine though that may be, but it is wasteful of its own space while that of the Palazzo Madama creates its own huge area and inhabits that without pretence or excuse.*

The other work of Juvarra which is on the same scale and in the same manner is the Superga, on a hill a mile or two outside Turin, built, it is curious to think, in thanksgiving for the delivery of Vienna from the Turks. But the Superga with its splendid portico and dome, as I have written of them elsewhere, 'in classical sonata form', is superb but yet it is uninhabited, spiritually, and very chilly. What a grand and hugely projecting portico at

---

* The monumental stairways of palaces and monasteries in Austria and Germany were built, it could be said, in awareness of the stairway of the Palazzo Madama.

the Superga, suggesting that there may be nothing much in the octagon of a church behind it, less still when you look up at the correctness of the dome, a prizewinner among domes, the whole of it finished and beautiful in detail and enlivened by a pair of belfries of less conventional design! In brief, La Superga is a true basilica with all of both the grandeur and the shortcomings of its kind.

Juvarra, also, designed the façade of the Royal Palace in Turin and some of the decoration of its rooms; the framing of the lacquer panels in a *Gabinetto Cinese* for example, no detail being too slight to attract his interested attention.* Juvarra designed the carved panels which are painted red and gold and enclose oval or square panels of black or gold lacquer, or panes of mirror, while the coved ceiling is painted by Claudio Beaumont, a Piedmontese painter of a lively talent. Stupinigi being a hunting-castle, he even made designs for the wall-sconces which had a stag's head for chief motif. At the exhibition of Baroque Art in Piedmont held in Turin in 1963 there was a room of *maquettes* of stage scenes cleverly reconstructed from the stage drawings of Juvarra, who even wrote out the title-page and drew the initial letters in the musical score of an opera for the sets of which he had been commissioned by the Holy Roman Emperor. It is evident that he was a theatrical artist of the highest quality, the equal of the brothers Torelli who were famous throughout Europe, or of Ferdinando Galli da Bibiena. His four churches in Turin show the more usual and current form of his genius, being fluent in the full late Baroque idiom of his Roman training without return to the monumental high Renaissance as in the Superga, or the pained striving through higher mathematics toward originality of Guarini. His talent was of easier flow; although in his church of the Carmine one critic sees a conscious influence from Northern or even German sources in the high open galleries and consequent greater areas of light coming into the nave, and another critic† traces the brick campanile with its serpentine sides to Borromini's Sant' Andrea delle Fratte, though it lacks the sculptural effect of that extreme invention.

Bombing during the last war unfortunately destroyed many traces of Juvarra's handiwork and left gaping spaces, but a place in which he may still be appreciated at his fluent best is in the Piazza San Carlo. It takes not more than a glance to distinguish as his the façade of Santa Cristina, one of the two churches on the south side of the piazza with a street between them. It is so much more animated and eloquent than its companion; with an interesting doorway, oval window flanked by statuary above that, and array of obelisks of fine design upon the skyline. The marvellous competence of the architect

* Illustrated in colour in the first volume of the Catalogue of the *Mostra del Barocco Piemontese* at Turin, 1963, pl. 1.

† Rudolf Wittkower, *op. cit.*, pp. 277, 278, and James Lees-Milne, *op. cit.*, pp. 182, 183.

shows itself in this façade; only a trifle from his vast output, but what confidence, what a delivery and what finished grammar!★

Juvarra is to be sought, too, in the Royal palaces of Venaria Reale, Rivoli, and Racconigi. At the Venaria Reale, the chapel, the stables, and the *citroniera* or lemon-house are by him. In addition he built at least four private palaces in Turin; and façades and altars for local towns like Chieri and Oropa and Vercelli, and for Nice and Chambéry which were still, then, included in Savoy. This extraordinary production is on a Handelian scale but without, it would seem, the nervous storms to which Handel was victim. He must have had, it is true, a large body or *équipe* of craftsmen who were able to carry out his ideas, and who could take on his work at diagram or sketch level and carry it to completion. The work must have been carried out through heads of departments, and the inscription on the menu in French railway dining-cars, 'présenté par le chef de brigade . . .' is the quickest explanation of what I mean. The workshops of the Royal palaces in and round Turin – in this most neglected part of all Italy by the art lover – must have been upon a scale only equalled at Versailles. The palaces, we should remember, besides the Royal Palace, the Palazzo Madama, and the Palazzo Carignano in Turin itself, included country palaces or villas at Racconigi, Rivoli, the Venaria Reale, Moncalieri, and Stupinigi.

Among these craftsmen, even though he may not have worked specifically for Juvarra, mention must be made of Pietro Piffetti (*c.* 1700–70), the *ebanista* – there is no exact English word for it – who worked almost exclusively for the Dukes of Savoy, whose pieces of furniture were one of the major sensations of the aforementioned exhibition of Baroque Art in Piedmont of 1963, and who in the words of the catalogue 'more than any other craftsman of the time characterises and glorifies the eighteenth century in Piedmont.' Two plates in colour in that catalogue illustrate his works; a cupboard with intarsia work in precious woods, mother-of-pearl and ivory, in the Queen's apartments in the Royal Palace, and another of the same materials with addition of tortoiseshell, now in the Quirinal, works of marquetry and inlay which should of their very excess of detail become odious but that by some feat of alchemy achieve the impossible and can invest a cupboard or a *prie-dieu* with the elegance and the wilful decadence of a Beardsley drawing.†

All of which leads with irresistible force to the Palazzina di Caccia, or Royal Hunting Lodge of Stupinigi. It is Juvarra's masterpeice and one of the most beautiful palaces in Europe, aesthetic beauty being a quality that must be denied to the palace of Caserta, and indeed beyond the grasp of an architect

★ The façade of Santa Cristina is in variation upon that of San Marcello al Corso, in Rome, by his master Carlo Fontana.

† That there were other craftsmen little inferior to Piffetti is proved in the little inlaid oratories of the King and Queen in the Royal Palace, several rooms of which are in no way inferior, though less famous, than the apartments by Cuvilliés in the Residenz at Munich.

of the calibre of Vanvitelli. Elasticity of imagination was one of the qualities of Juvarra, fortified and made more pliant by his theatrical experience and training, and indeed it is of his theatre drawings that Stupinigi is most eloquent. In designing it, Juvarra seems to have had in mind that half of Savoy was, then, French-speaking – Chambéry, Annecy, Nice were part of Italian Savoy until 1859 – and to have conceived of it in the first place as a French hunting château which he then converted into an Italian scene painter's version of the same with all the allurement of theatre scenery and *trompe l'oeil* painting, but in fact built solid and realised. It is an extraordinary work by this eclectic who could, also, essay the Michelangelesque at the Superga, the sub-Alpine Escorial on its hill above Turin. Certainly, standing in the forecourt of Stupinigi, without pre-knowledge of its history and identity one might hesitate between France and Italy, and with no definition of either settle for a theatrical amalgam or romantic mixture of them both.

The Great Hall or Ball Room below its domed roof surmounted by the figure of a stag is the unique wonder of Stupinigi. Those persons fortunate enough like the writer to have come here and seen it with snow deep upon the ground will never forget the sensation of entering into this palace of the *Sleeping Princess*. For it is that to an unimaginable degree. The dynastic appearances, the *front fuyant* of so many demi-Bourbon and demi-Habsburg countenances, with the blood of lesser and even stranger matrimonial alliance predominant, make the mere portraits on the walls into the *dramatis personae* of this dormant palace,★ together with the thought of the strange elder branch of the family, extinct in 1831, who preserved the old customs and etiquette even to the wearing of powdered wigs until well on into the nineteenth century. The huge hexagonal forecourt has the central body or rotunda of the château (which is the ball-room) coming out towards us with wings spreading out from it at obtuse angles to either side and continued even further in both directions by offices and other dependencies. On the far side of the castle the forest stretches endlessly into the distance. Juvarra must surely have seen with his own eyes some of the great Austrian and German palaces and monasteries, perhaps also Blenheim or even Castle Howard, and not merely studied them in plan. It is this that makes Stupinigi unique as though, which is the truth, it is neither in France nor Germany, and not quite or entirely in Italy either, but in French and Italian-speaking Italy which is a kingdom of its own and apart.

In the oval shaped ball-room we recognise the stag-antlered sconces upon the walls, and then look up at the chandeliers and into the fresco'd galleries and the apses and half-domes of this superb feat of theatrical art made

---

★ The pastel portrait of a beautiful young princess in one of the rooms on that day bore an almost uncanny likeness to the beautiful Queen Margherita of my childhood in Italy. She was, herself, by birth a princess of the Savoy family.

permanent. The scene-painters, for so they could be rightly called, were the brothers Valeriani. The four huge pillars supporting the dome and the gloriously curving, convoluting gallery carry the eyes to the painted artifice in every direction and to the ceiling of the dome which is fresco'd, most aptly, with *Diana Departing for the Chase*, and one could think the empty gallery haunted by the music of her hunt.

From this wonderful painted vision which surpasses anything ever seen upon the stage the Royal apartments lead forth or open out, most unexpectedly, in four directions. The King's apartment of four rooms is fresco'd with hunting scenes and the chapel attached to it is dedicated to St Hubert from whose abbey, deep in the forest of the Ardennes, three or four couple of the black hounds of St Hubert were sent yearly by the Abbot to the Kings of France. There is, too, the Queen's apartment where Queen Margherita lived near to the portrait that so resembled her, and with *The Repose of Diana* upon the painted ceiling; the beautiful silk hangings of one room at least painted with flowers and plants disappeared during the war; but there are still the set of rooms in 'Chinese style', and there is the Sala delle Scuderie with hunting scenes by Cignaroli. After all of which delights it is sad to think that the plans of Juvarra except perhaps in the central rotunda were never quite fulfilled in his lifetime. He died, as we have seen, in 1736; and it would seem that Stupinigi, six miles from the city (an hour's drive) was seldom inhabited by his patron Vittorio Amedeo II, and only completed in its present form by that King's son Carlo Emanuele III in the 1770s, having been left undisturbed, so to speak, in its first sleep for some thirty years which is the span of a human generation. Be that as it may, this palace still seems deep in the slumber that has now overtaken it for more than two hundred years, and one looks for the courtiers of King Florestan XXIV who should be sleeping here and there just where the spell came on them. This beautiful and most theatre-inspired of all palaces only lacks the music to bring it life, though it might fall to dust at the first sound of horns and trumpets and there would be nothing left. It is indeed difficult to take Stupinigi literally and think of it as stones and mortar. It has a quality of enchantment and is, itself, dormant and enchanted.

Racconigi, Rivoli, the Venaria Reale, Moncalieri, all have their share of melancholy – Rivoli, for instance, where Juvarra began a huge palace for Vittorio Amedeo which was only a third or a quarter built, and then became a barracks – but one or more of these country palaces was badly damaged in the bombing. There are the *Santuarios* and the *Sacro Montes* upon their hills; and churches and palaces in Turin and in country towns in Piedmont by several other architects of the time; one of the foremost of them being Conte Benedetto Alfieri (1700–67), cousin to the red-haired poet and tragedian whom no one living has ever read, who was so much reputed in his lifetime and married the widow of the Young Chevalier. The best work of this architect is said to be a brick church at Carignano, with an interior described as built on the plan of a horseshoe or a fan. But, above all, there are the little chapels and sanctuaries by Bernardo Vittone (1705–70), the successor to Guarini and to Juvarra, and the last of the great architects to work in and around Turin.

Vittone went to study in Rome, and returned to Turin the devoted admirer and posthumous disciple of Guarini who had been dead by then for nearly fifty years. This must have come to the ears of the Theatine monks probably through their administration in Rome, and Vittone was entrusted with the publication of Guarini's drawings, which had long circulated in print form. His long delayed *Architettura Civile* appeared, then, at last, edited by Vittone in 1737, before in fact Vittone's own chapels and sanctuaries had begun to be built. Like Borromini and Guarini, his architectural forbears, he was of pietistic temperament with mystical leanings of much force and depth. All accounts seem to agree on Vittone's sour and disagreeable character and his meanness in money matters. He was a bachelor of traditional, even Dr Coppelius kind, utterly absorbed in his contrapuntal studies if that term can be applied to his juggling with spheres and domes in the manipulation of which he was nothing less than the Cinquevalli of his kind.

His palaces in Turin are unremarkable, as, too, his church of Santa Maria della Piazza in the city. Even his little churches and chapels in the country towns in Piedmont are uninteresting as to their exteriors. His sanctuary at Vallinotto, near Carignano, has an outside, it is true, which from its curious shape looks as though something of interest may be going on inside. It is a little whitewashed octagon in three storeys with a lantern, and was built for the agricultural labourers of a rich banker, which explains its small dimensions. But through the hexagon of its first dome of open ribs like those of the cupola of Guarini's Sudario chapel, you look through two more domes into the lantern. These open ribs are, themselves, painted with flowers and angelic heads, and you look through them to the second dome which is also painted, and through that again into the third, and then into the lantern. It is like a peepshow or some elaborate game of optics.

The little church of Santa Chiara at Brà, only known to me from photographs, is described by Wittkower as 'Vittone's most accomplished work'. Here, again, the vault has windows through which the painted sky of the second dome with its angels and saints are seen. It could be interjected that for such feats of *trompe l'oeil* the services of better painters than were available to Vittone would be most necessary. Photographs of another of his little sanctuaries, that of San Bernardino at Chieri, show his juggling with favourite shapes of apse and half-dome, the window-like openings contrived in those and the fantastic lightness and airiness of his effects. The Assunta at

130

Opposite: Detail of Basilica of La Superga,
Turin, by Filippo Juvarra.

Riva, near Chieri, is yet another of his little works of genius where he juggles with four domes at once, three of which are octagonal. A chapel that few people can have gone out of their way to see, that of San Michele at Rivarolo, Canavese, is described by another critic* as 'one of the most fascinating architectures of the world' from its incomparable skill and lightness. There are several other little chapels and sanctuaries by Vittone in the smaller Piedmontese towns,† including the oval church of San Gaetano, at Nice of all places, planned originally by Guarini, but altered by Vittone on the lines of his church at Brà. It is to be noted that nearly all of his buildings are in small towns or villages where, normally, no one would go in search of fine buildings.

Vittone had never the sums of his money at his disposal that made it possible for Borromini or Guarini to startle and surprise the world. But within modest dimensions he produced extraordinary results, his speciality being the play of dome and counter-dome even to the point, as we have seen at Vallinotto, of throwing up four domes into the air at once and juggling with them .It is the art of a conjurer or *prestidigitateur*; and one could wish it were possible for Vittone to have built a planetarium and thus to have achieved movement and rotation as well. It is probable that this would have appealed, too, to his mystical theories and ideas just as he was interested, also, in the relation between music and architecture, thinking that therein lay the secrets of proportion. He was the last architect in a long tradition of invention and innovation based on mathematical knowledge and very different, therefore, from the free-hand eloquence and poetry of the architects of Southern Italy and Sicily. It was the application of an intellect and not at all of an ease and a grace to architecture, and in the exterior of Sant' Ivo alla Sapienza, in the brick tower of Sant' Andrea delle Fratte, both by Borromini; in the cupola of the Cappella del Sudario and the interior of that, by Guarini; as, also, in three or four of the chapels by Vittone it produced some of the most extraordinary effects ever produced by wilful architecture that never calls on the accidental or the picturesque. With Juvarra the genius was of another sort; an affirmative genius that enriched and put in order everything it touched, and that had an incomparable resource and fecundity, virtues in which he comes second only to Bernini. There was almost nothing to which Juvarra could not put his hand; and his strong theatrical talent must have seen in Stupinigi the opportunity of making permanent something which was of its nature stage scenery and a stage spectacle and could not expect or hope for longer life than that.

Vittone within the small compass of his chances produced effects which,

* Henry A. Millon.

† The hexagonal Chiesa Parrocchiale at Grignasco, and churches of similar plan at Vercelli and Borgo d'Ale. cf. Wittkower, *op. cit.*, p. 377, footnote 55.

131

Opposite: Interior of cupola of San Lorenzo, Turin, by Guarino Guarini.

G

mathematically or geometrically perfect, are a *trompe l'oeil* offering forbidden visions into the elysium of the next world, sometimes rendered not up to his best intentions by an inferior painter's hand. It was therefore a spiritual beauty that he was working for through mathematical and geometrical means, and in his interest in numbers it is no wonder that he took note of music. He is an isolated figure, the last of his long descent from mid-seventeenth century Guarini. He may have despised the theatre in his soul, but he could not but be influenced, too, by the achievement of Juvarra in the ball-room or great hall of Stupinigi. There, something transitory was given the same permanence as the eternities he was trying to depict by breaking through a false dome into a higher one, and into another beyond that, and then into the lantern. And in the end, both of them, the ball-room of Stupinigi and the four domes of Vallinotto are theatre or artifice, and that far removed from nature.

6

'A new country of pagodas and Indian temples'

THÉOPHILE GAUTIER, *l'Espagne*

The towns of Cáceres and Trujillo, both of them in Estremadura, gave birth to many of the conquerors of Mexico and Peru, following on which both towns have their *casas solariegas*, town manor-houses of the Conquistadores, with forbidding doorways of granite and ponderous coats-of-arms above. Upon the façade of an old house in Cáceres, the Casa de Toledo-Moctezuma, you may see the heraldic achievement of this family, descendants of a daughter of the last Aztec Emperor; while in Trujillo, some thirty miles from Cáceres, was born Francisco de Orellana, first explorer of the Amazon, but, as well, Francisco Pizarro the conqueror of Peru, a sanguinary ruffian compared to whom Hernan Cortés, Conquistador of Mexico, stern warrior that he was, shines almost as a knight-errant or paladin.

In Trujillo I have seen the roof-less, cyclopaean hovel with huge round-arched doorway where was born Pizarro; and in the church of Santa María de la Concepción by the flicker of matchlight we saw the kneeling figure of an armoured knight in stone. This is the tomb of Pizarro, conqueror of the Incas, who was assassinated 'by the traitor Herrera' in the end; the son of a swineherd, suckled according to legend by an Estremian sow, but a being to whose lot fell the most unlikely adventures that have befallen man. In the temple of the Sun at Cuzco had he not seen the twelve golden lifesize statues of the Incas; the sacred garden sown with corn plants that were of gold, 'as well the stems as the leaves and corncobs'; and 'more than twenty llamas of gold with their young, and the shepherds lifesize, with their slings and crooks to watch them . . . all made of gold'? But all they meant to him was bullion and he had them melted down. Of all the treasures of the New World, or Other Indies, what is left? A feather ornament, fan or headpiece of green quetzal plumes, at Vienna, and a crystal skull or two, which may, most typically, be German Renaissance of origin, and not Mexican at all. Of the Incas even less is left than of the Aztecs.

One of the several *solares* in Trujillo is the Palacio del Marqués de la

Conquista, still belonging after more than four centuries to descendants of Pizarro. On the morning we saw this house there was blue sky and clear light and the barred windows, three floors of them, threw their shadows like bird-cages on the sunlit walls. Within those cages nothing hopped or fluttered. No green parrots of the mock-Indies and Amazon. But, at the corner of the Palacio de la Conquista, the chains much in evidence, there were figures of manacled Indians, in the words of Richard Ford, 'fit badges of the Conquest, and of the plunder and murder of Atahualpa'. They are half-figures, three rows one above another; but indeed they are hardly human of aspect and more like monkeys of the forest, their close-cropped heads jutting from the very angle or corner of the Palacio de la Conquista, making the cutting, sharp edge of it like a ship's prow with carved figures slicing into the waves. The cornice on which this rests is upheld by twin pilasters with busts emerging from the plinth of each pillar and out of the space between them. Busts of whom? For they could be effigies of the Roman Caesars (Trujillo claims Julius Caesar for its founder), or more Indians. Or, again, what are the little figures seated on the parapet of the Palacio, upon its very skyline? Above the frame of the figured prow or cut-water of the palace there is what looks to be a giant helm in stone; and blowing back from all this are wild feathery scrolls of stone that lie against the wall like a symbol or abstraction of the voyage, and that are of course repeated upon the other wall or angle of the palace that we cannot see. That is, at least, one interpretation of its ornament; and I have chosen the Palacio de la Conquista for opening of this chapter because I have thought it symbolic of the Spanish conquerors of the Nuevo Mundo and their origins, also for the reason that it illustrates facets of the Spanish character responsible for the ineptly and indeed misnamed buildings, the churches and palaces that we are about to examine.

For just as no one can go from Madrid to Andalucía or to the Levante crossing the dreary and monotonous steppe of La Mancha and not be reminded of its immortal knight-errant on seeing the windmills at which he tilted, so it is only necessary to have entered the hovel in which Pizarro was born in order to understand why Estremadura was the birthplace of so many of the Conquistadores. Why, in fact, they were ready and anxious to leave their homeland, yet had the energy and stamina to conquer a New World. Perhaps it was necessary to have been nurtured on the hard face of Estremadura in order to enter upon and endure the Altiplano of Bolivia and Peru. In contrast to which upbringing the exuberant ornament of the Palacio de la Conquista, which must be early seventeenth-century in date and built by the descendants of Pizarro two generations after the time of the Conquistadores, is as a liberation or freeing of the libido. They have made their fortune and returned home; better still, perpetuated their own dignity and self-importance even if these are set forth in somewhat flamboyant terms.

Spanish dignity, the trait or character of their nation in all tradition, even the wearing of black their colour of predilection in hue of austerity and self-restraint, must have, also, its opposite and antithesis. Hence, the processions in Holy Week of black-cowled *penitentes* but, also, the lights and dancing of the Feria. In Spain, if there is the Escorial, there are as well buildings gayer in tone, demonstrative of that exuberance and gaiety which the austere Herreran in the Spaniard has suppressed and hidden.

That it would be wrong to attribute this lightening of mood to gentler, balmier airs from Andalucía and the Levante is proved in many towns in Northern Spain, not least in Salamanca and in Santiago de Compostela. Revisiting this latter city in the summer of this year (1966) has only strengthened the impression from three previous visits that Santiago is a city nearly unique in Europe for the unity of its buildings and the beauty of its architecture. That this unity of co-ordination is due to one architect in particular is so obvious as to be scarcely, if ever mentioned though it is a fact which impresses itself at every viewing and upon each occasion one walks round the outside of the Cathedral looking up at its pinnacled or obelisked parapets and its three glorious towers. It was Fernando de Casas y Novoa, a local Gallego or Galician, who built the great West front or Fachada del Obradoiro of Santiago between 1738 and 1750, who would seem to be responsible for this. Yet the quadruple stairway below El Obradoiro is not his. It is a century and a half earlier and dates from 1605; and looking once more from the foot of that processional stair up the huge height of that giant façade to the pair of superb towers (230 feet tall) that frame it in from either side, we walk round the outside of the cloister, turn left past the south door or Puerto de las Platerías, up a wide flight of steps to the square behind the Cathedral which is known as the Quintana.

This is a marvellous place from which to look back at it all and the wonderful architectural movement and activity that it has about it. The third tower of the Cathedral, the Trinity or Clock Tower, or Berenguela, now reveals itself in all its splendour of fantasy, even taller than the other pair of towers and yet more fanciful and absorbing to look up at and try to study. But neither is this the work of Casas y Novoa. On the contrary it is by Domingo de Andrade and was finished in 1680, and it is a great part of the achievement of Casas y Novoa that he worked in with what had been begun before him, made an entity of it and finished it. The Berenguela has been described, not ineptly, as 'mainmast and voice of the basilica' and as 'one of the finest towers in Christendom' which it is indeed without fear of contradiction. One can look up at it again and again in admiration, beginning from the four early stone statues on its lowest gallery, and then up to the wonderful imaginativeness of its balconies and the little *templetes* or cupola'd pavilions marking each storey up to its belfry. The achievement of Casas y Novoa was to complete this whole body or entity of the Cathedral of Santiago, not only with his Obradoiro or 'work of gold' worked in the hard Galician granite of his high frontispiece between the pair of towers, but to back that with the granite embellishment of what is after all the exterior of the high altar, above the Puerta Santa which is only opened by the archbishop in solemn ceremony in jubilee years. This architectural enrichment takes the form of granite balustrading, three tiers of it masking or clothing the Romanesque vessel of the church that lies within with more pinnacles and obelisks than one can remember ever to have seen in any other place. But the three tiers of it are at different levels and above chapels of different shape which varies and enhances the effect of it all and its impact upon the skyline. For richness of effect, yet in mood of sobriety, it would be true to say that there is nothing to compare with this view looking back over the Cathedral from this third of its plazas known as the Quintana, with the tower of the Berenguela in front of us and the huge convent wall of San Payo behind us, except that moment of standing in the Court of the Doge's Palace, looking up at the Scala dei Giganti with the leaden domes and howdahs – it is not the first time I have made use of this phrase but I can think of no better – it could almost be said, kneeling and rising in the background. Somewhere behind this revetment or re-facing and its array of pinnacles and obelisks, masked at the present time by scaffolding where repairs of sinister import and much chiselling and hammering are in progress, must lie the doorway through which the eight *gigantónes* in the guise of pilgrims from different lands make emergence, totter through the crowds to the square in front of the towering El Obradoiro and on occasion dance a few steps, and go back to their seclusion.

Coming down the flight of wide steps again from the Quintana, the temptation here being to wander to and fro, and relinquishing that wonderful view of all three towers of Compostela in order to stand again before the façade of the Platerías with its Romanesque doorway and round-arched windows below the balustrade and obelisks of Casas y Novoa, the co-ordinator of Santiago, we are back by the outer wall of the cloister and can admire the Isabelline interlacing of its granite cresting, looking like the repetition of floreated lettering and with more than a hint of the Manoelino from nearby Portugal. All is of granite; and in the sunlight of this last visit gleaming in patches as though with a dusting of powdered crystal upon it, but at other times and on most days and evenings of the year, wet, and darkened, for Santiago has the rainiest climate in all Spain. And turning now with our back to the Platerías, in this city of fine architecture with its four plazas of the Cathedral each with its own façade and three other buildings, we have in front of us at the bottom of the steps, that most original of Compostelan edifices, the Casa del Cabildo (of 1758), a small granite palace in the local or regional Baroque, a sort of *Plattenstil* 'with ornamentation of purely abstract design, unrelated to any previous forms, very simple, bold, and well suited to granite.'* Seen on a previous occasion, rain was pouring down from the Casa del Cabildo, but pouring from cannon-mouths for its water-spouts are in the form of naval guns; but now on this golden evening we can see it to advantage and may admire the way in which it adorns and fills this lower landing of the square. But it is strange indeed on closer examining, given richness by the shadow channelled in its recessed pilasters, with most odd-shaped scrolls or elbows below its windows, and a most imaginative skyline of balustrading and high pinnacles, culminating in the middle above its uneventful doorway with a most highly stylised, framed set-piece of ornament that rises to a thin pointed obelisk on top of all. The architect, Clemente Fernández Sarela of resounding name, was greatly daring in competition with such neighbours, but his boldness holds and keeps its place. Not only that, it lends greater interest to the granite arcades of the side street even in the wet splashing of the Compostelan rain. The arcades here are as much for shelter as they are for shade.

Retreating up the steps again through the square of the Platerías, and now that of the Quintana, right round the back of the Cathedral past the Cruz dos Farrápos on whose arms the pilgrims hung their ragged clothes worn at the pilgrimage, changing them for others handed to them at the door near by, we come into the fourth plaza of the Cathedral known as the Azabacheria after the workshops where the jet ornaments were carved which the pilgrims bought to take home with them. The façade in this one of the Cathedral squares is by Ventura Rodríguez (1765–70) and is the least successful of all this complex of buildings though, even then, it is no insignificent contribution to the whole. But this is not the only reason for completing the circuit by walking through all four plazas of the Cathedral for the building opposite across the Azabacheria is the huge Benedictine convent of San Martín Pinario, with relief over its door of St Martin dividing his cloak with the beggar, a subject that for ever interprets itself and dictates its own form once one has seen it rendered by El Greco. The architect Casas y Novoa was much involved at this building, probably on its main cloister, perhaps even with what Ford characterises as its 'handsome fountain with three falls and satyrs' heads'. Certainly the huge *retablo* in the church is his, where, Ford says, 'Santiago and San Martín ride together in a fricassee of gilt gingerbread', in

* Mr Bernard Bevan in his *History of Spanish Architecture*, 1938, pp. 164, 165, and in his Introduction to *Muirhead's Blue Guide to Northern Spain*, 1958, p. ciii. I call the Casa del Cabildo the most original of such structures because the oft-quoted façade of the convent of Santa Clara, in this same *Plattenstil*, by yet another local architect, Simón Rodríguez, is in truth dull in comparison, with for crowning ornament the stone semblance of a log in place ready for the sawmill. Depressing in the green-greyness of its granite, this seems an unreasoning insistence on calling attention to itself. It could have no other purpose. According to Mr Bernard Bevan, *op. cit.*, p. cxix, there is a 'stupendous retablo' in Santa Clara, akin to that in San Martín Pinario, but the chapel is locked and no one has the key.

just the phrase expected of him and the date at which he was writing.★ But it is in fact a remarkable and strange production of its kind, rather resembling the transformation scene in an old pantomime but made of solid wood, not lath and plaster or painted canvas. It is at the same time a sort of transparency with openings practised in it so that the action of the *retablo* is not all at the same depth. It is not backed against the wall as are most *retablos*; it comes right forward bearing down upon you with the assurance of some big vessel when you are nearly underneath it in a small boat. The main body of it has even something of a hull's shape about it up there above the first cornice which is the waterline. Equestrian figures of St Martin and St James are perched incongruously where the lifeboats should be slung upon the gunwale as of both decks; there are figures, flag in hand, higher still, manning perilously the top-gallants; and the pair of domed pulpits, far down below, move slowly forward like a pair of tug-boats soon to drop their tow-ropes and return to port. In short, therefore, if there must be gilt *retablos* this of San Martín Pinario is among the most original, perhaps in the same category of fantasy as the *Trasparente* of Toledo Cathedral – which is not a *retablo*, but indeed a special term or appellation should be minted for it – and apart from the other *retablos* of Spain or of Mexico because it works not alone in height but depth, adding thereby another dimension to its golden possibilities.

This does not exhaust the buildings of its date in Santiago. At the back of San Martín Pinario lies another huge convent, that of San Francisco, with a sunken court and double stairs in front of it, a building of earlier date but recast in grandiose style. Besides which there are smaller buildings of interest and fantasy such as the little chapel at the corner below the Palacio Consistorial and between that and the Hospital de los Reyes Catolicos, but at the lower level coming up into the square. Could it be by the architect of the Casa del Cabildo? Certainly it has interest and always meets the eye.

All in all, where the later buildings are concerned, and it is these which give the town its character, the towers of Santiago make the unforgettable impression; and the clock tower, or Berenguela or Reloj tower of Domingo de Andrade, in particular, to be looked up at in wonder at the balconied window in the body of the tower, at the open pavilion above that with the little domed *templetes* at its corners, at the taller octagon over it where the bells hang with four more of the *templetes* at its corners, and above that to where it rises into the sun or mist or rain, the more impressive because of the three-tiered masking of the old back of the Cathedral with its concentric lines of obelisks and balustrades which make the setting for the Reloj and climb in

---

★ Ford, in all else so sound and sensible, says of Sarela, architect of the Casa del Cabildo, who had 'tampered with' the Azabachería, that 'he ought to have been cast into his namesake's river hard by'. It seems a hasty and unconsidered verdict on an architect who obviously thought for himself and built accordingly.

Opposite: A blue-and-white church tower at
Écija, Andalucía.

their eminence to some half its height. Once again it must be emphasised that it is this view of the Cathedral from the square of the Quintana, if one can stand so as to get all three of its towers within one's vision, that is even more impressive and yet more of an architectural treat than to stand in the main plaza looking up at El Obradoiro and its central panel or Espejo. It is, too, the Reloj or Berenguela Tower which was copied, albeit in more simple form, in so many of the Galician towns and villages as one approaches or comes away from Compostela.

By the time we reach Orense, the capital town of a province and till the expulsion of 1492 a flourishing commercial centre of the Sephardim, or Jews of Spain, since then stagnating, the shadow of Santiago has lifted and works of our period include a fantastically exuberant chapel in the left transept of the Cathedral – almost as if what is implied by *flamenco* had penetrated into the precincts with its handclappings and raucous shouts, here made manifest in noisy, vociferous gilding – and the façade of a small church facing up the street towards the Cathedral which at a glance could be by the architect of the second of the cloisters at the old Benedictine abbey of Celanova with the 'bad taste' scrolls and volutes of its balcony or *poleiro*. Astorga, which is in fact in León, not in Galicia, has its late seventeenth-century Baroque west doorway, and over that for weathercock a leaden figure of a Maragato in his baggy breeches much resembling a leaden garden statue; and Maragatos appear again as Jacquemart figures on the Town Hall clock, an agreeably unusual building of the date, looking on the plaza where on Corpus Christi and Ascension the Maragatos, what few are left of them, still dance the 'curious' *cañizo*.

More interesting than either of these towns is Lugo, the capital of Galicia, with a Cathedral which has all the aura of a holy place, and where by special privilege the consecrated Host is always exposed or *manifestado*,[*] to which end, and I think the custom is still continued, 'two priests are always in attendance, night and day, at faldstools on either side of the *capilla mayor* in front of the altar', which high altar is here 'enclosed in glass in a tawdry theatrical manner', but it must have been for the priests' protection who otherwise would be dead from cold and damp on those long nights of wind and rain. Be that as it may, the Cathedral at Lugo is still crowded at all hours to the extent that it is difficult to walk about in it. But the particular interest is that it contains the earliest known work of Fernando de Casas y Novoa (1711 – 14), which is the beautiful one-storeyed cloister, of elegant design if a little retarded in date for in England it would be called 'William and Mary' and attributed to the 1690s, being indeed the Spanish equivalent of the quadrangle of an Oxford College, yet with something unequivocally of Spain about it as

---

[*] Ford, *op. cit.*, 'the incarnate Hostia is always lighted up and manifested in a glass *viril*; one made by Juan d'Arfe [a celebrated silversmith] was given in 1663 by Bishop Castejon.'

Opposite: View of the Clerecía at Salamanca, by Andrés García de Quiñones.

H

we thought on seeing the same pair of snuff-taking priests still deep in conversation when we looked into the cloister again more than an hour later.★ There are very curious high *retablo*-like carvings on the walls near the doorway into the cloister; and then we come to the other work of Casas y Novoa, the circular Lady Chapel, and it is this into which it is difficult to get entry because of the crowd of worshippers. But, in fact 'circular' is too easy a term by which to describe it for the Lady Chapel is a circle, and again an outer circle, with semi-circular lobes worked in the space between those like indeed the petals of a dog-rose or eglantine. The stucco work is of dazzling intricacy, on a par almost with that in the *camarín* of Priego de Córdoba. One carries away from this Lady Chapel at Lugo an unexpected impression of holiness and beauty not least from its singularity of design. Coming out from it by a side door and walking round the back of the building, the array of balusters and obelisks on the exterior of this Rose Chapel, as I would like to call it, reveals it in all clearness as the work of Casas y Novoa because of its entire resemblance to the system of balustrading on the back of the Cathedral of Santiago, to that view of it, aforementioned, from the third of the plazas or the Quintana, and to that ranging of obelisks and balusters in tiers at different levels that had one the wish to parody this considerable architect one could compare for effect to a series of gasometers raised or sunk at different levels of fullness out of their pits or wells.

Coming away now from Galicia, a province with a character as different from the rest of Spain as Wales from England – its fields marked with upright slabs of stone, its windy heaths where the genista was firing huge patches of hillside in September with its yellow spikes, and from the whine of the ox-carts with solid axles of wood slowly crawling along the roads – we passed a circus train halted high on the mountain as though to get its breath. There was not time to get out and look at the lorries of lions and tigers, or at the caravans where their keepers lived. But I think I could have known the clowns, even in their day clothes, from the circus posters on the walls of every town we went to in Northern Spain. These posters, minor works of art, are a lasting memory of Galicia – and the other memory! – the towers of Compostela, the village versions of which have by now long faded from the landscape. Nothing more of that sort was to be seen until Logroño, centre of the rich wine district of the Rioja. Here is the recessed portal of Santa María la Redonda, an architectural exercise in rare form, with graceful sculptured figures and bas-reliefs within its hooded portal; but, also, this church is conspicuous for its pair of towers by another local architect, Martín de Beratúa; moreover, they are beautiful from the point of view of a lover and ·

★ G. Kubler and M. Soria, in *Art and Architecture in Spain and Portugal*, Harmondsworth, 1959, p. 60, write of this cloister as 'decorated in the manner of Domingo de Andrade', architect of the tower of the Reloj at Santiago, and rightly speak of it as 'a grandiose and cheerful enclosure of light and air'.

connoisseur of the steeples of Wren's City churches, an unlikely and improbable discovery along the roads of Northern Spain.

Were there a book, not of castles but of towers in Spain,★ to cover all the kingdom from the Giralda of Seville to the Mudéjar towers of Teruel, it would surely, include this pair at Logroño. But, also, not far from there is a still more beautiful example, the detached tower of Santo Domingo de la Calzada, by the same architect Martín de Beratúa, and of date (1762–7) to relate it to those latest of the City steeples, to St Giles-in-the-Fields by Flitcroft, or to St Leonard's, Shoreditch, by George Dance the Elder, to both of which indeed it bears resemblance but, also, to my much lauded tower of the Reloj at Santiago, which the architect must certainly have seen and studied. The base or shaft of his tower at Santo Domingo is ribbed with pilasters, above which the octagonal bell-chamber has domed turrets at its corners, taller, more elongated than those of the Reloj, with round openings above the bell-windows flanked by Corinthian pilasters, over which the transition to the smaller stages, still octagonal, but with smaller openings, becomes circular at last, and richly pilastered, and loses itself into a point that in the blazing sunlight we can scarcely see. It is of course Spanish in colour, not the white Portland stone, but it is an amalgam of Wren's and his disciple's bell-chambers or steeples and of the Reloj of Santiago, and makes all the stranger that moment of going into the church and beholding in the first moment of entry the white cock and hens of Santo Domingo in their iron cage of the fifteenth century, now floodlit, high on the transept wall.†

But it is time to speak of the city and the dynasty of architects who lent their name, unwittingly, to this vernacular or native style of Spain, of which a first taste could be in the chapel of Santa Tecla in the north-west corner of Burgos Cathedral. This is harmless enough and not likely to arouse comment. It is difficult to detect the floreated decoration high upon the mediaeval vaulting, by a disciple not a member of the 'heresiarch' family; but Salamanca is the city in which the works of the Churrigueras are to be seen in competition with the late Gothic and the Plateresco, where, in fact they surprise by their dignity and sobriety.

The differing identities of the family are indeed an entanglement of Churrigueras, a name that in itself, as I once wrote, 'calls to mind a sort of fluttering of edges'. But it is ironical that this very effect, the flutter and dazzle of cornices, applies really to other architects, not practising in Castile, whose work must have been quite unknown to the Churriguera family.

★ I am thinking of a mid-Victorian phenomenon: *The Spires and Towers of England*, by J. Wickes, London, 1853–4. El Burgo de Osma, near Aranda de Duero, with a splendid mediaeval Cathedral, has a late Baroque tower (1739–44) much resembling that at Santo Domingo de la Calzada, by a pair of architects with Basque names. This, too, would call for inclusion in a book of towers.

† For a fuller account of the white cock and hens in their cage at Santo Domingo de la Calzada see my *Truffle Hunt*, 1953, pp. 298, 299.

Doubtless it was their name, merely the sight and sound of it, whether written down or spoken, that incurred the blame and laid it at their door. It seems to have been spelt Xuriguera in early days, which simple form of it might have absolved them. But it was the accretion or multiplication of r's that doomed them, for the truth of which it is only necessary to have heard a Spaniard rolling his r's in *charros*, – a term denoting the country folk of the province of Salamanca, prototype, incidentally of the *charro* horsemen of Mexico in their huge sombreros, gorgeous jackets, glittering harness, and great saddles with stirrups to match. Once you have heard an old Spaniard mouthing the word *charros*, you can think of what several generations of Spaniards would make of the double r's in Churriguera!

There was Alberto, Joaquín, José Benito – the first of them, born in 1665 – José Simón, and Manuel Lara, and there may well have been others. It would be hopeless, were it even possible, to follow their careers in detail. Most renowned of the family was José de Chirruguera, who began like most of the family as a carver or designer of *retablos*; and his rare buildings are eminently, even dully respectable, in particular his model village and church of Nuevo Baztán, the latter of Herreran severity in boring reminder of the sombre splendours of the Escorial. But it was Alberto, youngest brother of José, in whom the originality of talent showed itself; in the Plaza Mayor of Salamanca – though with assistance, or perhaps the position was reversed, from García de Quiñones, member of a dynasty of architects as muddling to sort out as the Churrigueras – a square which is arcaded in great part, where bull-fights were held until a hundred years ago, which is reminiscent of the Plaza Mayor in Madrid, but of a dullness and stiffness that do not bear comparison to the earlier Place Vendôme, or the later Place Stanislas at Nancy. But this is Salamanca, and neither Paris, nor Madrid; and we are to expect different effect made of its pale golden stone.

The marvellous play of this material in the hands of the late Gothic or Isabelline, and the Plateresco architects makes it hard even to imagine what Salamanca can have been like before Marshal Marmont (in 1812–13) in the words of Wellington – and who would disbelieve him? – 'destroyed thirteen out of twenty-five convents, and twenty of twenty-five colleges which existed in this celebrated seat of learning . . . the western portion of Salamanca is consequently one heap of ruins', the area of the walled city in the Middle Ages, when it had ten thousand students, having been rather larger than Oxford and Cambridge together. But just as the Plateresque merges into the late Gothic without fuss or argument in this wonderful old city so the Churrigueresque, which here belies its name for fantasy and hysterics, takes place in the general harmony without false note or dissonance. Prime example of which is the work done at the New Cathedral by Alberto of the name. This is manifest in his stone choir-screens in the nave, forming that central fort or redoubt of the *coro* where Spanish magnificence runs riot in every cathedral to keep the canons warm in winter and cool in summer at their chanting. Within the *coro* are the choir stalls, the work of José Lara de Churriguera from his brother's drawings,★ which but for their joint authors would take their place among the most splendid of church furnishings in Spain. It was Alberto, the elder brother, who designed the octagonal lantern of the New Cathedral, a skilful exercise in structural or realised perspective in the theatrical sense. But then, had not Alberto de Churriguera started his career when twenty-four years old with his design for a catafalque for the first wife of the pallid imbecile Carlos II, last of the Spanish Habsburgs, which design was in the strict Fratel Pozzo, Bibiena theatrical tradition? Had he, also, designed the gilded organ-case with those horizontal, salvo-firing pipes in the true Spanish fashion? Considering that he began as a carver and maker of altar pieces it is not improbable. Or had a hand in the sacristy, described by one authority as 'bright with Venetian mirrors'? On retiring from his post at Salamanca, Alberto de Churriguera worked in freer vein as in the parish church at Rueda where his façade is placed between round drum towers, and the frontispiece itself seems to show the influence of the villain of the piece Pedro de Ribera, the real renegade or hero of the Churrigueresque, particularly in his fantastic and notorious doorway to the Hospicio Provincial in Madrid which was indeed built some twenty years earlier than this portal at Rueda. It is the same doorway simplified, at Rueda, with round eye-shape or ocellus over it, lifted cornice, statue in a niche above that, and the top of the frontispiece showing against the sky. But Pedro de Ribera we must return to later. For the rest at Salamanca there are doorways by members of the family, and the grand and beautiful sunken court of the Clerecía by Andrés García de Quiñones, collaborator in the Plaza Mayor. This cloister of the Jesuits is superb and solemn with its giant columns, and is of Roman grandeur, most unlike in temperament to the 'excesses' of the native style. But this is a judgement that holds true of most of the buildings of its date in Salamanca. The extravagancies in golden stone are of the late Gothic and the Plateresque; they are the beauty of Salamanca but not to be ascribed to this family of architects who get all the blame. Who could think, standing in this courtyard of the Clerecía, that the splendid dome and pair of towers which could be Roman of the late sixteenth century are by Andrés García de Quiñones, partner or pupil of Alberto de Churriguera?

But an attempt must now be made to narrate the *Trasparente* of Toledo Cathedral, the sculptor or architect of which – Narciso Tomé – could as well be called the author or choreographer. The *Trasparente* caused an enormous sensation at the time of its dedication (1732), an occasion celebrated with

---

★ But was he in fact José de Lara Churriguera, or more simply José de Lara? There was a Manuel Lara de Churriguera in the family. No one seems to know or care.

public rejoicing, a bull-fight, and more prosaically, the appearance of a poem *Octava maravilla cantada en octavas rimas* by Fray Francisco Rodríguez Galán.★ Such details show that the *Trasparente* was no mere doorway or new sacristy. But it is difficult to put into words what the *Trasparente* is, or what it was intended for. Its purpose was to celebrate the gift of the Holy Communion to mankind but, then, again, how can it be described? For it is not an altar, nor a chapel; neither, precisely, could it be called a *pièce montée*, under which term could be grouped Bernini's *Ecstasy of St Teresa* (Santa Maria Vittoria, Rome), his baldacchino, or the Cathedra Petri in St Peter's, or the progeny-altars of Bernini in churches in Bavaria by the Asam brothers. The *Trasparente* is a phenomenon nearly alone and unique of its kind, but surely nothing if not theatrical in intention and effect. From the floor upwards it begins modestly enough; the whole of 'this chapel without walls'† being supported to all appearances by the pair of small white marble angels who are standing on the altar. This is but the beginning of a vast deception. At this moment it is but a simple altar with a seated figure of the Virgin, and bronze bas-reliefs on either side, but the ends of the cornice above her curve outwards like a pair of cow's horns, and are the air-strip or touch-down for a whirlwind of angels flying and diving with more than the energy of a shoal of dolphins among the shafts of a sunburst issuing from the windows of a little hidden *camarín* where the Eucharist is exposed, a small chamber reached by a little stairway that is concealed behind the marble panelling at the back in fact of the high altar, or *altar mayor* of the Cathedral. The golden sunburst and the rays coming out from it are the point or focal centre of the *Trasparente*, above which is a bas-relief of the Last Supper carved in alabaster, over which again the afore-mentioned 'ventilator shaft' – there could be no fitter term for it – adorned with paintings of the history of Gideon, the Lamb of the Seven Seals, the Twenty-four Elders of the Apocalypse, and more besides, loses itself into the heights, like looking up a great chimney-shaft, the kitchen chimney in the ruins of Glastonbury for instance, but distempered and plastered, and then handed over to the fresco painters.

Such is the *Trasparente* of Toledo Cathedral, starting from nothing and ending as an experience, not to the taste of everyone, but without parallel; at once a sunburst, a whirlwind, and the 'flying dream' of the psychoanalysts,

★ Let it not be thought that it is only Spaniards who take up their pens on such occasions! cf. *Urania: or a description of the top of the theater at Oxford*, by Robert Whitehall, 1669, an epic poem inspired by the painted ceiling of the Sheldonian Theatre by Robert Streater, Sergeant-Painter to King Charles II; or the epic poem on Sir James Thornhill's *Judgement of Paris* upon the staircase ceiling at Charborough Park, Dorset, by the Rev. Christopher Pitt (d. 1748), rector of Pimperne, and translator of *The Aeneid*.

† George Kubler and Martin Soria *op. cit.* This is their phrase; and they describe how by removing one entire rib-vault of the fabric 'in order to augment the light', Narciso Tomé contrived 'a light-trap rising high above the Gothic vaults like a ship's ventilator'. How well they write!

mixed so much with metaphor and allegory, and so much adorned and interrupted by the passage of headlong Archangels and by flying cupids that the mind refuses and can take in no more. However, on nearer examination it yields a point and reveals a tell-tale date. For the columns to either side of the figure of the Virgin and Child have their marble casing in shreds and tatters to reveal their fluting, a piece of symbolism of elusive meaning, but the *Trasparente* emerges with the cupids' heads upon those columns as having not only Bernini for ancestor, but for collateral and contemporary, Caffieri, Meissonier, Oppenord, and other craftsmen of the reign of Louis Quinze. A typical example just as involved in imagery, is the clock called *la Création du Monde*,★ destined by Dupleix for the King of Golconda, but never given to that potentate after the fall of the French Indies. The world is being born from the roaring seas in a whirlwind of clouds, under a burst of sun-rays. This astonishing object is just as wild in imagery as the *Trasparente*, which is therefore not quite alone of its kind but had its smaller scale equivalents during the Rococo decade or two of the reign of Louis Quinze. Only it is the difference between a clock or snuff-box and an object with the dimensions of a minaret or factory chimney.

But we come now to the true heresiarchs or exponents of the native style, of whom Pedro de Ribera (1683–1742) is best known, though one of the least interesting. He seems to have been drawn away from the Churriguera family – he may have been a pupil of José of the name – by the influence of the Court architect, a German, Teodoro Ardemáns who built the palace of La Granja, and was hostile to the Churriguera family. Ribera worked almost entirely in Madrid, building several palaces of no outstanding particularity, churches several of which were damaged in the Civil War but none of them of much interest, and leaving two monuments of outstanding curiosity in Madrid to keep his name alive. The nine-arched Puente de Toledo, across the Manzanares, with its great cylindrical cut-waters and the extraordinary. Aztec-looking, stone-canopied shrines along its parapets† make this bridge of noble proportions more suited to Mexico City than to Madrid. Churrigueresque as it may be, to use that misleading term, the Puente de Toledo could well have been built by a Spanish-trained Indian or *mestizo* architect in the first or second generation after the conquest. The other building is the portal to the Hospicio Provincial which, also, would not look amiss among the teeming six million population of Mexico City. It has the full repertoire of *estípites*, inverted pyramids, hooded shell-niches, and so on, to relate it to Tepotzotlan, Taxco, Guanajuato, and other places described in the chapter on Mexico. The portal is of coarse brown stone set in a long

---

★ Illustrated in a colour plate in *L'Oeil* for September, 1966, pp. 30, 31. The clock is at Versailles.

† Ford *op. cit.* calls attention to 'the hideous statues of San Isidoro and his wife looking out for water'. What would Ford have thought of the statues of saints along the Charles Bridge at Prague?

building which is otherwise without interest. But the theatrical pre-occupation of this strange portal is further emphasised and drawn attention to by looped-up curtains hanging from the cornice, ready to let fall their folds at any moment to hide the tall inverted pyramids or *estípites* and mask the grotto'd doorway. The portal of the Hospicio is violently and dramatically picturesque as though invented by a scene painter of wide experience to portray a palace doorway in a wholly imaginary and unknown country. But it is true to say that it is modest in both expression and dimension compared to the Churrigueresque of Mexico to which it may serve as introduction, but which it anticipates by some twenty to forty years.

This being an architecture which of its nature interprets and illustrates the sunlight, apart from regional instances such as the granite churches and arcades of Santiago, or the towers of that same city and its satellite towers as that at Santo Domingo de la Calzada, it is to be expected that it should attain to its profuse flowering in Andalucía and the South of Spain. Some attention having already been paid in another chapter of this book to the façades of Valencia and Murcia this is now the moment in which to discuss the Churrigueresque, or native style of Spain as I would prefer it to be described, in Seville and Granada, not forgetting Córdoba for some of the most interesting buildings of their kind are in the province of that name. When considering such buildings it must ever be kept in mind that Andalucía is opposite North Africa, 'the promised land of the Moors' – more apposite to the argument than the proximity of Dover to Calais – and that innate memory of the Mosque at Córdoba and the Alhambra of Granada, not forgetting the Giralda of Seville and its Arab court of orange trees, must be behind the mind of all Andalucians. Who could think otherwise on knowing the 'white towns', or *villes blanches*, like Tarifa or Vejer de la Frontera, whence can be seen the Moroccan coast and the mountains of the Rif – or Mojácar, too, another of the 'white towns' where a few of the old women still wear the Moorish veil – *villes blanches* that insinuate themselves into the same pigeon-hole of the memory and imagination as the 'white towns' of the Greek Islands, isles of the Cyclades and Sporades – Thira on Santarin, Mykonos, Pholegandros, Skopelos – and that become inseparable from thoughts of those extremities of Europe near to the domes and minarets of the Turks and Moors.

The first building of the date in Seville likely to obtrude itself upon our attention is the Sagrario, and after that the Palacio de San Telmo. The Sagrario or parish church attached to the Cathedral will delay no one for more than a moment or two who is on his way through the Court of Oranges to the Gothic wonders that lie beyond. It is of the date: that is enough and there is far more to see. If it reminds one of the Sagrario of the Cathedral of Mexico City which is by Lorenzo Rodríguez, who was born at

Spain

Corner of Palacio de la Conquista at Trujillo,
decorated with rows of manacled Indians.

Above: Detail of Santa María at San Sebastián.
Opposite: Façade of Santa María at San Sebastián.

Santiago de Compostela in the mist.

Dome of cathedral of
Santiago de
Compostela.

Twin west towers of
cathedral of Santiago de
Compostela above the
Isabelline cresting
of the cloister.

Façade of Santa Clara
at Santiago de
Compostela.

San Frutuoso at
Santiago de
Compostela.

Façade of the Clerecía at Salamanca.

Opposite: Doorway of the Hospicio Provincial at Madrid by Pedro de Ribera.
Below: Cloister of Lugo Cathedral by Fernando de Casas y Novoa.

Right and below:
Two views of
camarín of
Cartuja of El
Paular, near
Segovia.
Opposite:
A detail of the
same building.

Portal of Palacio de San Telmo, at Seville.

Doorway of Archbishop's Palace at Seville.

Sagrario of the Asunción at Priego de Córdoba.

Guadix and came from Cadiz, so much the better but one misses those two exterior façades of red *tezontle*. The Palacio de San Telmo is another matter. It is on the outskirts of Seville near the Guadalquivir, and nearly next to the Tobacco Factory of *Carmen* where the *cigarreras* long ago were 'nearly superseded by machinery', though it is not possible to pass it by even now and not have in one's ears the muted strings of the violins in the cigarette girls' chorus early in the first act, a sound which Nietzsche likened to a breath from the garden of Epicurus. The long brick front of the Palacio de San Telmo is interrupted by its three-storeyed entrance in most flamboyant style with coupled pilasters on all three floors, a half-dozen of statues on the first landing to each side of a balcony which looks empty in their absence, and this extremity among façades rears up its last storey to no practical purpose against the sky, a feature for which it has been condemned by purists but it is not pretending to be more than a fantasy and an extravagance. It is not inappropriate that perhaps the strangest and most extreme of all El Greco's paintings, his picture of *Laocoon and his Sons*, now in the Metropolitan Museum in New York, should have been for a century or more in the San Telmo Palace when it belonged to the Duc de Montpensier and his descendants.

The architect of this far-fetched frontispiece was the Sevillan, Leonardo de Figueroa (1650–1730). Did he, also, or one of his sons, one may think in passing, design the box of the Maestranza in the old Bull Ring of Seville, in the shadow almost of the Giralda, familiar from the lithographs of J. F. Lewis, *Sketches of Spain . . .* (1833–4)? The columns of this huge box, its cupola and broken cornice, hold more than a hint in them of the Palacio de San Telmo and Leonardo de Figueroa. He, also, built a number of churches in Seville, of which the most interesting is San Luis. Its interior is the best place in which to sample the Sevillan style. In this city of old convents, with Mudéjar tilework and *artesonado* ceilings* it is a surprise to enter a church that shows so many signs of careful planning. In the first place San Luis is most painstaking and elaborate in lay out. You enter into its domed circle only to see it is not a rotunda at all. It has four semi-circular lobes or petals at the cardinal points of its circumference between which chapels or apses there are altars; and the interior, once grasped, is no less ingenious in its scheme of decoration. Salomonic, or twisted columns in pairs frame in each altar, and support the archway into each apsidal chapel; while above these altars, at the foot of what are really the portions of wall that carry and support the dome, and below its cornice, are bronzed or gilded grilles of one-nun, bulbous protuberance in their middle, and over that again and above the cornice the

---

* Santa Clara, San Clemente el Real, Santa Paula, Santa Catalina, and others. The restored chapel of San José is a little masterwork of the Sevillan Baroque style, in its small area no less than a *multum in parvo* of the city of *Don Giovanni*, of *Carmen*, and *The Barber of Seville*.

I

regular *loges* or opera-boxes of the nuns. Further there is adventitious aid from inlay of blue glass on portions of the altars. There are other churches of the date in Seville, but San Luis is the best of them; and there is the staircase of the Archbishop's Palace, next to the Cathedral.

But more beautiful than Seville itself, because unspoilt, are country towns like Carmona and Écija, or Osuna; the last named if only as a *ville blanche* and at the thought that in the days of Richard Ford the balconies of its houses were 'ornamented with superb carnation pinks'. Carmona is another matter. It is a treat to walk about its streets with their feel of a Roman origin and Moorish upbringing, and to look into its churches; San Pedro, for instance, where the chapel or *sagrario* leading out of the church could have been designed on purpose as a white and gold refuge from, and yet interpretation of the heat. But Écija is the prize of all the little towns of Andalucía. It is an excitement merely to be approaching Écija, with its renown as the town with the hottest climate in all Europe; and from having read the account of it in Théophile Gautier's *l'Espagne* (1845) who writes that he had come 'to a new country of pagodas and Indian temples, with strange porcelain monuments and statues'. What a delight to be visiting Écija, in the imagination at least, with the devotee of Fanny Elssler, lover of Carlotta Grisi, and author of *Giselle*! And if admitted to his friendship there would be much to discuss in broken English and bad French. There do seem indeed to be some eight or nine towers rising from the town as we come nearer to it. Écija, incidentally, is not one of the *villes blanches* of Andalucía. Its prevailing colour is terracotta, and once within its walls we find that it has three church towers that are lined with *ajulezos* and several china monuments and fountains.★ One brick tower at least is shaped like a pagoda; and induced perhaps by its climate, some kind of Oriental vision or delusion seems to have haunted the minds of the architects of Écija.

But the country palace of the Marqués de Peñaflor is beautiful indeed in a different mood, with its curving street front, window-boxes in full flower along its curving balcony, and portal with Salomonic pillars. So beautiful is the Peñaflor Palace that it would seem to have musical associations all its own. The *fandango*, if of stately sort, heard in Count Almaviva's palace, and the heavenly simplicity of the country dance that follows upon it – is the stage direction really of insistence that they should be heard in the town palace of Count Almaviva? The palace of the Marqués de Peñaflor at Écija would seem to be their ideal setting. The arias, even the famous march, are another matter. They breathe the sophistication of great stairs, gilt salons, and golden

---

★ Mr James Lees-Milne in *Baroque in Spain and Portugal*, 1960, pp. 114, 115 mentions 'the diminutive *sagrario* of San Juan . . . with its inner open dome through which another dome is seen, brilliantly and invisibly lit'. He calls it 'a gem of Baroque art', by an unknown architect, but unfortunately it has eluded me.

theatres. But from the country music of the *Nozze di Figaro* this little palace at Écija, once seen, is inseparable for ever more; even though the dog-days of August be too hot, and Mozart might not have approved when Ford writes that 'some of the best bull fights in Spain take place' in this Andalucian town of porcelain towers and Indian pagodas.

The Baroque of Granada and of Córdoba is more interesting and more adventurous than that of Seville, perhaps for the reason that the Alhambra and the Mosque of Córdoba were of a character sure to assert itself in any mind; and then again, probably because of this very factor, both districts produced one, if not two most original and outstanding geniuses in their sort; architects, but lately disinterred from oblivion, but beside whom the Churriguera family and even Pedro de Ribera are but ordinary and tame, in sequence to which some of the smaller churches of Granada well repay a visit, and more especially those churches that possess a *camarín*, a sort of holy-of-holies, more often than not with some of the attributes of a lady's boudoir, being in fact the dressing-room where the robing of the holy images takes place and where the robes are stored. As a poetical symbol or concept this had a particular appeal to the Granadine mind, a fair instance of which is the *camarín* of Santa Cruz la Real, now called, confusingly, by another name.★ It is a curious little upstairs apartment formed from three apses round a domed shrine in the centre; the whole coruscating, even ricocheting with lights and reflections from the misted panes of mirror of different shapes set in its walls and ceiling, and with an inlaid floor of remarkable elaboration, in fact an intricate stone carpet laid in different colours.

However, all this is but trifling in effect compared to the *sagrario* and *sacristía* of the Cartuja de Granada. But one almost ignores the *sagrario* for all its walls of porphyry and jasper and the tabernacle in the middle with its Salomonic columns that lies beyond it; of mysterious origin, too, for work on it only started some years after the death of the architect who, nominally, designed it. He was Francisco Hurtado y Izquierdo (1660–1725), a native of Lucena in the province of Córdoba, who repaired early to Granada. And the stucco work of intricate and dazzling whiteness now proves to be the handiwork of Luis Cabello; while Luis de Arévalo to whom at one time the *sacristía* was attributed *in toto* was but the stonemason. Work was only completed much later, at some time between 1771 and 1783, which adds to the mystery. And now another claimant to being designer of the *sacristía* has been brought forward of recent years in the person of Francisco Xavier Pedraxas, who was only born at Priego, between Granada and Córdoba, in 1736, eleven years after Hurtado died, and who most surely to judge from

★ Santa Escolastica. In the Penguin Book, *Art and Architecture in Spain and Portugal*, 1959, p. 57, the joint authors cite the small Andalusian town of Estepa, near Osuna, for its *camaríns* in Granadine style; the Carmen, the hexagonal Asunción, and the octagonal Remedios. They could well be beautiful.

his other interiors must have had some hand in it. Hurtado, at any rate, finished the *sagrario* in his lifetime. But the *sacristía*? Is it his; or the work of Pedraxas? For the *sacristía* was finished nearly four decades after Hurtado's death. The doors and vestment cupboards of ebony and tortoiseshell inlaid with mother-of-pearl and silver, and with silver handles, were the work of a Carthusian monk who was engaged on them for more than thirty years (1730–64). Work, then, continued on it until late in the century, as we have seen; till not much more than fifty years before Théophile Gautier saw it and was first to appreciate its intended rivalry with the stucco arabesques of the Alhambra. The tall, facetted pilasters of this extraordinary interior in all their dazzling whiteness, and the Beardsleyesque flutter of its cornices make a visual experience of unique sort that haunts the memory.

But, also, Hurtado has designed *camarín* and *sacristía* in another Carthusian monastery far away in the pinewoods near Segovia, the Cartuja of El Paular. Hurtado had been entrusted by the prior with the design for this in 1718. Work began two years later, but here again Hurtado died before it was finished, and the authority who discovered and disinterred Pedraxas from oblivion★ would attribute the *camarín* of El Paular to his protégé, and perhaps with reason. Pedraxas, it is known, put down the inlaid floor of the *camarín* at El Paular – perhaps, also, that of the *camarín* of Santa Escolastica at Granada? – but on visual evidence from what we will see of his other work, is it not more probable that the plans of Hurtado were completed and carried through after he had died? The style and manner are that of Hurtado's lifetime, not the Rococo of Pedraxas. Also, the *camarín* at El Paular is in hard materials, not in stucco. At Granada it is the mystery of how stuccowork after Hurtado's designs can possibly have been continued for years after he had died. On the strength of which we would see the hand of Pedraxas in Granada, and less so at El Paular, an interior which is extraordinary enough in all conscience.

The *camarín* of El Paular is a domed octagon, called the *Trasparente*, behind the high altar, in the shape of a Greek cross, with the tabernacle in the centre. This, which is circular, rises high into the dome and has Salomonic columns of beautiful and unusual colour.† Out of this *camarín* a red and gold lacquer door leads through a screen of interlacing arches, *à la Mezquita de Córdoba*

★ Mr R.C. Taylor, who has written of F.X. Pedraxas in the *Art Bulletin*, 1950, and the *Architectural Review* for July, 1952. cf. also, Antonio Gallego y Burín, *El Barroco Granadino*, 1956. But it is pleasant to record that Mr Taylor allows the extraordinary doorway of the Castillo de Bibataubín, that fantasy-barracks at Granada, to the displaced Hurtado. His, then, are the statues of grenadiers in tall half-sugar-loaf hats, with their hair in pigtails, fierce moustachios, and muskets on their shoulders, guarding the balcony over which sits a lion on a stone cushion, brandishing a drawn sword, and wearing a crown. And why not, to put it tersely? But they were damaged in the Civil War and are on guard no longer.

† Mr James Lees-Milne, *op. cit.* p. 122, writes of these that they are 'of a brilliant coral colour, only matched by the rushing waters of the Pisuerga river in an April spate after torrential rains'.

and most obviously of that derivation, into the *sagrario*; the screen in itself being one of the curiosities and anachronisms in all architecture for in default of a name to whom to attribute it one can only think of Guarino Guarini who it is probable had seen the mosque at Córdoba while he was in Spain. Anyone who has admired Guarini's ceilings in the chapel of the Santo Sudario or that of San Lorenzo, both at Turin, with their intersecting ribs of obvious mathematical-Moresco derivation would see this screen at El Paular as their near relation. The *sagrario*, again, is cruciform in plan with chapels between the arms. It has been said that this pair of apartments, the *camarín* and the *sagrario* of El Paular are more beautiful, if less remarkable, than the *sagrario* and *sacristía* of the Cartuja of Granada, and this is perhaps the truth. But their use of Moorish motifs is more profound than the flutter of the cornices and fretted pilasters at Granada, more thoughtful and less fascinating, and suggestive to my mind, at least, less of Pedraxas than of Hurtado.

But now another complication arises for it appears that Hurtado, who was born at Lucena, and married a lady from Priego, both towns being in the province of Córdoba, had his workshop at Priego and even worked there on his plans for the Cartuja of El Paular.★ And it is at those two Andalucian towns of Lucena and Priego that we are now to investigate the buildings of Pedraxas. They are indeed of recent discovery, being quite unknown when I wrote my book on Spain in 1949; and I was only able to visit Priego and see its churches in August, 1962. But a first contact with Pedraxas many years ago was with the choir stalls of the cathedral at Guadix, the town with a Gypsy suburb of Gypsy caves resembling the *Thebaid* of Hieronymus Bosch, and even that long ago I thought those red wood choir-stalls peculiar and almost Mexican in style. Mr R. C. Taylor now attributes them to Pedraxas. They have, at least, the hint of his surpassing fantasy and strangeness for the full taste of which it is necessary to have visited Lucena,† and better still, Priego.

It is an exciting drive from Córdoba to Priego, starting before the morning gets too hot, down the Paseo del Gran Capitán and across the Guadalquivir, and after a time to a white town up and down a hill, of a dazzling lime-kiln white, with streets that were once mule tracks now become flights of steps. Impossible, too, on leaving Córdoba, that town of the two Senecas and of Lucan, of Averroes and of Luis de Góngora, not to have memories of the white alleys of the Barrio de la Judería, so much more beautiful and unspoilt than the whitewashed alleys of Seville. By which time we may have been going for an hour or more past hills *capitonné'd*, there is no other word for it, with olive trees from top to bottom, hills that are olive-tufted, olive-quilted;

★ Mr James Lees-Milne, *op. cit.*, p. 125.

† The *sagrario* of the parish church at Lucena is by Pedraxas. But the town, pleasantly enough, is better known for its apricots and olives.

and then desert, and after that a rocky gorge, and a water-mill, it must be, with flowering balconies. And we have arrived. It is Priego de Córdoba; where we go first not having breakfasted, and led thither by the traffic policeman who has quitted his conductor's desk for the purpose, to the *Bar los Colorines: especialidades: Jamón serrano y vino de Montilla*; and there were ten or fifteen of the hams hanging from the ceilings, hams from the real mountain swine, our driver told us. This was no Italian espresso bar; no Orvieto, or sweet vermouth, no *cannelloni* or *tagliarini*, but only olives and Montilla, the local sherry with a dry and salty taste, and soon thin slices of *jamón* were brought, pierced with wooden toothpicks, and two or three wafers in a paper napkin. The Feria was to begin next day and last all week; there were to be bull-fights, dancing, and speeches from the balcony of the town hall; and we went to look in the church of the Asunción which was being swept out and made ready for the morrow.

This church is the masterpiece of Pedraxas. The interior which is very tall and high, and shimmering with a greenish light, has a screened and mirror-hung *sacristía*; but it is the two-storeyed octagonal *sagrario* which is altogether unique, bringing this building in a small town in Andalucía into the same category as the palaces and churches of Lecce and Noto; and indeed to Bavarian masterpieces such as Wies or Zwiefalten. The balcony that runs round this octagon above the fantastic *stucchi* of the cornice leads the eye to windows at the back with beautiful wreaths and scrolls of stucco to surround them, but it is the stucco panels to both sides of the entrance into this octagon that are not of Europe, not even of Moorish Spain, but are almost Khmer or Cambodian in their absorbed intricacy, and multiplicity of figures. And the arches of the octagon above that balcony have again that Beardsleyesque movement or flutter, that nearly imperceptible guitar-like twanging or trembling of their decorative motifs that we learn to associate with that extraordinary apartment in the Cartuja of Granada.

There are fountains in plenty in Priego de Córdoba, but no palaces. Another of the churches is San Nicasio, known to the inhabitants as *La Aurora*, the only church in Priego with a façade in the sense that word is understood in much of Italy and Sicily. In scale it is but a one-aisled chapel, but with an interior richness of decoration that it is difficult to credit to the date (1771) and to a time when for instance both Gainsborough and Romney were in the full practice of portrait painting.[*] But, then, the *sagrario* just seen is later still, of 1782. *La Aurora* is by a heavier hand, the heavily stucco'd bosses of its ceiling reminiscent of the barrel-vault of Santo Domingo at Oaxaca in southern Mexico which is festooned with grapes. Behind its altar, I had been led to believe, was a *camarín* of theatrical effect 'with inlay of heart-shaped mirrors', and fresh from the *camaríns* of Quito in Ecuador and of

* The interior of *La Aurora* is illustrated in my *Monks, Nuns and Monasteries*, 1965.

churches in Mexico was disappointed in what I found.

Perhaps the Virgin of the Carmelites is the best of the other churches in Priego. It has a *sagrario* of that unusual greeny whiteness peculiar to the interiors in this Córdoban town, and could be due to some local mineral ingredient in the paint or stucco. In shape it is a pillared oval carried out with an elegance and lightness of hand that are lacking in *La Aurora*, and it has the 'fluttering cornices' of Pedraxas. Then, there is the church and hospital of San Juan de Dios belonging to an order of white-robed nuns, with an appropriately snowy or Sierra Nevada-white interior wherein the pupils, at least, of this 'last epigone of the school of Hurtado' must have had a hand. Another chapel of *La Aurora*-like category and dimension, that of Las Angustias, is reminiscent in little touches of that snowy interior in the Cartuja two or three days away on horse or mule-back in Granada, with for additional fantasy the nuns' grille that is of nature lacking in a Carthusian monastery. A white church above and on the outskirts of the town has a pastel-blue *camarín* for high altar, set like a piece of old stage scenery with a pair of doors and a stair above that to the figure of the Virgin standing in what is none other than a glittering boudoir or robing-room with free-hand flower paintings upon its walls. And this account of Priego should end at the green Rococo pulpit and its flower paintings and the, for once, coloured or polychrome *camarín* of San Pedro; but in an hour or little more we were gone from Priego: 'Lecce, Noto, all no more than a glass of wine and a few minutes to wait, in a world of wonders.'

7

Estilo Mejicano

That there is a '*style mexicain*' in architecture, just as surely as to the gringo's discomfiture and defeat there is a Mexican cuisine coming only after the French, Italian, Russian, and Chinese schools of cooking is the argument of this present chapter. Of this I was convinced long before I had the actual knowledge, and now on the strength of two or three sightings of most of the buildings mentioned I think it is indisputable that this is true. For I must explain that I wrote of Mexico in a book published as long ago as 1924, making its finale into a fanciful expedition into this country which I had read of, but where I had never been. But I remembered, and can never forget now, John L. Stephens' *Incidents of Travel in Central America, Chiapas and Yucatán* (1841) which was in my grandmother's library when I was eight or nine years old, with Catherwood's mysterious and wonderful drawings of the stone pyramids and carved monoliths of the Mayans, and had only to read them again for an account of huge old churches, five or six of them seen in a day's ride through the lush but impenetrable savannah. So I may claim early initiation into passages of his narrative like his riding, 'armed to the teeth', into the arcaded plaza of Quezaltenango; his sailing along the coast of Costa Rica and Nicaragua, and seeing eight or nine smoking volcanoes at the same time; or his climbing up into the ruins of a temple, opposite the island of Cozumel, carved with human figures all of them in immense plumed head-dresses, and seeing below him in the clear water at the cliff's foot a great fish eight or ten feet in length gliding along.

It was Madame Calderón de la Barca's *Life in Mexico* (1861), reprinted in the *Everyman Library*, that inspired this re-reading. And about the same time (1920–1) I found Baxter's *Spanish Colonial Architecture* in the library of the Victoria and Albert Museum, and Terry's *Guide to Mexico* fell providentially into my hands. Thus equipped I was ready to start, and could begin writing. But in fact it was not so easy, and progress was achieved more through poetic licence than by dull fact. For there was but little information to go upon. There were the, already, twenty-year-old photographs in Sylvester Baxter's book, and beyond that but little that was factual except the name of

Estilo Mejicano

The semi-tropical façade of La Soledad at Oaxaca.

Above: Two tiled panels, 1698, by Miguel Gonzales celebrating the capture of Mexico by the Spaniards. They show Cortez's entry into Mexico city (*left*), and the reception of Moctezuma there, while the Indians dance on their canoes on the lagoon.
Opposite top: Poblano (country) church at Tlaxcaltzingo with two tiled domes.
Opposite bottom: Balcony at the side of the basilica of Santa Prisca at Taxco.

Top left: Belfries of Santa Prisca, Taxco.
Bottom left: Carved frontispiece and bases of towers of Santa Prisca, Taxco.
Right: One of the belfries of the Santuario de Ocotlán.
Opposite: Side view of the Poblano (country) church of San Francisco Acatepec.

Above: One of the three golden *retablos* of La Valenciana at Guanajuato.
Opposite top: Carved stone doorway of the Templo de Cata at Guanajuato.
Opposite bottom: Semi-barbaric relief from the porch of the church of
Guadalupe at Zacatecas in northern Mexico.

Tresguerras, the architect, as it was then conjectured, of the two convents of Santa Rosa and Santa Clara at Querétaro. What was important to establish was the existence and individuality of a Mexican style, to which the 'Indians' themselves, the landscape and its volcanoes, the flowers and cacti and humming-birds lent accents of their own.

This I had to try to do from instinct, not from knowledge, for I was not able to get there in person for another thirty years, until 1952, and then only for six days during 'Thanksgiving', a blessed respite from a lecture tour in the United States. During that short visit however I visited everything I wanted most to see with the exception of Querétaro and Guanajuato; and I have been twice to Mexico again since then. How astonishing it is to think that when I wrote of Taxco in 1922, it was still three days' ride over the stormy mountains of the state of Guerrero!★ For now it is distant from Mexico City rather less than two hours on a motor-road! And it is so thick with tourists that you can hardly see the cobbled pavement, though nothing can mar the beauty of the postcard view of Taxco with the narrow street winding down and then up again to the twin towers of the church. Mexico City, itself, must have eight to ten times its population of all those years ago. Yet it is still and will always be Mexican; and even though it is a little Americanised by now it is more that the Mexicans have Mexicanised the 'Norte Americanos'.

Where else could we be but in Mexico before the flower-stalls by the railings of Chapultepec? Or in the court in front of the shrine of the Virgin of Guadalupe among the stalls that sell the medallions, 'the ribbons giving the exact measurements of the lady's head', and the score or more of smoking, ambulating kitchens? Is it necessary to write again of the *calaveras* or death's heads made of sugar, which skulls are sold in the Indian market on All Souls' Day, which I have said are as typical of Mexico as the fan and mantilla are of Spain? But in fact nothing of more importance than the three tiled domes of the church of Carmen, each of a different colour, in the suburb of San Ángel, could be anything other than of this origin, and it is not enough to say of them that they are 'in the Mudéjar style', or that they are reminiscent of the coloured domes of Murcia in Spain. For they are indeed most typically Mexican, no less so than the white-shirted and trousered 'Indians' at the stalls in the square outside under the fine old trees.

The church of El Carmen is Mexican alright, but the Spanish influence in Mexico, so far as it is Spanish, had more serious beginnings. An American scholar has lately published a book, the result of many years travel and research, his subject being the *capillos dos Indios*, or open air atriums attached to churches to hold the large Indian population that had compulsorily become converted after the Conquest. There are a large number of these,

---

★ Or, as it was once, five hours' ride on horse or mule-back over the mountains from Iguala, which town is some hundred and forty-five miles from Mexico City.

Opposite: Tiled steps, porch and dome of the Santuario de Ocotlán, seen from an interior courtyard.

running almost into hundreds, many of them in remote parts of Mexico, and the energy there displayed on the part of the priests and friars is hardly less astonishing in scope than the martial feats of the Conquistadores. They are mid sixteenth-century in date, in the colonial Franciscan manner, impressive in scale, and with 'documentary' sculpture of teaching intent, being for this very reason although peculiar to Mexico different altogether from the '*style mexicain*' it is sought to establish, which dates from a time when the Indian population had long been converted and were themselves taking a hand in it.

But this was a manifestation that was late in date and only established itself towards the middle of the eighteenth century, founding itself upon the latest models come straight from Spain. Of which there is a prime example in Mexico City in the twin façades of the Sagrario Metropolitano or separate parish church attached to the Cathedral, begun in 1749, which façades are the work of Lorenzo Rodríguez, an architect from Guadix in the province of Granada. This pair of frontispieces are in Spanish *retablo* manner like the carved high altars of their churches. But it is the walls of red *tezontle* rising up in a flight of bold and increasing curves and edged with white stone, with beautiful windows set in them and framed in the same white stone, more still the wall of red *tezontle* connecting the two fronts that is typically Mexican and by that more interesting than the Cathedral itself. Another church, that of La Santísima Trinidad is a later work of the same architect with a front of three storeys, framed in a multitude of pilasters and inverted pyramids, with side walls again of the red *tezontle*, the building material that we begin to appreciate for being Mexican. The cupola of the tower is in the shape of the triple crown or tiara of the Popes, but this allusion does not obtrude itself and is allowed to reveal its meaning in its own time. The interior of La Santísima has been wrecked, its golden altars melted down for the gold they contained; which has not been the case happily at the church of Santo Domingo, another church built in the phrase of Terry's *Guide*, of 'a porous amygdaline, stained a light red', or in fact once again the red *tezontle*.

If we want to be sure of the '*style mexicain*' it is only necessary to enquire for the Casa de los Mascarones of 1766–71, sometimes attributed also to Lorenzo Rodríguez – by then become Mexican as to the manner born, if still of Spanish accent and pronunciation – the unfinished one-storeyed palace of the high sounding Don José de Mendoza, Conde del Valle de Orizaba; an eight-windowed building broken by elaborate cupid-supporting pilasters that, traffic and noise problems apart, cannot but connect itself in the romantic imagination with the unfinished, one-storeyed palace upon the Grand Canal in Venice, were if not that this and the works of art it contains are now the Palazzo Guggenheim. Perhaps the ideal resident for the Casa de los Mascarones in Mexico City would have been that nobleman of Spanish descent, Don Carlos Rincón Gallardo, Marqués de Guadalupe y Duque de Regla, prime and last example of the *charro* horsemen in their huge sombreros, gorgeous jackets, glittering harness and great saddles, a costume dying out in Mexico despite his efforts to preserve it. This old gentleman, who only died in 1950, was to be seen riding in the streets of the capital in his beautiful costume with a *charro* attendant following, and had even adapted a black *charro* dress with silver ornaments for evening wear. How one would have liked to see him issuing forth from the Casa de los Mascarones with its high barred windows for his morning ride; better still, maybe, on his way to dinner down the moonlit streets!

The Shrine of Guadalupe is of necessary mention after its titular scion, less for the church itself than for the Capillo del Pocito or 'Chapel of the Holy Well'. This is in fact a pair of chapels, a bigger and a smaller like a mother and daughter, both of elliptical shape with domes of blue and white tiles, and with the ribs of the domes outlined in yellow. Below this, the walls of maroon-coloured *tezontle* have star-shaped windows framed in white stone. This pair of domes with their twin lanterns and tiled cupolas in the same chevron pattern somehow suggest the bubbling, if gaseous spring beneath them, and they make a strong visual impression that helps to form the picture of this country in our minds. Which said, and the noise and dirt forgotten, the Indian markets make the strongest memory of this city of six million people.

Two persons, widely travelled but of different tastes, the one a Russian scholar the friend of Tolstoy and of Gorki, the other an authority on the operas of Mozart, have told the present writer that in their opinion two of the beautiful cities of the world were Kiev and Puebla. They concurred in this; and if, not having seen Kiev, I would for my part put Prague as its alternative and replacement, I would be inclined to agree with both of them about Puebla, particularly on arriving there at the heat of mid-day, sitting in a café in one of the arcaded plazas and listening to a marimba band. This instrument with two players is of thrilling sound at the first hearing, like a vastly improved Gypsy dulcimer or cymbalom, but it is the melancholy truth that the music they play is of such inferior sort that it soon palls. Often, and again, it is the same experience, and a marimba band however eagerly anticipated is nearly always disappointing. In this welter of old ragtimes and cheap waltzes and mazurkas there is no opening for a Bartók or a Kodály; and in the disillusionment one might start to wonder if the buildings of Puebla would begin to go the same way. But they do not. And already it may have begun to become apparent that this is another facet of *le style mexicain* quite different from what we have seen in Mexico City, but not less purely and entirely Mexican. That it will prove to be a city of churches and convents is probable in the common knowledge that in this country where the monks and nuns were dispossessed by the laws of 1857, nuns were found living secretly and practising their vows in a certain convent, that of Santa Mónica, some eighty years later than this in 1935.

Without direct comparison which it would be ridiculous to carry to its furthest point it is probably true to say that there is more of coloured architecture in the sense that colour is used in its buildings, in Puebla than in any other city in the world except Isfahan. And it is providential for our argument that most, if not all of them, come within the time limits of our theme. Not that particularly subtle use is made of this colour for in fact these are domes and façades of china, and this is a china architecture. But, certainly, it makes its effect. One traveller of a century and a half ago goes so far as to say that 'in the splendour of its churches . . . Puebla must take the first rank in the Christian world' and that he who would wish to see the pomp of religious ceremony should visit this city' where the service of tenebrae in the Cathedral surpassed in magnificence all he knew of the pomp of Courts'. Can Puebla de los Angeles, as it was called, really have contained sixty churches, nine monasteries, thirteen nunneries, and twenty-three colleges? But, at least, this early traveller and precursor thought of another and original word by which to describe it when he speaks of 'houses and churches many of which are covered with glazed tiles, or delft of various colours'. So delft let it be, which is a change from tiles or *azulejos*! And as for the domes and cupolas of Puebla! La Concepción is in delft of blue and white; San José has a treatment of blue and yellow; the dome is yellow, blue and orange, while the house of the parish priest, nearby, has a dome of white delft with blue designs upon it, bands of yellow delft as ribbing for its dome; and a lantern of white and light blue, alternating with yellow and dark blue. The Cathedral has twin towers of great height covered with yellow and red delft, and a dome glazed yellow and dark green.

Two other instances are still more spectacular. The Templo de San Francisco is indeed most peculiar; a stone frontispiece in three storeys and a final row of finials, set in red brick with four tiled flower pictures like playing-cards, and then the red brick wings fold forward just like a house of cards. The flower motifs are in blue and yellow delft upon a white ground, and these panels are repeated, four again to each side, as the wings of the façade lean forward and fold towards us. The church of Guadalupe, outside the town, has a façade of delft in zigzag bands of orange, blue and green, that alternates with white. The angelic figures in the spandrels of its frontispiece have yellow gowns and orange wings. The towers are in red and green delft, and the four tiled subjects are framed in blue and white. Over them are the sun and moon in delft, with orange bodies and yellow rays upon a blue ground. It will be seen that this is a china architecture, granted the sunlight, of brilliance and reverberation, if not of the very highest taste.

As to the interiors, not all of them have been gutted of their golden altars. La Soledad has two huge gilded altars; Santa Catarina has no less than eight of them, in extreme state of dilapidation and not in any case the finest specimens of their kind. Here, to this present, they are but the echo of what is to be seen in Spain. As is, also, the sacristy of the Cathedral, more like the drawing-room or club-room of the canons where they gather to chatter and take snuff, though it cannot compete for faded luxury with the sacristies of Toledo, or of La Seo of Zaragoza. But, perhaps, all said and done, it is to the exteriors of Puebla that one returns in mind, and that this is in the main a memory of red tiles, as to which the delft phrase would be mistaken and misleading. Not, as I have said, that much subtlety is expended upon the tones of red. But both bricks and pottery, after all, are made of clay; and without much reflection upon the problem both brick-kilns and tile-factories, of which latter there were no fewer than thirty at work in Puebla by the middle of the eighteenth century, seem to have been working to the same ends. Brick and tile become, as it were, unified or amalgamated to the extent that before certain specimens one has to debate in one's mind as to whether they are tile or brick.

And for an instance of this, take the interior patio or cloister of Santa Mónica, the 'secret convent' of nuns aforementioned, which is a two-storeyed affair where the tile decoration is of the simplest, but the all-over effect is of a maroon-red background with inlay of blue quatrefoils set into a white ground. It is a red patio, red is its characteristic. A red patio with blue inlay forming false arches and outlining the real. It is a true example of the Pueblan style. An old house in the town, the Casa del Alfeñique (meaning 'almond-cake', and therefore fancy work or 'ginger-bread') is of the same manner. It is framed with the same red tiles forming a matt or unglazed surface, into which little rounds of blue tile with surrounds of glazed white, are inlaid like so many studs or nails. It is in fact a house of red delft with a rich and fanciful confectionery cornice in white plaster, and on the second floor the windows have rich and heavy window frames of white in the Spanish barocco taste. The Casa del Alfeñique with 'Indian' touches is spiritual companion to that fantasy barracks at Granada, the Castillo de Bibataubín.

A tiled kitchen in one of the convents of Puebla is of the same character,[*] the unconscious brain-child of the same parents as the patio of Santa Mónica, and of the Casa del Alfenique, which is no more than to say that it is in the vernacular of Puebla, and has the identical ideas and converses in the same Poblano patois. Which brings us to a subject typically and specifically of Mexico and no other country. For it was in the kitchen of Santa Rosa in Puebla that *Mole Poblana* was perfected, most horrific of nunnish inventions

* The information in the paragraph following is derived in part from the weekly publication, *Esta Semana*, Mexican counterpart and shadow to *La Semaine de Paris*. This should be consulted for where-abouts of the red, green, yellow, and perhaps most alarming of all, black *moles*, while details are given, also, of regional handicrafts, and of such localized products as the cochineal-dyed *sarapes* of Oaxaca, and even of the local flower-markets.

and *chef d'oeuvre* of the Churrigueresque cuisine; twice-boiled turkey in a sauce of cacao, liquorice, sesame, chillies, amaranth, cinnamon, and eleven more ingredients. A dish said to have been concocted by one of the nuns in the beautiful, blue-tiled kitchen of Santa Rosa, when preparing for a visit of the Archbishop. But in pursuit of the true Mexico there is no need to stop at that. Further south, in the town of Oaxaca where the churches built of *cantera verde* unlike the 'delft' churches of Puebla turn a beautiful green after rain and the carnival is 'celebrated with enthusiasm', green, yellow, red, and black *moles* are served, washed down with 'devil's blood', a drink made of *tequila* (distilled from the maguey cactus), chillies and orange-juice; while if by good fortune you are still further south at Tehuantepec, upon the isthmus, 'weddings usually take place on Sundays, and anyone may attend at will, by simply paying the sum of one peso. For this, he is entitled to a glass of mezcal, a loaf of bread and a slab of chocolate, everything adorned with a coloured tissue-paper flag. He can also have the typical dish of beef, and dance the whole day'! What further need is there to know we are in a semi-tropical climate than that in the church at Pátzcuaro, on the lake of that name, which town was once famous for its tapestries made chiefly of the feathers of the humming-birds (*picaflores*) – or is *huitzitzilin*, the Indian name for these, more beautiful and evocative? – there was an image of the Virgin made of corn-stalks, for which reason it was very light in weight and glued together with a substance obtained from orchids; or that lower down, hotter still, and near the coast, not far from Vera Cruz, there is a town of which the local specialities are given as gardenias and exotic hair-do's! And we take leave of Puebla with a last admiring look at the wall-paintings of bullfights in the shops where *pulque*, a much stronger cactus liquor than *tequila* is on sale, wishing to have seen its streets and plazas when enlivened with the china *poblana* dress, and hoping yet once more to hear a marimba band playing outside a café under the hot arcades.

Several of the villages round Puebla have churches in this local or Poblano style; and most notable among them San Francisco Acatepec, seven miles outside the town, approached through a red brick Mudéjar gateway with a façade which is of rich design in tile mosaic, outdone however by the base of its two towers which are of 'delft' in daring colours, while the right hand belfry has blue and yellow spiral bands that wind around the double columns at its four corners. In these, the blue and yellow 'delft' on a glazed red ground reaches to the height of fantasy attained in the 'flush-work' of coloured flints on the exterior of St Michael Coslany and other Norfolk churches. In the interior of San Francisco Acatepec the doorway to the baptistery is almost Manoelino in convolution, and reminiscent of the pair of doors of coral inspiration in the abbey of Alcobaça, though the motifs are not marine but vegetable, and the date not 1520, or thereabouts, but round 1730. Scarlet poinsettias, six or seven feet high, and in full colour in December, give additional excitement. Atlixco, another village rather further from Puebla, in a valley famous for its fertility with the snowy cones of Popocatépetl and Ixtaccihuatl within view, and yet more scarlet poinsettias, has a pair of Poblano churches. One of these, La Merced, has a statue of the Virgin in a niche over its doorway, her cloak upheld by midget angels, more vegetable than human, and the impressed or moulded richness of the stucco has reminded more than one observer of pressed wax or marzipan.

But if these are bucolic instances, and so long as the Mexican air and atmosphere are now established, we can betake ourselves, to one of the prime examples of *le style mexicain* which is the Santuario de Ocotlán, on a hill a mile outside Tlaxcala. I first saw it in 1952 on the way back from Puebla to Mexico City, recognising it from afar but unable to believe my good fortune for in the excitement of seeing Puebla, the snowy volcanoes and the Mexican landscape in general including the superb towers and bastions of white cloud for ever sailing and drifting in the high and fathomless empyrean of this inspiring country, the *primus inter pares* of both Americas, I had not realised we would go near Tlaxcala. But the Santuario de Ocotlán it was; and devotees of the Baroque and Rococo should approach this, the most pleasing if it is not the most serious building in both sub-continents, in the same spirit in which they are initiated into the pavilion of the Amalienburg or the pilgrimage church of Wies. Certainly, while a derivative of the local Poblano style, – so different again from that of Mexico City, or from what we will see at Taxco, Guanajuato, or Querétaro, all of which are in local manners or idioms of their own – the Santuario de Ocotlán is almost startingly original and unlike anything one has seen before,* and it is with mounting excitement that we climb near enough to take in its detail.

The façade itself and the twin towers are of a dazzlingly white stucco. But the base of the towers, with the swelling in each of them which holds the stair and projects therefore like a column or member up each base, is sheathed in hexagonal glazed bricks, scarlet in colour, and set in brilliant white mortar as in the meshes of a net. The effect, therefore, is of scarlet shark's skin or shagreen. But not in all lights. For on a second or third viewing the scarlet bricks may take on a more pinkish colour, or show orange-red. Indeed as with certain hues of red hair in human beings that may vary in mood or circumstance from coppery to apricot, or even to vermilion – and as, in parenthesis, with the china-tiled domes of the mosques of Isfahan – it is not possible to be categorical as to the colour. It can be one thing on one day and

---

* The façade of the church at Tlaxcala, down at the bottom of the hill, must be by the same hand. It merits inclusion in the long awaited album or anthology of façades. More so, still, the Santuario upon its hill.

in one light; and on another day, another. But I see it, myself, as pink-scarlet shagreen.

Between the pair of towers, the façade or frontispiece of dazzling white is in two storeys under a huge recessed shell which springs forth in protection of the figures and ornaments below. The first storey has two pilasters to each side of the door, and between each pair, a pedestal carrying a winged archangel, with busts of the Fathers of the Church above them. The upper storey has for its centre a window shaped like a double star, fringed stucco curtains, and in front of its light a statue of St Francis holding three globes that support a statue of the Virgin. To either side are pillars with more winged archangels; and above the star-shaped window the cornice carries yet another pair of archangels. With its pilasters and *estípites*, or inverted pyramids, and its statues, this whole façade is a golden *retablo* of Spain, or the still more golden Mexican *retablo*, translated and adapted into snow-white stucco.

As to the pair of white towers, they are in two storeys also. They have triple or bunched pilasters at each corner, of even dodecagonal effect, with the addition of obelisks upon the upper storey, and the flutter of so many cornices and the wreathed or flowering pilasters add to the whole effect. The only incongruity is the little belfry for the clock, over the snowy frontispiece, that spoils the curving cornice of the huge scroll ornament below. That apart, there is no impediment, and nothing now to delay our entry into the Santuario in order to see the *camarín*, a little octagonal room behind the high altar which a pure blooded Indian craftsman, Francisco Miguel, is reputed to have spent twenty-five years in decorating, and as is usually the case where there are such stories, he spent too long there and overdid it. Most of the hierarchy of the heavens are upon the carved and painted, the even lacquered ceiling, full length, but under life-size statues with metallic tints upon their robes. Not only the walls and ceiling, but the doors, the chairs and tables and the cupboards, are ascribed to his hand. It is a wooden grotto, all gilded, but patient and ant-like, of little inspiration.

It is its exterior which is the interest of the Santuario de Ocotlán. There is nothing to compare with it in Europe where, decidedly, there is no church with shrimp-coloured bases to its towers and a snow-white frontispiece sheltering under a shell-motif of Caribbean or Pacific origin. And for once the much maligned label of 'Churriguerismo' is not to be tied upon it, for if the two storeys of its twin towers are touched by that persuasion, again there is no colour precedent in all Spain for their bases. The frontispiece, of Spanish *retablo* derivation, has been converted from an interior to an exterior feature, becoming native or Poblano in the process, and the Indian or *mestizo* has taken over to the extent even that were it established that a craftsman of pure Spanish blood was responsible for the façade it could be said nevertheless that he was working in the semi-Indian manner. One who like the present writer

Opposite: Golden interior of the Rosário Chapel in Santo Domingo at Puebla.

has spent much of a lifetime in seeking out the Baroque and Rococo in all its manifestations in many countries of the world cannot but come away from the Santuario de Ocotlán with the feeling that this is an unique specimen with a semi-exotic beauty and poetry that is all its own.

But the most famous monument of its date in Mexico and the perfect example of the Churrigueresque is the church at Taxco. So much so that its obvious beauties in the way of elegance and dignity, and its suitability to both purpose and environment are enough to convert those who would never have thought to find themselves admiring a building of this kind. It is of course much helped by the beautiful little town in which it stands and that to a far greater extent than Ouro Preto in Brazil could qualify as the national monument of all Latin America. Its red-tiled roofs, steep winding streets and pebbled pavements in mosaic, give to it the aura of some old forgotten town in Italy or Spain, rare indeed in the new world, the Nuevo Mundo; but now anything but forgotten or deserted for its streets are as full of tourists as Stratford-on-Avon or Siena. It was a mine-owner of Spanish origin, José de la Borda, who arrived penniless from Europe and made a huge fortune from the silver mines of Taxco, who built the church of San Sebastián y Santa Prisca, where work was begun in 1751. It was the wool and cloth merchants, it should be said in parenthesis, who built the churches of Suffolk and the Cotswolds; just as the church here at Taxco, and another at Guanajuato, were built from the proceeds of a silver mine. The churches of Ouro Preto were of like origin. What has gone wrong with the world? Why is there nothing to show from the gold mines of South Africa and Australia? Is it a symptom of the world disease that has destroyed most of the living arts and involved itself in two world wars? This may well be so. However that may be, one cannot forget the first sight of the twin towers of Taxco rising above the tiled roofs into the deep blue and golden sky of Mexico, and the glitter of the sunlight from off its dome of blue and green, and orange and white tiles.

The material of San Sebastián y Santa Prisca is a pinkish-golden stone that can be 'rose-coloured' as Pál Kelemen describes it, or it can be dark golden like the tidal sands just uncovered by the waves, depending on the slant of the sunlight or on a sudden shower of rain. The façade is in two storeys with two pairs of Salomonic (twisted) pillars in the higher of them, and its central feature is a bas-relief of the Baptism over which is the customary window. The base of the towers is plain but for the four circular windows in each with their rich window frames, one above another; while above that the towers grow very elaborate and are, themselves, in two storeys, all their four faces on each floor having balconies that are supported by grotesque masks. Indeed the twin towers of Taxco, now become a familiar feature to thousands of tourists from towns in North America, are among the triumphs of their 'debased' school of architecture and of an unsurpassed natural affinity to

187

Opposite: Detail of tiled façade of San Francisco Acatepec.

K

their landscape setting. Were one to criticise this by now almost too familiar transmutation of the arts of Spain it would be to accuse it of a self-conscious elaboration of its own importance, as though it had been told it was to be the golden lodestone of its remote valley for which reason, as to its façade and pair of towers, it shakes itself in all its ruffles as it comes up out of the hillside, a comparison drawn without apology in translation from the Spanish word *espedaña*, used to denote a belfry or 'the ornamental extension of the façade above the roof line', and derived apparently from the verb *espedañar*, 'to spread the tail feathers'.★

Inside San Sebastián y Santa Prisca there are no fewer than twelve gilded Churrigueresque altars or *retablos*, such an array of them as exists nowhere else in the world, and in view of that more than a little overpowering. Moreover, in this as in the subsidiary arts in general by then established for more than two centuries in New Spain, there were different schools of *retablo* carving according to locality and among those demi-Indian academies of fantasy this of Taxco is some way from being the most fanciful of all. But for respite from the stalactitic cavern the sacristy should be seen for its large vapid paintings, the work of a Zapotec Indian, and for its fantasy chairs and tables, and coming forth again the organ is most beautiful, a bunched column of long pipes like stalks for its centre, fringed gold curtains draped above these and the lesser pipes to each side, and masks and cupids wherever there is room for them on pedestals and brackets. Moreover, the balustrading of the organ-loft has a choir-organ placed, or rather hung or fastened upon it like a golden brooch, the smaller counterfeit or clavichord, we could say of it, of the louder array of pipes behind; while even the bell-racks on the rail to either side have been treated and given the shape of lanterns. Coming away, we may feel that the organ and the twin towers are the lions of Taxco; the organ taking a high place even beside the salvo-firing organs of Spanish cathedrals with their great gilded cases and broadsides of level pipes, or beside the more delicate, satyr and mermaid-figured organs of Portugal; while, as for the rose or golden towers of Taxco that alter in colour according to your fancy, they are not less beautiful than any towers in Spain, than the towers of Compostela with weeds and snapdragons lolling from their cornices, or, of Mudéjar accent, the green-tiled towers of Teruel.

After San Sebastián y Santa Prisca of Taxco and after the Santuario de Ocotlán, the third of the four outstanding Churrigueresque buildings of all Mexico is the Seminario de San Martín at Tepotzotlan, built as a novitiate for the Jesuits some thirty-five miles from Mexico City on the road to Querétaro. But much has happened here since I first saw Tepotzotlan in 1952! Only as little a time ago as that it was, I think, still in use as a church. The best view

★ Pál Kelemen, *Baroque and Rococo in Latin America*, New York, 1951, p. 44; who notes that the *espedaña* 'is a feature that found a most interesting application in Latin America'.

of it was from over the wall surrounding the conventual estate which had inverted circular openings or dips through which one could admire and study the façade. To one side on the slope leading to the church, as I well remember, there were one-storeyed houses with awnings whence the pounding of maize tortillas could be heard and there was an alfresco restaurant. Now all that has been swept away. There are rows of what could be almshouses, or ticket offices, or both, or either; and the façade of the church, that I recall as being dark golden in colour, has been cleaned and scraped into a grey-whiteness;* all for the sake of secularising the church and turning it and the buildings of the convent into a Colonial Museum. I think it is nc possible to say that it has been improved upon in the process.

The façade and tower of Tepotzotlan, and the really wonderful altars or *retablos* we are about to see, all date from the decades between 1730 and 1760, only a few years before the Jesuits were expelled. The façade is in three storeys; and the first cornice, as I wrote of it many years ago, has a level flat line like a breathing-space below the greater elaboration of its upper storeys. It is a mass of statues and *estípites* or inverted obelisks, with garlands, medallions and heads of flowers. The tower – there is only a single tower at Tepotzotlan – is in two storeys with double pilasters at each corner. It is not as fantastic in design as the towers of Taxco; though the façade here by an unknown architect is, I think, even more successful and fanciful in design than that of San Sebastián y Santa Prisca, yet I am unable to believe or accept that the colour of the stone is the same as it was when I first saw it. It seems very different and much less beautiful.

But the interior of Tepotzotlan, though secularised and for that reason dead and not alive, is dazzling beyond anything that can be imagined for it has five of the huge golden altars, 'like knights and castles ready to move', as I wrote of them all these years ago, and they do indeed seem to stand tottering under their load of gold dust, ready like the dancing towers of Nola to move if only the better to show off their glittering coats-of-mail. To the amateur of the Spanish *retablo*, those for instance before the high altars of Toledo and Seville which are among the wonders of all Spain, the five *retablos* of Tepotzotlan will come as a revelation for there is no such array of them under one roof anywhere else, and also it is a tradition that had been dead for nearly two centuries in Spain, and it might have seemed impossible but for the Indian or *mestizo* craftsman that this tradition could have been carried on. They are towering, great golden structures that touch the ceiling and seem to have the attribute of movement like the dropping or showering from within

---

* Elsewhere, the stone is described as 'ivory-like in colour'; but no ivory is so dead, or has that limestone whiteness. The restaurant, newly opened in the cloisters of Tepotzotlan, is a place in which to take on trial the splendours and miseries of the Mexican cuisine. It is a temple of the national cooking, where red or green *moles* can be assayed and eaten.

a golden cavern. Nor is this all. To one side, there is the *camerino*, or chapel of Loreto, which if anything is still more extraordinary, though the figures of negroes holding baskets of flowers and fruits are rudimentary of execution, but the *camerino* has much red in it as well as gold, and its vaulted ceiling with winged angels lifting their hands to carry the beams of the ceiling are a beautiful and poetic invention, let us imagine, of the *mestizo* mind. The five golden altars of Tepotzotlan and the *camerino*, too, though less so, are of a golden intricacy only matched, where the carving is in pink sandstone, not in wood, thereafter gilded, by the carved ornaments and motifs of the outer chapels of Angkor.★ Which is the most glorious of the *retablos*? That of the high altar, the *retablo* of dedication to St Ignatius Loyola, or to the Virgin of Guadalupe? It is only possible to look at them in wonder, and walk away.

Having been familiar with photographs of the fourth of the transcendental Mexican churches for nearly half-a-century, I am not to be deterred from writing of it because I have not been there. It is the church of La Valenciana three miles outside the town of Guanajuato, where during the eighteenth century in this country where anything could happen, it was discovered that there was a vein of silver running under the village. This came to the surface in three mines, La Valenciana, La Cata, and Las Rayas which was the richest of them, and had in addition to its silver, a strata of amethysts in crystal form.† Soon there were seventy thousand persons living in Guanajuato; including three thousand Indian and *mestizo* peons who went down, on alternate days, fifteen hundred feet in the Valenciana mine. The famous German traveller and explorer, Humboldt, describes the palaces of the mine-owners and the mud-huts of the miners in Guanajuato. But besides the huts and palaces there were the churches; two of them in the town itself, La Compañía of the Jesuits and San Diego; the latter with a fine Churrigueresque doorway in the Spanish manner, all pedestals, medallions, and *estípites*, but of great height and marvellous technical virtuosity in carving.

The silver magnates built their churches outside the town. One of them, Vicente Manuel de Sardeneta y Legaspí, Marqués de San Juan de Rayas, even built his church at the mouth of the silver mine where it fell into decay with the working out of the silver, until a few years ago when, almost as improbably as its being built at all, it was transported stone by stone into the city and rebuilt half a block from the main street by the Rotary Club of Guanajuato. It is due to them that the façade of San Juan de Rayas rises again with its obelisks or *estípites*, and the flaunting of its *espedañas* or tail-feathers of stone upon the skyline. Another mining church in or outside the town, that of La Cata, third of the silver mines, would appear from photographs to have a carved stone doorway replete with minute figures crawling among the

★ Those of Banteai Srei, in particular.
† cf. Pál Kelemen, *op. cit.* p. 90, 91.

tropical flowers, the foliage, the obelisks, the fluttering cornices and, so on, of a Hindu or Dravidian intricacy worthy of the stone carvers of Halebid in Mysore.*

The church of La Valenciana stands, too, near to its silver mine among the rocks and slag-heaps of the old workings. The hill on which it stands, and the surrounding hills as well, are pitted with mine-shafts and ore-heaps. Its builder was the Conde de Valenciana, richest of the silver magnates; but, also, the miners themselves gave part of their daily wages – according to one account the value of a piece of ore called the *piedra de mano*, a stone the size of a man's hand, at the end of every week, and as well they worked on it during their holidays without pay. All of which need not be taken too literally; or that they were forced into it, for it was at once their recreation and their insurance policy, and there was little else for them to do. Now it is deserted and in the charge of one lonely, plain-clothes priest; unless La Valenciana, too, has been secularised and made over into a museum.

Perhaps the church gains a little like some broken statues from having only one completed tower. It allows at least a clearer view of the tiled dome. The façade is in two storeys with an *espedaña*, or cresting; the whole of a flat, almost Plateresque relief, only some few inches in depth, with a wooden doorway of unashamedly Mudéjar pattern. Its extreme picturesqueness is helped by its eminence upon the steps it stands on, also, by the windows in the base of the towers; that, at least upon the middle or second floors could be the window from a house or palace in Salamanca. The *espedaña*, above all this, is fluttering and dangling, and the whole is as much a monument to dead silver mines as, in due proportion, the cyclopaean walls of Cuzco to the gold of which they are the massive and silent ghosts. Inside La Valenciana, an interior which must be a little spoilt by its stamped and incised white stucco, there are three more of the splendid and towering golden altars. These again are like processional towers and look as though ready to sway forward and advance a few steps into the body of the church, a feeling heightened by the many statues looking and gesturing in our direction as though halted for the moment on a huge golden float, and by the garlands and flowers of the fiesta which are even painted in bunches on the panels of the back. The golden *retablos* of La Valenciana suggest the floats of a seraphic carnival and the processional cars, in a gilded and wooden rendering, of the temples of Southern India.

Very different in spirit is Querétaro, a town as full of churches as Puebla, but with more of the Andalucian and less of the *mestizo* in it. There are houses, we will call them colonial mansions not palaces, that would not look out of place in the whitewashed alleys of Córdoba or Seville. The house of the Marqués de la Villa de Villar del Águila is typical of these, with its patio and

* cf. *Arte Mexicana: Epoca Colonial*, by Pedro Rojas, Mexico City, 1963, p. 100.

cuspéd arches that are Moorish, or almost Moghul in pattern, and show the affinity of all things Moslem from Agra or Delhi all the way to Granada, but reached to Mexico without the filigree or stalactite. Very curious indeed is the cloister of the Augustine convent in Querétaro, odder still when we know its date, and that it was built by two Augustinian monks in the middle of the eighteenth century. It has even been suggested that the caryatids on the upper storey 'are making the signs of the deaf-mute alphabet with their uplifted hands'. More peculiar still, at the base of the dome there are angels with huge plumes which were perhaps intended for figures of Indian *caciques*, and there are more of these Indian dancers, if that was the intention, at the base of the unfinished tower.

But the interest of Querétaro is its pair of convents, Santa Clara and Santa Rosa de Viterbo, When I first wrote of these more than forty-five years ago it was the custom to attribute both convents to the neo-classical architect, Tresguerras, who in fact expressed disapproval of the side altars for 'their intemperate extravagance' and for the sculptor Roxas' carvings of a type of nymph (or angel?), 'always useless, idle'.[*] Besides which, Santa Rosa was completed in 1752 and Tresguerras was only born in 1745; so Tresguerras is no longer, as I thought all those years ago, the hero of Querétaro.

How could Santa Clara, even if it was the biggest conventual building in all Mexico, have sheltered as many as eight thousand nuns? Its church in any case is smaller than that of Santa Rosa. Many of the nuns, of whom only a small number can possibly have been of pure Spanish blood, worked in the convent sugar plantations and in the fields. The more skilful of them worked with their needles. No more than a few score of them can have found accommodation in the chapel. But there are wonderful things to see in Santa Clara, even if they seem less marvellous in the light of later knowledge of for instance the marvels of Bavarian Rococo. In particular, the nuns' tribune or grilled opera-box above the doorway leading to the sacristy and into the nunnery is a conception of deep romance and poetry. The grille is a close masterpiece of wrought iron work, and its supporting gold woodwork and the shell-like ornament over the grille but heighten the romantic, sacred harem feeling which is further enhanced by the wooden screen or grille above the nuns' choir, of interlacing pattern and genuine resemblance to the lattices, *moucharabiyes* and other devices by which the Muslim seek to keep their women inviolate and to themselves. The six golden *retablos*, not so towering in height as the floats or chariots of La Valenciana, clutter the nave of the chapel with their golden silhouettes and seem of themselves to illumine it with their brilliance and glitter.

The chapel of Santa Rosa de Viterbo at Querétaro, a scene over which I let my enthusiasm run wild when writing of it from hearsay in 1920–1, even in

[*] Pál Kelemen, *op. cit.*, pp. 95, 96.

more sober judgement is something exceptional, but then I had not seen convent-chapels such as that of Santa Clara in Oporto, or the Neapolitan San Gregorio Armeno. Or, I might add, the chapel of the Ursuline nuns at Straubing on the Danube, or the Convent of Jesus at Aveiro; all of which would suffice to alter their inter-importance in one's eyes. In respect of which, I now find Santa Rosa less Mexican, as I had thought it to be, and more like an exceptional, if not transcendental chapel of the nuns in Southern Italy or Spain. In places such as those mentioned one's eyes go at once to the nuns' choir; and at Santa Rosa this takes the form of a grille of chain-mail, as it looks to be, with cupids at the sides pulling back a stucco curtain which at a glance was never wide or long enough to draw across the opening. Just over this, the space below the *coro alto* or upper gallery is filled by a number of portraits of saints, all separately framed but coalescing together into a golden reredos, above which the screen in feminine complement has been given not only the centre piece and the handle but even the slats of a huge openwork fan. The French soldiery, great melters of golden religious objects under both Napoleons whether in Mexico or Spain, burned down the high altar of this chapel for the metal it contained, but leaving altars that could hardly be less splendid. Other beautiful features in Santa Rosa are the screened balconies of wrought-iron for the Mother Superior, and the confessionals. These latter are pulpit-fronted; the sides appear to be derived from some fantasy on the plaited palm-fronds of Palm Sunday; the canopy is in the form of a gilded shell, and the interior of this static or immobilised sedan-chair is painted with flowers in carefree, light-hearted mood. Very curious, too, is the painting of the *Hortus Conclusus* or Walled Garden on the wall of the sacristy. This is indeed most touchingly and appropriately beautiful of subject for its convent setting.

In the foreground, within the gateway of the garden, the Virgin is sitting with cupids hovering over her head and lambs playing at her feet. The lambs are receiving white roses from Her which they carry to the Crucified Christ in the foreground of the garden, to be turned red by the blood from His wounds. A winged angel holds up a vase of lilies and roses to receive the stream of water and of blood from His side, so that the water falls on the white lilies and the blood upon the roses. It is, therefore, in part the legend of Santa Rosa. As backcloth to all this is the far wall of the Hortus Conclusus with its recessed arches and urns on columns, its parterre, and some of the fruit trees of the walled garden. There are figures of one or two nuns carrying jars of water, or kneeling at a fountain. But in the foreground, where there are flowers growing and more fruit trees, we see the nuns of Santa Rosa and their pupils working in the garden, one of the latter with a parrot on her shoulder. In the right hand panel the nuns are looking away from us into the flowerbeds, but in the left half of the canvas two of them are facing us in their habits and coiffed headdresses, one of them resting a water-jar on the painted balustrade. Nothing could be more appropriate to a nunnery than the theme of a *Hortus Conclusus*, and even if it is not a great painting it is more acceptable than most of the Mexican school of painting and is indeed among the peculiar delights and pleasures of monastic art.

Such are the principal buildings of *le style mexicain* throughout the land, though there must be hundreds of those background pieces that give beauty and interest to any film or photograph, as for example the scenery for 'Westerns' when filmed in the states of Chihuahua or Sonora. There is romance and the call of the unexpected over the border. The late R. B. Cunninghame Grahame has told me more than once of how as a young man he would swim his horse across the Rio Grande just in order to sleep in Mexico. In that northern region contiguous to the United States there are no more than Misiones and village churches for six hundred miles until you get to Zacatecas which is the real beginning. Here, the church of Guadalupe with its semi-barbaric façade looks from photographs almost incredible as work of the two first decades of the eighteenth century. Already, at San Luis Potosí a hundred and fifty miles to the south, the tone has altered and there are golden *retablos* in the Cathedral. From photographs, again, the twin side portals of the nunnery of Las Rosas in Morelia, and the recessed portal of La Salud in San Miguel de Allende are, alike, improbable and 'retarded' cases of architectural development.★

But another provincial city, Salamanca in the State of Guanajuato, has only had justice done to its buildings by one writer. Here, San Agustín, the church of the Augustinian Fathers, of unpromising exterior, has four golden *retablos* of unprecedented splendour, the peers, it would seem of those of La Valenciana but different in style, and according to documents not long discovered, the work of the sculptor Pedro de Roxas, of whose altars the neo-classical architect Tresguerras was disapproving in the convents of Querétaro. The high altar was long ago destroyed; but one pair of the four side altars is distinguished by having five sculptured groups, the two lower and the central scenes surmounted in both *retablos* by huge golden crowns. That in the centre above a fringed curtain about to drop upon the minutely painted and carved group below, set as though into a little room or canopied balcony, having huge open lobes to its crown, above which a winged archangel is poised in the light that pours in through a window. The golden *retablos* of Salamanca must be among the finest works of art of Spanish derivation in all Mexico.

★ Compare the recessed portal under a hooded shell at the church of San Juan de Dios in Mexico City. The provincial example is some half-century later in date than that in the capital. For these, as for Salamanca, cf. Pál Kelemen, *op cit.*, pp. 94–6. A colour plate of one of the golden altars of San Agustín is in Pedro Rojas, *op. cit.*, pl. xxii.

And these notes can end at Oaxaca, the most southerly town of any importance in Mexico, where the overcrowded, barrel-arched ceiling of Santo Domingo, festooned with bunches of grapes in stucco and far too loaded with busts and figures, pales in interest beside the church of La Soledad, up steep flights of steps and splendid of façade, in three storeys, many-statued, but advancing or coming forward like a house of cards. But indeed the greater interest of Oaxaca is its climate; the nearness of Monte Alban of the tombs, and golden ornaments found in them – even the *sarapes* of the Zapotec Indians, dyed scarlet, as to the original specimens, from cochineal insects that live in the cactus plants. Oaxaca, such things considered, is well and truly in the semi-tropics.

Having written at some length in these pages of the Churrigueresque for which I prefer the term *le style mexicain* and, later, of the Baroque and Rococo in Brazil, this is the moment in which to state what there is pertaining to our subject in the rest of Latin America. All in all it is the result of five journeys; to Brazil; to Peru and Bolivia and Ecuador; and to Guatemala, Mexico and Yucatán. But of these different countries there is none to compare with Mexico where architecture is concerned, nor in point of the attendant arts. There, not one but half-a-dozen local styles were evolved, some two or three of which qualify for the term invented for them. The others are the early 'Franciscan' Spanish of the missionaries, coming soon after the Conquest, or the Spanish – pure, but not so simple – of contagion, we may imagine, from the climate and from the earliest drops of Indian blood prevailing.

Peru could not be more different from Mexico where building is concerned. Cuzco is like a Spanish provincial town in a Tibetan setting. A cathedral and a church of the Jesuits such as one might find in Cáceres or Badajoz; not the slightest touch of Churriguera. Not even in the glass altars of the *mestizo* nunnery of Santa Clara! But what an extraordinary race were the Spaniards in their great century! Ayacucho, a Peruvian provincial town with twenty churches; Trujillo, another town with sixteenth- and seventeenth-century churches; and Cajamarca, yet another! All three of them hardly more than names. In these, and others, the buildings are in retarded Spanish Renaissance with, of course, local features, to culminate in the Andean *mestizo* buildings of the Altiplano, particularly round Lake Titicaca, a style in which the Indian, the Quechuan or Aymaran blood by now predominates.* Perhaps only persons of origin from the inhospitality of Central Spain, from the very Cáceres and Trujillo of the Conquistadores, both in Estremadura, could have made a new life for themselves in a land such as

---

* This architecture is ably dealt with by Harold E. Wethey in *Colonial Architecture and Sculpture in Peru*, Cambridge, Massachusetts, 1949; besides which, it is amply illustrated and written of by Pál Kelemen, *op. cit.*

Bolivia, and in such a place as Potosí of the silver mines, nearly fourteen thousand feet high, and some fifteen hundred miles inland either way from Lima or Buenos Aires, but under their aegis to increase early in the seventeenth century to a population, mostly slaves of course, working in the silver mines, more numerous, it is said, than that of contemporary London or Paris. The better to understand Cuzco or Puno (on Lake Titicaca) you have to have seen the aforesaid Cáceres and Trujillo.

Quito in my view is more interesting and agreeable than Cuzco. And Quito, alone of South American cities with the exception of Ouro Preto if, that is to say, we exclude the mere gilded woodcarving, the *capelas todos de ouro* of other Brazilian churches, has some of the luxuries, as apart from the necessities of architecture. I shall never forget the Otavalo Indian we used to see every Saturday morning – only on Saturdays, what was he doing the rest of the week? – selling scarves and woven stuffs like his kinsmen of Quito and Guayaquil, along the cement crescent of Copacabana, to be known at once by his aquiline features and red skin, his pigtail, white hat and poncho and white pantaloons. He was as a wanderer from another world in Rio de Janeiro; in reminder that there was more of interest and an ancient and indigenous civilisation on the other coast of South America, in Ecuador. Among the luxuries of Quito was its school of sculptors;★ but their statues and figurines apart there was something peculiar to Quito, or, at least, better seen there than anywhere else. This is the *mampara*, a carved and gilded screen erected under the choir loft, just inside the door. There are two superb *mamparas* in Quito; one of them in the Sagrario or parish church attached to the Cathedral, and the other in the Jesuit church of La Compañía. The first is in red and gold with carved columns like the stem of a candelabra, but these have pierced or openwork pilasters to each side which are carved so as to be seen with the light coming through them; and the volutes of these pilasters have cupids hiding among the golden leaves. This is a feature I have not seen elsewhere. The other *mampara*, in La Compañía, has its columns festooned with bunches of grapes, and is in gold on a white lacquer ground. It is the Quiteño churches that according to legend have scarlet lacquered interiors. La Compañía, which has the finest classical façade in all Latin America, designed by a German Jesuit in 1722 in full-blown Baroque, does give the sensation that its walls and ceiling are in red lacquer, but this is only that a pattern is cut into the stone of the piers, and incised or stencilled on the stucco in gold upon a scarlet ground. And the little chapel of the Rosário, built on an archway or bridge over the street, or it is in fact the *camarín* of the church of Santo Domingo where the clothes and jewels of the Virgen del

★ Pál Kelemen, *op. cit.*, devotes a whole chapter to the sculptors of Quito. Several of them, as we would expect, were of *mestizo* or Indian blood; but it could be said of them in general that the smaller. their sculptures were, the better.

Rosário are kept, to be approached theatrically up a hidden staircase, makes use of every known device to add the last touch of theatrical brilliance to itself, including panes of mirror and touches of scarlet or carmine in its gilding. Of such are the scarlet lacquered church interiors of Quito, but it has one or two other buildings besides La Compañía that are worthy of an Italian, even almost of a Roman setting.

For the rest, it is an affair of fine and noble sacristy rooms; at San Agustín in Lima and La Merced in the same city, in better taste it could be added than the club-room sacristies of Brazil, of São Bento in Rio or the church of the Carmo in Bahia. Or there are splendid organ-lofts like the golden casket or bird's nest of La Merced in Quito which true to the lacquer tradition is on a dark red ground. By the same token there are beautifully carved pulpits or confessionals, that of San Carlos in Lima for example with *bombé* front and canopy in Rococo manner, but in execution as perfect as English mahogany carving of the school of Chippendale. Other, and remoter examples on the Pacific side of South America are almost sure to be the work of Indian or *mestizo* craftsmen. And in Brazil there are the vestment presses, and for secular use the chairs and tables and cupboards of jacaranda wood in its three tones or colours from Bahia which are almost certainly the handiwork of negro carpenters and joiners. The best of these are unsurpassed in workmanship. But any, or all of them are outdone by what can be seen in Mexico. That handful of names, the churches of Taxco, Ocotlán, Tepotzotlan, La Valenciana, almost certainly San Agustín at Salamanca, with their Indian tones or undertones emerging through the Iberian idiom, are in appendix to what is best of their date in Europe, which is to say in Italy, Bavaria, or Spain.

8

'Je suis Brésilien, j'ai de l'or'

MEILHAC AND HALÉVY, *La Vie Parisienne*

A steamy, detestable morning of immense length building up to a cross luncheon and a wasted afternoon, not able either to read or sleep on deck owing to the foggy, hot dampness that dwindled slowly to a taut and feverish night of endless tossing and turning, trying to avoid the draught from the electric fan. The day in fact when we crossed the Equator sailing on a French vessel to Brazil; and the next day, or it may have been the morning after that, we had a forecast of its landscape when we passed the long horseshoe-shaped island of Fernando de Noronha, our first landfall and to be remembered therefore, but chiefly for pitying the United States' scientists stranded for atomic reasons on its antipodean rocks. Our ship left a long curving wake behind it as if to afford a full view and foretaste of where we were going. And for some twenty minutes Fernando de Noronha unrolled itself in all its bareness with its awkward hills, and then passed slowly out of sight. Some two days after that we arrived in Rio on a wet and pouring day, and drove through tunnel-like, straight streets of shops and offices under tall palm trees, through a real tunnel loud with motor-horns and out onto the huge cement crescent of hotels and apartment houses that is Copacabana.

We had arrived, and there is reason to remember we had crossed the Equator in order to do so. There are great cities like Rio de Janeiro and Buenos Aires, and Johannesburg and Melbourne and Sydney, that lie south of the Equator but none of them are famous for their buildings or their works of art. Perhaps they have not had time. And it is to be noted that, alike, the ruins of Angkor and those of the ancient Mayan cities lie north of the Equator. Only the temple-mound of Borobodur in Java, the island of Bali, and the ancient cultures of Peru are south of that line. The land masses are not so huge, it is true; nor the aboriginal inhabitants so susceptible or creative in the arts. The most interesting by far of the cultures mentioned being the last named; or, indeed they were a series or layer of cultures with for aesthetic climax the woven and embroidered ponchos of Paracas, a desert peninsula in the south of Peru, mantles of spun cotton or of vicuña hair found wrapped round the mummies, exceedingly curious in pattern and technically among the finest and most elaborate textiles ever made.★ That was south of the Equator true enough but on the Pacific coast of South America. We are at the moment on the other or Atlantic coast where there was little or nothing before the white man came.

Certainly there is little indeed along the concrete crescent of Copacabana, half-a-mile long at least, with thousands of bodies bathing daily from the sands but a few yards across the road, and more than that number still on Sundays, though the sands at night are quite deserted but for a fire or two flickering from an earthen pot far out, which we are told is for some Voodoo incantation or act of vengeance. The scene when you get away from Copacabana is beautiful with its broad new boulevards, avenues of palms, and areas of land reclaimed from the sea, being transformed, some of them, into tropical landscape gardens from the expert hand of Burle Marx. It is from here that there are wonderful and astonishing views of the bay and of the mountains; Sugar Loaf Mountain and Corcovado which has the Christ on top, hills of strange and barbaric shape belonging to the new world and of which there was the foretaste at Fernando de Noronha; and then, but turning round, the terrible shelved terraces of the *favelas* or negro slums of Rio which seem always about to slide down into the city, which they some-times do in cascades of mud and rocks and taking bodies with them.

About halfway between the tunnel leading out of Copacabana and the old part of Rio, on a little hill with a staircase leading up to it, is the little tiled church of Nossa Senhora da Glória do Outeiro, of elegant and elongated oval interior,† with pretty blue and white *azulejos* of obvious import from Portugal the mother country, but quite truthfully of no more importance architecturally than fifty or a hundred churches in villages or small towns in Portugal. It is pretty, and prettily sited, but little more than that. Nor is the far bigger church of São Bento, down in the old town, proportionately, of much deeper interest. It is one of the golden caverns of Portugal, of authentic Brazilian gold as to its contorted woodwork; but the carvings are by heavier hands and altogether lacking in the fantastic grace and elegance of the gilded caverns or grottos as they are to be seen at their best in São Francisco or at the convent of Santa Clara at Oporto, which are among the wonders of Rococo anywhere in Europe. Perhaps the answer is that São Bento more

★ For the textiles of Paracas and those of Tiahuanaco, which is in Bolivia, cf. my *Golden Wall and Mirador*, London, 1961, pp. 41, 42 and 43, 44.

† A hexagonal nave with curving corridors or open ambulatories round it, rather as in the plan of Wies or other of Dominikus Zimmermann's churches in Bavaria. But white rough-cast walls, stone pilasters and string courses, and a pinnacled skyline make it very typical of Northern Portugal.

resembles the Lisbon churches than those of Northern Portugal, a theory which is borne out in the Madre de Deus and the Paulistas, about the only churches in Lisbon that survived the earthquake of 1755. There, again, the style and handling are dull and heavy compared to what is to be found around Braga and Oporto; and retarded, too, when we read that the interior of São Bento was 'ready for gilding' as late as 1734.★

Other churches in Rio, those of Sant' António and the Penitencia are no better and have little beyond rich gilding to offer to their Cariocan congregations, and after one or two excursions to the old town, expensive, too, because of the distance involved, we came to confine ourselves to the reinforced concrete of Copacabana. On several mornings during that fortnight in February there were fogs more easily associated with evenings in Westminster or Pimlico, and it was strange to look down from the cement balcony past the pair of dachshunds lying out on the balcony beneath, giving a feeling of vertigo whenever we saw them for this was on about the fifteenth floor, and find one could hardly see down as far as the serpentine black and white mosaic pavement which is indeed the flag of Copacabana's fame.

But neither is this the place in which to sample the orchids or humming-birds of Brazil. There are pieces of virgin forest it is true only a few minutes above the town; and on the way up to one of the beautiful villas on the hills outside Rio we saw fluttering in front of us a blue Morpho butterfly, iridescent as the headlamp of a motorcar and about the size of a folded evening newspaper. Perhaps the only compensating feature of the sands of Copacabana were the children's kites, sold neatly folded, but opening into an eagle's head and pair of wings in varied colourings. Fog or sunshine, alike, there was ever a squadron of the bird-kites at balcony-height upon the wing. Talk, too, of humming-birds to be seen in the streets and gardens of Petropolis, the summer capital of Dom Pedro, but they were not visible. And rumour of still more humming-birds at Therezopolis; named after the Empress, and yet higher in the mountains, but we did not on this occasion go so far afield.

We had come to Brazil in order to visit the Minas Gerais and see the famed churches of Ouro Preto; and the best way of reaching them is to fly to Belo Horizonte and go from there by road. Belo Horizonte, which one may scarcely have heard of before, being somewhat of a surprise in itself for it has a population of half-a-million, good shops, a skyscraper hotel, and a colony of Japanese who work the market gardens. We eat our luncheon at that very typically Brazilian invention, a *churrasqueria*, where the grilled meats with pepper and hot sauces are indication not of indigenous origin but that the dishes are of derivation from Portugal with its non-tropical, more northern

★ *The Age of Grandeur*, by Victor L. Tapíe, London, 1960, pp. 245, 246.

climate. The *churrasqueria* is a huge hall which could be easily adapted for theatricals or religious meetings. Nothing in Belo Horizonte holds any hint of where we are going. One has only the sensation of being far inland in a country so huge that in effect on looking at a map one has hardly covered any distance in it at all. There is a school, imitating in shape a pen, an inkpot and a blotting-pad, by Oscar Niemeyer, and one or two other modern buildings in Belo Horizonte; and there is the touch of the Wild West about it, but with Brazilian accent.

Some way out of the city we pass a country club by a good modern architect, built somewhat in the shape of an eagle's wings hovering over some chasm in the mountains, and it is indeed on the very edge of an astounding view stretching away for miles over it would seem almost uninhabited country. We come down in the heat through red, rocky hills as though, which is the truth, we are in ironstone country, halting for a moment or two at a spring of nearly Castalian purity and coolness; and after driving for another hour or two the first sign of anything different comes at the small town of Sabará. Here we are taken to see the little church of Nossa Senhora de O, standing in a square where a few mangy dogs are the only living creatures to be seen. There was an interval during which it looked as though we would never get inside this little church we had come such a long way to see. But now people began to appear. Everyone here was a mulatto, and we had arrived among the former gold mines of Minas Gerais. Of which Nossa Senhora de O was both a symptom and a premonition.

It is tiny in size, not much bigger in area than a side chapel in most other churches, overlaid of course with the local gold, of a carat that seemed almost to flash at one out of the darkness, but with something strange in the detail of the carving and painting which is that in this town, miles away from anywhere – always, unless you come from it yourself – the ornament is 'Chinese', or 'Indian', if we prefer that, for this is only to the extent that European-made lacquer is 'Chinese'. Not that it is particularly good lacquer, or of a notably high degree of craftsmanship, but it is in fact, and not vaguely, chinoiserie, and of early appearance even if most things you see here are a generation later than they would be in Europe. The little decorative motifs in a lacquer technique in Nossa Senhora de O are therefore to be compared to early attempts at lacquer chinoiserie in old houses in England such as Bolsover Castle, where they may date from as early as the reign of James I, even if here in remote Minas Gerais they may be as much as four human generations later in time. The lacquered panels of this little interior are in red and gold with painted motifs in a darker blue and gold. 'Lacquered' interiors such as that to the Jesuit church of La Compañía in Quito, many hundreds of miles away from here in Ecuador, where there are scarlet lacquered walls and ceiling, are at least nearer geographically to China; though again in this last instance it is not really lacquer at all but only a pattern stamped or incised into the plaster, and then painted and varnished scarlet. The name of Macao, the ancient colony of Portugal in China, is of course always brought up in connection with Nossa Senhora de O, but it may be thought doubtful indeed that there was any association however remote between them. Nossa Senhora de O is a little curiosity of uncertain provenance and little more than ephemeral interest. But is it really, as the leading authority upon the old churches of Brazil would have it, 'un joyau de l'art baroque . . . tout entier de l'époque D. João I'; which would compare it to the three great lacquered halls, a light green, then a darker, and then a shade like that of orange Niger leather, of the library at Coimbra?

Sabará may be the first introduction to another phenomenon, the achievement and renown of the sculptor and architect António Francisco Lisboa (1738–1814), 'O Aleijadinho'. He was the illegitimate son of a Portuguese father and an African mother, a mulatto, therefore; and the legend is that he contracted leprosy at about the age of forty, lost eventually the fingers of both hands, and had in the end to work at his carvings with his chisel bound to the stumps of both hands. Fired with the pathos of this legend there was a tendecy to attribute carvings and churches alike to 'O Aleijadinho', who was promoted to universal genius of the Minas Gerais. Many of the records and original documents have been destroyed which was nothing unusual among a population the majority of whom could not read or write, and it is now difficult to establish the truth about what is, or is not from his hand. Above all it is not clear, or indeed established with any degree of certainty, whether he was in fact architect as well as sculptor.

But at Sabará there is the undoubted hand of 'O Aleijadinho' in the church of Carmo where the carved doorway of typical *pedra-sabão* (soapstone), the stemma or coat-of-arms above that, and the pulpit are indubitably by him; and perhaps this is the place before we see more of 'O Aleijadinho' to keep our heads and not give in to the indiscriminate praise now lavished on him in compensation for his sufferings. These carvings by him at Sabará are in fact extremely pretty, though not by far his best work, which is to be seen in two churches in particular, of confusing name for both are dedicated to St Francis of Assisi; respectively, at Ouro Preto and at São João d'El Rei.

But that is for the next day or two. For the moment all attention is taken up by the enormous eight or ten-wheeled lorries upon the road, carrying iron ore from the mines of Minas Gerais, taking up all the road and going at terrifying speed round the corners. Indeed, departure from this district of Minas Gerais on an overlong drive to get back to Belo Horizonte long after dark was made really frightening by these 'goods train' lorries which kept in front unyieldingly for long miles together, or provided thrilling dual-track racing, side by side, for agonising moments to our one-eyed driver. Luckily

Opposite: Church of São Francisco de Assis at Ouro Preto.

on this day of arrival in Minas Gerais it was not dark yet, and by way of distraction if brave enough one could look off the road down into the ravines which had generally banana-palms, papaya, or other sub-tropical fruit trees growing in their depths. And now we were nearing Ouro Preto, and in some natural degree of expectancy as to what we were to see. For this is perhaps the most remote part of the world to which our school of architecture and the applied arts was to penetrate. Such Latin-American cities as Cuzco or Potosí may look more remote on the map, but Cuzco had been capital of the Inca Empire and had been for centuries a centre of large population, its altitude notwithstanding; while Potosí early in the seventeenth century had a hundred and sixty thousand people living in it, a larger number of inhabitants than contemporary London or Paris, however long and arduous the trans-Andean journey may have been. Goa and Macao, two other seemingly distant places, were in direct communication by sea with Portugal their mother country, being indeed like Tangier, Bombay, Ormuz, typical Portuguese forts and trading-posts, for the Portuguese unlike the Spanish Conquistadores kept to the coast and did not march inland. Ouro Preto and the subsidiary towns or villages are in fact the one exception to this rule. There is no Cuzco or Quito, no Mexico City or Antigua in the Portuguese Empire which was maritime more than military. But the reason for it, as always in Latin America whether Spanish or Portuguese, was mineral. The life and death of Cuzco was its gold. Potosí was the silver mine of the world. But the reason and excuse for Ouro Preto was the discovery of gold. Ouro Preto was in its day the Klondyke, the Johannesburg, the Ballarat, the gold rush of Brazil.

The gold was first discovered there in 1698, and soon royal decrees were issued from Lisbon declaring the whole district a closed area and forbidding in particular the religious orders to set foot within it, the reasons for which are mysterious for the Kings of Portugal were nothing less than lavish in their patronage of the monks and nuns. Was it the secular clergy in Brazil itself who were jealous; or did such a paragon of extravagance as João v of Portugal wish to keep some of the flow of gold and diamonds for himself and have more to spend at home? Whatever the cause, a curtain of secrecy descended upon the Minas Gerais,* behind which the lay-confraternities of the Franciscans and Carmelites, of São José and of the Rosário, whites, blacks and mulattos alike, sought to outdo each other in religious processions, in carnival events, and on the exterior and interior of their churches. That this was the only form of popular entertainment open to them does nothing to lessen the contrast between their activities and those of other mining centres mainly of Anglo-Saxon derivation which leave nothing behind them more solid than

* No strangers were permitted in the Minas Gerais; agriculture and industry were forbidden; and schools were not allowed. Only gold mining was encouraged until the gold ran out.

Opposite: Carlos III of Spain at Dinner (detail),
a fantasy by Luis Paret y Alcázar (1746–99).

some streets of wooden shacks, a 'hotel', and the wreck of its saloon bar, or, in fact, the ghostly setting for a 'Western'.

Instead, and now on the outskirts of Ouro Preto, called before and for good reason Vila Rica, we are nearing one of the more extraordinary epidemic centres of community architecture, of that sort which presupposes a certain remoteness from the larger centres of human life. Such was the case in England with the mediaeval churches in Norfolk and Suffolk and the fen country, and with the 'wool churches' of the Cotswolds; and elsewhere, the Rococo of Bavaria, of the churches and palaces in towns in Apulia, and in the Modica-Ragusa and the Noto areas of Sicily. Another such Arcadia which has come down to living times with music added must be the isle of Bali. But of them all Ouro Preto must be the most remote and distant, and the more exciting therefore after thirty years and more of expectation to be arriving in it.

The first impression of Ouro Preto is a little disappointing because of the difficulty of the terrain; also, perhaps, because one had anticipated a more tropical background. Instead, it is built on a steep declivity with ten or a dozen churches all looking alike, with a frontispiece between twin towers standing on spurs of the hillside at different elevations, the finest of them in fact being below and out of sight from the old house or *pousada* where we were staying. Another of the churches stood on a terrace above our heads only a few feet away. And round the corner of this road straight in front of us, and then up or down the steepest of hills, night and day came lorry after lorry every few minutes, carrying iron ore, noisy in proportion to the load they carried with them. This particular corner of the town was no place for quiet contemplation of the façade just a few feet above us, even if one climbed up onto the terrace. And indeed the church was locked most of the time we were in Ouro Preto. We only once got inside it.

But there are at least ten other churches in Ouro Preto, though probably the first place one is taken to see will be the Museu da Inconfidencia, in a large old building in the chief square. This is interesting because of the evidence it affords of the civilised life led in this far away town, old dresses, fine furniture of jacaranda wood, musical instruments,★ and so on. There are, also, sculptures by 'Aleijadinho' though these do not show the sculptor at his best for the forte of 'Aleijadinho' was on the external cresting or coat-of-arms on the front of the church, or with the altar structure or holy water stoup inside. He was not, at least in the writer's opinion, a good woodcarver in the round.

It is perhaps natural enough that one of the first impressions to strike the

---

★ Records have recently been issued of eighteenth-century music from the Minas Gerais, 'mainly sacred works written by mulattos and negroes for use in local churches'. The music was found in the cellar of an old house in Ouro Preto. As to the rest of the contents of the museum, none of the horror always attaching to articulated statues is spared us in the armoured statue of St George by 'O Aleijadinho', a nearly lifesize figure resembling a puppet from the Sicilian marionette theatre.

visitor to Ouro Preto, more particularly one who has already seen Mexico and Peru, Bolivia and Ecuador, is its Portuguese or Lusitanian character without any of that admixture of the Indian, the place of which in Minas Gerais is taken by the hint or shade of the mulatto. So many of the craftsmen employed on the churches, the 'Aleijadinho' among them, were of this origin. And the next impression on approaching nearer to the churches is how different they are from the heavy Baroque of Rio or of Bahia; of São Bento in the first named, or São Francisco in the latter. Instead, they seem to have been planned and built under an influence from the North of Portugal, having much of the grace and elegance of that Arcadian Rococo. But in fact it is a characteristic of all such Arcadias, wherever situated, whether in a hundred villages and small towns in East Anglia or the Cotswolds; in the sub-Alpine meadows and fir-woods of the Pfaffenwinkel; or in the orange-groves of Noto; that the fire of enthusiasm has lifted them out of their remoteness into the forefront of their age, even if on occasion there is some-what of a timelag and they must be judged against the whole of the age they ornament and not the first and earliest of its pioneers.

This is decidedly true of Ouro Preto where, as we shall find, some of the work is so retarded in time that it dates from after the turn of the century and into the eighteen-hundreds. Meanwhile, on our way to the churches, as well as the veranda'd houses there is occasion to notice the wall-fountains which are a special feature of Ouro Preto, the Portuguese *chafariz* being a beautiful word for them, all more or less of the same design, with large scrolled volutes like the back of a chair, generally with a shell motif within that, and the water trough or drinking bowl below. The first church one is likely to be taken to is the best, which is that of São Francisco de Assis. It could be called indeed the pattern church, alike, of Ouro Preto and of 'O Aleijadinho', standing, as has been said, some little way downhill and offering at first sight the most characteristic possible of 'Aleijadinho's' carved soapstone doorways.

The exuberance begins above the door proper with the pair of cupids perched upon the broken cornices, and continues above that with an elaborately garlanded medallion of the Virgin, and over that again rather in the manner of a locket with a necklace hanging from it, resting on the cornice, a still larger circular medallion of St Francis on his knees receiving the stigmata. This doorway is the 'Aleijadinho' style in its excelsis; and his hand is to be seen again in the triple-bason'd lavabo in the sacristy, a fine large sculptured composition with a standing figure of St Francis with cupids at his feet above it, though doubt has been expressed as to whether 'Aleijadinho' actually designed it, or took more than a share in certain details of the carving. But, then, the same doubts have found expression as to how much he was responsible for the plan of the building, or whether indeed he was an architect at all. But M. Germain Bazin with all the authority at his command maintains his argument and gives 'O Aleijadinho' all credit for the plans of São Francisco, with which from first to last he was involved from 1766 until 1792. It is even thought that the painted ceiling over the nave by Manoel da Costa Ataíde (1762–1837) which all would agree is to date the *chef d'oeuvre* of Brazilian painting, painted as astonishingly late in date as 1810 while 'O Aleijadinho' was still living, may have been submitted to him in detail for his approval. It is known that this lighthearted and beautiful decorative painting of the Virgin in glory with angel musicians had been scrutinised and passed under the microscope, as it were, by the ecclesiastical authorities, a test from which it emerged with amazing buoyancy and freedom.

We must have gone inside nearly all of the eleven churches of Ouro Preto, and after São Francisco the finest of them is the Carmo with again a pretty door by the master's hand, and prettily shaped Rococo window above it; though the dull looking towers are unworthy of him, and neither is the lavabo in the sacristy by 'Aleijadinho'.* That, unlike some of the Bavarian masters, he could make beautiful and detailed drawings is proved in designs preserved by him in the Museu da Inconfidencia at Ouro Preto, and in view of these it seems impossible to disown him as architect, though the generality of his talent is surely exaggerated by M. Bazin who, speaking of São Francisco, says of him: 'Even in Italy, where so many artists were simultaneously architects, painters and sculptors, there is not one monument like this, which expresses every aspect of a man of genius.' This is almost to attribute the painted ceiling by Manoel da Costa Ataíde by default to 'O Aleijadinho'; and the argument in favour of his universal genius wears thin again when perhaps the prettiest single object in Ouro Preto, the winged statue of the Archangel Michael in delayed Louis Quatorze masquerade dress with three plumes like an Indian *cacique* in his hair, standing in a beautifully contrived niche over a doorway with half-shell canopy for roof in what M. Bazin calls full Joannine or João v of Portugal style outside another church, that of São Miguel or Bom Jesus de Matozinhos, is called by him a hybrid work and removed therefore in large measure from his hand.

And this is perhaps all it is necessary to say about Ouro Preto.

On another day we went with the charming and intelligent director of the museum through not particularly interesting country to see the churches at Mariana, another mining town not many miles away. Two churches here, both of them in the main square, are of some little interest because of the touches of chinoiserie in their woodwork and painted decoration; but in the main the importance of Mariana is in proving the eminence of 'O Aleijadinho'

---

* The Carmo is the church standing on a terrace just above the house where we were staying. The church of the Rosário built by the lay brotherhood of that name to which only negroes were admitted, with its *bombé* front and double oval plan with curvilinear walls, is the most beautiful building in Ouro Preto after São Francisco and the Carmo.

in his absence, and perhaps one would never have felt so certain of that without this negative experience of visiting churches where only his shadow and not his handiwork is seen.

Early the next morning we left Ouro Preto for a long day of sightseeing which was only to end late at night, racing the sixteen-wheel iron-ore lorries on the road to Belo Horizonte. The first objective was 'O Aleijadinho's' twin masterwork to São Francisco at Ouro Preto – if that is not too high a term for both or either of them – his doorway and frontispiece to São Francisco de Assis at another town of the difficult name, São João d'El Rei. Certainly it is a finely carved and worked ornamental doorway of green soapstone, of a type to be admired, with less fuss made about it, in Northern Portugal.* The blazon over the doorway of the arms of Portugal and of the Franciscan Order is necessarily more laborious of execution but it compares with the armorial paintings upon Meissen porcelain; and is it better than those just because it is bigger and in more intractable material? This doorway and its carvings which are thought to be largely from the sculptor's own hand are considered nevertheless to show deviations, as though ordered to make alterations from his own designs. It should be added that this church at São João d'El Rei stands impressively on a platform down a tall avenue of palms, and that the interest of its interior is heightened by a pair of ghostly altars, painted white, in sign that they are late in date, after 1820, and that the gold dust of Brazil was running out.

The problem some hour or two later was Congonhas do Campo, of which if for euphony only it is irresistible to add that it is the sanctuary of Bom Jesus de Matozinhos. And not only is it a sanctuary, but in a sense a *Sacro Monte* and a sacred garden in its own particular sense, if without flowers or flowerbeds, and the acclaimed masterpiece and *chef d'oeuvre* of 'O Aleijadinho'. It is of course on the pattern of the terraced staircase with chapels on its landings of Bom Jesus at Braga in the mother country, and of the yet more beautiful 'sacred garden' with its obelisks and columns outside Lamego. But the situation is that quite simply 'O Aleijadinho' was by now too ill and crippled to do justice to himself. Whereas the doorways of the two churches of St Francis at Ouro Preto and at São João d'El Rei are of almost exactly the same years 1774–6, his statues at Congonhas do Campo date from the last ten years of his life in the seventeen-nineties and the early eighteen-hundreds. It was in 1772 that he was first attacked by his mysterious illness. 'O Aleijadinho' died in 1814, and already by 1831 a German traveller was writing that the statues at Congonhas were carved by a man who had lost his hands. Even before that an Englishman was stating the same thing;

---

* cf. the façades of the Malheiros Reimões chapel at Viana do Castelo, which is one of the architectural delights of Portugal, a doorway with a 'Chippendale' window over it standing like an arrowhead at the apex of two streets to face its public.

and it was the same story that Sir Richard Burton told in 1868. 'O Aleijadinho' was then thirty-nine years old at the time that his illness began,★ and in that very year there is the record of a payment made to two negroes who carried him at Ouro Preto in a litter. According to his biographer Brêtas writing in the eighteen-sixties who knew his still living wife, he lost all except the thumb and forefinger of each hand. Mention is made, too, of his African slave Mauricio who fastened the chisel to the stump of his hand, and on occasion carried him upon his back. The poor sculptor had to crawl along upon his knees; he lost all his teeth, his chin and lower jaw became distorted giving him a horrifying expression which frightened all who saw him, he became bitter, and morose, and wore clothes which concealed his deformity and hid his face. For the last four years of his life he became too infirm to work; and given the extraordinary details of his career it is no wonder that legends grew up about him after his death.

The church at Congonhas do Campo is approached by a double stair and terrace on which are grouped over lifesize stone statues of the twelve apostles, making a gaunt, bare effect which indeed gives an impression of physical suffering and pain. Below this are the six chapels of the Via Crucis containing the *passos* or groups of wooden statues by 'Aleijadinho' and his pupils or workmen, sixty-six figures in all, of varying merit, some of the wooden polychrome statues being preferable to the stone figures of Apostles on the terrace. But I found it difficult, myself, to admire them whether in wood or stone. In fact I found Congonhas do Campo painful, even agonising in the extreme, and my thoughts went back to the wretched mulatto sculptor in his happier days before his dreadful infirmity had begun when he was master of the light and graceful Rococo doorways of the Carmo at Sabará, and of the churches of São Francisco at Ouro Preto and at São João d'El Rei. Those, I think, were where his real talent lay; augmented, if such is the case and his existing ornamental drawings showed him capable of it, by his talents as architect of two or three churches which in the mother country of Portugal are a beautiful if forgotten commonplace.

But the sad aura attaching to Congonhas do Campo had as relief and recompense the true gem or delight of the Minas Gerais which is the Church at Tiradentes of the unromantic name.† This, too, has the distinction where

★ 'On hésite entre le mal de Hansen ou lèpre récessive, la syphilis héréditaire ou le rheumatisme déformant. Brêtas nous propose le choix entre une maladie epidémique, la zamparina, ou l'humor gallico provenant d'excès vénériens et compliqué de scorbut.' cf. Germain Bazin, *l'Architecture Réligieuse Baroque au Brésil*, Paris, 1956, vol. 1. p. 186. The details which follow are taken from M. Bazin's translation of the original account by Brêtas, first published in a local newspaper of the Minas Gerais in 1858.

† Tiradentes means in fact just what it says; dentist, i.e. tooth-puller, long before that evolved into the art of the dental surgeon. Joaquim José de Silva Xavier, whom we may term a surgeon-dentist, was a patriot who was hung by the authorities in Rio in 1792, and his head sent to be displayed in Ouro Preto. His hometown had its name changed to Tiradentes in his honour.

my own personal mythology is concerned of seeming more remote and far away than anywhere I have ever been in my life with the exception only of an excursion into the deep countryside made from Puno on Lake Titicaca, in Peru. That these were on the same South American continent seemed incredible until one remembered that Tiradentes was in the negro and *métis* or mulatto shadow thrown from Africa, but how different again from that in Alabama or Tennessee! Remote it may be, but the way to it is marvellously tropical across *barrancas* heavy with banana palms and paw-paw trees, very unlike the ascetic rigours of the Altiplano of Peru; and when at last you see the church tower, the road, or rock-track rather, intent on heightening anticipation, goes the longest possible way round to reach it, and even after that there is quite a walk to reach the church door. Inside there is, I think, the prettiest interior we saw in all Brazil with a wooden ceiling, of boards, not beams – that is to say – most elegantly and lightly painted in Venetian furniture style, as though the craftsman whoever he may have been had not only seen such painted furniture but by some feat of extrasensory perception was acquainted with the interior of St Mary's church at Whitby, but of mind not fixed upon the whalers sailing from that northern port for Arctic seas, but dilating from that to some sort of inappropriate pleasure barge for non-existent Brazilian inland waters. How else, except for sheer high spirits, to explain the painted carpentry of that extravangantly long and unnecessary bridge-like gallery leading from half-way down the nave towards the organ-loft. Still less, the organ itself with its columnar pipes, gilt swags and garlands, and the trumpet-blowing cupids under the roof astride the cornice. Surely the church at Tiradentes, more than Nossa Senhora de O at Sabará, is the authentic 'joyau de l'art baroque en tout Brésil'.

We shall see whether, or not, this opinion was confirmed by further experiences in Brazil. For now the problem was Bahia, or São Salvador, the former capital until the King Dom João VI removing himself in 1808 from Napoleonic aggression in the form of Marshal Junot and his troops, chose to disembark and stay in Rio. For long after that date Bahia may have remained in just the state we see it in the drawings by Jean-Louis Debret, the French drawing master and pupil of David whom the King sent for from Paris to head the academy of painting. Negro slaves were in great number (slavery was only abolished by the liberal Emperor Dom Pedro II in 1889). The rich whites were carried round in litters and palanquins – the mother of a friend of the writer, living in Bahia, used to be taken in a sedan-chair from the upper to the lower town and thought she must be the last living person to be so carried, for after all a sedan-chair is different temperamentally from a pedal-cycle or rickshaw. For the rich, climate apart, Bahia must have been a pleasant if enervating place to live in. It has often been described, and more than once in the writer's experience, as an earthly paradise. It was full of churches, convents and old buildings, and we had to go there.

I shall never forget the heat at the military aerodrome where we arrived, or the long and thrilling drive into the town past those deep gullies full of tropical trees and plants, by bamboo glades, and then along the seashore past beaches of snow-white sand, with nothing between us till the mangrove shores of Dahomey, or maybe, the Bight of Benin. Then came the houses, the streets and squares, and the hotel built by a good architect on the open plan with one huge glass-walled room on the first floor, and the dining room with coloured waitresses in the turbans, white lacy shirts and full white skirts of the Bahian costume. So we were in Bahia. But the hotel was the only place where we saw the local dresses all the week we were there, and they were not for sale in any of the shops, though it is said they are still worn in towns and villages around the bay. The large negresses selling glutinous-looking drinks and skewers of grilled meat in the streets had but the hint in them of what Bahia must have been only fifty years ago. In a museum in the lower town built out over the sea are other relics of the city's golden past, the carved prows of fishing boats in the guise more of rocking-horses; and painted wooden mermaids with fair hair for the fishermen to throw for luck into the waters. The silver collars were there, too; and rope or liana hammocks of an exquisite whiteness and of lascivious import as of whom one would like to find lying there, a yellow parrot of Amazon on her shoulder in the darting and whirring of the humming-birds or *picaflores*, slung from the boughs of some tropical and sweet-smelling tree. Hammocks of just this pattern and whiteness are on sale in the marketplace.

The days in Bahia were hard and bright with heat, and the nights made lively with torrential rain and thunderstorms. We had been given letters of introduction to persons who we were assured would show us the old town and the *quintas* outside it, where certainly there would be fine Bahian furniture to be seen. But the *dolce far niente* or its equivalent of the Brazilian doldrums was in force and the introductions did not materialise. So we saw Bahia unaided, by ourselves, and set off to do so morning and evening in the scarecrow taxis of the place, where the taximeters jumped and panicked like the seismograph before and during a bad earthquake. First of all, and nearly always, we would go down steeply into the old town past the church of Conceição da Praia, the fishermen's or sailors' church, whence we once saw a most extraordinary religious procession issuing forth with a woman dressed in purple – as the Magdalene? – weeping and wailing in ecstatic fashion – but the church itself is most uninteresting.

Then, past or through the fish-market where the negro porters on most mornings were talking or sitting amid the fish-debris with sacking over their heads in the ceaseless rain, past the factory of Suerdieck where the Bahian

Brazil

Carved porch by 'O Aleijadinho' to the Carmo church at São João d'El Rei.

Opposite: São Francisco de Assis, façade by 'O Aleijadinho' at São João d'El Rei.
Left: Head of a prophet in front of the church of Bom Jesus at Congonhas do Campo.
Below: Double staircase leading to São Francisco de Assis at São João d'El Rei.

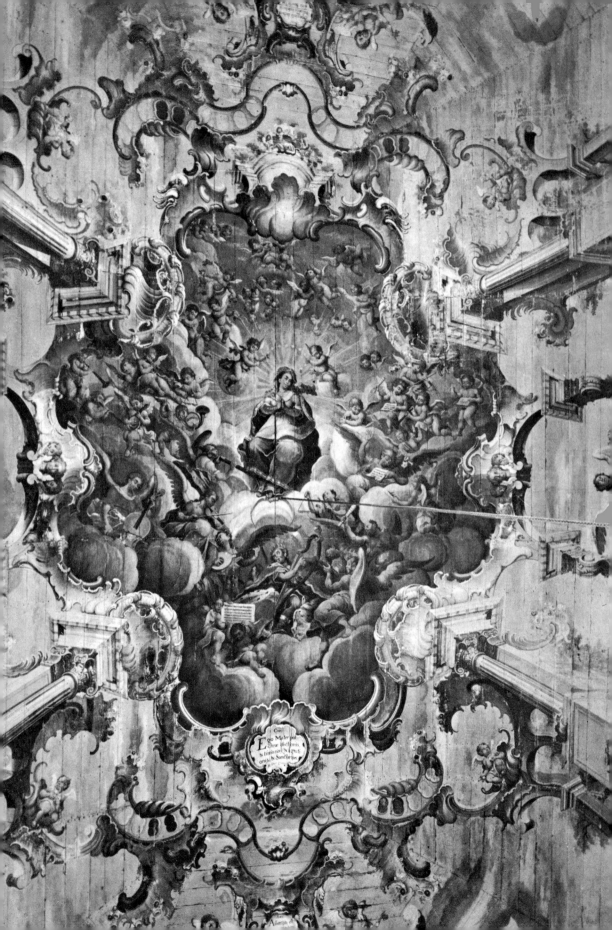

Above: Gallery in the church at
Tiradentes.
Left: Elegant pelmented balcony in Nossa
Senhora da Conceição dos Militares,
one of the sixty-two churches of Recife.
Opposite: Painted ceiling by
Manoel da Costa Ataíde in São
Francisco, Ouro Preto.

Above: Detail of façade of the church of the Third Order of the Franciscans at Bahia.
Opposite: Gabled façade of the church of Nossa Senhora do Carmo at Recife.

cigars are sold and by the black market of the money-changers, along the stalls of the snow-white hammocks and by an elegant pink building of about 1815–20 date in Adam style which was the Bourse, and up into the old town again, bound for the golden lion of Bahia which is the church of São Francisco, entrance to which was always painful because of the beggars sitting or lying outside it. The interior is one of the golden caverns of Portuguese contrivance which indeed would have been impossible for them but for the gold of Brazil. For dazzle and metallic glitter it is to be preferred to São Bento in Rio, but on the other hand how inferior it is in fantasy and imagination to the 'golden caverns' of São Francisco or Santa Clara of Oporto, at home in Portugal! The detail is coarse and heavy, and there is none of that lightness of hand and elegance that can make of a simple pelmet or picture frame a positive and glittering work of art. The double-storeyed cloister of São Francisco has *azulejos*, but not particularly good ones; and it is the much earlier looking façade of the chapel of the third Order of the Franciscans, next door to the big church, which is the best building in Bahia, though again in a provincial town in Portugal it would not attract much interest to itself.

The church and convent of Carmo is much the same as São Francisco, except that the accent is less on gilding than on the silver altar-front and fittings and benches of jacaranda wood. Its sacristy is a glorious apartment with multi-coloured stone floor, side-tables, chairs, consoles and statues, retarded seventeenth-century in date but like a Renaissance club-room by Sir Charles Barry.★ It must in its day have been the most comfortable and congenial apartment in all Bahia. Of the other churches in the town not much more need be said. The blue church with the twin belfries down the sloping Largo do Pelourinho deep in the negro quarter was to my taste almost voodoo-dark inside; and no less so another church near by at the top of a steep and sordid flight of steps.

The convent towers are on the skyline in all this part of Bahia; Nossa Senhora da Lapa of the Poor Clares and Santa Clara do Desterro among them. The Franciscan nuns of the latter convent who were drawn from the noble *hidalgo* families of the town being famous throughout the eighteenth century for their dissipation, real or exaggerated, the feasts and balls they gave, and even the *comédies d'amour* in which the young nuns took part. Today it seems a depressing building with long dark passages, but the nuns are still celebrated as the best makers of sweets in Bahia, a few of these no doubt dating from the time when black slaves working in the kitchens under the instruction of the

★ M. Germain Bazin, writing of the Third Order of the Franciscans in Rio, has this to say. 'Encore aujourd'hui, celui qui visite à Rio le siège de l'établissement, dit "de la Pénitence", impressionné . . . par la profusion d'or de l'église, par le luxe du consistoire, croit pénétrer dans une sorte de jockey-club réligieux.' *op. cit.* vol. I. p. 13.

Opposite: Church of the Third Order of Carmo at Recife.

nuns invented some of the excellent, if over dangerous triumphs of the Bahian cuisine.★

Perhaps the finest things in Bahia in point of workmanship are the presses of jacaranda wood with silver handles in many of the churches, as for instance in the sacristy of the cathedral which belonged formerly to the Jesuits. There were superb woodcarvers in Bahia during the eighteenth century who made chairs and cupboards of jacaranda wood in its three tints or colours which could be indicated roughly as the 'gold', the 'lavender' or 'silver', and the dark wood streaked with henna. Is it unreasonable to suppose that the unforgettable beauty of the jacaranda trees in flower together with the quality of the jacaranda wood became symbolic to the Sephardic Jews in exile from Portugal of a promised land? The old synagogue of the Sephardim in Curação has a tabernacle and presses of jacaranda wood; and so have the synagogues of the Portuguese Jews in Amsterdam and at Bevis Marks in the East End of London. This must have been the most precious and valuable wood they could procure. It is true that Malay craftsmen working under Portuguese, and then Dutch influence at the Cape and in Ceylon made superb furniture, but the finest of all 'colonial' furniture was from Bahia. In a private collection in Rio there were tall cupboards and settees of this provenance which equalled any works of English cabinet-makers of the best period. And for gem of his collection this amateur owned a 'bi-sexual' table, a splendid sideboard of jacaranda wood with ball and claw legs, a scroll or cartouche in the middle of the panel, and what was obviously a representative of the male and female emblem to each side of that. This curious object, which we were told was not unique of its kind, came, and this was odder still, from one of the nunneries of Bahia.

We were not able to see any of the *quintas* round Bahia, nor the Church of Carmo at Cachoeira some forty or fifty miles inland from Bahia up the Paraguassu river. The church looks from photographs to have splendid and romantic gold balconies or opera-boxes with pelmets over them in more or less the Bahian manner. Is it perhaps at Cachoeira that the turbans and white shawls and wide skirts of the old Bahian costume are still worn; or is it in towns and villages nearer the coast? In any event it will be gone in a few years like the yellow, horned turbans of Martinique, and the 'earthly paradise' of Bahia will be the poorer for this loss.

The contemporary, if rusty Pompeii of Brasilia not being within this present context, the search for Baroque and Rococo only took us to one more town which was Recife. This has the distinction of being about the nearest landfall to Europe from the South American continent, but a look at the map will show that it is far below the Gulf of Guinea and on the same

★ On both coasts of South America, in Lima as in Bahia, this still goes on, cf. my *Golden Wall and Mirador*, 1961, p. 53.

parallel as Luanda in Portuguese West Africa. Personally, I found Recife more to my taste than any other town in Brazil. For some quarter of a century (1630–54) while Portugal was ruled by the Kings of Spain, before it regained its independence, Recife or Pernambuco was a Dutch possession colonised by Prince Maurice of Nassau who later was to return home and build the Mauritshuis at The Hague. He had even contemplated removing the majority of the Dutch population to safety in Brazil. He took with him two painters, Albert Eeckhout who spent eight years in Brazil and made sketches on the spot from which after his death the set of tapestries was woven known as the *Texture des Indes*, and Frans Post who on the strength of what he painted there and on his return home is known as the painter of Pernambuco. Recife has indeed even now in spite of great commercial development many of the elements of a Dutch water city. It has lagoons, wide canals and many bridges.

On a fine and beautiful evening we drove out of Recife towards the old city of Olinda. And gradually the landscape in spite of its tropical trees took on the golden light of classical antiquity, the *aprica littora* almost of Tarragona which intensified as the old settlement came into sight upon its hill. From near distance Olinda is the Tarragona, the Arles or Nîmes of South America, an impression only tempered and not diminished by a church on the slope of the hill in which in spite of the growing darkness, and not being able to approach the high altar because of High Mass, we could make out the golden ceiling and the revetment of blue and white *azulejos* typical of all Portugal. When we got into Olinda it was too dark to see anything more, and of the ten or a dozen churches listed by M. Germain Bazin we had seen the interior of that one alone. But in the semi-tropical twilight there was the hint of old houses with gardens behind high walls and what must have been convents. Olinda was unforgettable in that falling darkness. It was there, had one the choice, that one would wish to live in Brazil, with the feeling even that the light of morning need not dispel that first impression in the semi-darkness.

Recife is very different from Olinda. Seen from afar, or even from near to, it is not a city with any romance at all attaching to it. Indeed it is not incomparable to Rotterdam. That is, until you notice there are semi-tropical trees growing along the streets and in the squares. And then the façades of churches, several of them, begin to surprise one with their gracefulness, their gabled frontispieces and fine towers, and not only are they, even from the outside, more carefully kept than those of Rio or Bahia, but it is apparent that there is considerable difference of style. But neither is there any resemblance to Ouro Preto and to the doorways, escutcheons and medallions of 'O Aleijadinho'. A typical church of Recife is that of the Third Order of Carmo. It has a gabled front; or, in the phrase of Mr Pál Kelemen, the pediment is 'drawn high' and given a window which, as he says, recalls the opening in

Dutch or Flemish gables through which merchandise was pulled up into the attic, and this gable has rich scrolling round it reminiscent even of the old guild houses in the Grande Place at Brussels; while below this in the main body of the façade the three windows over the doorway have statues in niches standing between them. The Rosário is another church with a gabled front; but it is the church interiors that are very fine indeed and of a quality surpassing anything to be seen in Rio or in Bahia. The Rococo pelmets from Portugal make their appearance here without any of the heavyhanded treatment and execution of the *Baroque tardive* of those other cities; and there is a feature peculiar to Recife of very high windows for coolness with a gallery running beneath them, the heat of the semi-tropics being, as it were, masqued in any case by shade from the adjacent buildings. The gilded interiors of at least three or four of the churches of Recife qualify for their inclusion among the *capelas douradas* of all Portugal even if M. Germain Bazin, their apostle, is carried a little far in his enthusiasm when he calls the, in truth remarkable enough, ceiling of the Conceição dos Militares at Recife, 'la Chapelle Sixtine de la Rocaille'.★ This '*rocher incrusté de coquillages*' is indeed more reminiscent of the marine-garden motifs of the Bom Jesus de Braga.

His is an excitement in no need though of sedation when M. Bazin writes of his discovery of the church of Nossa Senhora da Corrente de Penedo on the left bank of the São Francisco river, after traversing three hundred kilometres of *mato* only inhabited by a few *vaqueiros*, garbed in leather driving their herds along, and his arrival at this lost town where the only food at the inn was a ragout of *jacquare*, an evil-sounding fish from the São Francisco. Before this interior, 'cette merveille de civilisation raffinée' he is reminded of entrance into the Sainte Chapelle of Paris. That there are not lacking other beautiful and more accessible buildings in this part of Brazil must be the case at João Pessoa, the old capital of the state of Paraiba, just north of Recife, where the church of São Francisco has a walled court in front of it, a tower faced with pale blue tiles, and a gabled façade with three splendid balconied windows above no fewer than five doorways each with its latticed, wooden, Moorish-looking door.† One has to imagine this court and the church beyond it thronged with hundreds of turban'd negro slaves in their local variant of the beautiful Bahian costume, and then the lavishness of the scale explains itself.

Our last experience of Brazil, which was at Recife, was of markedly different character, and in as it were another idiom, but so unlikely was it that it is perhaps worth mentioning. We were staying not in the city itself, but at Bomfim, a beach resort a mile or two outside the town. The rigours of beach life were, it is true, mitigated by one or two Gauguin-style restaurants

---

★ *op. cit.* vol. I. p. 287.

† Pál Kelemen, *op. cit.* pp. 244, 245, and plate 166 (b). Penedo, referred to above, is in the state of Alagôas, about half way between Bahia and Recife in this incredibly huge country.

in thatched huts of palm leaves hidden in the tropical forest just behind the hotels and shops. On the way to one of these, and than again returning quite late at night, the same ancient crone was begging under the arches of the hotel, and there was something familiar in the way she held herself and the way she walked. She was not begging, or not exactly begging but muttering in some strange tongue, and when rebuffed walking off with that peculiar stride. Often I had seen that wide-limbed walk before, but where? And I remember, too, wondering what she was doing here, and whether she lived in a hovel of palm leaves among the semi-tropical trees.

Next morning when we drove to the airport with our only acquaintance in Recife who spoke not a word of anything but Portuguese, we came round the corner into the main square of the little suburb of Bomfim and the whole of that empty space was one huge Gypsy encampment. There must have been ten or a dozen huge low tents of black or dark brown canvas. In an instant we were in the midst of a crowd of them who came rushing to every side of the car, the old crone among them. One could hear a din of hammering from within the tents; and as more of them came pouring out, the crash of dropped pots and pans like the noise of falling trays, or indeed the clash of cymbals. They were Rumanian *calderarii* or coppersmiths; grandchildren, supposedly, of the Tchorons and Demeters who were the leading families among the coppersmiths who suddenly appeared in England in 1911 to the great interest and excitement of all lovers of the tsiganes or ciganje, and some of whom are known to have gone subsequently to Brazil. We were surrounded by the flashing eyes and smiles of the Gypsy Lotharios and their *romīs* or young maidens. We had no camera and could not photograph them, had that even been possible in all the excitement and among so many furtive hands. We could not even ask how long they had been there; where they were going, or where they came from. Neither have I been able, though I have tried, to get anyone to follow them up. Probably they were gone by next morning. To João Pessoa, who knows? Or to Penedo, a hundred and eighty miles from anywhere? Where, again, at least they would have a background of architecture worthy of them in the glittering, coruscating Rococo of Brazil.

9

The Castrati, and Others

'October 2nd 1850', we read in an old diary, 'Flexmore (clown) calls for annual song'; and for 4 September of the next year, 'Flexmore comes in chaise with Madame Auriol about pantomime'. Do not these few words give us the smell of the theatre in our nostrils? Of the most romantic part of London, still left, which is that round Drury Lane and Covent Garden? They are from *The Life and Reminiscences of J. L. Blanchard*, 1891; and reading further, there are accounts of George Wieland, the imp or sprite, whom Blanchard considered to be the greatest exponent of the lost art of panto-mime, speaking from personal memories of Grimaldi, Bologna, and all the famous pantomimists of his time. Above all, there are no less than magical, if in the end tragic accounts of Tom Ellar, the harlequin, and of James Barnes, the pantaloon. Little wonder that Blanchard, remembering all this, writes of himself, that 'one, at least, of the passengers along the streets sees more spectres arise out of the pavement as he passes the modern buildings than will stir the imagination of belated pedestrians a hundred years from now.' I could write, and indeed have written, more upon this theme.★

There could be few better subjects for the writer, and the present person among them, than the old theatre or opera house. Beautiful as a theme, if only for the reason that little else than that can be done about it now that actors and audience alike are long since dead, and contingent again to this present, because the theatre like the roundabouts of the fairground from the time of their beginning until a very few years ago belonged by tradition, and

---

★ Dicky Flexmore, the son of a comic dancer, was not only a clown. He burlesqued the famous dancers of the Romantic Ballet. When he died in 1860, of consumption, *The Times* said of him that he was especially noted for his close and natural imitation of leading dancers of the day, such as Perrot, Carlotta Grisi, and Cerrito. In 1848 he revived *Esmeralda*, playing the part of Gringoire the rôle created by Jules Perrot, the greatest male dancer of the age, and Madame Auriol took the name part. In the next year he produced *Les Patineurs*, to the music of Meyerbeer, and in the same year he married Madame Auriol who was the daughter of the French clown, Jean-Baptiste Auriol. Wieland who died aged thirty-seven, played the part of Asmodeus in *Le Diable Boiteux* (*The Devil on Two Sticks*), the old ballet by Coralli whose dances are still admired when we see a performance of Giselle. cf. pp. 253–8 of my *The Hunters and the Hunted*, 1947, which are a fantasy and entr'acte upon Blanchard's *Reminiscences*, and on the theatre of his time.

of their very nature, to the age of gilt and stucco. So many of the old theatres
are gone; as to those others that are still standing, they have their nostalgic
interest in plenty, from the old theatre I saw this year in Toronto – it may be
the oldest building extant, as it is certainly the most romantic, in that new
born and sprawling megalopolis of the Great Lakes – to that most nostalgic
part of London, just now invoked round Covent Garden and Drury Lane,
not forgetting the Lyceum. The old Lyceum Theatre, least of the three; and
now, and for long since, a dance-hall, but it has seen better days; and impossible on passing it not to think of at least one night in its history, that of
15 April 1886, when Franz Liszt attended the gala performance of *Faust* with
Irving in the leading role. In the interval the orchestra played a Hungarian
march by Liszt, and the applause was so great that he had to come to the
front of the Royal box with Ellen Terry. Afterwards, Irving entertained him
to supper underneath the theatre, in the rooms of the Beefsteak Club, of
which Sir Martin Harvey gives so fine a description in his *Memoirs* –
mysterious, underground vaults leading to rooms hung with stage armour,
passages haunted by Kean and still trod by actors who had known and could
imitate his walk, while Irving his host, had no less ghostly a tread. So much
for one evening of theatrical history, and a performance of *Faust* by a great
actor attended by the greatest virtuoso and executant in human history who,
in himself, combined so much of Dr Faustus and Mephistopheles, of Lovelace
and of the Gypsy *primas*. Impossible to pass that theatre without thinking of
Liszt arriving in the gaslight, and of his banquet afterwards with Irving in the
vaults below. It was his farewell tour. He was seventy-five years old, and he
was to die, a few weeks later at Bayreuth with the word 'Tristan' on his
lips.★

And now with that smell of the theatre in our nostrils, we come out of
one theatre only in order to enter another. It is a little further away, in the
Haymarket, and will be the means of our meeting with actors and musical
virtuosi no less, indeed still more extraordinary than those just encountered.
The theatre is Sir John Vanbrugh's Opera House, but unfortunately no print
or drawing of its interior has survived. It came in date between Castle
Howard and Blenheim, and from Defoe's account it must have been plain
and simple on the outside. Within, it was an affair of columns and much
gilding. It had a huge proscenium, probably framed with pillars, and what
would seem to have been a foyer of huge dimensions, the whole resembling
perhaps the Painted Hall at Greenwich Hospital. Vanbrugh wrote his play
The Confederacy for it. It was the biggest theatre yet built in London but with
impossible acoustics. The actors could not make their voices heard. However,

★ A few sentences are quoted here from my *Life of Liszt*, 1936, pp. 323, 326. In parenthesis, the writer
remembers seeing that wonderful singer and superb actor Chaliapin passing the statue of Irving
outside the National Portrait Gallery, and taking off his hat to it as he walked by.

it was here that the great Italian singers were introduced to London, the acoustics being suited in mysterious fashion for music but not for drama. At the Opera House in the Haymarket, the *castrati* were imported for the first time into England. At first the operas given were only *pasticcios*, but Handel produced *Rinaldo*, the earliest of his operatic ventures at the Haymarket. Nicolino, the mime and singer, and Senesino, the greatest of human singers after Farinelli, made their debut at the Opera House. The rage had begun. Nevertheless, it was unprofitable for Vanbrugh and he lost his money.

The adulation of the *castrati* singers was one of the more curious aberrations of the Augustan age, if rivalled and indeed excelled by the vagaries of millions all over the world in their pursuit and applause of long-haired drummers and pop-singers. Dr Burney has this to say of the process of their manufacture.★ His sentences have been oft-quoted, but may come as new to some readers.

I enquired throughout Italy at what place boys were chiefly qualified for singing by castration. I was told at Milan that it was at Venice: at Venice that it was at Bologna: but at Bologna the fact was denied, and I was referred to Florence: from Florence to Rome, and from Rome I was sent to Naples. The operation is most certainly against the law in all these places, as well as against nature; and all the Italians are so much ashamed of it, that in every province they refer it to some other. However, with respect to the Conservatorios at Naples, Mr Jemineau, the British Consul, who has so long resided there, and who has made very particular enquiries, assured me, and this account was confirmed by Dr Cirillo, an eminent and learned Neapolitan physician, that this practise is absolutely forbidden in the Conservatorios, and that the young *castrati* come from Lecce in Puglia; but before the operation is performed, they are brought to a Conservatorio to be tried as to the probability of voice, and then are taken home by their parents for this barbarous purpose. It is said however, to be death by the laws to all those who perform the operation, and excommunication to everyone concerned in it, unless it is done, as is often presented, upon account of some disorders which may be supposed to require it, and with the consent of the boy.

But Dr Burney goes on to say that M. de la Lande† was more fortunate, having ascertained that 'there are shops in Naples with this inscription: *Qui si castrono ragazzi*, but I was utterly unable to see or hear of any such shops during my residence in that city.' The story seems improbable: but, for all that, and wherever operated, it was only necessary to set foot in one of the four Conservatorios of Naples to find *castrati*. In that of Sant' Onofrio, Burney found 'sixteen young *castrati*, and these lie upstairs, by themselves, in warmer compartments than the other boys, for fears of colds, which might not only render their delicate voices unfit for exercise at present, but hazard

★ *The Present State of Music in France and Italy*, *1771*.
† M. de la Lande was author of *Voyage en Italie*, Geneva, 1790.

the entire loss of them for ever.' In the accounts of this same Conservatorio, there is mention of 'a suit of clothes for one Sebastiano, eunuch of Andria . . . the clothes of black material since the eunuchs are always dressed in black.'★ Andria it may be noted, was in Apulia, not far from Lecce. Another town where the operation was performed was Norcia, which is near Spoleto. Caffarelli, the rival of Farinelli, had the operation performed upon him at Norcia. But it was the surgeons from Bologna who were famous for this, and may have been practising their trade both in Norcia and in Lecce. And not only in Italy. When Dr Burney went to Ludwigsburg in 1772 the Duke of Wurtemberg had no fewer than fifteen *castrati* in his opera company, and two surgeons from Bologna in his employment but, then, Duke Eberhard Ludwig, a pluralist if ever there was one, had a private troupe of opera singers and ballet dancers, a topic upon which Casanova in his memoirs had salacious things to say.

The *castrati*, then, were a superfetation and something of an anomaly; one of those unnecessary things tinged with cruelty; like the nightingales' tongues of the Roman banquets; like the grain rammed down a goose's throat to give it a diseased liver; like the livers of hyenas that were the *foie gras* of the Egyptian Pharaohs; or the blinded linnets that were let loose in churches in Naples and Southern Italy on certain saints' days, the theory being that they sang more passionately with their eyes put out; or, perhaps most horrible of all, the 'Old Jacksons' a breed of fighting cock in the Southern States, once of great celebrity, and having the reputation of fighting better after losing their eyesight in the main.

The sources of supply, then, were Lecce – a city of which so much has been said in these present pages if for other reasons, but not forgetting its great singers – and Norcia, a small town that with some little bearing on our previous paragraph is famous for its black truffles. Norcia was in fact of sinister, double reputation for this reason. And from the four Conservatorios of Naples, Sant' Onofrio, Pietà dei Turchini, Santa Maria di Loreto, and Poveri di Gesù Cristo, but chiefly from the two first named, the eunuch singers went forth to seek their fortunes. Very different of inclination were the musical Conservatorios of Venice, where the orphans were girls and Dr Burney saw a young and pretty nun conducting the choir and orchestra with a sprig of pomegranate blossom tucked between her coif and hair.

It is surprising to learn that in Rome, the fulcrum and place of issue of excommunication, there were more than two hundred *castrati* singing in the churches,† and that it was not uncommon for *castrati* to go about in women's

---

★ But at the Pietà dei Turchini, another of the Conservatorios of Naples, they wore red belts and 'Turkish berets' (perhaps fezzes?). cf. *The Castrati in Opera*, by Angus Heriot, London, 1956, p. 41; and Salvatore di Giacomo: *I Quattri antichi Conservatorii di Napoli*, Palermo, 1925.
† Angus Heriot, *op. cit.*, pp. 25, 27.

M

clothes all the time. But that, at least, was of their own volition, and in proof of the silliness of their neuter gender. In Japan, on the other hand, the *onnegata*, or actors playing female roles in the *Kabuki* theatre, had to wear feminine dress and live as women off the stage. They even entered public baths by the ladies' door!★ It is enough to have seen the *Kabuki* theatre once only to remember the falsetto voices of the *onnegata*; and interesting to be told that the *geisha* come to the theatre 'to learn from the *onnegata* how a woman of distinction should dress and behave'. One of a family of great Japanese actors has said 'that if actresses were now introduced on the Kabuki stage they would do no more than imitate the *onnegata* of the last century.' This is something which it is difficult for a Western audience to understand; as it is, also, that so many of the conventions of the *Kabuki* stage were influenced by or adopted from the *Bunraku* or puppet-theatres of the Japanese. The affectations and the interminable warblings and vocalisations of the *castrati* singers would probably be found unbearable, but the most famous of them must have been great artists, as well as being technically, in range, in expression, and in acrobatic agility the most consummate singers there have ever been. It is their vocational absurdities, surgically induced, so to speak, and the artificial-nightingale aspect of their singing that would make them interesting were we enabled through some alchemy of time to hear them sing today.

The reason for the *castrati* was a simple one, that women were forbidden to sing in churches, and either forbidden or at the least not encouraged, to sing upon the stage. But neither were tenors, the legendary heroes and matinée idols of Italian opera, given any importance. Opera in the eighteenth century, even when it was written by Germans, by Handel or by Hasse, was Italian opera, and this meant *castrati* in the principal rôles until Gluck started to reform opera and bring it into shape with the classicising tendencies of Winckelmann, and it could be said, with the beginnings of archaeology in ancient Greece and Rome and their effect upon the art and architecture of the time. Gluck may have been only to some little extent aware of this in himself, but it was in the air and was instinctive in his search for truth and real emotion in his operas. It was the Napoleonic Wars and the inrush of new ideas and French logic into Italy that put an end to the *castrati* as an archaic relic and an anachronism. It was the end of them in the sense that no more of them were made. But the surviving *castrati* continued to sing. Velluti, the last of the great eunuch singers of Italy appeared in London in 1825 when, according to Lord Mount Edgcumbe, no singer of his description had appeared in England for a quarter of a century. Excitement was intense, and the theatre hushed as he came on. 'The first note he uttered

★ *The Kabuki Hand books*, by Aubrey S. Halford and Giovanna M. Halford, 1956, p. 391. A most fascinating and enthralling book about the great actor families and their plays.

gave a shock of surprise, almost of disgust, to inexperienced ears; but his performance was listened to with attention and great applause throughout, with but few audible expressions of disapprobation speedily suppressed.' It is curious to think that the opera in question, *Il Crociato in Egitto*, had been written for Velluti by Meyerbeer, this being the last historical instance of the chief rôle in an opera being written for an eunuch singer – Meyerbeer, the nascent 'Michelangelo of music' as he was later to be considered, then finishing the first or Italian phase of his phenomenal career before his removal to Berlin, and subsequent career as creator and arbiter of grand opera in Paris – all dust and ashes, now, and not one of his operas performed in any theatre! – and more curious still that one admirer of Velluti's singing in this opera by Meyerbeer should have been the Duke of Wellington of all unlikely persons.★

If, as has been suggested a little way back, the theatre and more still the opera house belong of tradition to that Italian world of gilt and stucco, and never more so than when it is an Italian enclave, almost an independence upon foreign soil, then, as much as the tenor, the *torero*-equivalent of the footlights, it is the forgotten *castrati* who should be thought of and re-membered in context with the golden opera houses and their tiers of boxes. Nicolino (Nicola Grimaldi) was in fact the first of the *castrati* to appear and make the success of *Rinaldo* which was Handel's first opera in London (1711); Nicolino who, in *Idaspe fedele*, an opera by another composer, delighted his audience by his fight with a lion, a ludicrous scene often encored which had great appeal to George Hogarth as a specimen of foreign silliness and affectation, and which moved even Lady Mary Wortley Montagu to write that she 'was last Thursday at the new opera, and saw Nicolini strangle a lion with great gallantry'.

The two greatest of the *castrati* who sang in London were Senesino and Farinelli. But the career of Senesino and the account of him as an artist are insignificant beside the extraordinary career and achievement of Farinelli. Besides which, owing to unique circumstance, it is possible as we shall see to form in one's mind a very accurate picture of his manner and appearance. Farinelli (real name Carlo Broschi) was born at Andria, in Apulia, his father being a minor government official, which makes it the more surprising that he should have submitted his son to be operated upon. There is some slight mystery about this, as in other details to do with Farinelli's life and even his choice of name, which have never been explained. At an early age he was sent to Naples and put under the care of Porpora, to judge from his pupils the greatest teacher of singing there has ever been, through whom he came

---

★ It may have been because Velluti had sung the previous year in Florence at the private performance of an opera by Lord Burghersh, a musical amateur who was British Minister to Tuscany, and had married Wellington's niece.

into contact with the Abate Metastasio, the librettist of opera, who became his lifelong friend and whom he often visited in Vienna. After phenomenal successes in Italy and in Germany, Farinelli came to London in 1734 and stayed here for three years where by his appearance in operas of Handel and various Italian composers he created, by comparison to any phenomenon of our own time, far more of a popular and social furore than that attending the London seasons of Diaghilev's Russian Ballet. Handel apart, the only other foreign musician besides Farinelli who has created anything of a comparable sensation until the arrival of the American 'pop-singers', or birth of our own by improbable process of parthenogenesis in the cellars of Liverpool, will have been Haydn on his visits to London in 1791-2 and 1794-5. And it could be argued that Farinelli's three years here combined in themselves some elements of all those others put together.*

It was in 1738, the year after he left London, and for some twenty after it, that Farinelli attained the most phenomenal stage of his career in the service of the melomaniac Philip V, grandson of Louis XIV, and first of the Bourbon line of Spain. It seems to have been at the instigation of his second wife, Isabella Farnese, that Farinelli was invited to Spain where he quickly gained the King's confidence, and by his singing and through his personality had a decided influence upon the melancholia from which the King was suffering. It was a curious predicament. Isabella Farnese wanted the Duchy of Parma to which she was heiress, and also the Kingdom of Naples which belonged to Spain, for her own children, although they had an elder half-brother Fernando, the child of Philip's first marriage, and his person barred her children from the throne of Spain. She cannot have foreseen that the same melancholy that she set out to cure in her husband would one day destroy the stepson, although it had been for some time kept under by the same audition of music which relieved his father, and that by the stepson Fernando VI's death, her own son Carlos III would be recalled from Naples to rule over Spain. The story that Farinelli sang the same four songs (two of them by Hasse) nightly to the King may be no more of a distortion or exaggeration than my own meeting with a tame parrot in Cuernavaca which sang the whole of *One Enchanted Evening* (from *South Pacific*) all through, when, in fact, all it did was to start off in romantic vein with the first few bars. What is more important is that Farinelli soon became virtual, if not in fact, prime minister, and was entrusted with numerous schemes for irrigation, dredging of rivers, plans for agricultural improvement, and the like, all of which he carried out with great success. The stepson the Queen disliked, the Prince of Asturias, later to be Fernando VI, had for wife the Infanta Barbara of

---

* Another, and a comparable theatrical sensation of a hundred years later, was the appearance of Taglioni, Grisi and other dancers of the Romantic Ballet at Her Majesty's Theatre, also in the Haymarket, in the eighteen-forties.

Portugal, of musical descent through her grandfather the Emperor Leopold I, and through her paternal ancestors, Afonso VI and João IV, as well. Of dwarfish build, dark and mulatto-like of complexion, with thick lips in the semblance of her great-aunt Catherine of Braganza, Queen of our Charles II, this Royal lady was a person of great musical talents, and the pupil of her music-master, Domenico Scarlatti.

The accounts of Philip V's melancholy madness in letters of the time from ambassadors and others make unpleasant reading. He wandered about unshaven and refusing to change his underclothes; also, it would seem, emitting loud humming noises which were his imitation, emulation may be the better word for it, of Farinelli's singing. Only a year after his arrival at the Spanish court Sir Benjamin Keene writes home '. . . the King himself imitates Farinelli, sometimes air after air, and sometimes after the music is over, and throws himself into such freaks and howlings that all possible means are taken to prevent people from being witness to his follies. He had one of these fits this week, which lasted from twelve till past two in the morning. They have talked of bathing him, but fear they shall not persuade him to try that remedy.'*

There is downstairs in the Prado in Madrid, an immense painting of Philip V and his family by Van Loo, in which every member of this strange group of related and interrelated human beings is portrayed. It is for the record; but they are hardly characterised or given personality. There was opportunity here for a stranger and yet more interesting *Las Meninas*, but only the genius of Velázquez was missing. There is something about the attitude and the hunching of the shoulders in the King's portrait which hints at his melancholia. But, of course, the truth must have been much stranger or less palatable than this collection of princes and princesses in their silks and velvets, ablaze with Orders. It is improbable indeed that the King was ever induced to sit still for long enough to have his portrait drawn; still less likely that he would ever sit down with even one member of his family at a time. The truth as to the bearing and physiognomy of this grandson of *le Roi Soleil* would have been different indeed, and not a little frightening, if less terrible than pathetic. But it was only a hundred years later that after Waterloo,

* In the booklet accompanying the new recording by Miss Joan Sutherland of Rossini's *Semiramide* (1823), an *opera seria* to which some aura of that past in which the *castrati* sang still clings, the part of Arsace, 'a young captain of the Assyrian army', being taken by Miss Marilyn Horne, *en travesti*, there is a short history of the opera. Under date 1831, it says: 'During a visit to Spain on one memorable occasion Rossini was present when the King's brother, Don Francisco de Asís, performed the part of Assur "with suitable gestures, in a salon of his palace, to the infinite amusement of his Royal wife."' I think this is a mistake, for Don Francisco de Asís, the future, ineffectual husband of Queen Isabella II, was only born in 1822. It was probably his father, Don Francisco de Paula (b. 1794), married to a Bourbon princess from Naples, who was brother to the reigning King of Spain, Fernando VII, and also to Don Carlos. Don Francisco de Paula would have been a great-grandson of Philip V. One wonders just how funny his singing with 'suitable gestures' may have been!

when the great coinage of Pistrucci was struck at the Mint under the aegis of the Prince Regent, his father George III, then a poor old lunatic man with a long white beard, was portrayed as a clean shaven, bull-necked Roman Emperor à la Diocletian or Domitian.

When Philip V died and his son Fernando VI succeeded him, the same situation repeated itself in even aggravated form, as regards, that is to say, the musical climate of the reign. More operas were performed at the Spanish Court, then, than have been given since in Spain, where Madrid, the capital city, still lacks an opera house. Fernando VI was a weak-minded, lunatic-fringe type addicted to music, but the Infanta Barbara now become Queen, a virtuoso musician herself, though she may have been uncouth and uneducated in other respects, was a musical patron of a sort that did not appear again until the 'madness' of King Ludwig of Bavaria in his support of Wagner. The feminine foibles and pettinesses of the *castrati* seem not to have been present in Farinelli who never took advantage of his situation and continued to hold it without arousing the jealousy of his rivals. This state of affairs lasted from 1746 until 1758, when Queen Barbara died; her husband died a few months later of 'melancholy madness', his half-brother Carlos III arrived from Naples to become King, and Farinelli was honourably and it would seem gratefully 'retired' and left Spain to go and live in a villa he had bought some years before outside Bologna. Here he lived until 1783. In 1770 he had been visited by Dr Burney who had long talks with him, and heard him play on several of his harpsichords, including the one given him by Queen Barbara which must often have been played upon by Domenico Scarlatti.

Such was the extraordinary career of the greatest virtuoso in singing there can ever have been, who as an executant in his art is to be equated with Liszt and Paganini. His appearance therefore, especially because of the peculiar physical condition attaching to it, is of no little interest. The evidences of this are to be found in the large oil-painting by Amigoni, of Farinelli, his friend the Abate Metastasio, and the female singer Teresa Castellini, formerly in private possession, and now in the National Gallery at Melbourne. It will be seen from this how agreeably good-looking was Farinelli, and indeed there does not seem to be anything particularly strange in his appearance. He had not the jealousies and foibles of the other *castrati*, which two things taken together and coupled with his good manners, tact, and high level of intelligence, made possible the political side of his career. But it is not to be expected that the physical aspect of this greatest of singers should pass without comment, and the proofs of this are in the album of caricatures preserved in the Royal Library at Windsor Castle. This had been the property of Consul Smith, the somewhat shady dealer and collector through whom King George III acquired so many of Canaletto's drawings and paintings. It contains numerous caricatures of singers, many of them by Marco Ricci, the nephew of Sebastiano Ricci, and others by the collector and amateur, Count Zanetti, a friend – and where caricature was concerned – copyist of Marco Ricci. His drawings must be a part of the set of caricatures 'burlesquing the features, persons and stage attitudes of all the actors and actresses of repute who have appeared at the five theatres of Venice since he first began to frequent them, that is, 40 or 50 years ago.' And the Frenchman Clément goes on to say, which shows the pre-eminence, then, as now, of the London theatre, 'What a fine companion piece to this collection could he have made for himself in London! I do not know if he is still alive.'* (This was in 1751, and Zanetti in fact died in 1767.) The Marco Ricci drawings, too, may, or may not, have been a part of a collection of caricatures of singers which belonged to the famous amateur Count Algarotti, a friend of Consul Smith's, which later disappeared.

In any event, from this vast and profitable field for caricature there are few enough, too few remaining. There are seven drawings of Farinelli by Marco Ricci in the album; but although letters from Zanetti have been preserved in which he mentions his own caricatures, 'almost portraits' of Farinelli, none of them are in this album. There is such a drawing, however, in the Print Room at the British Museum, in which it is seen how closely Zanetti imitates Marco Ricci even, as Mr Croft-Murray points out, in his caricatural elongation of the feet. But this must have been very decidedly a feature of Farinelli, then a very thin and tall young man for both Ricci's and Zanetti's drawings of him date from before 1730 when Farinelli will have been no more than twenty-five years old. He is described in the catalogue as 'in gala dress', which includes a cocked-hat under his arm, a sword at his side, and a long stick or cane dangling from his right wrist. The queue of his wig is exaggerated in Zanetti's drawing, as is the size of his cuff, and of course his immensely long, most typically Spanish-clown-like feet. But the 'gala dress' surely means no more than that Farinelli is off-stage and in his best clothes, which are not, it is to be remarked, very different from the best of Ricci's caricatures in the Windsor album, that showing Farinelli 'in an Oriental rôle' with his right arm and right leg not drawn at all. He is a 'captive in chains' in any case, but his characteristic and strange physiognomy is to be seen; his small head in proportion to his height, strongly marked eyebrows, and in the other drawing by Marco Ricci, the one of a pair, his very prominent front teeth. In the companion drawing of the *castrato* with his back turned, we get again the smallness of his head, his immensely long back, the braiding of his tail-coat spaced almost like the ribs of a skeleton, and his elongated boots.

* P. Clément, *Lettres critiques*, 1767, quoted from *Venetian Drawings at Windsor Castle*, by Anthony Blunt and Edward Croft-Murray, London, 1957, p. 148. It is Mr Croft-Murray's rendering of the original sentences in French. cf. also, p. 146 and p. 139.

Farinelli is immediately to be known and recognised from this drawing although we see only the back of his head.★

There are many drawings in the Windsor album of Senesino, the nearest rival to Farinelli, who sang in London in many of Handel's operas, then quarrelled with him and joined the rival 'opera of the nobility' which had Porpora for its composer. The most famous of the *castrati* after Senesino, of beautiful name but implying only that he came from Siena – Senesino, himself, being a long way behind Farinelli in fame – were probably Caffarelli and Egizziello. The first of these exhibited in his person all the tiresomenesses and affectations of which the *castrati* were capable, but calmed down as he grew older, the Calabrian estate and Dukedom of San Donato which he bought for himself being perhaps the greatest assuagement to his nervous pride. An interesting moment in his career, and one which is contingent to the developing of this present chapter was the invitation from King Dom José 1 of Portugal to attend the opening of the new Opera House in Lisbon in 1755. It is Dom José whose equestrian statue stands in 'Black Horse Square', the old sailor's name for the Terreiro do Paço, riding proudly forward to the water's edge, his helm magnificently plumed, and his cloak falling from his shoulders to the horse's flanks, perhaps the most beautiful equestrian statue of the eighteenth century, but a product less of warfare, even of joust or tournament, than of the theatrical masques and entertainments of this music-loving court. Dom João v, the father of Dom José, of an extravagance backed by the new found gold and diamonds of Brazil, was the builder of Mafra and of the lacquered library at Coimbra; it was he who ordered the altar-fittings, the sacred vessels and the vestments for the chapel in São Roque, and who drove in the golden coaches of Belém. In addition, he maintained the singing at the Royal Chapel as on the basis of an opera house, hiring for this purpose the greatest Italian singers of the age, his only rival in this respect being the Elector of Saxony and King of Poland when the Royal chapel and opera at Dresden had among its contracted artists half the famous singers of Europe.† The opening of the Opera House in Lisbon was a new departure. It was for its time the finest theatre in Europe, so quickly to be destroyed by earthquake that next to no mention of it at all is left. The opera performed at this opening night of Dom José's Opera House, and it is to be remembered that he was brother to the Infanta Barbara, the pupil and scholar of Domenico Scarlatti, was *Alessandro nell' Indie*, by the Portuguese composer, Perez. It was dedicated to Caffarelli, and a whole troop of horses appeared on the stage, with a Macedonian phalanx. One of the King's

★ What a portrait must have been Dantan's caricature-statuette of a headless Duke of Wellington, to be known from his stance, without his nose or chin! It would seem that no cast of it has survived.

† Angus Heriot *op. cit.*, p. 60 and footnote, on information derived from Dr Burney, *The Present State of Music in Germany*, 1773.

riding-masters rode Bucephalus to a march which Perez composed to the *grand pas* of the most beautiful horse from the *manège*. So much for the opera performed; but of the theatre itself there is little more known than the sentence or two devoted to it in the recently published *Journal of Lord Hervey*.* The opening was in April, and the disastrous and terrible earthquake at Lisbon was in November of the same year (1755). By a curious coincidence Dresden suffered a very similar disaster from the bombardment by the Prussian troops of Frederick the Great, only four years later in 1760, in the Seven Years' War, a catastrophe in which for instance all the scores of Hasse's operas were destroyed. They had been collected there in order that they should be engraved. All the works of art in the Palace at Lisbon perished in the earthquake, including the library, the musical collection, and it is thought, paintings by Van Eyck, fruits of his mythical journey to Portugal. Nearly all the churches in Lisbon were destroyed. It was a total disaster. Yet, as late as 1787, Beckford writes that 'the Queen of Portugal's chapel is still the first in Europe, in point of vocal and instrumental elegance; no other establishment of the kind, the Papal not excepted, can boast such an assemblage of admirable musicians.' Egizziello, whose very name suggests the warbling of these artificial nightingales – it is disappointing to learn it is derived from Domenico Gizzi, the singer under whose tutelage he was placed at eight years old! – was probably the greatest of these singers. He went to Lisbon in 1743 and stayed there for ten years, thus escaping the earthquake of 1755 by his absence, while Caffarelli who was still in Portugal, having stayed on after the opening of the Opera House, escaped it by luck for he happened to be away at Santarém. Lord Hervey, who gives 'Bibiena' as the name of the designer of the new Opera House, does not further particularise among the clan, and it would be unfair to expect more precision from him. Was it, then, Giovanni Carlo Bibiena who later designed the uninteresting Memória church at Belém, near Lisbon, not, as might be thought, in memory of those killed in the earthquake, but in thinksgiving for Dom José's escape from assassination in 1758. Pombal is buried there; and the mere linking of his name with the Memória church would make it certain that condign retribution was given those accused of the attempted murder. No one who has read Portuguese history will forget the appalling fate of the entire family of the Duke of Aveiro, on the obviously trumped up charge that they had plotted the King's assassination. That was in 1759; and later still in the 1780s a wretched Italian was tortured and torn limb from limb by wild horses at a spot near the Terreiro do Paço for the same offence, once again at Pombal's command in order to strike terror into his political opponents.

Was it then the same Carlo Bibiena who designed the interior of the old

---

* Lord Hervey, later third Earl of Bristol. His Journal, edited by David Erskine Kimber, was published in 1953. He was a naval officer and amateur Casanova.

Opera House at Bayreuth between the years 1745 and 1748? He was one of the less famous of the family, it is true, being neither Ferdinando or Francesco who were brothers, nor Giuseppe or Antonio who were sons of Ferdinando.★ But the two first mentioned, who were born in 1657 and 1659, were in the full tide of their work by the end of the century, at about which time it is probable that Carlo or Giancarlo Bibiena was born. There was a third, even a fourth generation of the family, if we allow Giovanni Maria Galli da Bibiena (1619–65) as its founder. If, as stated in the footnote, the surviving theatres of the family are a disappointment, the fame of this sept or clan of theatre-builders and scene-painters must remain a legend but for the interior of the old Opera House at Bayreuth. And the wanderings of this nomad family of theatrical artists all over Europe must excuse this rapid transference from the capital of Portugal to a small Franconian Duchy.

It was part of theatrical tradition that the audience came, as much to stare and be stared at, as to direct their glances on the stage. It was for this reason that the rows of boxes were designed in such fashion that each of them projected slightly forward, one after the other, allowing for an uninterrupted view of the stage and in order, too, that the occupants should be seen to every advantage from boxes near by and from across the theatre. But, also, in such a theatre as the old Opera House at Bayreuth, in order that the audience should stand and face towards the Royal box which for this reason, and regardless whether the Royal personages got a good view of the stage, or not, was always placed in the centre of the first tier. At Bayreuth, because of this turning of all eyes towards them at their entry and departure, the box for the Margrave and Margravine – she was the Margravine Wilhelmine, sister of Frederick the Great – was, itself, made into a miniature stage with little steps or platforms on either side for the heralds to sound their trumpets at the right moment. The Margrave's box was another stage – a theatre within a theatre – or almost another altar; and it is to be surmised from this that the actual performances were in all probability dull and long. The elaboration of the painted scenery by the Bibiena and their school was in order to carry the opera or play which but for this would become intolerable.

What would be our reactions on hearing and seeing an opera by Handel or by Hasse with this scenery, and two or three *castrati* singing in it? The male contralto or soprano voices could not but make a strange effect, the more so for their interminable ornaments and roulades and their simulated passions. Their voices will have been very curious indeed at a first hearing, and would

★ Surviving theatres by members of the Bibiena family are the oval Teatro dei Rinnovati by Antonio Galli da Bibiena, 1753, in the old Sala del Gran Consiglio on the ground floor of the Palazzo Pubblico in Siena; the Teatro Comunale at Bologna, 1756–63, by Antonio of the name; and the Teatro Filarmonico at Verona by Francesco Bibiena, 1716, but restored in 1760. Not one of those three theatres as to its interior can be described as anything but disappointing.

come upon one with as much of a surprise as those first moments of hearing the *Joruri* reciter at the puppet or *Bunraku* theatre in Osaka. He recites accompanied by the *samisen* orchestra, stringed instruments of the oddest possible effect until the ear gets used to them. But as to the ravishment in the tones of the *castrati* there can be little question; and in their singing of dramatic rôles instinct may have supplied what they could only partly, but not entirely feel though it is to be realised many of them had fervid, if never wholly satisfying love affairs. They were not incapable of love. Quite to the contrary; but they could get little, or only partial satisfaction from it. When Goethe says of them: 'a double pleasure is given, in that they are not women, but only represent women. The young men have studied the properties of the female sex in its being and behaviour; they know them thoroughly and reproduce them like an artist; they represent, not themselves, but a nature absolutely foreign to them', he is echoing almost word for word the remarks quoted a page or two back about the *onnegata* or female impersonators in the *Kabuki* theatre of Japan. Goethe even advocated that the *castrati* should take the place of actresses, not only in operas, but in plays; and seems to have considered them to be better natural actresses than actual women taking the part of women on the stage. But of course their voices had neither the timbre nor the meaning of women's voices. They were boys' voices, artificially prolonged and subjected to most intensive training, including, doubtless, many tricks and turns of technique now lost for ever.

It must not be forgotten that Rossini said in his old age in Paris during the Second Empire that one of his reasons for ceasing to compose was that there were no more good singers, now that the *castrati* no longer taught singing in their retirement. Or did Rossini imply by this that he thought the *castrati* were the greatest singers? It is not impossible. He was born in 1792, was in his full genius as composer of operas by 1813, and in time therefore to have heard the last of the great *castrati* singers. The first generation of great woman singers was, it could be said, but just beginning; and he who recalled, and had still in his ears their unearthly warblings and their interpretation of embodied, yet disembodied passions, might well think that ordinary women singers could not supplant them; and that of their very nature women could not undergo so prolonged and terrible a training, for it is certain that a great deal more than mere surgical inhumanity went into the musical education of the *castrati*. It was a time when a child's education was severe beyond belief, and what else could be expected for these trained acrobats of the larynx?

To someone who has seen and known the *skoptsi* droshky-drivers of Galatz and Bucharest it would be of interest to know more about the physical appearance of the *castrati*.★ Besides the portrait group of Farinelli and his

★ cf. *Roumania.*, 1938, pp. 77–81, for my account of the *skoptsi* and of the *skapetz* cabman, Pedracchi.

friends by Amigoni there are other portraits, including one of Carestini which, curiously, is by Knapton who painted the members of the Hell-Fire Club, but there is nothing in the mezzotint to make it different from Knapton's other portraits. The truer pictures of the *castrati* are in the caricatures by Zanetti and by Marco Ricci. Here they are to be seen in what convention prescribed for them as Classical, i.e. Heroic, or in Oriental dress; the Classical which covered all rôles from the heroes of antiquity to the paladins being an adaptation of Roman armour; and the Oriental, the conversion of the same into something else by addition of a scimitar and turban.

But there exists one great curiosity and theatrical relic which is the portrait of the castrato, Carlo Scalzi as *Sirbace* in Porpora's opera of *Rosbale*.* Scalzi, who sang in Handel's operas in London, was not particularly famous as a singer. In the portrait he stands pointing with his left hand to the plumed cap and aigrette on a table. He is small and insignificant-looking with pug-dog features and thick lips, and his left hand rests in silly gesture behind his back. But his hand is really lying on his balloon-like coat-tails which are wide as a crinoline and look springy to the touch as though they had whalebone in them. Both his jacket and coat-tails are gorgeously embroidered; his jacket has a kind of gold-chain design round the collar; while the front of his tails have a panel of scallop-shaped pattern in, one would surmise, gold embroidery with heavy tassels lying on it; or, indeed, it is a kind of conventionalised cloud-pattern as impalpable as the *Barricades Mystérieuses* of Couperin, and flourished round its edges and along its crinoline-circumference with scrolls and arabesques worked into the silk or cloth of which his dress is made. His breeches and stockings are unremarkable, but he wears elaborately laced boots; and has in addition a drapery which falls from him to the ground. It is difficult to know from the painting whether this is part of a curtain, or some further garment which he is wearing. It would appear from this portrait, as must have been the case, that there were theatrical tailors and embroiderers who worked only for the stage. Certainly one has never seen such clothes in any other painting of the time; not even in the astonishing portrait of the dissipated young rake in the huge feathered hat by Fra Galgario (in the Poldi-Pezzoli collection at Milan). Looking at this portrait of the *castrato* Carlo Scalzi, and knowing that he and his like sang in London† during the

---

* This portrait is in the Wadsworth Athenaeum, Hartford, Connecticut. Alfred Loewenberg in *Annals of Opera*, 1943, gives the opera as *Sirbace*, first produced at Naples in 1723, with music not by Porpora but by Francesco Feo. Metastasio adapted the libretto for Porpora whose version was given at Naples in 1725, and at the Teatro San Crisostomo in Venice in 1737. There is no mention of *Rosbale* as an opera.

† Angus Heriot *op. cit.* p. 179, points out that fifty years after Farinelli, Senesino and Egizziello had been the rage of London, another trio of *castrati*, Pacchierotti, Marchesi and Rubinelli, caused an equal furore in the 1780s. Two of these singers, it may be remarked, were still living as late as 1829, by which year, be it remarked, Byron, Keats and Shelley, all three were dead.

Farinelli fever, one can understand the fun made of them by Hogarth in Scene II of his *Rake's Progress.*†

With the arrival of Carlo Bibiena to carry out the interior of the old Opera House at Bayreuth in 1745 – its exterior is by the Frenchman Joseph St Pierre who, also, built the Eremitage outside the town – it is reasonable to assume that Italian carpenters and painters came with him. The setting up of a theatre interior of this sort with its carving and gilding, all of which is in front of the curtain, and then the most important part of all which is behind the scenes, cannot have been accomplished in three years by a solitary, probably non-German-speaking Italian, however talented and however much steeped in theatrical tradition. He must have had workmen with him who spoke his own language for this enterprise which was as specialised as the setting up of china-works or glass-factory. It is to be remarked that the theatre interior is in full blown Baroque and must have been old fashioned in its day. The beautiful and Rococo Residenz-Theater in Munich by Count Cuvilliés, the Court dwarf, dates from 1751–3 but could belong to a different generation from the old Opera House at Bayreuth. But so was Johann Sebastian Bach old fashioned in his time. The theatre at Bayreuth seems to be of his generation; and the Residenz-Theater which was begun only three years later in 1751 could belong to the age of Mozart who was not born until 1756. But the Italian theatre architect at Bayreuth was working in his family profession which at that time was nearly a century old from the death of his great-grandfather G. M. Galli da Bibiena in 1665.

10

Music-master to the Infanta Barbara: Domenico Scarlatti

It is at once inspiring and consoling when there comes the moment to look again and try to finish something long ago begun. I say 'try to finish' because nothing of the sort can be 'definitive', least of all a project attempted along these particular lines, and indeed the closer the detail attempted the more certain it is only to reveal its shortcomings and mistakes. But I wrote a little book *A Background for Domenico Scarlatti* which was published in 1935 for the two hundred and fiftieth anniversary of the composer's birth in 1685. That is already more than thirty years ago; and during this interval of time I have had all of his music available to me pretty constantly in my attention and do not think it will be taken amiss if I now set down what I believe I have learned from it and about it. His more than five hundred and fifty keyboard sonatas are an inexhaustible mine or treasury of mingled fact and poetry in proportions of, so to speak, a water or carat not often to be discovered in the works of any other human being.

The circumstances of Domenico Scarlatti's life and career were unique and unlikely enough in themselves. Unique, if only because of their extraordinary contradictions; so little being known about his life and character; whereas, so much is ascertainable, is, almost, visible even now, about the frame or setting of his private, and yet professional career. Into all this we will begin enquiring in a few moments. But, first of all, I had better set down my own qualifications for the task, such as they are, and detail the one or two advantages that have fallen to my lot. Above everything else I had the privilege of hearing that wonderful musician Mrs Violet Gordon Woodhouse on literally hundreds of occasions from the time I was nineteen years old. This was in the winter of 1916 in the middle of the first world war. It was an experience beyond parallel that continued until a year or two before her death after long illness in January 1948. I propose later in these pages to give a few details of her career lest these should go unrecorded. For it must be explained at this point that Violet Woodhouse was throughout her life an amateur and not a professional performer, and as an artist the more untired and unspoilt because of this. We may conclude that the unsurpassed beauties of her playing and its incomparable freedom and freshness of approach were due to her not having to endure the fatigues and frustrations of a touring virtuoso. Above all she was the ideal performer of Domenico Scarlatti, and this for a particular reason which was, as we will see later, because of her approach to his music, and her understanding of it, from a Spanish angle.

My other qualification in which, it will be noted, there are points of similarity enough to form a parallel, lies in being the owner of twenty-six long playing records containing no fewer than three hundred and twelve harpsichord sonatas by Scarlatti, played by that superb performer, Fernando Valenti. He was born in the USA but of origin from Spain, his family having come, I believe, from the island of Majorca. His instinctive attitude to the music is, therefore, that of a Spaniard so that in some of the sonatas performed by him I can hear the perpetuation, as it were, of Violet Woodhouse's playing. The advantage to a non-musician like myself of having such a corpus of this marvellous and ever improving music ready to hand and always available is something so incalculable that I find it difficult to put my gratitude into words. Of that dead performer of genius, for she was unquestionably nothing less than that, I have memories that I know will last me all my lifetime. The playing of the other, and living one is constantly, almost more often than not, beneath my hand. Of the interpretation of both of them I will be writing later in this chapter, and at some length. And now having set forth my ignorance and my deep love for his music I feel I can begin.

Domenico Scarlatti, sixth of ten children, was born at Naples on 26 October 1685. Johann Sebastian Bach and Handel were born, too, in that *annus mirabilis* of music. The father of Domenico was Alessandro Scarlatti, who was famous in most branches of the art but more especially for over a hundred pieces written for the stage. He was born in Palermo, and the grandfather of Domenico was born in Trapani, so they were Sicilian in origin. It is to be assumed that Domenico learned the rudiments of music from his father, but relatives on both sides of the family were professional musicians. He lived in a musical household frequented by opera singers, and what is more important than who taught him is what he taught himself. Naples was, then, the capital of the world's music and in particular of the art of singing. Dr Burney has this to say about it:

It was at Naples only that I expected to have my ears gratified with every musical luxury and refinement that Italy could afford . . . I came hither animated with the hope of pleasure. And what lover of music could be in the place which had produced the two Scarlattis, Leonardo Leo, Pergolese, Porpora, Farinelli, Jommelli, Piccinni, Traetta, Sacchini, and innumerable others of the first eminence . . . without the most sanguine expectations? . . . In the manner of their executing music there is, at Naples, an energy and fire not to be met with elsewhere, perhaps, in the whole universe: it is so ardent as to border upon fury, and from this impetuosity of genius, it is common for Neapolitan composers, in a movement which begins in a mild and sober manner, to set the orchestra in a blaze before it is finished. Like high bred horses, they are impatient of the reins, and eagerly accelerate their motion to the utmost of their speed, as Dr Johnson says that Shakespeare, in tragedy, is always studying for an occasion to be comic.

Thus, Dr Burney whom we have already accompanied in his inquisitiveness at Naples into the conservatories of the *castrati*. But could his analysis of the Neapolitan style in music be bettered as an account of many of the sonatas of Domenico Scarlatti? And for another view of the Neapolitan school, the late Edward J. Dent has this to say of Domenico's father:

The best pupil of Alessandro Scarlatti, we may safely say, is Mozart. Almost all those characteristics of style that we are accustomed loosely to consider as essentially Mozartian, were learned by Mozart from Italians of the preceding half-century. Indeed, Mozart to some extent repeated the work of Scarlatti, uniting in himself the massive strength of Leo, the sweetness of Durante and Pergolese, the swift energy of Vinci and the racy humour of Logroscino, together with that divine beauty of melody which belonged to [Alessandro] Scarlatti alone.★

These are forgotten names, of no import but to a few scholars. 'The massive strength of Leo, the swift energy of Vinci, the racy humour of Logroscino', these are perhaps recaptured a little if we listen to a further sentence of Dr Burney. 'Having the honour, this day, of dining at our Minister's, I was very much entertained in the afternoon by the performance of a fat friar of the order of St Dominic, who came there to sing *buffo* songs; he accompanied himself on the harpsichord in a great number of humorous scenes from the burletta operas of Piccinni and Paesiello, which he sang with comic force, little inferior to that of Casaccia, and with a much better voice.' It was a golden age of music that permeated the population and descended down to street level. The street singers and street musicians of Naples we may think we can distinguish in not a few of Domenico Scarlatti's sonatas when the echoes of those lost and forgotten composers have fallen on deaf ears. This is what Jean-Jacques Rousseau has to say in his *Dictionary of Music* at the word *Genius*: 'Va, cours, vôle à Naples' – 'Go, run, fly to Naples.' Both Paesiello and Piccinni, the defeated rival of Gluck at the Parisian opera, belonged to a later generation than Domenico Scarlatti, it is true, but the musical tradition, the golden age of music at Naples was of long duration, perhaps the final expression of its popular or *buffo* appeal as of the songs sung by the fat friar to Dr Burney being *La Danza*, which Rossini wrote for the great basso, Lablache, and which is said to reproduce his style in singing, a tarantella that must have sounded out all over Naples, sung to the tinkling mandoline, as

★ *Alessandro Scarlatti, his Life and Works*, by E. J. Dent, London, 1905.

The Castrati, and Others

Carlo Scalzi as Sirbace. The sheet of music is from the third act of the opera.

Caricatures from a sketchbook by Marco Ricci: (*top left*) Farinelli in an Oriental rôle; (*top right*) Farinelli in walking dress; (*bottom left*) Senesino and Faustina; (*bottom right*) Valentino Urbani in an Oriental rôle.

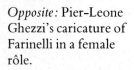

Opposite: Pier-Leone Ghezzi's caricature of Farinelli in a female rôle.

Farinello Napolitano
famoso autore d'opere de
canto nel teatro di S. Eliseo nell'Anno 1729.
fatto da me Ant. Maria li 2 Marzo 1729

Amigoni's portrait of Farinelli with the miniature fleet of Aranjuez in the background.

Frontispiece showing a scene
from Metastasio's *Demofoonte*.

Riot at the Haymarket Theatre
during the performance of an
opera.

Cornelis Troost, *Harlequin as Barber*.

Venetian glass figures of two actors playing *morra*; from the Rosenborg Castle at Copenhagen.

Drawing of an actor by Stefano della Bella.

BALLI DI SFESSANIA
di Jacomo Callot

Cap. Cerimonia.   Sig.r Lauinia

Cap. Spessa Monti.   BaGattino.

Cap. Esgangarato.   Cap.o Cocodrillo

Fracischina.   Gian Farina

Pasquariello Truonno.   Meo   Squaqua

Scenes from the *Balli di Sfessania* of
Jacques Callot.

Riciulina.   Metzetin

Pulliciniello.   Sig.ª Lucretia.

Cap. Mala Gamba.   Cap. Bellauita.

Cap. Babeo.   Cucuba.

Cap. Cardoni.   Maramao.

Taglia Cantoni.   Fracasso.

Above: Ceremonial carriage with paintings by Solimena.
Opposite: View from the royal box of the theatre at Caserta.
Below: Ceremonial barge constructed by the town of Naples for the arrival of
Carlos III of Spain. The painting on the canopy is by Francesco de Mura.

Above: Drawing by E. Q. Asam of a round chapel.
Opposite: Interior of the Fenice Theatre, Venice.

Left: Virtuoso staircase in a theatrical set designed by Filippo Juvarra for the theatre of Cardinal Ottoboni in Rome.
Left below: Opera house at Bayreuth by Carlo Galli da Bibiena: the proscenium.
Opposite: Ceremonial box of the Margrave and Margravine in the opera house at Bayreuth.

Above left: Portrait of Domenico Scarlatti, in the museum at Alpiarça, Portugal.
Above right: Infanta Barbara and her brother Dom Pedro, by G. D. Duprà.
Below: Group portrait by Amigoni, with Metastasio, Teresa Castellini, Farinelli, the painter, and an Austrian archduke.

did indeed *Funiculi-Funiculà*, another tarantella with for theme the funicular railway up Mount Vesuvius, belonging to Messrs Thomas Cook & Son, when I first remember Naples.*

The father, Alessandro Scarlatti, may have been *maestro de cappella*, to the Spanish Viceroy of Naples; the infant Domenico, 'Mimo' as he was to be nicknamed, may have been held at the font by the Principessa di Colabrano, the Viceroy's wife; but their family circumstances were not so grand as it all sounds; we may assume that Domenico was largely self-taught, and that it was suddenly noticed and realised in the family that he had talent. At Naples he remained until his father took him to Florence in 1702, when he was between sixteen and seventeen, hoping to get employment for him from Ferdinando de' Medici, eldest son of the Grand Duke (and brother of the dreadful Giangastone, last of the male line), a prince who divided his time between Pratolino where he had a private theatre and the Palazzo Pitti. Nothing came of this beyond a stay of some months in this 'art city', which would probably have had little effect upon someone of Domenico's temperament and interests – in so far as these are known to us, but in fact nothing is known and it is all assumption. Florence was in any event, its agreeableness and ease of living apart, a dead or moribund city at that time compared to Naples or Venice, or to Rome – and after these few months Domenico returned to Naples where he had been appointed organist in the royal chapel and had begun a half-hearted career as opera composer in the footsteps of his father.

The next move, and it must have been both pleasant and inspiring, was to Venice where his father sent him in 1705 at nineteen years of age in the care of the famous Nicolino (Nicola Grimaldi), the greatest *castrato* singer of his generation, who was later to cause a *furore* – that good old theatrical term and a physical experience to be so much envied by mere authors – in Handel's *Rinaldo*, where the unmusical Addison describes him as 'exposed to a tempest in robes of ermine, and sailing in an open boat upon a sea of pasteboard'. It was Nicolino, too, as may be remembered from a previous page, who in another opera had the fight with a lion, 'a poor biped in a lion's skin . . . breathing a love-tale in the pseudo-monster's ear, and at last fairly throttling him upon the stage', a scene which so amused George Hogarth.† But his successes in London lay in the future. Nicolino was the idol of Venice at the time he arrived there with the young Scarlatti. He had sung in many of Alessandro's operas and was much beholden to the father.

---

* In like vein, a last echo of the golden age of music in Vienna when, as I say, it had permeated the population and come down to street level, was the performance of *Fiaker-walzer*, Viennese cabmen's waltzes, sung to his own accompaniment by the late Victor Beigal, an Austrian singing-teacher long settled in London. It is a pity indeed that this was never recorded.

† cf. George Hogarth, *Memoirs of the Musical Drama*, London, 1838.

It needs not to be stressed that Venice was, then, the pleasure city of Europe. Having arrived there in the company of the great Nicolino, we may take it for certain that Domenico will have visited probably all four of the opera houses, and attended concerts at the celebrated Pietà where was the choir and orchestra of female orphans with the famous Gasparini as choir-master and Vivaldi, *il prete rosso*, as his coadjutor and assistant. Because the names of the musicians in question are better known to us it might seem that the musical life in Venice was of a higher order than at Naples, but this might well be wrong. It was Naples, not Venice that was the musical capital, but Venice must have been an experience always to be remembered. Nearly seventy years later Mozart, then at the impressionable age of fifteen, was in Venice with his father for the carnival of 1771; and we may think we hear the echoes of this experience in his music especially in *Il Seraglio* – where else could he have seen Turks and other Orientals wandering about the quays and narrow streets? – and the Venice of 1705 will not have been lost upon Domenico Scarlatti either, whether he was the silent introspective character we would think him to be, or, in contradiction, the hopeless gambler he is reputed to have turned into in his old age.

But also, in Venice he was to enjoy musical experiences of unforgettable kind for he met and made friends with Handel who, according to legend, he first encountered 'playing in his visor on a harpsichord' at a masquerade. They were to meet later in Rome and may have travelled from Venice to Rome in each other's company. Handel was barely inferior to Scarlatti as a performer on the harpsichord and he surpassed him in organ-playing; and so great was his admiration for Scarlatti that we are told the mere mention of his name, even in his very latest years, was sufficient to cause tears to come into his eyes. Scarlatti was no less susceptible to the name of Handel, for we are told by Mainwaring, Handel's first biographer,[*] that 'it was mentioned but lately . . . by two persons . . . who came from Madrid, that Scarlatti, as oft as he was admired for his great execution, would mention Handel, and cross himself in token of reverence.' And Mainwaring refers to him as 'Domenico Scarlatti, now living in Spain, and author of the celebrated lessons', when in fact he had died three years before, in 1757. But 'the two persons' were lucky indeed for at least they had heard him play.

The other friendship formed by Domenico Scarlatti in Venice was more curious for in the words of Ralph Kirkpatrick in his study of the composer, 'it is the only account we have of his playing during his entire life, beyond brief mention'. No account that is to say, after he was twenty years of age, for of course he never gave a concert, or played in public. This other friend was Thomas Roseingrave, the Irish musician of tragic destiny, who later was to become organist at St George's, Hanover Square. For the rest we have to

[*] John Mainwaring, *Memoirs of the Life of the Late George Frederic Handel*, London, 1760.

quote from Dr Burney:

Roseingrave having a few years after this fixed his affections on a lady of no dove-like constancy, was rejected by her at a time when he thought himself most secure of being united to her for ever. This disappointment was so severely felt by the unfortunate lover as to occasion a temporary and whimsical insanity. He used to say that the lady's cruelty had so literally and completely broke his heart, that he heard the strings of it crack at the time he received his sentence; and, on that account, ever after called the disorder of his intellect his *crepation*, from the Italian verb, *crepare*, to crack. After this misfortune, Roseingrave was never able to bear any kind of noise without great emotion. If, during his performance of the organ at church, anyone near him coughed, sneezed or blew his nose with great violence, he would instantly quit the instrument and run out of church, seemingly, in the greatest pain and terror.

In the end Roseingrave had to resign his post and retire to Dublin, where Archdeacon Cox tells us 'he was perfectly rational upon every subject but the one nearest his heart; whenever that was mentioned he was quite insane;' but still played superbly upon the harpsichord, especially extempore, and was well enough not only to write music himself but to edit, after Scarlatti's death, his friend's *42 Suites of Lessons*. Roseingrave was blamed in his lifetime for crude harmony and extravagant modulation, epithets sufficient in themselves to draw interest to him from a modern audience.★ And in fact I have in my possession a letter from Serge Diaghilev stating his intention of producing some of Roseingrave's music as a ballet, and enquiring from me who should be asked to orchestrate it. But the death of Diaghilev intervened.

We must revert to Roseingrave's, the only contemporary account of the twenty-year-old Scarlatti's playing, with recourse once more to Dr Burney:

Being arrived at Venice on his way to Rome, as he himself told me, he was invited as a stranger and a virtuoso, to an accademia at the house of a nobleman, where among others, he was requested to sit down to the harpsichord and favour the company with a toccata, as a specimen 'della sua virtù'. And, says he, finding myself rather better in courage and finger than usual, I exerted myself, my dear friend, and fancied by the applause I received, that my performance had made some impression on the company. After a cantata had been sung by a scholar of Gasparini who was there to accompany her, a grave young man dressed in black with a black wig, who had stood in one corner of the room, very quiet and attentive while Roseingrave played, being asked to sit down to the harpsichord, when he began to play, Rosy said he thought the ten hundred d – ls had been at the instrument; he had never heard such passages of execution and effect before. The performance so far surpassed his

★ Quoted from my little book of 1935. Now, all these years later, Roseingrave is beginning to be performed. It is curious that another great English admirer of Scarlatti, Charles Wesley, who seemed destined to be the musical genius the family were always attempting, should have met with a dreadful accident, falling into a hole in the street, which disaster affected his brain. He was organist at St Marylebone Old Church.

own, and every degree of perfection to which he thought he should ever arrive at, that, if he had been in sight of any instrument with which to have done the deed, he would have cut off his own fingers ... Roseingrave declared he did not touch an instrument himself, for a month.

It was Roseingrave, it should be said at this point, who started the enthusiasm for Scarlatti among English musicians and amateurs. His continuing friendship with the composer gave rise to the apocryphal story of Scarlatti's visit to London in 1720 when his opera *Narciso* was produced at the Haymarket Theatre and Roseingrave conducted. There is a story, too, of his visiting Roseingrave in Dublin twenty years later in 1740, which may have been given rise to by the edition of Scarlatti's harpsichord sonatas or *Essercizi* published under Roseingrave's editorship in London in 1739. Signs of this continuing cult in England for Scarlatti, although it is fairly certain he never came here, are the transcription of some of his pieces for string orchestra by Charles Avison and the continuing support and presence of such a figure as Dr John Worgan who also published an edition of his sonatas, and among whose pages, in the British Museum, three unpublished sonatas by Domenico Scarlatti were found as lately as 1938,[*] and who in Dr Burney's words:

was impressed as a youth with a reverence for Domenico Scarlatti, by old Roseingrave's account of his wonderful performance on the harpsichord, as well as by his lessons; and afterwards he became a great collector of his pieces, some of which he had been honoured with from Madrid by the author himself. He was the editor of twelve at one time, and six at another, that are admirable, though few have now perseverance sufficient enough to vanquish their peculiar difficulties of execution. He is still in possession of many more, which he has always looked upon as Sibyls' leaves.

From which quotation two things are deducible, that Dr Burney – 'I, who have been a collector of Scarlatti's compositions all my life', as he writes of himself in another context – envied Dr Worgan his possession of those pieces in the master's autograph, and that, as there is also further evidence to show, Scarlatti was not completely out of touch with musicians in the outside world during the twenty-eight years he lived virtually *in clausura*, in the strange circumstances shortly to be related, as music-master and *virtuoso da camera* to the Queen of Spain. We come back now to the 'grave young man, dressed in black with a black wig, standing in a corner of the room very quiet and attentive', and although only twenty years of age already a prodigious

---

[*] The present writer will never forget being rung up from the British Museum by their discoverer Mr Richard Newton, one summer morning in 1938, in a great state of excitement to say he had only a few minutes before found two unpublished sonatas by Domenico Scarlatti among Dr Worgan's manuscripts. And he telephoned again after luncheon to say he had discovered one more.

performer on the harpsichord. It would be pleasant to believe that from the wonderful experience of eighteenth-century Venice, its masquerades and its musicians, he travelled back to Rome in the company of Handel. According to Mainwaring, Handel's biographer, 'Handel used often to speak of this person with great satisfaction', and, *ante*, 'he followed him all over Italy, and was never so happy as when he was with him'. Yet, once they had parted in Rome, they never met or corresponded again.

The length of Domenico's stay in Venice is not known, but he lived in Rome from 1709 to 1719, for ten years that is to say, during which time he entered the service of the Dowager Queen Maria-Casimira of Poland,★ and was later choir-master of St Peter's. For Queen Maria-Casimira he had to compose operas for performance in her private theatre in the Palazzo Zuccari, and at St Peter's he had to play the organ and compose Masses and Salve Reginas; in quantity for both places, and it is clear that he had a competence but not an aptitude for either. Both employments must have bored him, though it is interesting to note that Filippo Juvarra designed the scenery for her private theatre, as, also, for that of Cardinal Ottoboni where the milieu must have been more interesting; where his musical contest with Handel took place, and where he must have met musicians like Arcangelo Corelli who had an apartment in the Cancelleria, Cardinal Ottoboni's palace; or like Pasquini the composer, and Scarlatti's only rival as executant, but in an earlier and old-fashioned style of playing.

Queen Maria-Casimira, often accused of setting herself up for posthumous rival as patroness of the arts to that other exile, of her own volition, Queen Cristina of Sweden, had another harmless and inept interest, typical of its day, in the Accademia degli Arcadi. Here, the Roman nobles masqueraded as classical shepherds and shepherdesses under fancy names – Queen Maria-Casimira for instance being called Amarisca Telea – meeting in their various palazzi, called 'huts' for the occasion, or in the 'pastures' which were their cypressed gardens, with an ineptitude only rivalled by the *tziganes* of Kalman's tuneful *Fürstin Maritza* or his *Czardasfürstin*. The secretary of the Arcadi was G.M.Crescimbeni whose lyrical minutes of their pastoral meetings ran to several volumes, and who had his town headquarters at an old house in the Corso. Alessandro Scarlatti, Domenico's father, was admitted member or rather shepherd in his Arcadia, under the name Terpandro. Domenico, never, though one of his operas was given a pastoral performance, and there is not

---

★ Born, Marie La Grange d'Arquien, married to Jan Sobieski, the hero of the war against the Turks, who was elected King of Poland in 1674. She was exiled to Rome by her son in 1699, returned to France in 1714, died there the next year; and was grandmother to Clementina Sobieski who married Charles Edward Stuart, the Young Pretender. Mr Ralph Kirkpatrick mentions Winckelmann, David, and Sir Joshua Reynolds as later inhabitants of the Palazzo Zuccari, which, also, as he remarks, served as setting for some episodes in D'Annunzio's *Il Piacere*.

even mention of him in Crescimbeni's reporting. But then something happened through the unlikely medium of the Arcadi which was to affect and alter all Domenico's career. It came about through the insistence of Dom João v, King of Portugal, on presenting the Arcadi with their Bosco Parnasio or Parnassus on the slopes of the Janiculum, where his portrait still hangs and the little open air theatre of the Arcadians can still be seen in its deserted garden. It was all part of the campaign of the insensately extravagant Dom João, rich from the new found gold and diamonds of Brazil, to extract certain privileges from the Pope and get the goodwill of the Roman nobles to this end. Successive embassies were sent to Rome, until in the end he got his way, and Benedict XIII made the Cardinal of Lisbon into a Patriarch and allowed him to officiate in vestments resembling those of the Pope, and his canons in imitation of those of the cardinals. Although not a priest, Dom João even received the Pope's permission to say Mass. Finally, in the last year of his reign, the title of 'Fidelissimus' or 'Most Faithful' was conferred upon Dom João to tally with those of 'Most Christian' and 'Most Catholic', attributed to the Kings of France and Spain. After this, Dom João died, perhaps satisfied. The other side to his character was his long liaison with the nun Paula Teresa da Silva, known as Madre Paula, of the convent of Odivelas in the outskirts of Lisbon. He had another mistress, a French nun; and by the pair of them he had three illegitimate sons, the 'Meninos de Palhava', meaning 'children of nothing at all', or 'worthless straw', whose palace in Lisbon, now the Spanish Embassy, is still reputedly haunted by them. One of them, Dom Gaspar, was Archbishop of Braga, while Dom José had been made Grand Inquisitor. The history of Dom João is full of curious contradictions.

The initial move in this new orientation of Domenico's life came with the departure of Queen Maria-Casimira to France when he was appointed *maestro di cappella* to the new Portuguese ambassador, the Marquês de Fontes, and in 1714 composed a piece to celebrate the birth of the Crown Prince of Portugal, the future Dom José I. Two years later came the fantastic mission to the Pope of this same Marquês de Fontes in the three huge gilded coaches that are still to be admired at Belém. They were built in Rome and had therefore only to make the journey from the Embassy to the Quirinal; but there was the return journey by land all the way round the shores of the Mediterranean at a not much greater pace than that of the two miles an hour of the otherwise invisible Japanese Court ladies in the bullock-carts from which they dangled their sleeves in only sign of human occupancy in *The Tale of Genji*. The journey back to Lisbon took several months. The three golden coaches have ivory fittings, curtains of gold brocade, and huge allegorical sculptures of Neptune and the sea-gods in evocation of Portugal's past supremacy over the distant seas. They were drawn by horses of *haute école* training, while uniforms of indescribable splendour were worn by the coachmen and the lacqueys who walked beside them.★

In the meantime Dom João was collecting singers and musicians for his new Patriarchate and for his own private chapel, among them Domenico Scarlatti who gave up being choirmaster at St Peter's in order to go to Lisbon in 1719. For the first few years of his stay in Lisbon he continued with the Masses, religious pieces and serenades of his Roman curriculum and there is little of interest to report. But Dom João, who like George IV has been much abused for his expenditure, was not only a great patron of the arts but there was musical talent of marked sort in his family. His grandfather Dom João IV was a composer of merit and collector of a musical library of vast size which perished in the earthquake of 1755. But, as well, Dom João V had married a daughter of the Habsburg Holy Roman Emperor Leopold I, who behind features almost in facsimile of those of Alfonso XIII, the last King of Spain, was a distinguished composer. It would seem not impossible that Dom João should have musical talent among his children, and this occurred in the person of the Infanta Barbara, his daughter, who was born in 1711. She must have early become his pupil at the harpsichord, and it is probable that he gradually relinquished his other work in order to give more time to her for it is clear that she was, herself, a most remarkable performer. When she was about fourteen years old she became betrothed to Fernando, Prince of Asturias, and heir to the throne of Spain, and their marriage took place four years later in the strangest, but grandest circumstances in January, 1729. It was to be a double wedding. Not only was the Infanta Barbara to marry the Prince of Asturias, but his sister the Infanta María-Victoria de Borbón was to marry Dom José, the future King of Portugal.

Dom João, at once father and father-in-law of the double wedding, spared no expense. The Portuguese and Spanish Royal families met at the frontier; the latter 'after a nine-day journey through deep snows' to Badajoz; and thence to the frontier, 'much fatigu'd with the bad weather, which had scarce ever ceas'd from the time they left'. Dom João had built a palace of fine stone to accommodate the Court for one night only especially for the wedding. The two families met at the frontier on the river Caya; the Portuguese on their side of the river arriving in a cavalcade of one hundred and eighty five coaches and six (more than eleven hundred horses), each with fifteen or twenty servants in the richest liveries, one hundred and fifty chaises, and six thousand soldiers. But the Spaniards much to their mortification

---

★ In the epoch of napalm, nitrogen bombs, and Polaris submarines it is pleasant to enumerate the other extravagancies of Dom João. They include the sacred vessels and vestments for the chapel in São Roque, all made in Rome, and unparalleled for richness; the palace-monastery of Mafra; the lacquered library at Coimbra; and the breakfast service in gold by François Thomas Germain, the greatest of French silversmiths, with many hundreds of other pieces by Godin and by Cousinet. Much else which is unrecorded must have perished in the earthquake of 1755.

were forbidden to wear gold braid upon their uniforms and were mostly in the traditional black of Spain.

The marriage contracts were signed by both parties in a pavilion built across the river Caya so that 'the two Kings might meet without ever going out of their own territories, entering just at the same instant, step by step', which must have been an excessively curious sight to see. Sir Benjamin Keene, the British Ambassador, describes the ceremony;[*] 'I had placed myself very conveniently yesterday to see the first meeting of the two families, and I could not but observe, that the princess' figure, notwithstanding a profusion of gold and diamonds, really shocked the prince. He looked as if he thought he had been imposed upon. Her large mouth, thick lips, high cheek bones and small eyes, afforded him no agreeable prospect; but she is well shaped and has a good mien.' Since both Courts took their musicians with them to the wedding it is probable that Scarlatti not only witnessed but took part in these proceedings. And then, or shortly after, he went in the suite of the Infanta Barbara, now Princess of Asturias, to Spain.

Eight or nine years of Scarlatti's life had been spent in Portugal. During this time he must have obtained permission to return to Italy on more than one occasion for he saw his father Alessandro in Naples before the death of the latter in 1725, and at forty-three years old he married a girl of sixteen in Rome in 1728. He was still in touch with Hasse, then studying in Naples, and with Pasquini, Corelli, Gasparini, and the musicians who lived and worked in Rome. In the next, or Spanish phase of his life he was to be far more isolated, and in the absence of other influences, exposed to those he had made or invented for himself. In Portugal these did not exist or were not perceptible so that his musical thoughts were those of his Neapolitan childhood and youth, or of adolescence and young manhood in Venice and in Rome. And from choirmaster and musical journalist in the sense of composer of Court circular character, he was settling down into music master, or *virtuoso da camera* to give it a more elegant name, to the Infanta Barbara and to her uncle, the Infante Dom António, the King's younger brother.

It would be idle to look for influences of native Portuguese music in the sonatas that Scarlatti may, or may not have written while he lived in Portugal.[†] For the native idiom hardly existed, if at all; and if in the next phase of his composing there are abundant traces of Spanish music and even of incipient *flamenco*, no one has yet claimed to find a *fado* either of the Lisbon or Coimbra kind in the five hundred and more sonatas of Domenico Scarlatti. Of more interest is his meeting with Carlos Seixas (1704–42), the composer of an apocryphal nine hundred toccatas, nearly all of which, if

[*] *The Private Correspondence of Sir Benjamin Keene*, Cambridge, 1933.

[†] Mr Ralph Kirkpatrick on the authority of Santiago Kastner, claims Sonata K238/L27 as a folksong from (Portuguese) Estremadura.

their total ever existed, are still unpublished. Seixas was born in Coimbra, where his father was organist, and at fourteen years old succeeded him; or according to other accounts became organist at Braga. The Archbishop of Braga was Primate of the Kingdom; and at sight of the twin organ-cases, the most elaborate of any in Portugal, and their golden riot of dolphins, tritons, mermen and satyrs, one is tempted to contravene historical probability and prefer it that Seixas should have been organist as a young boy at Braga. In any case whether from Braga or Coimbra he was soon transferred to the Sé Patriarcal at Lisbon; and it was at Lisbon that at the instance of the Infante Dom António he played to or had lessons from Scarlatti. The few pieces by Seixas that I have heard do not particularly suggest the influence of Scarlatti; far less so than the sonatas of the Spanish friar Antonio Soler who comes much later into the story. Is there no influence at all? Or did, perhaps, Seixas and Scarlatti have some influence on each other? There is hardly enough of personality in Seixas, or of what little by him is known to me, to form a decided opinion either way and the hearing of dozens, perhaps even scores of other toccatas by him would but confuse the issue. A strange, if more tangible relic of his near decade of years in Portugal, was the visit of the traveller Barretti to the palace-monastery of Mafra in 1760 – thirty years after Scarlatti had left Lisbon – when the bell-ringer performed 'the most difficult lessons of Scarlatti' on the carillon.★ But times have changed. When a friend of mine, now deceased, went to Mafra the bell-ringer, warned of this impending visit from an official of the British Museum, ascended to the carillon tower and welcomed him with a rendering of *The Merry Widow* waltz.

Within a few weeks of the wedding, that is to say early in 1729, Scarlatti must have arrived in Seville where the Court was to remain for the greater part of the next four years, and the Alcazar of Seville will have struck anyone nurtured on the buildings of seventeenth-century Rome with its Moorish undertones in *azulejo* panels and *artesonado* ceilings. The old Royal palace at Sintra which has Moorish-Manoelino touches is but a half-hearted Orient compared to the tiled courts and whitewashed alleys of Seville. It was here in Andalucía that he must have begun to listen to popular music, and where in his own pieces for his instrument he, in Dr Burney's words, 'imitated the melody of tunes sung by carriers, muleteers, and common

---

★ cf. *A Journey from London to Genoa, through England, Portugal, Spain and France* by Joseph Barretti, 1770. The clocks in the towers at Mafra are set in motion by immense cylinders covered with spikes, there being upwards of two hundred tons of metal in the pair of towers. The works of the clocks, chimes, and bells were ordered in Holland, but the manufacturers refused to supply them fearing that the Kingdom of Portugal could not bear the charge. João V wrote back with typical gesture saying that he had made a mistake in the order and that he wished twice that amount to be incurred, and with his letter he prepaid all expenses.

P

people'.* Scarlatti had, as music master, to accompany the Court on its progresses, and must certainly in this way have heard the guitar music of Cadiz, the ancient home of *cante hondo*, the songs and dances of Granada, and softer music of the Levante.

After four years in Seville the Court left for Madrid and the palaces near there. This was in 1733, and now a routine of life was established divided between the various palaces which was to continue for some quarter of a century until Scarlatti's old age. The routine, as established by Mr Ralph Kirkpatrick, was: January to mid-March, El Pardo; at Easter, the Buen Retiro in Madrid; April to June, Aranjuez; end of June, Buen Retiro; July to October, La Granja; end of October to early December, the Escorial; and Christmas at Buen Retiro.† To which these details may be added, that the Pardo is the old hunting lodge, some eight or nine miles from Madrid, now lived in by General Franco, and so much enlarged by Carlos III in 1760 and onwards that not much remains of it as known to the Infanta Barbara and her *virtuoso da camera*; that of the Buen Retiro, in Madrid itself, which was burnt down in 1734 with terrible destruction of paintings by Titian, and it has been said as many as two-thirds of all the paintings by Velázquez, there is no more than the huge fresco by Luca Giordano on the vaulted ceiling of the main hall, of the *Founding of the Order of the Golden Fleece*, an important fresco but degraded in its present setting; while Aranjuez with its gardens and La Granja with its fountains are too well known to call for description, the latter perhaps less so than the former so that it is not out of order to declare the fountains of La Granja superior both in beauty and in their mechanism to the fountains of Versailles. Scarlatti will have had his lodgings in the palace dependencies of La Granja and Aranjuez; in probably the Escorial itself; and he had, as well, his own house in Madrid.

Yet all this time there is hardly a mention of him, and not a single word of description from anyone who heard him playing. Indeed almost the only time even his name occurs is in a report to Paris by the French Ambassador in 1746, who writes 'the only Italians here that deserve attention are two musicians, one a harpsichord player named Scarlatti, the other a singer named Farinello. I believe I have already told you somewhere that the first was a favourite of the Prince of Asturias, and the second of the Princess. Since the change, the latter has gained the upper hand over his colleague.' The 'change' in question was the death of Philip V and the accession of Fernando and the Infanta Barbara to be King and Queen of Spain. By which time Sir Benjamin

---

* The carriers and muleteers were often in those days Maragatos, people of Berber origin living in the moorland villages around Astorga. It would be interesting to know if there are echoes in any of Scarlatti's sonatas of their songs. For further details of the Maragatos, when the noise of their castanets could be heard at the distant railway station, cf. my *Spain*, 1950, pp. 55, 79.

† Ralph Kirkpatrick, *Domenico Scarlatti*, Princeton, 1953, pp. 91, 92.

Keene, the British Ambassador, who had seen them married all those years ago in 1729, had changed his tune: 'From the bottom of my heart I do assure you, that we may apply to her whole deportment, what we used to say of her dancing in particular, that if she had been born a private person, she must have made her own fortune. Upon my word her qualities, great as they are, are her *own* and she is less beholden to *Royalty* than Princess ever was ... Nothing was ever so free, so ready at a distant hint, and so perfectly condescending as she is.' What is interesting here is the reference to her skill in dancing. She could have made her own fortune as a dancer, if she had been a private person. But not a word about her skill as a musical performer, and no mention whatever of her private teacher and musician.

The only word about Scarlatti in Spain comes in fact from outside, through the information gathered about him from all available sources by Dr Burney. By this time, too, at the age of fifty-three in 1738, he had published his *Essercizi per gravicembalo,* which appeared in London (and not as thought before in Venice); and he had been honoured by being made a Knight of the Portuguese Order of Santiago, a distinction which must have been requested for him by the Infanta Barbara from her father. It is perhaps typical that it should have been a Portuguese and not a Spanish honour. Isabella Farnese was still Queen of Spain, the Infanta Barbara was only Princess of Asturias and reluctant to ask a favour from her mother-in-law. Did she obtain the honour for him from her father the King of Portugal in view of the forthcoming publication of his *Essercizi*; or was it coincidental, which seems more likely in view of the reticence of Domenico Scarlatti and his apparent inability or unwillingness to draw attention to himself? He seems, still and always, 'the grave young man dressed in black, standing in a corner of the room very quiet and attentive', a picture of him which it is difficult to reconcile in our minds with the 'agreeable man in society, so much addicted to play, that he was frequently ruined, and as frequently relieved in his distress by his royal patroness' of Dr Burney; or who had, in the words of a biographer of Farinelli, 'miserably dissipated in gambling the fruits of his talent and the gifts of royal generosity', the informant in both instances being Farinelli himself, who must have known the truth about Scarlatti, and who even 'assured' Dr Burney that 'his widow and three daughters were left destitute at his decease'. But Scarlatti was only a member of the Royal household and the Queen's music-master. Farinelli was potential prime minister, and not long after Fernando's accession became Knight Commander of the Order of Calatrava which was one of the highest honours that could be conferred in Spain. The difference in their respective stations in life is very plain to see.

It is reasonable to think that a few at least of the *Essercizi* of 1738 will have been pieces dating from his youth, and perhaps from as far back as when he dazzled Roseingrave and made friends with Handel through the wonders of his playing. In 1708 or 1709, that is to say, in Venice, which was already thirty years ago. But, then, Chopin, Liszt, and other pianist composers were writing music characteristic of their talents while in their teens; and what poet collecting his works for publication has not included poems written by himself at an early age! We should expect therefore to find in them a large proportion of his 'Neapolitan' sonatas, pieces inspired by the clatter and hustle of a huge city, the tarantellas, the buffo or 'patter' songs of popular opera, together with graver memories of Pasquini, Corelli, and of the great musician who was his father. During the nine years of his life in Lisbon immediately prior to publication of his *Essercizi* he was exposed to no new musical influences, and the pieces written during that time, many of which will have figured in the *Essercizi*, are more likely to have been keyboard exercises or 'lessons' in the old meaning of that word, of inspiration, that is to say, merely from looking at or considering the keyboard; or as the writer or poet will sit down at his desk and from long practice turn something to account; or, in the toils of the other profession, write in order to bring out some particular point in fingering and in execution. And now and again, as with the poet – for even poetry is something one can train oneself to write – there will come something of apparent difficulty which resolves itself in high spirits and retains in itself something of the exhilaration with which it shaped itself and was set down on paper.

It is permissible to think that the few melancholy pieces among the *Essercizi* may have been written in Portugal where Scarlatti found himself in a sea-city which was like Naples, but which was not Naples, and that lacked most if not all of the inspirations and amenities of the siren bay. He must probably, that is to say, have been bored in Lisbon, where he may have felt forgotten and that his time was wasted. It cannot have been interesting enough to let him forget Italy and the lures of Rome and Venice. Court ceremonies and the golden coaches of Belém up and down the cobbled hills of Lisbon were not enough to fill the emptiness of nine years. Lisbon was provincial, but Spain beginning with Seville was an old and curious civilisation of its own with elements he could make much of and which meant something to him.

It was before the present Royal Palace in Madrid was built, and after the death of Philip V, that his widow Isabella Farnese took up her residence at La Granja with its fountains; building, as well, another palace at Rio Frio near Segovia, and, it was her intention, not only a palace, but a monastery of Discalced Franciscans with their church, barracks for the bodyguard and the Walloon Guards and a troop of infantry, a theatre, an orchard, gardens of different kinds, and a large park with groves of trees.* Such was the state

* *The Royal Palaces of La Granja de San Ildefonso and Rio Frio*, by Marqués de Lozoya, Madrid, 1964.

kept by a Dowager Queen of Spain; and such the long corridors and the ante-rooms, we may be sure, of eternal waiting for this greatest of virtuosi and supreme composer for his instrument, who for the little mention made of him could have been the man who came round the palaces weekly, to wind up the clocks. Apart from his home in Madrid, his having married again meanwhile, and his attendance at El Pardo and the Buen Retiro, Scarlatti's spells of duty took him to Aranjuez and to the Escorial. He was once more in a surrounding of music, but it was now the Court opera and the Italian singers organised for the new King and Queen by Farinelli: operas more often than not with libretti by Metastasio and music by Hasse, Jommelli, and lesser Italians. The theatre was the Coliseo at Buen Retiro, with the great saloon or El Casón painted, as we have seen, by Luca Giordano with, to give it greater detail:

in the principal apartment of the roof Hercules giving the Golden Fleece to Philip the Good, Duke of Burgundy; Pallas and the Gods subduing the Titans, answering to which the Majesty of Spain appears ruling the terrestrial globe, in a subordinate compartment of the ceiling; an antechamber containing the Conquest of Granada; and from the great saloon we go to the garden by a little oval cabinet, covered entirely with looking glass, in the ceiling of which is represented the Birth of the Sun, with people of all nations worshipping the rising deity, whilst the priests are engaged in offering sacrifices. This, likewise, is by Giordano.★

But, of it all, only the painted ceiling of the great hall is left. Scarlatti must also have taken part in the extraordinary removals and returns of the Court to and from the Escorial which with their military escorts, gilded coaches, and long lines of sumpter mules may often have been in snowbound parody of a trans-Saharan caravan.

Aranjuez was the spring and summer resort where we may be sure that the asparagus and wild strawberries for which it is still famous were not neglected. Here, also, there was a theatre where operas were performed. The Tagus which runs through the gardens was provided at the instance of Farinelli with a miniature fleet and there were serenades and displays of fireworks.† It would be idle to suppose that nothing of this superficial splendour had effect upon Scarlatti or influenced him in the music that he wrote. It seems, rather, to have inspired a particular kind of melancholy in him, in which you may think you sense all the splendours of the world passing before him, and his tiring of them and rejecting them. But, as well, and of direct Royal palace application as it were, are the handful of 'military'

★ *A Journey through Spain in the years 1786 and 1787*, by Joseph Townsend, London, 1791.

† Ralph Kirkpatrick, *op. cit.*, p. 113 and footnote, gives details of a volume in the library of the Royal Palace at Madrid which describes the operas given at Buen Retiro and the 'diversions of the flotilla at Aranjuez, decorated with watercolours illustrating the flotilla in detail.' Farinelli had three copies made; one for the King, one for the director of the opera, and another for himself which he took with him to Bologna. It would be pleasant to see these published.

sonatas which can only have been inspired by the Walloon Guard or other martial body beating the tattoo directly below the window in the forecourt, or more distantly on their own parade ground. The Trooping of the Colour in front of the Horseguards at Whitehall on the Queen's birthday is about the only living relic from the military ceremonial of every Royal Court in Europe from Potsdam to St Petersburg and from Copenhagen to Madrid. And it is to be noted that the music in question would be a matter of trumpets and drum-taps. There were few military marches for military bands and that is exactly the effect of this particular group of sonatas by Scarlatti.

It must have been during the Royal sojourns at the Escorial – 'end of October to early December', or, with greater concision, during the winter months of November – and towards the latter years of his own life, that Scarlatti came into contact with Padre Antonio Soler, who was organist there. Soler was of Catalan origin, born near Gerona in 1729, and therefore in his early twenties when he became a monk of the Escorial in 1752. It is sad that none of Scarlatti's English admirers went to Spain to see him, for Lord Fitzwilliam visited Padre Soler at the Escorial in 1772*, and brought back with him twenty-seven of Soler's harpsichord sonatas. Soler must certainly have been well acquainted with some of Scarlatti's pieces and may have had lessons, or at the least, conversations with him. Among the seventy sonatas for the instrument by Padre Soler there are some that are very close indeed to Scarlatti particularly the two or three of them that in part reproduce the rhythm of the *zapateado*. They are very like to Domenico Scarlatti, and yet just in their divergences there is a world of difference. Soler has not the quick wit and dazzling change of subject of Scarlatti. He has not the fire and the experience of the world of Scarlatti who had been born and bred in the fulcrum of Italian music, and known the greatest singers of the day.

The only account, and then not in a direct way, of the old age of Scarlatti comes again through the medium of the indefatigable questioner, Dr Burney. When in Vienna in 1774, he called on Dr L'Augier, one of the principal physicians to the Imperial Court, and an ardent amateur of music. It was Dr L'Augier who informed Dr Burney of the extent to which Scarlatti had been influenced in Spain by the music of the people:

M. L'Augier [Dr Burney writes] in despight of uncommon corpulency, possesses a most active and cultivated mind. His house is the rendezvous of the first people of Vienna, both for rank and genius; and his conversation is as entertaining, as his knowledge is extensive and profound. Among his other acquirements he has arrived at great skill in music, has a most refined and distinguishing taste, and has heard *national* melody in all parts of the world with philosophical ease.

* Padre Soler died at the Escorial in 1783. The Spanish *Marcha Real*, which was performed of old in the court of the Royal Palace at Madrid, is said to have been sent by Frederick the Great with advice that it was to be performed on silver flutes. This inspiring tune was given an orchestral setting by Balakirev in his *Overture on two Spanish themes*.

He has been in France, Spain, Portugal, Italy, and Constantinople, and is, in short, a living history of modern music. In Spain he was intimately acquainted with Domenico Scarlatti, who, at seventy-three, composed for him a great number of harpsichord lessons which he now possesses, and of which he favoured me with copies. The book in which they are transcribed, contains forty-two pieces, among which are several slow movements, and of all these, I, who have been a collector of Scarlatti's compositions all my life, have never seen more than three or four. They were composed in 1756, when Scarlatti was too fat to cross his hands as he used to do, so that these are not so difficult as his more juvenile works, which were made for his scholar and patroness, the late Queen of Spain, when Princess of Asturias.

M. L'Augier, the Infanta Barbara herself, and perhaps Scarlatti, all three were immensely fat, though the latter certainly shows no signs of it in his lately discovered portrait, shortly to be described. But did Scarlatti live to be seventy-three years old? Nor can it be considered likely that he should have composed all forty-two of these pieces especially for M. L'Augier. And there is little or nothing further to add to this, except that in a letter written in 1752 to the Duke of Alba, the composer describes himself as ill and unable to go out of his house; that he died in Madrid five years after this in 1757, and the Infanta Barbara his patroness a year later in 1758, leaving her harpsichord and all her manuscript sonatas to Farinelli, then living in retirement at Bologna.

It would be through this will of the Infanta Barbara, in which she bequeathed two thousand doubloons and a diamond ring to Scarlatti who, we have seen, had predeceased her, that the two sets of Scarlatti's manuscript sonatas found their way to Italy. One of these sets, in fifteen volumes decorated in coloured inks, and in one of its volumes with titles and other marks illuminated with gold, all bound in red morocco stamped with the arms of Spain and Portugal, is in the Biblioteca Marciana in Venice. Another set of fifteen volumes, less luxuriously written out and bound, is at Parma.★ These are the major sources for the Scarlatti sonatas. Another set with more than three hundred of them once belonged to Brahms. But not one autograph sonata of Scarlatti has been found. The huge edition of Scarlatti's keyboard works amounting to five hundred and forty-five of the sonatas, edited by Alessandro Longo, appeared in 1906; and since then, with some rejected and others found, the total has gone up all told to five hundred and fifty-five. But Longo attempted no chronological order, separated sonatas which had obviously some connection together, and committed other errors which prompted the new numbering of the sonatas based on close examination of the manuscripts and a common sense view of historical and musical probability. In the course of this Mr Ralph Kirkpatrick has established that no fewer than three hundred and eighty-eight are arranged in pairs, and at least

★ Ralph Kirkpatrick, *op. cit.*, pp. 137, 138.

twelve more of them were arranged to form tryptychs in groups of three. Of this I have taken notice wherever it has been possible, but granted my own limitations it has not made any easier the task I have tried to set out to do. My only excuse is that in the little book published in 1935 I think I was the first person to attempt the arranging of this wonderful music into groups that may have been inspired by particular moods and subjects. Even Mr Ralph Kirkpatrick in the Preface to his great work on Domenico Scarlatti, published in 1959, describes himself as 'inspired in part by Sitwell's little book', and started upon his ten year task in 1943. Another authority, Miss Kathleen Dale, in her article in *Music and Letters* for April, 1941 attempted to divide the sonatas into ten categories of style, Street Scenes, 'Perpetuos', Adagios, etc: but although she includes a section 'Dances' among them, has most curiously omitted to notice the peculiarly Spanish idiom that is the fascination in so many of them.

Having said which, and paid tribute once more to that one of the two musicians to whom I owe all and any access to this most wonderful music, I must fulfil my promise to set down a few details of her life and career. Violet Gordon Woodhouse was born on St George's Day, 23 April 1871, and came of the Sussex family of Gwynne of Folkingham. Neither of her parents was musical. But she was taught music from her earliest years, and when in London was taken regularly to concerts and to the opera. She showed early talent as a pianist, but as early her career took a different turn when Arnold Dolmetsch, later to become famous for his re-creation of old musical instruments, persuaded her to drop the piano and play the harpsichord. She was, thus, one of the first of English musicians or, for that matter, of musicians in any country, to revive the playing of music on the instrument for which it was originally written. There was for a long time a prejudice against this, particularly on the part of those whose musical training had been in Germany. It must be mentioned again at this point that Violet Woodhouse was throughout her life an amateur and not a professional musician. She would give up playing for many weeks at a time, and resume it again though there were days when, in her own words, the notes sounded like 'a packet of needles'. But so do 'words, words' sound in the ears of an author. What, then, was her stature as a player? It is one of those mysteries into which strength and power of personality enter as much as with an actor. She was decidedly as good, and often better in some directions, than Wanda Landowska who was her only rival; and to compare musical sensations that are of their nature and degree incomparable, Ferruccio Busoni, all of whose London recitals I attended in 1920–2, in his very different way, in Beethoven and in Liszt, was the only musician I have heard to produce musical sensations of the same order. But the one was for the concert hall, the other for 'room music' and had the magic that could hold an audience of a handful of persons spellbound for an hour or more not wishing to move or stir.

This was more particularly in her later years when she preferred to play the clavichord, having in fact in the decade between 1920 and 1930 persuaded Dolmetsch to create the small clavichord for her that is the only type now made.★ And about this time, or a little later, Thomas Goff had begun to make his incomparable instruments in both dimensions, big and small, which happy occurrence gave a new zest and interest to her playing. It was only natural that, dating from her first conversion from the piano to the harpsichord, she should have played English folk tunes, then being collected by Cecil Sharp and others, together with the pavanes and galliards of Byrd, John Bull, Orlando Gibbons, and their contemporaries, music reheard again after being virtually dead and extinct for some three hundred years. But the obvious composer for her to play with her revived instrument in mind was Johann Sebastian Bach, of whom she was an incomparable performer though not of the sort who would play his *Goldberg Variations* all through at a sitting, but a prelude and fugue or two, then perhaps an English or a French suite of Bach, and then a Mozart sonata. But I am here to speak of her playing of Domenico Scarlatti and must ignore, alas! and omit the rest! It has to be said that both in Scarlatti, in J.S. Bach, and indeed in all her playing there was another and a different accent or intonation from the ordinary, in the sense that her approach to this music was not Teutonic, or even French, but came from Spain.

This was largely because of the influence upon her of Rubio,† her Spanish music master, and of his friend Fernández Arbos, long resident in London, the pair of them having been friends and companions of Albéniz when they were music students in Berlin. The three of them were so poor that at one time they had only one pair of trousers between them which was respectable enough to go out in. Violet Woodhouse, it should be said in parenthesis, played pieces by Albéniz to perfection. Fernández Arbos, who taught music for many years at the Royal College of Music and lived in London from 1894 to 1916, also influenced her and wrote a Spanish piece, a *Seguiriya Gitana*, which he and Rubio performed with her. She had met Sarasate, the great Spanish violinist who was supreme in the classics but played his Spanish

★ Mabel Dolmetsch in part 8 of her *Personal Recollections of Arnold Dolmetsch*, published in No. 14 of *The Consort*, for July 1957, p. 15, says: 'It was at Violet Gordon Woodhouse's suggestion that he produced in 1913 the smaller model of clavichord, having a compass of four octaves, in place of the large five octave instruments which had prevailed hitherto.' For a few details in the next page or two I am indebted to my brother's *Noble Essences*, 1950, pp. 245, 246 and 259.

† The cellist Agustín Rubio was born at Elche, in Southern Spain, in 1856. Before coming to England he had toured the continent with Adelina Patti, and had played in many European capitals. He died in London in April 1940 having, as my brother remarked, survived long enough at any rate to see the end of the Spanish Civil War, cf. *Left Hand Right Hand*, 1945, pp. 197, 199.

dances as encore pieces, being taken to meet him in Arbos's rooms in Savile Row in 1893 or 1894 by his only English pupil, Nettie Carpenter. Sarasate, who must have had much of the personal charm and magnetism of Paderewski, used to tell Violet Woodhouse that she should have been his daughter. Arbos and Casals were frequent visitors to her house before the 1914 War, as later was Segovia. I remember as typical of the advice given her by Rubio, that she told me he had said to her when playing the *adagio* of a sonata by Mozart, always to remember that it was the music of a young man who had been in love with opera singers. And she, herself, told me that in her interpretation she had always in mind the singing of de Reszke whom she heard when a young woman, and who was the finest artist she had ever heard; in curious footnote to which it could be recalled that the great pianist Anton Rubinstein said that the supreme influence upon his playing had been the singing of Rubini; that he tried to play, in short, in the way the great tenor sang.

Such in but a few lines was this great amateur musician and player upon harpsichord and clavichord, Violet Woodhouse whom I was able to hear during all the years 1916–46 in the houses where she lived in London at different times, and at Nether Lypiatt in Gloucestershire. I should add that there were always a number of sonatas by Scarlatti in her repertoire, but latterly I think I kindled her enthusiasm for him, and in the last year of the war I was able to obtain for her the complete Longo edition of his sonatas from the widow of my old and dear friend, the pianist Frederick Dawson. Within a few weeks she spoke to me on the telephone to say she had learnt eighteen of the sonatas which she had never played before. I was, also, able to obtain for her with difficulty, during that last year of the war, some pieces by Carlos Seixas. I think she never came across the music of Padre Soler whom she would have found more interesting still. At this time in her seventy-fifth year, perhaps her strength was failing, and she played wholly upon the clavichord, or, rather, on one or other of her clavichords; this being in her own words, 'the most beautiful solo instrument ever invented, and the study of a lifetime'. I think that all who heard her play preludes and fugues by Bach or sonatas by Scarlatti, on the clavichord, would agree with her.

My long experience of hearing this music is my one qualification for this task; and I have another advantage in the possession of the twenty-six long playing records containing three hundred and twelve sonatas of Scarlatti played by Fernando Valenti.* What I have attempted to do is to arrange such of the sonatas that I know by ear into the groups to which they seem to

---

* They are Westminster records, announced as a 'complete recording' but when resumed after long interval for one more record, the twenty-sixth of the series, the scheme appears to have lapsed again. Only another sixteen records would be needed to complete it with the five hundred sonatas, which is all that need to be recorded.

belong, without arrogating to myself any pretence to secret knowledge as to their subject or meaning. In addition to those sonatas played by Valenti I know of course a good many more, say, three hundred and thirty in all, out of the five hundred and fifty odd that form the total. But of these some twenty or thirty were really organ or violin sonatas, so that the real sum would be not far above five hundred sonatas; of which I may claim some hearing, if not knowledge, of three hundred and thirty or so, which makes for more than three-fifths of the grand total. There is the superb edition of sixty of Scarlatti's sonatas recorded by Ralph Kirkpatrick himself; and it is only alas! that there are but sixty of them, in place of three hundred and more, that opens the wider field and gives more facility for the ear to play upon with the recordings by Valenti.

I will now go ahead with the attempted classification of the sonatas, only dallying for a moment with what are in effect a pair of footnotes, but owing to their contingency they deserve a longer hearing. The first is in connection with the painter Jacopo Amigoni who was much in contact with both Farinelli and Domenico Scarlatti; and the second is with the lately found and little known portrait of Scarlatti which is of the very greatest interest. Jacopo Amigoni (1675–1752) was born in Venice, worked for some years for the Elector of Bavaria, notably at Schleissheim, and came to London in 1730 where he stayed, on and off, till 1739. Here he painted frescoes and portraits, and the altarpiece at Emmanuel College, Cambridge, is from his hand. It will be noted that Farinelli was in London during the four years 1734–7. Amigoni returned to Venice in 1739, and in 1747 went as Court painter to Madrid. The allegorical frontispiece – and allegorical it certainly is! – to Scarlatti's *Essercizi* of 1738 is by Amigoni, with low flying cupids holding the stemmas of Portugal and Spain over an altar; above which an angel, or perhaps a virtue, holds an open book of music and displays it to a female who touches a manuscript sheaf of music with her right hand. In the year of his arrival at Madrid Amigoni was painting scenery for the operas Farinelli produced in the Coliseo of the Buen Retiro (see p. 271); but, besides, he painted at least three portraits of Farinelli. One, is of the *castrato* seated being crowned by his Muse, a roll of music in her other hand, with a wreath or indeed a *lei* of roses already round his waist and shoulder, while four cupids frolic in the foreground, one of them reading aloud to the other in infant precocity, and a trumpeting female with trumpet or horn in either hand reclining on a cloud just behind his head. The other portrait, present whereabouts unknown, is in effect a beautiful portrait of the *castrato*, dressed most elegantly, with white wig, and wearing all his Orders, playing with a pug-dog which has cropped ears; and it is this portrait which has the miniature or toy-flotilla of Aranjuez in the background.

The third, and most interesting of Amigoni's portraits is in the National

Gallery at Melbourne, and shows the *castrato* seated, with his friend Metastasio and the singer Castellini.* The history and origin of this painting are unknown; but it must be presumed to have been taken back to Bologna by Farinelli when he returned from Spain, and to have hung in his villa where Dr Burney saw him surrounded by three harpsichords he had brought from Spain, by portraits of the Royal Family, and the paintings made by Amigoni for his opera productions. There is, also, what has been assumed to be a portrait of Scarlatti, though his figure is so much in the background as to be almost unrecognisable, in a huge group of the Spanish Royal Family by Amigoni, now known only from the engraving, for the oil-painting has been lost or has disappeared. There is the usual allegorical winged figure overhead and in fact indoors near the ceiling, and King Fernando VI and Queen Barbara are standing in full Court dress with an ermine robe arranged near them. There are numerous other figures, a sentry musket on shoulder, and in the other corner of the painting three or four ladies in waiting or maids-of-honour, and above those a balcony with musicians among whom Farinelli is recognisable, and a figure holding a sheet of music who, it is thought, may be Domenico Scarlatti. But in effect it is hardly a portrait and little more than a musician with a roll of music in his hand. But it could be Scarlatti, even if it tells us next to nothing about him; and this must have been Amigoni's most ambitious portrait group, if it lacks the interest of his big painting of Farinelli with Metastasio and Faustina Bordoni, and has none of the charm of Farinelli with the pleasure flotilla of Aranjuez in the background. Amigoni was, at the least, luckier in Spain than other painters. He came away with a fortune; while G. B. Tiepolo fell from favour largely at the instance of Raphael Mengs who derided him as old-fashioned. Tiepolo must have died, disillusioned and sad, after his glorious career in so many parts of Europe, while even Mengs 'called to Madrid by Charles III and magnificently rewarded', suffered too; and in the eloquent phrases of Fuseli's notes to the Rev. M. Pilkington's *Dictionary of Painters*, 1810, 'Excess of application, and some disgusts, which too often are excited by envy of distinguished merit, threw him into a state of marasmus', and he returned to Rome.

The long lost portrait of Domenico Scarlatti is another matter altogether. It had belonged to Scarlatti's descendants whom Mr Ralph Kirkpatrick visited in Madrid, and was sold by them long before that, in 1912, through a dealer who, they thought, had sent it to London. Thereafter, all trace of it was lost. But it had been bought from the Madrid dealer by Senhor José Relvas, former Portuguese Ambassador to Madrid, and taken by him to Portugal. Senhor Relvas, who died in 1929, had placed it in the Casa dos Patudos, his collection of works of art which he left to his native village of

---

* This figure was thought, mistakenly, by Dr Burney to represent Faustina Bordoni, wife of the opera composer Johann Adolf Hasse.

Alpiarça near Santarém, and there it was found a few years ago by the Portuguese art historian, Professor Reynaldo dos Santos. The portrait is uniquely interesting. The mid-Victorian lithograph of Domenico Scarlatti which is universally reproduced is of unknown origin, and may well be entirely fanciful. But this portrait is of the importance of Delacroix's head of Chopin, only much more detailed; and it is a work of art where the recently discovered daguerreotype of Chopin, pitiful as to his state of illness in the last years of his life, is but a photograph. In the portrait the composer holds a letter in his left hand, addressed 'Al Signor D. Dom Scarlatti', and his right hand rests upon a harpsichord. His coat is described as 'grey-brown with cuffs of gold with green embroidery', and on a red ribbon he wears the Order of Santiago, set in diamonds, so that the portrait was painted after he was given the Order in 1738, and about the time, therefore, when his *Essercizi* was published. He would, then, be fifty-three years old which is how he appears in the portrait.

Appendix:
Notes on three hundred and more Sonatas by Domenico Scarlatti

My attempted arrangement of Domenico Scarlatti's keyboard sonatas according to mood and subject begins with those sonatas played by Mrs Violet Woodhouse which make their appearance again in the albums recorded by Valenti. Although the complete Longo edition was only in her possession for some eighteen months before her last illness prevented her from playing, some kind of natural instinct directed her towards those pieces that were particularly suited to her. One early summer evening at 11, Mount Street in 1946 she played to me for some two hours on end, and I lost count at somewhere between twenty-five and thirty sonatas by Scarlatti. It is safe to assume there were perhaps three dozen sonatas by Scarlatti in her repertoire towards the last year or two of her life. But among those pieces that I note down as characteristic of her style of playing I do not include that most brilliant of his pyrotechnic sonatas Kirkpatrick 113 Longo 345 – the well-known sonata with the handcrossing – because it is not directly evocative of her personality in performance. To be included, rather, in his pieces of inspiration from the Siren city and the towns around the Bay of Naples, she gave a brilliant rendering of its returning and cumulative attacks and advances but it is a virtuoso piece of ubiquitous and irresistible appeal, and so I do not include it in her personal and particular category of performance.

This particular group of sonatas set down and established, we move on to that section of them which seems to me to be of Italian inspiration, and Southern Italian, at that, as of Naples as a cosmopolis, or indeed the old kingdom of the Two Sicilies. Accurate and invaluable as may be Ralph Kirkpatrick's new numbering of the sonatas upon broad lines and on general principles of commonsense it must be obvious that it cannot be individually correct as to the numbering of every sonata, whether singly or in pairs. There must be for instance sonatas that he wrote in Portugal reminding himself of Italy; none of which categories of time or place take account of course of those pieces which are in the true sense 'lessons' or 'exercises' and inspired by the keyboard, the run of notes, or in order to exhibit or put to practice certain effects or tests of playing. Those, also, it seems to me, are in a class to themselves; and among them the famous 'handcrossing' sonata (K113/L345) just mentioned, though, too, it is a virtuoso piece for only top-rate performers.

A third and fourth group, modest in number of its components, is of tarantellas and Siciliennes the cerebral origin of which is not to be disputed; there is a further section of sonatas inspired by bell-sounds, the ancestors if in varying·mood of Paganini's *La Campanella*; there is another group mostly of dances, not particularly either Spanish or Italian in feeling; a section of 'military' sonatas, one or two of them of a dazzling brilliance, others perhaps a little obsessed by processional, even funereal muffled drums and funeral paraphernalia; a collection of the typical, 'high speed' sonatas of Scarlatti irresistible for their high spirits and which are in popular opinion the basic or prototype Scarlatti; yet another section of his *adagios*, among the most beautiful of all his works, some of them doubtless inspired by the wonderful singers he had so unique an opportunity and experience of hearing; a section of pastoral or bucolic pieces of quiet and peaceful intent; a most exhilarating, and at the same time romantic group of sonatas inspired by the sounds and sights and thoughts of hunting, something not encountered again in music until the *Wilde Jagd* of Liszt and the Romantics, to end indeed with *La Chasse Royale* of *Les Troyens*, even down to César Franck's *Le Chasseur Maudit*. And to end with, the group of his sonatas that seem to be, and many of them are indubitably, of Spanish origin, though it would be the greatest mistake to treat of them all as Spanish dances. True there are *jotas Aragonesas* and *zapateados* among them, not forgetting a Portuguese fandango and 'a typical song or dance tune (*balada*) from Portuguese Estremadura', but in fact there are Spanish pieces in a whole gamut of different moods and feelings from deepest melancholy and introspection to wild gaiety. A large number of them are directly inspired by the Spanish idiom in music which was then just beginning to form itself. It was in these that 'he imitated the melody of tunes sung by carriers, muleteers, and common people', and that we hear, as against the mandolines of the Bay of Naples, the guitars and handclappings, the castanets and finger-snappings of incipient *flamenco*. But, also, if it be not too fanciful to suggest it, the singing of the *castrati*, of the artificial nightingales if they may be called that, of the Buen Retiro and of Aranjuez. At the hands of this great musician the popular Spanish music was given a form and a perfection of shape that it has never had since, while there are pieces as poetically beautiful as Debussy's orchestral evocation in *Ibéria* of a land he had never seen with his own eyes. By my own count among the three hundred and thirty sonatas known to me there are some hundred of Spanish feeling and inspiration, and of course there are others. There is no such other body of Spanish music anywhere in existence; and in conclusion one could only wish that the Infanta Barbara his patron, become Queen of Spain, had loaned him for three years or so to Prince Esterházy. Then we could have had pieces written by him in Hungarian, even in Slovakian rhythm; he would have heard the Tsigane cymbalom, and it would have been one more of the supreme fascinations in all music.

1 *Sonatas by Domenico Scarlatti played by Mrs Violet Woodhouse, and listed here as typical of her musical personality*

Kirkpatrick	27	46	53	54	84	141	201	263	285	328
Longo	449	25	261	241	10	422	129	321	91	Suppl. 27

Kirkpatrick	341	387	400	451	492	524	531
Longo	140	175	213	243	14	283	430

It would not be wrong to consider these seventeen sonatas to be among the most beautiful of all those by Scarlatti, and I have suggested that the taste and instinct of the great musician with whom I associate them in my mind led her unerringly to them. She was a person of instinct and not a scholar. Four at least of them, K27/L449, K141/L422, K328/Longo Supplement 27, and K531/L430 are the complete epitome of her playing. We take the most beautiful of them in order, according to Mr Kirkpatrick's new numbering, that is to say:

K27/L449	A reflective piece, as of someone standing aside to watch the splendours of the world go past him, which may indeed have been his mood when writing it, with run or descent back into reality at each close.
K53/L261	Not actually in Mrs Woodhouse's repertory, but so completely in tune with her temperament and style of performance that I list it here as though she played it.
K84/L10	Virtuoso start, with sighing aftermath of great beauty.
K141/L422	Begins with a reiterated, woodpecker hammering, a quintuple touching of the note, exactly, though with other intent, as in the second or quick section of Liszt's *Sixth Rhapsody*, but here it is no Gypsy cymbalom; breaking after that into wonderful depth of sentiment and feeling, then the 'dotted line' and back to the virtuoso beginning. This sonata of mandoline inspiration.
K328/Longo Supplement 27	Exquisitely moving and beautiful, and in the four final notes of each section, thrice repeated, justifying of itself Kirkpatrick's discovery that in both its manuscript sources (in Parma and in Venice) 'it bears complete indications for what are evidently change of manuals', and is therefore to be considered as an organ piece.
K387/L175	A playful theme, almost a '*jeu de notes*', then augmented and embroidered, and commented upon within itself. Most beautiful.
K400/L213	Underlying melancholy of exquisite experience.
K492/L14	Starts, as with a flourish or fanfare of hunting horns, then breaks into 'Catherine-wheel' ornaments of dazzling effect, with an introspective section in the middle; and on the whole is decidedly to be classed with the Spanish sonatas. Kirkpatrick classes it as last of a trio of sonatas intended by Scarlatti to be played as a triptych. They would then read: K490/L206, K491/L164, K492/L14.

K531/L430   A perfectly beautiful piece of music.

2 *Neapolitan sonatas*

K	2	13	14	17	20	29	60	125	259	377	388	430	445
L	388	486	387	384	375	461	13	487	103	263	414	463	385

Thirteen in all, and it will be noted that eight of them are given early numbering in Kirkpatrick's new notation, thus bearing out the assumption that the bulk of them were written in Italy before Scarlatti left for Portugal and Spain. It is the case, that seven of them, K2, 14, 17, 20, 259, 388 and 430 were included in Tommasini's arrangement and orchestration of Scarlatti sonatas for Diaghilev's ballet *The Good Humoured Ladies* which was given a Neapolitan setting. Diaghilev will, himself, have played through a great number of the sonatas to make his selection, and the writer of these notes who knew him well and greatly admired his musical judgement finds further confirmation in his instinctive selection of those sonatas which are early in date before Scarlatti went to Spain. One of them it is true, K17/L384, is described by Mr Gilbert Chase as 'full of guitaristic effects and resembling the style of Albéniz', but this is a matter of personal taste. Not only does it *sound* Italian and not Spanish, but its early numbering, one may think, precludes it from being composed after Scarlatti had heard the Spanish guitar.

3 *Tarantellas*

K	54	103	323	413	519
L	241	233	95	125	475

Of these, K103 has hunting-calls in addition to tarantella time, with a beautiful and passionate second section. K323 is sheer cantering and galloping. K413 is another tarantella with hunting-calls. K519 has brilliant octave passages at end of each section. All four are among his masterpieces.

But are they, in fact, tarantellas? K413 begins in tarantella rhythm and almost immediately hunting-calls begin and cantering and galloping of horses. A little masterpiece of compression. K519 no less so.

4 *Siciliennes*

K	125	132	398	513	521
L	487	457	218	Suppl. 3	408

Outstanding among these beautiful pieces in a metre, so to speak, that was in Scarlatti's blood and that he must have remembered from childhood is

K513/Longo Supplement 3, a late sonata written probably thirty years after he had left Southern Italy for good. It evokes the droning bagpipes of the *zampognari* and the strident flutes of the *pifferari* when those shepherd-musicians come up from Calabria to play before the crib or *presepio* at Christmas; or so they did as I remember them forty years ago at Amalfi on winter days when I was young 'and frost was on the tangerines'. Their echoes are heard, too, in Handel in his *Concerti Grossi* and in *The Messiah*. He must have heard the *zampognari* in his Roman days (1707–9) when he heard Calabrian shepherds sing and play their Christmas song.* The particular sonata referred to is marvellously evocative and beautiful. But its magical entertainment, as ever with Scarlatti, is over in a few moments, ending gaily, even frenziedly, as in Jacques Callot's *Neapolitan Dances*, or *Balli di Sfessania*. It is curious indeed how this concluding piece of reminiscence – as much that as the *Valses Oubliées* of Liszt – gives the visual effect of being seen very small and far away exactly as in the distant, end-of-village street dances of the *Balli di Sfessania*.

5 *Sonatas based on bell sounds*

K	145	398	503
L	369	218	196

6 *Dances* (not of Spanish character)

K	40		42	77	137		172	258		441	471		554
L	357	Suppl. 36	168	315		Suppl. 40	178		Suppl. 39		82	Suppl. 21	

In this section K258/L178 is solemn and curious, with sudden interpolation of a *Schuhplattler*, almost a clog dance, surely not of Italian or Andalucian inspiration. It a little resembles the unfinished *Catalonia* of Albéniz. Had Scarlatti ever set foot in Holland I would say he had heard one of the barrel-organs in Amsterdam.

K554/Longo Supplement 21 is a kind of *passepied* or step dance.

7 *Military Sonatas*

K	140		335	360	380		420	487	499	515	520
L	107	Suppl. 10	400	23		Suppl. 2	205	193	255	86	

The too famous Cortège sonata, now as well known as Scarlatti's Pastorale, is K380/L23. Another, and better military procession of ceremonial, not funereal effect, is K140/L107. But the most brilliant of all the military pieces is K520/L86, a late sonata and no more than two minutes of intoxicating effect – a piece inspired by the mounting of the guard below the Buen Retiro, or other palace window, but reaching to ultimate heights of fantasy.

* cf. Percy M. Young, *Handel*, J. M. Dent and Sons, *The Master Musicians Series*, 1947, p. 188.

8 *High speed 'velocity' sonatas (nearly always played too fast)*

K	113	120	177	180	203	403	445
L	345	215	364	272	380	470	385

One of the most delightful of them is K203/L380 which could hardly be bettered for liveliness and sparkling entertainment.

9 *Adagio Sonatas*

K	19	32	34	53	69	86	87
L	383	423	Suppl. 7	261	382	403	33
K	148	158	164	238	279	287	291	310	324
L	64	4	59	27	468	Suppl. 9	61	248	332
K	328	331	356	462	472	478	481	544	546
L	Suppl. 27	18	443	438	99	12	187	497	312

Of these K32/L423 is marvellously beautiful and poignant.

10 *Pastoral or bucolic sonatas*

K	109	114	230	255	296	429	489	490
L	138	344	354	439	198	132	Suppl. 41	206

Among these could be cited K490/L206 which is enchanting and spring-like in its freshness.

11 *'Hunting' Sonatas*

K	140	177	256	313	323	372	403	477	491	494	519
L	107	364	228	192	95	302	470	290	164	287	475

I would add to these K103/L233 and K413/L125 in both of which the galloping, cantering transforms into a tarantella.

K491, it will be noted, is second of the triptych of Spanish sonatas K490, 491, 492. I can still hear in my mind a 'hunting' sonata played by Violet Wood-house, but the identity of which is now lost to me. The fanfare of its opening, and the quickening, cantering gallop of the hunt are in wonderful evocation, though only in memory, of 'the little dark musician of genius' that she was. Miss Kathleen Dale gives K477/L290, which is unknown to me, as so full of horn-calls that it evokes the introduction and opening scene of Act II of *Tristan and Isolde*. Another sonata, K519/L475, can only be described as a little masterpiece in its own genre. K413 must be mentioned again here as a hunting piece with interpolation of a tarantella, most hauntingly beautiful. Those who listen in this group of sonatas for *Un appel de chasseurs perdus dans les grands bois*, in that marvellous line of Baudelaire from *Les Phares*, will often hear their quarry.

There is a well defined group of virtuoso sonatas in which one of the star pieces is that most famous of his sonatas K113/L345, where handcrossing occurs with cumulative effect of utmost firework brilliance; though Kirkpatrick says of another sonata K120/L215, perhaps a little impulsively, that it has 'the wildest handcrossing of all'. It will be noted how near together these two sonatas are in date of composition according to Kirkpatrick's numbering. They should date from his Roman years when he astonished Handel with his playing. Another virtuoso piece is K427/L286 in which the rapid flow is interrupted with fascinating effect as by a trumpet alarm or call. But I could hardly agree with Kirkpatrick that this or its companion sonata is Spanish. There is, too, K255/L439, a piece inspired surely by that clash, or diphthong, or even triphthong of three notes. Kirkpatrick suggests that this, too, like K328 was for organ. Can it, then, be in the 'classical guitar style' of Gilbert Chase? Also, there is a particular group of sonatas that is full of whirring effects:

K	56	103	124	237	395	403
L	356	233	232	308	65	470

A *feu de joie*, or whirling firework of high spirit is K146/L349, a sonata which Mr George Malcolm plays inimitably.

And a group with glissando passages, unprecedented elsewhere in music until Liszt:

K	216	229	275	302	515
L	273	199	328	7	255

These pieces make one regret more than ever that Scarlatti never heard the Hungarian cymbalom. The first named sonata is most brilliant and exciting.

There is, as well, another group of sonatas to be classed as among the most beautiful of all though different again from that group described as being typical of Violet Woodhouse's playing. These would include K147/L376, K251/L305, K359/L448 and K461/L8, all of which combine virtuosity with intense feeling and are hardly even eighteenth-century in form or content, and anticipate not so much Chopin as Brahms or Liszt. This group would comprise:

K	147	159	193	213	251	359	461
L	376	104	142	108	305	448	8

The last named is the most like Bach of all Scarlatti's sonatas known to me.

A tentative list of one hundred and one Spanish sonatas by Domenico Scarlatti

K6/L479	Resembles a zapateado or cobbler's dance, but how does it come so early in Kirkpatrick's numbering?
K9/L413	The well-known 'Pastorale'. Is it really in 'early guitar style'?
K17/L384	I have put this in the Neapolitan section, but Mr Gilbert Chase describes it as 'full of guitaristic effects and resembling the style of Albéniz', so it must be included here.
K26/L368	Mentioned in the postscript.
K27/L449	*Vide* account of his among the sonatas played by Mrs Violet Woodhouse. It is strangely and hauntingly beautiful, if of underlying melancholy.
K28/L373	Guitar effect. One of the most charming and sprightly of all the sonatas. Fascinating with its runs and glissandos in alternate and opposing directions. More Spanish than any piece by Albéniz or Granados.
K38/L478	Very curious effect with glissandos and sweepings of the strings.
K46/L25	Spanish in mood and dignity, and very reminiscent of the manner of Mrs Violet Woodhouse in her playing.
K54/L241	Opening in tarantella rhythm, with lovely and heart-warming later section. Much handcrossing. This sonata is most marvellously beautiful.
K56/L356	A transcendental, firework sonata, with very distinct development into a zapateado. A very grand work with glissando effects and all sorts of interest.
K57/Longo Supplement 38	Tapping and drumming, and smashing of the hand on the back of the guitar. On the whole, though, melancholy and sad.
K64/L58	'In popular style', with military undertones. March-like, and more Handelian than Spanish.
K96/L465	Spanish, but with flourishes of hunting horns. Kirkpatrick hears 'bells, guitars and castanets' in it as well.
K99/L317	A zapateado, if only rather more than less; or, maybe, a fandango.
K105/L204	Very Spanish indeed. Curiously early in numbering according to Kirkpatrick. Perhaps, therefore, written in Portugal.
K107/L474	Grinding effect like a hurdy-gurdy. Very full of feeling and expression. But this was one of Diaghilev's mistakes. When I first heard it in his Neapolitan Scarlatti ballet in 1918 I recognised it as Spanish, long before I knew that Scarlatti had spent so much of his life in Spain. A most beautiful sonata.
K109/L138	A pastoral sonata.
K115/L407	Grand and sad, with Spanish thrumming and drumming.
K119/L415	Unashamedly flamenco in approach and action. One of the most exciting, if not most beautiful of the sonatas.
K124/L232	Whirring effect. Brilliant and seemingly both Neapolitan and Spanish in effect. Whirling, whirring ornament, then sudden dramatic break into breathtakingly beautiful passage redolent of Spain. Outstanding among the sonatas.
K132/L457	Opens in the guitar language. A marvellous guitar piece all in all.
K133/L282	Unagressively Spanish. Rather like one of Sarasate's Spanish dances for violin.
K135/L224	Another zapateado. Agile and sprightly beginning, then delightfully fluid and brilliant second section, followed by the zapateado, which is very like Sarasate, but more intellectually brilliant and imaginative.

K140/L107	Processional in effect, with echo of distant trumpets. A splendid ending.
K141/L422	See my account of this beautiful sonata as played by Mrs Violet Wood-house.
K146/L349	Very typically Spanish, as much so as any piano piece by Albéniz.
K147/L376	Slow and profound. Wonderfully Spanish in instrumentation, if not in idiom.
K152/L179	A Spanish dance of beautiful and decisive tang and flavour. Probably a fandango.
K159/L104	One of the most beautiful of all Scarlatti sonatas, and very Spanish in feeling. With curious break or pause very full of weight and meaning. Dazzling fireworks and Catherine-wheel ornaments. Gilbert Chase says this has a pronounced rhythmic analogy to the theme used by Lalo in the rondo of his *Symphonie Espagnole* written for Sarasate, but I fail to see the resemblance.
K161/L417	Spanish, but in gentle mood with guitar strumming.
K175/L429	Said by Gilbert Chase to resemble Turina's *Andaluzua sentimental*. Certainly very Spanish in effect.
K202/L498	'Replete with Catalonian dance rhythms, and resembling the popular music of Sicily', so writes Mr Gilbert Chase. It is certainly true that the Sicilienne section in the middle of it is rather different from the bagpipe music of the *zampognari* in K513/Longo Supplement 3. But where are the 'Catalonian dance rhythms'? There is no sign of the Sardana.
K206/L257	Grand and tragic, with passionate feeling. One of the most beautiful of all the sonatas. But little proof of the simulated castanet effects mentioned by Mr Ralph Kirkpatrick.
K207/L371	Unknown to me.
K208/L238	Poignant, and a good deal more than merely poignant.
K209/L428	A jota on vigorous, emphatic lines. Courante and galante as well; a dance, more than a jota, with pleasing second section which may have lost its meaning in the passing of time, as has happened with much of Couperin. Not particularly Spanish, and perhaps should not be here at all.
K212/L135	Very close to de Falla's Spanish songs and dances.
K214/L165	A sad and stately Sicilienne of slight Spanish accent. In his sleeve note Valenti speaks of this sonata as a Spanish dance.
K215/L323	Suggestive of an outside guitar with deep notes of almost bloodhound baying.
K216/L273	Gloriously beautiful and inimitably Spanish. Grinding hurdy-gurdy effect and Catherine-wheel ornaments, but whirling, not whirring in effect. A good deal of Lisztian preluding, followed by the Spanish whirling and grinding.
K222/L309	Spanish in battery and percussion of guitar notes.
K229/L199	Much grinding of guitars, working both ways, in six flights, as it were, of glissandos. Very exciting, if sombre, and very Spanish indeed.
K237/L308	Very tense and complicated, with marching progress up the keyboard.
K238/L27	'A balada, or folk dance from the Portuguese province of Estremadura', but it is uninteresting.
K239/L281	This sonata reminds Kirkpatrick of a procession of *gigantes* and *cabezudos*, pasteboard giants and big-heads, through the streets of some Spanish provincial town. But it is among the delights of music that it can and does suggest anything to anybody.

K251/L305 A marvellous work of art with a sort of shutter of guitar sounds coming down upon and cutting off its mood of melancholy and introspection. An inimitable two minutes or so of music and poetry. Marvellously passionate and beautiful.

K264/L466 Another jota, with melancholy, ringing start. The jota is in the second section, but not very marked in rhythm.

K275/L328 Grinding hurdy-gurdy effect with glissandos as well.

K288/L57 Only slightly Spanish.

K291/L61 With 'the Andaluz descending fourth', but imperceptibly Hispanicised, and suggestive of a game of musical 'nap' with purposeful slowing down, and then the sudden pounce and collecting of the hand of cards.

K303/L9 Trills resembling bird-songs and gentle guitar strummings.

K309/L454 Has an emphatic second section with whirling roulades for ornament and self-expression.

K360/L400 Trills and simultaneous touching of notes, indeed triphthongs, so called.

K367/L172 Guitar effects. Very strongly tinged with music for the guitar. One of the grandest of the Spanish sonatas. Much strumming of guitars – not the tinkling of mandolines. Brilliant, showy, almost sequin-spangled, one could say, with its coruscating whirling guitar sound.

K369/L240 'A minuet, really a jota aragonesa'. Very Spanish, and much more elaborate than its description by Mr Gilbert Chase would suggest. Reminds a lover of the *Nozze di Figaro* of the sarabande at Figaro's wedding in Count Almaviva's palace at Seville. It is tempestuous in Lisztian fashion – with a bleak background, anxious and emphatic, and then bleak again. It has deep preluding followed by quick runs like bird-ritual dances, with a very marked guitar beat. There are numerous variants of the jota. Learned opinion for instance describes the sixth of the *Spanish Dances* of Granados as being a jota of Alcañiz, a slower variety of jota than that of Zaragoza, but differentiating this again from the jota of Valencia.

K377/L263 The so-called *Bourrée d'Aranjuez*. To my instinct more Italian than Spanish, and it certainly sounded southern Italian in the Neapolitan ballet of Scarlatti's music mounted by Diaghilev.

K380/L23 This is the well known, too well known Cortège, so called, which is far too long.

K383/L134 Dramatic, high tension Spanish.

K385/L284 Very beautiful change of key in opening section, and very poignant in succeeding section.

K390/L234 A sonata of courante, fluent effect, but difficult to define as more than a little 'Spanish', and perhaps should not be included here.

K395/L65 Marvellous play of rapidity, with all kinds of interest, not to say fascination. A second section opening almost like a Spanish cavatina is followed at once by fireworks and high spirits.

K397/L208 A jota aragonesa, which Gilbert Chase describes as having pretence to be a minuet, though I do not follow what he means. This is very beautiful, and perhaps Spanish more in shape than substance.

K400/L213 Typically and nostalgically Spanish.

K414/L310 'In classical guitar style', but unknown to me.

K419/L279 Beautiful, but intensely and reflectively melancholy.

K420/Longo Supplement 2 Spanish, with military overtones.

K426/L128	According to Gilbert Chase 'in tonadilla style'. That seems an exaggerated statement. It may be so, but the fact that it is a tonadilla does not obtrude.
K427/L286	This is the 'running' or 'courante' sonata with the alarm or trumpet call in the middle. But it is difficult indeed to think of this delightful invention with the call to arms in the middle of it as being Spanish in intention.
K435/L361	Cited by Kirkpatrick for its counterfeit of castanets and their 'dry clattering'. I would have thought it more Neapolitan than Spanish in feeling, and to be grouped with the Italian sonatas; but its companion does
K436/L109	strongly suggest a band of guitars, though with no accompanying castanets.
K442/L319	Very Spanish indeed, with much syncopation. Beautiful opening, then much plangent and feverish counterfeit of guitar playing.
K443/L418	Military and processional – but it is not a military funeral.
K447/L294	Smooth progression into a sprightly dance. Octave leaps and other terpsichorean feats.
K450/L338	Mr Gilbert Chase calls this 'a typical dance from the province of León'. Mrs Violet Woodhouse told the writer that she played an English folk tune closely resembling this to Rubio, the Spanish cellist, who immediately recognised the tune as Spanish.
K460/L324	Begins like a figure in dancing – then comes preluding of great beauty, and the sonata has a beautiful, skilful and agile ending.
K476/L340	Very Spanish indeed in its second section, with the crisis-making, accumulating nervous tension of guitar-strumming that only Scarlatti can achieve in so short a spell of time.
K490/L206 K491/L164 K492/L14	These three sonatas form a triptych, surpassingly beautiful, beginning in Spanish grandeur and solemnity, and continuing through the tarantella to the dazzling 'Catherine wheels' at the end.
K503/L196	Spanish echoes and undercurrents. Beautiful.
K507/L113	Another jota, but slow to take fire, and conceived more as a vehicle of thought than for a dance. Interesting to compare with the jotas of Padre Soler.
K509/L311	This has pleasing touches, particularly in its latter half.
K514/L1	A zapateado. Extremely curious. Very distinctly and gloriously Spanish and with curious, dying echo, almost, as it were, in its second sentence. The dying echo, itself, made into the subject of the second section – then grinding of guitars, but the echo comes back again and has the last word, if twice repeated.
K515/L255	Sprightly, with scampering at the start.
K516/Longo Supplement 12	Impressive, but not startling.
K517/L266	A jota, with touches of the zapateado. Courante and lively. But the zapateado has a slow fuse and delays before it catches fire.
K518/L116	Of Spanish grandeur. But, in fact, being one of the late sonatas, Spanish from long association; when Scarlatti instinctively wrote as a Spaniard, but not forgetful of his Italian past.
K519/L475	Neapolitan high spirits, but with no roulades or cartwheel reminiscences of his Italian youth.
K521/L408	Very strongly suggestive of the guitar. Pastoral opening, followed by big wild leaps in contrary motion between the hands. But by no means the wildest leaps of all.
K527/L458	Prim musical-box start, then beautiful and full-throated.

K528/L200	Of unheralded Spanish idiom at the start; but how Spanish can you be before the end, with full guitar effects! Enormous leaps and broken octaves.
K529/L327	Grand and pleasant. The guitar stress or beat in the second section is markedly Iberian. Repeated handcrossings in both directions. Very brilliant.
K532/L223	Proud and beautiful in flamenco manner with much grinding of guitars.
K533/L395	Spanish, but in the mood of the well known sonata K113/L345 with the handcrossing. This, if anything, is more syncopated and livelier still.
K534/LII	Solemn, with much thrumming and grinding.
K537/L293	Very curious. Unusual and strange verse, followed by chorus of guitar, and dance termination.
K540/Longo Supplement 17	Simple start, but grows plangent with guitar stress four times over in doubled version.
K544/L497	Spanish, with grinding of guitar, 'Catherine wheel' displays, etc.
K545/L500	Very wild and furious, with slapping of backs of guitars in counterfeit.
K546/L312	Profound, and deep, but dull.
K548/L404	Most fascinatingly, poignantly beautiful. Among the loveliest of all. One of the last of Scarlatti's sonatas, and a glorious, if poignant exit for his genius.

In addition:

| K297/Longo Supplement 19 | Played by Ralph Kirkpatrick in his album of records, where it is given as 'Autentica balada: un canto de la Estremadura Portuguesa'. It is in truth more than a little boring. |
| K504/L29 | Cited by Kirkpatrick as 'a fandango from the Portuguese province of Estremadura'. Beautiful, curious, and very intricate in shape and sound. Exceptional and apart in the whole run of the sonatas. |

The selection of those sonatas which are Spanish in feeling and in idiom is no easy matter, depending, as it must do to some large extent, on personal taste and preference. I have listed the hundred or so sonatas which seem to me to be Spanish in atmosphere and inclination. Mr Gilbert Chase in his *Music in Spain*, New York, 1941, pp. 111, 112, gives a list of Scarlatti's Spanish sonatas of which only two, as will be seen in my notes, are unknown to me. With the exception of these sonatas – and I give their numbers, K207/L371, K414/L310 – all the others on this list I have heard frequently and know pretty well, my sources besides Valenti, being recordings by Luciano Sgrizzi, John Beckett, Huguette Dreyfus, George Malcolm, Ralph Kirkpatrick, and Horowitz.

There are some hundred sonatas listed here as being Spanish out of, as I have said before, the three hundred and thirty, or so, sonatas with which I am fairly familiar. The remaining two hundred and twenty-five of Scarlatti's sonatas making up the total of five hundred and fifty-five, must of course have other sonatas in all categories which could be added to my lists. There are evidently subtle shades of difference between the Spanish and Neapolitan, as could be said in parenthesis, of the counterfeit on another instrument, the harpsichord, of guitar or mandoline. Taking into consideration that their evident and obtrusive Spanishness would thrust many of the sonatas into the foreground and draw early attention to themselves, there must still be many others among the hundred and eighty or so sonatas that I have perforce left unexplored, if we leave out from the grand total a few which are early pieces of no consequence, others which were really intended as violin sonatas, and so on. Perhaps in all there could be as many as a hundred and fifty, or a hundred and sixty sonatas in the Spanish idiom and feeling.

POSTSCRIPT

Since writing the above, some of the sonatas unknown to me which I most wanted to hear have been played to me by Mr George Malcolm. This is an experience which I owe to the kindness of my old friend Thomas Goff. Thanks to it, I was able to identify immediately the 'Hunting' sonata K477/ L290 as that played to me so often by Violet Woodhouse. Miss Kathleen Dale, who describes it as 'so full of horn-calls that it evokes the introduction and opening scene of Act II of *Tristan and Isolde*', does not exaggerate. It was a strange experience to hear again that opening flourish as of some hunting party in Queen Mab's Kingdom, after a silence of twenty-one years since the early winter of 1946. This sonata is pure magic.

Mr George Malcolm then played K172/Longo Supplement 40, a masterpiece of different kind, but hardly of another order. This is best described as a transcendental dance, but no more intended for dancing than the gorgeously dressed children's dolls with their high headdresses and flowered *obis* in the doll-shops of Kyoto are meant for children to play with and pull to pieces. This is a sonata of Neapolitan kind, comrade to the *Balli di Sfessania*, and the tarantella is never far away.

Next, Mr Malcolm played K450/L338 which it will be remembered is the 'typical dance from the province of León' of Mr Gilbert Chase. This, also, I found to have been in the repertory of Violet Woodhouse so that it was familiar to me. It is, emphatically, a Spanish dance, if not of Andalusian sort. But after this came one of the two 'finds' or discoveries of the afternoon, K26/L368 which is indeed an astonishing tour-de-force. This sonata seems to contain in itself everything that has ever been heard or said of the guitar, an over exaggerated musical instrument except as a poetical idea and because of its association with such peaks of musical poetry as the serenades in *Il Seraglio* and in *Don Giovanni*, no less so in *Il Barbiere*. But the sonata is not evocative of a solo guitar, it suggests a guitar band; and all of which that should be capable as a poetic concept. It is an astonishing and transcendental sonata, never to my knowledge performed or recorded but hidden away in the eleven volumes of Longo as closely as though buried in the tomb.

An even more remarkable and exceptional work of art was sonata K211/

L133 of which it could be said, in brief, that it does for the mandoline of the Bay of Naples what K26 does for the Sevillan guitar. Swinburne's 'leaves that tremble like lute-strings, or like fire' are evoked in this transcendental two minutes of music that for a virtuoso piece is not dissimilar from Liszt's étude on Paganini's *La Campanella*, except that the other is a work of virtuosity and this is a work of art. The long rallentando rattling of the mandoline is wonderfully evoked. Two other sonatas that Kirkpatrick cites as suggestive of mandolines, K298/Longo Supplement 6 and K143/Newton Sonata 2 proved to be, if charming, of very much less importance as works of art. The mandoline sonata of Scarlatti, K211 and its balancing, if not paired guitar-companion K26, would seem to be quite unique among the sonatas, and to describe them in the nature of a 'find' or discovery is not exaggerated.

Mr George Malcolm played one other piece which was unknown to me, K363/L160, a sonata decidedly Spanish in intent and purpose. This makes one more Spanish sonata to be added to the total, which will now amount to one hundred and two in all. But, as I have said, there must be others; and here I must end these notes which are up to this point, as complete as I can make them. As I finish writing these lines I have once more in my ear that hunting fanfare or flourish which I never thought to hear again, and am reminded through the playing of Mr George Malcolm of that musician of genius who is long since gone away.

Further listening has added a few more sonatas at the last moment; and it is now possible, I think, to establish a mandoline section of Neapolitan-Spanish inspiration, but differing in conception from those sonatas that seem based on the guitar. This section would now include:

Kirkpatrick	14	141		143	211	298	435	455	555
Longo	387	422	Newton Sonata 2	133		Suppl. 6	361	209	477

of which sonatas one or two appear, as of right, in the Spanish section. K141/L422 is particularly beautiful.

The Spanish section to include these further sonatas:

K20/L375 — The extravagant quickness and lightning turns in this sonata could be described as in the mood of Callot's *Balli di Sfessania* which almost certainly Scarlatti had never seen.

K24/L495 — This is number 24 of the *Essercizi*, and could be termed a giddy dance in prestidigious form, with leaps and landings in the language of the guitar.

K125/L487 — I have transferred this from the Neapolitan section, because despite its early number and Neapolitan affinity it has guitar-like terminations and declensions.

K193/L142	One of the most lovely of all. Wonderful opening, like a pushing off from shore into the 'trembling of the lute string'. A rare poignancy, and force of guitar-like chords in their surging and their dying.
K201/L129	Decidedly among the most beautiful of all the sonatas, and very reminiscent of Mrs Woodhouse's playing.
K203/L380	A 'question and answer' start, followed by brilliance and coruscation but of a minor sort. A beautiful specimen of Scarlatti's imagination.
K213/L108	A transcendental piece of heavenly length. Guitar-like strummings of deepest melancholy, the poetry of which only emerges in full force on the instrument for which it was written, and not upon the piano.
K263/L321	Long and reflective – Extremely beautiful.
K271/L155	Minor, and controlled whirlwinds or catspaws. Delightful of effect, and uniquely Scarlattian.
K386/L171	Of Spanish descent beyond argument, and beautiful indeed.
K455/L209	Mandolinesque, with repeated and busy twanging of the strings.
K520/L86	Military sonata of great brilliance.
K555/L477	A neat 'Northern' start, then change of climate to the serenading south. A beautiful work of art.

Of these thirteen additional Spanish sonatas, K193/L142, K201/L129, and K213/L108 are exceptionally beautiful.

With the exception of the two specified previously I have heard all the other sonatas mentioned. These two included, this makes a total of 115 Spanish-sounding pieces. But among the three hundred and more to which I have had access there are certain to be a few omissions. It again raises the question as to how many more Spanish sonatas may be among the two hundred or so which are not known to me. As I have said above, the grand total seems likely to be upwards of a hundred and fifty in all.

In a last word on the subject, taking into consideration all the different facets in his huge and varied output, it would seem that Domenico Scarlatti did not anticipate the development of the modern pianoforte. His bias would appear to have been towards the progression and perfection of mandoline and guitar subjects, but in directions and dimensions of which those instruments in themselves are incapable. His Latinity, of Sicilian and Parthenopaean origin, and of Roman and Venetian experience, found its fulfilment in the Spanish setting. And now it is time for a farewell to this greatest of keyboard composers and executants, always excepting Chopin and Liszt of whom he is the peer and equal.

6 June 1967   SACHEVERELL SITWELL

Index

Churches and other buildings are listed under the name of their town; paintings are under the name of the artist.

MARTIN GOTTFRIED

HARRY N. ABRAMS, INC. · PUBLISHERS · NEW YORK

In Person

THE GREAT ENTERTAINERS

CONTENTS

ALONE AND ALIVE

The entertainer works alone. Presenting himself for approval, he steps through the curtains to dare the spotlight, and it plucks him from the darkness that might have kept him safe. Armed only with material, he hurries to satisfy the audience, or at least to survive it. He may sing, dance, or tell jokes, but whatever the routine he is a gladiator, and whether he performs in the Roman Colosseum, at a king's court, in a vaudeville theater, or on a nightclub floor, the room he is working is his arena. That is where he does his act.

"Act" and "performance" were not used to describe variety routines until the modern era of American vaudeville. It was an interesting development in word usage, for both can be applied to stage as well as personal behavior: "act" as a display of affectation and as a bit of business, a ploy (or "routine"). In theater-derived slang we "clean up our acts" or "get our acts together." An act can even be an identity. Bob Hope, for instance, is a comedy act. And we, too, are our acts. In that sense, our act is the personality we send forth as a facade, a social self to hide behind. We are known by that facade, for who can see within us? It is a self we think (or hope) will seem confident and appealing to others. The performer develops or polishes his act or facade to such an extent that his inner and outer selves become confused. Which is real? He closes the dressing-room door behind him and, exhausted by self-promotion, lays himself to rest like a shadow on a chair. If he is a top star, even that respite is denied, for, having received so much approbation, he is willing to invest his soul in the image and exploit his self for show.

Samuel·Beckett based the leading characters of his great play *Waiting for Godot* on the low comics of the English music hall. These *naifs*, archetypes of mankind, clown their way through life's misfortunes and frustrations, laughing lest they weep. Like Beckett's Estragon and Vladimir, every entertainer needs a courageous naiveté in order to stand before an audience and attempt to amuse it, without company for protection. This book pays tribute to such solitary courage and celebrates every performer who ever stepped through a curtain to tumble, tap-dance, or sing his way to survival. None of them did it just for the money, but neither did anyone ever entertain simply to make an audience happy. Entertainment is a selfish act, performed because of a positive need to show off and be appreciated. The entertainers brave criticism and rejection in exchange for a spot on the bill and the ritual reward of hand claps.

Alas, they are a fading tribe. The vaudeville theaters and nightclubs are dark, abandoned, razed, converted, and gone. The casino showrooms of Las Vegas are overshadowed by newer ones in Atlantic City, where there are stages only for performers who can attract audiences that can afford to gamble high enough. Others in the shrinking circle of elite entertainers perform in cavernous concert halls where they attempt to reach audiences of four- or five-thousand people. Soon, still fewer stars will attract even larger audiences, while rock acts play arenas and

OPPOSITE:
Frank Sinatra

ABOVE:
Al Jolson

stadiums. Finally, there will be no performer-audience confrontations at all.

Television is America's major entertainment medium, but television is a demagnetizer of live performance. The presence and energy of the entertainer are lost in the electronic transmission of his image, for life disappears along the circuit boards, somewhere between the transistors and the microchips. High-fidelity recordings and equipment never can really sound like live music, being different in nature, and there is a similar eeriness in comparing the performer who prances before the camera with his electronic image on the nearby studio monitor. The image does the dance, sings the song, and smiles the smile but no energy is exchanged between performer and audience. The image on the screen is not a person. It is a composition of blips. The image has phosphors for flesh.

During television's first years, unemployed vaudevillians were willing to settle for phosphors and blips. All the jugglers, the magicians, the eccentric dancers were "between engagements," as they put it with customary bravado. In those formative years of television, network executives considered the medium a branch of theater. They scheduled many variety shows, and the entertainers were resurrected from vaudeville's grave to stock them, but it was only a midnight revel. Vaudeville might be imitated on television, but it could not be re-created because it required the spirit of live communion. Too, popular entertainment reflects the mood and style of an era, and jugglers, magicians, and eccentric

Slapstick comedy takes its name from the "slap stick," a noisy, therefore funny, stage prop used as early as the seventeenth century in the Italian commedia dell'arte. The slap stick consisted of two strips of wood tied at the handle, which when slapped against somebody would make a sharp cracking sound. In this reproduction of a print of 1689, the comic servant Columbine applies the slap stick to Harlequin. The improvisational nature of commedia dell'arte provided chances for solo turns within an ensemble.

dancers simply weren't in the 1950s fashion. But most devastating of all was television's fast-revealed and frightening ability to wear out performers and material. The phenomenon came to be called "overexposure," but the term was double-edged. For the living-room screen was watched at point-blank range. It *uncovered* the act. Even when new material was turned out, audiences quickly saw through the routine to the heart of the brave faker.

And so acts that might have been devised, tested, rewritten, polished, and then performed for years on the vaudeville circuits were done a couple of times on television and then were scrapped. The stages for the army of able, professional, working performers were almost all gone. Soon there would be nowhere "to work in one," a theatrical expression that means playing in front of the first (number one) curtain, straight out to the audience. In drama, few actors ever work there. They perform on a set that is farther back on the stage. They feign reality, and so as protection they can enjoy an imaginary fourth wall that rises between them and the audience. Only occasionally do plays require actors to come forth and address the audience. Thus, performing "in one" is generally associated with variety entertainment, with personal appearances.

Making a personal appearance, performing an act, the variety entertainer puts himself on the block. If he is a success, nobody else can share in it: all fantasies are realized, he is hailed and beloved. But if he is disapproved, given the hook, and pelted with tomatoes, then he can blame no playwright, no director. He is personally responsible for the outcome, and the absolute nature of this is reflected in show-business jargon: the entertainer who succeeds "slays them," the one who fails "dies." How strange is this ritual of exaltation and sacrifice, and how inarticulate the audience's responses: hand claps for approval, hoots for rejection. Such judgments might be expected from gorillas.

The psychological basis of this behavior must be buried deep in human psychology. Why is the comedian's role so hostile, bringing laughter but not happiness? Why does the singer seem such an innocent, so earnest and vulnerable? Why is the dancer a pet? Why is the juggler clever, the acrobat not? Why are audiences threatening, even heartless? That last question is the least perplexing. Perhaps audiences know that the urge to perform is reckless. Perhaps the power to reject encourages sadism. At the Colonial Theatre, one of New York City's first vaudeville houses, there was a ritual called the "Colonial clap." Whenever a performer was failing, the audience would begin to applaud rhythmically and the noise would build until the humiliated entertainer was forced to break off his act and flee. What primitive ritual could be more barbaric?

Except for a brief survey of origins, this book will not cover the entire history of variety entertainment (the interested reader is referred to the bibliography). It would be impossible to describe every professional act performed in America's speakeasies and cabarets, on its burlesque and vaudeville stages, in its nightclubs and concert halls. Nor could all the notable entertainers be included here, among the photographs or in the text. Apologies for the inevitable oversights are extended in advance.

Rather, this book is offered as an appreciation of the peculiarly American variety turn and of the solo entertainer, who is surely a metaphor for human individuality and bravery in facing up to life's hazards. It is presented with the rueful awareness that the end is at hand, for almost all of the stages have vanished or been rendered obsolete. And so, a hail and farewell to the array of lively acts and routines and foolish turns that past performers invented: magic tricks and contortions; bicycling; showing trained seals and bears and dogs; singing and dancing; doing impressions; telling funny stories; clowning; performing acrobatics; juggling; stripping; impersonating the opposite sex; playing musical instruments or nonmusical ones like saws, glasses, bells, and washboards; jumping on trampolines; turning somersaults; whistling. Of all God's creatures, only humans do such silly things.

Entertainers are often called children. They have traditionally been considered immoral, or merely raffish. They have lived the lives of gypsies. Wandering minstrels—vagabond variety performers—were known long before mime was introduced to Greek and Roman drama about 200 B.C. "Mime" did not then mean charades in leotards but was rather what we would now call improvisational theater: brief comedy sketches extemporized between the acts of Greek tragedies and Roman comedies.

In England during the first centuries of the Christian era, another sort of light entertainment was developed. Each Anglo-Saxon tribe had a "gleoman," who accompanied himself on the harp as he sang songs (or "lays") about local heroes and history. *Widsith*, perhaps the first poem written in English, describes the life of a fourth-century gleoman. But the most famous of their compositions is, of course, *Beowolf*. Composed by an eighth-century gleoman, it is almost the only epic of the Old English period that survives.

Mimes and gleomen had made their appearance in response to a demand for lighter entertainment, but even they proved too stuffy for some audiences. Rowdier performers were already on the way, fellows who specialized in country dances, acrobatics, and a variation on the fireside chant that came to be known as "the telling of obscene stories." The comedian had arrived.

In northern France, the wandering minstrels were called "jongleurs" and the gleomen "troubadours." The latter, like their English colleagues, sang ballads about military battles and royal romances, but the Norman troubadour enjoyed a higher status than the English gleoman. He was a fellow of respectable, even noble, birth who traveled on horseback with an entourage of jongleurs trotting behind. Arriving at a castle, he was welcomed by the lord, not as an itinerant player but as an equal. He was shown to a comfortable lodging and entertained at the host's own table. Hardly theatrical riffraff, he enjoyed the show himself. Next day, the lord's retinue of knights and ladies might gather in a meadow, beneath encircling trees festooned with ribbons and flowers. Outdoor banquet tables would already have been laden with refreshments for the local gentry. Again the jongleurs would perform. At last the troubadour himself would deign to sing. So, the star.

But it was his jongleurs, the working performers, who most closely resembled our own vaudevillians. Like the circus performers of later times, these common players made up for their lack of charisma—*star quality*—with an abundance of talent. They did cartwheels, wire-balancing acts—almost anything that might be asked for in the way of eleventh-century entertainment. In one medieval press release, a jongleur advised:

I can play the lute, the violin, the bagpipe, the syrinx, the harp, the gigue, the gittern, the symphony, the psaltery, the organistrum, the regals, the tabor and the rote. I can sing a song well and make tales and fables . . . I can throw knives in the air and catch them without cutting my fingers. I can do dodges with strings and balance chairs.

And for an encore he would throw a somersault and walk on his hands. *Ann-Margret*

After the Norman Conquest, jongleurs swarmed across the English countryside. These foreign gleomen performed at weddings, baptisms, and knight-dubbings. Now female performers were permitted on the English stage for the first time, and these "glee maidens" accompanied the gleomen on lutes and sometimes were even permitted to join in the acrobatics and tumbling.

New variety entertainments emerged among these common jesters: puppet shows, hoop-leaping. The occasional little troupe even traveled with a lion or a camel. The trained bear proved a particularly successful addition, although Ben Jonson was perhaps overly enthusiastic when he wrote, "Good performing bears can dance at first sight and play their own tunes if need be."

Some jongleurs improved their lowly status by specializing in magic. These *tregeteurs* could make flowers and even lions seem to disappear. They would also hammer nails through their hands or snip off their own noses—an illusion accomplished with the help of "a piece of spunge with some sheep's blood in it, to be retained privately."

In 1572, because of a handful of troublemakers and ale-swillers, the merrymaking was dampened and the reputations of all itinerant players were besmirched. In a mood of moral zeal Parliament passed an Act (oh, irony of terms) decreeing "fanciers, bear-leaders, common players, minstrels and jugglers that wander abroad without license from two justices of the peace at least, should be taken, adjudged and deemed rogues, vagabonds and sturdy beggars." The unlicensed minstrel was made punishable at the stocks and the whipping post. Undaunted, the rogues, vagabonds, and sturdy beggars persisted in cartwheeling about the country, even adding comedy sketches to their increasingly popular repertoires of joke-mongering and gross obscenity.

They also found new places to work. The seeds of cabaret were sown in the courtyards of inns and taverns, where itinerant performers entertained for tossed coins. The drinking men called these entertainers "buskers," a term that would be exported to the New World with the Pilgrims. Country fairs offered an even more festive milieu for variety performance. Originating in the thirteenth century, they grew in number during the next several hundred years, providing open-air markets for goods of all kinds. A general holiday spirit prevailed, offering a natural opportunity for entertainers. The most famous was held outside London, the annual Bartholomew Fair, for which Ben Jonson's play was named, so-called because it traditionally opened on August 24, St. Bartholomew's Day. This and other great pleasure fairs offered midways where ballad-singers, conjurers, stilt-walkers, and bear-leaders could perform. The exhibition of freaks and other human oddities, while nearly as old as mankind, became institutionalized there. Other secondary attractions—"sideshows"—included the likenesses of public figures, a medieval wax museum. There were pantomimes, too—musical renditions of children's stories—and one never knew what famous actor might show up in them. For when the doldrums settled upon London Town, leading players could pick up extra pennies at one or another of these fairs. Edmund Kean himself once performed in a pantomime at Bartholomew Fair. There was no shame in it—in fact, after the theaters that the Puritans closed in 1642 had reopened, Bartholomew Fair became a prime showcase for new works. John Gay's *Beggar's Opera* was produced there in 1728.

But the two strains of entertainment, the legitimate stage and variety shows, were separating, the former appealing to the cultured, the latter to the masses. When drama moved to the indoor theaters for the winter,

the variety acts found housing in London too. Before the music halls were opened, the storytellers and clog dancers and singers of funny songs performed in the saloon theaters of such popular London pubs as the Grecian Urn and the Eagle Tavern. By 1870 there were a dozen music halls in London, with names like the Pavilion and the Eastern Music Hall. A decade later there would be opulent music halls in Drury Lane and on Westminster Bridge Road. Variety entertainment had arrived. It would fast become a fixture of British life and be exported to America.

However, comic monologues were performed in America before the turn of the century. "Girlie" and "leg" shows had for some time been popular attractions at beer halls, and in 1840 William Valentine opened the first New York variety theater. It was a modest establishment, more saloon than theater, but the idea caught on and soon similar auditoriums were popping up in storefronts across the nation. Known as "honky-tonks" or "free and easies," they combined the attractions of the saloon, the theater, and the gaming house. Then at last, in 1871, H. J. Sargent organized Sargent's Great Vaudeville Company in Louisville.

The origin of the term "vaudeville" has confounded academe. The French phrase "voix de ville" (voice of the city) would seem the likeliest source, but some scholars have speculated that the term comes from "chanson du vau," as the ballads of the early troubadour Olivier Basselin were called, or the "vive vaude" entertainments of thirteenth-century France.

It seems probable that the saloon ambience had kept variety entertainment from becoming the national rage, for there is no mass entertainment without the family trade. That would soon change. Vaudeville became America's popular entertainment. The troubadours and conjurers of the past evolved into our singers and magicians. The tellers of obscene tales, bless them, continued to tell them as comedians. The medieval jongleur who proudly advertised his multiple talents found counterparts in the vaudeville entertainers, who could do almost as much. A journeyman American vaudevillian named Sylvester Schaffer, for instance, could juggle, sharpshoot, do drawings, prestidigitate, tumble, perform with trained animals, whips, and ropes—and dance a bit. All the high-spirited vaudevillians—running breakneck, elbowing for stage space, shoving and joking and clowning—found a prance to do in the spotlight.

The spotlight is now all but snuffed out. This book was made to provide the setting, the moment, and the audience for just one more prance.

The cruel tradition of heckling originated not in variety entertainment but in the legitimate theater, and it began as actual physical punishment. Here spectators hurl potatoes at actors who dared to displease. Rotten tomatoes —less dangerous but presumably funnier—were the preferred ammunition of American vaudeville audiences.

Alone and Alive

ENTERTAINMENT STAGES

Men, women and children, who cannot live on gravity alone, need something to satisfy their gayer, lighter moods and hours, and he who ministers to this want is in a business established by the Author of our very nature. P. T. BARNUM

In America's towns and cities during the second half of the nineteenth century, it was not uncommon for a man to unwind, after a twelve-hour work day, with a schooner of beer at his local honky-tonk. The larger places seated about three hundred of these thirsty fellows on uncomfortable folding chairs, but then comfort was not the main attraction. Beer was, and so were a rowdy male atmosphere, dance hostesses, games of chance, and continuous entertainment.

Having paid a token admission, these fellows would stop at the wine room or bar and then the gaming tables before coming in for the show. By then, some were doubtless giddy from cuddling with the bar girls, for whom they'd bought carbonated sugar-water at an exorbitant four dollars a bottle, thinking it champagne. Some of the bar girls were female impersonators, and the occasional discovery of this deception would prompt a round of rattled indignation, bluster, and ribbing. Other customers might have won or lost a few dollars at roulette, faro, poker, or spindle (an arrow-spinning game).

Once inside the makeshift theater, they would jostle and crowd their ways over the wooden chairs that were lined up in rows to face the stage. As we know from saloon scenes in countless Western movies, the drop curtain was divided into boxes containing elaborate advertisements. These six-by-two-foot rectangles, leased out at two dollars a week, touted funeral parlors, beers, liver pills, and trusses.

The raucous audience would be hushed by the bar girls as a man edged out in front of the curtain, to be greeted by good-natured whistles and catcalls. This stagehand, known as the "thespic altar boy," held a long, flaming taper with which he ignited one footlight and then the next until the skirt of the curtain glowed warmly in the orange light, reflecting it back into the eager faces in the first rows.

One of the three basic sets was in place behind the curtain. If the first sketch was to be melodramatic, the sinister "dark woods" set, with gnarled trees and twisting branches, would be there. If romance was in store, the theater would call for the "light woods" set, meaning the idyllic scene, a sunny glen painted on muslin. If the sketch was to be comic, a kitchen interior would do. Meantime, the actors would be making up with flesh-tinted greasepaint, highlighted by brilliant rouge on the cheeks and good thick black lines for wrinkles. A heavy hand on the makeup was required to make an effect in the dim gaslight.

At curtain's rise, a typical show in one of these honky-tonk theaters would begin with a chorus line of three or four buxom young women in corsets and bloomers. A song-and-dance act might follow, then a singing quartet, a contortionist, or a comedian like Jack Murphy. Murphy

OPPOSITE:
The 3 Gormans, an act with Haverly's touring minstrel show.

ABOVE:
Sophie Tucker

Entertainment Stages

was representative of his trade. He had made his debut in Philadelphia, breaking in with the Log Cabin Varieties. Given his chance, he developed a solo turn, playing the banjo while telling funny stories:

"Judge, this man came home the other night, took down the front door and hit his wife with it." "No case at all," said the judge. "Any man has the right to a-door his wife."

A dramatic sketch might come next, and then another solo turn—a singer, perhaps. And as many as fifteen acts followed, stretching on until dawn. The closing number, called an "afterpiece," was a racy sketch—racy at least for the era—with a title like "After the Shower" or "The Art of Flirtation."

As these honky-tonks grew more popular, they became fancier. Some added private boxes for good customers, with sitting rooms curtained off in the rear. The business conducted back there, it has been reported, ranged from slightly advanced cuddling to outright prostitution.

The honky-tonk shows grew more elaborate. The solitary pianos of the early days were augmented by banjos and occasional clarinets. Yet professional as these places were becoming, they remained exclusively male sanctuaries. A woman contemplating a visit could anticipate not only a tarnished reputation but an evening spent fending off mashers. Ladies and children had to go elsewhere for entertainment: to a riverboat or, if no river was handy, to a Wild West or minstrel show.

The minstrel show was essentially racist, based on impersonations and caricatures of black slaves. As such, it has become a skeleton in our theatrical closet, and that is unfortunate because minstrelsy was an otherwise elegant form of musical theater. The masks and stock characters looked back to the Italian commedia dell'arte of the seventeenth and eighteenth centuries, but the shows also offered a classic and formal basis for the vaudeville bills to come. As ensemble pieces, however, they are peripheral to this appreciation of the soloists of the variety stage. When they disappeared after the Civil War, doomed by the plantation mentality on which they were based, the kind of entertainment a man could bring his family to became a very rare commodity.

Outside the cities, in the farmlands where most Americans lived, practically the only professional entertainment available was the itinerant medicine show, and that was most definitely unfit for the young and the pure. For the medicine show was only half show business. The other half was booze business. Alcohol was the only effective ingredient in the nostrums, potions, and panaceas peddled from the back of the horse-drawn wagons by teams of buffoons and straight-men–spielers. The comedy routines that they played out came quickly to the point: a sales pitch and prompt sampling.

Midway through the nineteenth century, the God-fearing in farm and city remained wary of the corruptive influence of theatricals. Show-going was considered wasteful and show folk disreputable. Why, it was practically sinful just to seek entertainment for the family.

This general attitude did not seem likely to change when one Antonio Pastor opened a new honky-tonk theater in New York City. The diminutive and ebullient Pastor was a former circus ringmaster who had moved over to the business end of show business. His Music Hall, at 199–201 Bowery, was more elegant than the usual honky-tonk, but at first its shows remained resolutely low in tone, aimed at the masculine trade. As far as Pastor was concerned, women and children could go to the museums for amusement, and that was exactly where they *did* go. For it was a "museum" that Phineas Taylor Barnum opened in 1842 to attract

them: P. T. Barnum's American Museum, on Ann Street in New York.

Now here was a bit of hokum worthy of the soon-to-be legendary showman. Barnum realized that no business could be big business until it capitalized on the family trade, which seems today as close to an eternal verity as anything in popular culture. The educational exhibits that Barnum provided to legitimize his museum were no more than a few stuffed animals in the curio section on the main floor, leftovers from the five-story museum he'd converted. However, his new exhibits were carnival sideshows and human oddities—most particularly, popularly, and sensationally, the twenty-five-inch-tall Charles S. Stratton, billed as "General Tom Thumb."

General Thumb was to sell millions of tickets, and they would be sold at a dime apiece. Outside the "dime museum," a barker—called the "Professor" but no different from his fellows on a carnival midway—would lure customers with promises of giants, midgets, bearded ladies, armless wonders, and assorted beastfolk—leopard-, bear-, snake-, and gorilla-people. Barkers would also promote such exotics as Bertha Mills, whose feet were size nineteen, and even real freaks like the original "Siamese twins," Chang and Eng.

Also on the exhibition floor of Barnum's American Museum were "platform" acts that required little space, featuring sword-swallowers, strong-men, and magicians. On the floor above was a House of Wax, filled with replicas of wife-killers, train robbers, former presidents, and, when applicable, their assassins. These kinds of exhibits had changed little since their origin at England's pleasure fairs and would remain the same in more modern days.

On the top floor of the museum was a small variety theater where brief bills of entertainment were performed hourly. Barnum's taste tended to the carnival midway. Rather than vaudeville entertainers, he favored sideshow midgets like Admiral Dot, Queen Mab, or Boston Littlefinger. To his surprise, though, audiences favored the variety shows. By the 1870s one of his bills of entertainment might have included a juggler, a clog dancer, a pair of acrobats, and a musical instrumentalist. The finale, borrowed from the honky-tonks, was an afterpiece.

Many showmen imitated Barnum's successful dime museum—opening New York's elegant Eden Musée and popular Crystal Palace; Boston's Austin and Stone's; Chicago's Epstein's; and Minneapolis's Wonderland. The museum aspects varied. Some advertised stuffed mermaids; others promoted suits of clothes made of blown glass. Soon there was tough competition for the entertainment dime and, in addition to the curio museums, by the 1880s New York also had scores of handsome honkytonks. Besides Tony Pastor's Music Hall there were Harry Hill's in lower Manhattan, Jack Berry's Varieties in Greenwich Village and, farther uptown, in Chelsea, the Alhambra. These little theaters proliferated so quickly that performers could book themselves all the way to California and command steady salaries of as much as two hundred dollars a week.

Meantime, Pastor's new Bowery theater was a success, and he had even organized a touring company of his own. As the 1880s began, theaters were being built especially to house such shows: handsome auditoriums like the Tabor Grand in Denver, the Adelphi in Chicago, and the Howard Atheneum in Boston. Pastor built his own place, the jewel-like Fourteenth Street Theatre. Its opening date was February 8, 1881, and the featured attraction was a lengthy spoof of Gilbert and Sullivan's *Pirates of Penzance*. The Savoy operas had become the rage and, unprotected by copyright, they were shamelessly bootlegged. Rather than blatantly steal them, the more respectable producers presented

OPPOSITE, ABOVE:
Its immediate popularity led Barnum to expand his American Museum, at Ann and Fulton streets. Freak attractions were his favorites. He was surprised by the success of the variety shows on the top floor.

OPPOSITE, BELOW:
Tony Pastor's Fourteenth Street Theatre, birthplace of modern vaudeville, in 1895

pastiches. Pastor's was called *The Pie-Rats of Pen Yan* and it featured a favorite of his, a pretty young dumpling named Lillian Russell. She would of course go on to stardom, but at this stage she was no great attraction and business was only fair.

Pastor, who had once worked for Barnum as a tumbler, clown, and ringmaster, then had an inspiration, an inspiration frankly borrowed from Barnum, whose success with the family trade was now considerable. He struck boldly, eliminating his dance hostesses and bar girls. He closed his theater's liquor, wine, and beer bars. He posted a sign back-stage warning performers against the use of such words as "slob," "sucker," "damn," "hell," and—who knows why?—"socks." Plainly he meant business, and it was to be big business. Pastor's name for it was "polite vaudeville," and the concept was revolutionary: variety enter-tainment for a mixed audience of men and women.

The opening date for the first show under Pastor's new policy, "entertainment clean as a hound's tooth," was October 24, 1881. The night was rainy. At the other variety theaters business was bad, but not at Tony Pastor's. The new Fourteenth Street Theatre was packed and, for the first time, with an audience that included decent women.

The little showman had of course prepared that week's bill with spe-cial care, eliminating all but the most respectable of his regular acts. Ellie Wesner opened with a couple of songs and then launched into her monologue. The Leland Sisters followed with sweet and playful duets. Pastor had slotted Dan Collyer to follow; his songs were silly ones, but

Seen here c. 1891, Lillian Russell, a Tony Pastor protégée, was in the first wave of female singers popular in the early years of American vaudeville. Pastor publicized her hourglass figure.

they had tinges of the old raciness—for instance, "Tommy, Don't Wriggle the Baby." Pastor probably sighed with relief when it got by.

Mack and Ferguson raced on stage as if to distract the audience from Collyer. They were a popular Irish dialect comedy team and their routine was well known and beloved, all the way to its climax, when Mack buried a hatchet in Ferguson's skull. Even though Ferguson wore a padded fright wig to cushion the blow, years of playing the act would leave him deaf. Lillie Western followed with her musical varieties (banjo and concertina), and then Frank McNish closed with low comedy. As a surprise finale, Pastor himself appeared in his traditional ringmaster outfit to sing a half-dozen of the thousands of songs in his repertoire.

That first night was triumphant but not revolutionary. It would not be so easy to overcome one of the major proscriptions of Western civilization and make regular theatergoers of women. The initial audience of curious women did not return, and the male customers, upon whom the day-to-day business depended, were pressing Pastor to resume traditional shows, booze, and girls. Business sagged but the showman was resolute. He compromised by designating one performance a week as Ladies' Night. At that performance, every female customer would receive a free box of chocolates. None came. He offered flowers, food (hams and bags of flour). Still they would not come.

In desperation he advertised that the first twenty-five women to buy tickets for the special ladies' show would receive free silk dresses. Silk dresses did it. Twenty-five were hardly enough. Scores of women were in line before the box office even opened. Virtually every study of American variety entertainment marks the birth of vaudeville with Pastor's silk-dress promotion.

Tony Pastor's clean-up campaign was doubtless necessary to overcome the historically sleazy reputation of variety entertainment, but his eagerness to avoid even a hint of the risqué would ultimately lead to excessive prudishness. A practically priggish conservatism developed in vaudeville that detracted from the ribald spirit that had always provided a certain dash. Vaudeville paid the price for acceptance by upholding a level of decency not merely fit for women and children but sufficient to satisfy the demands of an inquisitor. As a result of this self-censorship, a curious blend of low urges and high morality would for decades characterize *all* American entertainment—theater, the movies, television. Stage invective would be limited to juvenile epithets; in the movies, not even married couples would sleep in the same bed, and life would go on without bodily functions; television entertainment would be sanitized as if for an audience of children exclusively.

Perhaps the show makers of Pastor's time as well as our own endured these limitations because they were seeking not only family business but professional and personal acceptance. It was not many years, after all, since they had been barred from polite society; certain hotels and communities still excluded them. Perhaps for all these reasons, vaudeville was to become puritanical beyond the dictates of plain sense. There seemed to prevail a basic fear that one blue joke or sexual innuendo, one off-color sketch or frank expletive would not merely alienate the family trade but destroy the hard-won offstage respectability. It would be back to the honky-tonks and the fleabag hotels for the rogues, vagabonds, and sturdy beggars. This, then, was the bargain: the hypocritical acceptance of a moral code to which neither performers nor audiences actually adhered.

Pastor's Fourteenth Street Theatre became the most famous vaudeville house in America. Its roster of performers was brilliant, for only the best could play polite vaudeville, only the best could be thoroughly entertaining without smuttiness—and only the best played Pastor's: Harrigan and Hart, Weber and Fields, the Four Cohans, Buster Keaton, Nat Goodwin, and of course Lillian Russell. Audiences flocked to see these ascendant stars and doubtless to see Pastor himself as well. He appeared in the lobby at almost every performance in his tails, high-heeled boots and collapsible top hat. On a lucky night an audience might even find him strolling on stage to sing his theme song:

> *Are you going to the ball this evening?*
> *No, not this evening! Some other evening!*
> *Good evening!*

They loved him, they loved his high spirits and good humor, and so did the performers who worked for him. Pastor was said never to have "closed" —that is, fired—an act. His attitude toward performers was so sentimental that when reminded of his house band's ineptitude he once remarked, "I know they're terrible but they're my old boys and they can die here." And he could well afford to be magnanimous. He had vaudeville all to himself. The competition was still in Boston.

Benjamin Franklin Keith had cut his teeth in show business as a "candy butcher," hawking chocolates and racy gazettes during intermissions at primitive Boston variety houses. He had a real talent for discovering (or inventing) freaks, and when he left burlesque to open a curio museum he revealed another gift, a knack for naming them: the Dog-Faced Boy (a youth with a badly splotched complexion); Baby Alice, the Midget Wonder (a premature baby); and the Three-Headed Songstress (an optical illusion).

Keith found an ambitious and energetic young partner in Edward F. Albee—whose grandson is the well-known playwright—and expanded operations, acquiring a second museum and putting up a variety theater in Philadelphia. Soon he replaced his freak shows with popular acts and low comics. In 1893 Keith and Albee opened a theater just blocks from Pastor's and took advantage of what Keith perceived as Pastor's weaknesses. Their Union Square Theatre was bigger than the Fourteenth Street Theatre and they offered higher salaries to lure the best performers, leaving the sentimental Pastor with every worn-out and needy entertainer who begged him for a booking. Pastor had also cut back to two shows a day, and Keith and Albee began running continuous shows.

Still Pastor lorded it over the competition. Did not songwriters still clamor to have their latest numbers aired at his place? Introducing a song at Tony Pastor's, it was believed, could guarantee it national popularity. Influential as Pastor was in popularizing songs like the smash hit "Wait Till the Sun Shines, Nellie," the little impresario considered comedy acts the key to variety success. Though he avoided the cruder ethnic sketches that were attracting the crowds to Keith's theater—"The Sport and the Jew," "Irish by Name but Coon by Birth," and "The Merry Wop"—by today's standards his comedy acts were, as Joe Laurie, Jr., dryly remarked in *Vaudeville*, rather less than witty:

In those days the corn was very green. Actors laid them in the aisles with such sparkling chestnuts as, "I sent my wife to the Thousand Islands for a vacation—a week on each island." Or, "Are oysters healthy?" "I never heard them complain." Or, "You can drive a horse to drink but a pencil must be lead."

And any gag employing false teeth or hair, a wooden leg or a mother-in-law panicked the house.

For thirty years, Eddie Foy starred in both vaudeville and legitimate theater. In 1913, at the age of fifty-nine, he came out of retirement to form the most famous of all family acts, "Eddie Foy and the Seven Little Foys." Here he does his youthful vaudeville turn, "Why Do They Call Me a Gibson Girl?" in the Broadway show The Orchid.

Plainly and regrettably, the line between popular entertainment and the higher theatrical arts was one no self-respecting writer would cross.

Albee hounded Pastor as if the entire vaudeville business depended on the New York market. Although he was supposedly Keith's executive assistant, it was he who wielded the power. He raised star salaries higher and cut the admission price to fifty cents. In response, Pastor dropped

his own admission to thirty cents and remained confident enough to take a full-page advertisement in the Christmas edition of the *Dramatic Mirror*, boasting that his Fourteenth Street Theatre was "the first specialty and vaudeville theater in America catering to polite tastes," and that its clientele included "the best families of the metropolis."

Albee pressed Keith to build more and bigger theaters: the Keith Colonial in Boston, the Palace in Cleveland, a second house in Boston, and another in New York. Relegating his chief to the background, and ever more aggressive, ruthless, and now widely despised and feared, Albee was fast becoming czar of vaudeville and the Keith houses the most important "wheel" (booking circuit) in the country. Only the top acts played it. This, now, was the big time.

The expression, "big time," like "small time," is an outgrowth of the vaudevillians' use of the word "time." An act would sign a contract for a certain number of work weeks on one of the vaudeville wheels. Such a stint was known as "Keith time" or "Orpheum time," and, then, as "playing the Keith time." Because these were major wheels that offered the most comfortable theaters, the biggest and most polite audiences, the highest pay, and the best working conditions, playing them was known as playing the "big time." The "medium" and "small" times referred to lesser circuits with smaller salaries and meaner conditions.

Moving from one circuit to the next, as if on meshing gears, an act could be booked as far as two years in advance without scheduling the

The tiny Anna Held, another reigning queen among vaudeville's lady singers, was married to the great Flo Ziegfeld, who boasted to the press that she took daily baths in fresh milk.

same theater twice. Thus a comedy sketch, dance routine, or set of songs could remain unchanged and provide a performer's livelihood for years. No wonder, then, the addition of even one joke to a routine was considered a major revision. Vaudevillians would wait for remote engagements to test new material so that no harm would be done to the dear-as-life act, should the new material fail. In this way, routines were protected as they were polished—as well they might be, for an act was all a performer had. It was his living. Naturally, anyone who stole material, even so much as a joke, was considered vile. Vaudevillians even established a central office where, after being written out and sealed, acts could be registered so as to establish their true and original authorship.

The Keith wheel was considered the biggest time of all because it paid the highest salaries and offered the best working conditions in the largest, most luxurious, and greatest number of theaters. Its performers played only two shows a day—Albee having reimposed that on Keith, though hardly out of sympathy for performers. Albee simply believed it to be efficient scheduling as well as an argument for lower pay: once he had performers dependent upon him he slashed their salaries.

On the medium time, the grind might be four performances a day, and on the small time an act could work for six or even eight performances a day, with the pay as little as twenty-five dollars a week. This was known as the "death trail," or "the aching heart" to those unfortunate enough to be playing storefronts, virtually honky-tonks, in one-night stands in the boondocks.

Depressed by Albee's competitive tactics, Tony Pastor retired in 1908, but by then Keith had other Eastern competitors: F. F. Proctor, Marcus Loew, Klaw and Erlanger, and William Morris. As for the rest of the country, Martin Beck's Orpheum circuit shared the Midwest with the Kohl and Castle wheel, while Considine-Sullivan and Alexander Pantages controlled the West Coast.

This, then, was the start of vaudeville's brilliant era. A host of motley jesters was to blanket the country, confidently booking themselves hundreds of performances in advance, the top stars earning as much as several thousand dollars a week. The center stage was in New York City, now the country's entertainment capital. There, splendid theaters boasted a peak-caliber eight-act variety bill, which had developed a ritualistic quality.

As Bill Smith explained in *The Vaudevillians*, an eight-act show began with a "dumb" (silent) act—an acrobat, or a bicyclist, or perhaps an animal-trainer. The second place—traditionally the worst spot on the bill because it was the first talking act, performed while the audience was usually still arriving—was filled by a newcomer, a minor comedian, or a female singer. There followed a "tab" show (a tabloid, or abbreviated, version of a recent Broadway success) or a "flash" act, meaning an act with a large company, elaborate costumes, and its own scenery.

The fourth and fifth spots on this typical agenda were usually filled by a solid performer, perhaps an established comedy team, or by a rowdy act like "School Days," one of Gus Edwards's kiddie groups, or perhaps the Marx Brothers' "Fun in Hi Skule." Sixth on the bill was approaching the cream of the show, and this niche called for a class act, perhaps a dance team. Then came the headliner, *always* seventh and next to last. The closing spot, considered a throwaway since many customers left after the star turn, was usually another dumb act.

If the program was ritualized, the acts were not. Their variety was limited only by the performers' imaginations, and there were no limitations on originality, brilliance, or chutzpah. Entertainers trotted on stage

seeking no less than to overwhelm the audience, and whether the reaction was enthusiasm or contempt, nothing they did was ever ludicrous enough to be truly surprising, for the ludicrous was merely everyday and some acts were magnificently preposterous. The Cherry Sisters, for instance, were billed as "The World's Worst Act." They once sued a newspaper for libel on the basis of an insulting review, and after watching the act the judge ruled against them. A net was stretched across the stage whenever Effie and Addie Cherry played Hammerstein's Victoria Theatre in New York, to protect them from tossed eggs and tomatoes. Beginning as five farm girls and ending as two, the Cherry Sisters insisted that they were supposed to be *good*. They enjoyed a thirty-year vaudeville career on the premise of being awful and not knowing it.

Other curious acts might show up on a bill, such as "Francis White, the World's Smallest Dancer," or "Willard, the Man Who Grows." Willard would chat with audience volunteers while the backdrop behind him inched downward. The strong horizontal line that was behind him at waist level when he began would end up around his hips—hence, growth. McNaughton, the Human Tank, swallowed frogs, and Charlie Chase ate lightbulbs. Swain's Cats and Rats raced around a track, the cats astride the rats, and The Lunatic Bakers jumped in and out of ovens. Cantor Joseph Rosenblatt sang "Molly Machree" and the armless Lutz Brothers assembled an engine with their feet. The team of Marguerite Webb and Jack Connelly played the piano with fruit. Annie May Abbott, the Georgia Magnet, defied anyone in the audience to lift her.

Tops among the odd acts, believe it or not, was Helen Keller, assisted by Annie Sullivan. They were more sober personages in later years but in those cheerful and halcyon days they headlined in vaudeville, Keller using her fingers to read the lips of audience volunteers. Nobody considered this disrespectful or insensitive. Show business was a leveler. And in such sweet times, beyond chastisement, playing the Keith circuit became a fair mark of success.

Yet, several successful theaters in New York notwithstanding, the frustrated Albee could not establish a flagship house there. First Tony Pastor had taken center stage, and then Oscar Hammerstein grabbed the spotlight. A multimillionaire inventor of cigar-making machines, Hammerstein was a fellow with a history of failed theaters. He had indulged his enthusiasm for show business by building auditoriums: first, in 1880, the Harlem Opera House; then, in 1895, the Columbia, uptown on East One Hundred Twenty-fifth Street; and after that, the plush Olympia Music Hall, on Broadway at Forty-fifth Street; and finally, in 1906, the Manhattan Opera House, on Thirty-fourth Street. These various white elephants were done in by architectural errors, cost overruns, and disastrous programing. Hammerstein's love of lavish entertainment, grand opera in particular, was not supported by business sense or even a reliable showmanship (only by his cigar-making machines). One of his grandiose notions, for instance, was a vaudeville version of a three-ring circus, with three acts performed simultaneously. In 1893 he accepted a bet with conductor Gustav Kerber and in forty-eight hours composed a grand opera, *The Koh-i-Noor Diamond*. Kerber refused to pay on the grounds that Hammerstein's opera was terrible, but the ingenuous impresario produced it anyhow, on the stage of his Harlem Opera House. *The Koh-i-Noor Diamond* attracted a pathetic four hundred dollars in ticket sales at its single performance.

When in 1898 Hammerstein's $350-thousand Olympia was sold out from under him, he was left destitute. Friends organized benefits at the various music halls he'd built and lost. The undauntable Hammerstein took the money and, a hopeless case, put up yet another theater, the 1,250-seat Victoria at Seventh Avenue and Forty-second Street, and for once his gamble paid off. The Victoria became America's premier vaudeville showcase, known to entertainers simply as "the corner." It would ultimately earn Hammerstein five million dollars and during the next seventeen years provide a stage for the country's greatest performers.

Of course, it was not Hammerstein who was responsible for the Victoria's success. It was his son Willie, a fellow as reserved as his father was flamboyant. Behind Willie's dour facade, however, were the gaudy colors of an inherited showmanship, and the colors showed where they mattered most: in the operation of the theater. For instance, Willie had no qualms about advertising the farewell appearance of the fabled cooch dancer Carmencita, six years after her death. Audiences accepted the impersonator as if deception were a normal part of show business, which of course it was. Over the big auditorium, Hammerstein built another called the Paradise Roof. There he promoted "Hy-Tone Vaudeville," with acts more refined than those in the music hall below. The afterpieces, however, were usually played by performers who had just finished the show downstairs.

Willie Hammerstein served refreshments in the glass-walled Paradise Roof. He installed as hostess a young black woman, whose expression was even grimmer than his own. Known as Silent Sue, she glared at the customers and they were dared to make her smile. Silent Sue could not smile supposedly because her facial muscles were paralyzed. Spreading such a rumor was typical of Hammerstein's showmanly style.

Another example of it was hiring Evelyn Nesbit to appear at the Victoria. Miss Nesbit was the beautiful wife of Harry K. Thaw, who in a jealous rage murdered her lover, the prominent architect Stanford White. Thaw had been committed to a state hospital for the criminally insane. Evelyn capitalized on the tragedy by performing in vaudeville. Such appearances by notorious public figures were known as "freak acts" and Willie Hammerstein was given credit (or blame) for originating the genre. He booked prizefighters and explorers at the Victoria too, but along with his audience he seemed to prefer swindlers like Barney Bertsche, forgers like George Schroeder, bank robbers like Ed Morrell, and just about anyone involved with murder.

As 1913 began, Hammerstein was scheduling these and otherwise accomplished performers far in advance as he prepared to deal with the mighty competition of the Palace Theatre, rising some five blocks to the north. When that plush 1,700-seat auditorium was originally announced, he had been less concerned, probably feeling confident on his home ground. The builder was Martin Beck, the Midwest vaudeville entrepreneur, who was hoping to crash the New York market. Neither Beck nor Hammerstein, however, had reckoned with Edward Albee, who was half crazy on the subject of the Keith circuit's being without a flagship theater in New York. The Palace apparently snapped his tolerance. Albee just would not countenance an outlander's strolling in with a "palace" and gaining squatter's rights to the territory in the bargain. So he simply saw to it that no performers were available to Beck. This wasn't hard to do, as his United Booking Office controlled every major act in the country. And when that happened, Beck's financial backing van-

Swain's Birds, an early vaudeville act

ished and Albee took control of the big theater, the most beautiful vaudeville house in the nation.

When the Palace finally opened later in 1913, its marquee bore the Keith nameplate, and Albee had his flagship theater. It was to become a legend. No name is so closely identified with top-flight vaudeville as the

The last of Oscar Hammerstein's huge theaters was the Victoria, at the corner of Seventh Avenue and Forty-second Street. Thanks to the showmanship of his son Willie, it was the first of the old man's elephants that was not white. Because of the popularity of Willie's "freak acts," the Victoria became known as the "nut house."

Palace Theatre, and to this day, "playing the Palace" means being at the very top as an entertainer.

But for a while Hammerstein's Victoria remained New York City's premier vaudeville house. Just to be near it, performers liked to hang out on the street in front and talk show business. The Palace's managing director and booking agent, Eddie Valentine Dowling, floundered for an entertainment policy to distinguish it from the crowd and from the Victoria particularly, and nothing seemed to work. It was as if Hammerstein had cornered the showmanship market. Eventually, Dowling was inspired to import Sarah Bernhardt from France to star in a one-act play (playlets were not uncommon in vaudeville). The Divine Sarah insisted on being paid in gold coin immediately after every performance, but she was worth every karat. For with her engagement, the Palace would become identified with vaudeville that was prestigious enough to rank with the legitimate theater.

Now, the difference between vaudeville and the Broadway legitimate theater was simple: vaudeville was a program of variety acts that was performed two (or more) times a day and changed every week. Legitimate theater was a musical or dramatic show that played only eight performances a week, running unaltered as long as audiences supported it. Broadway's musical revues might resemble vaudeville in offering a

After vaudeville audiences had lost interest in the scandal that rocketed Evelyn Nesbit to notoriety, she was faced with either oblivion or the development of an act based on some talent she had not yet displayed. The beautiful former chorus girl found a dance partner in a boxer named Jack Clifford, with whom she performed at B. F. Keith's Alhambra Theatre.

series of entertainers and sketches, but they aimed to please a more sophisticated taste; they offered new songs; the program never changed; and there was not the variety—the jugglers, magicians, acrobats, and comedy acts—that gave vaudeville its tempo.

For performers, however, there was a much more significant difference between vaudeville and the legitimate theater: prestige. The legitimate theater was the *legitimate* theater. The Palace would change that, but while the Victoria reigned, deluxe it may have been but vaudeville it still was.

At the new Palace, the rules of propriety were as strict as they had been when Tony Pastor first introduced polite vaudeville. "Remember," a sign backstage read, "this theater caters to ladies and gentlemen and children. Vulgarity will not be tolerated. Check with manager before using any material you have any doubt about. Don't use the words hell, damn, devil, cockroach, spit, etc."

After Eddie Dowling announced Sarah Bernhardt's imminent appearance at the Palace, Willie Hammerstein countered by signing his favorite freak act, Evelyn Nesbit, for a return engagement at a considerable three thousand dollars a week. It seemed, initially, as if for once Willie had miscalculated. This woman who had inspired murderous jealousy no longer seemed able to inspire audiences. Business at the Victoria was slow until, by a coincidence still difficult to believe, her ex-husband, Harry Thaw, escaped from Matawan State Hospital.

When Thaw was found in Canada, Willie had a friend up there send a wire signed "H.K.T." which contained a threat to kill Evelyn plus a threat to sue the theater if the name of Thaw was not instantly removed from the billing. Thaw did not come back to New York but largely due to the way Willie Hammerstein ballyhooed the news of his escape, Evelyn remained the box office draw at his theatre for eight weeks, attracting $175,000 during that run. (Charles and Louise Samuels, *Once Upon a Stage*)

The stunt was to be Willie's last, for he died the next year, and without his wonderfully sobersided flamboyance the Victoria faded and was sold and razed. The Palace, now without any real competition, rose to glory and its weekly show became an event. Afficionados would attend the Monday matinee just to be first to see the new bill. They would catch the classic sketches repeatedly, searching for refinements. Tickets weren't cheap (a dollar and a half for an orchestra seat), but there in the plushest showcase for the country's favorite entertainment medium the top entertainers in the country played before the toughest audiences. The Palace was the ranking stage in a field of thousands from tents in the farmlands to other Palaces that had sprung up in emulation of the first, in cities from coast to coast.

The one and only original Palace Theatre featured only the best. The great women singers who had dominated show business since the turn of the century—Eva Tanguay, Nora Bayes, Elsie Janis, Sophie Tucker, and other troupers in feathers and hats—were the backbone of its original roster. The wonderful funnymen played there, such teams as Smith and Dale; Burns and Allen; Clayton, Jackson, and Durante. True, Ed Wynn, Bert Lahr, and the other great clowns favored the legitimate theater, but clowning was a European tradition as was the theater. America's great innovation was the monologist, and these fearless talkers grew up on the Palace's stage—Julius Tannen, Lou Holtz, Milton Berle, Joe Frisco, Fred Allen, Frank Tinney, and the greatest of all, Jack Benny and Frank Fay. (Bob Hope played the Palace too, early in his career. He was so discouraged that he had to be talked out of quitting show business.)

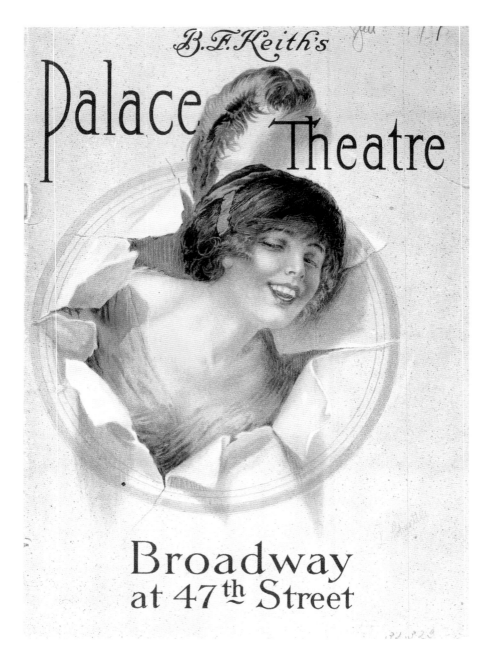

B.F. Keith's

Palace Theatre

Broadway at 47ᵗʰ Street

OPPOSITE, ABOVE LEFT:
Evelyn Nesbit was one of Willie Hammerstein's "freak acts," offering not talent but notoriety. What Evelyn was notorious for was sex appeal.

OPPOSITE, ABOVE RIGHT:
If Eva Tanguay had been tempestuous but untalented, Elsie Janis was just the reverse—meek but perhaps the most gifted of all the vaudeville actresses. A headliner in her teens, she could sing, dance, perform acrobatics, and do impressions, but she achieved her most glorious successes in troop shows, entertaining American doughboys overseas. It was there that she discovered and sponsored (and, some say, fell in love with) Maurice Chevalier.

OPPOSITE, BELOW LEFT:
Imposing in her brimmed hats and endless boas, Nora Bayes was nevertheless victimized by her own romantic and emotional soul. She talked too much about her private life onstage and backstage and complained so much about her competitors that Eddie Dowling, the Palace's managing director, once pushed her out the stage door and didn't let her back in for the show.

OPPOSITE, BELOW RIGHT:
Although she was born in Warsaw, Anna Held's specialty was playing the French coquette and singing (into a hand-held mirror) such songs as "I Just Can't Make My Eyes Behave." Married to Flo Ziegfeld, this great singing lady never appeared in his Follies.

OVERLEAF, LEFT:
Irene Foote was a New York debutante when she met and married a little-known English song-and-dance man named Vernon Castle. As a team, personifying elegance and romance, Vernon and Irene Castle became idols of the American stage. They built a beautiful nightclub and called it "Castles in the Air." Irene's hair and dress styles set the fashion for a generation of women. As romance would have it, Vernon became a World War I pilot and died in a flaming crash.

OVERLEAF, RIGHT:
The dance team of Fred and Adele Astaire, one year after turning professional. It was 1905, he was five, she six, and they were already touring on the medium time.

There were other big-time vaudeville houses in New York City—the Riverside and the Riviera on upper Broadway, and Proctor's Fifth Avenue downtown, and the Orpheum in Brooklyn—but for a first-class evening of first-class entertainment in a first-class setting, as lavish and special an evening as any Broadway theater might offer, the Palace was guaranteed gala, and tickets were scalped outside almost every night.

The beginning of the end came with the Wall Street Crash. Suddenly, there was little money available for frivolity. The radio networks were already established, and a depressed population preferred to stay at home and hear the best entertainers for nothing rather than go out and pay for second best at a local vaudeville theater. Many city-dwellers who still wanted to go out for an evening preferred the activity of dancing along with the new orchestras to the passivity of theatrical spectatorship. Too, hard times inspire a certain physical recklessness that can serve as a vent for frustration, nervousness, and rage. Dancing is a readily available and acceptable outlet. It thrived in the Crash years as it would in wartimes.

The Palace's downfall began in 1929, when a three-on-Sundays policy was instituted. Then Albee was forced to lift his ban on radio performers, bringing in Eddie Cantor and George Jessel for eight weeks each in

Miss NORA BAYES

The Theatre Magazine Co.

1930. By 1932 the operation was fraying at the edges. The great theater stooped to four shows a day, alternating with movies. Within months, the shows were dropped. The golden age was over.

Personal entertainment is a performing art without strict form. Each entertainer creates his own form; he is the art as well as the artist. His creation, his show, his act cannot be read or hung on a wall, or be re-created by anyone else. It must be performed on a stage in front of

The greatest star and the hottest attraction in all of vaudeville was Eva Tanguay, the "I Don't Care Girl," who by her own admission could neither sing nor dance. Early in her career, Tanguay socked another chorus girl who was upstaging her and discovered the value of publicity. Her sexual adventures, fiery temper, and unpredictable stage behavior kept her in headlines and business.

ABOVE:

Though in her day vaudeville was striving to shed its risqué reputation, Sophie Tucker was insistently, exuberantly, and triumphantly bawdy. She started out, at the turn of the century, singing in blackface, a "coonshouter" in a New York beer hall (some consider this the first cabaret entertainment in America). Tucker found regular work as a rollicking and lusty act. Pictured here in 1914, she had progressed in vaudeville to the big time of Oscar Hammerstein's Victoria and B. F. Keith's Palace. Always unique, "The Soph" survived after the other singing ladies of early vaudeville went out of style.

BELOW:

By professional consensus, at the very top of the vaudeville class were Jack Benny and Frank Fay. Fay's ego, awesome in good times, was just as inflated when its owner was under siege. Late in his career, when things were going badly, Fay returned to the Palace to share emcee duties with his wife, the glamorous movie star Barbara Stanwyck. After two weeks of a three-week engagement that everyone in show business knew was thanks to Stanwyck, Fay skipped out, leaving her to finish alone (Gus Van stepped in as his replacement).

an audience. Without that stage and audience, he and the act do not exist.

As America's thousands of vaudeville theaters were shutting down, entertainers were pushed to huddle in the few remaining spotlights; on the last stages. But in the youthful time of vaudeville, as in all youthful times, decay and change and death itself lay ahead, in a future not only unforeseeable but unimaginable. America's great entertainers still had time, while there still was time, to caper across the great vaudeville stages.

AL JOLSON
The Greatest Entertainer in the World

If anyone epitomizes the singular excitement of live performance and its ephemeral, unrecordable nature, that figure is Al Jolson. Billed as "The World's Greatest Entertainer," he probably was just that. By almost every available account, his performances were electrifying and his appeal crossed all boundaries of taste and intelligence.

To say that he was a singer is to call Fred Astaire a dancer, Jack Benny a comedian, or Liberace a piano player. He invented a new kind of singing and a new kind of song—big numbers done in big, overwhelming ways. Jolson would move up stage and down, from one wing to the other, dancing, skipping, getting down on one knee and wringing his hands, then rising to spread his arms in exaltation. Song singing, a passive and nearly inane activity, had been made into performance.

He had a voice of size, a rich baritone that landed on each note with bell-like purity; his rhythmic impulse was metronomic; and his musicianship was influenced by the improvisations and slides of Dixieland jazz. But the songs themselves were an utterly new sort. Soaring numbers conceived for theatrical effect, they were designed especially for the Jolson style; high-stepping, expansive, and totally American songs: "Swanee," "My Mammy," "Rockabye Your Baby with a Dixie Melody," "Toot, Toot, Tootsie," "There's a Rainbow 'round My Shoulder," "I'm Sittin' on Top of the World." Nobody had ever sung such extroverted numbers before, at least not with the dominating verve that Jolson flashed. Theater music had been light and cheerful until then, or else downright florid. And nobody had attempted the flat-out bravura that Jolson demonstrated as he ran on stage (he would never just walk) to grab the spotlight as if with his hand and not let go of it, rocking and socking. Future star singers and theatrical belters who had never seen Al Jolson would owe their careers to him, for he invented big singing.

Al Jolson's movies and records provide few clues to the effect he created onstage, the effect of a man possessed, according to the critic Gilbert Millstein. But there are enough descriptions available to piece together an impression of what it must have been like to be in this performer's shock range.

Jolson had, in 1909, left a trio (which included his brother Harry) to go out as a single. After a year in vaudeville's medium time, he felt cocky enough to take full-page advertisements in the theatrical newspapers announcing, "You never heard of me but you will!" He left vaudeville for the prestigious Dockstader's Minstrels, and there he developed the black musical and verbal intonations to go with his blackface makeup. The Minstrels led to a small part in *La Belle Paree!*, a musical comedy that was opening the palatial Winter Garden Theatre on Broadway. The overlong show received dismal reviews, none of which singled out the twenty-five-year-old blackface singer. At the third performance, the audience had been decimated by walk-outs when he made his usual entrance. Pearl Sieben, Jolson's biographer, describes the occasion:

He walked to the center of the stage. The single spotlight hit him. He shaded his eyes with one hand and gazed out to the audience.

"Lots of brave folks out there," he said. "Either that or you can't read." There was a spattering of uneasy laughter. "Come to think of it," he went on, "after the reviews we got, there's a lot of brave folks up here on the stage." The laughter increased. It was infectious. Al pointed to the audience. "Hey," he said, "I know you. You was in the audience the last time I played Brighton

Beach. You used to like my act. What's the matter, you come into this classy joint you think you shouldn't have a good time? C'mon, this place ain't so much. I remember when it was the Horse Exchange." A wave of laughter spread through the audience. "That's better. Now I got a few songs to sing—if you'll listen."

The next day's papers told of a new star who had captured the sophisticated Winter Garden audience.

Talent, if not the least of it, is only one key to a performer's success. The way that the talent is used, how it is communicated, how it is packaged counts just as much, and Jolson had already developed idiosyncracies enough to distinguish him from all the other blackface singers. It was certainly brash to break character in a musical comedy and chat with the audience; and it was risking annoyance to be arrogant about it. But he was "Joley" to everyone now and everyone was a "mug" or a "kid" to him, and his casual style was disarming. Audiences always sense an entertainer's pleasure or ease onstage, and they share in it.

Although *La Belle Paree!* had a Jerome Kern score, it was common in the musical theater of the time to interpolate additional songs, and Jolson added a Stephen Foster medley that included "Oh, Susanna," "Camptown Races," and "I Dream of Jeannie." He would ever after be expected to interrupt his shows and announce that he was going to treat the audience to some singing, and the hell with the plot. They came to count on it (as the actors in the cast came to resent it), awaiting Jolson's tag line, "You ain't heard nothin' yet."

He wore a nappy wig over the blackface makeup, a dark blue suit that was short at the cuffs, a floppy bow tie, and white gloves. Those gloves would develop a life of their own as he introduced an entire vocabulary of hand language—palms up or down or out, fingers jabbing, fists punching—to go along with the poses and gestures that added choreographic flair and drama to the mere act of singing. Jolson was becoming an entire act. He would skip, shuffle, leap down into the audience and dash up one aisle and down the other, stopping to serenade a pretty girl, an old woman, a child. Corniness works—don't forget it. Then he was back onstage, turning away from the audience but never letting it out of eye contact. Now his eyes were rolled into the corners of the sockets, staring, winking. He would freeze in that pose and then pop into a fast soft-shoe or a buck-and-wing, until the suspenseful beat began. Then he would segue into a melodramatic, incantatory recitation.

> *Mammy, I'm-a-comin'*
> *Sor-sorry that I made you wait,*
> *Oh mammy, mammy, I'm comin'*
> *Oh God I hope—I hope I'm not too late!*

It wasn't over yet. He would clap his hands and jab a finger, and then he would tilt his head back, arch his spine, roll his eyeballs heavenward, and spread-eagle his arms to climax.

> *Mammy, don't you know me?*
> *It's your little baby!*

And finally, punching and peaking,

> *I'd walk a million miles*
> *For one of your smiles,*
> *My ma-aaa-my!*

ABOVE:
Al Jolson sheet music cover

BELOW:
Al Jolson's career was resurrected by the hugely successful 1947 film The Jolson Story. *Here he rehearses for a comeback appearance at a New York movie-presentation house.*

GEORGE JESSEL

The California branch of vaudeville's top comedians—the group that had succeeded in radio—was an arrogant lot. George Burns, Jack Benny, Groucho Marx, Milton Berle. They were competitive and argumentative, but there was one thing they agreed on: the funniest man of all was George Jessel. The problem with Jessel, the consensus seemed to be, was that he spread himself too thin. He was an actor and a singer as well as a monologist. He could come through onstage (there were comedians' comedians who couldn't) but he never was as funny in performance as he was among fellow funnymen. For instance, Burns couldn't get over Jessel's impromptu cold-war crack, "You guys think the Russians can't invent an atom bomb just because they dance sitting down." And Eddie Cantor loved Jessel's ad-lib at a White House luncheon, "Never before has so little chicken served so many."

Jessel had starred on Broadway in *The Jazz Singer* and had worked regularly as a monologist in vaudeville. His opening line was among the most famous: "Hello, mom? This is your son Georgie. You know. From the checks." But between a love of fun and perhaps too easy a flow of natural talent, he let his career go to flab and, while he never wanted for work, neither did he ever win from the public an acclaim commensurate with that of his colleagues. Instead, he became a caricature of himself, ultimately to be better known as a subject of impressions than for his own great gifts.

As the Palace began to show the first signs of decline, vaudeville mogul Edward Albee was forced to lift his ban on radio performers, hiring George Jessell (left) and Eddie Cantor for an extended engagement as co-emcees.

*George Jessel at the Palace, doing
his impression of Eddie Cantor*

CLOWNING AROUND

A performer watched an opening act. A comic barrelled onstage with a red nose a blue wig, green makeup, teeth blacked out, baggy pants, funny hat, a loud vest, slap shoes, an outsized checkered coat and a big heavy watch chain. "By the looks of that guy," the performer said to the stage manager, "he must be a very funny comedian." The stage manager replied, "That's the straight man."
JOE LAURIE, JR., *Vaudeville*

The wild and raucous comedians who had been doted upon by the honky-tonk audiences were perhaps pioneers but they were also the cavemen of comedy. Their senses of humor were too broad and (though it's hard to imagine) sometimes even too ethnic for the more refined audiences of "polite vaudeville." The early crowds at Tony Pastor's had enough of the honky-tonk in their blood to be amused by the mayhem of Mack and Ferguson, but not for long. Soon they were asking for more sophistication than a hatchet in the skull. Dialect provided it. Almost any accent was considered funny: Italian, Jewish, Russian, Irish. And Dutch:

A: I am delightfulness to meet you.
B: The disgust is all mine.

This inspired exchange was dreamed up by Joe Weber and Lew Fields, a star dialect-comedy team that did make the successful transition from honky-tonk to vaudeville. They too had started out as a knockabout act, "The Skull Crackers," but the two twelve-year-olds worked out the characters of Mike (Weber) and Myer (Fields) and soon discarded the bludgeon of slapstick for false whiskers, checkered suits, flat derbies, and the drier pleasures of verbal riposte.

Mike: I receivedidid a letter from moin goil but I don't know how to writeninin her back.
Myer: Writteninin her back! Such an edumuncation you got it? Writteninin her back! You mean rotteninin her back! How can you answer her ven you don't know how to write?
Mike: Dot makes no nefer mind. She don't know how to read.

It is difficult but not impossible to envision the circumstances that made such dialect jokes hilarious, but we can certainly understand why audiences were amused by this classic exchange:

Myer: Who was that lady I saw you with?
Mike: That was no lady. That was my wife.

OPPOSITE:
The Marx Brothers' stage identities were established early. They lavished a wealth of career time developing, mining, and finally becoming these characters.

ABOVE:
Jimmy Durante

Fat and skinny was the formula for teams. The straight man was skinny because fat presumably looked funny. About the same height and build, Weber and Fields used padding and elevator shoes to create the impression of fat and skinny, and by the turn of the century they were earning two thousand dollars a week apiece with such material as:

Myer: Tell it, vot is you playing?
Mike: Pool, ain't it?
Myer: You got to name vot ball you shoot.
Mike: Good! I name it Rudolph.

Such routines could be used for years as an act looped one circuit before hooking onto the next. Probably no routine was ever plied more continuously than Joe Smith and Charles Dale's classic "Doctor Kronkite." This was essentially a prototype burlesque sketch, calling for a comic, a straight man, and a dumb blonde. Smith and Dale squeezed a buxom actress into a nurse's uniform and took the doctor's office sketch to the top of vaudeville.

Smith (the patient): I've got a rheumatism.
Dale (Dr. Kronkite): Where do you have this rheumatism?
Smith: On the back of my neck.
Dale: That's a good place for it. Where would you *like* a rheumatism?
Smith: On the back of *your* neck.

Although Joe Weber (left) and Lou Fields broke up their act while young, they periodically reunited and at one point even bought their own Broadway theater.

Smith and Dale were so popular they were able to play repeat engagements without changing the act, for knowing every line and bit of business seemed only to heighten the fun. It was no longer the humor of the exchanges that delighted afficionados. Rather, they savored the ritual of the Smith and Dale routine and the refinements of its presentation.

Dale (singing): Take off the coat, my boy
                  Take off the coat, my boy
                  Take off the coat, my boy
Smith and Dale (together): The coat is off.

What's *that*? Such strange humor is a uniquely American eccentricity. By and large, our professional monologue comedy is a comparatively straightforward affair, with codified joke patterns, logical sequences, and punch lines that are based on conventional elements of surprise and truth, but an earlier strain of offbeat and even anarchic humor, dark with the bizarre, lends our low team-comedy rich glimmerings of madness. For those who look, it can be found in the modern era too: for example, in Laurel and Hardy, Martin and Lewis, Dan Ackroyd, and the late John Belushi.

Anarchy but not madness lay at the heart of the Marx Brothers' vaudeville act. Their earliest routine, "Fun in Hi Skule," was one of countless schoolroom sketches that kept stagestruck youngsters from tap-dancing in the streets. According to Joe Adamson's *Groucho, Harpo, Chico and Sometimes Zeppo*, "It was a wild, bounding, violent, disordered, post-adolescent act that the Marx Brothers hit vaudeville with, week after week, town after town, for fifteen years . . . witnesses swear that they

(Joe) Smith and (Charles) Dale in their classic "Dr. Kronkite" sketch

destroyed props, backdrops, costumes and sometimes promoted physical damage to the theater." Yet the Marx Brothers' humor, for all its rambunctiousness, was essentially *verbal*, based on intelligence and the lucidity of literal-mindedness:

Groucho: What are the principal parts of a cat?
Gummo: Eyes, ears, neck, tail, feet.
Groucho: You've forgotten the most important part. What does a cat have that you don't have?
Gummo: Kittens.

It was unusual for Gummo to have a punch line since he was the straight man in what was otherwise a barrelhousing act.

The premise of "Fun in Hi Skule" was no more than to set the Marxes running amok. When these inspired zanies outgrew that setting, they created a new act that involved a policeman searching for stolen silverware. Having won the cop's approval, Harpo would unwisely offer to shake hands. Promptly, a dozen knives would come clattering out of his voluminous coat sleeve. This got such a laugh that Harpo gradually increased the number of knives to about two dozen, producing a grand jangling crash. He even added a coffeepot as a final salvo. The bit was so funny

The Marx Brothers in their moppet act,
"The Four Nightingales"

that, years later, he repeated it in the film *A Night at the Opera*.

The explosion that was the Marx Brothers, then, was one of ordered chaos rather than outright anarchy. Effective comedy must have energy, but it also requires structure, editing, shape, and timing. There is a difference, after all, between inspired creativity and formless abandon. The Marx Brothers seemed instinctively to sense that difference. They also worked with a purpose: their unique mixture of high verbal comedy and low pratfalls was aimed at puncturing pomposity. It was this sense at the core of nonsense that invigorated their work. When in 1924 they moved from vaudeville to Broadway, they were suddenly discovered as artistes by the intelligentsia. That show, a revue called *I'll Say She Is*, merely incorporated the routines they had developed on the variety stage. (Artistic status did not go to their heads, though Broadway did give them the respectability their mother, Minnie, so dearly desired. Already headed for Hollywood, the Marx Brothers performed in several more Broadway shows, but their days of in-person performance were all but ended.)

It is probable that no act in all of American variety entertainment surpassed the Marx Brothers' high-spirited and inspired lunacy. While their work in such movie classics as *Horse Feathers*, *A Day at the Races*, and *The Coconuts* is preserved and can continue to regale new audiences, it is not an equal exchange for their personal appearances. If value is the cost of replacement, the very dearness of the live entertainer lies in his ephemeral quality. What makes the entertainer precious is his mortality and the uniqueness of each performance.

For that reason, the team of Bert Williams and George Walker was worth a fortune to see. They did not work together for long, and there are no recordings of their act, which was one of the biggest in vaudeville. They were black men in an era of primitive racism, when discrimination was an everyday part of life (Walker himself was badly mugged during New York's 1900 race riots).

Walker was the straight man. He played the part of a hustling smoothie. Williams was the slow-witted clown, whose clear logic proved funny.

Williams: And what am I to do with this satchel?
Walker: All you got to do is bring it to me at a place where I tell you.
Williams: When they come to count up the cash and find it short, then what?
Walker: By that time we'll be far, far away—where the birds are singing sweetly and the flowers are in bloom.
Williams: And if they catch us they'll put us so far, far away we never will hear no birds singin'. And everybody knows you can't smell no flowers through a stone wall.

While Walker and Williams were definitely a "colored act" and even had to wear blackface makeup to look like stage darkies, they didn't play in exaggerated minstrel style. An articulate man, George Walker spoke his mind. "The one hope of the colored performer," he said, "must be in making a radical departure from the old, 'darky' style of singing and dancing . . . there is an artistic side of the black race and if it could be properly developed on stage I believe the theatergoing public would profit much by it." This was courageous and perceptive for 1910 but Walker did not live to see his dream realized. He died in 1911, a victim of extravagant living as much as of disease. The team was at its peak and he but thirty-nine. Bert Williams went on to become one of the *Ziegfeld Follies'* greatest stars.

Another major ethnic comedy team in big-time vaudeville was Willie and Eugene Howard, a Jewish (or "Hebe") act. Although the Howard Brothers' dialect and visual clowning betrayed their origins on the honky-

tonk stage, their comedy was not quite as simple-minded as that of Weber and Fields, and, unlike Smith and Dale or Weber and Fields, the Howards did not do the same act repeatedly. As a matter of fact, for some afficionados of vaudeville, the Howards represented the ultimate in team comedy. On tour they might perform a sketch about Arctic explorers surviving on matzo-ball soup, or recruit a couple of chorus girls to join them in an operatic quartet where the men were less interested in the aria than in the sopranos' cleavage.

The best of the routines was "Tomorrow Comes the Revolution." In this, a pathetic looking Willie, with his tiny frame, old clothes, and burning eyes, was perfect as a Communist agitator lecturing a crowd from a soapbox. He promises them relief from those bloodsuckers who have always exploited the poor, the greedy capitalists. "Tomorrow, like them, you will eat strawberries and cream." Whereupon one of his listeners pipes up, "But I don't like strawberries and cream." Willie scowls, scarcely believing his ears. Then he thunders, "Tomorrow comes the revolution, you nothing. Tomorrow you will eat strawberries and you'll like it." (Charles and Louise Samuels, *Once Upon a Stage*)

Such material may not seem particularly amusing today, but comedy is the product of material and delivery and the tone of the times. Since such tones change with fashion, most comedy dates quickly and badly. If so many people admired Willie and Eugene Howard, we can only accept the praise as deserved. Yet, explain this: some of the earliest of the George Burns and Gracie Allen routines remain funny. Even on paper.

Originally, Burns had been the comic, with baggy pants and a turned-up hat, and Gracie the straight, or "feeder." The act failed, but "even Gracie's straight lines got laughs," Burns remembered. "She had a funny delivery, very sharp and quick and cute." The success or failure of a team could ride on a decision as simple as switching roles, and once Burns and Allen had switched theirs, he concentrated on tailoring the material to her silly sanity. Vaudeville surely produced few writers of comedy superior to George Burns.

Bert Wheeler (right) never found a steady partner. Here he works with Bob Woolsey. Wheeler had his start in one of Gus Edwards's kiddie troupes, as did performers as diverse as Eddie Cantor, Sally Rand, and Groucho Marx.

ABOVE:
Bert Williams (left) and George Walker

BELOW:
The blackface comedy team of (Jim) McIntyre and (Tom) Heath topped variety bills for fifty years, starting out in the honky-tonks and winding up at the Palace.

George: I've got an idea. I'm going to ask you something, then you ask me the same thing. In other words, I am going to be the comedian.

Gracie: I know what you mean. You're going to be the funny fellow.

George: That's the idea.

Gracie: Well, go ahead. Be funny.

George: Well, I might have a little trouble, but this is what I mean. If I should say to you, "Why are apples green?" all you have to do is repeat the same thing. You say, "I don't know. Why are apples green?" Whatever I say, you say.

Gracie: I get the idea. I repeat what you say and then you tell the answer.

George: That's it. Well, here we go. What fellow in the army wears the biggest hat?

Gracie: I don't know. Why are apples green?

George: Now don't be silly. When I say, "What fellow in the army wears the biggest hat?" you must say: "I don't know. What fellow in the army wears the biggest hat?"

Gracie: Oh, I got it. Yeah, you're the comedian.

George: All right now. What fellow in the army wears the biggest hat?

Gracie: The fellow with the biggest head.

George: I certainly am the comedian.

Gracie: I think so. Try another one.

George: All right, here's another one. What is it that sings and has four legs?

Gracie: Two canaries.

George: I picked out a good game.

George Burns succinctly describes this sketch as a "streetcorner act"—a comic and a straight simply standing there, exchanging setups and punch lines. The writing is his and it is flawless. There is no waste. The straight

George Burns and Gracie Allen combined the high comedy of the monologist with the low comedy of the vaudeville team and came up classics.

Eddie Jackson (left), Jimmy Durante (center), and Lou Clayton lived out the movie cliche of facing a break-up because only one of them (Durante) was offered a chance in Hollywood. Durante took his partners west with him, making them his managers. The trio continued to revive their act at benefits and private parties.

lines, patiently repeated, set up not just the jokes but, more important, the audience. Even throwaway lines aren't throwaways—"That's the idea" and "I get the idea" provide flow, while "You're going to be the funny fellow" and "You're the comedian" are double-edged. The lines also point out to us that we are being given a lecture-demonstration on comedy technique, all the way to the wry final line, "I picked out a good game." It is difficult to imagine a comedy routine more perfectly written than this example. George Burns has always seemed modest and a gentleman, crediting Gracie Allen with doing all of the work. The truth is, the act would not have succeeded without her character and it would not have succeeded without his material. It took them far from the ethnic clowning of Weber and Fields, the burlesque of Smith and Dale, the lampoons of Willie and Eugene Howard. Most of the top vaudeville teams would be left behind after the dawn of the radio era—Bobby Clark and Paul McCullough, Ed Gallagher and Al Shean, even the popular blackface team of Jim McIntyre and Tom Heath. Radio was a medium of talk, and not only were Burns and Allen a talking team but their talk was deadpan. They were a two-part monologist. There would continue to be teams in older styles, such as the burlesquers Bud Abbott and Lou Costello and, a good many years later, Dean Martin and Jerry Lewis. But the future was unmistakable: low-comedy teams were destined for oblivion, among the first wave of entertainers to slip out to sea with vaudeville.

Clowning Around

THE FIRST FUNNY TALKERS

Of all the entertainers, none is braver than the monologist because the audience lies in wait for him and he knows it. For him the house saves the most devastating rejection: a stony silence in the face of ever more desperate efforts to amuse. The person who tries to make us laugh is at the tough end of a dare. Perhaps this hostile relationship can be explained by the abstractness of humor and the involuntary nature of laughter. The person who tries to make us laugh is someone to fear because he can literally disarm us—lower our rational defenses and, at that, merely with words. The laugh he "gets" is one he forces from us; it is a laugh of reflexive comprehension, won despite our resistance, leaving us momentarily out of control of ourselves mentally and physically. For "helpless with laughter" is not just an expression. There isn't much else that you can do when you are laughing.

No question, the laugh the monologist is after has nothing to do with happiness. The laugh of happiness comes from the heart, and even the laugh a clown gets is cheerful, but there is no joy in a monologist's laughs. They come from the head. And these are probably all reasons why there is tension, armor, and hostility in his vicinity.

When he wins, when he does get the laugh, the victory is only a temporary one. He must repeat the trick if his act is to succeed, and repeat it to the end. If the audience wins, if it finds him unamusing, its victory is sour. It glares in grim superiority while he sweats, squirms, and even strikes back:

These are the jokes, folks.
What is this, a cemetery?

The clown has it easier. A descendant of the court jester, he cuts an endearing figure. His appearance, his behavior, his facial expressions, his clothes are all funny-looking. He is either a fool or a child and is free of blame should he fail to get a laugh, because he is an innocent. Even when he succeeds, when he makes us laugh, we are pleased. The audience has no sense of being outwitted by an Ed Wynn, a Bert Lahr, a Sid Caesar; there is no sense of domination, and so people love the clown and would trust their children with him. But who would trust a child with a monologist or, still worse, his angry successor, the stand-up comedian?

Although monologists can be traced to the medieval tellers of obscene

OPPOSITE:

A startling photograph of the young Bob Hope, dancer-like, stylized, and almost foppish. He was devastated by the tepid reception given his first appearance at the Palace.

ABOVE:

Harry Langdon

stories, the ones at the turn-of-the-century honky-tonks were considered lesser performers than the clowns, the team zanies, and the buffoons. The honky-tonk monologist was, in fact, employed only before the show, to settle the rowdy audience. He might be permitted a few of the clown's devices, such as blackface or dialect, but once the show began only the guileless funny man and his pratfalls were considered funny.

If the monologist is defined as a man who attempts to amuse an audience simply by saying funny things, then one of the first to perform on a main bill at a honky-tonk was Walter C. Kelly. A transitional figure, Kelly is unfortunately remembered as the racist who in 1909 refused to work on the same bill as Bert Williams. But Kelly's act was a major and popular one. It was called "The Virginia Judge." He would stride on stage in judicial robes, sit down at a desk, and slam the gavel. He would then play the roles of various attorneys and defendants, using Italian, Dutch, Jewish, or Irish dialects. Here was the start of the modern comedian's confrontation with the audience. It would ultimately lead to the vaudeville monologist who faced up to the public with only words and ideas in his defense. The challenge was clear: make them laugh—or die in the attempt.

Sensing the awful risk in this, the great clown Ed Wynn created a routine on the subject, introducing it on March 24, 1913, on the opening-night bill at the brand-new Palace Theatre, where—ironically enough—the uniquely American monologist would be bred and developed. Wynn's act, called "The King's Jester," was about a grouchy king who was doomed to die unless someone made him laugh. All the jesters in the realm were summoned to try and save his life. Those who failed were put to death—a neat metaphor for comedy's life-giving energy and the comedian's death-defying task. (Wynn's perceptive sketch deserved a better ending: the jester finally gets a laugh out of the king by whispering a joke in his ear and adding, "I didn't know you wanted to hear *that* kind of joke.")

The Yiddish dialectician Joe Welch came even closer than Walter C. Kelly to direct storytelling. Welch would shuffle miserably on stage in shabby clothes, as forlorn as a beggar. Standing stooped, his shoulders hunched, he would stare balefully at the audience, blink back tears, agonized and despairing. Only then would he utter his opening line: "Maybe you t'ink I'm heppy?"

As sight gags, dialect, and outlandish costumes were displaced by verbal humor, monologists grew conservative in dress and sober in manner, a style borrowed from the straight men of burlesque. They would eventually wear business suits and speak carefully, as if taking the part of sanity, logic, and the audience. Good diction was originally used to contrast with the clown's dialect and foolishness. It was now essential, for the laughs depended on the words alone and this resulted in the ornate manner of speech that would characterize monologists for many years. A detailed, almost Dickensian kind of storytelling went along with it. An early example by the popular vaudevillian George Fuller Golden was reconstructed by Joe Laurie, Jr., in *Vaudeville*:

One day I was riding on top of a bus in London with my friend Casey. I was nearly worn out with several hours of sightseeing, and the bustle and excitement of the London streets, the hoi polloi, the Billingsgate and the rattle were becoming unbearable when we came in sight of Westminster Abbey. Just as we did so, the chimes burst forth with joyous melody and I said to Casey, "Isn't that sublime? Isn't it glorious to hear those chimes pealing and doesn't it inspire one with renewed vigor?" Casey leaned over with one hand to his ear and said, "You'll have to speak a little louder, George. I can't hear you." I said,

"Those magnificent chimes. Do you not hear them pealing? Do they not imbue you with a feeling of reverence? Do they not awaken tender memories of the past?" Casey again leaned forward and said, "I can't hear you. You'll have to talk louder." I got as close to him as possible and said, "Do you not hear the melodious pealing of the chimes? Do they not recall the salutation of Old Trinity on the Sabbath morning? Do they not take you back to the dim vistas of the past when the world was young and touch your heart with a feeling of pathos?" Casey put his mouth close to my ear and said, "Those damn bells are making such a hell of a racket, George, I can't hear you!"

Monologists were to prove especially welcome in vaudeville because they could double as masters of ceremony. They were the only "civilians" on the bill, working in street clothes and speaking like normal people. Of course the suit and tie were the monologists' equivalent of baggy pants; careful diction their version of dialect. But, taken straight, the act would do for a master of ceremonies.

Among the first generation of vaudeville monologists, Roger Imhoff and Julius Tannen are credited with originating the basic style of appearance and performance. Sober in mien and conservative in dress, Tannen was positively mortician-like. "Pardon me for being late," he'd begin grimly, "but I squeezed out too much toothpaste and couldn't get it back in." Most monologists imitated this subdued and understated style. "Senator" Ed Ford would introduce himself by saying, "Although my name is Ford and I was assembled in Michigan, I am in no way related to

Only the most sophisticated clowns could survive vaudeville and follow radio and America into the era of monologists. The great Bert Lahr was one of the survivors. He created his classic routines for Broadway revues.

A Palace headliner, Frank Tinney was thrown and eventually destroyed by radio.

Ed Wynn "The Perfect Fool."

that obscure Middle Western manufacturer who put a radiator on a roller skate and called it an auto."

Although every monologist considered his act topical, most concentrated on the general. The idea was to develop humorous possibilities by threading a line of reason through the loopholes of improbability. Calmness and a straight face were considered powerful attributes, the smile a tool to be used only at the punch line, to cue the audience and give it a laughing start. Smooth continuity was the basis of the craft, linking the anecdotes with logical connections rather than rattling them off in arbitrary order. Frank Tinney was an exemplar of the style. He would amble onstage and, with mock innocence, tell an intentionally bad joke such as, "I asked an acquaintance, 'Lend me a dollar for a week, old man,' and the fellow replied, 'Who is the weak old man?'" The audience would groan at the awful pun, and Tinney would give them plenty of time to do so, lighting a cigar and puffing at it a couple of times. Then he would plead the merits of the joke with the conductor in the orchestra pit, suggesting that the only thing needed to make it funny was the appropriate musical accompaniment.

Joe Cook was another sedate headliner.

I will give an imitation of four Hawaiians. This is one. [He whistles] This is another. [He strums a mandolin] And this is a third. [He taps a toe] I could imitate four Hawaiians just as easily but I will give you the reason I don't. You see, I bought a horse for $50 and it turned out to be a running horse. I was offered $15,000 for him and I took it. I built a house with the $15,000 and when it was finished a neighbor offered me $100,000 for it. He said my house stood right where he wanted to dig a well. So I took the $100,000 to accommodate him. I invested the $100,000 in peanuts and that year there was a peanut famine, so I sold the peanuts for $350,000. Now why should a man with $350,000 bother to imitate four Hawaiians? [Exit]

Other front-rank monologists were George Jessel, Jack Benny, Lou Holtz, Milton Berle, Frank Fay, and the unique Joe Frisco. Frisco had begun as an eccentric dancer, with a peculiar number he called the "Frisco Shuffle." Eccentric dancing is a good example of the abstract humor that runs through American comedy. Funny because perverse, it was the antithesis of the graceful movements that traditional dancers aspire to. Frisco's jerky dance steps, angular but engagingly awkward,

ABOVE LEFT:
Walter C. Kelly is generally credited with having launched the all-talking comedian of American vaudeville with his act, "The Virginia Judge."

ABOVE RIGHT:
Julius Tannen was the first comedian to discard the funny clothes and makeup, and run the risk for laughs on wits alone.

A youthful Milton Berle, wisecracking with the conductor at the Palace Theatre about 1937. Berle must be ranked with Bob Hope and Jack Benny among the most enduring of America's monologists. His career spanned half a century and he was perhaps the most versatile of all, a stand-up, a sketch comedian, and a clown. His willingness to do anything for a laugh and his obliviousness to all else around him in a single-minded devotion to the audience made this man an almost expressionistic figure.

were a choreographic version of his own deadpan comedy. Like his hat tricks and fancy cigar-smoking, eccentric dancing was a way of doing monologues without speaking. In fact, Frisco did everything but talk, for when he finally did speak it was clear what he had to be silent about: Joe Frisco was a stutterer. Speaking proved to be like doing his eccentric dance—it was an affirmation of his own style as acceptable and appealing, even though it was different from everyone else's. Only then was he able to use it freely and without embarrassment. In time, Joe Frisco gained such confidence that he was recognized as one of the fastest and most original comic minds on the vaudeville stage. As for the stutter, it came to be his trademark.

Even in company as brilliant as Frisco's, one stand-up comedian stood apart: Frank Fay. George Burns said, "He was the greatest single monologist I've ever seen." Fay was the first monologist to abandon all exaggeration of appearance and speech. The garrulous Lou Holtz and George Jessel had a hint of the Yiddish in their styles; Milton Berle couldn't resist clowning and making faces; Jack Benny played the violin; and Fred Allen and W. C. Fields still juggled.

Tall, lithe, Frank Fay would stroll on stage, the essence of debonair. He was stylishly dressed, he moved like a dancer, and his wavy red hair was a show in itself. Audiences were mad for him. His voice was resonant, his diction crystal clear, and his hands did figure eights as he wove arch and sophisticated patterns of finely drawn anecdote and fantasy. He was the consummate professional, as his colleagues readily agreed. But he was not their favorite human being. For one thing, he had a reputation for anti-Semitism, which did not endear him to the many Jews in vaudeville. For another, he was an overbearing egoist, a trait possibly acceptable in a field that fundamentally involved ego, except that Fay's conceit was untempered by humor and his cruelty to other performers was a byword. It was not unusual for Fay to sadistically whisper an insult to an entertainer waiting in the wings to go on.

He could do wonderful and novel routines—an imitation of John Barrymore doing the Charleston, or of Enrico Caruso singing "Darktown Strutters Ball." According to George Burns, "He was a master performer. Fabulous. Everybody copied him. Jack Benny came from Fay's school."

But he became the biggest vaudeville name to be destroyed by radio (except for a brief comeback as the star of the Broadway play *Harvey*). Although nightclubs might have kept him busy for years, Fay's ego was crushed, and a performer without an ego is like (or perhaps exactly the same as) a pilot who is afraid of heights.

Some years after Fay had retired to obscurity, abandoned by his wife, Barbara Stanwyck, to his arrogance and anger, Burns recalled:

He was asked to be master of ceremonies at the May Fair in Hollywood. The May Fair was a big thing where everybody went. We all wore tails, Jack Benny in tails, myself in tails. And they asked Fay to be master of ceremonies, and nobody greater. And Fay got up there that night and he looked around and everybody was working but him. That's when he was at his greatest. With sarcasm.

As he said something, somebody heckled him. And he stopped and he said, "Who said that?" And at the table they said, "Groucho Marx." He said, "Oh?" And he said, "Groucho, come up here. We'll talk, you and I." And Groucho wouldn't get up. And Fay looked over to him, very charmingly, and he said to him, "You do need Zeppo, don't you?" That's how great he was. "You do need Zeppo." That's Fay at his best. Or anybody at their best.

Frank Fay's debonair appearance and his vanity about it had set him off from the other monologists in vaudeville. Trademarks were eagerly, even desperately, sought out by these fast talkers: anything to separate them from the crowd. W. C. Fields's style was boozing and misanthropy. George Jessel was remembered as the fellow who was always making telephone calls to his mother. Fred Allen juggled. Jack Benny began as a musical act, and even after concentrating on comedy he leaned on the violin for recognition.

Benny had originally called himself "Ben K. Benny" (his real name was Benny Kubelsky). He did a double with a pianist named Lyman Woods, and in 1917 they'd even played the Palace. It was the second slot, worst on the bill, but it was still the Palace. The act was essentially musical and Benny's comedy was limited to mugging while he was fiddling, or holding the violin in funny ways.

When he decided to go it alone, he billed himself as "Ben K. Benny —Fiddle Funology" until the bandleader-comedian Ben Bernie complained about the similarity of names. The central office that had jurisdiction over such disputes judged Kubelsky the imitator. His act became "Jack Benny: Fun with a Fiddle," then "A Few Minutes with Jack Benny," and finally "Jack Benny: Aristocrat of Humor."

Aristocratic his humor was, and early on, too. When he began developing comedy about stinginess, he did not depend on mere jokes. Tone of voice or a mild hint might be trigger enough for a humorous connection. For example, telling about a dinner date he'd had, Benny would say, "She got so excited she dropped her *tray*." Pauses and timing were devices that Benny used early in his career. He would recount an evening of fun at the greyhound races. He had bet two dollars, pause. On the rabbit, pause. To show.

By 1924 Jack Benny was headlining at the Palace. Two years later he turned to the legitimate theater, appearing in the revue *Great Temptations*, and for the next several years he worked only in big-time vaudeville. Whether it was he who had influenced Frank Fay or the other way around, the pair were to represent the most highly developed form of monology known to vaudeville.

As for the low comedians, most were fading into burlesque and then oblivion. The survivors—Ed Wynn, Bobby Clark, Bert Lahr, Bea Lillie

Jack Benny at fifteen. His first solo act contained more fiddling than "funology."

—performed in the legitimate theater, but it was only by sheer dint of greatness that they endured, genius transcending fashion. The clown, low comedian, and cut-up, no matter how inspired, was too broad a performer for increasingly sophisticated tastes, and blind radio hastened his demise. The comedian's world, like the movies, was entering an era of all-talkies.

HARRY LAUDER
The Original Scotsman

Harry Lauder is the only evidence needed to prove the unpredictability of show business. In 1907 this little fellow arrived from Scotland to make his first American appearance. He was already thirty-seven, ancient for a debut. To the drone of bagpipes, he strolled on stage wearing a plaid kilt and high stockings. He leaned on his crooked walking stick and smiled warmly at the audience, and what in the world were these tough New Yorkers to make of him? His knobby knees were exposed. A tam-o'-shanter was perched on his head. A stock Scotsman? This was the original.

For 24 minutes, Mr. Lauder stood before the footlights as a woebegone youngster, looking over the mutilated toys removed from several pockets . . . he recited a meeting with an old man and instantly would become the old man. . . . While as a boy, Mr. Lauder sang "The Softest of the Family." . . . For the opening the Scotchman did a party (where different persons were called upon) concluding with "Stop Your Tickling, Jack!" and "My Scotch Blue Bell." . . . For the finale, a pretty blonde girl came stealing upon the stage and was introduced as "That's her," his Scotch blue bell. The audience believed just what Mr. Lauder said. He is never "on the stage" during the act. . . . After a speech and tumultuous applause, Mr. Lauder sang "We Parted on the Shore" dressed as a sailor who had never been to sea. . . . Booked to remain in New York for five weeks, he could remain for six months.

An ovation never equalled on the variety stage was his reception. (Sime Silverman, *Variety*, November 9, 1907)

Harry Lauder would make twenty-two cross-country appearances in America, the last half-dozen billed as "farewell tours." No matter how long he was onstage, and sometimes it was as much as an hour and a half, audiences never wearied of him. His bag of stage tricks—singing, telling anecdotes, confiding personal feelings, reenacting incidents from his past—simply *worked* on them. (Skeptics beware! Contrivance is no sin on the stage. All show business is hokum.)

Harry Lauder only played in his own show, never in the *Ziegfeld Follies*, and never on any vaudeville bill—except for the greatest show he ever was a part of. It was the opening night of his 1911 national tour, and the black-tie audience was already assembling in the huge Manhattan Opera House, but Lauder's ocean liner had been delayed by stormy Atlantic weather. His agent, William Morris, began to telephone performers all around New York, with the idea that they would entertain in an emergency all-star vaudeville show until the ship tied up and Lauder could get to the theater.

Some twenty volunteer acts showed up, including Blossom Seeley, Leon Errol, and the Dolly Sisters. Between numbers, the audience was kept apprised of Lauder's progress—how far out at sea the liner was, when it was being met by the tugboats.

The parade of acts continued. Carter de Haven was the master of ceremonies. The great monologist Frank Tinney arrived toward midnight, still in blackface, having finished his evening's performance at the *Ziegfeld Follies*. Irving Berlin sang, accompanying himself on the piano.

When de Haven announced that Lauder had arrived at the Battery, had been met by a limousine, and was on his way uptown, a great roar arose in the theater. Was not this evening laced with the excitement of the once-in-a-lifetime?

At one o'clock in the morning, still in street clothes, Lauder strolled

on stage to a tremendous ovation. He was carrying a sheaf of music, the orchestra parts for his act, all he'd been allowed to take from the ship's hold. He walked to center stage. The applause and cheers were unrelenting. He smiled and waved to the audience and then held his arms up high, gesturing for silence. The excitement, though, was too invigorating to be easily relinquished. Finally hushing the exhilarated crowd, Lauder said in his familiar and beloved burr, "Aye, aye, I'm tellin' you, it's been a verra frantic rush. But now, if you will bear with me, I will go through the program of songs I did at the ship's concert out in the Atlantic last Saturday night."

He sang and chatted, told stories, murmured confidences, and even did a Highland reel. As a special treat, he included two new songs, "Every Laddie Loves a Lassie" and a number destined to be an enormous hit, "Roamin' in the Gloamin'." Evidently, he had no trouble meeting the challenge of following twenty major acts and a three-hour introduction.

How to account for Lauder's success? The explanation lies in the chemistry between performer and spectator. Harry Lauder could have happened at any time. An audience is always capable of unleashing its enthusiasm, ever waiting for a Pied Piper.

Harry Lauder was the prototype Scotsman.

HARRY LANGDON

Harry Langdon is best known for work in Mack Sennett's movies, but he first established himself on the stage. A graduate of medicine shows and dime circuses, he dropped blackface makeup to develop a vaudeville act that played, almost unchanged, from 1906 until 1923. Langdon would drive on stage in a car that promptly broke down. He would then work at fixing it, and the comedy lay in his tempo—which grew slower through the years—as well as in his physical responses to the situation. He would caress the stalled car, kiss it, warn it with a wagging finger, and all the time look back and forth from auto to audience. In this increasingly stylized act, whiteface makeup would make Langdon's baby face seem rounder, his eyes ever wider. He was a pantomimist as much as comedian. Though his Hollywood success was great, film could never capture the precisely timed and controlled exchange between the innocent onstage and his charmed audience.

OPPOSITE:
Harry Langdon as mime

ABOVE:
Harry Langdon doing his impression of Harry Lauder.

ZIEGFELD
MOULIN ROUGE

(Formerly NEW YORK THEATRE)

KLAW and ERLANGER - Lessees -

Management F. ZIEGFELD Jr.

THE ZIEGFELD FOLLIES

Although entertainers historically suffered from social snubs and second-class citizenship, they also created their own rankings of prestige. In vaudeville, for instance, there were strict classes of billing that applied both to a show's running order and to the size of a name on the poster. (The term "billing" originated with the bill of acts that was posted in front of a variety theater, but it came to refer to any mention of a performer's name.) Honky-tonks were considered above dime museums but two steps beneath vaudeville; burlesque was one step down, the legitimate theater of Broadway one step up. There was always some gauge to determine greater or lesser prestige, and if there wasn't, then one would be created. Part of this was theatrical snobbery and egotism but the larger part was defensiveness, for the distinction between performance and ego is a blurry one. You are your act—protect your act—protect yourself.

One issue was never resolved: whether the acme of stardom was playing the Palace or the *Ziegfeld Follies*. The Palace, of course, was the pinnacle of international vaudeville, but vaudeville it remained, while the *Follies* was the legitimate theater. Some of the entertainment royalty, such as Al Jolson, Bea Lillie, and Bert Lahr, felt they'd finessed the Palace versus the *Follies* issue by performing only in Broadway musical comedies and sharing the stage with no other acts. Harry Lauder, too, toured only with his own show. The niceties notwithstanding, one thing was certain: star billing in the *Ziegfeld Follies* was a measure of great accomplishment, and those who earned it were an elite among American entertainers.

Producer Florenz ("Flo," or "Ziggy") Ziegfeld presented the first of his shows in 1907. It was a "revue"—the French spelling of "review" was considered fancy; the French spelling of *anything* was considered fancy. A revue was a series of acts not unlike a vaudeville show except that instead of being changed weekly, the bill would remain the same as long as the public continued to buy tickets. Songs would be written for it, and original comedy sketches—not low comedy but humor aspiring to some sophistication. To all of this, Ziegfeld added resplendent production numbers featuring beautiful young women. Indeed, they were the theme of the *Follies*, which was subtitled *Glorifying the American Girl*. Beautiful girls distinguished the *Follies* from all other Broadway revues.

Twenty-one of these flamboyant and elaborate shows were presented under Flo Ziegfeld's aegis between 1907 and 1932, and while another four were done after his death it is a striking coincidence, I think, that the last of the *Follies* personally produced by Ziegfeld opened in the same year that the Palace concluded its top-flight vaudeville policy. Our most prolific era of personal performance had come to a conclusive end.

Most of the *Ziegfeld Follies* were presented in the beautiful New Amsterdam Theatre on Forty-second Street. Among the stars were such singers as Ruth Etting, Nora Bayes and Jack Norworth, Eva Tanguay,

OPPOSITE:
Ziegfeld Follies *poster*

ABOVE:
Marilyn Miller

Sophie Tucker, the Dolly Sisters, and Marilyn Miller. But the era belonged to the comedians, and they were the biggest *Follies* stars: Will Rogers, W. C. Fields, Fanny Brice, Ed Wynn, Eddie Cantor, and, perhaps the greatest of all, Bert Williams.

When Williams's long-time partner, George Walker, suffered a mortal illness, the Nassau-born comedian became a single and was booked to star in the 1910 *Ziegfeld Follies*. It was an awesome measure of his success because, although there had been black performers in white vaudeville (Charlie Case, notably), they were not common and certainly not headliners on the big time. However, Flo Ziegfeld was no Branch Rickey and he backed out of an original plan to include Williams with white performers in a comedy sketch. Williams was only allowed to do his solo spot. He brought down the house. Even racist audiences forget their bigotry in the presence of the live entertainer.

Bert Williams worked as a tramp clown in seedy formal clothes. He wore a battered top hat and shabby tails. He had his trousers too short and his shoes too big, with blackface makeup over his own tan skin, just as it had been when he'd worked with Walker. He opened his act leaning against one side of the proscenium arch, a baby spotlight on his outstretched white gloves. Then he brought the audience along with monologues, songs, and mime. He might play all the parts in a silent poker game—dealing, betting, glancing up and down or at the other fellow's cards. Or, if he spoke, his manner would be confidential, his voice friendly and subdued, the shuffling style and Southern intonations mocking.

Where I'm living now is a nice place, but you have to go along a road between

ABOVE:
Joseph Urban's rendering of his proposed Ziegfeld Theatre. The celebrated Viennese architect also designed the interiors for this Manhattan showplace. It was razed in 1967 and replaced by an office building.

OPPOSITE, ABOVE:
Florenz "Flo" Ziegfeld with his chorus girls

OPPOSITE, BELOW:
Nora Bayes (Leonora Goldberg) was already a headliner when she met, married, and teamed up with the song-and-dance man Jack Norworth. They wrote their own theme song, "Shine On, Harvest Moon," and sang it all the way to the Ziegfeld Follies. But "The Stage's Happiest Couple," as they were billed, was threatened by Jack's philandering and Nora's jealousy. On one occasion, she insisted on their being billed as "Nora Bayes, Assisted and Admired by Jack Norworth." He ultimately left her and, to make things worse, teamed up with her competitor, Trixie Friganza. Thereupon, Nora changed her billing to "The Greatest Single Singing Comedienne in the World."

The dancing Hungarians, Janszieka and Roszika Deutsch, better known as the Dolly Sisters, headlined in the Ziegfeld Follies *as well as in Broadway revues and operettas.*

BELOW:
The creative and original Bert Williams, shown here in the Follies of 1910

In Person:
The Great Entertainers

two graveyards to get to it. One night last week I was coming home kind of late and I got about halfway home when I happened to look over my shoulder and saw a ghost following me. I started to run. I run till I was 'most ready to drop. And then I looked around. But I didn't see no ghost, so I sat down on the curbstone to rest. Then out of the corner of my eye I could see something white, and when I turned square around, there was that ghost sitting alongside of me. The ghost says: "That was a fine run we had. It was the best running I ever saw." I says, "Yes. And soon as I get my breath you're going to see more."

According to Eddie Cantor, Williams was "close to genius . . . the greatest comedian I ever saw," but "comedy" doesn't seem to describe his act precisely.

> *I ain't never done nothing to nobody*
> *I ain't never got nothing from nobody, no time*
> *And until I get something from somebody, some time*
> *I'll never do nothing for nobody, no time.*

This was "Nobody," Williams's theme song, his own composition. In a hobo's sentimental ballad he conveyed the bitterness of a black man forced to grin and play the darky. Yet there was no talk of anger in the act. Had there been, it would have been disastrous. Even offstage, Williams was circumspect about bigotry, though he had constant cause for anger (the white Ted Lewis had developed an act so similar as to involve

As both singer and dancer, the beautiful Marilyn Miller was adored by Follies *audiences. She starred in two editions.*

a battered top hat and tails and even a lonely theme song—"Me and my shadow/All alone and feeling blue"). Racial slurs seemed to be a normal part of life. On one occasion, Williams was complimented backstage by a fellow performer who added, "And what's more, you know your place." By chance, John Barrymore and Spencer Tracy were watching the show from the wings and overheard the remark. Williams nodded to the two great actors and whispered, "That's right. I know my place. Dressing Room One."

Ziegfeld was ultimately encouraged by Williams's popularity to include him in a racially integrated sketch. It was a minstrel number, hardly a daring choice, but it was one with such minstrels as Eddie Cantor as Tambo and the fabulous singer-dancer Marilyn Miller as the interlocutor. Yet implicit in even so classy a routine was Williams's color, for the all-star cast had to be in blackface if he was in it. Even Booker T. Washington's accolade was condescending. Williams, according to Washington, had done "more for the race than I have. He has smiled his way into people's hearts." Small wonder the great comedian was bitter. One evening after a performance, Eddie Cantor suggested that they meet at his hotel before setting out for an evening's partying. "Okay," Williams replied. "I'm on my way to the back elevator." He paused before adding, "It wouldn't be so bad, Eddie, if I didn't still hear the applause ringing in my ears."

Williams's achievement was more than rising above racism. With stardom so casually bestowed nowadays, it is difficult to grasp the extent of his fame, or for that matter, the success of his fellow *Follies* stars. In an era of tough competition among many entertainers, the performer had to preserve the unique notion of himself that had first motivated him; had to keep generating the power that he had first produced onstage; had continuously to refine the craftsmanship that had been developed over the course of thousands of performances. And, not least, all his new material had to meet the audience's expectations of him.

The down-home style of Will Rogers so charmed and disarmed audiences that they forgot how much talent, expertise, and experience had gone into his act. Starring in seven editions of the *Ziegfeld Follies*, he too was at the pinnacle of the entertainment world. The one-quarter Cherokee Indian had come to New York in 1905 as a "dumb" act with a Wild West show, silently performing rope tricks. There were fifty of them in his repertoire but the best one turned out to be unrehearsed: Rogers lassoed a nervous steer that was aiming to charge the audience at Madison Square Garden. It put him in the newspapers, and the publicity resulted in a booking at Keith's Union Square Theatre. Within a week he was playing Hammerstein's Victoria, where one night he impulsively said, "I am going to throw two of these ropes at once, catching the horse with one and the rider with the other. I don't have any idea I'll get it but here goes." Once the audience laughed nobody could shut Rogers up until he died in a private-airplane crash thirty years later. By then he had become one of the most popular and beloved entertainers ever to appear on an American stage, transcending show business to become a national hero. Rogers would write a nationally syndicated column of political satire and even address Congress.

"All I know is what I read in the papers" was his tag line, and the newspapers were where he got his material. Rogers would amble on stage wearing a ten-gallon hat and riding chaps, twirling his rope and drawling about politics and economics or whatever events of the day interested him. The costume and routine were suited just so to his down-to-earth style and common-sense humor. Congress was "the house that

OPPOSITE, ABOVE:
The "Great White Hope" prizefight was reenacted in the 1910 Follies, with Billy Reeves as ex-champion James Jeffries and with Bert Williams, in blackface makeup, as Jack Johnson.

OPPOSITE, BELOW:
The Ziegfeld beauties were divided into three categories: the tall "show girls," who were displayed in elaborate and sometimes outlandish costumes; the "ponies," who did the dancing; and (shown here) the "mediums," who did a little of everything.

jokes built," the "national joke factory." If Prohibition was good for anything it would at least put an end to snake bites, because "no man is going to let a snake bite him after liquor goes out." His was a gentle twitting, social criticism that deflated without the sour taste of malice. "The woman who used to faint and be revived by a nip of brandy will just have to struggle along without fainting."

Rogers knew humor and vitriol are not good for each other. When he

Will Rogers managed to be showmanly without compromising his intelligence, and he demonstrated that audiences can follow a humorist's lead to rather high comedy levels.

chose to express himself with feeling, he cut the comedy. "Here is what Washington missed out on by not living to be 199 years old.... He would have seen our great political system of 'equal rights to all and special privilege to none' working so smoothly that seven million are without a chance to earn their living.... He would see 'em handing out rations in peace time that would have reminded him of Valley Forge."

Just as Rogers gradually replaced his cowboy costume with a crumpled business suit, so, when he died, he had transcended show business to become a part of American lore, and yet he never pretended to be anything but an entertainer. For most people in the world of show business, vanity and phoniness come with the greasepaint and the spotlight. The only ones who seem to escape this are the stars.

Could Fanny Brice have possibly been more different from Will Rogers? A tall, slender, elegantly plain Jewish girl from Brooklyn, she haunted amateur contests until at seventeen she landed a chorus job in burlesque, at the Columbia Theatre on Broadway. At the turn of the century, burlesque was raunchy but not lewd. There were certainly chorus girls and low comics but the show consisted mainly of brief musical sketches with a variety show in the middle.

On the night that Brice was asked to substitute for the soubrette (the leading lady), another of the chorines recalled: "You never saw a performance like it. Think of a one-man show with thirty people onstage. Fanny rolled her eyes, she winked, she kicked, she sang loud enough to wake the whole state of Ohio. She was all over that stage and they brought her back for seven encores."

Incongruous costumes are a staple of clowning, and what could be more incongruous than the folksy cowboy Will Rogers in drag? Brandon Tynan is spoofing David Belasco, the producer who affected a priest's habit, in this sketch from the 1920 Ziegfeld Follies.

The Ziegfeld Follies

After that, the management gave her a singing part in the variety section of the show. Irving Berlin was working for the Columbia Theatre at the time and he wrote "Sadie Salome" for her, spoofing with Yiddishisms the ongoing rage for Salome dances. Berlin suggested that Brice make the song funnier still by singing it with a Yiddish accent, and that started a career routine of hers.

After two years with the burlesque show, the nineteen-year-old was discovered by Florenz Ziegfeld himself, and he put her into the 1910 *Follies* singing a "coon" song written by the show's musical composers (themselves black) Joe Jordan and Will Marion Cook.

> *Lovey Joe, that ever lovin' man*
> *From 'way down south in Birmingham,*
> *He can do some lovin' an' some lovin' sho'*
> *An' when he starts to love me*
> *I jes' hollers for mo'.*

Twelve encores.

Fanny Brice was somehow able to combine serious singing with comedy. Most comediennes are sexless parodies of women, raucous and vulgar, perhaps trying to prove they are not women at all and thus are admissible to the all-male club of comedians. Yet away from the stage, humor in a woman can be very sexy. Brice's clowning was broad but not unfeminine. It seems to have been extemporaneous, a giddy urge. She could go from torch singing to clowning without a jolt. In one *Follies* she began to sing "You Made Me Love You" with total earnestness, then did the second chorus in Yiddish dialect. Singing the same song in London, she found the audience restless and so,

grabbing the curtains, Fanny began to swing on them while she sang. Swinging, she kicked her long legs, she winked at the orchestra leader, she leered, she rolled her eyes, she beckoned to the men in the audience to join her upstairs. She didn't stop grimacing or kicking or clowning until the audience was hers. (Norman Katkov, *The Fabulous Fanny*)

Despite such antics, she could spellbind an audience with a song, and it was invariably "My Man." Ziegfeld had commissioned an English translation of the French "Mon Homme" just for her, and when Channing Pollock wrote the new lyrics Brice rehearsed it for the 1921 *Follies*. Her notion was to look French while singing it. Her idea of French was a black silk dress and a red-fringed scarf drawn around her shoulders. And a red wig. Stark and somber in this melodramatic costume, she stepped out of the upstage shadows and stalked down the Winter Garden stage to rehearse the song. A pianist waited at the upright. Somewhere in the darkened auditorium, Ziegfeld sat and watched.

Now in the lone spotlight, Brice leaned against the piano. She pulled the red scarf tightly around her arms and with a pat made certain that the wig was in place. Then, just as she nodded for the rehearsal pianist to begin, Ziegfeld loomed out of the darkened rows of seats. He climbed the short flight of steps leading to the stage. He walked silently and purposefully toward her and without uttering a word he snatched the wig from her head. Then he pulled the scarf from her shoulders. He tossed it off into the wings. Then he took hold of her dress at the neckline and yanked it until it ripped. He shredded that dress until it hung in tatters and then said, "Sing it."

Oh my man I love him so
He'll never know . . .

Fanny Brice as "Baby Snooks" with
Bob Hope in the 1936 Follies

Her private life was public. The tabloids were reporting every detail of her marriage to the gambler Nicky Arnstein and lately the details had been grim. He was in Washington, out of prison on bail between trials.

She stood on the bare stage with the lights turned down low and the piano softly leading her on. She stood without moving once, holding her bare left arm with her right hand. She sang it straight, with no frills and no flounces and no invention and no tricks . . . she sang it ten thousand times after that . . . but she never sang it without caressing her arm and closing her eyes.

> *What's the difference if I say*
> *I'll go away*
> *When I know I'll come back on*
> *My knees some day.*
> *For whatever my man is*
> *I am his forever more!*
>
> (Norman Katkov, *The Fabulous Fanny*)

It was Fanny Brice who encouraged the fledgling Eddie Cantor. There have been stars so unique as to seem positively peculiar, and Cantor was certainly one of them. The little fellow was a comedian-singer with a tenor so light it was nearly soprano. According to Brice, "He couldn't dance a lick," and she told him so on the opening night of his first *Ziegfeld Follies*, the 1917 edition. According to Cantor, "We laughed so hard we had to hold each other up. . . . I relaxed and lost my fright and tenseness."

But she had probably meant it, because he *couldn't* dance a lick. In Cantor's own words, "It is hard to explain in cold type what audiences consider funny. Gestures, subtle inflections of voice, fleeting changes of expression, an upward roll of the eyes may turn a dull line of material into sparkling stage humor."

That was the main thing he did, roll his eyes. And clap his hands. He had made his stage debut one amateur night at Miner's Bowery Theatre, after a pal had said, "Look, even if you get the hook you get a dollar along with it." As Cantor recalled, "Two players had already been yanked in by the huge iron hook and the audience let out a bloodthirsty howl."

He was exaggerating. The hook was neither huge nor iron. It had been devised one amateur night in this very burlesque theater when a young singer worked vainly to amuse the boisterous crowd. Backstage the manager came across a prop cane with an unusually large crook in its handle and was inspired to lengthen it by attaching a long pole. He extended the pole behind the tyro so that it was in the audience's sight but not the performer's. Then, hooking the already despairing fellow by the neck, the manager yanked him off stage. The audience roared.

The cruel hook became part of theatrical lore, a reminder of the entertainer's risks in appearing alone onstage before the savage audience. The hook symbolizes the constant threat of rejection that the entertainer must deal with.

Eddie Cantor avoided the hook that amateur night by stealing Walter C. Kelly's "Virginia Judge" act and playing a series of characters in various dialects. Then he joined one of Gus Edwards's kiddie groups, "Kid Kabaret" with George Jessel and Lila Lee. He finally worked out his own act for a vaudeville debut on a small circuit owned by two ex-furriers, Adolph Zukor and Marcus Loew. The two future movie tycoons suggested he do a sketch, but instead the nineteen-year-old Cantor went blackface. By his own admission, he hadn't an original idea in his head and Jolson was the rage.

Fear of getting the burnt-cork makeup in his eyes led Cantor to leave great circles of skin unblacked, and he covered these with white-rimmed spectacles. The look was to become his trademark and he used it in his first *Ziegfeld Follies*, skipping across the stage, rolling his eyes, clapping his hands and singing

> *If you knew Susie*
> *Like I know Susie*
> *Oh, oh, oh, what a girl . . .*

But he felt that a crucial decision he had been pondering was now inevitable and wrote about it with an articulateness and eloquence unusual in star memoirs.

I had made my resolve that the old black face must die. This dark mask had helped me to success. Now the audience knew only this cork-smeared face while I stood hidden behind it, wondering what would happen if the blacking came off. . . . I had made my mind up . . . I was not going to be a slave to a piece of burnt cork for the rest of my acting days. For the *Follies* of 1918 I prepared a scene in white face. My agent asked Ziegfeld to let me try it and he agreed, but in an evasive way. . . . On opening night, Ziegfeld refused to let the scene go on, saying there was no room for it. . . . But this change meant more than my job to me. It meant my future and freedom from the black label. The second night I gave him an ultimatum, "Either the scene is in or I am out." Ziegfeld gave in and it was the first time I felt revealed to the audience and in personal contact with it." (*My Life Is in Your Hands*)

Cantor would don blackface only a few times after that. He didn't know it at the time but he had taken the step that would make the difference between his dying with vaudeville as a blackface singing act and thriving in the radio era as a personality comedian.

> How you gonna keep 'em
> Down on the farm
> After they've seen Paree?

Cantor sang this World War I song in the 1919 *Follies*, a show that he

Eddie Cantor's trademark was black makeup, and it made him famous in the Ziegfeld Follies *of 1917. But in the 1918* Follies *Cantor refused to go on in blackface, seeking to rescue his own identity, and in the process he rescued his career. It was this integrity that suffused his stage personality and made him popular, for Cantor's talents were not in themselves spectacular.*

considered "the greatest of its kind." He co-starred with Bert Williams and Marilyn Miller, and they introduced such great Irving Berlin songs as "Mandy" and "A Pretty Girl Is Like a Melody." Said Cantor, "If you were a hit in a show like that, you were a hit!"

The zest and ringing honesty of Cantor's recollections are the best possible clue to solving the mystery of why this apparently undistinguished and often even silly entertainer went so high. Surely he communicated in his work this selfsame enthusiasm, high spirit, and benevolence. That is what witnesses recall. Through sheer good will he maintained amiable relations, on- and offstage, with otherwise difficult and unpredictable stars, for if the act is the ego, a hugely successful act makes for a huge ego. Solitariness and powerful self-definitions are natural to even such unspoiled stars as Cantor worked with—Fanny Brice, Will Rogers, Bert Williams, and W. C. Fields.

Fields recalled a charming practical joke that he played on Cantor and Rogers during a performance of the 1917 *Ziegfeld Follies*. The prank began when Fields visited Rogers backstage not long before curtain time. Lounging idly with nothing seemingly on his mind, Fields puffed on his cigar and with some relish told Rogers a new joke he'd just heard. The Germans, it seemed, had let loose a new cannon that was so powerful it could shell Paris from thirty-five miles away. This did not frighten the always patriotic American military. "That's nothing," was the reaction of the brass. "Uncle Sam's now got a gun that can shoot everyone in Berlin, right from Staten Island, and all those Germans it don't kill it takes prisoner!"

Rogers enjoyed poking fun at American jingoism and said he would use the joke that very evening at the end of his monologue. Satisfied, Fields left cheerfully and strolled over to Eddie Cantor's dressing room. He told the same joke and got the same response. Cantor said that it was such a good joke he was going to close *his* monologue with it.

Fields had a busy time of it, that show, keeping Rogers distracted and away from the wings while Cantor (who went on first) was onstage. The joke went over wonderfully and an unsuspecting Rogers clapped Cantor on the back as the little fellow trotted into the wings after his final bow. Soon Rogers was himself onstage, doing beautifully as usual. He then launched confidently into the joke about the new German cannon.

"Well? How did it go?" asked the tickled Fields with a bright grin as Rogers strode into the wings after his act. The cowboy looked irritable, which only amused Fields the more. "Strange," Rogers muttered. "It sounded like a funny line to me but nobody laughed except the musicians."

The Ziegfeld Follies did not have a monopoly on elaborate revues. Eleanor Powell, considered by many the best of all female dance acts in vaudeville, worked without her taps in George White's 1932 Music Hall Varieties.

W. C. Fields—William Claude Dukenfield—is the beloved bad boy of American entertainment, one of the great favorites of both audiences and professionals. Like Bert Lahr, he sought out burlesque when low clowning went out of fashion in vaudeville. Billed as "The World's Greatest Juggler," he had quickly learned that juggling wasn't enough. "Somehow, even though I was a kid I had sense enough to know that I must work with my mind and not just my hands. If I hadn't realized that, I'd be laid on the shelf today. People would be saying, 'Bill Fields? Oh yes, he used to be a juggler, didn't he?'"

He used to be the best juggler of all, it's still said, at a time when the stages of vaudeville were crowded with great jugglers. They juggled knives, flaming torches, and bowling pins while Fields worked with hats, cigars, bananas, and even white mice. The comedy of this aside, jugglers will tell you that their great challenge is not just the number of objects tossed together in the air but the diversity of their weights.

Fields's comic style was misanthropy delivered in a stewed literary style, and the combination of clowning, acid, and education was bracing. Groucho Marx's mixture alone is comparable. Additionally, Fields had struck upon so comic a stage persona that, like Jack Benny, he could skip the jokes and mine the resources of the W. C. Fields image. All he needed to do for a laugh was mention a child (he could not bear kids) or

ABOVE:
A Ziegfeld showgirl

OPPOSITE, ABOVE:
After the regular Follies *performance was over, a late show called a "Midnight Frolic" was sometimes produced in the roof cabaret atop the New Amsterdam Theatre. This scene is from the 1915 edition, featuring Oscar Shaw and the Dolly Sisters.*

OPPOSITE, BELOW:
Sybil Carmen and the Kidder Kar Girls in a Ziegfeld "Midnight Frolic"

booze (he could not get enough of it). In his delightful decadence he surely influenced the nightclub comedian, Joe E. Lewis.

Though the following anecdote may be apocryphal, Fields amusingly recalled the time when he was asked to stand in for an indisposed burlesque actor. The role was as the heavy in a sawmill melodrama. The heroine, as usual, was tied to a conveyer belt that was advancing her writhing body toward a fiercely whirring buzz saw. This particular actress, it seemed, had been repeatedly rejecting Fields's romantic advances. Now, as the conveyer drew her nearer to the buzz saw it suddenly became clear that this villain was not kidding. Her shrieks, as Fields gleefully recalled, were rattling the rafters of the theater when he finally called the moving belt to a halt. It had brought her perilously close to the saw. "One of my most superb performances," he said. "From then on, ingenues treated me with respect and fear, which is as good as love and usually ends up in the same place."

Even among originals, W. C. Fields was striking, and that was necessary if one meant to be a star in an era so abundant with entertainers. His special ability meshed with a special performing personality in a way that magnetized an audience and disarmed its hostile defenses. By transcending juggling, Fields became a comedian, but by making an artistic creation and an ongoing character of his comic sensibility, he became an immortal entertainer. To greater or lesser degrees, the other stars of the *Ziegfeld Follies* were in his class: Bert Williams, Will Rogers, Fanny Brice, and even, in his own sweet exuberant way, Eddie Cantor.

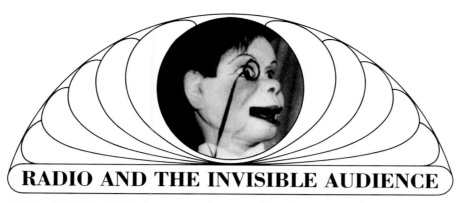

RADIO AND THE INVISIBLE AUDIENCE

I n 1922 DeWolf Hopper made himself a place in the history of show business by agreeing to perform his rendition of "Casey at the Bat" on radio. Most stars considered the budding medium beneath them, and lesser performers who were tempted by it were frightened off by the Keith circuit's terrible-tempered Edward Albee and his threats never to hire any vaudevillian who ventured into a broadcast studio. Albee was wise to be fearful, for radio and the movies would prove vaudeville's undoing. More was at stake, however, than mere vaudeville. Moving pictures, radio, and phonograph records were threatening the very nature of the live entertainer as a physically present performer confronting a physically present audience.

Hopper found performing on radio unnerving. "It was a peculiar and dramatic sensation," he said, "speaking to thousands upon thousands you couldn't see. It was the hardest thing because I couldn't gesticulate." He spoke for a generation of vaudevillians who would be confused and even destroyed by the microphone and the unseen, unresponsive audience. The distance between the entertainer and the entertained, chasm enough when merely the size of a nightclub floor or an orchestra pit, was now infinite. Radio broadcasters tried to comfort their performers by inviting spectators into the studio, but this audience was not the target audience. *They* were at home. (*What* audience? *Where* at home?)

In 1926 the National Broadcasting Company inaugurated the first network, thereby creating a coast-to-coast home audience. This national radio hookup produced a sense of national community that had never existed before. Radio shows happened for all of America at the same time.

The earliest entertainment broadcasts were musical shows, fifteen-minute variety programs with orchestras and comedian-announcers. Such a program was "The Coo Coo Club," originating in Cleveland, which featured a seven-man band playing such favorites as "The Little Clock on the Mantel," "The King with the Terrible Temper," and "The Three Trees." Art Herske introduced the songs, spicing his announcements with humor:

I heard your mother-in-law was dangerously ill.
Yes, but she's dangerously well again.

It was not until "The Happiness Candy Stores," however, that network radio was truly launched. This immensely popular show was aired on Friday evenings from seven-thirty until eight o'clock and featured Ernie Hare and Bill Jones. It ran for almost six years, and, when the run was through, radio had become a national habit.

Musical shows were the programing of choice because they were essentially aural. They generated radio's first home-bred stars, the crooners. These new romantic singers were products of the jazz and dance bands, whose hotel and casino engagements were popularly broad-

OPPOSITE:
Milton Berle held his own in the movies and radio, but his audacity in leaping into television when it was new, raw, and scorned by top-drawer show business paid off for him in historic ways. Nightclubs and movie theaters emptied out on Tuesday nights, when his "Texaco Star Theater" was broadcast. The man who made *television became a national hero, playing to the studio audiences with a reckless exuberance that was positively daring, as if he were back in vaudeville. As television technology matured and the medium prospered, such freedom of performance would be undercut. The dehumanizing process of electronic transmission would suppress the personal element entirely.*

ABOVE:
Charlie McCarthy

cast by remote hookups. Microphones and the inherent intimacy of radio led the crooners to tone down from the more full-bodied voices of vaude-ville stars Gene Austin, Nick Lucas ("The Singing Troubadour"), and Arthur Tracy ("The Street Singer"). The radio singer's audience, after all, was but a few feet from the loudspeaker.

The era of the crooner began when Rudy Vallee's radio program achieved national popularity, and from that day, vaudeville's star singers were fin-ished. The top American singers for the next decades would be male romancers, performing in a soft-voice style popularized by Russ Columbo and Bing Crosby.

With radio proving itself quite able to manage without the vaudevillians, Albee lost his power to keep the comedians off the airwaves. By that time, however, the broadcasters no longer wanted all of them. Many of the great clowns were considered too visual, and others simply felt un-comfortable in the blind medium. Bert Lahr, perhaps the greatest clown in the legitimate theater, told his biographer John Lahr, "In those days, I was a fellow who was always moving. When I got in front of that micro-phone and had to hold a paper in my hand, I had fear. . . . I was always ahead of my script. I couldn't read it because I wanted to move all the time."

LEFT:
The comedian DeWolf Hopper, a longtime associate of Weber and Fields, found radio "unnerving" because he "couldn't gesticulate."

OPPOSITE, ABOVE:
The first network radio program to become a national rage was the "Clicquot Club Eskimos." Named for its sponsor, a manufacturer of club soda and other mixers, this musical program established radio in 1926 as a medium for vaudeville to reckon with.

OPPOSITE, BELOW:
Every new mass-entertainment medium needs a star, for it is not technology that generates audience enthusiasm but a performer. The public buys the technology to reach the star. For radio, the new star was Rudy Vallee and, in turn, the "Vagabond Lover" reaped the rewards of novelty, drawing vast crowds of adoring women wherever he appeared in person.

ABOVE:
The "Texaco Fire Chief," Ed Wynn

BELOW:
This photograph was taken purely for promotional purposes since Charles "Andy" Correll (left) and Freeman "Amos" Godsen hardly had to blacken up for a radio broadcast. Theirs was not a blackface act but a black-voice, or dialect, act—and for many years "Amos 'n' Andy" was among the most popular of all radio shows.

ABOVE:

Al Jolson failed in radio for the same reason that he had succeeded on the stage: his performing style, which had electrified theater audiences, was outsized for the fireside medium. His show did poorly, and not even such guest stars as Cantor could rescue him from the oblivion into which he was slipping.

BELOW:

Singers are ideal supporting acts for comedians because they don't compete for laughs and, even better, because they soften up audiences for comedy. Thus, radio comedians often worked with vocalist protégés. Jack Benny promoted Dennis Day. Edgar Bergen introduced Jane Powell. Here is Eddie Cantor with his discovery, Deanna Durbin.

Another great clown who had his travails was Ed Wynn, "The Perfect Fool," although for a couple of seasons, as the "Texaco Fire Chief," he too was successful on radio.

Announcer Graham McNamee: Say, chief, I read in the papers that you had an explosion on the farm.
Wynn: Oh, I had a terrible explosion on the farm . . . my pet hen ate some popcorn and then sat on a stove.

This was a merry madness, but Wynn, like Lahr, had sight gags in mind and would even wear costumes for his studio audience. This did not bode well for radio success and his show faded quickly.

Other funnymen made the radio plunge only to drown in the attempt, unable to cope with the medium's idiosyncracies. The most startling failure was Frank Fay's—startling because he was considered vaudeville's supreme monologist. George Burns analyzed it this way:

The reason [Fay] didn't make it on the radio was that he did the whole thing himself. He did a radio show for a half hour where he did the commercials, he sang the songs, he did all the talking. And he wouldn't pay for writers. That would be beneath Frank Fay. He didn't think anybody could write.

Like other reproductive media, radio reproduced indiscriminately. In performance, entertainers try to re-create themselves, but movies and radio (and later, television) short-circuit that, the lens and microphone transmitting every word and expression. Audiences want their performers to be not only entertaining but *nice*, and radio revealed Fay for the conceited and mean-spirited man he was.

Frank Tinney was another top monologist whose career was destroyed by radio. An understated and intelligent raconteur, he not only needed laughs for timing and feedback but couldn't even bring himself to believe that anyone out there was *listening*. He returned to vaudeville a demoralized and defeated man. Even his theatrical audiences sensed this and turned away.

Yet there were others who thrived in the new medium, and some were even inspired by its idiosyncracies. For if presence and visual impact no longer mattered, then of sudden new importance was personality and the quality of one's voice. Indeed, these characteristics often seemed more significant than the material itself. The comedian didn't have to be a funnyman.

With appearance irrelevant, a group of average-looking, rather than funny-looking, comedians rose to prominence, their humor based on vocal personality. They were dryer than vaudeville's clowns, but their speaking styles were more colorful than vaudeville's raconteurs, and also more personal, as befitted the intimacy of the new medium: Jack Carson, Jackie Gleason, Freeman Gosden and Charles Correll ("Amos 'n' Andy"), William Bendix, Danny Thomas, Joan Davis. They did not address the audience directly but performed in half-hour sketches that would come to be known as "situation comedies." And this was the start of the end of solo entertainers in radio. The showman was becoming an interpretive artist rather than a creative one, performing the material of others instead of doing his own act, an actor playing a part in a show rather than *being* it.

Radio needed more than musical and comedy shows to fill the hours of its days. New forms of programing were devised: quiz shows, dramatic anthologies, mysteries, discussions, news programs, game shows. All of these suited because, unlike stage entertainment, they could be enjoyed unseen. And yet the entertainer would not die; radio continued to be dominated by those vaudevillians who had been able to manage the transition from the variety stage: Jack Benny, Milton Berle, Fanny Brice, George Burns and Gracie Allen, Eddie Cantor, Fred Allen, and, of all things, a ventriloquist. In 1938, according to the Hooper ratings, the Edgar Bergen–Charlie McCarthy program was the third most popular in all of radio, behind only the Jack Benny and the Fred Allen shows.

The idea of a ventriloquist on radio was positively surreal. The premise of such an act, after all, is to create the illusion that a doll is alive. Diverting the audience's attention to the colorful dummy, supplying it with a voice and personality, the ventriloquist completes the effect of life by seeming to listen, with lips compressed, while the doll (the funny one) does most of the talking. The result is a one-man comedy team, the ventriloquist playing straight man to himself.

Radio obviated the technical feats of ventriloquism since it hardly made any difference whether or not the artist's lips moved—nor did he

have to drink water or smoke while his dummy talked (to mention but two stock routines). Indeed, with no dummy to be seen there was no need for a dummy at all: a voice would do. Edgar Bergen's genius, then, lay in the creation of a character so vivid that the home audience could visualize "Charlie McCarthy" and accept him as totally human. This made Bergen the ultimate ventriloquist, a creator of life. He was so complete, magnificent, and perfect in the execution of his act that he left the competition behind. Nobody ever came close. He was not a ventriloquist but *the* ventriloquist.

Charlie McCarthy's features had been modeled on a newspaper boy spotted on a suburban Chicago street, but Bergen's stroke of genius was Charlie's costume: top hat, white tie and tails, and a *monocle*. No explanation was given for all this finery. This was simply Charlie, dapper, neurotic, sassy, vulnerable, an ageless adolescent, a teenage bon vivant with urban complexities and anxieties. With his silky city toughness, he was sardonic and bitchy, even campy, and yet palpably sensitive.

Bergen (coming upon a humming Charlie): Charlie?
McCarthy: Bergen, you frightened me.
Bergen: I'm sorry.
McCarthy: Lately, I'm just a bundle of nerves.
Bergen: What brought all this on, Charlie?
McCarthy: Oh, it's unquestionably overwork. Schoolwork, homework, tests, and examinations. Oh, I tell you, it's simply driving me mad.

Fanny Brice's adaptation to radio was successful but sadly limiting, because, in order to achieve it, Brice replaced her wonderful mixture of burlesque clowning and torch singing with the silly, one-dimensional "Baby Snooks" character.

The average adolescent does not complain about being a bundle of nerves; he doesn't cultivate world-weariness. But Charlie McCarthy's character was based on a tension between sophistication and innocence.

Like most comedians of the era, Bergen could not resist insult humor. It was certainly appropriate and irresistible when the notable child-hater W. C. Fields was a guest on the show.

Fields (singing): Give me my boots and my bottle.
McCarthy (to Bergen): Here comes W. C. You're a walking ad for black coffee, Bill. Hello, Mr. Fields, hello.
Fields: Hello, my little chum. I was thinking about you only yesterday.
McCarthy: No! You were!
Fields: Yes, I was cleaning out the woodshed. Reminded me of you.
McCarthy: Mr. Fields, is that your nose or a new kind of flame-thrower?
Fields: You'd better come out of the sun, Charles, before you come unglued.
McCarthy: Do you mind if I stand in the shade of your nose?

Drier still, by consensus, was the work of Fred Allen. Born in Boston as John Florence Sullivan, he had developed a juggling act that carried him through the lesser wheels of vaudeville under the billing "Paul Huckle, European Entertainer." When Huckle added jokes to the act, he became "Freddie St. James" and then, "Freddie James, World's Worst Juggler," a joking reference to W. C. Fields's billing as "The World's

ABOVE:
Edgar Bergen was the ultimate ventriloquist. He did it perfectly, succeeded absolutely, and there really was no point in anyone else's even attempting to be a ventriloquist after that. In fact, when Bergen added a second dummy, Mortimer Snerd, to his radio act, he proved that he could not improve upon what he had already done. Snerd, seen here with his creator, was amusing, but he was no Charlie McCarthy. For Charlie McCarthy lived.

BELOW:
When W. C. Fields, who seemed as much of a caricature as Charlie McCarthy, got together with him on his immensely popular radio show, even Bergen disappeared, as if he felt out of his depth with those superbright smart alecks. The ventriloquist's act is to disappear. How much suppressed cynicism and sarcasm, one wonders, was Bergen able to release through McCarthy?

Fred Allen, who played the Palace with his wife, Portland Hoffa, described that famous theater as "the towering symbol of vaudeville . . . a Palace program with an act's name on it was a diploma of merit . . . an act that played there was booked unseen by any theater manager in the country."

Greatest Juggler." By 1920 he was "Fred Allen," working steadily in the big time and then graduating to the legitimate theater.

Radio, however, proved Allen's true métier and, given his own show in 1932, he used it to showcase his unique style of topical, bone-dry skepticism. The program's format was conventional: a company of stock players in half-hour situation comedies designed to set off the star's

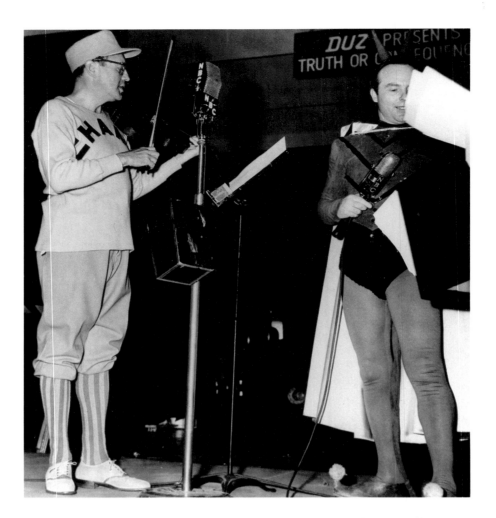

sense of humor. The following segment from a typical Fred Allen program satirized the advertising agencies that packaged most radio programs, as well as the Hooper and Crossley rating services that had recently emerged as the virtual arbiters of which shows would be continued or canceled. Allen played an adman worried about the "Kenny Dank Show," now down to a minus rating.

Allen: Not only every radio listener in America isn't listening to Kenny Dank. Two hundred thousand people who haven't got radios aren't listening either.
Secretary: But how can people without a radio not listen?
Allen: Don't question statistics, Miss Yuck. The entire advertising business is founded on surveys. The first man who questions a survey will topple the advertising game like a house of cards. (To Dank) Figures don't lie. Here's the Crossley report. Here's the Hooper that checks to the Crossley. Here's the Dooper that checks to the Hooper. And the Booper. According to the Booper, Hooper, Dooper you are down to minus two point two.
Dank: Well I was on opposite two [of FDR's] fireside chats last month.
Allen: You can't blame him for everything.

Allen conducted an ongoing "feud" with Jack Benny, much as Bob Hope did with Bing Crosby. Mere references to the other fellow could draw laughter and provide an outlet for good-natured insult humor. Benny and Allen were certainly a disparate pair. Benny presented a benign character and made himself the butt of the jokes. Allen was a faultfinder, a carper—and however sagacious his satiric thrusts, they made him seem crotchety. Benny was downright *maternal*. His humor, in contrast to Allen's, was forgiving and therefore endearing, dealing, as it so often did, with his own vanity and ego, punctured. It avoided the topical, which inevitably dates. It was also better written.

The clown element in Jack Benny's work went largely unnoticed in radio because it went unseen. But Benny could still express this comic impulse for the benefit of the studio audience, as here, with Ralph Edwards as a guest, on the popular "Truth or Consequences."

Youthful Mickey Rooney and Judy Garland. Late in the 1930s, both Hollywood and vaudeville lowered their guard and allowed their stars to perform in the new medium of radio.

Announcer Don Wilson: Mary [Benny's wife] told us that Warner Brothers were going to make a picture about your life.

Benny: Yes, sir, the same studio that made the life of Emile Zola, the life of Louis Pasteur, the life of Mark Twain and now the life of Jack Benny. [A pathetic fanfare, two shabby trumpets] *Now cut that out.* Smart-aleck musicians.

Bandleader Phil Harris: You know, Jackson, I can't understand any studio wanting to make a picture of your life.

Benny: What do you mean?

Harris: *I'm* the guy. Color, glamor, excitement. That's what they should make: the life of Phil Harris.

Benny: Phil, the story of your life wouldn't pass the Hays [censorship] office. So don't be ridiculous.

Harris: All right, so what's interesting about your life?

Benny: Mine is a story of adventure and courage. The real true life of Jack Benny. [Once more, a pathetic trumpet fanfare] Now stop with that. Enough's enough.

Jack Benny was the Mozart of comedians, elegant and perfect. Yet his success in vaudeville had not been immediate. Audiences had to acquire a taste for his deadpan style. Mack Lathrop, a fellow performer, recalled that "onstage in the hinterlands . . . the audiences didn't understand him. And he would be out there dying. And he would look off into the wings and make comments that would have us hysterical with laughter, but the audience wasn't laughing."

Radio seemed created just for Benny, providing a private, intimate audience that could concentrate on subtext—on what Benny did *not* say (he needed only to be asked about vanity or miserliness to get a laugh). Relying on the continuity and exposure, he patiently impressed a com-

plete character upon his audience. He was able to spend a career capitalizing on this awareness of his foibles and quirks. At the end, a mere silence ("Your money or your life . . .") was all that was necessary for a laugh.

If Jack Benny was the happiest example of a vaudevillian adapting to radio, Bob Hope was the ultimate radio-bred comedian. The archetypal stand-up, he was probably more concerned with being funny (or afraid of not) than any of vaudeville's monologists. This may have been rooted in a terrifying awareness of how easily a radio-station dial could be turned. Hope's was the comedy of jokes, gags, one-liners, and wisecracks—as compared with the monologist's anecdotes, inference, and subtext. Shunning the traditional sober precision of the vaudevillian delivering a monologue, Hope rattled away, ignoring the traditional discipline of sequence and logic. Vaudevillians would denigratingly call him a "comic" rather than the loftier "comedian," but he would, in fact, become the

ABOVE:

Dinah Shore (shown here with conductor Gordon Jenkins) was one of the first singers born of radio. The Blue Network was the National Broadcasting Company's. NBC established a second (Red) network, which it subsequently sold to the new American Broadcasting Company.

BELOW:

The tenderness of the young Frank Sinatra's singing and the intimacy of his radio performances created an image that was difficult to reconcile with the brash Sinatra of later years.

most popular comedian in the history of American show business. His brashness and energy were natural to the America of the twentieth century's middle decades.

Bob Hope made his stage debut at twenty-one, with Fatty Arbuckle's comeback vaudeville act of 1925. Within three years he was starring on

Broadway in musical comedies. He would seldom again work before live audiences, except for his celebrated troop tours. His career would be spent in radio, the movies, and television. Doubtless it was because of such media performance that he came to seem so cool and distant in his work, but he mastered these fields as did nobody else, for he devoted his career to them.

Hope began his radio career on September 27, 1938, and, just as he continued to sing his theme song,

> Thanks for the memory
> Of this our opening spot.
> Oh! I practically forgot
> You'll love the show next Tuesday.
> There's a scene where I get shot
> You'll like that so much...

with various lyrics, his style would remain virtually the same for the next fifty years.

My uncle just left town... he was here with the American Legion. It was a nice, quiet convention. The second night, the boys at the hotel gave the house detective twenty-four hours to get out of town. But I want to thank the American Legion for getting me a half-day off, last week at Paramount. They came over to the set I was working on, and took the camera with them as a souvenir. Paramount didn't mind that so much, but they'd be very thankful if the fellow from Texas would please bring back Dorothy Lamour. And the parades were wonderful. One thing I noticed, the women look different this year...

It was the rapid-fire style in full force. "American Legion" and "Texas" were catchwords for laughs, along with the idea of naughty boys abducting movie star Dorothy Lamour. None of this was based on character, situation, or comic logic, and as a result the writing showed. Hope even reduced the familiar connective "but speaking of" to the token "I want to tell you," and on occasion to a mere "but." He would never endear himself to the intelligentsia because his style was so aggressive. Too, his material had no point of view, though it was topical. There were no teeth in this satire, and a joke about one political candidate could as easily have been made about another. Yet Hope's popularity was immense, his success stupendous, and there is a weight and approval in that which must be recognized. However, among his colleagues, perhaps Hope's only champions have been the brainy Woody Allen and the fast-witted Johnny Carson. There are few comedians sharper than Allen and Carson, so perhaps that is a minority worth listening to.

It is a pity that Hope so rarely faced the challenge of the live audience. It might have saved him from the complacency that later marred his work. There is no way of knowing how different his career might have been had he plunged into the crucible of in-person performance. Surely no faster comic mind ever worked before a microphone.

America's transition to television was a comfortable one. Many of radio's familiar stars made the switch as smoothly as a monologist changing subjects: Jack Benny, Burns and Allen, Groucho Marx. Others, like Edgar Bergen and Fred Allen, could not manage it, their momentum irretrievably geared to the spoken word and the mind's eye. Although television at first seemed to promise a resurrection for vaudevillians, it only provided temporary work for the variety entertainers. The medium was even more dehumanizing than radio. The performer was now a mere picture of himself, dancing on the face of a cathode-ray tube.

By 1938 Bob Hope had developed the wise-guy style and the machine-gun delivery that would give his career an astounding fifty-year momentum.

THE SEX QUEENS

It was the priggishness of vaudeville that launched American burlesque, for as variety entertainment was being sedated for the family trade, the rowdy comedians and their equally rowdy audiences were forced to find new homes. They found them in such burlesque houses as the Comique in Washington, D.C., Boston's Old Howard, Philadelphia's Olympic, and New York City's Miner's Bowery Theatre. There, entertainment remained cheerfully unpretentious and lowdown.

By 1905 the Chicago-based Sam T. Jack was touring burlesque shows south to Texas and New Mexico, and soon afterward there were two full burlesque wheels, the Columbia in the East and the Empire in the West. On these circuits could be found many of the clowns who had been displaced by vaudeville's refinement—Weber and Fields, Clark and McCullough, Jack Pearl, Gallagher and Shean, and the great Bert Lahr.

While there was plenty of bawdiness in the early days, there were no striptease dancers. Burlesque consisted of one-act plays that lampooned current comedies or melodramas and, between the acts, an "olio," or variety show. This would include not only comedy teams and pratfall clowns but also many of the other acts continuing in vaudeville, such as contortionists, magicians, and jugglers. So there was a certain amount of overlap between the two stages. Because of burlesque's later identification with strippers, some of the fine performers who played it were subsequently embarrassed by the connection and disowned it.

Burlesque became the arena for broad and boisterous comedy. The props to be found backstage would likely include slap sticks, fright wigs, pistols, and all manner of baggy pants. Onstage, there were countless courtroom sketches with slammed gavels and spritzed seltzer bottles. Cheating wives were familiar figures, concealing their lovers in armoires while comedian-husbands sputtered in impotent jealousy.

Primitive musical theater came to dominate these early burlesque shows while lampoon went out of style. A typical production of 1910 might begin with a blare from the pit band as the curtain rose and the chorus girls burst energetically from the wings. After this opening number of song and dance, the leading lady (or "soubrette") would be introduced, and then the comedian would barrel on stage. The plot might have the chorus girls coaxed into trying champagne and getting tipsy, or offer other developments of similar moment. It made no difference at all because the audience was not demanding. And in this cheerful, energetic setting a series of musical and comedy numbers would be linked, helping to introduce Broadway's great era of musical comedy. Irving Berlin wrote for such shows and Fanny Brice got her start appearing in them.

The middle act occasionally offered its own surprises. For a time, a curious taste developed for "purring matches," in which one man kicked another in the shins until the fellow couldn't take it anymore and con-

OPPOSITE:
The young Ann Corio

ABOVE:
Little Egypt

ceded defeat. Otherwise, the variety entertainment in burlesque differed
little from vaudeville except for the broad and leering comedy. That was
all the sex there was in early burlesque, until the arrival of the girls from
Chicago.

Cooch dancing, that infamous craze, was originated at the 1893 Chicago World's Columbian Exposition by a unique performer appearing on

the Midway Plaisance. Her name was Fahreda Mahzar Spyropolos, but she billed herself as "Little Egypt." Her costume consisted of a fringed and brocaded bolero jacket and harem pantaloons. Her face was veiled but not her abdomen. To an insistent and insinuating drumbeat, chains jiggling at wrists, ankles, and hips, she wriggled and gyrated and shook her belly and fanny until she rocked the country. At once, "cooch dancers," "hootch dancers," and "hootchy-kootchy dancers" were titillating audiences in burlesque shows across the country. Billed as "Extra Added Attractions," they were saved for the end (a) so as to keep audiences from leaving and (b) so they could be easily deleted should the authorities arrive unexpectedly. Police raids, of course, made for wonderful publicity.

Cooch dancers were not the first females to expose their charms on the American stage. As early as the 1850s there had been theatrical presentations of "Living Bodies" that on the pretext of replicating great works of art presented nude, but motionless, women in such *tableaux vivants* as "Adam's First View of Eve," "The Expulsion from Eden," or "Rodin's 'The Kiss.'" Modest as these sensualities were, some audiences could not be restrained. At one performance, a number of men came to the theater carrying, according to a slumming critic,

prodigious opera glasses and pocket telescopes. The audience as a whole was made up of sensual old rakes, scoundrels around town and, yes, a few bankers and brokers. In one instance, the gentlemen left their seats and jumped over the footlights, forcing the terrified models backstage and into their dressing rooms.

This surely was as nothing compared to the night in 1928 that a beautiful chorus girl named Hinda Wasau went on a Chicago stage to do her shimmy dance. She was having costume trouble and, unable to manage a quick change, found herself onstage with one costume half off, the other half on. A trouper, Wasau proceeded as best she could, trying to pull away the wrong costume while still shimmying. Unfortunately, or perhaps not, both costumes came off, piece by piece, and although Wasau stopped well before nudity, the audience (according to reports) was most expressive in its enthusiasm.

Here are two of the best in burlesque, comic Jimmy Savo spritzing the vivacious Margie Hart who, according to stripper Ann Corio, "had a yen to take it all off."

At roughly the same time in Cleveland, a hefty interpretive dancer named Carrie Finnell also discovered the suspense value of disrobing, one garment at a time. However, she announced her intention in advance. Moreover, she promised that the disrobing process would continue indefinitely. Carrie Finnell managed to extend that engagement for fifty-two weeks. The invention of the striptease dance is credited to these two pioneering women.

After Finnell had established her act and shortened its duration, she continued on her innovative path by inventing the fine art of tassel-twirling. It seems that the revelation of an entire breast was morally acceptable so long as the nipple itself remained unexposed—doubtless, because of its maternal connotations. To preserve the image of mother-hood unsullied, the "pastie" was created, a small circle of sequins glued over the nipple with a tassel attached for decoration and emphasis. Bearing these badges at the tips of her pendulous breasts, Carrie Finnell promoted herself as "The Remote Control Girl," who could move her breasts while remaining otherwise still. According to one journalist who preferred anonymity, "She trained each generous bust to twitch on cue, jump to attention and do just about everything except sing 'April Showers' in Swahili."

From a more technical point of view, Finnell

would start one tassel on one bosom slowly, like a propellor revving up on a World War I plane. Faster and faster it would spin while its fellow tassel lay limp and neglected on the other bosom. Then the other tassel would come to life. It would start spinning slowly, while the first tassel was at full speed. . . . She would walk across stage with the tassels swirling in front of her and the applause would ring out . . . she could make one go slow, the other fast. She could spin the left in one direction and the right in the opposite direction. She could lie on her back and somehow keep the tassels elevated and twirling. (Ann Corio, *This Was Burlesque*)

Any performer has sex with an audience in a metaphorical way. A stripper is in the business.

Within a few years the Minsky family established a chain of twelve burlesque theaters in New York City. Louis ("Little Ziggy") Minsky replaced the voluptuous strippers with slimmer beauties, and in the thirties striptease dancing became standard burlesque fare. The showmanly Minsky even brought the girls into the audience, dressing his usherettes in Scheherazade costumes. Many gifted comedians would get their start on his and other burlesque stages—Phil Silvers, Jackie Gleason, Bud Abbott and Lou Costello, and Red Skelton, who began his act by strolling through the curtain with a grin on his farmboy face, saying, "Hello, everybody!" He would keep on strolling until he crashed into the orchestra pit.

While comedy bits like Skelton's were wonderfully zany, and while the sketches were sometimes rich and earthy, too often the routines were heavy-handed, parceled out to the comic and the straight man. As described by Ann Corio (*This Was Burlesque*),

The straight man was an elegant character in a seedy way. He wore the right clothes for a gentleman, but somehow they just didn't look right. Compared to the baggy-pants comic, however, he was a tailor's dream. His job was to dominate the comic, to scold him, to get the better of him with the girls, to try to take his money unfairly. When the comic won out, everyone enjoyed his victory.

The straight man also had to be master of the double take, which in burlesque is called "the skull":

OPPOSITE, LEFT ABOVE AND BELOW:
Burlesque at the turn of the century relied more heavily upon songs, broad comedy, and costumes than upon the enticement of nudity, but the aura of bawdiness invited disrepute, nevertheless.

OPPOSITE, RIGHT ABOVE:
Little Egypt started it all in 1893 at the World's Columbian Exposition in Chicago.

OPPOSITE, RIGHT BELOW:
In an unsubtle and surely uncomfortable pose, the redoubtable Carrie Finnell, noted inventor of twirling tassels

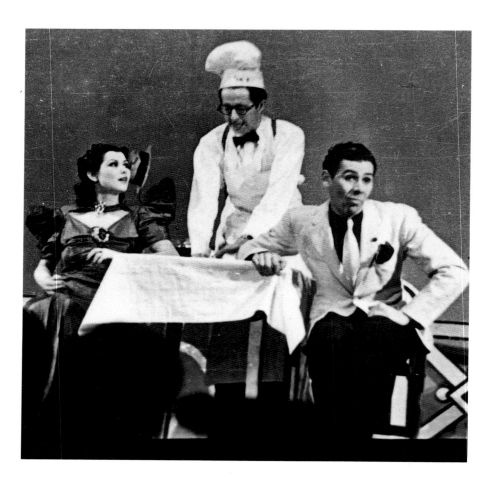

Straight Man: Without a doubt you are the most illiterate person that I have ever met.

Comic: That's right. Build me up.

S: When I say illiterate, I mean you're dumb. You haven't the intelligence of my youngest child.

C: You have a child? How long have you been married?

S: Three years.

C: That's good. How many children do you have?

S: Six!

C: Married three years and you have six children?

S: Yes.

C: That's damned good! How do you account for having six children and only being married three years?

S: I attribute it to the reading my wife did.

C: Reading? What's that have to do with it?

S: Well, the first year we were married, my wife read a book entitled *One Night of Love* and at the end of that first year she presented me with a baby boy. The second year, she read a book entitled *A Tale of Two Cities* and at the end of that year she gave birth to twins. The third year, she read a book entitled *Three Men on a Horse* and at the end of the third year she presented me with triplets. That makes six altogether. See?

C: Let me get this straight. The first year you were married your wife read a book called *One Night of Love* and at the end of the year, bang, there was a baby boy. The second year she read *A Tale of Two Cities* and gave birth to twins. The third year she read *Three Men on a Horse* and gave birth to triplets.

S: Yes.

C: I'll see you later. I have to rush home and stop my wife.

S: Why?

C: She's reading *The Birth of a Nation*.

Such material was less than brilliant. Despite much insistence by nostalgic fans, the comics were not burlesque's reason for existence. The sensationalism of the strippers gave burlesque its excitement.

Phil Silvers (center) in burlesque at the Apollo Theatre on Forty-second Street

A burlesque theater of the 1930s had a standing company that included a motley chorus line and a house singer who doubled as master of ceremonies and straight man. The star comedian and stripper would vary. The performance began with a production number featuring the chorus line, a group not to be confused with the Rockettes. Traditionally, one of these girls was clumsy, but it was hard to tell which one was working at it. A comedy routine followed, a simple one because it was early in the show. Comedians often became favorites in a particular theater. Mike Sachs, for instance, was identified with the Howard Atheneum in Boston, a house that was never called anything but the "Old

Ann Corio

Howard." He did the same sketches so often that he continued to do them at the Old Howard for years after going blind.

The first stripper on the bill would generally be a novice, a girl from the chorus line who had apprenticed as a "catcher," hovering in the wings to snare the garments wafted offstage by the headliner. When the beginner had finished her strip, more elaborate comedy sketches would follow, tasty items about short-winded traveling salesmen and insatiable farmers' daughters. A typical sketch was "The Gazeeka Box," named for an invention that the straight man sold to the comedian. When the straight man demonstrated it, the big box worked beautifully. It produced the wonders that were promised, usually a beautiful blonde. After the comedian bought it, of course, nothing happened at all. Or else a cop came out.

No question, as strippers grew more popular, burlesque comedy declined, but the price may have been worth it. For striptease dancing, while it lasted, was a solo performance unlike any other. Dealing as it did with sex and arousal, it traded in feelings of the most intimate kind. The living presence of a willing, eager, hungry goddess could not remotely be approximated by the same act on film. For adolescents, a stripper was often the first experience of a truly sexual woman. Not unlike a virginal visit to a prostitute, this event was heightened by its theatricality and the permeating sense of private passion within a community of aroused men. There were also occasional women of nerve and independence who visited a burlesque house to know the heat of sex; to learn the bumps and grinds; to discover the secrets of passion from the only authorities there seemed to be.

The strippers of burlesque were erotic queens in an era of sexual cover-up. Unlike the moist-lipped but virginal sex goddesses of Hollywood, these women were present, they were forthright, they were available. No doubt about it, they would come through. The tease was fulfilled onstage in proud exposure of the female bodies of men's dreams.

As described by Ann Corio, one of the most beautiful and famous of all strippers, the striptease was truly a rite of sexual arousal. "The various steps," she explains in *This Was Burlesque*, "were known in succession as 'the flash,' or entrance; 'the parade,' or march across the stage in full costume; and then 'the tease,' or increasing removal of wearing apparel while the audience lusts for bed and body; and the strip to G-string and pasties."

There is no known origin for the term "G-string." It is a sequined triangle of cloth covering the pubes and fastened around the waist with a string. G-string and pasties were all a stripper wore at the end of her act. That was as inevitable as the death at the end of a bullfight.

The basic outline of a stripper's act was ritualistic, too. She would appear fully clothed in the opening "flash" (a term derived from vaudeville's costumed "flash acts") so as to establish her act's uniqueness, dressed as a Southern belle, perhaps, or a bride. She would almost immediately strip to a "panel" dress, which had strips of material in the front and back with the sides left open to allow quick glimpses of thigh and breast. The real excitement came with the strip down to G-string and pasties, not because of the nudity but because of the bumps (thrusts of pelvis) and grinds (twists of hips and fanny), all simulations of lovemaking.

In this was the essence of the act and the heart of the stripper's talent. Her job was convincing the audience that this was for each of them, personally; that they so excited her she lost her senses onstage; against her wishes and despite every ounce of her professionalism, she was helplessly and violently caught in the driving urges of passion. This was a wonderful pornography. Her temples would go pale and her cheeks

Gypsy Rose Lee at work

flush as she rubbed against the curtain or lobbed a sash or her hair or anything between her legs. Her eyelids would lower under the weight of desire as she slipped into a trance of throbbing hunger, body heat rising. To the darkened and dream-filled balcony, the stripper of burlesque offered the prostitute's hot lewdness in the magnificent body of a dream woman, not for a price but from heavy urgency.

Asoak in this passion, adolescents, young men, fathers, and grandfathers sat in shoulder-to-shoulder fraternity. They gaped at these aggressive seductresses so hungry for the shy, so available, so womanly. These throbbing queens who thrived on the fantasies of the frustrated, came to fulfill sexual longings and starvations at a time when wives and girl friends wore bathrobes until the bedroom lights were out, and then stripped down to pajamas.

In show business as elsewhere, golden ages become golden only when they are over. The golden age of striptease dancing lasted from 1930 until 1950. Gypsy Rose Lee was probably the best-known stripper of the era, projecting sexuality by performing a cool and aloof act. A beautiful and smart young woman, she developed a striptease that depended more on style and humor than on disrobing and gyrating. Although famed as a stripper, she did not actually spend many years in burlesque. She capitalized on her publicity to build a career in the legitimate theater.

Among the more committed strippers, Ann Corio rates Margie Hart as the raunchiest—"a knockout redhead with a yen to show it . . . the most daring stripper of them all." Hart went naked whenever she felt like it, which evidently was often.

Another star stripper of the era was Georgia Sothern, who roared on stage, bumping and shaking to "Hold That Tiger." According to Corio, Sothern "did an act that no one who ever saw it would forget. She was a cyclone of sex and she literally blew the walls down." Georgia Sothern was indeed unforgettable. She would sit back on a park bench, facing the audience. The music would beat. She would fix a warm and moist smile on her lips, her eyes half-closed. She would slowly, urgently undo a long silken handerchief from around her waist. I think it was green. With a firm thrust she would tuck an end of it beneath her G-string. It would drop from between her spread legs to the floor.

She would sit on the bench, gazing profoundly at every man in the audience. Her arms would extend on either side, hands resting lightly on the bench-back. The weight and substance of her flesh—flat and muscled flesh of a dancer—was full on the bench. The rhythm of the music increased and the handkerchief would begin to move. And then *it would wave in rhythm to the music.* Carrie Finnell might twirl her tassels, and every other stripper in burlesque too, but Georgia Sothern . . .

Other strippers had other specialties. Sherry Britton, Lili St. Cyr, Peaches LaVerne: glorious creatures with exotic, self-mocking names that conjured up illicit hungers. When Mayor Fiorello La Guardia closed down New York City's burlesque theaters in 1937, these sex goddesses were forced to take their exquisite feathers and veils and silky negligees to seedy theaters and strip joints on darkened streets in small cities unworthy of their incensed fantasies. They continued in such sorry circumstances for another decade.

It is difficult to appreciate what La Guardia accomplished. In hindsight, his moral zeal appears politically motivated, and his persecution of the Minsky family seems unconscionable. We have hardly benefited. Today, sleazy sex shows proliferate in New York City, where once these magnificent creatures quickened our pulses, transporting us with such innocent lust.

OPPOSITE, LEFT ABOVE:
Since there was no way of improving on the fine simplicities of stripping, gyrating, and thrusting, each girl sought to stand apart from the crowd by developing a gimmick. Sally Rand's was the fan dance.

OPPOSITE, RIGHT ABOVE:
The porcelain Rose La Rose, born Rosina de Pella, died in 1972 at the age of fifty-three, leaving an estate of two million dollars. She had been living in Toledo, Ohio, where, a reporter friend recalled, "she decorated her home beautifully and expensively but it looked like something from a Hollywood set." Rose La Rose had told him, "Burlesque is dead." Understandably among the last to admit it, she added, just in case there might still be a chance, "but I'm not going to be the one who says it." The reporter wrote to a friend, "It's kind of crazy, Rose dying here in Toledo. It certainly wasn't her town, even though she tried to be one of the girls. She never quite made it with the neighbors. She tried to be a hausfrau but she didn't know how." No initiate who had ever watched Rose La Rose from the balcony would have been surprised.

OPPOSITE, LEFT BELOW:
Tempest Storm

OPPOSITE, RIGHT BELOW:
Lili St. Cyr's gimmick was based on the sex appeal of not undressing but dressing. Her act opened in a bathtub.

OUT OF A HAT

Perhaps of all the lost entertainers, none are more irreplaceable than the magicians. To do magic, what an act! Their performances were so stylized as to be ritual. We can still see the ghosts —elegant and graceful, elbows high and white gloves poised like the hands of conductors—waving magic wands to produce roses and doves from top hats, glowing cigarettes from thin air, and coins from behind the ears of ecstatic children. How could we have let such wondrous creatures depart? Fantasy, drama, suspense, mystery, surprise, glamor, and high spirits were combined in the exotic person of a man wearing a Vandyke beard, dressed in white tie and tails, making miracles before our eyes.

Like acrobats, magicians have always seemed foreigners. There is something European about the calling. They traditionally took exotic names—sometimes a single word, like Blackstone or Mandrake (yes, there was a Mandrake the Magician); sometimes, in Barnum fashion, a more complex concoction—"The Great Lafayette," for instance. Italian names were always popular in magician circles: Dante, Cardini, Rosini. At the turn of the century, the most revered among his fellow magicians was Kellar, and his prestige carried over to a protégé mundanely named Howard Thurston.

A few of these performers earned lifelong reputations among their colleagues for originating classic illusions. There were but two requirements for a trick to rate this distinction, and unbelievability was but one of them; the other was showmanship. Although magicians are wonderful in making us forget that we are watching entertainers, not wizards, *they* never forget it. They can hardly afford to. The apparatus of their tricks may be painstakingly mechanical and tedious, but it must be perfectly concealed beneath an appearance of miracle. Nowhere in all of entertainment, including the theater, is the synthesis of illusion and reality so flawlessly maintained. And of course that is necessary; the reality of illusion is the magician's very act.

Horace Golden was the first to saw a woman in half. Sam DuVries introduced levitation. It happened on the stage of Hammerstein's Victoria Theatre. Some of us are still awed by the sight of a woman seemingly afloat in the air, a hoop being passed around her body to prove that no strings are suspending her. We murmur, "How did he do that?" and who among us knows? In our hearts we suspect that the woman is truly afloat.

Some magicians, trying to separate themselves from the crowd and carve out a niche on the crowded vaudeville bills, became hypnotists. Often presented as a scientific demonstration, their acts invariably fell back on audience volunteers, who were stretched across the backs of two chairs—rigid! The mind readers had themselves blindfolded and tried to identify objects held aloft by the audience. There were even comedy magicians, best-known of whom were Frank van Hoven ("The Mad Magician") and Carl Ballantyne ("Ballantyne the Great"), whose tricks always backfired.

OPPOSITE:
Poster advertising the great magician Kellar

ABOVE:
Doug Henning

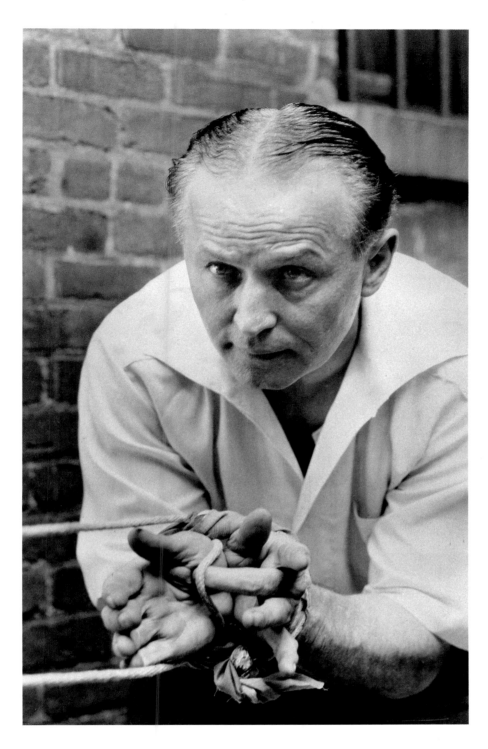

OPPOSITE, ABOVE:
Mastery of illusion is not a guaranteed ticket to success as a magician. Houdini's tricks, marvelous as they were, dazzled the public because he decked them in showmanly trappings.

OPPOSITE, BELOW:
Milbourne Christopher's variation on the Sam DuVries illusion of levitation. His 1950s stage presentations, Now You See It *and* Christopher's Wonders, *were the first Broadway shows devoted entirely to magic.*

ABOVE:
Bound hands posed no problem to Houdini. He would reveal no more than what this photograph shows, aware that a magician's very existence rides on the most important illusion of all—that he is working magic.

Escapes were the novelty that established the most famous magician of all, Harry Houdini. Born Ehrich Weiss, in Budapest, he began as a trapeze artist, and it was his athletic agility that made possible his great feats of escape. At first he worked with his brother Theo in a conventional magic act called "The Brothers Houdini," taking the name from the French conjurer Robert Houdin. When Theo left the act, Harry devised an illusion called "The Metamorphosis." He would have himself tied up and put inside a trunk, which in turn was locked and bound. When the escape was made it was not Houdini who emerged but his wife, Bess. (The traditional presence of a lovely assistant in magic shows seems based not merely on the reliable appeal of beauty but also on the historic association of women with purity and honesty.) "Metamorphosis" has since been performed by many magicians, but by far the most inventive has been the young Canadian Doug Henning, who developed a career in magic long after magicians had become obsolete. As Henning has pointed out, the wonder of "Metamorphosis" is that "it has elements

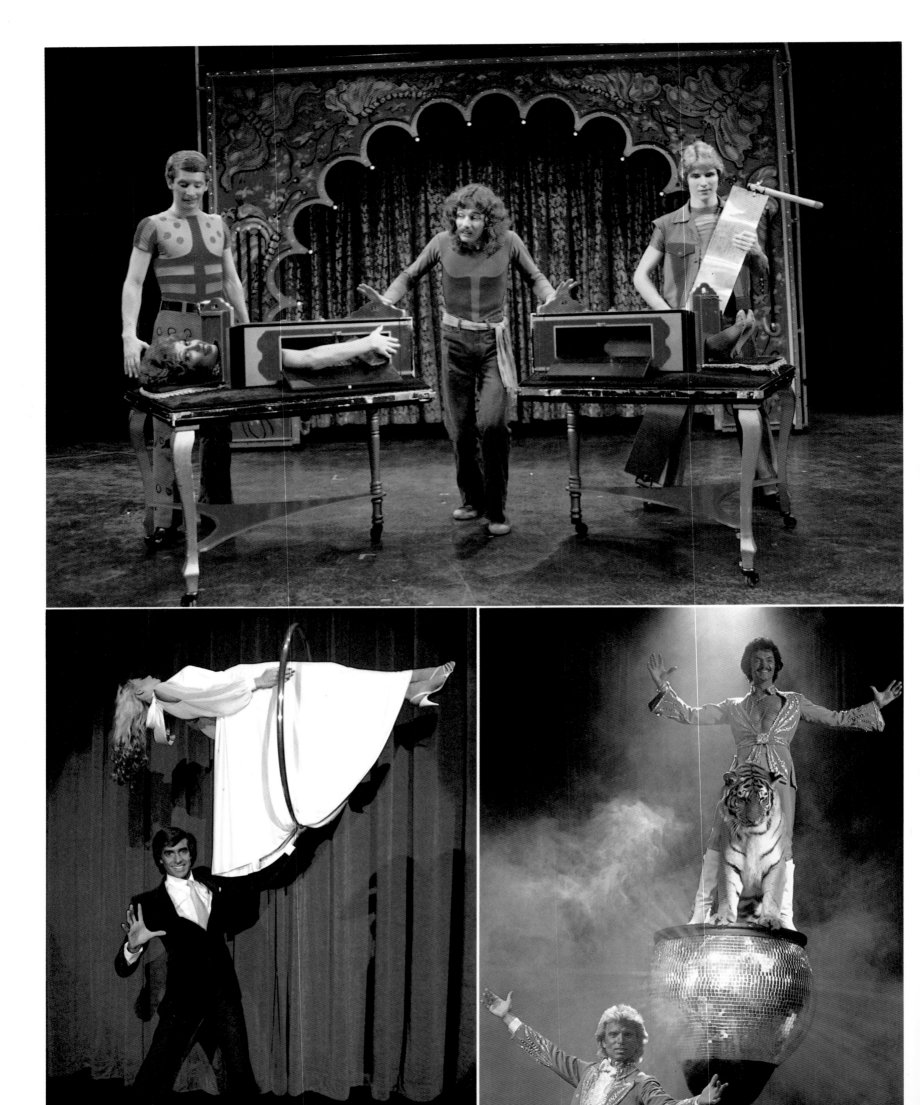

of both escape and magical illusion. The fast escape is athletic and ingenious, but the showmanship of it lies in the switch of person and, even more crucial, the change in *gender*."

Houdini often performed his feats of escape as free public demonstrations until they had received sufficient coverage in the newspapers. This flair for publicity elevated him from performer to public figure and provided the leverage to demand extraordinary fees. In Manhattan on July 7, 1912, Houdini had himself handcuffed and his legs manacled. He was then locked in a box and tossed into the East River. Less than a minute later, he emerged from the water. When the box was raised and brought to the pier, it was still nailed shut. And when it was finally pried open (by a team of burly carpenters) the manacles were still inside. Several weeks later Houdini opened at Hammerstein's Paradise Roof and did the same trick, this time in a giant tank of water. "My Challenge to Death," as he called it, filled the house with curiosity-seekers who had missed the East River performance and were eager to pay top dollar to see it. Few entertainers have had such a genius for showmanship. Houdini proved that a magician is not merely a master of sleight of hand, distraction, and illusion, but primarily an entertainer, who must dress up his performances with effects and theatrics. Crafty illusionist and a brilliant escape artist he certainly was, but his showmanliness was what made Houdini the most famous magician of all. He never merely escaped from a trunk; it had to be immersed in a roaring river, or suspended above a deep gorge. Or he might have himself locked and chained in a jail cell, or tossed into the water strapped in a straitjacket. Gifted with a sense of what would thrill the public, he developed billing that read like circus posters. "Metamorphosis," for example, was subtitled, "The Exchange of Human Beings in a Locked, Sealed, Corded Trunk." Of course, this was only window dressing, but so much of theater is window dressing.

Houdini did not restrict himself to escapes. His feats of illusion were treated with similar dash. As he himself described one astonishing piece of legerdemain, "I swallow—if one's eyes are to be trusted—anywhere from fifty to one hundred and fifty needles and from ten to thirty yards of thread. Then, after a few seconds, I bring up the needles. All threaded." Allowing himself a showmanly boast, Houdini added, "In Boston, at Keith's Theatre, it was presented at a special performance to over a thousand physicians and they were never able to explain it." And if a *doctor* couldn't explain it . . .

When Doug Henning performed his version of Houdini's "Metamorphosis" on a 1975 television special, his own showmanship made it even more theatrical. As Henning described it, "The safety man who holds the ax, to chop the water tank in case anything goes wrong, wears a black executioner's hood. At the end of two and a half minutes, the curtains [dropped to cover the tank during the escape] are removed. The tank is empty and I had vanished! The executioner figure—who had been in full view through all the proceedings of locking me upside down in the water-filled tank—would remove his hood. And it would be me."

The magician is the only performer who should be called "incredible," and yet his astonishing illusions are produced by a series of quite practical exercises and some quite concrete and businesslike equipment, like hidden pockets, collapsing flowers, and false-bottomed pitchers. But compared to modern technology, the magician's tricks are as nothing. This is an age of space shuttles and microsurgery. We are too sophisticated now for rabbits and doves that emerge from top hats. With the primary exception of young Henning, a magician today cannot pull a career out of the air.

OPPOSITE, ABOVE:
The technique and showmanship Doug Henning displayed in his imaginative versions of traditional illusions made him a sensation first on Broadway and then on national television in an era when magic acts had become obsolete. Perhaps his best trick was success itself.

OPPOSITE, BELOW LEFT:
David Copperfield built his Broadway act on good looks and sensuality—that is, a modern version of the traditional, Mandrake type of magician. The Dracula-like sensuality of those moustached wizards was not lost on Copperfield.

OPPOSITE, BELOW RIGHT:
The magicians have abandoned their traditional costume of top hat and tails in an effort to modernize the profession and to redeem it. Most contemporary magicians, those that are left, work in dark suits, although some perpetuate the flamboyant taste of the past—and why not? After all, magic acts harken back to sorcery. Doug Henning wears colorful, hippie-style costumes, and in this photograph Siegfried (left) works in circus-ringmaster regalia.

THE STAND-UPS

Humor can be dissected but the thing dies in the process. It has a certain fragility, an evasiveness which one had best respect. Essentially, it is a complete mystery.

E. B. WHITE

The stand-up comic is a funnyman stripped of his baggy pants and makeup, denied the slapstick and the pratfall, laying his wits on the line before an audience of skeptics. The show he puts on is all talk—the mind as an act.

"Act," in its first definition, is a verb. The comedian is the only performer who doesn't *do* anything. What he does is himself, as we do ourselves in daily social intercourse; selves that cope, even charm, so as to get by in life, and in work, and in love. The comedian does himself-the-act as a public ritual. He claims that a funny thing happened on the way to the club; or that he was with no lady, he was with his wife. The audience understands that he is just joking but goes along with the conceit, accepting the fiction as its contribution to the entertainment transaction. Whether it continues to accept what the comic offers depends on his ability to keep what is nonsensical plausible. That is the equation of the humorous.

The comic is usually an ordinary fellow—neither good-, bad-, nor funny-looking, except for comediennes, who are traditionally unattractive. Audiences accept good-looking singers, acrobats, jugglers, and magicians. They are not threatening. A comedian dares an audience to keep from laughing and, when working in the nightclub style, he can be quite hostile. Were he good-looking, he would have almost no chance of success because audiences know that attractive people can hurt. Too, attractiveness would be inconsistent with an act that, at core, is attempting to prove that charm can win affection and attention. The idea is to amuse the audience and win it over without the use of anything but the mouth. That is the "look, no hands" of the stand-up.

The difference between a monologist and a stand-up comedian is the difference between a theologian and a Holy Roller. The concern is the same, but one approaches it with dispassion and the other with headlong hysteria. Vaudeville's monologist was devoted to sobriety and eloquence because he was distancing himself from the low comics of the honky-tonks. Dignity was his costume and formality his routine. His offspring, the stand-up in the saloon, however, was a desperado, a con man shot into the arena like a rooster in a cockfight. The fellow's aggressive-defensive stance could not have been more effectively designed to provoke resistance. The spotlight was there, he trotted into it and was *on*. The battle for survival had no preliminaries, no warm-up. At mere arm's-length from his audience, the fellow had to come out slugging, for it was either slaughter them or die, and silence was the dreaded judgment, the resonant and echoingly mute announcement that a joke was unfunny. Only a wisecrack like Jackie Mason's "I never saw dead people smoke before" could cut that tension.

Vaudeville's monologists had been raconteurs. They told leisurely anecdotes and outright jokes. The stand-up in the saloon was part of a
newer, faster world. He had to create patterns of humor, spin comic
filigrees in the smoky air, play upon the audience until the smiles could
be parlayed into heady and uncontrollable laughter. This might involve
weaving the most bizarre narrative tapestries, but if the comic was rolling,
then for the length of his routine the audience would roll with him.
Before absurdism became familiar in drama, stand-up comics were trad-

*"Sam, you made the pants too long,"
rasped Joe E . Lewis, ever the
irresponsible and irrepressible imp,
at his headquarters, New York's
Copacabana.*

Jimmy Durante was neither a stand-up nor a sketch comic. His singing was funny, his looks were funny, and his act was simply to be adorable. From the start he was a legend.

ing in it. Without any pretentions to art or culture they were night-flying to fancy in wondrous and scary solos.

These kamikazes of show business were bred in the saloons while radio was in the process of eliminating the vaudeville monologists. Those elegant raconteurs had escaped the ethnic comedy and fright wigs of early vaudeville only to stand unwanted by this new and ironically *verbal* medium.

In 1935 no less a monologist than "The Great Faysie" was reduced to hosting an amateur night at Hollywood's Trocadero nightclub. "Frank Fay and His Undiscovered Stars of Hollywood," it was called, but the main attraction was neither Fay nor his undiscovered stars. Rather, customers came in hope that such moviefolk as his ex-wife, Barbara Stanwyck, would be in Fay's audience. Trouble was, those who had suffered from his arrogance and cruelty were rather enjoying Fay's sorry times, and there wasn't much of an audience in the Trocadero on the landmark evening when Joe Lewis strolled on stage to introduce the era of the saloon comic.

Lewis's history was melodramatic. Ten years earlier he had been a singer-monologist nicely launched on the speakeasy circuit. In 1925 he had summoned up the nerve to quit the first steady job he had ever enjoyed as an entertainer—a year spent as master of ceremonies at a Chicago club called The Green Mill—for a run at the competitive New Rendezvous that not only included more money but provided a chance to escape the mobsters who were his employers. Accepting the offer did not endear Lewis to those gentlemen, and he was warned, "You'll never live to open."

The New Rendezvous was jammed for his opening night, November 2. It was the kind of audience that watched suicide leaps. Word of Lewis's imminent demise had obviously gotten around. The room was ringed with Chicago police as the comedian walked on stage, a red carnation in the satin lapel of his tuxedo. He would always work in formal clothes.

ABOVE:
Nightclub entertainment was personal. As when jesters played for kings, the experience was nose-to-nose. Doodles Weaver's act involved eccentric singing voices. Up close it was odd.

BELOW:
In 1932 at Harlem's Cotton Club, Cab Calloway sang and pranced in front of his orchestra, anticipating the bandleader-as-performer by a decade. Working musicians tend to be quiet, letting their instruments speak for them, and Calloway's extroversion would remain unusual.

Later, all comics would. The waiters tiptoed through the room, cringing in anticipation of sudden gunfire. Lewis began his monologue. Everyone in the room seemed to flinch whenever a dish was dropped. It was not an atmosphere conducive to comedy, yet nothing untoward happened. In fact nothing happened for a week. Then, Lewis's throat was cut from ear to ear and he was left for dead.

Ten years later, his face scarred and twisted into a permanent grin, his voice a croak, he was trying again, but strictly as a comic, for he could hardly sing. He was trying to make a comeback at that shabby amateur night run by a demoralized Frank Fay, who was not getting many laughs with his torch songs for Barbara Stanwyck.

Lewis finally came on for his spot, on visibly quaking legs. It had been years since he faced an audience, and the things he used to do no longer were working. He fidgeted, put a hand in one pocket and then took it out, leaned against the piano. He lighted a cigarette. All of this, designed to create a casual impression, instead revealed a man patched together with bravura, and audiences do not laugh at nervous comedians. They prefer their martyrs brazen.

After the show, the owner of the Trocadero spared the distraught Lewis none of these observations and yet insisted on the completion of the full week's engagement. Lewis went on to play the Trocadero for fifty-nine consecutive weeks, taking over the master-of-ceremonies assignment from Fay. Unerringly he seemed to choose the most gifted amateurs—Deanna Durbin, Martha Raye, Tony Martin, Judy Garland, Mary Martin. His voice grew stronger, the rasp no longer interfering with his intelligibility. From the handicap he created a unique stage persona. He would later say, "I'm a lucky bum. If I hadn't been cut up I would have been just another comic. The knife sharpened my brain, made me slow down too, improved my delivery."

As the entertainer in the image of his audience, the scarred and vocally maimed Lewis reflected the wising up of America, its transformation from a naive and provincial society to a cynical, urban one. His philosophical acceptance of the assault reflected the hoodlum mentality that generally characterized nightclubs, lending them a heartless and illicit glamor.

This second career progressed swiftly. "I'm not Joe Louis the boxer," he would begin, "so stop fighting me already." They loved it. He moved on to the Chez Paree in Chicago and an audience attracted to late nights, bright lights, flashy girls, and famous names from sports, show business, and the underworld. Entering to his theme music, "Chicago (That Toddlin' Town)," he was the charming wastrel, a man-child happily wallowing in every working stiff's dream—a world of betting, broads, and booze. There were limits to his decadence, however. He never stooped to the sanctimonious hypocrisy that characterized later saloon comics. They might mutter about the good Lord after an evening of crudeness. Lewis would just head for the craps game.

His trademark was a glass of Ambassador's Scotch and the racing toast "It's post time," and audiences delighted in his amoral, cynical, and hedonistic tone. To them, there was a new and refreshing candor in Joe E. Lewis (he added the initial to distinguish himself from Joe Louis, although he would insist he'd borrowed it from the movie actress Lizabeth Scott). Thus originated not only the saloon comic but the saloon-style entertainer, the wise guy in the tuxedo who dominated floor shows for the next several decades, from Frank Sinatra to Sammy Davis, Jr. Where if not in Lewis would Dean Martin have found such happy inspiration?

Lewis's act was strictly of and for nightclubs. He seldom worked in radio, having a heartfelt contempt for its family style, which he considered unfit for adult consumption. On the rare occasion that he did accept a guest spot, his material usually misfired because it targeted the wrong audience and he could not bring himself to pander to the virtuous. Lewis would not work in the movie-presentation houses either. The grind at those screen- and stage-show palaces was unsuited to his sleeping habits and he didn't need the money. By war's end, he was the dean of stand-ups, the highest-paid entertainer in American nightclubs, earning five thousand dollars a week at the Copacabana, on East Sixtieth Street in New York City. Those were the golden years of American bistros. Concrete and neon meccas rose from the marshes and the deserts: twin El Dorados in Miami Beach and, in the West, Las Vegas.

Nightclubs meant more than drinking and watching a floor show. They symbolized what would later be called a "life style." "Cafe society" was now a metaphor for a middle class freshly released from wartime proscriptions and prewar class distinctions. The nation had entered World War II a farm-oriented, moralistic society intimidated by the culture of Europe. It was emerging as the watchman of the world. With our system triumphant, confident of our righteousness and strength, having attained a healthy standard of living but still without the culture or maturity quite to handle it, how could we not be brash, materialistic? Joe E. Lewis was this nightclub world incarnate, and, though ascent and eclipse lay ahead in Las Vegas, for the moment he held court in the Mount Olympus of saloons, the Copacabana. That was where every act in every tank-town club and provincial hotel aspired to. Comedians sweated through nasty audiences and miserable conditions with this one dream, and goal, and certainty in mind: the Copa was but a joke away.

In the years to follow, those acts successful enough to play the Copacabana would defer to Lewis: Frank Sinatra, Danny Thomas, Lena Horne, Billy Eckstine, Nat Cole, Eddie Fisher, Dean Martin and Jerry Lewis, Tony Martin, Sammy Davis, Jr., Peter Lind Hayes and Mary Healy. Only Joe E. Lewis could open the Copa's season in the fall, and he would get top pay. That was not mere respect. Saloon performers owed their very trade to him.

His style was recklessly cheerful but had an underlying hostility that would influence other cabaret performers. Lewis was perfectly capable of silencing a noisy critic with a modest comic device ("Please sir, watch your language. There are musicians present"), but more likely, he would be abusive ("Are you the victim of sex experiments?"); or he might even walk over to the offending customer, pick up a drink, and throw it in the fellow's face. Drunk or misguided hecklers could receive tongue-lashings far more severe than they deserved or than was necessary to silence them. Perhaps the explanation lies in the psychological profile of a typical comedian—a physically and mentally unexceptional person who has long felt inadequate and unloved; a person needing attention but lacking the conventional skills for getting it (academic, financial, artistic, athletic); a person with a lifetime of pain chits to cash in. Being funny can release and resolve this hostility through a burst of ego reward: the joke, the laugh. And since every laugh is potentially scornful (laugh with me? laugh at me?), the comedian is always abutting the self-contempt so close to home. His act, then, is thoroughly, and consistently, and brutally engaged with rejection.

"Please forgive me for drinking onstage," Lewis would say, "but it's something I like to do while getting drunk." There was a terror there, a comedy of self-destruction. "I know you're wondering about the cane," a limping Lewis once told his audience. "Yesterday afternoon I went

Phil Silvers, a sketch comic rather
than a stand-up, graduated from the
burlesque stage to the movies. He and
another ex-burlesquer, Rags Ragland,
had put together an act and got
themselves booked into the Copacabana
when Ragland suddenly died. Frank
Sinatra stepped in as emergency comic.

over to Dean Martin's house to play some checkers. We drank some hot
chocolate, then put on some Lawrence Welk records. That's when I
spotted this spider on the ceiling. Without thinking, I stepped on it.
That's how I happened to hurt my leg."

Lewis was to do for Las Vegas what Jack Benny had done for radio and
what Milton Berle was in the process of doing for television: establish
the franchise. He single-handedly gave the desert gambling resort status
among high rollers. When he began playing the El Rancho Vegas Hotel
in 1951 he brought cachet. By the time he was through, the strip of flash

in the desert had become America's Sin City. One hotel opened after another and hired top stars to perform in their great entertainment rooms at salaries that nightclubs elsewhere could not match, for the gambling casinos subsidized the floor shows and it was not necessary for the food and liquor receipts to carry the star freight. The Copacabana was paying Lewis five thousand dollars, while El Rancho Vegas was giving him twenty-five thousand. Entertainer loyalty could not be relied upon indefinitely, and it would only be a matter of years before the nightclub business went out of business.

Dreaming in the dark, a host of young comics was preparing for that business, a brazen and fearless brigade of tuxedoed, cigarette-smoking wise guys. These would-be Joe E. Lewises were to find other venues. Buddy Hackett would ultimately become a lewd panda rolling on stage at a gambling casino; Alan King, fit and handsome, would stroll out to confront his Westbury Music Fair audience with the aplomb of an insurance executive; the black sheep among these saloon tyros, Lenny Bruce would abandon the fast crowd to play to intellectuals, wearing jeans as pale as his troubled face. These and the other stand-ups following Lewis's star were not as diverse as first it might seem. They were New York boys mostly, and most of them, like Lewis, were driven by a street urge to be funny. They were sidewalk survivors living by their wits. "Funny" had streetcorner prestige because it was related to survival and bravado. "Funny" rode on wheels of attack.

The funniest among these fellows went to a curious school for comics:

Low comedy was not the nightclub crowd's cup of tea. The broadest any comedy act got was the Ritz Brothers, who were the smart money's version of the Three Stooges. Cafe headliners through the 1940s, they were a versatile team of zanies who could sing and tap dance and do fast-paced comedy routines.

a school tucked away in the Catskill Mountains of New York State. Most middle classes seem to be summer-swarmers. Parisians go to the south of France, Londoners to the beaches of Spain. In the decade before World War II and in the years to follow, the Jewish middle class of New York City went to "the mountains." The reference was not exactly to the Catskill Mountains, a range of gentle hills, the highest rising just above four thousand feet. More precisely, "the mountains" meant a sizable group of resort hotels, family camps, and bungalow colonies clustered around the towns of Liberty and Monticello about ninety miles north of New York City. The only topography significant to *these* mountains was the height of the waiters' chutzpah and the depth of the dessert menus, for such resorts catered to vacationing families in search of Kosher-style food and a Kosher-style atmosphere. The area came to be known as the Borscht Belt and it was said that the road leading there had a center stripe of sour cream.

Inevitably, entertainment was offered at these holiday resorts. It began on makeshift stages set up in the dining rooms after Saturday dinners. The audiences sat on folding chairs. The lighting and sound systems were primitive. The headliner was given ten dollars for a performance and a week's room and board. If he was already staying at another hotel, then he was paid a flat twenty-five-dollar fee.

As the area became more popular, some of the larger hotels built barn-like structures to house the shows. These were called "cassinos," after a card game played in the halls in the afternoons. By the outbreak of World War II, even the most modest bungalow colony was presenting a comedian at a Saturday-night show. After this casual start, the Catskills became a showcase for nightclub entertainers, the minor leagues for the saloon singers and comedians who would be the stars of the 1950s and 1960s.

Often these entertainers began as waiters or busboys, doubling as "tummlers" (a Yiddishism for someone who is playful, a clown). The tummler in a Catskill Mountains resort hotel was a daytime entertainer whose job it was to distract the guests between the gargantuan meals that were the hotels' main attraction. Most guests spent the days either anticipating or digesting them. Tummlers would make merry at poolside,

Alan King was the closest thing to a raconteur that the Catskills produced. Not unlike the gentlemen monologists of vaudeville, King appealed as a decent and intelligent fellow who could point out the humorous side of everyday life.

ABOVE:
*Catskills resorts followed the lead of
Las Vegas hotels in replacing relatively
intimate traditional nightclubs with
large-capacity showrooms such as the
Imperial Room of the Concord Resort
Hotel.*

BELOW:
*A Catskills hotel publicity shot: from
right to left, golf pro Jimmy Demaret
with nightclub headliners Dean Martin
and Buddy Hackett*

if necessary jumping in fully clothed. In short, they did whatever was necessary to divert the guests from the pangs of hunger or heartburn. This called for a manic energy that later characterized the antics of former tummlers Danny Kaye, Mel Brooks, and Jerry Lewis. Tummlers, the descendants of the minstrels and court jesters, are overdue for medical study.

In later and more pretentious times, the tummler, born again as "social director," would amuse the guests in more refined ways, but while games of Simon Says and finger-painting classes may have appealed to the more culture-conscious hotel owners, such diversions were unworthy of the true tummler, and his moment of glory was onstage in the nighttime show, introducing a comic or—dreams realized—as the comic introduced.

The comedy that worked in the mountains could not always be brought down to the nightclubs in the cities. Comedians can't resist tailoring material. Laughs, always torn from an audience, tear easier when the jokes are local, lewd, and ethnic. In the Catskills, a comic didn't even have to be Jewish to be *Jewish*.

A pair of black comedians ran into each other at the Red Apple Rest, which was the traditional lunch stop on the long drive to Monticello. "What are you doing here?" one asked the other. "Working the holidays," the fellow responded with equanimity, meaning the fall Jewish holiday season surrounding Rosh Hashanah and Yom Kippur. They sat down at a table and, over bagels and lox, one of these black funnymen asked the other what kind of act he was doing. "Well," the man began, "I open with 'Eli, Eli,' and then I go into 'Bei Mir Bist Du Schoen,' 'Joe and Paul,' 'Rumania-Rumania,' and 'Pincus the Peddler.' Then I do my tribute to Israel and the 'Hatikvah.' I beg off with 'Let My People Go' and do 'The Anniversary Waltz' for an encore." The other fellow stared in disbelief. "You son of a bitch," he finally gasped. "You stole my act." (Anonymous)

The ambitious comedian knew that such parochial material was undesirable in the nightclubs and that only those who developed general (meaning gentile) approaches would be able to join the world beyond this blintze Brigadoon. But the basic training had to come first: the development of the nerve to face an audience, and writing and practicing and rewriting (or buying) material that could get a laugh every ten or fifteen seconds and hold an audience for twenty-five minutes, the length of an opening act.

Borscht Belt audiences were tough. These vacationers were show-wise New Yorkers who judged even the greenest novices by professional standards. A lackluster comedian might encounter restless and even brutal audiences who simply stared at him. But the fellow who was funny could count on club work in the fall because New York's booking agents covered the mountains like moss, and the word on a newcomer spread quickly. It was said that comedienne Totie Fields, for instance, had her contract renewed halfway through her first opening night in the Catskills.

As the hotels prospered, some became immense compounds that were open the year round. The most prestigious of these were Grossinger's Country Club and the Concord Resort Hotel. On only a slightly less exalted plane were such country inns as Brickman's Hotel, Brown's Hotel, the Evans, Kutscher's Country Club, and the Anglican hostelries, the Raleigh and the Windsor. Even this was but the tip of the mountains for, with war's end, a boom was on. Americans were climbing into their first new cars in years, to go out and enjoy themselves again. It was the dawn of the saloon entertainer's day, and no matter that this sun rose, with the early show, at 10 P.M.

The comics who sauntered down from the mountains must have seemed brash compared to established comedians like Jack Benny, Burns and Allen, Edgar Bergen, and Fred Allen, and to such radio funnymen as Bob Hope, Danny Thomas, and Jackie Gleason. These newcomers were certainly gaudier than their predecessors, but then postwar America was gaudy. Ruralism and Protestantism were no longer social imperatives. Vaudeville's Jewish comics had affected ministerial speaking styles, but war had freed the country's minority groups for diversity and the city boy could be himself. Joe E. Lewis's time had come. Thus were born the feisty, fast-talking saloon stand-ups, their punch lines adorned with rim shots from the drummer: Buddy Hackett, Alan King, Lenny Bruce; such hard-driving comedians as Jan Murray, Red Buttons, Jack Carter, Dean Martin and Jerry Lewis, Don Rickles, "Fat" Jack Leonard, Jackie Miles. They had been learning their trade onstage, from one hotel to the next, playing to a big or noisy crowd one night and a slow crowd the next. Some nights they did more than one performance—an early show in one hotel, a late show somewhere else, perhaps even another at dawn in a third hotel's lounge rather than the big room. Sometimes they opened for a singer or headlined in a bungalow colony. The occasional veteran was in their midst. A big hotel might, for the Fourth of July or Labor Day, engage Milton Berle, Harry Ritz, George Jessel, or Myron Cohen, but home-grown comedians were the rule: young and scrappy newcomers, fast-talking and sharp, honing themselves to professional smoothness by sheer backbreaking practice. They were the winking and finger-snapping imps, street urchins outfitted by Times Square haberdashers, pushy spielers in ruffled shirts and velvet lapels.

There was a future they had in mind, a long-range future in the big city nightclubs: Chez Paree in Chicago, the Latin Quarter in Boston, the Chase Hotel in St. Louis, Versailles and the Latin Quarter in New York, the Miami Beach hotels, and, at the end of the rainbow, New York's Copacabana. But even at first there was work available. These comics, already a notch above the "strips" (strip clubs) that were strictly for raw beginners, could move from the Catskills to the small clubs like Buffalo's Town Casino and Chez Ami, the Three Rivers in Syracuse, La Martinique in New York City, the Vine Gardens in Chicago, Blinstrom's in Boston, the Monticello in Framingham, Massachusetts, the Preview Lounge in New Orleans, the Triton Hotel in Rochester. Why, in Brooklyn alone there were clusters of nightclubs that hired mid-range comedians, clubs with such exotic names as the Capri, the Bali, and the Pink Elephant.

Comedians operate in a field of nervous energy. Abundant work only enriched the heady atmosphere, and the funnymen scrambling for this work were a sociable and rascally lot who dealt with their profession obsessively and compulsively, for in real ways they had made their work into a sexual rite.

The relationship between stand-up comedy and male sexuality is unmistakable. The singer gets the girl with his good looks, but the laugh extracted by the plain man is lustier. Funny-business has traditionally been a male occupation. The occasional female comic is usually impelled to make herself into a travesty of a funnyman, the performing equivalent of a tomboy, one of the guys—Martha Raye, Joan Davis, Imogene Coca, Joan Rivers, Phyllis Diller, Totie Fields. Such gifted comediennes as Fannie Brice, Gracie Allen, Mae West, Elaine May, and Lily Tomlin succeeded in remaining recognizably female but they have been exceptional.

The male comic struts for women's attention. If the men in the audience are not to be alienated, he must win their identification. Seducing

In the early 1950s Dean Martin and Jerry Lewis were the highest paid nightclub act in the country. Never before had a team so perfectly blended high (verbal) and low (physical) comedy. Their wisecracking appealed to urbanites, their pratfalls to provincials. When the team split up, Lewis's low comedy lost the balancing effect of Martin—and it showed.

with humor, after all, is nothing new ("Make me laugh and I'm yours"), and the grand tradition of dirty jokes reveals the basic tie between comedy and sex. The comedian is a homely peacock, a would-be frog prince, a hero in female eyes for having risked and won in the terrifying arena of the floor show.

The innumerable accounts of sex-on-the-run between comedians and backstage dancers, chorus girls, and strippers—accounts often puerile and sometimes pathetic—combine to create a professional image: comedians making love as fast as they rattle off jokes, grabbing girls in the alleys between shows; desperate for love—blind and groping, reaching, grabbing, much as they do for laughs. Their acts are sexual lures. Frank Fay, the suave matinee idol; Bob Hope a sharpie, the traveling salesman; Alan King, the paternal figure; Woody Allen, boyish and intellectual; Buddy Hackett, cute; Lenny Bruce as Peck's Bad Boy. All these are familiar seduction approaches and even when the ploy is one of helplessness, it communicates a machismo, for it is surrounded by the glamorous aura of show business. Comics get their girls. Funny has always been sexy and in the spotlight it is probably all but irresistible.

The sexual energy that impelled the performance of the fast-talking nightclub comedian (how far, after all, is a seduction line from a carnival spiel?) was short-circuited by television. A stand-up's aggressiveness and sexuality proved harsh and even frightening on the home screen. Television invited the lower-keyed performer, and better suited to this intimate medium were such understated monologists as Bob Newhart, Bill Cosby, George Gobel, and the dazzlingly weird Jonathan Winters. For the most part, they played Thurberesque family men—with amusing eccentricities, but family men nevertheless. They were not of the cities (a euphemism for Jewish) because television was a nationwide medium. They did not cater to the mood of the nightclub but, rather, to a split-level Middle American consciousness: formica over flesh. *That* was the real television network, a coast-to-coast mental suburb. The cigarette and highball glass of the naughty saloon gave way to the milkshake of the Eisenhower era, and there were no dirty jokes on television.

Following an initial flirtation with variety entertainment, television programmers—like radio programmers before them—discovered that soloists did not best suit the medium. Home audiences did not want to be confronted. They wished to be unobserved, to look in on something that was not looking back at them, and so television monologists did not endure unless (like Danny Thomas or Bob Newhart or Bill Cosby) they found a niche in situation comedies. Several sketch comedians of genuine artistry did develop on television: Sid Caesar, Jackie Gleason, Ernie Kovacs. But they could not work toe-to-toe with an audience—none performed successfully in person, or even just facing the studio audience. Among those monologists who became popular in the first wave of television variety-programing, only Alan King managed to extend his career to live performance, and he had developed his technique in the Borscht Belt and merely rubbed a goyish television patina on his satiny and professional nightclub technique. King, in fact, was probably the smoothest monologist since the heyday of Frank Fay and Jack Benny.

A recurrent theme of this book is the entertainer as a reflection of his time. The funnymen of the 1950s were products of a homogenized and wary McCarthy-era America. They were restrained performers who shrank from the stand-up's traditionally hostile challenge, his death-defying courage, his sexual energy. They were hardly the macho rascals of the nightclub floors. But the following decade was contrastingly active, hot, and energetic. That mood, too, found reflection in comedians' styles.

OPPOSITE, MIDDLE ROW,
LEFT TO RIGHT:
Shelley Berman was a comedy actor who, along with Mike Nichols and Elaine May, emerged from Chicago's celebrated Second City company. Berman was considered a bright but "sick" comedian, one of several who became popular in the mid-1960s. It is a measure of those times that "sick" meant daring and realistic.

Martha Raye at the Paramount Theatre, New York. Comedians are usually plain men who strut and punch for the approval of the ladies in the audience. To hold her own in so stag a club, a comedienne had to become brash, mocking her own gender.

America's conservative turn following the heady activism of the Vietnam years was reflected in the success of Joan Rivers, an extremely funny woman who reverted to the one-of-the-boys mugging of prefeminist comediennes.

OPPOSITE, BOTTOM ROW,
LEFT TO RIGHT:
Sid Caesar was an inspired sketch comic, one of the great television discoveries. He was left gaunt by years of relentless pressure for new material. Like other great actor-comics, from Lahr to Gleason, he could not work "in one," up close to an audience, and so he turned to Broadway plays.

Red Skelton cleaned up his burlesque act so successfully that he became part of Americana.

"When you worked on Broadway," George Burns said in conversation, *"if you did seventeen or eighteen minutes, that meant you had a very good spot on the bill. If you only did twelve minutes, you were on number two. So when you'd meet an actor on the street—let's say he's playing Proctor's Fifth Avenue—and you'd say, 'Jim, how you doing at the Fifth Avenue Theatre?' he wouldn't say 'Good' or 'Bad.' He'd say, 'Eighteen minutes.' That meant he had a good spot on the bill."*

OPPOSITE, TOP ROW, LEFT TO RIGHT:
Specializing in insult comedy before Don Rickles was "Fat" Jack Leonard. "You got a nice personality," Leonard would say, "but not for a human being. . . . Some day you'll go too far and I hope you stay there."

Ernie Kovacs was a bright zany who made inspired use of television technology in the 1950s, when the medium was still undeveloped. In his own fashion, Kovacs could work as a monologist with a live audience, a talent that would have served him well, but he died young, in a car accident.

Danny Thomas was one of the rare nightclub comics who succeeded with sketches. He made his fortune in a television series and retired into eminence.

In Person:
The Great Entertainers

146

OPPOSITE:

Jackie Gleason was another brilliant sketch comic who had trouble with stand-up routines. He attempted to sidestep his discomfort by doing monologues in character, here for instance as "Joe the Bartender," an act he created for television. It didn't work.

ABOVE:

Like Will Rogers, Mort Sahl drew his material from the newspapers; in fact, he carried a furled newspaper on stage with him as a prop. Sahl spared neither major American political party his gibes. He was one of the first comedians to exploit the college market, playing university auditoriums, where his educated and sophisticated humor was likely to be appreciated.

RIGHT:

"My mother tried to kill herself with an overdose of Mah-Jongg tiles. Many members of my family are eccentric. My wife was an immature woman. I'd be in the bathroom taking a bath and she would walk right in and sink my boats." Woody Allen's stage persona— a lusty Jewish intellectual who is well-adjusted to his neuroses—was complemented by his stage style —restless and aggressively defensive. Through sheer funniness, Allen made an audience feel that it was on his own high intellectual level. As a movie director and writer, Allen keeps this stage character of his alive on film but he no longer works as a stand-up comic.

The Stand-ups

The John F. Kennedy years inspired idealism, respect for intelligence, and vitality in the country, and the energy flow continued after his assassination into the Vietnam years of unrest, protest, and rebellion. With the issues of war and race firing up the country, a group of thinking-man's comedians arrived, and their material was political, psychological, and socially conscious. Enough Americans were by then college-educated to support novel and bright comedians like Mort Sahl, Dick Gregory, Mike Nichols and Elaine May, Shelley Berman, Woody Allen, Robert Klein, and the Smothers Brothers. Lenny Bruce plunged down from the Catskills, surreal in his daring. Intelligence and wit came into style. Will Rogers, who had found that treating mass audiences with respect, as if they were intelligent, brought out their respectability and intelligence, might not have been pleased to find his successors scorning America's vast majorities and its traditional values. But then, the comedians of the 1960s and early 1970s were trying to be both rebellious and popular—quite a trick. They had to work on tougher turf than Rogers had known, in a show business that had been reconditioned by saloon entertainers; moreover, Las Vegas had wiped out the nightclub, and so these performers had to find new stages.

Of all the "sick" comedians who startled America in the late 1960s, none had a more deviant humor than Lenny Bruce. He satirized sacred cows from organized religion to presidents; he imagined Hitler in show business and stewardesses jettisoning infants from overloaded airliners. He used obscene language when other comics dared no more than "darn" and "heck"—and Bruce took off at them too. Yet if his material was radical, his delivery betrayed a schooling in the Catskills resorts, for he was as sharp and urban as any fast-talking stand-up. Then he became a cause célèbre. Intellectuals egged him on, and law enforcers rushed to protect the public from him. Possessed merely of a sensationally funny spirit and a need to make people laugh —and to be paid for it—Bruce was pushed to a sorry and dreadful end. Nightclub owners do not look for police trouble, and as they shied away from him Bruce's career collapsed. So did his front. Revealed was the frightened bravado of the essential comedian. Hounded, prevented from working until he was professionally destroyed, he retreated into narcotics and died of a heroin overdose. Not many years later, Eddie Murphy was using language and material that would have made Lenny Bruce seem an innocent—and that he had been.

RIGHT:

It seems that George Carlin was created to be what an unneurotic and luckier Lenny Bruce might also have become. For, as Bruce's was, Carlin's appoach is countercultural and he was strident in his crusade to justify scatological language. But Carlin lacked Bruce's attraction to martyrdom and was too self-disciplined to explode. His subjects are adult and diverse, his style educated, and his wit fleet. He connects with audiences from casino showrooms to college campuses.

OVERLEAF, LEFT:

In an era of outspoken black comedians, Bill Cosby suppressed his anger. His amiable manner has made him very popular and durable.

OVERLEAF, RIGHT:

A mugger, a pratfaller, a sketch comic, and a monologist too, Steve Martin onstage was among the most inspired of contemporary comedians. His brainy foolishness was rooted in the tradition of great clowning. In another era he would have transported live audiences but in our electronic age he swept past personal appearances into cable television, the networks, and then movie space.

Those new stages were college auditoriums (work pieced together in one-night stands—the "concert tour") or the handful of intimate clubs aimed at the college crowd, such as New York's Village Vanguard or San Francisco's Hungry i (i for "intellectual").

The thinking-man's comedians thrived on live audiences, and their comedy was not so recondite as to be ungraspable. After all, it is not in the comedian's interest to be obscure. As long as their audiences got the joke (and here they were no different from George Jessel or Bob Hope), Mike Nichols and Elaine May could joke about Béla Bartók, and Woody Allen about Kierkegaard. Their audience got it, and laughed in person. Theirs was a flesh-and-blood constituency, though a dwindling one, for America had, for the most part, turned to electronic showmen.

These wits opened doors for stand-ups who worked in original and even eccentric ways. George Carlin, Robin Williams, Eddie Murphy, Steve Martin, Lily Tomlin, and Richard Pryor introduced a personal comedy that met the highest standards of show business, and yet they

could deal with matters of substance or more adult whimsy. They found ways to combine fantasy and invention with sure technique. How the delightful and cockeyed Rodney Dangerfield fit into this group was both inexplicable and delicious.

Today, the shrinking market for live performers and the lure of movie and television money quickly removes the gifted from live audiences. The older saloon comics work the few remaining casino nightclubs, but the young and exciting comedians seldom face up to audiences. Soon face-to-face may be gone and the dreaded last laugh will have been had. There are many small comedy clubs around the country, clubs that allow young comedians to test their material and themselves, but to what end? These clubs pay virtually nothing and there are no paying clubs to move up to. Except for the almost extinct talk show there is only one place in television to aspire to—situation comedy, and that is no place for the stand-up. Was it symbolic that the gifted, weird Andy Kaufman went from stand-up, to a television series, to a premature death?

It may be that all our jesters are about to die, and that would be tragic. The mortal who teeters on the edge of disaster with just a mind and a mouth to keep his balance is speaking for all of humanity. More than the soldier or statesman, he is the hero of the mortal crowd, the symbol of human optimism, good cheer, and endurance. If this jester has in fact had the last laugh then that laugh will surely have been the worst.

ABOVE:
"Feuds" were good business in radio. They created continuity and provided a rich lode of harmless insult comedy in a medium that devoured material. One of the two most famous fictitious feuds in radio was Bing Crosby's with Bob Hope. (Jack Benny's with Fred Allen was the other.)

LEFT:
Rich Little is doing Richard Nixon. Impressionists were among the last of vaudeville's variety artists to go under. One performer seeming to be another is an act that has the appeal of wonder and an element of magic.

OPPOSITE, ABOVE LEFT:
Dick Gregory was a comedian with a conscience. As the era of black assertion began, he found it trivial to entertain in nightclubs. Instead, he devoted himself to marches and demonstrations and went on a hunger strike on behalf of black rights.

OPPOSITE, ABOVE RIGHT:
Vulgarity and toilet humor in Las Vegas: Charlie Callas at the Landmark. An opening act or lounge comic might resort to such gross business, but he had to be a desperate man.

OPPOSITE, BELOW LEFT:
Vulgarity and toilet humor in Las Vegas: Godfrey Cambridge at the Aladdin

OPPOSITE, BELOW RIGHT:
Richard Pryor was cheerfully sardonic from the start, dealing with the pimps, drug dealers, and winos who were fixtures in the world of growing up black. Pryor was unprejudiced in his disrespect, and behind his broad-reaching good humor was the mind of a disciplined performer and writer.

ROGER RIDDLE
Working Comic

You go on stage, you work the worst clubs, you live in terrible hotels, sometimes don't work at all. You're emotionally naked, you're psychologically rejected. Nobody goes through life like a comedian does.

ROGER RIDDLE

The stars are only a few of the working entertainers who carry on the torch, what is left of the flame. The larger group of this honorable breed does not plunge into stretch limousines; is not surrounded by flunkies; has no private planes, no bodyguards, no television specials. These are the fellows with a patent-leather shoe in the spotlight and a sandal on line at a Burger King, which was where I stood with Roger Riddle one warm September evening in 1984, on the way to a play-date at Brown's Hotel in the Catskills.

He handed the bandleader sheet music for "The High and the Mighty" and "Auld Lang Syne," the accompaniments he wanted toward the end of the act. He knew better than to ask for music earlier than that. Playing for dancing, the musicians expected a coffee break during the comedy routine. In fact, the bandleader's first question was how much time did they have for coffee?

Riddle has never appeared on television, in Las Vegas, or in Atlantic City. Virtually unknown except to the agents and managers who handle the day-to-day entertainers for the Catskills resorts, he is a professional who works almost two hundred engagements a year, almost all of them one-night stands, and who earns between seventy thousand and one hundred thousand dollars a year.

Scores of comedians like Riddle are supported by the Catskills hotels. The flashy euphony of their names does not (as intended) conceal but, rather, betrays their origins and their stations—and tells still more about them. The names suggest men who have bought a show-business dream: Dick Capri, Freddy Roman, Lee Allen, Lenny Rush, Marty Brill, Sal Richards, Vic Arnel, Roger Riddle. They are names without families, names born of nightclubs in Pittsburgh and St. Paul, Montreal and Fort Worth. Unknown, these fellows do not trot on stage to fanfares and applause. They are perennially up-and-coming, the journeymen of show business, flashy wise guys with savvy and street smarts, focusing their energies, their physical bodies, their wits, and crumpled bits of material upon the audiences of two hundred, five hundred, or even nine hundred vacationers spending saved money, vacationers who get a show with the price of a room and have nothing to lose by slamming an exit door in a comic's face. If being a comedian is the toughest and loneliest and most frightening thing a performer can do (and that is one thing virtually all performers agree on), nothing is tougher, lonelier, or more frightening than doing it as a journeyman. They are bruised but resilient, the gallant facing the lions with black ties and gags.

Riddle's dressing room is a bare cubicle the size of a monk's cell. He can hear the opening act vocalizing next door. Tonight it is to be a tiny, middle-aged, blonde soprano who can also belt from the chest. Her act is twenty-five minutes, as all opening acts more or less are. Riddle goes on at ten-thirty. He isn't nervous. At fifty, he has spent half his life in show business, the last six years doing the same act. He knows it works.

In Person:
The Great Entertainers

156

Roger Rosenthal (alias Riddle) was born in Manhattan into a troubled but well-to-do family, his father a Park Avenue surgeon. A college clown, he took a summer job as a tummler at a resort hotel and then, as "Jolly Roger," developed a kiddie act. Weeknights he emceed at strip joints until he talked his way into a four-month stint on a cruise ship. "I didn't know what I was doing, but I'd get away with junk," he remembers. "Polish jokes, gay jokes, ship jokes. Like, 'My room is so small I put the key in the door and broke the porthole.'"

After six years of such apprenticeship, he landed his first respectable booking in a New England hotel. Feeling that he was on his way at last, he brought along a current girlfriend, sat her in the front row, and then strolled on stage, beaming and quick. He had material. He had been developing it over the years in other strip joints, other cruise ships. Now he began. The Polish jokes, the gay jokes, the ship jokes. Elegant.

Out of the corner of his eye as he talked and grinned and gestured onstage, he saw the hotel owner walk out of the wings. He continued the act. The audience was dead silent. They stared at him. The owner approached and then, *apologizing* to the customers for the comedian, took Riddle by the elbow and walked him off stage. "You," the man said, "are the worst comedian I have ever, ever had on my stage. Ever seen on *any* stage. You'd better pick another line of work."

On the Catskills hotel circuit, Roger Riddle's dressing room was, more likely than not, a cubicle with a bulb-lined mirror.

As Riddle recalls, still cringing at the memory, "I wept when it happened. My girlfriend was there and I wept. Nobody can describe the pain, after working in a profession for six years (no matter *where*—I was working), and someone who is in a very class situation, with a middle-class audience in a hotel, tells you, 'You're the worst I've ever seen.'"

Actors flee their emotions, comedians show them for laughs.

"I decided he must have been right. That's when I started figuring out what the hell I was doing. To me, the true comedian is the one who can come out and have a character, an attitude, and a point of view. I decided that my attitude was, I was always in pain."

Riddle looks spruce in his mohair tuxedo with its white lining, his blue formal shirt, the crimson handkerchief flaring from his breast pocket. The 1,400-seat nightclub is three-quarters filled, a round room decorated in chandelier, mirror, and whorehouse-red flocked wallpaper. Asking for applause for the orchestra, he excuses the eight musicians and begins talk-

Roger Riddle at the Raleigh Hotel,
1985

ing about his birth, his childhood. "My whole life has been inundated with pain and, with your permission, I would like to share it with you. . . . Why should I suffer alone?"

"Pain," he says with a groan. "Pain" is the litany, and after a while the audience murmurs the word along with him. They are plain people, men in zipper jackets, women in slacks and sweaters. Elderly, undrinking. He pulls the microphone from its clamp and paces the stage.

Riddle is sympathetic toward his fellow comedians. The only one who annoys him is "the cuff-link comic. That's the guy who looks great in his well-cut tuxedo; he can do everything—sings a little, dances a little, he does impressions; he's learned an hour's worth of gags, jokes, *non sequiturs* and one-liners, some funny, some not; he has good timing, the mechanics are impeccable." Riddle goes on, "And the audience says to itself, 'He acts like a comedian and he looks like a comedian so he must be a comedian.' But they don't remember a thing he said."

A compulsive talker, Riddle has other theories. He has no urge to be funny offstage and shakes his head over the curiosity of that. Instead, he has an urge to be serious. He thinks that the difference between an ordinary performer and an *entertainer* is vast and yet simple. "I bet you one day Liberace was onstage, playing the piano as usual, when all of a sudden, for no reason at all, he turned around toward the audience and gave them a big grin and waved at them with one hand while he kept playing the piano with the other. And that was it. He was a showman."

He tells the audience about his mother marrying his stepfather and his father marrying his stepmother and nobody wanting him around. "I never learned to defend myself because my parents sent me to Jewish boarding schools. So nobody fought. They just sued each other." There are other outright jokes. This is, after all, a comedy act. He talks about a doctor "so young his surgical gloves were pinned to his shirt." But also, "I talk about the pain in my life and I even talk about with all the pain and all the sorrow I could die of it. And then I do die. And then not only do I die but after I die I prepare my own funeral. And then I envision somebody delivering my eulogy. I eventually go to heaven."

Delivering this routine is hard work for Riddle. He paces the stage, bending, turning, stretching. The physical strain leaves him awash in perspiration but the effort succeeds. The audience is attentive, even rapt. A stretch in mid-act exaggerates senility for comic pathos. This is risky business under the best of circumstances, and the audience at Brown's is an older audience, making it even riskier. Riddle gets a standing ovation.

He returns to comedy and is winning laughs about every fifteen seconds. After fifty minutes he gets to the funeral section. The band is back in time for "The High and the Mighty." Then he is off, having cut the eulogy and "Auld Lang Syne" because the laughs were steady, and better not to stretch.

The response is warm, the show went well. Nevertheless, Riddle does not stay to mingle with the audience. It pays off in wedding and bar-mitzvah dates, but Riddle can't bring himself to do that. Nor can he fawn over headliner singers who might make him their opening act. Instead, he scrubs off his makeup, changes clothes, and—it is nearly one in the morning—heads toward his car for the two-hour drive back to New York City. His tuxedo is in a garment bag slung over a shoulder. Guests compliment him as he passes. "You're original," one says. "I've seen them all but I've never seen anyone like you before."

Riddle has this repeated for my benefit. "I'm the best," he tells me. "Peerless."

INTERNATIONAL GLITTER

There can be no entertainers' hall of fame, no building with pictures and recordings and memorabilia, no museum with mannequins and preserved costumes. Not even film clips or videotapes can conjure up the vitality and magnetism of the top star in live performance. Such an entertainer is a legend of the moment, his very presence mythic. Every performance is, for every person in every audience, the event of a lifetime.

The greatest of the entertainers are not singers or comedians but showmen. They are the show themselves. Animate phenomena, they are raised to a higher scintillation than most humans; raised to glory and triumph as they come to life in the spotlight. They not only survive but emerge triumphant throughout careers that often endure for decades. In show after show, before infinitely diverse audiences, they prove themselves beyond vogue or nationality. Such stars have no generational boundaries, their styles no moments of fashion. In an era when a television series can create an overnight superstar who will be forgotten next season, we may well be reminded of this marathon of success, this grueling gauntlet. For if every entertainer faces his day of judgment anew at each performance, the international headliner must face it knowing that anything less than greatness will be a letdown.

Popular entertainment seldom travels well. Language is only one reason for its unexportability. Even in countries with a common tongue, communication with an audience can be hindered by slang, patois, even simple accent. But more crucial to communication than even language is a turn of mind, a cultural wavelength. This is at the heart of entertainment, and a turn of mind is usually untranslatable. *That* is why they don't get the jokes.

The international star is rarely a funnyman. Nothing is so parochial as humor. Sid Fields, an adored British music-hall comic, never attempted to work in America, and even those of our stand-ups who did perform abroad, such as Bob Hope or Jack Benny, never reached Englishmen as they did Americans (and Hope was *born* in England). The singer of songs is more likely to transcend cultural boundaries because music is truly universal, but even he must offer more than songs. Maurice Chevalier is a good case in point. His assets were modest. His singing voice, although musical and certainly agreeable, was a light and even raspy baritone. His stage movements and dance steps were slighter still. But in his manner—oh, and in his style—the fellow could not have been more endearing. The entertainer, then, as myth: Chevalier became, for his audience away from France, the epitome of Gallic charm.

He started out as, of all things, an acrobat. Injured in an early accident, he turned to dancing and became successful enough at it to perform regularly in the music halls of Paris. By 1904 he was appearing at the Folies Bergère and there he met the celebrated chanteuse Mistinguett. A romance began and after World War I Chevalier became her dancing partner, but by then he had greater ambitions and added songs to his dancing. "My influence," he would later say, "was the American music hall," by which he meant vaudeville. He came under that influence when he joined Elsie Janis in the 1919 London revue *On the Level, You're a Devil*. There Chevalier developed the manner and the costume that would become his career trademarks: a straw boater and tuxedo, an air of gay sophistication, flirtatiousness, and insouciance.

Within ten years, this French song-and-dance man was a generic "entertainer" on the international circuit. He starred in New York's *Midnight Frolic*, a sophisticated revue that Flo Ziegfeld presented on the New Amsterdam Theatre roof after performances of his *Ziegfeld Follies* had ended in the main auditorium below. Just as Harry Lauder had created the perfect Scotsman, so Chevalier was now the thing itself, the French troubadour. With his crumpled suit, his affectedly awkward pigeon-toed step, and a boater hat lifted in midair, he raised invention to archetype.

> *Every little breeze*
> *Seems to whisper, "Louise."*
> *Birds in the trees*
> *Seem to twitter, "Louise."*

Even his signature songs—"Mimi" by Rodgers and Hart and "My Ideal" by Richard Whiting—seemed singable only by him. He would translate American songs into French ("Isn't It Romantic?") and French ones into English ("Valentina"), and traditionally he concluded each performance with his theme song, "One Hour with You." Mistinguett said, "He put the song over as if he were humming it for his own pleasure, with a rhythm and sureness of touch that took my breath away."

Although Chevalier seemed French from his twinkle to his wink, "What I did," he said, "was mix the American novelty and the old French humor so that even to the French I was something new." But this sweetheart relationship ended abruptly after World War II. Not only was Chevalier accused of having been a Nazi collaborator because he had sung on Radio Paris for the Pétain regime; he was simultaneously criticized as being a Communist sympathizer for having endorsed the antinuclear Stockholm Peace Appeal. To be caught in such an absurd political sandwich would suggest not wrongness or opportunism but political naiveté. The America intimidated by Senator Joseph McCarthy was not, however, disposed to forgive, and the troubadour was denied a United States visa until 1955, when he made a comeback appearance on Broadway.

He worked on a big stage, unpretentiously accompanied by a lone pianist. He ran through his songbook between chats with the audience. Typically, at one evening performance he walked to the edge of the stage and, shielding his eyes from the spotlight, scanned the audience. "Oh," he remarked conversationally, smiling and waving as if at an old friend, "I don't know your name, but I have the impression you are my friend because the first time I sang here in New York, in the Fulton Theatre, you were sitting in the same seat." This was much the sort of thing that Jolson had done thirty years earlier. "And," Chevalier continued, "your wife—I remember her too. Yes. Oh, that's very nice to see you both here tonight. . . . You have not changed at all, you know. Oh, you have got a bit grayer over there—but so am I. I don't know anyone who gets younger each year."

It was an indefinable patter, not humor. It was Chevalier's act, confidential and wry. Producer Billy Rose was captivated. "There's plenty of

OPPOSITE, LEFT:
Marlene Dietrich

OPPOSITE, RIGHT:
Maurice Chevalier

gray under that jaunty straw hat now," he said, "but when he begins to sing, he's still the gay young man of France . . . when Chevalier is on, the other actors might as well be dealing pinochle in the dressing room." But the *New York Times* drama critic Brooks Atkinson, a man of keener political sensibilities, could not in principle accept Chevalier simply as an entertainer. "There is something a little sad," he wrote, "in seeing him again. There are too many ghosts in the wings and backstage." The review did the entertainer no harm, however, and Chevalier played New York regularly and successfully for many years thereafter. Having begun as a romantic figure, Chevalier would conclude his run of fifty years on a note of nostalgia and grandfatherliness. Of all modern performers, only Frank Sinatra can match him in staying power.

Briefer by far was the cabaret career of Marlene Dietrich, and yet thinking of Chevalier calls her to mind both because they were friends and because she too was among the few Europeans to captivate American audiences. There was also a certain formality that they shared onstage, as if a courtesy paid to audiences by visitors from another country, although Dietrich kept her distance to the extent of being remote. She had developed this style as a film actress and it paid off handsomely as a stage manner. Whereas Chevalier was intimate and endearing, she was a figure of icy glamor. She loomed as if out of a mist—dramatic, cool, erotic—snubbing age in an evening gown that revealed every pulse beat on a death-defying youthful body that was well past fifty when she began her in-person career—a career that from the outset was on the international level.

Any great star develops an aura of legend. Audiences gather as if in appointment with history. A performance of Marlene Dietrich's had an even more solemn, ritual-like tone. The audience came to worship her, and without fail the final curtain of every performance brought flower-bearing admirers to her feet. Her biographer Sheridan Morley observed that

while Dietrich's Hollywood contemporaries drifted into elegant postwar obscurity, Dietrich took herself into the theatre, there to become not an actress nor precisely a singer but simply a solo star, able to command a minimum of $5,000 a week for an appearance which was to become one of the great recurring theatrical happenings of the 1950s and 1960s. (*Dietrich*)

She still had longish flaxen hair that tended to slip over one eye, framing her high cheekbones and setting off her alabaster complexion. Pencil-hard eyebrows arched over ice-blue, experienced eyes—but the core of the Dietrich allure lay in her brutally red lips, curling in the trace of a smile. Sneering? Cynical? Hers was the face of moral decadence, beautiful but arrogant and heartless. (Wasn't this a wonderful act?) Her beauty seemed total, her stance as intimidating as her face. Dietrich's costumes were probably more essential to her act than any other singer's, from her signature men's clothes to the famous creation she wore for her Las Vegas debut in 1959, a see-through gown of gauze, dappled with more than two hundred thousand hand-sewn beads, fitted to paint her skin. In a dispatch to the Paris newspaper *L'Etoile*, Paul Tanfield swooned: "She swayed to the microphone with that lubricated walk which is as old as Eve. Her hair was a cascade of spun gold. Her dress fitting closer than close, her figure like a debutante's. Age, Shakespeare said, cannot wither her. He was speaking of Cleopatra but the same goes for Dietrich, the soignée, the indestructible fifty-four-year-old butterfly."

Actually, she was a fifty-eight-year-old butterfly at the time of the Las Vegas debut. Born Maria Magdalene Dietrich in 1901, she was by then

Marlene Dietrich

known simply as "Dietrich" and, with theatrical flair she signed her autograph that way. Dietrich's second career as a performer was to last fifteen years, and her act remained virtually unchanged throughout. Whether at a Broadway theater, a Las Vegas hotel, or the Edinburgh

Danny Kaye had the gestures of a dancer.

Festival in Scotland, she did ninety minutes of songs without pause or intermission. When she spoke, she was brief and when she sang, she hardly moved. Her voice was a growly baritone, her appeal tantalizingly, voluptuously androgynous.

> They call me naughty Lola,
> The wisest girl on earth.
> At home my pianola
> Is played for all it's worth.

The other songs in her repertoire were similarly insinuating, a curious mix of American and European tastes: "La Vie en Rose," "The Laziest Girl in Town," "Falling in Love Again," "The Boys in the Back Room." Her musical director during the 1960s was the young Burt Bacharach, who, faced with developing a song program for a non-singer, framed and presented her with the skill of a true accompanist, sympathetic and supportive. The act was severe, as Dietrich herself was. There was none of the solo singer's usual patter or special material, none of the production values or back-up dancers. The show was Dietrich, only Dietrich, and it brought out the devotee even in intellectuals. The critic Kenneth Tynan, for instance, wrote with melodramatic ingenuousness, "It seemed as if whatever hell you happened to inhabit, she had been there first, and survived."

No performer was ever more an act than Dietrich. Audiences gave her that special tribute of the world-class star: the credit that she was onstage precisely what she was offstage. When Dietrich at seventy-three finally did stop performing, her audiences could not believe that age was the reason, even though the two nasty spills into the orchestra pit that did it were plainly age's fault. Until then, her gallant routine had been nothing less than the defeat of time.

To imagine Marlene Dietrich sitting down to dinner in Paris with Maurice Chevalier and Danny Kaye may seem a star-struck fantasy, yet that is exactly what she was doing when Prince Rainier of Monaco telephoned one evening. Seems a gala was being planned, a little party at the palace, at which, the prince hoped, a favorite entertainer of his wife's might appear. Princess Grace's choice was not Chevalier, nor was it Dietrich. It was Danny Kaye. As Kaye continued to decline the offer, perhaps in trepidation after many years away from live audiences, Rainier's offer rose from ten thousand dollars to twenty-five thousand dollars. And still he refused ("I am having too much fun in Paris to leave now").

Such conversations with such people would have seemed beyond all imagination in the lower-class Brownsville section of Brooklyn where, as David Kaniel Kominsky, Kaye was born in 1913. Kaye set his incredible escape in motion by becoming a tummler at a summer-resort hotel. Better than any other in recent memory, Kaye's international career illustrates the bloodline from the medieval gleoman—troubadour—wandering minstrel to the topflight twentieth-century entertainer.

Kaye's first winter work was as one of "The Three Terpischoreans," a dance act that did not get very far in New York but compensated for that by going all the way to the Far East on a seedy tour. There, an onstage tumble gave him his first laugh, and he was hooked on comedy. Instead of returning home, he went to London as a comedy-dance act, booked for eight weeks at the Dorchester Hotel. For this engagement he assembled special material from numbers he had developed as a tummler, including the song "Dinah."

Only it was not pronounced "Dinah." Oh, it was sung properly. It was even sung endearingly. But the title was pronounced "Deenah," as were all the rhymes, such as "feenah" and "Caroleenah." To compensate for a certain degree of limitation in this number, Kaye sang the second chorus in high-speed double-talk. Summer-resort audiences had enjoyed that somewhat more than did the Dorchester crowd. Another of his tummling numbers was Cab Calloway's "Minnie the Moocher," an audience-participation piece that in Kaye's version also led into double-talk. The Dorchester engagement was not a watershed in the annals of British entertainment.

Unsurprisingly, Kaye found himself back on the resort circuit that summer, and there he met Sylvia Fine while she was helping to write a show called *The Straw Hat Review.* It was brought to Broadway in the enthusiasm of summer, but what had been refreshing and delightful in the mountains in July proved amateurish on Broadway in the fall. After a ten-week run, the revue closed. Surviving were an enthusiastically received Kaye and his newfound writer-wife, Sylvia Fine. Kaye was the discovery of the following season, working at a New York nightclub, La Martinique, and singing his wife's clever and deft patter songs, such as the spoof of French hat-designers, "Anatole of Paris".

Kaye was, then, from the outset an entertainer rather than a mere comedian. His purpose was not to get laughs but to delight. He was unique, and his material would have been leaden in any other hands. Even though the La Martinique engagement was his last personal appearance for many years, he inspired writers to tailor material for him and in that way entertained in solo even while working in musical comedy. For the 1941 Broadway hit *Lady in the Dark,* Ira Gershwin gave him "Tchaikovsky," in which Kaye rattled off the names of scores of Russian composers. But he still had enough of the tummler in him to be restless doing the same show eight times a week. Eddie Cantor, engaged at the time in a musical version of *Three Men on a Horse,* recalled:

Danny played at a theatre next door. He had a break in his show at the time I did a number with six chorus boys. It would have taken Danny a little advance time to plot this one but one night [he] slipped out of his own show, made a split-second change into a chorus boy costume and pranced out on stage behind me. I was singing. As a grace note he took along a banana, which he ate during my routine. My number got laughs it never had before. What was up? I knew something must be happening behind my back. Every time I turned around the banana disappeared. I examined each boy sharply. Funny, I thought; that new chorus boy looks like Danny Kaye. The new chorus boy eyed me mildly with an affectionate look, the sort of look you get from a loving but not too bright cocker spaniel. I looked harder. Danny looked more lovingly and tossed first one foot and then the other, all in perfect timing with my own dance routine and the rest of the chorus. Finally I caught on—it broke up the show—it was too funny—it was a riot. Everyone loved it. (Kurt Singer, *The Danny Kaye Saga*)

Kaye had two distinct careers. His early fame and success rested on a series of movies (*Up in Arms, The Secret Life of Walter Mitty*), in which he played a bumbling innocent. These capitalized on his charm but not on his talents. The telephone call from Monaco may well have played a part in spurring Kaye into his second phase, which reinforced his original impulse to solo as a live entertainer. Simply by chance (or not) he

A rare photograph of Danny Kaye in drag, doing a takeoff of the ultrasophisticated Kay Thompson for a 1948 "Frolic" at the Los Angeles branch of the famous Friars' Club

was vacationing in nearby Cannes at the time of the Monaco gala and he impulsively stopped in at the palace on the night of the party. Recognized and admitted at once, he was introduced and called to the stage, where he performed impromptu and for nothing. Perhaps this reminder of the excitement of a live audience caught hold of him because soon afterward he accepted an engagement at the prestigious London variety theater, the Palladium.

The managing director of this famous house, Val Parnell, was going through a phase of booking American movie stars (Hollywood was suffering from the competition of television, and many famous actors were underemployed). The taste of the Palladium's audiences, unfortunately, was extremely British, and the American performers who ventured on that enormous stage did so at their peril. Just before Kaye arrived, for instance, Mickey Rooney had been unenthusiastically received and, before that, Rita Hayworth had played a calamitous engagement. Popular enough as a movie star, Kaye was virtually unknown in England, at least as a stage performer, when, on February 2, 1948, he stumbled out from the wings in a city where he had flopped only ten years before. (He stumbled out, as the story goes, because, frozen by panic, he had to be shoved.) As Kaye's biographer Kurt Singer describes it, that performance made him a cult figure.

He sang scat songs, told of his trip to England, lamented his fears and thrilled the audience with a voice of surprisingly good quality and a scintillating wit. He jockeyed the mood of the British to the point of seldom-experienced lunacy. He lured the audience to sing with him, to imitate his voices, noises and ugh-ughs. Without a pause for fresh air or sensible syntax he mimicked the Nazis and the Russians.

The audience was completely under his spell. The heartbeat of the performance gathered momentum. There appeared to be no way to break up the show. The audience stood clapping, smiling, laughing, stamping and refusing to go home.

The Royal Family came to see the show, as did Winston Churchill and even the archbishop of Canterbury. "With each new performance," according to Singer, "his popularity grew. A legend of enormous and almost embarrassing proportions was growing." At Kaye's last performance, the English were not about to part with him. He was to remain onstage for two hours, and the audience, at the end, rose and sang "Auld Lang Syne." Next day a newspaper headline lamented, "Our Danny's Gone Away."

In 1950 Kaye participated in an extraordinary benefit show in honor of the late Sid Fields, the beloved English music-hall comedian. The variety bill began at midnight and did not end until five o'clock in the morning. The fifty stars included Orson Welles, Judy Garland, Vivian Leigh, and Laurence Olivier. Even in such company, Danny Kaye was the main attraction. A series of annual visits followed and he became a British institution, a frequent visitor at Buckingham Palace, an intimate of Princess Margaret.

His prestige was now too great for conventional engagements. The showcase he sought was a New York equivalent of the Palladium. He found it in Broadway's Palace Theatre, and the entertainment "concert" he gave there—a solo performance in a theater—proved a pioneering concept, a way for entertainers to play to immense audiences without the distractions—food service, smoke, drunk customers—of nightclubs.

In 1956, when Kaye played an eight-week engagement there, the Palace had long since been abandoned to movies, but it was destined to be regularly rescued from oblivion because of its marketable legend as the stage for greatness. At forty-three, Kaye was still trim and youthful, and though he had never been handsome there was something of the willowy jester about his looks. His lithe, six-foot frame was topped with a head of golden red hair, and his movements were a dancer's, loping and graceful. Aging zanies tend to a barely concealed nastiness symptomatic of an awareness that what they do ill suits an adult. Kaye had little of that. At the Palace he seemed simple and charming. He dressed casually in a sports jacket and contrasting trousers, usually in shades of brown, his preferred color. He sang songs from his films, notably the recent *Hans Christian Andersen*, which many considered his best. With such enchanting Frank Loesser songs as "Inchworm" and "The Ugly Duckling," he reduced adults to children, lullabying them with his sweet and gentle, almost Irish, lyric tenor. A tummler to his fingertips, Kaye

Young, undamaged, and wonderful Judy Garland—never quite five feet tall. Of all the Hollywood stars, she most surely could have made it just as successfully on Broadway.

returned to routines he had done in the Catskills, organizing the audience into sections for participation. Now, with his reputation behind it, the material that had bombed years earlier in Britain worked beautifully.

He ambled to the apron of the stage and sat down, his feet dangling into the orchestra pit. Lighting a cigarette, he confided in the audience, chatting about his daughter, or the English, or (seemingly) whatever happened to pop into his head. He even reminisced about Harry Lauder, plainly aware that the casual act he had developed, with its confidences and anecdotes, and the bond with the audience upon which it rested, bore a startling resemblance to the working style of the great Scotsman.

Kaye had little patience with prepared and rehearsed routines. Even for the most accomplished ad-libber, the hour or so of a headlining act requires organization and polish. The seemingly most casual of acts are as carefully memorized, rehearsed, drilled, and timed as a full-length play. They leave very little room for the impromptu. For Kaye, however, having grown up on improvisation, "the written word doesn't mean a thing," he told biographer Dick Richards. "It's not till I start playing with the words, mouthing them, shaping them with my hands, kicking them around, winking at them, that they begin to excite me."

Kaye's engagement at the Palace was ultimately extended to fourteen weeks, but afterward a kind of retirement was inevitable. He toured the show around the world, but part of any performer's compulsive psychology is perpetually to top himself. Las Vegas hotels could pay his fees, and he played in them, but for Kaye, that was a step down from the prestige of the Palladium and the Palace. It was possible for exotic European stars like Marlene Dietrich and Noel Coward to play Las Vegas comfortably because there was novelty and humor in it, and because the stupendous casino salaries were irresistible to those underpaid and overtaxed Europeans. Danny Kaye, however, must have felt that he needed neither the money nor the nightclub environment. He then devoted himself to the United Nations International Children's Emergency Fund.

Kaye must have served as an example for Judy Garland when, in 1951, she too found her movie career in recession. Like Kaye, Garland had begun as a variety entertainer, in her case in a vaudeville act called "The Gumm Sisters." Her last stage appearance had been in 1938 at New York's Loew's State Theatre, a Times Square presentation house, where between movies she did twenty-five minutes of songs to promote her next release. Though her career problems were complicated by personal troubles, Garland now faced the same frightening question as had Kaye: had movie work drained her of performing blood? Did she still have the drive and energy and magnetism to attract and ignite an audience? Could she sing in person, sing to an audience and connect with them after thirteen years of recording soundtracks in Hollywood? What kind of stage personality would she project now?

America was not the place to find out. If things turned out badly, better badly far away. For Val Parnell of the Palladium, still reveling in Kaye's stupendous success, Garland's possibilities must have seemed limitless. What neither he nor anybody else could have suspected was that Garland's travails—the publicized battles with alcohol and pills and nerves that had broken her film career—would become *the very basis* of her stage act. Audiences were to gather not merely for Garland, the singer, but for Garland, the survivor. It was to be an emotional aerial act with the star risking nervous collapse onstage at each performance.

The audience's role was to be an active one: more than perceiving the risk that was being run, they would also respond to it, not as voyeurs but as participants. Suicide-watching was not a part of it, however, at least

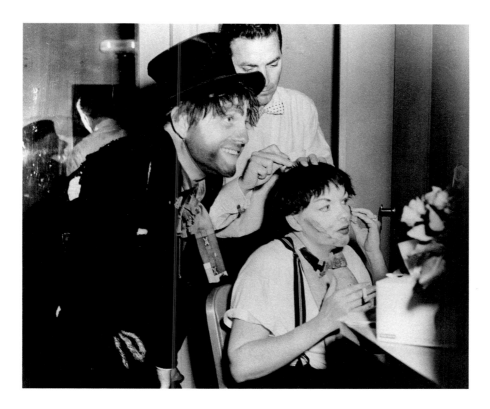

not at the start. At the start, the audience was survival-watching. It would cheer Garland on at every performance as she brought herself to the brink of breakdown. The very timbre of her voice conveyed past and present pain, and the unique gestures that she developed expressed an indomitable spirit transcending terrible agonies. This tightrope act, combined with high-powered songs and the volunteered emotionalism of her audience made for an electric atmosphere.

Garland brought her crisis-studded life to a London that had always been Tabloid City. Indeed, the newspapers had long been filled with stories of her demons, real and imagined. Now at the Palladium she was starting anew, and though it seemed as if she'd been a movie star for a lifetime, she was only twenty-eight. Parnell billed her as "America's Singing Sweetheart," but she was no longer the teenager lost in Oz, the Judy Garland who had so virginally co-starred with Mickey Rooney. She was a strange and striking mixture of ingenue and bag lady, a young woman brought low by circumstance and emotional ogres.

On opening night at the Palladium, the orchestra struck up the overture, a medley of songs associated with Garland. The volume and tempo and intensity of the music seemed to build as the star's appearance grew imminent. When the orchestra segued into "Over the Rainbow," the audience rose to its feet, reminded of the innocent girl, her promise, her broken dream—Garland's life story as movie script. Cheering and applause had built during the overture and now intensified. As Lorna Smith described the scene in *Judy with Love*, before Garland even appeared, the audience was in a state of frenzy, a state that fed on itself.

Making a nervous entrance [she] hovered hesitantly near the wings . . . clasping her hands in front of her and then behind her, standing first on one foot and then the other. She was clearly overcome as the applause continued. It was some time before she collected herself sufficiently. . . . Nervously she started to sing, and despite the crescendo of applause, she kept right on singing with hardly a pause between songs.

Then Garland *stumbled and fell down*. Was this the feared collapse? Was she drunk? Drugged? Dying? The pianist, the musician nearest

Backstage at the Palace in 1956, Alan King watches Judy Garland make up for "A Couple of Swells."

her, slid from his bench and stepped quickly to her side. He leaned down and grasped her elbow, whispering. She looked dazed but then smiled and nodded. He helped her to her feet. Pale, unsteady, smoothing her clothes, she reached for the microphone. The pianist touched her one last time, as if pushing a glass safely away from the edge of a table, and then stepped back to his place at the keyboard. She resumed her singing, the audience resumed its roar, if possible more intensely than before. "I wanted to cry," she later recalled. "But I laughed instead and the audience laughed with me."

The act was an ambitious one. The songs she'd been associated with in Hollywood were sweet and girlish: "For Me and My Gal," "The Boy Next Door." But the songs she added to her program were outsized and dynamic, such Jolson songs as "Swanee" and "Rock-a-bye Your Baby with a Dixie Melody." Even her quieter numbers were calculated to create emotional, if not musical, electricity in their implied references to her troubled life: Irving Berlin's "How About Me?" or Noel Coward's "If Love Were All":

> *I believe*
> *The more you love a man*
> *The more you put your trust*
> *The more you're bound to lose . . .*

The ambitiousness of her act, then, lay in the combination of whopping song and whopping emotion. Garland was attempting an emotional exhibitionism so intense, and a relationship with the audience so intimate, that the love would come through in waves, rush over her and wash away her griefs. The audience's participation was necessary in this and if, in the process, a certain hysteria was needed to convince her of their love, then she would do whatever was required to provoke it. Since some in the audience brought a need to be part of this transaction, and others arrived eager to be hysterical, Garland's slightest show of grief or panic was cue enough for roaring responses and accolades.

None of this can detract from her awesome talents as musician and entertainer. According to her Palladium conductor, Gordon Jenkins, she was a "tremendous musician, the whole band could tune to her pitch. Those electric crescendos are far beyond the scope of any mortal teacher." But Garland's stage power was more than merely musical. She instinctively made theatrical choices of songs, but then so did other singers. Was it her stage manner? Garland invented an entire vocabulary of gestures; her limbs became the supporting cast. She would reach and grope painfully for the rafters, or struggle to touch the wings, or wrestle one arm down with the other as if it were straining of its own will for some higher place of safety; or she would caress the microphone, crooning into the rhinestone sleeve she'd had it fitted with. This was real showmanship, but not just showmanship. To quote Jenkins again: "I believe that people cry at Judy for the same reason that they do at sunsets, or symphonies, or cathedrals. When one is confronted with greatness, it is impossible not to be touched."

The comparisons are embarrassing, and yet we do thrill at and are transported by such performances. Did she actually achieve greatness? The word is too big for mere entertainment but our responses to such performers do spill over. Our eyes well up with tears. We shiver. Whatever it means, even if it is a shallow response to stimulus, the performing energy is there to provoke it. Of course it is easier to respond to theatrics than to real life; easier and less costly in true emotion and depth of feeling. These tears are salt-free. But they are tears.

Judy Garland's last performance at Madison Square Garden

By the time Garland returned to America—again following Kaye's lead, to play the Palace—she had assembled the components of an act that she would perform for the next fifteen years. In a real way, the act and its audiences would, as promised, save her life. Although her career as a performer appeared to be based on her movie fame, she only *acted* as if her life were over, as if the present were but reminiscence and deathwatch. In fact, concertizing was to be the major part of her career in both duration and impact. Ironically, it was in concert that she kept her ingenue self alive, playing its artlessness and vulnerability against her taut and ravaged present self. Thus, the phenomenon of Judy Garland was no more attributable to her voice alone than Kaye's huge charm was to his comic sense, than the magnetism of Dietrich was to her singing voice, or than Chevalier's stage presence was to his songs.

Garland opened at the Palace on October 16, 1951. The Palladium story seemed to have preceded her because once more the applause began during the overture. Then the great crimson curtain soared upward and a chorus of eight male dancers stepped briskly into a number called "Judy" that had been specifically written for the occasion. Then the star appeared upstage, her hands cupped around her mouth. She strode straight toward the audience and then she grinned and yelled, "Hello!"

Her songs came in bunches. Some were plainly confessional: "I Don't Care," "Some of These Days," "My Man." Others conjured up her movie self: "The Boy Next Door," "You Made Me Love You," and of course "The Trolley Song." She changed into tights and a fedora for "Get Happy" and then teamed up with one of the chorus boys to do "A Couple of Swells." By the time she actually sang "Over the Rainbow," the Palace was hers, and she stayed there for nineteen weeks. The engagement established her as one of the top attractions in show business, but in dealing with her troubles as an implicit part of her act, the hook when all other love-lures failed, she made them the heart of her life. Her Palace triumph was jolted, four weeks into the run, when she collapsed onstage and had to be rushed to a hospital. So it was throughout the concert years: any Garland performance might be aborted because of physical-emotional collapse. That was the unwritten number on the program, the ghost part of the show. The main part?

In 1956 Garland returned to the Palace, giving the young comedian Alan King the opportunity of his career by making him her opening act. She would watch from the wings, already wearing the clown costume for "A Couple of Swells"—baggy pants, checkered coat, a fright wig. She would stand and cheer and clap her hands for him. When she returned to London the following year, the demand for tickets forced her to book a bigger theater, the 3,100-seat Dominion, and on closing night the audience simply would not let her go. "More! More!" the roaring crowd demanded. Back and forth she strode across the stage, finally so excited that she started singing without the microphone. Lorna Smith quotes Gordon Jenkins, her conductor, as having asked if they should begin "from the top."

"We will *not*," said Judy. "Six 'Swells,' four 'Swanees,' we'll be here all night." "We've got plenty of time," someone called out. "No," she grinned, "we'll take it from 'I loves ya.'" The closing ovations were shattering and Jenkins said, "That was one of the greatest performances of all time."

Garland's relationship with her audience was a mixture of need and fear on her part, love and threat on theirs. It was a grotesque exaggeration of the merely emotional relationship that exists between all audiences and performers. In her case, the audience's enthusiasm and friendship were laced with the menace of cries for more. What, we wonder, is the implied "or else"? How dangerous could this audience become, were it denied what it required?

Now Garland organized grand tours, following Danny Kaye's lead, but unlike Kaye, Garland was in financial straits and could not afford to remain aloof from nightclub work. When she played Las Vegas during the 1957 Christmas holidays, she walked out on the New Year's Eve show, blaming the noisy crowd. For a while a huge new Brooklyn club called the Town and Country made a run at matching the Las Vegas salaries, and when Garland played there the Copacabana's fate was sealed. Perhaps hers was too, for her appearances and condition were now unpredictable, and from time to time her young daughter Liza Minnelli was brought on stage to perform in place of the dazed mother.

The next year in Las Vegas, Sammy Davis, Jr., introduced her at the Sands Hotel as "the greatest entertainer in the world," but 1958 was to be a disastrous year for a Garland besieged by hepatitis, laryngitis, alcoholism, drug dependence, back taxes, back problems, money problems, and, because of all this, escalating emotional problems. Work was impossible, but essential. As she memorably remarked, "Wind up the Judy Garland doll. Get her on."

And the crowds grew bigger, noisier, even more threatening in their adoration. Writing in the *Chicago-American* in 1961, Maggie Daly said that as Garland's concert "reached its crescendo, the audience seemed incapable of absorbing any more emotion . . . that is, until she finished. They raced to the footlights by the hundreds to touch her foot, or her hand, or her perspiring face." She attracted fourteen thousand people to the tennis stadium at Forest Hills, Queens, and nineteen thousand to the Hollywood Bowl. She was playing giant auditoriums now, the opera houses in San Francisco and Chicago, the Shrine Auditorium in Los Angeles. An hour-long first act, a thirty-minute intermission, and then back for an hour and a half. Thirty songs in all. It was as if the point were not to celebrate performance but to survive it. The ordeal seemed devastating. The dumpy lady who had played the Palladium now weighed 103 pounds and less with every show. "By the time she reached the encores," as Lorna Smith tells it,

Judy was so totally winded and exhausted that she sometimes barely managed to walk to the wings between songs. Once there, she would mop up, square her shoulders, shake her head and take deep gasps for breath in much the same way a boxer does after a near knockout punch, then take a deep, deep breath before resuming a relaxed-looking smile and returning to face her deliriously happy audience who were calling for "More! More!"

"More! More!" The audience craves to mourn the *slain* gladiator, their martyr. "More!" Garland seemed to have sensed the perversity of their worship when she told a Chicago audience, "I keep having this terrible dream. I'm about eighty-seven years old and I'm wearing lots and lots of white beads and white orchids and I sort of creak onto the stage on my cane and I sing something like this." She emitted a few strangled notes. "And you're all there and you're just as old as I am and you clap and cheer and say, 'That's our Judy.' "

She toured the world. ("Adult men and women jumped on their chairs to applaud"—*Leicester Evening Mail*.) She played a command performance for the queen of England, kicking off her pumps while singing "Swanee," and she finished the number with the shoes in her hand.

ABOVE:

*Victor Borge's "comedy in music"
appealed to international audiences for
decades. He exemplified the enduring
professional who hones his materials
to perfection. No matter how often
Borge placed his sheet music upside
down or slammed the piano lid by
mistake, he made it seem as if he
himself were still amused by it all.
And if he was amused, so were we.*

BELOW:

Noel Coward in Las Vegas

Financial pressures were unrelenting but they were not the only reason for her brutal schedule. She was probably only alive when onstage. She gave a legendary concert in New York's Carnegie Hall, a concert whose recording captures the fabled hysteria. Her usual costume was a sequined white or green pantsuit, but this time she put on a black Norman Norell sheath with a blue satin jacket.

Singing is a static act. Singers must invent their show, using patter and gesture to add a theatrical context. Garland's repertoire had taken on the Jolson style, and also like him she ruled the stage physically. She would rarely stand still before the microphone unless a moody ballad demanded it. Even then, her bony fingers might be spread before her face, or her hands would be thrust defiantly on her hips, the feet apart and flat on the floor. Or her head might be thrust back, her eyes closed, and the back of a hand to her brow. Or she might lean into the spotlight, hands raised to shoulder level and straight out in front of her, as if about to applaud. She might shoot an arm straight up, along a beam of light, as if reaching for the bulb and its comforting heat. She might snatch the microphone from its clamp and stride the width of the stage, great forceful steps from one wing clear across to the other. Others—Jolson, Cantor—had worked the stage with comparable energy, but Garland's act assumed an expressionistic vividness and unreality. She was a puppet, a stab of color with the tension of bottled explosives. How strange, such compression in someone ready to fly apart.

In 1964, skeletal and hollow-eyed, she toured Australia, momentarily triumphant in Sydney only to crash-dive in Melbourne, where she stumbled onstage to croak through several songs before calling an intermission. Thirty minutes later she returned to face the restless, excited, resentful, eager, angry audience. She stammered through a few more songs before concluding with Arthur Schwartz and Howard Dietz's "By Myself." Then she murmured into the microphone, "It's so lonely by myself. Goodnight," and hurried off in tears.

The audience snarled.

Her last five years were cruel. She concertized sporadically, fitfully. In London she unexpectedly sang at a midnight benefit for the Actors' Orphanage. She was supposed to simply sit at one of the onstage tables and watch the proceedings. The elite of British drama were the main attraction—Laurence Olivier, Edith Evans, Robert Morley, Richard Attenborough, Michael Redgrave, Flora Robson. But when Garland

Edith Piaf's growls and whimpers for lost love had an essentially sophisticated appeal. Her admirers comprised an elite international club.

made her entrance, the audience would not stop cheering until she said, "All right, what do you want to hear?" and then struggled through "Swanee," accompanied by an unprepared pianist. Her last concert was in Copenhagen in 1969, and three months later she died, ancient at forty-seven.

International stardom beckons only a small and elect group because the requisite talent, success, and durability are so rare and also because its logistics were fully developed only after World War II. Before 1945, it was extremely difficult for an entertainer to orbit the globe on performance tours, although some (Harry Lauder and Elsie Janis, for example) certainly managed it. Had Charlie Chaplin ever elected to return to personal appearance he would surely have achieved world success. Other performers likely to have appealed to audiences across national boundaries were Jolson, who was uninterested in travel, and Fred Astaire, who stopped dancing before live audiences in order to star in stage musicals and then in movies.

Among those American and European entertainers who have achieved international status is the honey-voiced Harry Belafonte, a balladeer with a magnetism in live performance that made him perhaps the sexiest man in show business. His counterpart in that respect was Lena Horne, whose international career—like Garland's and Kaye's—only began after the demise of traditional Hollywood. The sexiness and blackness of Belafonte and Horne undoubtedly contributed to their success. Much of the European world continues to see blacks as exotic figures, perhaps not quite as exotic as Josephine Baker seemed a half-century ago but still *earthy*, as if that were a genetic quality. However absurd the attitude, these entertainers wisely capitalized on it.

European performers who have crossed America's wavelength are not abundant because our arrogant provincialism has required that all entertainment be in our own language. Edith Piaf had but a limited success in America. Bea Lillie and Noel Coward achieved greater popularity, although they, too, played for only very sophisticated audiences, until Coward made sophistication a part of everyday life in Las Vegas. Among foreign entertainers, aside from Chevalier and Dietrich, perhaps only Victor Borge reached the mass American audience.

Of course there are international rock stars, and probably no act even approached the Beatles in popularity. At the arena- or stadium-level, the concept of live performance assumes new and awesome connotations, but the nature of an act performed before as many as a hundred thousand spectators belongs in its own category.

Today, the showman has less and less reason to make international appearances. The rewards of movies and television are tremendous. Why should Barbra Streisand or Bette Midler bother to undertake the hard work and constant travel of an international tour, even though it is safe to suppose that they would excite audiences everywhere and achieve tremendous success? In the past, vanity, ego, and ambition would have been reason enough, but today such qualities are considered naive and the money can be made in easier ways. Nevertheless, some showmen are still invigorated by the challenge of performance abroad. Frank Sinatra, Diana Ross, Peter Allen, and Liza Minnelli, for instance, continue to make such tours. But even when they do, they are physically so far removed from their audiences—think of Radio City Music Hall, the arenas, and even stadiums—that the "personal" quality of the appearance is insignificant. The entertainer becomes smaller as he gets farther away—less human as his voice booms out from scores of speakers —and finally he will be gone.

OPPOSITE, ABOVE:
In the 1940s pop singers aspired to movie careers, and Lena Horne found roles early in her career. The era's bigotry relegated her to cameos, however. It was not until much later that she was able to establish herself as a star act.

OPPOSITE, BELOW:
Harry Belafonte in performance at Madison Square Garden with singer Miriam Makeba. Belafonte's honey voice, his choice of catchy folk melodies and calypso tunes, his wonderful looks, and his radiant sexuality were the ingredients of international superstardom. Although he wore his shirts only modestly unbuttoned, the women in Belafonte's audience invariably left his performances convinced that the shirt had been open clear to the navel.

JOSEPHINE BAKER
and Exotic Harlem

"She resembled some tall, vital, incomparably fluid nightmare which crossed its eyes and warped its limbs in a purely unearthly manner; some vision which opened new avenues of fear, which suggested nothing but itself." This was Josephine Baker as described by the poet E. E. Cummings. Baker had traveled far from the Deep South. Having set out in show business as a teenage dancer with the Dixie Steppers on the black vaudeville circuit in the 1920s, she slithered and swiveled her way to the Plantation Club above the Winter Garden Theatre on Broadway. When the French painter Fernand Léger suggested to his friend André Daven, director of the Champs-Elysées Theatre, that a Negro show would excite Paris, they had the New York cabarets scouted for talent. Baker, according to biographer Lynn Hanley in *Naked at the Feast*, "kicked out of the line of hoofers shaking and shimmying . . . adding a touch of eroticism with a series of bumps and grinds." She was brought back to Paris, where she became the rage.

Josephine Baker was without a country rather than international, too American to be Parisian and too Parisian to be American. An exotic in France, where blacks were rare and romanticized, she exhibited her body as an artwork and sang her songs with the aura of sophistication that distinguished the popular culture of Paris during the 1930s. In the world of Cole Porter and Noel Coward it was chic to be ebony, to be a Negress.

Cummings went on to say with melodramatic license, "It may seem preposterous that this terrifying nightmare should have become the most beautiful star of the Parisian stage. Yet such is the case." Subsequently, Josephine Baker returned to America for brief appearances but she was more a legend in her homeland than a popular favorite. In an era of expatriates, she had become a European.

OPPOSITE:
After years as an expatriate, Josephine Baker returned to America and performed triumphantly at a Carnegie Hall concert.

ABOVE:
Josephine Baker, staying on too late in her career, as do many stars

POPULAR MUSIC AND POP STARS

Unless you have a desire to live, to live a good deal apart from yourself, from that overbearing self-concern, you can't play.   ARTIE SHAW

Entertainers are poets of performance: they express the self through action. Like Shakespeare's fools, they not so frivolously mimic the tragedies of the times and in this way help make life bearable. They are mirrors that reflect the mood and style of an era, its human factor.

In the 1920s, music makers caught America's rhythms: the get-rich-quick fever of Wall Street, the machine-gun violence of Chicago's gangsters, the jittery exuberance of Prohibition speakeasies. Orchestra leaders became the magicians of popular music. They could wave a wand and set the world to dancing. The lyrics' sweet inanities made blue skies a nightly promise. There must have been an urgent belief that the dance could go on forever.

That was the time when it was important to know how to dance. There had always been light music for social dancing. Early in the 1800s, slave orchestras played for polite dancing and then the black musicians partied afterward, themselves dancing the cakewalk and the bamboula. In the 1860s dainty steps were set to chamber orchestrations of Stephen Foster's airs. Forty years later the elite syncopation of Scott Joplin's ragtime urged a quicker pace.

There were concert bands in the Midwest, and Dixieland jazz bands in the South. The circles and partners and whoops of country and square dances were accompanied by small fiddling ensembles, so the notion of an orchestra playing for dancers was nothing new. What was novel in the 1920s was an orchestra playing popular tunes for individual dancing, rather than patterned ensemble dancing. Americans replaced the rituals and group movements of the court or country dance with the improvising couple, and the music written for them was something all our own, something never heard before.

Modern American popular music did not exist until Jerome Kern wrote "They Didn't Believe Me" in 1914. It was a revolutionary song, coming as it did at a time when popular taste was exemplified by Harry von Tilzer's "Only a Bird in a Gilded Cage." A generation of songwriters was launched: George Gershwin, Cole Porter, Vincent Youmans, Richard Rodgers. Why, Irving Berlin was already writing about dancing:

> *Ev'rybody step*
> *To the syncopated rhythm*
> *Let's be goin' with 'em,*
> *When they begin*
> *You'll be sayin', "Yes sir, the band is grand.*
> *He's the best professor in all the land."*

The quickening pace of life was echoed in the fast dances of the 1920s:

OPPOSITE:
Michael Jackson's 1984 "Victory" concert tour commanded the highest performance fees ever charged: a million-dollar guarantee for every show. Vast auditoriums were booked to accommodate the crowds of ticket-buyers who made such fees thinkable. The production effects of "Victory" proved unimpressive to audiences accustomed to the fancier video tricks of musical television, but Jackson's instincts as a singer-dancer-showman were tested as he worked live to this television-bred audience and he withstood the formidable competition of his own video image. This child-singer had grown into a spectacular performer.

ABOVE:
John Lennon

the Charleston, the Peabody, the Black Bottom, the Castle Walk, the Negro struts, the tango. With the more sophisticated 1930s, a new step was invented to suit, and it was cheerfully called the "fox-trot." The times were depressed and gloom was masked by bravado. Weren't Fred Astaire and Ginger Rogers swooping and gliding in a lucite Venice? Wasn't Cole Porter's "Anything Goes" proof enough of American confidence? High-toned numbers swept out of Broadway's musical comedies, and the society orchestras played them for the Astaires from New Rochelle and the Rogerses who worked in Woolworth's—lightfooted couples who were even better escape artists than Harry Houdini. Depression could be danced away.

The sentimental syncopation of the fox-trot was the ritual rhythm of the bandstand Pied Pipers. In New York City, a fantastical palace arose in Central Park, built just for dancing. It was called the Casino in the Park. Located near the Seventy-second Street transverse, it featured the first true society orchestra, Leo Reisman's. Under his baton, those who would banish depression trotted, glided, and dipped to "You Do Something to Me" and "Life Is Just a Bowl of Cherries"—and they danced with an elegance and a freedom from care that would ever after set the standard for gaiety.

When Reisman's pianist succeeded him as head of the orchestra, the dance band became a star vehicle. The pianist was Eddie Duchin, and on Saturday nights in 1931 his performances were broadcast over the radio, making the debonair musician a favorite, for these broadcasts from dance floors—"remotes," they were called—became immensely popular. Radio transmitted not only the music but the shuffling of the dancers' feet, the buzz of conversations, the party atmosphere. Life itself seemed to be gliding along only because the handsome pianist-bandleader waved it onward from his keyboard, enticing fantasizers through radio's grille cloth with jaunty and irresistible rhythm.

> *I know that you know*
> *That I go where you go . . .*

Some of the bandleaders had higher aspirations than others. Jimmy Lunceford, Duke Ellington, and Fletcher Henderson took their jazz seriously. White orchestras adopted and modified this new "swing" for dancing. Paul Whiteman attempted to elevate the vaguely disreputable reputation of all jazz by commissioning concert pieces from George Gershwin and Richard Rodgers. Whiteman also featured a tight-harmony singing group, The Rhythm Boys, whose soloist was the young Bing Crosby, but star singers still lay in the future. In 1933 Benny Goodman organized the first swing band, and as it achieved national success, along came Tommy Dorsey, Artie Shaw, and Glenn Miller. A modern age of skyscrapers, industry, and autos was reflected in this streamlined white jazz played by "big bands," as they came to be called, and radio spread the news.

In 1936, Goodman played the Paramount Theatre in Times Square and drew his young audience out of their seats—out of the protective, passive, secure anonymity of spectatorship. They were up on their feet, in the aisles, dancing the jitterbug to Goodman's syncopating clarinet. By 1938 it must have seemed as if *everyone* was dancing to these orchestras' honey saxophones and toodling clarinets, their blasting trumpets and thumping bass fiddles. "Big band swing," the white, commercialized, danceable form of jazz, was what the country was stepping to, and although this was to be America's music for only a decade it would capture

OPPOSITE, ABOVE:
"Is everybody happy?" was Ted Lewis's tag line. A clarinetist and bandleader, he took the outcast-clown routine originated by Bert Williams. It enabled him to quit the music business and succeed as a vaudevillian. His comedy could be a bit strange.

OPPOSITE, BELOW:
Frank Sinatra sings with the Harry James band at the Roseland ballroom in 1939. Radio broadcasts of hotel engagements brought a sense of party into the home and helped establish popular music as entertainment.

and reflect a national sensibility—the mood, the tastes, the style and attitude of the country—as perfectly as any popular music ever would.

On the surface at least, the national outlook was homogeneous. As the 1940s began, America was a world complete in itself. Minority groups were unthreateningly in the minority, and, presumably, everybody was eager to be assimilated into the white, Protestant paradise. The big bands reflected the prevailing unity and harmony in tightly orchestrated arrangements that swung, but not too indecorously. These arrangements were muscular, straightforward, and, if it can be said of music, unneurotic. It is still possible to hear in them an American camaraderie, a national sense of moral certainty, and, as the war years approached, an open-hearted and quite wonderful patriotism.

> Don't sit under the apple tree
> With anyone else but me
> Till I come marching home.

Big bands and their singers and the popular music of the era marched us off to war dancing the boogie-woogie, the jitterbug, and the lindy hop. Because of this association with the arm-in-arm of war effort, there will probably always be something touching and valentine about our memories of Benny Goodman, Artie Shaw, and Glenn Miller; about the bobby-soxers of Frank Sinatra; about the crooning of Bing Crosby and the finger-snapping of the Andrews Sisters.

It was the bands that provided the basic *live* entertainment of the 1940s. Vaudeville had disappeared and nightclubs were subdued in the war years. Comedians performed on the radio or in the movies. Most star singers preferred radio, records, and, when they could get it, movie work to personal appearances. There was more money and prestige in performing for the mass media, and so except for armed-services tours, the stars seldom sang before the public.

By forfeit, then, the live entertainers of the 1940s were the big dance bands. They played not only for dancing in hotels but also as acts in the five-a-day movie presentation houses. From the classic brass of the Dorsey, Miller, and James organizations, and the reedy swing of Goodman and Shaw, to the bounce of Sammy Kaye, Guy Lombardo, and Freddy Martin, the greater and lesser bands appeared *live and in person* at the Roxy, the Capitol, the Strand, the State, and the Paramount theaters along Broadway, and in similar movie-vaudeville theaters across the country.

But with an occasional exception like Cab Calloway, the bandleaders were musicians, not entertainers. They had scant experience as showmen and little inclination to acquire any. What they did provide was music personalized so that the audience could identify the numbers with the faces. For instance, "Sleepy Lagoon" and "Ciribiribin" conjured up the handsome Harry James, while "Opus One" and "The Sunny Side of the Street" evoked the fatherly and academic look of Tommy Dorsey. Despite Dorsey's genial appearance, "The Sentimental Gentleman of Swing" had a nasty temper and tongue. Benny Goodman, another apparently amiable fellow, was known among musicians as "The Ray," a comic-book epithet inspired by the fiercely disapproving glare that Goodman directed at his band whenever his back was to the audience. (Symphony orchestra conductors, too, tend to the tyrannical. There must be something about leading a band that fosters tyranny.) These dance bandleaders did little onstage other than play their instruments and make perfunctory gestures conducting, but in popular entertainment audiences have a tremendous need to focus enthusiasm on an individual, and the bandleaders satisfied their need.

OPPOSITE, ABOVE:
Harry James playing for servicemen in 1943

OPPOSITE, BELOW:
Sooner or later, every Benny Goodman set would feature the band's great drummer, Gene Krupa. Positioned upstage center, at the apex of the band pyramid, his gear spread around him like a feast of snares and cymbals, Krupa would be spotlit so that his shadow was thrown, high and awesome, against the rear wall of the hall. Then he would pound away, a theatrical phenomenon.

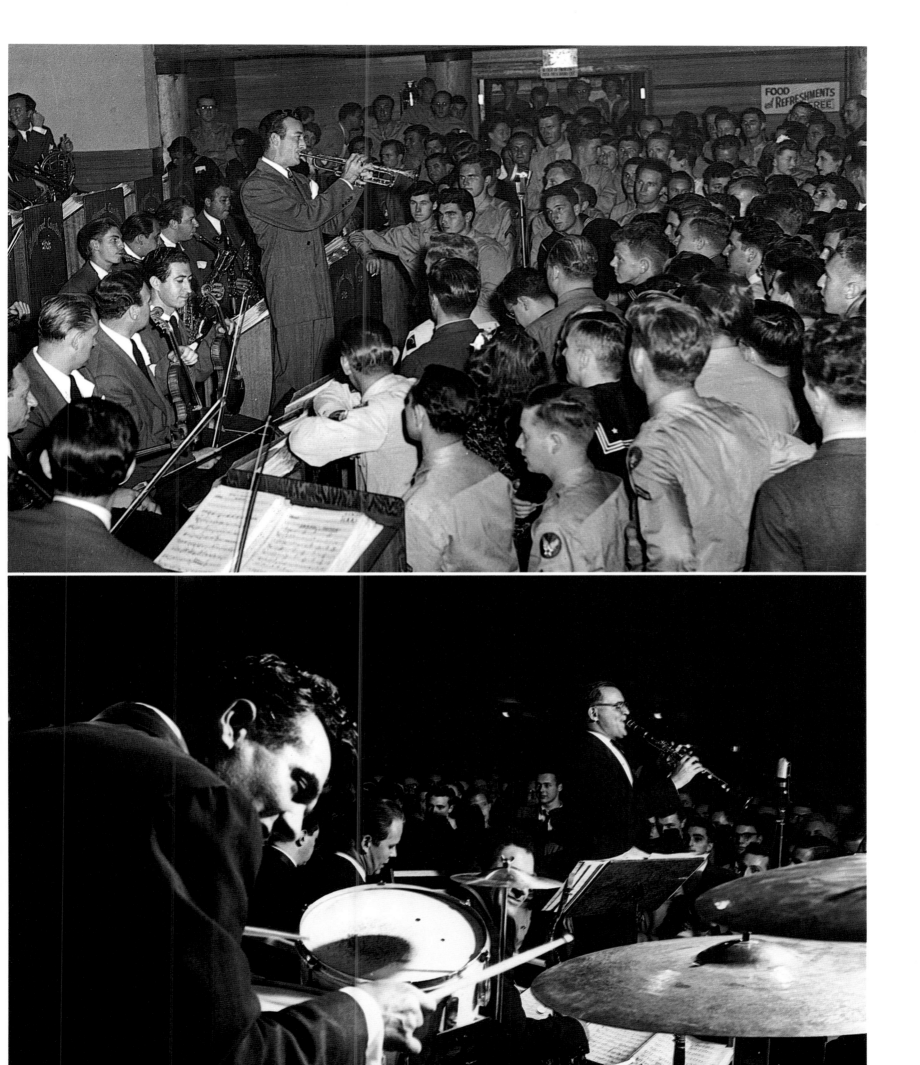

The band music could be heard on radio and records, but, just as with classical music, the listening experience was different when live. The physical proximity of the musicians, the ambience, and the social aspect of being part of an audience made attending a big-band performance an experience entirely different from hearing these songs on the radio or a record.

In order to make the event more of a show, dance bands developed companies of performers—boy and girl singers, a clowning musician (usually one whose instrument seemed funny and left his mouth free, like the drums or a ukelele), or small vocal groups, such as Glenn Miller's Modernaires or Tommy Dorsey's Pied Pipers. All of this made American popular music a genuine branch of show business, a branch that in the rock era would reach mammoth audiences.

In Person:
The Great Entertainers

190

ABOVE:
The handsome and charismatic pianist
Eddie Duchin at Atlantic City's Steel
Pier in 1935. He turned leading a
band into a personal act.

BELOW:
The key to the Andrews Sisters' success
was singing as if they themselves were
a dance band.

During World War II, taste in popular music shifted from dance bands to singers. The psychology of this seems obvious. There were almost no boys left for the girls to dance with and there was a lot that needed to be expressed: "They're Either Too Young or Too Old," "Saturday Night Is the Loneliest Night in the Week," "I'll Be Home for Christmas."

There had, of course, been popular singers before the war: Al Jolson and Harry Richman, who played the legitimate theaters; Gene Austin, Nick Lucas, and Arthur Tracy ("The Street Singer"), who performed in vaudeville; and the various radio singers—Rudy Vallee, Russ Columbo, Bing Crosby, and Kate Smith. After the war, with the emergence of popular records as a mass medium of entertainment, solo singers began to dominate the popular music of America: Perry Como, Dick Haymes, Dinah Shore, Tony Martin, Nat Cole, Vic Damone, Peggy Lee, Jo Stafford, Doris Day, Margaret Whiting, and Gordon MacRae. Why, even the Andrews Sisters disbanded when Patti decided to go it alone.

The most individual of these singers by far, and the most representative of the era, was Frank Sinatra. Bing Crosby had symbolized the small-town, home-and-hearth, white America of the prewar years, but Sinatra, even in his travails—his fall from favor and resurrection—was emblematic of a new and young country, hard-bitten and feisty. Minority groups had come of age on the battlefields and in the army hospitals, and you no longer had to be white and Protestant and Anglo-Saxon to be American. Individuality had replaced assimilation as the ideal. Sinatra reflected the new ethos. This swinger was urban, not rural, and unashamedly Italian. He was off the streets and he represented the aggressive and confident mentality that was taking postwar America to prosperity. He also had the sweetest, most beautiful, and tender voice that had ever been (and probably ever would be) heard singing a popular song.

Like his contemporaries, Sinatra outgrew the bands, and by 1945 he was America's first pop star. Adolescent girls, honey-sweet in their innocent sweaters and bobby sox, would scream and sob and faint at his feet,

Young, impressionable band singers identified with the instrumentalists they traveled with and thought of themselves as musicians, too. Musicality influenced the singing styles of Frank Sinatra, Doris Day, Dick Haymes, and, shown here with Benny Goodman, Peggy Lee. Her launching hit with the band was "Why Don't You Do Right?"

OPPOSITE, MIDDLE ROW,
LEFT TO RIGHT:
*Dick Haymes was Frank Sinatra's
successor in the Tommy Dorsey band.
When Sinatra quit to go it on his own,
popular music had become so big that
replacing him was a major event, a
ritual of succession in which Sinatra
himself participated (his introduction
of Haymes can be heard on record).
Haymes had a wonderful voice but
lacked the charisma that made Sinatra
a star.*

*Perry Como left the Ted Weems
Orchestra and parlayed a Crosby-
influenced singing style and a
congenial manner into a success that
seemed as effortless as the image he
presented. Perhaps no other singer
slipped with such ease into the ethereal
realms of radio and television.*

OPPOSITE, BOTTOM ROW,
LEFT TO RIGHT:
*Handsome Russ Columbo, "The Romeo
of Song," joined Bing Crosby in
introducing a modern American style
of singing in the early 1930s. Radio's
built-in amplification and close-up
home speakers invited a quieter style
than the vaudeville stage or hotel
bandstand, but Columbo's romantic
obbligato was traced by some to his
origins as a violinist with the Gus
Arnheim band. Crooning "I'm Just a
Prisoner of Love," he was Crosby's
only serious challenger. He died at
twenty-six, the victim of an accidental
gunshot wound suffered, it was said,
while he and a friend were cleaning
an antique dueling pistol. Thousands
came to the funeral. Crosby was one
of the pallbearers.*

*Nat "King" Cole was a top jazz pianist
who made a reputation singing the
soulless, rhythmless popular music of
the postwar era. His great success with
such songs as "Mona Lisa" and "Too
Young" was based on the irresistible
combination of a white singing style
and a buttery and mellow, flawlessly
pitched voice. Any black performer
during those years was faced with
either a compromise of this sort or an
obscure career in the strictly Negro
market. Cole became one of the elite
attractions at the Copacabana.*

RIGHT:
*Billie Holliday was, for many, the
ultimate jazz singer.*

OPPOSITE, TOP ROW, LEFT TO RIGHT:
*"Hold Back the Hands of Time" was
an appropriate song for Eddie Fisher,
the last crooner. Although his sweet
tenor voice brought him fame, his
chosen genre was sterile and its fans
were aging. Popular music had become
young territory, and these young were
ready to rock 'n' roll.*

*Vic Damone at the Flamingo Hotel in
1959. Never a superstar, Damone was
one of a group of solid, popular
entertainers with staying power.*

setting a model for teenage fans ever after, and initiating a crucial change
in American popular culture, of which adults had traditionally been the
arbiters and consumers. Before the war, children had either observed or
partaken of it obediently, and as a result mass entertainment remained
at a relatively mature level. There was a real sophistication in our movies,
radio programs, and popular music then. Inexpensive phonograph records arrived on the scene with a more permissive society, and the American popular-music makers became the first industry to perceive and
respond to the youth market, and later to cultivate it aggressively.
Ultimately, a plummeting age-taste quotient would deposit all of our
popular arts at the preteen level.

Postwar prosperity was making America a cozy place. The war had necessitated Spartan restraint. The country had prospered, but there had been nothing to buy. Peace revived luxury and fun, and making it nicer was the savings account that could buy it all. This condition, historians say, created a mood of self-satisfaction and conservatism; a determination to hold fast to every gain achieved. So began the Eisenhower years—the 1950s, synonymous with complacency, which the popular music of the time reflected. The songs were spineless, the singers bland. This was musical carpeting for slow dancing, until the beat and the dancing disappeared entirely.

When the dancing stops, it is usually because the music has lost drive and vitality. American popular music between 1945 and 1955 was dominated by nonsense songs ("Mairzy Doats," "Ragg Mopp"), wimpy ballads ("Too Young," "Because of You"), sentimentality ("The Old Lamplighter," "Harbor Lights"), novelties ("Chatanooga Shoeshine Boy," "The Old Master Painter"), and listless versions of Broadway tunes such as Perry Como's "A Bushel and a Peck" (*Guys and Dolls*) and Eddie Fisher's "You've Gotta Have Heart" (*The Pajama Game*).

The world of popular music was now filled with sons of Crosby, milky crooners, and curiously assertive girl singers, but none of them sang in person because the prestige, the money, and the work remained in radio, records, and, at the end of the rainbow, movies. All of show business was now in reproduced media.

The big bands had returned from the war to find themselves as obsolete as the zoot suits with the reet pleats in which they'd enlisted. Once so virile and earnest, they were now forced to play musical mush in hotels that would soon decay like the vibrant inner cities, like the simplicities of wartime life, and like the bands themselves. Although its leader had died in a wartime air crash, the Glenn Miller Orchestra was

It was not rock 'n' roll that killed traditional American popular songs. It was musical decadence. In the 1950s a burgeoning music business looked for profit not in live performance but in hit records. Creative control was transferred from composers and singers to record producers, who created not songs but "product" and who condescended to the public rather than trusting to the appeal of good songs and good singers. The final generation of old-style vocalists was caught in this maw of gimmick music: Georgia Gibbs, Frankie Laine, Guy Mitchell, Patti Page, Kay Starr, and, shown here, Johnnie Ray.

resurrected to replicate the hits of a sweeter and richer time, and so a nostalgia for the 1940s developed. Nostalgia would ultimately become a national plague, choking off life's breath from the present as the dark mockery of camp replaced sincerity and enthusiasm.

The entertainer's performance is a metaphor for daring to live, for asserting individual character, for self-expression however frightening the risk. The studio-bound singers of the 1950s were not taking such chances; they and their music reflected the passivity of the time. They did *not* express themselves or assert any individuality. They sang the songs as written, and as directed by the record producers. They were obedient, and obedience was the tenor of the times. The record was the end product. Frankie Laine, Johnnie Ray, Guy Mitchell, Patti Page, Les Paul and Mary Ford—these popular singers would be used in the recording studios as elements in packages. Even Frank Sinatra and Perry Como were pressed and labeled like the discs. More records were being sold than ever, but there was less music on them. *Popular* music—music of the people, music that people sing—had disappeared. Who ever sang "How Much Is That Doggie in the Window" or whistled "Ghost Riders in the Sky" and "Mule Train"? The record machine had replaced the musical artist.

The beatnik movement of the 1950s rushed to fill the vacuum with jazz, and in the process restored the live musician to life. In bebop, jazz had evolved into a style so esoteric that few but musicians could appreciate it. But the high folk art that jazz is for blacks seems forever doomed to dilution and commercialization by the white music business. Thus the jazz that the postwar college generation embraced was "cool" (and white) jazz, as abstract as bebop but of a more accessible nature, easy and modal. It seemed to echo the sought-after personal style of the first hippies, the beatniks.

Jazz clubs cropped up from New York to San Francisco, from Birdland to the Blackhawk—and they featured such young and popular performers as Chet Baker, Stan Getz, Gerry Mulligan, and Dave Brubeck. Small clubs in college towns offered poetry read to jazz. Plainly, performance music still had appeal, and audiences still could be reached by musician-entertainers, but this jazz was so cool it had no beat. Rhythm remained the elusive factor in popular American music and teenagers fiddled with their radio dials, restlessly seeking a pulse. They found it in race music.

"Race music" was the term privately used to describe what the record business publicly called "rhythm and blues." It was, in fact, music for the Negro market, a gospel-derived popular music written, performed, and consumed by blacks. When white youngsters discovered this rollicking, popular style, they danced with the joy of those who believe they have discovered something new under the sun. In exuberant epidemic, the music swept across the lifeless landscape of American popular music. "Rock 'n' roll," it was renamed, a black slang expression for "sex," and sex was its unmistakable message. White America was appalled. Blacks were still superstitiously feared as reefer-smoking bacchanalians, unleashers of animal instincts. Scrubbed white American teenagers were shuffling, gyrating, stomping, and bumping to such non-Crosbys as Fats Domino, Chuck Berry, and Little Richard and to groups with improbable names like the Platters and the Penguins. Soon, inevitably, there were white imitations.

In every generation, in every era, parents fear their children's loss of innocence—that is, sexuality, whose development brings the end of dependency and childhood, the end of the joy of parenting. The fads and crazes of youth symbolize and herald the onset of puberty. A sexual

ABOVE:
Although rock 'n' roll ended the classic era of American popular song, an elite of sophisticated audiences and performers remained devoted to the music of Cole Porter, Rodgers and Hart, and the like. Perhaps no performer has been so closely identified with this genre as Bobby Short, the supper-club singer-pianist par excellence, who is seen here performing in 1983 at Maxim's in Paris.

LEFT:
Lena Horne still presented herself strictly as a singer when she toured with Tony Bennett in the early 1970s. But when she realized she was an entertainer, she could carry the show alone.

OPPOSITE, ABOVE LEFT:
"Good Golly Miss Molly." Little Richard was an audacious and exuberant rocker whose big songs were "covered" (imitated and recorded) in a diluted rock-'n'-roll style by singers like Pat Boone, so as to reach a mass (that is, white) market. Frankly effeminate in his outlandish hairdos and heavy makeup, Little Richard was willing to endure ridicule rather than change his outrageous style.

OPPOSITE, ABOVE RIGHT:
In 1959 Elvis Presley, fresh from the army, came home to Tupelo, Mississippi. He would not perform live again for ten years.

In Person:
The Great Entertainers

harbinger and a sexual threat like the flapper fad, the jitterbug, and Frank Sinatra, rock 'n' roll shook the foundations of Eisenhower America while the kids took to the dance floors, and small bands began to play in local bars, and new dances called the "twist" and the "frug" and the "monkey" set those youngsters to boogying. This touchless dancing implied a physicality considerably more erotic than the prissy embraces of the fox-trot.

Bestriding this pulsating and shaking world was the most shocking image of all—truly greater than life-size—a jerking, twisting, thumping rock-'n'-roll cowboy in motorcycle leather, his hair greasy and his sideburns dangerous. Was he not a father's nightmare? The classic bad boy was Elvis Presley. He gyrated and he shook—and perhaps his lyrics were unintelligible, but his message was not. Presley's message was sex, no different in this from Sinatra's or even Rudy Vallee's; but because the message was being delivered by a punk, a greaser, a rocker, a poor white from the Deep South, the message was of course unspeakable, unthinkable, and irresistible.

The machine called the American entertainment industry has an ability seldom realized outside of horror movies: the ability to make products of people, the ability to ingest naive, vigorous, original, creative talent and spew it out as homogenized, salable pap. The supreme achievement of 1950s materialism—the neutering and polishing of Elvis Presley —began as soon as his commercial potential became apparent. He had

emerged from a musical ambience that had not yet lost its lusty vigor. In the South, from the roadhouses to the Grand Ole Opry, singers still sang on stages—before audiences—not as disembodied voices but as present performers who could set the blood to flowing. There, popular music was still a folkloric experience, a performance art—and Elvis Presley was a natural. His rich baritone voice hammer-tripped on syncopation, the counterrhythms jiggling in his shoulders and thighs. The young man put on a show. He would wind up and explode in the space of a chord progression while his hips swiveled and his knees did a hummingbird dance of their own. This display was what made him thrilling to watch, and it was the first thing he was deprived of. Much was made of Presley's television censorship, the networks' refusal to show him in action below the waist. It is not far-fetched to call this symbolic castration. With the rescue of twenty million virgins came the elimination of Presley's virility as a performer. Then he was whisked off to Hollywood to be taxidermized in celluloid. King Kong.

Of course that could not stem the tide of rock 'n' roll. According to Jerry Wexler, the musicologist and record-company executive, "Elvis Presley was the one person who changed the music. He was the apostle. In this vessel, black music came to white America." Like a Colonel Blimp at Armageddon, the entertainment establishment scoffed at the revolution in popular music. They and their audiences had an investment in the status quo. From Las Vegas to New York City, nightclub stages were denied to rock 'n' rollers, who, ironically, were the first live-performance-oriented singers in generations. The establishment was (insanely? audaciously?) trying to stem the changes of time. With the crisis-filled 1960s already on the way, the Nero-like club owners persisted in featuring the singers and comedians of a past they would not part with.

Meanwhile, youngsters were feasting on jazz, rock 'n' roll, even folk music. It was not the folk music of Pete Seeger or Woody Guthrie but a smoother, catchier, newly written kind of folk music. Guitar-strumming groups like the Limelighters, the Kingston Trio, the Tarriers, and Peter, Paul and Mary grinned and plunked about social issues. While the harmonies were sunny, the intent was to say something, *anything* but the inanities of 1950s popular songs. Theirs was exuberant folk music, and they were performers. They joked, they entertained.

Nightclubs employed *them*. They were white.

To this ferment was added something that changed the face of America: a bizarre war in Vietnam that tainted the Johnson Administration in the eyes of the country's youth, threatening the record-buying generation with the military draft. As rock 'n' roll developed into sophisticated "rock" music, a new breed of performer-songwriter sang of the new issues rather than of the romance of yore. The Haight-Ashbury section of San Francisco came to symbolize a youthful linking of idealism, mysticism, drug experimentation, and an ardent fury with the war. This was the era of flower children and hippies, an era expressed in the music of groups with image-drenched names like the Jefferson Airplane, the Quicksilver Messenger Service, the Grateful Dead, or Big Brother and the Holding Company. Rock 'n' roll had evolved into any kind of music that the creators chose to write.

Even though the Beatles assiduously avoided the political in their music, these English youths stood at the forefront of the American musical flowering. For in their experimentation and development they had opened all the musical doors.

Were the Beatles an act? Like all raw rock bands they began by playing in bars. The concerts they gave in the first flush of their fame were

ABOVE:

In the 1950s, Bill Haley and the Comets gentrified and broadened rock 'n' roll with his "Rock Around the Clock" and similar blockbusters. American popular music was being hit by its own version of the atomic bomb.

MIDDLE:

Possessed of a shining mezzo-soprano, Joan Baez was among the first of the popular folksingers to bring politics into performance.

BELOW:

Peter Yarrow (right), Paul Stuckey, and Mary Travers were among the top folksingers of the 1960s, along with Bob Dylan, Joan Baez, and Judy Collins. The trio's "folksongs" were actually new ("If I Had a Hammer," "Blowin' in the Wind"). Such songs of social protest were the door out of banal popular music, the door leading to the Woodstock era.

OVERLEAF, LEFT:

Rod Stewart at Jones Beach, New York

OVERLEAF, RIGHT:

The Rolling Stones started out as a scruffy alternative to the Beatles, but the band's lead singer, Mick Jagger, evolved into one of rock's flashiest showmen. Rock performers devoted much more effort to live performances than did their predecessors in popular music, whose media were essentially radio, records, and movies. Working live in concerts and clubs was a regular part of a rock performer's career, prompting the development of personal choreography, costumes, lighting, and showmanship. Mick Jagger's dancing style was modeled on that of the great James Brown, "King of Soul." Brown's act was based as much on dancing as on singing, and Jagger drew on that joyously funky bopping.

ABOVE:

Ray Charles was greeted by catcalls at a jazz concert given in Carnegie Hall in the 1950s. Purists considered any rhythm-and-blues singer beneath them. Less than a decade later Charles was hailed by jazz afficionados as the best of all soul singers and a jazz genius. Here he is with his band and the Raylettes at the world-famous Apollo Theatre in Harlem. It was a ghetto showplace for such entertainers as Ella Fitzgerald, Lena Horne, Billy Eckstine, and countless choreographed rhythm-and-blues groups, from Gladys Knight and the Pips to the Temptations.

BELOW:

Because of his showmanship on the podium as well as his television appearances as teacher and raconteur, conductor Leonard Bernstein transcended the hothouse of classical music and became well known to the general public. Other classical musicians, perhaps less extroverted than Bernstein, have also been world-class entertainers. Vladimir Horowitz and Van Cliburn do not merely play the piano; Isaac Stern and Itzhak Perlman do not merely fiddle; Luciano Pavarotti, Placido Domingo, and Joan Sutherland do not just sing. Their greatness, like any star's, lies in the sum of talent plus charisma and showmanship. Anyone who ever saw Maria Callas knows the difference between a singer and a star.

In Person:
The Great Entertainers

204

OPPOSITE, ABOVE LEFT:

Like Mel Torme, Bobby Darin was a musician-singer who could compose and arrange. Darin played guitar and piano. He was as comfortable singing primitive rock 'n' roll ("Splish Splash") as he was with theater music ("Mack the Knife") and jazz ("Bill Bailey, Won't You Please Come Home?"). As a solo performer he was ingratiating, clever, and magnetic. A brilliant talent, he died young.

OPPOSITE, ABOVE RIGHT:

Wayne Newton started out in show business as a chubby young man singing high and sweet on the Sunday-night Ed Sullivan television variety program. He was transformed by nightclub magic into the quintessence of Las Vegas machismo, and even though he was never a national star in concert or on records, he became box-office royalty in the casino showrooms, an attraction ranking with Frank Sinatra and Dean Martin.

OPPOSITE, BELOW LEFT:

Steve Lawrence and Eydie Gorme playing Atlantic City. Her voice was as good as any in pop music, with flawless pitch and sensitive phrasing. Lawrence's baritone was also a thing of beauty, and early on he relaxed and revealed an appealing sense of humor and a genial wit. A balance of brightness and musicality helped the two performers project a dual personality that made their act a routine of show-business and domesticity. They finessed rock 'n' roll to become a major showroom act.

OPPOSITE, BELOW RIGHT:

Sammy Davis, Jr., became a top-rank song-and-dance man long after such acts had gone out of fashion.

hysteria-driven rallies, where it was impossible to see or sense an act, if one was there. The charming personalities of Paul McCartney, John Lennon, George Harrison, and Ringo Starr emerged in their movies. The Beatles thrived in the record studio, where they spearheaded and exploited a revolution in sound techniques, capping it with "Sergeant Pepper's Lonely Hearts Club Band," the ultimate flower-era rock album. Their unpredictable songs spurred a generation of creativity. The music that resulted made for an era of rich artistic expression, and this rock music had an influence on public moods and attitudes on a scale never before approached. The era reached its climax with the Woodstock, New York, concert of August 16, 1969, when rock triumphed in all its musical, theatrical, communal, and political guises.

And so rock 'n' roll, which had begun as an illiterate drone justified by a lusty beat, became by 1970, rock—a cast of mind, a system of values, and, only incidentally, a musical medium limited merely by the imagination of the performer. Popular music was now restored to the creators who were writing it and performing it, and it was music to be heard in person and watched in performance. Rock records sold, but concerts were the main event.

The role that psychedelic drugs played in this creative explosion can easily be deduced from the band names themselves. Timothy Leary and Ken Kesey were the cult heroes of the day, proselytizing for LSD as the drug of choice, the doorway to nirvana. The rock bands buzzed and whined and spun out musical dreams reflecting the color drips and un-folding flowers of psychedelia. They wore elaborate hippie costumes and held forth in such rock emporia as the Fillmore East in New York City, or in the great dance halls of the West Coast such as Wonderland and the Fillmore in San Francisco. They performed in front of light shows that simulated hallucinations as patterns were projected on stage scrims and as stroboscopic lights were flashed across the audience. Amplification systems for the rock concerts made previous performance sound seem like the hum of transistor radios. Mammoth speakers were stacked one upon another, bellowing and radiating sound at ear-shattering levels, never too loud for the youngsters.

All of this created a theatrical experience that made the listener a participant, and roughly from 1967 until the early 1970s there was no entertainment in America that could compare to the rock experience in terms of creativity, productivity, and sheer energy. It was also frightening, as the energy expenditure and drug abuse destroyed such powerful per-formers as Janis Joplin, Jim Morrison, Jimi Hendrix, and, ultimately, Elvis Presley.

The entertainers who survived were perhaps the more conventional, certainly the luckier: Bob Dylan, Elton John, Paul Simon and Art Garfunkel, Mick Jagger, Paul McCartney. These reflections of an era's youth had matured into middle-aged professionals by the late 1970s. The smoothness of their performances could not obscure the tremen-dous energy they continued to radiate after *decades* of success. These people had learned how to perform before audiences the size of which would have addled ordinary entertainers. Or is it more difficult to per-form for half a dozen people in a living room than for seventeen thousand in Madison Square Garden?

The question may be moot. By the 1980s, American popular music had once again submerged into a passive, reproduced form. McCartney and Jagger and the other elder statesmen of rock music seemed posi-tively antiquated alongside new performers who seemed to be from outer space—performers who were working primarily on records and in the

OPPOSITE:

When they idolize performers, audiences often idealize them and credit them with qualities beyond the power to entertain. No performers have ever benefited from this tendency to the extent that the Beatles did. They were seen as summing up the best in humanity. Their music was, of course, catchy and sophisticated but it was the personalities they presented as their act that brought them an unprecedented popularity. The dynamic era of the late 1960s and early 1970s, with its powerful social and political upheavals, seemed distilled in them.

Although the Beatles started out as a club act, and performed the first of the colossal rock concerts, that 1965 Shea Stadium performance was their final live group appearance. During the rest of their reign as international stars, they performed reproduced—on records and in movies.

Paul McCartney, the matinee idol among the Beatles, wrote their sweeter and catchier songs, such as "Yesterday" and "Michele." His cheerful lyricism perfectly complemented the sardonic wit and toughness of John Lennon's songs ("Strawberry Fields Forever," "A Day in the Life"). The two wrote virtually the entire Beatles catalogue. Onstage too, it was McCartney and Lennon who set the style and tone of the group.

BELOW LEFT:
Singing with Big Brother and the Holding Company in 1968, Janis Joplin performed at a level so intense she could not sustain it. Joplin was one of a number of sensational rock stars who were self-victimized by drugs and alcohol abuse. Others were Jimi Hendrix and Jim Morrison.

OPPOSITE, ABOVE:
Romance was the essential subject of American song until the idealism of folk music merged with the drive of rock 'n' roll. Then a substantial kind of popular music evolved to reflect the serious concerns and the intensity of feeling that characterized America's cathartic Vietnam years. Among the most prominent singers of such songs was the team of Art Garfunkel and Paul Simon.

OPPOSITE, BELOW:
Flamboyance and showmanship were demanded of rock stars who performed in huge auditoriums with the competitive support of flashing light shows and gaudy simulations of drug hallucination. Elton John, one of the most musicianly of rock stars, was also among the most flamboyant and showmanly.

In Person:
The Great Entertainers

new field of musical videos. These musical television movies, with their bizarre imagery and synthesized sounds, became the prime launching pad for popular music. In many of them, the singer would not even be seen singing the song. Instead, the video movie would embellish, illustrate.

Such videos could hardly be duplicated in concert, nor could much of the electronically synthesized music, but it was the look that came to matter more than the performance or the song.

These new stars of pop music, with names like Duran Duran or Frankie Goes to Hollywood, embarked on periodic concert tours. The essential medium for their music, however, was the record or the tape cassette or the television set. The audience was listening. It was watching a screen. It was not singing. It was not dancing.

The world had turned electronic.

Popular Music
and
Pop Stars

BIG BANDS

The leaders of the big bands were father figures, at least to their audiences. Glenn Miller, Tommy Dorsey, and Benny Goodman seemed humorless in their silence. They wore eyeglasses, their era's symbol of studiousness and wisdom. That they stood apart from and above their orchestras was always clear. Conducting, they would make the merest downbeats, tucking clarinet or trombone beneath an elbow, as if it were a teacher's pointer. Yet their musicians, their boys, wore costumes (matching tuxedos) and sat behind monogrammed music stands. Was this not an act?

In *The Big Bands*, George Simon writes, "Whenever the band played, the kids would scream for "In the Mood," and Glenn [Miller] always responded with quite a show, winding up with the trumpets waving their derbies [mutes] and the trombones whisking their horns high in the sky."

Of all the big bands, the one most closely identified with God and country was Glenn Miller's, and by 1940, two years after being organized, it was the nation's favorite, instantly identified by the "Miller sound." This musical signature was created by a clarinet playing the melody line and a tenor saxophone duplicating it an octave higher. Jazz men derided this as bland and monotonous, but the public never tired of it.

Major Glenn Miller disappeared over the English Channel on December 15, 1944, while flying to Paris to play in a concert celebrating the city's liberation. His orchestra had existed but six years and yet in that time it became a musical metaphor for the entire era, representing America's wartime harmony and determination. Miller's death created an impact of myth and for many decades after, the bandleader's records sold abundantly. He had conducted for a national prom that may have been the most sentimental era in American history. With no trouble at all, his enduring records of "Tuxedo Junction" and, of course, "In the Mood" made this era into folklore.

The Glenn Miller Orchestra was the archetypal big band. In the World War II years, it had an almost historic aura.

They danced in ballroom dreamlands beyond the cities, such exotic locales as New Rochelle, New York (the Glen Island Casino), and the suburbs of Chicago (the Aragon Ballroom). City ballrooms were less romantic but livelier: the Savoy in Harlem (Chick Webb and his orchestra, with vocalist Ella Fitzgerald) and Roseland, of course, where Woody Herman played. But the real places to dance in New York were the hotels, and each had its "room." Benny Goodman's band was stationed in the Manhattan Room of the Hotel Pennsylvania; Harry James and Tommy Dorsey played alternate engagements at the prestigious Astor Roof; over at the New Yorker's Terrace Room, Jimmy Dorsey's band played for dancing, along with the boy singer Bob Eberle and the girl singer Helen O'Connell. All band vocalists were boys or girls, there were no grown-up band singers. Doris Day was the girl singer with Les Brown and the Band of Renown at the Green Room of the Hotel Edison, and waltzers convened at the Hotel Roosevelt Grill to dance to "the sweetest music this side of heaven," played by Guy Lombardo and his Royal Canadians.

When Artie Shaw was in New York, he would play for dancing at the Blue Room of the Hotel Lincoln, but smooth and respected as the Shaw band was, its leader was troubled. "I'm cursed with a serious-mindedness," he said, an intellectual who might have been speaking for all entertainers distracted by brains. "I know that you can take yourself too seriously." Shaw's problem was like Hamlet's: to master his own complexity and inhibitions in order to *act* (that word again)—to become an extrovert single-mindedly devoted to performance. This conflict was reflected in his elaborately arranged swing music, which was sophisticated jazz pulled to tension between romp and self-consciousness.

Jimmy Dorsey at the Hollywood Canteen

BING CROSBY

For a long time, Bing Crosby was America. For fifty years he was one of its most popular movie and record stars. So powerful was his image as both a crooner and a film personality that often overlooked was the purity of his baritone and the musicality of his instincts. Yet once he had left Paul Whiteman's Rhythm Boys, he ceased being a live performer except on rare occasions, such as troop entertainments. Although his career was awesome in its duration and heroic in its reputation, it was bloodless and without human connection. Spending virtually all his working years isolated from audiences—in radio, records, and films—Crosby developed a performing style so private, so small in scale, and so removed from those who watched and listened to him that he evolved as a model of detachment. This is profoundly ironic, since no figure in American entertainment so well reflected the country's times as Bing Crosby.

In 1977 he embarked on an international tour to celebrate his fiftieth anniversary as a performer and he found that, although he was a giant among greats, he barely existed for live audiences. This proved most painful on the night he opened his New York engagement, the last stop on the tour. The Uris (later to be renamed the Gershwin) was a cavernous theater. There had been a desultory advance sale for the twelve-performance booking. Crosby simply was not a New York act. The city likes tough entertainers: Frank Sinatra, Lena Horne, Peter Allen. It is not laid back. It is not mellow. It is of the streets, whether those streets are Queens Boulevard, 125th Street, or Madison Avenue. And yet even for the New Yorkers who came, there was something out of the ordinary in the evening. Bing Crosby sang "I Surrender Dear," "Don't Fence Me In," "Pennies from Heaven," "Just One More Chance," "Moonlight Becomes You," "I'll Be Seeing You." The past was rushing by, brushing the cheek. "Accentuate the Positive," "South of the Border."

> I'm gonna settle down and never more roam
> And make the San Fernando Valley my home.

The audience sang along, uninvited, under its breath, sweetly. This was memory come to life, a childhood beside the radio. "You Are My Sunshine." Old songs bring the past into painful proximity. This voice was itself the past, and it was difficult to believe that the source of the sound so familiar, the *whistling*, was without a doubt that well-remembered face on the stage.

Yet what was there was not the man; it was a replica of a movie image. Crosby had no stage substance. He had refused to come and sing for the people and the people had become accustomed to it. They accepted him on his terms, media terms, the voice disembodied and the face a photograph. That finally became his legacy. His recordings and movies were the reality. Still, it was sentimental and nostalgic, even startling, to find that he existed in the flesh.

His show was amateurish, how could it not be? He was inexperienced. It was listless, under-rehearsed, and loosely written. The opening acts were embarrassing. Mrs. Crosby performed an interpretive dance. The theater itself was only three-quarters filled, and any show-business tyro knows that on the first night of an engagement, with all the press and television coverage, the appearance of a sold-out theater must be maintained, even if drunks have to be dragged in from the Bowery and propped up in their seats. But Crosby had been too proud to spend money on advertising. All the proceeds were being contributed to charity.

Crosby croons.

He had insisted that every opening-night ticket be paid for, which had effectively kept his publicist from ensuring a full house.

From Crosby's point of view, the world had waited so long to see him that it would break down the doors at the opportunity. From the world's point of view, it no longer cared. His years of distance had taken their toll. He was a myth, yes, but in show business even myths need promotion.

Still, when he sang "White Christmas" the audience hushed and became babe-like. There was no sing-along now. This wasn't just another nostalgic song. This particular song sung by this particular singer was linked with the past of anyone who had been alive in the 1940s, the 1950s, or the 1960s. "White Christmas" didn't recall merely a moment or a period but an entire era—for some, the best time of their lives. Bing Crosby singing "White Christmas" in person was the closest anyone could get to a time machine, and the hush of the theater reflected the awe at being hurtled back to so long ago—to a way of living, a way of thinking, and a trust in America, in religion, in moral absolutes and traditional values.

May your days be merry and bright
And may all your Christmases be white.

This was really something to give an audience. Crosby had finally developed an act.

Bing Crosby, shown here with the Boswell Sisters, followed Rudy Vallee into radio, where the studio microphones and intimate home speakers made crooning possible.

BOB DYLAN

Probably no entertainer has ever had so profound an influence on the lives of his audience as Bob Dylan. His power would have been calamitous had he been a demagogue, but Dylan was a preacher of idealism. His "Blowin' in the Wind" was the very anthem of a generation that would not only make a stand against fighting in a cruel and senseless war but actually drive a president from office. The valor of his conscience inspired a youth weary of parental cynicism and self-interest. When Dylan abandoned folk music for the electric guitars of drug-oriented rock, his followers might have been mistaken for powerful blocs warring over questions of international moment. During a 1964 concert at the tennis stadium in Forest Hills, Queens, Dylan was thunderously booed when he brought on an electrified rock band and sang such uncharacteristic new songs as "Mr. Tambourine Man" and "Like a Rolling Stone." This was the music of the folkies' rock-'n'-roll enemy, the brainless teenagers.

Dylan had sensed that rock music was developing beyond boogie-dancing and doo-wop lyrics. He pioneered the development of image-drenched, free-form lyrics that some academics compared to James Joyce (and others to the random typing of pretentious simians). With Presley kept under celluloid in Hollywood, Bob Dylan, a natural showman, became the most important and dramatic performer in American popular music. Like any star, he brought the quality of legendry to his concerts. Alone before a microphone that windy night in Forest Hills, he let his tuxedo jacket blow and snap against his lean frame, its crimson Broadway lining a punch line for his sexy jeans. He faced colossal rejection, yet he sang into the teeth of the hateful gale. The crowd strained to hoot out the despised rock sounds, but Dylan persisted and in that persistence rose to a showmanly stature from which he would never descend.

Like Garbo, Bob Dylan created tension by blending the heat and intimacy of celebrity with a personal, cool remoteness. The biggest of rock stars, and one of the first, Dylan became the political and social conscience of an era, and mythic figure was the role he played.

NIGHTCLUB CITY

*Frenzy in an audience can be worked up if you work in a frenzy yourself.
Al Jolson knew that. People want you to work, to give your all. They
want sheer exhaustion.* LIBERACE

The last chapter in personal entertainment is being written on the concert circuit, the high-powered but final vaudeville wheel. At one time, acts gamely toured from one town and theater to the next. Then they moved up from roadhouses to strip joints, summer hotels, nightclubs. Today, caravans of production crews, like Egyptian slaves, bear limousine-throned superstars from stadium to arena, setting up and tearing down million-dollar technological extravaganzas. Here is the decadence of personal appearance, the ultimate stage for the live performer, and it is a tomb fit for a pharaoh. Leave it to show business —ever the flashy exit.

The last stars turn ghostly in these spotlights, the distinction blurring between the "live" of life and the "live" of videotape, for mere life size cannot deliver the thunderclap to dominate an arena or a football stadium. The audience, massed at a distance, must listen through arrays of loudspeakers and sometimes even watch on great television screens. Does anyone even know if that is the actual star who is being plucked from the darkness by the spotlight? Does it matter?

Simple multiplication suggests the immense revenues possible as abstract millions of magazine readers and television viewers materialize into tens of thousands who pay twenty or thirty dollars for a seat at a concert. No site can be too big when such profits are contemplated, and the audiences seem hardly to mind. This might be called the Woodstock Syndrome. No longer essential is the physical proximity, the magnetism that once lay at the heart of the in-person act. Frank Sinatra, it was said, seemed to make eye contact with everyone in his audience. That would hardly be possible in the Houston Astrodome. A modern solo performance for a very large audience is no longer a collective of such private communions but, rather, a social experience. The audience communicates with itself. Most are television children who have never experienced live performance and so do not miss it, and many know music only as records, radio, or tapes, heard only through speakers. In comparison, a gambling casino's four-thousand-seat showroom is intimate; it is also a penny-ante operation and hardly worth the effort of a star's appearance.

Only singers can play in sites bigger than concert halls because they need not be seen even clearly as long as they are heard. A comedian needn't be seen either, but who can be funny over a loudspeaker? That is why modern funnymen, if they wish to make a lot of money, abandon personal appearances for the movies. Steve Martin, Lily Tomlin, Richard Pryor, Robin Williams, Rodney Dangerfield, and Eddie Murphy rarely return to the audiences who first gave them recognition.

OPPOSITE:
Shirley MacLaine

ABOVE:
Carol Channing

Those who can attract the crowd play the concert and arena circuit for fees that in 1984 for top stars climbed beyond one hundred thousand dollars for a single performance (see table). Michael Jackson's 1984 "Victory" tour traveled to arenas at guarantees of one million dollars a show. Sometimes these performers seem starbursts, novas with careers of the instant. At the end of Jackson's tour, his popularity was already waning. Next year, another star will rise for the crowd in the concert hall, the sports arena, the athletic stadium.

A few among these last entertainers are relics from the age of live acts: Frank Sinatra, for example, or Liberace. There are occasional newcomers who seem eager to project the charisma of the live act even in vast show sites. Liza Minnelli, for instance, or Willie Nelson. There is presence in these performers. As for the likes of Barry Manilow, Neil Diamond, and Kenny Rogers, they are the children of simulation and electronics. They have never had the chance to develop and project humanity. They are traveling television shows.

Mammoth-scale performing has outpriced and overshadowed Las Vegas, much as that city of nightclubs earlier replaced the country's saloons, cafes, and supper clubs. Las Vegas is today's Palace, a ghost theater once legendary for having played host to the great; but just as the Palace became a travesty of itself, so has Las Vegas. Today the gambling resort is a desert Disneyland offering midway entertainment to tourists. East of the Mississippi, it is easier for a high roller to go to Atlantic City to gamble. No excursion is involved. In a cool age, the casino itself is the attraction, and entertainment but a sometime distraction. Even at that, the Atlantic City shows are something with which the Las Vegas hotels cannot compete. For they can no longer afford to pay the biggest stars, and their own heroes have been overtaken by age and mutations of style. (Oh, beloved Buddy Hackett, Sammy Davis, Jr., and Shecky Greene —replaced by Julio Iglesias, Lionel Ritchie, Barbara Mandrell!) Will the newcomers have the staying power that once was requisite for simply *becoming* a star?

The nightclub sensibility was intimate, personal, and sexy. Hot. A modern concert or arena performance is neutered by distance. The performers project a video cool and a sexual absence. This, too, is a mirror of contemporary values. Nobody can be sexy on television, because the warmth of flesh is missing, and that has shattered traditional concepts of rugged masculinity and kittenish femininity, and has invited the androgynous manner we see in such vivid performers as Michael Jackson, Bette Midler, Peter Allen, and David Bowie. Theirs are gaudy and campy acts, often comments on the bogus sincerity of the nightclub floor. The sexy performers of Las Vegas, they imply, were frauds. Why pretend that there is romance and intimacy between performers and audience? Low necklines and tight pants are ridiculous. Only outrageous glitter, therefore, is sincere because it is frankly off the level. Innocently decadent, these campy stars of our time—inside-outs of Sophie Tucker and Al Jolson —are the final performers, last of the extroverts, bigger than life.

One courageous entertainer introduced flash and made it acceptable before the word "camp" became common parlance. In 1943 this twenty-four-year-old musician finished a performance on the Normandy Roof of the Mont Royal Hotel in Montreal. He sat down in his room and plopped a pile of picture postcards on the writing desk. Scrawling the same note on each, he addressed them to nightclubs across America. He was doing the secretarial work himself so as to save an agent's fee, and the message he wrote was direct: "Have you ever heard of Liberace?" It could have been the plaint of every performer who ever yearned to be heard of.

Liberace at the Café de Paris, London, 1956. And in Las Vegas, 1979.

It was fair enough for him to ask. He had only recently shortened his billing from Wladziu Valentino Liberace, itself less than a household word. He was an intermission act, playing familiar classical themes and popular favorites between shows, one of a thousand such entertainers. His technique was respectable. Had he not made a youthful appearance with the Milwaukee Symphony? Other light pianists had similar credentials but Liberace's ambitions were greater than most, and he had imagination and originality as well as a pragmatic candor that would ultimately endear him to millions: "People say I'm prostituting myself by not sticking to the classics, but let's face it—there's more money in being commercial."

Soon after sending out the postcards, he received a telephone call from the entertainment director of the Last Frontier Hotel in Las Vegas, and within weeks was stepping off a train into a rural desert town with two rustic hotels on its outskirts, the El Rancho Vegas, built in 1941, and a few hundred feet of scrub away, Howard Hughes's brand-new Last Frontier. Liberace recalls these as little more than motels, yet the area would ultimately become the fabulous "Strip" of pastel-concrete hotels. In 1943, however, the only hint of that future lay in the entertainment offered, for improbably appearing in this remote outpost were Joe E. Lewis at El Rancho (show people abbreviate everything, as if having no time for mundane details) and, just closing at the Last Frontier, Sophie Tucker.

Liberace negotiated himself a $750-a-week contract and felt smug about it. He'd been paid but $350 in Montreal. On opening night the entertainment director felt obliged to confess that as Sophie Tucker had been paid $4,000 a week she would be embarrassed to offer less than $1,500. That would not be the last time anyone offered to double Liberace's salary. When the Flamingo Hotel opened in 1946, its managing director would try to lure him away. The owners, Al Capone and Meyer Lansky, were not folks to trifle with, but Liberace was spared the decision when the dealmaker Bugsy Siegel was shot to death for a New Year's present.

Definitely, then, the Las Vegas atmosphere was heady and the young pianist thrived on it. He was too restless to sit still on a piano bench. The strange circumstances of his birth seemingly prophesied that, for he had been born weighing an enormous thirteen pounds, while beside him, emaciated and dead, was a twin brother. "You see," his sister Angelina later mused, "my brother had taken all the vitality."

Vitality indeed. High spirits would be the key to his career. Inspired by a scene in a current movie biography of Chopin, he bought a second-hand candelabra and put it on his piano during an engagement at the Persian Room at the Plaza Hotel in New York. Finally, he moved up from intermission act to the show itself, where playing the piano became the least of it. He could as easily have been showing slides of table settings. The act was really the character he played, and it was daring: a sweet, virtually prissy matinee idol playing light favorites to the women in his audience. But it worked.

He made Las Vegas his headquarters. Its show-business aura was home to him. Like so many performers, the person he enjoyed being was too extroverted and in need of approval to operate at full throttle in ordinary society. Only on a stage was Liberace the self he needed to be. "Offstage," he once said, as if speaking for all performers, "I'm not too sure of myself but onstage I'm in command."

Yet it was television that was to launch him on a national stage. "The Liberace Show" began as a local Las Vegas program in 1951. The next year it was syndicated nationally, and then in 1952 something happened

OPPOSITE, ABOVE:
Caesar's Palace, Las Vegas

OPPOSITE, BELOW:
Casino showgirls

that changed the course of the pianist's career: he was signed to play the Hollywood Bowl, which was of course a most prestigious engagement for a cabaret performer. Because of his television exposure, the crowd he attracted was immense, some twenty thousand people. Preparing for the concert, Liberace confronted the problem of a mammoth audience and the distance that would separate him from it. How was he to be distinguished from an orchestra also dressed in black tie and tails? The solution was to decide his future. He would wear a *white suit of tails*.

All kinds of wonderful things began to happen and all kinds of semi-funny things were said about it. I was called "the new Cab Calloway . . . the hidey-ho man of the Hollywood Bowl." . . . The white suit didn't go unnoticed. And what's more, I noticed that it didn't. I saw the showmanship there is in daring to do something different, in challenging the conventional. I realized that just with the white suit I had lightning in a bottle. (Liberace, *Liberace*)

This remark clarifies the nature of stardom: it is not so much the product of superior talent as of a headlong drive to be different. *To be noticed.* No wonder reviews are called "notices."

By 1953 Liberace was a national craze, television's first, and sensing the importance of his discovery, he exploited its possibilities. He affected Edwardian clothes, with ruffles blossoming from cuffs and collar. Framed by candelabra and costumes, he smiled into the cameras and played to the housewives and grandmothers, bringing a kind and sentimental son-prince into their empty afternoons. Hardly handsome, he nevertheless was romantic, an unthreatening admirer dressed for daydreams.

Matrons were not his only audience, however. From the Cherry Sisters to Don Rickles and Howard Cosell, the performers people love to hate have been good box office. Nobody ever put this proposition to quite the test that Liberace did. His effeminate manner drove insecure males to frenzies of scorn. Unflappable, Liberace offered his classic rejoinder, "I cry all the way to the bank." The geniality of his cynicism won him widespread admiration, even from men. For not only did this fellow have the courage and the integrity to be what he was, he was also no fool.

The act now became a thing to be tinkered with, edited, honed, and polished. When in 1954 Liberace left the rebuilt and rechristened New Frontier for the Riviera Hotel, setting a Las Vegas salary record at $50,000 a week, his contract stipulated that he wear clothes topping anything he'd worn before. "From then on," he recalled,

it was Nellie bar the door . . . I was caught in a gimmick. I was a curiosity who had to come up with $50,000 of sensation a week. . . . Over the years I've used fur coats and fur trim, jewels of all kinds and diamond buttons that spell out my name. I've dressed as a hillbilly, a clown, a court jester. I've appeared in the styles of famous composers, worn hats, plumes and wigs of various eras. I even have a jacket that lights up and twinkles when the house is blacked out.

This was only an extension of national taste, for it was an era of tail fins and triple-tone superchrome cars, split-level ranch houses, and Cinemascope movies. When the Las Vegas hotels began to replace their nightclubs with theater-like "show rooms," Liberace made his entrance in a Rolls-Royce. A smaller car rolled out just to pick up his fur coat. Some years later, he appeared in star-spangled red, white, and blue shorts, twirling a baton. He might make an exit hoisted through the air on a wire, a sequined cape flaring and sparkling in the spotlight. His high spirits were indomitable, and when he billed himself as "Mr.

Showmanship," the title seemed deserved. He still played the piano, but it was really just an excuse for his costumes and patter. He would play a Gershwin medley, or selections from *My Fair Lady*, or a popular theme from a concerto. Winking at his audience, he would launch into boogie-woogie. Such humor was broad by sophisticated standards, but Liberace was not playing to sophisticates and knew that big careers are not built on small bases. Moreover, by this time his act had developed a life of its own.

He would lean toward those in the front rows and show off his diamond-studded, piano-shaped rings. "Heck," he would say, "why shouldn't you look at them? After all, you bought them." And he would chuckle, more amused than anyone by his frankness. As for his clothes, he would cheerfully concede, "I didn't come here to go unnoticed." Toward the end of a show, he'd admit, "I've had so much fun myself that honestly, I'm ashamed to take the money." After a pause worthy of Jack Benny or Harold Pinter, he would smile and shrug, "But I will." He used such lines for decades and yet his delivery always made them sound fresh. To most audiences, personal acts seem ad-libbed. Of course they are not. Acts are written, memorized, rehearsed, and practiced. The impromptu effect is dependent upon the writing, the direction, and most of all, naturally, the performance. If the routine sounds tired, practiced, or contrived, it will not work. Liberace's act grew smoother through the years, and four decades later it was a thing of beauty as he performed it for audiences of six thousand at New York's Radio City Music Hall during a week-long engagement in 1984. He played as personally to those in the faraway reaches of the upper balconies of that huge auditorium as he did to the people up front, and when he eased into "Let Me Call You Sweetheart" on the big concert grand, the audience sang along softly, without being asked. So, he had done what every super-showman does—brought the walls closer. Although he had once vowed that he would never play New York (perhaps in response to newspaper abuse, as we shall see), his warmth and star power took this audience as any. He put them in his pocket.

Then he was on his feet, attempting a few throw-away dance steps and panting, "I'm not good but I've got guts," and the audience adored the self-deprecation. Like any very great star he had about him the wrap of legend, and merely *seeing* him was the show; he could do as he chose.

It had not always been so. When he went to England in 1956, the *London Daily Mirror*'s pseudonymous columnist "Cassandra" called him a "deadly, sniggering, snuggling, giggling, fruit-flavored, mincing, ices-covered heap of mother love." Liberace sued for libel, perhaps feeling that as the highest paid act in the world he could afford justice. When the case came to trial three years later, he won a $22,500 judgment, but the price he paid was steep.

I'm No Homo Says Suing Liberace. (*New York Daily News*, June 9, 1959)

Twenty-five years would pass before performers could be flamboyant and campy without fear of insult. Liberace never made any declarations on the subject of homosexuality ("What am I supposed to do? Come out on the 'Johnny Carson Show'?"), but he grinned through much abuse to broaden general attitudes. As it's said, he paid the dues and took the heat so that others would not suffer as he had, and he did it with ability, pride, character, integrity, and good humor. "This is one of my sport coats," he would confide to an audience, the rhinestones positively blinding, "and don't ask me what sport."

Had it not been for this man of grace, who dared to be himself in an era of frightened conformity, Bette Midler would not have been able to go so easily from steam-bath performances to stardom, and Peter Allen could not have preened and wriggled and shaken his way to stardom with such delightful exuberance. "I'm just *this* far from a drag act," Liberace could finally say in 1982.

His forty years in show business had spanned a multitude of other changes as well, not the least of which was the rise and fall of Las Vegas as the self-proclaimed Number One Show Business Capital of the World. The neon oasis had come far from the scruffy desert town he'd found in 1943. Eleven years later, his switch to the Riviera Hotel made headline news in entertainment circles, for in that short time Las Vegas had become the main event. How long Frank Sinatra's contract ran, what was Dean Martin's salary, which performer played where—these were crucial matters in the place where the heart of America's nightclub life had been relocated, underworld aura and all.

Ever since Prohibition, cabaret performers had been linked with gangsters, for bootleggers had run the speakeasies. Repeal did not separate the underworld from show business. It was too profitable and too

All stars have a common denominator. It is the showmanly impulse, evident in this highly unlikely but irresistible team effort: the glamorous Dietrich and the earthy Louis Armstrong, seen at the Riviera Hotel in Las Vegas, 1962.

ABOVE:
After Gracie Allen's death, George Burns tried many partners. Here, in 1960, he dances with nineteen-year-old Ann-Margret at the Sahara Hotel in Las Vegas. He also teamed up with Carol Channing for a time. It was some years before he considered the possibility that he might actually be able to work alone.

RIGHT:
George Burns's amusement at Jack Benny in drag seems unfeigned—no surprise, since it is hard to even look at this picture without smiling. Benny had a priceless sense of absurdity and the wisdom to direct it at himself. Such clowning must be rewarded in heaven.

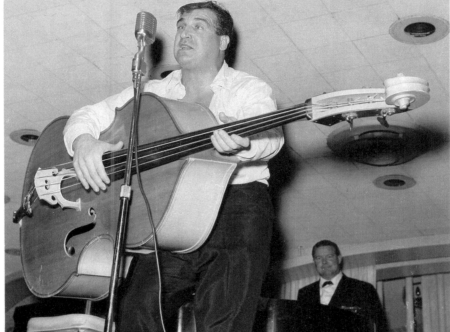

Tony Bennett was a musicianly singer, celebrated for his ballads but inclined to swing and always looking for songs with jazz qualities. There have been few popular singers to equal him.

A certain warping of perspective was required to bill a boys' club of entertainers as "The Summit at the Sands Hotel," but so enamored was the public of Frank Sinatra in 1960 that his pals' antics were major news. From left to right, Peter Lawford, Sinatra, Dean Martin, Sammy Davis, Jr., and Joey Bishop. They made a movie by day and entertained by night. Out of sight at ringside was young Senator John F. Kennedy.

Shecky Greene was one of the favorite comics in Las Vegas. He first played the lounges, later the main stages, but was never as popular elsewhere in the country.

Jan Murray, very professional and funny at the Riviera Hotel, Las Vegas, in 1967. Of all the stand-ups, he was the best-looking, the suavest, the most carefully modulated in his speech. Altogether a class act.

exciting. Now Las Vegas married nightclubs and gambling, one of organized crime's prime interests. In a sense, Fidel Castro had performed the ceremony. The baseball-playing, cigar-smoking revolutionary in military fatigues may have been a savior to the Cuban downtrodden and a threat to conservatives everywhere, but as far as show business was concerned, he was the man who made Las Vegas. When Castro shut down Havana as a playground for America's sharpies, the eyes of gamblers, swingers, and general fast-flyers turned to Las Vegas. From the mid-1950s through the 1960s, Vegas would be America's Sin City, show-business capital, and neon boom town. A flock of architectural spectaculars rose to form the glittering Strip. The Riviera set an altitude record at ten stories. It had gaudy neighbors in the Desert Inn, the Dunes, the Flamingo, the Stardust, the Thunderbird, the Tropicana, the Sands, and the Sahara hotels. America's biggest stars were on constant parade on their nightclub floors. Noel Coward, no less, played the Desert Inn, and so did Danny Kaye, Jane Powell, Gordon MacRae, and Eddie Fisher. At the Riviera, in addition to Liberace, the stable included Harry Belafonte, Tony Martin and Cyd Charisse, Juliet Prowse, and Louis Armstrong. The Flamingo had Mitzi Gaynor, Jack Carter, Pearl Bailey, Bobby Darin, Myron Cohen, and Ray Bolger. The Sands cornered the Copacabana alumni (its nightclub was called The Copa Room), and appearing there were Frank Sinatra, Dean Martin, Sammy Davis, Jr., Danny Thomas, and Lena Horne—but not Joe E. Lewis. The Flamingo had the dean of the saloons as well as Jack Benny, Judy Garland, Dinah Shore, and the Ritz Brothers.

Carol Channing's exuberant clowning was deftly transplanted from Broadway musical comedy to casino showrooms.

Even the lounges were star-studded. In these informal showrooms, where lesser acts played continuously and free of charge to come-and-go audiences, were the likes of Billy Daniels, Phyllis Diller, Vic Damone, Shecky Greene, Louis Prima, Harry James, Eartha Kitt, Sarah Vaughan, Della Reese, Don Rickles, Ella Fitzgerald, and Buddy Greco. Yet, though every well-known act in the country came at one time or another to Las Vegas in the 1960s, Liberace chose an unknown to open the show for him at the Riviera in 1962. It was a heady and daring thing to do.

His choice was a young New York singer and actress, Barbra Streisand, whom he had first heard in Manhattan's intimate Bon Soir cafe in 1959. She was eighteen years old at the time and earning $108 every week she was held over. A nearby bar in Greenwich Village had awarded her a one-week engagement there as a talent-contest prize, and that had paved the way to Las Vegas and her first professional booking. It would be extended for eleven weeks, beginning one of the fastest and most spectacular rises enjoyed by an American performer.

Barbra Streisand was a wise-cracking youngster off the Brooklyn streets, and her vulnerable confidence was engaging. "I'm a great singer. I always knew I could sing . . . I was given a sort of good voice," she said. "I suppose I'm going to be famous." A "sort of good voice," indeed. However sidewalk her speech, Streisand's singing voice was rich, accurate, powerful, and wide-ranging, and her use of it spanned the fast and slow, the loud and quiet. In 1961 she won a featured part in a Broadway musical and caught the critics' eyes, yet she insisted on moonlighting at

Barbra Streisand

New York's intimate supper clubs. "I never saw a nightclub until I performed in one," she told the *New Yorker*. "I'm doing this because I can sing the way I want to sing there. I can't do that in the show."

The next year she was working on a bigger and fancier nightclub circuit: Detroit's Caucus, Mr. Kelly's in Chicago, Basin Street East in New York, the Hungry i in San Francisco, and, in Los Angeles, the Coconut Grove, before going on to Las Vegas with Liberace. She seemed to relish the special nature of club work. "A great actress rides on emotion," she told a reporter. "She makes people feel the emotion behind the lines; a great singer does the same. You have to act to be a good singer. There's no trick in getting up in front of an audience and closing your eyes and singing. That's easy. But to get up there and keep your eyes open and look at your audience and make them feel what you want them to—that's hard."

Using a high stool as her only prop, she relied on dramatic numbers that could set off her soaring voice: "Where Am I Going," "Cry Me a River." She enjoyed resetting period songs like "Come to Me, My Melancholy Baby," or "If You Were the Only Girl in the World," and she had a taste for slowing down lively songs like "Happy Days Are Here Again."

Liberace went to Los Angeles for her opening at the Coconut Grove, loyal as well as professionally curious, and remembered with amusement:

She walked out onto the floor. She looked at the crowded tables in front of her. Then she looked to her right and saw still more tables full of people. To her left she saw another mass of tables and people. She took a deep breath and said, "If I'd known there were going to be people sitting on both sides of me as well as in front of me, I'd have had my nose fixed." (Liberace, *Liberace*)

By the time they opened at the Riviera, "her performance," he said, "was brilliant, electrifying." Ordinarily the entertainers in town had little opportunity to see each other perform since all show times were the same. To accommodate them, Liberace scheduled an occasional third show, late-late, "and the show people took her to their hearts."

Streisand was destined to abandon personal appearances quickly, perhaps successful too young to have developed loyalties to live performance. After her huge success at twenty-one in the Broadway show *Funny Girl*, she turned down offers to appear in gargantuan Shea Stadium and Houston's Astrodome. "As an artist," her manager said, "it wouldn't be right for her. All she'd make is money." But within the year Streisand was making money at Chicago's mammoth Soldiers' Field as well as at the 17,000-seat Festival Field in Newport, Rhode Island, and similarly cozy sites in Philadelphia and Atlanta.

Her concert performance had come far from the simple stool in a supper club. Now there was a thirty-five-piece orchestra onstage behind a scrim that was backlighted during the overture. She wore an orange and brown chiffon gown, with one shoe and one earring in each color, reflecting her early taste for offbeat, thrift-shop clothes. A short runway gave her the chance to stride into the audience, and for the second act she switched to a black, sequined evening gown and glossier songs ("I Wish You Love," "What Now, My Love?" "Autumn Leaves").

Already ranked with Frank Sinatra as not only the most popular but the best singer in America, Streisand was making a stupendous success with standard popular songs at a time when rock music was at its creative peak, and yet her drawing power was immense with all age groups. When she played the Forest Hills Tennis Stadium in 1965, the seven-dollar tickets were scalped at twenty-five dollars. Tickets to the Beatles'

OPPOSITE, ABOVE:
When Dean Martin and Jerry Lewis broke up their act in 1957, it was front-page news. The team's differences, it was reported, were not personal —rather, Martin was eager to relax and enjoy his success while Lewis was, in subsequent parlance, a "workaholic." It was taken for granted that Lewis had carried the team with his madcap antics and that Martin, at best a good straight man and a fair singer, would fade quickly from stardom. Instead, Martin went on to still greater triumphs on records, in movies, and on television. His most dazzling success, however, was as a live act for the gambling audiences of Las Vegas, where he was considered a box-office attraction comparable to Frank Sinatra alone. Martin's voice was a lush, husky baritone that had gone unnoticed only because he didn't seem to take it any more seriously than anything else. But it was his dry and often eccentric sense of humor that established his popularity. Like Joe E. Lewis, he presented himself as an overage adolescent interested only in booze and broads. This stage persona carried him through decades of popularity.

OPPOSITE, BELOW:
Tina Turner's energy is electric.

performance at Shea Stadium that same summer fetched only fifteen dollars. Making this either amazing or explainable were her looks. Traditionally, singers are supposed to be good-looking, but as Norton Mockeridge wrote in the *New York World Telegram and Sun*:

Barbra Streisand is just about the darnedest looking female I ever saw. . . . She's ungainly, she has scrawny legs, angular arms, a flat facade and a face that sometimes looks as though it came right out of *Mad* magazine. Her eyes perpetually seem to be peering at each other, her nose proportionally shames Jimmy Durante's, her gaping mouth slurs and twists and contorts when she sings, and her hair is a squirrel's nest.

There was something about Barbra Streisand's plainness that made her unique, even brave. Perhaps the combination of homeliness and magnificent talent gave hope to ugly ducklings everywhere. She was an individual, and in 1969 she won a truly impressive accolade, the Friars Club Entertainer of the Year Award.

Regular attempts have been made by the award industry to create prizes for variety performers, prizes that would rank with the Oscars, and Tonys, and Emmys, and Grammies; prizes as excuses for network television shows. One such effort resulted in the Las Vegas Entertainment Award, which fizzled after five annual presentations. Another, untelevised but more enduring, is the Friars Club award. This historic fraternity of variety entertainers has managed to retain the prestige of its annual accolade, doubtless because the flashiest of entertainers continue to be loyal Friars and because the award dinner has become famous for its "roasting" of honorees. Some twelve hundred guests bought their way into the Waldorf-Astoria's Grand Ballroom in May 1969 to watch Barbra Streisand become the second woman to win the Friars' appreciation (the first had been Sophie Tucker; in 1973 Carol Burnett would be the third). Danny Thomas was the master of ceremonies and Don Rickles said, "Barbra, I want to say this publicly and from my heart: I never liked you." In short, the fraternity gave her the same treatment it did the male stars.

Streisand's last live performing to date was done at the opening engagement of the International Hotel in Las Vegas, in June 1969. A third generation of hotels had, with Caesar's Palace, made the desert resort a skyscraper island. The International, with fifteen hundred rooms in its thirty stories, was then the world's largest resort hotel, and it was spectacular. Like Caesar's (as, of course, Caesar's Palace was known), it replaced the conventional nightclub with a 4,000-seat showroom, naturally called the Show Room Internationale. It was actually a theater, complete with balcony. The audience, like drip-dry Vikings, sat on either side of long, narrow tables. A wide stage replaced the traditional nightclub floor (from which floor shows had originally taken their name). Indeed, there was no dancing, nor was food served. There were no chorus girls either, nor any of the other conventional trappings of nightclubs. The nightclub, in short, was dead. Live entertainment was becoming bigger and grander, relying on large orchestras, awesome sound systems, and elaborate production. The intention, obviously, was to play for bigger audiences.

Not only was Streisand engaged to inaugurate this spectacular new hotel, she was signed up for a then-astounding five-year contract at one million dollars a year for four weeks of performance each year. On the first night of the hotel's first show, she sang for an hour. Her independent concerts had offered two acts, forty-five minutes each, but no hotel-casino will have its gamblers kept out of action for that long.

Raquel Welch had been written off as a vacuous Hollywood sex symbol who would not survive a few exploitation movies. Instead, she developed a spectacular command of showroom musical stages.

Wearing "clouds of fuchsia chiffon" (according to a *New York Times* report), Streisand opened her act mocking the extravagance around her by singing, "I've Got Plenty of Nothin' and Nothin's Plenty for Me." As prop snowflakes fluttered down for a rendition of "Jingle Bells," she joked about the unfinished hotel: "That's not snow, it's plaster." But the brash humor that had been so disarming a few years earlier now seemed snide. One of the more unfortunate side effects of stardom is egotism. We accept that, but allowing it to show during performance is unacceptable. Performing, however, plainly did not hold the charms for Streisand that once it had, and so perhaps she had no reason for good behavior. She'd once said, "The exciting thing about being a performer, the really creative thing, is going onstage or stepping in front of a microphone in a nightclub and creating something special just for the people who are there. You may be great or you may be lousy that night but that's the exciting thing about creating it all over again each time. The emotional quality is the thing I'm riding on, reaching out to the audience." But after this opening night, all she had to say was, "Whew! Only thirty-nine performances to go."

At least her disenchantment was conveniently timed. In 1969 every traditional American value was under assault and nightclubs, as bastions of materialism, were hardly excepted. Las Vegas had already put most of them out of business by offering higher fees, and now Las Vegas was replacing its own clubs with giant showrooms. These eliminated the personal communication of floor shows. At the same time, high-steppers in New York and Los Angeles were exchanging the spectator sport of entertainment for the participatory pleasures of dancing in a discotheque, a chic variation on the rock-'n'-roll dance halls of San Francisco with the same raison d'être: instead of sitting and eating and drinking and watching, the customer was himself the show, costumed in gaudy clothes and drenched in multicolored flashing and blinking lights. America's historic urge to dance, denied by the casino showrooms, was being exploited by the Daisy and the Factory in Los Angeles, and the Electric Circus, the Cheetah, and Arthur's in New York. But not in Las Vegas, where the drive was on to preserve the 1960s forever.

Streisand fulfilled her International Hotel contract, and that was the end of her live work. She had given the hotel its money's worth. In a town where the spectacular is everyday, she had launched the International glamorously; she had gotten it widespread press coverage; and she had practically sold out the huge new showroom for her entire engagement. Only the balcony had stubbornly remained unfilled. Only one performer ever *would* fill it, and he would fill it every night of his engagement, an engagement in fact that immediately followed Streisand's.

The marquee soared high above the hotel entrance. At night it shone like a heavenly monolith. The letters were giant, stark, black, and bold against the white background. They spelled out a single name. The name was "Elvis."

Three images form a triptych on which the vivid and tragic career of Elvis Presley was painted, and even though his immense fame was spread by records and movies, these pictures are of live performances because, as was evident all too late, Presley was first and most of all a showman, one of the most exciting and original ever produced by America. Probably no other entertainer in the country's history has been to such an extent conceived, nurtured, energized, influenced, and destroyed by the social and theatrical forces of his time. Probably none better deserves the now trite epithets "legendary" and "mythic."

The central and most triumphant of the three images is of Presley in Las Vegas, reappearing in 1969 as a live performer after a decade's submersion in movies and records. The earliest of the three images is the freest and most rapturous: Presley at the start, raw and untamed, a white-hot youngster who could sing black. This was the punk, the greaser, the country's first rock-'n'-roll star who so alarmed adult America, the sexual revolution incarnate. The final, cruel image is of Presley as a bloated, robotlike grotesque being lugged into arenas like a leaden parade float and then found drugged dead.

A carcass in a bathroom.

Broadway and the personal stage have always been very different places. On Broadway, individual talent is subordinated to the needs of a show, even when the show is a star vehicle. In person, the individual is the whole show. Carol Lawrence proved to be the rare entertainer who could play both Broadway and the showroom, achieving stardom as Maria in West Side Story *and then making a career in the nightclub big time.*

My first appearance after I started recording in 1955 was [with a touring Grand Ole Opry company] in an outdoor stadium. I was scared stiff. I came out and I was doing a fast-type tune and everybody was hollering and I didn't know what they were hollering at. Then I came offstage and my manager told me that everyone was hollering because I was wiggling. So I did a little more and the more I did, the more I got. (As quoted in William Allen Harbinson, *Elvis Presley: An Illustrated Biography*)

Like Liberace and his white tails, Presley had caught lightning in a bottle and knew it. "Wiggling" was to be his gimmick and, like Liberace, he appalled buttoned-up 1950s America. The management of the Grand Ole Opry had in fact been hesitant in the first place about the twenty-year-old country singer; had rejected his original audition in favor of Pat Boone, who would make a career of being the upstanding alternative to Presley's tomcat sexuality. But it was the tomcat's day. Marlon Brando and James Dean were swaggering across movie screens with vulnerable bravado, sending waves of body heat crunching in jackboots and rumbling with motorcycle engines. Presley already quivered and shook to his rocking music. Eager youngsters shrieked with comprehending joy. So did his first reviewer, a Memphis newspaperwoman: "I don't know what it is but he's got it. He moves, he struts, he shakes, he's mean, he's sweet. He's Sex."

Playing the Mississippi-Alabama Fair that year, still in a cowboy outfit, Presley brazenly opened his act with the decidedly un-country "Good Rockin' Tonight," and there was no doubt about what the "rockin'" referred to. A year later at the Dallas Cotton Bowl a ten-foot fence and a police cordon had to protect him from the twenty-six-thousand screaming fans trying to get at him in his pegged pants and draped jacket.

Presley had begun billing himself as "The Hillbilly Cat," but when his record "Heartbreak Hotel" became number one on the national popularity listings—not the country category but overall—he too left the hills. He indulged a taste for costumes that were part greaser and part black dandy: pink suits with white shoes, or green jackets with black trousers, cummerbund, and creamy boots. As the first rock star, he had no one to learn from. Those to come would model themselves on him. There were, to be sure, other performers on the same scent and they influenced him, country rebels like Jerry Lee Lewis, playing the piano on his feet and sometimes *with* his feet; or equally exuberant black singers like James Brown or Little Richard, leaping and stomping and flopping all over the stage. Presley surely shared their style, and yet he remained an original. He was the white boy who could dance and move and wiggle with the best of the blacks.

His style was not so smooth as to be slick, and he would always retain an amateur edge to keep his greaser credentials legitimate. His self-absorbed passion was like a stripper's, and yet a laugh hovered about him, providing a certain self-mockery to leaven the abandon.

He growls just a little, flicks the hair from his eyes, lets his heavy-lidded gaze burn up the front rows, raises his left hand...sways his body, shakes a leg, rolls his groin.... His hips begin to undulate, his head whips up and down and he seems altogether to be in some sort of trance.... His eyes are pencilled in and his fair hair dyed black to add demoniac qualities to his rough, romantic good looks. He does "Heartbreak Hotel" when the main lights are turned down.... He bends his left leg, supports himself on the right and then throws out his arms in appeal

> Well since mah baby's left me
> I've found a new place t'dwell
> It's down at the end of Lonely Street at
> Heartbreak Hotel.

It is more than they can bear—they are out of their seats—they are rushing for the stage and as the cops push them back he has already gone on to something else, crouching over, hands flailing. . . . He never fails to close with "Hound Dog." He falls to his knees, thrusts his groin in their faces, crawls

When Elvis Presley triumphed in Las Vegas, his white jump suit got as much publicity as most other entire acts.

over the stage like a snake, convulses, jerks upright, twists back to his feet.... And when he's finished he doesn't bow, never comes back for an encore, is just rushed away, shivering, sometimes crumbling from exhaustion. (W. A. Harbinson, *Elvis Presley: An Illustrated Biography*)

Presley's success was all but instantaneous. His records dominated American popular music—"Don't You Step on My Blue Suede Shoes," "You Ain't Nothin' but a Hound Dog," "Don't Be Cruel to a Heart That's True." The only hitch in this otherwise classic rocket ride to stardom was an engagement at the New Frontier Hotel in Las Vegas, where he was booked for two weeks in 1956 at $8,500 a week. The hotel had a reputation for offbeat choices. Liberace was one that had worked. In a couple of years, Mario Lanza would be one that didn't (failing to show up on opening night, then and there ending a tragic career). Presley's experience was almost as bad. Business was so poor that his act was nearly canceled. A hip-swiveling rock 'n' roller who symbolized a threat to the status quo was hardly what Las Vegas audiences, beneficiaries of the status quo, wanted in entertainment.

Presley struggled through his second week, and the rejection plainly stung. "I got no feeling from them," he later complained. "They just sat there and listened. They didn't respond." He was young enough to think that, given the chance, adults would like the same things teenagers did. He was also young enough to show his hurt. "I wasn't a flop," he insisted. "They don't keep flops two weeks, do they?" Later, in a more reflective frame of mind, he said, "I always wanted to play Las Vegas. So I did. Now I'll go on from here."

Liberace, once the reigning star of the New Frontier, tried to console Presley. Odd couple though these two might at first seem, they had their similarities. Both were nonconformists and both had a taste for the flamboyant. Presley, in his own way, was becoming as campy as Liberace. Both were blithely outrageous and both were sexual outlaws, threatening the traditional machismo symbolized by Las Vegas and embodied by such casino stalwarts as Frank Sinatra and Dean Martin. Liberace encouraged Presley to wear even flashier clothes than before, and they swapped gold lamé jackets for a backstage photograph.

There was something else that Presley and Liberace shared. Elvis, too, had been born with a dead twin brother, Jesse Garon Presley. That was eerie indeed. It was almost as if each of these driven entertainers had needed an extra life's energy, as Liberace said, "to work in a frenzy."

If Liberace's effeminacy was too much for the 1950s, so was the lustiness of "Elvis the Pelvis," as he had inevitably been dubbed. Both were too extroverted for the times, but despite all the indignation, they were extraordinarily successful. Plainly, the same suppressed sexuality that fostered public outrage prompted public adoration.

A great fuss was made over Presley's entering the army and having his hair cut short, particularly the infamous sideburns. Here, the castration symbolism and the parallels with the Biblical account of Samson's haircut and subsequent impotence are so apparent that it is embarrassing to take the opportunity to mention them. But, as Liberace says, I'll take it anyway.

Presley slipped unresistingly into a Hollywood maw of romantic musical comedies. It is not, I think, overly analytical to see in this a bargain struck, emasculation and dilution in exchange for the nirvana of movie stardom. His music and performance lost their hot sexuality, and with it their vitality and integrity. With the single exception of a 1961 benefit appearance for the Memorial Fund of the USS *Arizona*, Presley would not perform in person again for ten years. Had his movies not eventually

ABOVE:
Like many singers, only more so, Elvis Presley never developed a social assurance commensurate with his fame, and he virtually never went out in public. He made an exception, though, for Liberace's 1956 opening at the Riviera Hotel in Las Vegas, out of gratitude for the showman-pianist's support during Elvis's disappointing Las Vegas debut.

RIGHT:
Presley was the only star ever to sell out the gigantic showroom of the International Hotel in Las Vegas. And he sold it out for every show.

declined in popularity, he probably would never have been seen or heard from in the flesh again.

That is what made his return to the performing arena so suspenseful. It was not an elated Presley who arrived in Las Vegas in July 1969 to prepare for his opening at the Show Room Internationale. It was, rather, a somber Presley, who had reason to be uncertain about his ability to perform in person, uncertain about the appeal of his music—for rock 'n' roll had become white and sophisticated, dominated now by the Beatles —and uncertain about his ability to attract Las Vegas audiences, since he could hardly forget his 1959 debacle at the New Frontier.

Though a decade had passed, bringing rock 'n' roll to the forefront of America's popular music, none of its great stars had proved a popular attraction in Las Vegas. Ironically enough, Tom Jones, a slicked-up rock singer, had made a career out of what was essentially an impression of Presley in nightclub mufti. In turn, Englebert Humperdinck and Wayne Newton had drawn their acts from Jones. Yet as for the original "King of Rock 'n' Roll," the very continuation of his career was at stake, and he was too young to retire. Like all pop music stars since Frank Sinatra, he was struck by mid-career crisis when his teenage constituency grew up. If he was to continue, he would have to change.

Changed Presley had. It was an utterly new Elvis who showed up in Las Vegas that hot desert summer, a Presley designed to appeal to the fans who had (presumably) grown older with him and who (he hoped) were now the Las Vegas audience. He had always been a good-looking fellow but with a surliness through the cheek, an unpleasant sneer curling the lip, and a pasty softness about the face and body. Now, at thirty-four, he was broad-shouldered, slim-hipped, lean and taut. Maturity had given his features definition. His eyes remained soulful beneath the familiar lush eyelashes, and with long hair in style his sideburns seemed dashing rather than sleazy. Hardly a greaser, he was downright handsome.

The showroom's great golden curtain soared upward to reveal, dramatically silhouetted against a vivid red cyclorama, a fifty-piece orchestra already throbbing with rock-'n'-roll drive. The strings were massed and the rhythm section hefty—four guitarists and three percussionists beating out an opening vamp to set up the audience for show time. The vocal forces joined in this rhythmic overture, four white men singing back-up and a quartet of gospelizing black women, counter-clapping against the pulsating orchestra. The atmospheric opening that is so important to a showroom act was now rocking the big theater through the hotel's terrifying audio system, as out strode Presley in full black leather, his guitar a prop slung along his hip, to be thrust or jerked or hitched over his back.

The audience roared and the rhythm section delivered syncopating bursts of harsh trumpets against honking saxophones, propelling him through "I Got a Woman," a rhythm-and-blues song popularized by Ray Charles, but one whose momentum was pure Presley. Then "Polk Salad Annie," a country-and-western number with the classic Presley mix of Southern black and white. He crooned "Love Me Tender" to remind the audience of how rich his baritone remained, sweet as a choirboy's, which was where it had all started. Then back to the beat.

> *I'm proud to say*
> *That she's my buttercup.*
> *I'm in love*
> *I'm all shook up.*

He smiled into the resounding din and the big orchestra rocked behind him, pushing a wall of sound out at the audience. Then, as when young, he danced. The moves were not quite the same as when he'd first brazened it out before the nation. That had been thirteen years and the Beatles ago. Lately, he had watched Tom Jones sell stage sex in a style adapted, but updated, from his very own and he took the tip in return. His new moves, then, were up-to-date, yet characterized by his own vitality, and he was grinning with tremendous self-satisfaction—and then triumph. He was still the white boy who could dance with the blacks. He had survived everything that the forces of morality and conformity had contrived to make him a eunuch, and had emerged intact. The sexual electricity that had been the basis of his original appeal, and everything that had made him unique and special, had been suppressed but not eliminated. Like a butterfly wriggling and straining against its cocoon, he had won, bursting free to beauty and flight. It is neither romanticizing nor intellectualizing to call Presley's reemergence a triumph of individuality over a system.

The press did not miss the point. Presley's management made sure of that. It seemed as if half the International Hotel's opening-night audience was made up of invited media people. An airliner had been chartered merely for the East Coast rock writers. Restoring Presley's musical currency was a major purpose of this engagement.

And in that July of 1969, Elvis Presley was indeed restored. Not, however, by media manipulation. It is a myth that such things can be contrived. Our world may be fast and electronic, televised and publicized, but the artist must ultimately still do it by himself. Communicators may be flown in to spread the news, but the news must be made and the entertainer still has to go it alone to make that news.

Having exhilarated the entertainment world with his Las Vegas rebirth, Presley returned to the International Hotel six months later, this time wearing a spectacular white jump suit sparkling with sequins, brilliantly sashed, and slashed to the waist. This gaudy costume played a greater part in his act than even white tails had done in Liberace's. It was as if, in this costume, Presley had been reborn.

Movie work was more profitable than even the fanciest live engagement, but to Presley, playing Las Vegas meant much more. He was not only searching for validity as a live performer in the Beatles' era; he was not only revitalizing a sputtering career. A live act was the way Presley had begun. Audiences had all but conceived him, and plainly he felt at home with them, again sucking life and energy from them, vampire-like.

Alas, his triumph was to be short-lived. The "Elvis Presley Show" toured arenas across the country. Souvenir programs were peddled —pictures, posters, buttons, even replicas of the scarves that he tossed to fans in the front rows. The show would open portentously with the fanfare from Richard Strauss's *Thus Spake Zarathustra*, which had become a cliché in the wake of the movie *2001*. Presley would appear in an elaborate version of the Las Vegas jump suit, designed not quite artfully enough to camouflage the considerable weight he was gaining. In the huge auditoriums engaged for the tour he could only play to the eons of space surrounding him—without personal contact with the audience or feedback. The grossness of his body seemed to reflect a grossness in his work, as he postured grandiosely, as if to match his fame and reputation with the physical size of the arena. W. A. Harbinson, an Elvis enthusiast, described the resplendent decadence of his final appearances:

The drums begin to thunder . . . the strobe lights start flashing, the sound builds and builds, reaching deafening proportions and the stage lights pour down as Elvis slowly turns around, one hand on the mike, the other holding out the gold cape and it shimmers and flashes . . . and the BAM! BAM! BAM! Elvis' fist punches three times, the whole stage explodes and then, sudden crescendo, his right hand above his head, the incredible gold cape waving . . . and they've gone into the finale.

Glory, glory hallelujah
Glory, glory hallelujah

And as the last word builds, the stage lights come on full blast, the whole orchestra is standing and there, behind the band, stretching over the huge wall, lights flashing all over like the silver birds of truth, is an enormous and most garish Stars and Stripes. . . . And Elvis stands with legs parted, his head bowed, his arms outstretched and the lovely gold cape is a huge sun, burning up the whole auditorium, so they rise to their feet, their tears flow, their hands clasp and he falls to one knee, bows his head, crosses arms and wraps the gold cape around him like a shroud.

Shroud indeed. Audiences were appreciative, but the event was grotesque, its performer a bizarre parody of himself, no longer remotely the exuberant youngster with a jiggling leg and wiggle, or the glamorous Elvis who had survived to triumph in Las Vegas. Those, boy and man, were symbols of individuality and life; this was demonstration of commercial greed and ego crunch at work to subsume such individuality. He was a bronzed, dead pharaoh, hoisted on the throne and then borne to the arena where the fanfares and lights and blare might create the illusion of his existence. Dead-alive, he was displayed to the crowd.

In 1977, at forty-three, death came to Presley in a haze of madness and drugs, and it was followed by rumors and half-truths and speculations and investigations, but its basic meaning was not complicated. It merely made fact of a foregone conclusion: the vibrant, hot, dancing young man had not been able to handle the forces that attend immense stardom intellectually or emotionally, and so the entertainer had survived only at the expense of the individual. It was—was it not?—like one twin draining the life from another.

Stardom in show business invites an attention and a gratification for which the human ego is scarcely prepared. Emotional maturity, never common, is undermined by such forces. Is it inevitable that the self will crumble under such an assault as the public person becomes the only person? Is that why, in the modern show business of million-dollar one-night stands, the artist, ego inflated to the bursting, must die?

It is perhaps ironic that in these pages Frank Sinatra follows Elvis Presley, who could not survive the ravaging splendors of stardom; Presley, whose effect on adolescent girls and their aghast parents so resembled Sinatra's. "Rock and roll," Frank Sinatra said in 1955, "is phony and false—and sung, written, and played, for the most part, by cretinous goons." He had doubtless forgotten that Artur Rodzinski, director of the New York Philharmonic Society, blamed *juvenile delinquency*, no less, on the spell Sinatra had cast over teenagers in his younger days. Elvis Presley was doubtless the cretinous goon Sinatra had in mind, but the young rocker had his revenge. Upon Elvis's discharge from the army in 1959, Sinatra paid him half his television show's $250-thousand weekly budget for a six-minute appearance. Presley paid his own price: as a joke, he had to sing in white tie and tails.

The superstar is the individual distilled to legend. The crowd pays homage to that legend. Frank Sinatra became a star as a great and personal singer of popular songs, but it was not the voice or the songs that made him such a presence in our lives. Nor does the Sinatra legend rest on a unique personal quality such as Chevalier's gaiety, Dietrich's

glamor, Garland's emotionalism, or Kaye's charm. Frank Sinatra's legend is based on the tender heart we believe he has, consistent behavior to the contrary. Sinatra could sing like an angel and when he did, he *was* an angel. When he did not sing he got into trouble, and so he was us at our best, us at our worst; a man of confusion, inconsistency, and contradiction; cocky, vulnerable, pugnacious, classy, dangerous, and naive; an innocent with hoodlum tendencies; and the most attractive of singers, charismatic to distraction. Why do we think that someone who can sing (or dance or act or tell jokes) is also wise and informed, a great man (presidential material, perhaps)? Frank Sinatra's inability to handle power and fame suavely only made him seem as fallible as the rest of us. His melodramatic romance with Ava Gardner became the great and tragic love we all enjoy-endure at least once in our lives. His comeback from professional disaster was the ultimate show-business Cinderella story, and remember: Cinderella is a fantasy for the commoner.

Even were he not the finest singer of popular songs ever produced by America, Frank Sinatra's absolute presentation of self as show is reason enough to make him the closing act in this account of the great solo entertainers. As for his singing,

what few people, apart from musicians, have never seemed to grasp is that he is not simply the best popular singer of his generation, a latter-day Jolson or Crosby, but the culminating point in an evolutionary process which has refined the art of interpreting words set to music. . . . The secret of [his] technique lies in his uncanny gift for rephrasing a melody, his grasp of the nuances of lyric writing and his remarkably sensitive ear for a harmonic sequence. . . . Nor is there even the remotest possibility that he will have a successor. Sinatra was the result of a fusing of a set of historical circumstances, which can never be repeated. (Benny Green, *London Observer*)

Frank Sinatra's middle-class Italian family was not encouraging about his singing aspirations, but when as an eighteen-year-old he saw Bing

When Frank Sinatra played the Paramount in 1943, he discovered a new and powerful star-making market: adolescent girls.

Crosby in a Newark vaudeville house, in his own words, he turned a corner in his career. "I watched him. . . . He had such great ease that I thought, 'If he can do it that easily, I don't know why I can't.' That was one of the big turning points of my life." The next year, in 1934, Sinatra won an amateur contest in a local movie theater and with it an engagement across the river in New York at the Academy of Music on Fourteenth Street, where the early vaudevillian Tony Pastor had once reigned.

He joined a quartet, the Hoboken Four, and they came up winners on the "Major Bowes Amateur Hour," a radio program, going on to tour with a Bowes show. As a solo in the next few years, the slender young man with the lyric baritone and a startling clarity of diction plugged songs, performed in local clubs, and even sang for nothing on a New York radio station, just to be heard. Among the listeners was bandleader Harry James, who one June night in 1939 tracked him down in a New Jersey roadhouse where, as singing master of ceremonies, he was getting fifteen dollars a week. "I practically gave up," Sinatra later remembered, "because I felt I was getting nowhere. Someone said, 'That guy over there looks like Harry James.' I said, 'What would he be doing in a joint like this?'"

James had just left Benny Goodman to start a band of his own. He invited the skinny twenty-four-year-old to join him in an engagement at the Paramount Theatre in Times Square, the most prestigious of all the Times Square presentation houses. As James recalled, Sinatra accepted the sixty-five-dollars-a-week offer immediately. "We made a deal and it was as simple as that. There was only one thing we didn't agree on. I wanted him to change his name because I thought people couldn't remember it."

Once, observing Sinatra's nervousness in anticipating a review, James's band manager noted, "He wants a good write-up more than anybody I've ever seen." Sinatra's later imbroglios with the press may have originated in his need for approval and in his corresponding vulnerability to disapproval. In 1959, writing in the *New York World Telegram and Sun,* Scott Lawrence described Sinatra's retaliation against criticism as "swift and direct, whether [it] stems from a newspaperman, a heckler in a nightclub or the dissenting opinion of a friend. . . . When friends try to counsel, he will flare up. 'Don't tell me! Suggest! But don't tell me!'"

Any human being can be stung by criticism. The performer whose ego is exposed to the public seeks to prevent the considerable hurt which that can entail with a shield of bravado. Frank Sinatra never learned quite how to do that, not in fifty years of international stardom. Not learning made him famous.

From James's band, the young singer went to Tommy Dorsey's. As he remembered,

that night the bus pulled out with the rest of the boys at about half past midnight. I'd said good-bye to them all and it was snowing, I remember. There was nobody around and I stood alone with my suitcase in the snow and watched the tail-lights disappear. Then the tears started and I tried to run after the bus. There was such spirit and enthusiasm in that band. (As quoted in Robin Douglas-Home, *Sinatra*)

Despite Dorsey's reputation as "The Sentimental Gentleman of Swing," and his professorial appearance, he had a sharp tongue and a taste for fistfights. Sinatra had his share of scraps during this time, yet he always credited Dorsey's slide trombone as the inspiration for his own long-lined, swooping style. (Sinatra's musical expertise is considerable, and he has had a lifelong interest in opera, Puccini especially.)

His youthful distress at losing the security of the James band was doubtless allayed by a series of hit recordings with Dorsey ("I'll Never Smile Again," "My Prayer," "South of the Border"). Singing these songs in front of the band, on stands from New York's Astor Roof to the Hollywood Palladium, Sinatra established that his personal appeal—to women particularly—was obvious, instant, and amazing. After yet another hit record ("There Are Such Things") he quit the band to go it on his own. It was a daring decision in an era when singers were but appendages to orchestras, but his timing was perfect, for the big-band era was about to end; indeed, Sinatra would end it himself. He would become a phenomenon within four months.

His debut as a solo act came at the Mosque Theatre in Newark in November 1942, and it was there that Bob Weitman, managing director of the Paramount Theatre in New York, scouted him.

This skinny kid walks out on the stage. He was not much older than the kids in the seats. . . . As soon as they saw him the kids went crazy. And when he started to sing, they stood up and yelled and moaned and carried on until I thought, you should excuse the expression, his pants had fallen down. (As quoted in Arnold Shaw, *Sinatra: Twentieth-Century Romantic*)

Weitman booked Sinatra into the Paramount the following month as an "Extra Added Attraction" with Benny Goodman's band. "The King of Swing" was not a magnanimous man (in fact, it is beginning to seem as if few orchestra leaders are nice, whether popular or classical). Although Sinatra already had several hit records with Dorsey, Goodman claimed never to have heard of him. But the singer stayed on after the band's departure and business built. He was held over for four weeks and, according to Weitman, as quoted by Arnold Shaw:

During [that] first appearance at the Paramount, as the fever spread among the bobby-soxers, extra guards had to be retained to maintain order. Girls remained in their seats from early morning through Frank's last show at night. Some fainted from hunger, others from excitement. As his engagement lengthened, the windows of his dressing room had to be blacked out since the mere sight of him from the street below resulted in traffic jams.

The riot scenes were repeated during his appearances in Boston and Chicago. There had been matinee idols before, but as *Time* reported, "Not since the days of Rudy Vallee has American womanhood made such unabashed public love to an entertainer." There was, however, something new about these women. These "bobby-soxers" were adolescents. And he was "Frankie," "The Voice," the original pop star, the first teenage heartthrob, the first male singer to provoke plainly sexual responses from pubescent girls.

He was also nicknamed "The Swooner" (to Bing Crosby's "Crooner"), and the swooning might just as easily have been his as his fans', for, five-feet-ten-inches tall, he weighed only one hundred thirty pounds and would cling to the microphone as if for physical support. Seemingly burdened by the broad, padded shoulders of his draped jacket, he had only to smile, or adorn a note with a glide, to elicit shrieks of passionate despair from the hall. There were dark rumors that George Evans, his clever press agent, was paying some of the fans to instigate such demonstrations. Evans, in fact, once did rent an ambulance and park it outside the Paramount box office, but such stunts are futile if there is no show to back them up.

Sinatra's show was only beginning. In January 1943 he joined the popular radio program "Your Hit Parade." RKO Radio Pictures hired him to make a movie. Meantime, he performed in such night spots as New York's Riobamba. There, Robin Douglas-Home quotes him,

I had to open the show walking around the tables and singing. There was no stage and the dance floor was only as big as a postage stamp. I was nervous as hell but I sang a few songs and went off. Walter O'Keefe was the star of the show and he was to do his act last. That night he just walked on and said, "Ladies and gentlemen, I *was* your star of the evening. But tonight, in this club, we have all just seen a star born."

The real explosion was to come in October, when Sinatra returned to the Paramount for yet another engagement.

This appearance brought on the mightiest demonstration of female hysteria that any entertainment star had until then been accorded. When Frank arrived the first day for a 6 A.M. rehearsal, almost 1,000 girls were on line. By seven it stretched halfway down the block to Eighth Avenue. When the 3,000-seat theatre opened its doors at 8:30 A.M., enough youngsters were admitted to fill it to capacity. The picture preceding the stage show, *Our Hearts Were Young and Gay*, was utterly ignored. The bobby-soxers chattered, joked, exchanged Sinatra stories and intermittently sent up cries of "We want Frankie!" And after he was onstage, excitement reached such proportions that he had to plead for quiet or threaten to leave if the audience did not settle down.

The following day, a school holiday, was the haymaker. News reports spoke of "The Columbus Day Riot" at the Paramount Theatre . . . over 10,000 youngsters queued up in a line that, six abreast, ran west on 43d Street, snaked along Eighth Avenue and east on 44th Street. An additional 20,000, according to police estimates, clogged Times Square making it impassable to pedestrians and automobiles. . . . When the first show finished, only 250 came out of the 3,000-seat house. (Arnold Shaw, *Sinatra: Twentieth-Century Romantic*)

In this period of his career, the singer's image was boyish and even virginal. Occasional reports of tantrums were not played up in the innocent press of the time. The public Sinatra remained a frail singer of sensitive songs. "Try a Little Tenderness," "Put Your Dreams Away," "All or Nothing at All," and

> *I couldn't sleep a wink last night*
> *Because we had that silly fight.*
> *I had to call you up this morning*
> *To see if everything was still alright.*

He was a vulnerable young man with a floppy bow tie and a curl on his forehead, standing before the adoring audiences, smiling and holding the microphone as if for dear life. That was his routine, and women repeatedly expressed the conviction that he was singing directly to them.

Face it, singing is an act with limited visual possibilities. Unless the singer does *something*, he is going to look boring, or even silly, since it is difficult to appear adult and intelligent while vocalizing. In the vaudeville era, gesturing and dance movements made entertainers out of singers like Eva Tanguay and Al Jolson. In Sinatra's era of slow songs, such movement was inappropriate, and records and radio studios made it unnecessary. Singers became static performers, all the more so for being bound to their microphones.

Like other vocalists of his era, Sinatra simply accepted this, smiling occasionally and gesturing perfunctorily as he sang his songs. He spoke as little as possible, although he was always thoughtful about crediting

OPPOSITE, ABOVE:
When Hollywood's fat years were over, many star actresses attempted nightclub acts. Among those successful at it were Mitzi Gaynor, Debbie Reynolds, Shirley MacLaine, Raquel Welch, and seen here, Ann-Margret. She assembled an elaborate show —but not to disguise any lack of talent. Among the movie stars, in fact, none was more gifted, or more vibrant onstage.

OPPOSITE, BELOW:
Johnny Carson's career was made and largely spent in television, hosting the "Tonight Show." His heart seemed to lie with stand-up comedians, and he devoted much of his television time to them, even educating his audiences about their working methods. Carson particularly admired Jack Benny and Bob Hope, not only for their humor but for their professionalism. He was a professional himself, one of the quickest wits in show business, and when television commitments permitted, he played Las Vegas. One classic Carson line on the "Tonight Show" was: "In keeping with the holiday spirit, why don't you all turn to the person next to you, shake his hand and say, 'Howdy, stranger!' And that goes for you people watching at home in bed."

composers, and lyricists, and sometimes even arrangers. Yet it was still his person rather than just his marvelous singing that made him popular. Was it in his looks? He was hardly handsome, although it was plain at the start that women responded romantically to him. Some theorized that the skinny young man who clung to the microphone was appealing to the maternalism in all women, even young ones. His explanation was, "It was the war years and there was a great loneliness and I was the boy in every corner drugstore; the boy who'd gone off, drafted in the war."

Perhaps so, for at war's end his career slumped and sales of his records were declining precipitously by 1948. The public was turning to robust novelties such as "Ghost Riders in the Sky" and "Come-on-a-My-House." Sinatra, a wolf boy reared by musicians, had no taste for such gimmickry and by 1950 found himself without a movie contract or even a recording affiliation. Given a television variety show, he was slotted at the same time as Milton Berle, "Mr. Television," for whom all America paused. Sinatra's bad luck had become laughable. Forced, now, to return to live performance, he sang to the painful accompaniment of thin applause from sparse audiences at the Chez Paree in Chicago and even New York's Copacabana, a club that as a performer he'd once owned. Playing a New York spot called the French Casino, he tried to appeal with songs currently popular, but they were either mediocre ("You Belong to Me") or ill-suited to his voice ("I've Got My Love to Keep Me Warm"). He sank still lower with parodies that made fun of "Ol' Man Crosby":

He don't say nothin'
But he must know somethin'
For he just keeps singin' along.

It was as if he were blindly groping for the magic that made Crosby's success enduring, and then, surely in response to crisis, his voice went. The lyric baritone strained and then cracked as his vocal cords began to hemorrhage in the middle of a show at the Copacabana. He broke off, muttered a terse "Good night," and strode from the floor.

At the same time, his personal life was in disarray. Troubles somewhere, troubles everywhere. The tabloid newspapers scrawled his love life across their front pages as, not yet divorced, he romanced Ava Gardner. In the straight-laced 1950s, this was scandalous. For Sinatra it was also embittering. "Those newspapers," he said. "They broke up my home. They broke up my family. They ruined my life." And his life must indeed have seemed ruined, with his voice failing, his popularity fading, musical styles changing, and his marriage collapsing in the wake of a new romance that was itself rocky. Still only in his thirties, Frankie-boy was a has-been.

And so it was a fairy tale, a serial story, and altogether a show-business miracle that Sinatra was restored to wondrous fame and glorious fortune by a single stroke of his era's magic wand, the Academy Award. The story is inscribed in the holy writ of show-business press coverage: how Sinatra pursued a featured role in the movie version of James Jones's *From Here to Eternity*, how he was paid only eight thousand dollars to do it, and how a brilliant performance led to an Oscar, and a recovered voice, and hit records, and all things wonderfully golden. This was more than an ordinary comeback: it was to be the archetypal show-business comeback and the spine of the Sinatra legend.

That his renewed career was to outstrip his first was indeed marvelous, but, still more incredible, there was a critical difference between the two. The first Sinatra was a superb and magnetic singer. The second was, like all great entertainers, the one who brought his life onstage with him. He had been tested in the crucible and had emerged triumphant, manly, experienced—that was what he strolled into the spotlight with. Only with such personal revelation is performing greatness achieved. It is touching but absurd when such performers decry journalistic snoops. They want to keep the details of their personal lives private while offering the public their naked spirits. The gossip sought by the snoops is nobody's business, of course, but it is also small potatoes compared to the tremendous act of self-revelation that the great star performs onstage. As Presley and Garland so tragically learned, transcending mere "act" to achieve an ultimate self-revelation can result in the onstage self dominating private life, character, and finally existence. That is always a risk as the entertainer takes the final step toward legendry.

Sinatra's 1952 Academy Award was heaven on earth and all God's blessings. Transformed, he was no longer Frankie-boy. He had seen himself in the character of Maggio in *From Here to Eternity*—an Italian kid off the streets. Now he was willing to be his own adult self onstage. As his voice came back, tougher and surer, he put on a fedora, lighted a cigarette, and sang of experience.

It's a quarter to three
There's no one in the place
Except you and me.

Ironically, the popularity of rock 'n' roll forced him through a door that led to a receptive musical public. The market for single records was made up of teenagers who were uninterested in Frank Sinatra and traditional songs. But the just-introduced long-playing record created a new kind of product, an album that was one record. "Record albums," of course, were so called because they incorporated four discs in a book, or album. The long-playing record, which contained the same amount of material, seemed a much smaller investment. So Sinatra could record his kind of songs—classic American popular music—for an adult public, rather than futilely compete with rock 'n' roll. Sales of these new long-playing "albums" would become as important to the record industry as single hits. He was rolling lucky. Even long-playing records had been invented at the right time.

Resurrection was now his stock-in-trade. Because he was, after all, only a *singer*, his scrappiness and the rumors of gangland connections made him appealingly feisty, and newspapers doted on his every lapse. When he produced John F. Kennedy's inauguration show, the media even made his wardrobe a source of scandal because of reported quarrels with the designer. "This is the story of my life," Sinatra muttered with exasperation. "I buy some nice clothes and it becomes a crisis."

He occasionally reinforced his reputation onstage, and such moments were not pleasant. He interrupted a splendid concert to castigate a female gossip columnist with sexist slurs. Yet, in his increasingly triumphant career, even such mistakes made him seem human, and fallible, and all the more himself. He was one gritty customer, unsinkable, untamable, incorrigible. That was why he could sing the banal "My Way" and make it thrilling.

The decade following this rebirth Sinatra spent in movie and record studios, but even though records particularly let him be his best self, the musicianly singer, he was too much the child of live performance to live without audiences.

You know, I adore making records. I'd rather do that than almost anything else. . . . Once you're on that record singing, it's you and you alone. . . . Something happened [recording "One for My Baby"] which I've never seen before or since at a record session. I'd always sung that song before in clubs with just my pianist, Bill Miller, backing me up, a single spotlight on my face and cigarette, and the rest of the room in complete darkness. At this session the word had somehow gotten around and there were about sixty or seventy people there. . . . We had kept this song to the last track of the session. . . . [The] atmosphere in that studio was exactly like a club. . . . There was one take and that was that. The only time I've ever known it to happen like that. (As quoted in Robin Douglas-Home, *Sinatra*)

As television cut into Hollywood's popularity, reducing the number of movies made, he turned ever more to live performance. The times were his. John F. Kennedy was a show-business kind of president, and Frank Sinatra had the entree into the presidential circle. Las Vegas reflected his sensibilities, and he could appear there at whim. He was considered the ultimate attraction among high-rolling gamblers, and that made sense because he was a strong performer as well as a representative of the flash mentality.

When he was announced, a roving spotlight picked him up walking through the packed tables. . . . The deafening applause drowned out the music. A cool look at the audience, a snap of the fingers, a toss of the head and he was away into "The Lady Is a Tramp." Nobody in the audience moved—they just sat, staring with absorbed attention, at the man with the microphone whose voice rasped, flowed, blared, tiptoed, hovered and swooped through a score of songs from the poignant torch song with just a piano and a single spotlight on his face and cigarette to the exultant showstoppers with a full 40-piece orchestra and floodlights. His singing electrified that audience. (Robin Douglas-Home, *Sinatra*)

His love affair with the saloon and gambling set grew hot enough for him to acquire part-ownership in two Nevada casino-hotels, but when the Nevada State Gaming Commission revoked his gambling license in 1963, because of alleged underworld friendships, the romance ended. Sinatra was not to appear in Nevada until 1981, when he successfully won reinstatement of the license. In the years between, he entered the international concert circuit, triumphant across the country and around the world. He could appear whenever and wherever the fancy struck him and guarantee a sold-out house at exorbitant prices.

The golden songs of Tin Pan Alley, 1920 to 1940, were his personal territory as he became the musician's singer for all the world, master of the music of Richard Rodgers, Cole Porter, Jule Styne, Harry Warren, Harold Arlen, Jimmy McHugh, and James Van Heusen. With an instrumentalist's ear, he sought out the most inventive, surprising, and gratifying of popular songs, from the esoterica of Alec Wilder ("I'll Be Around") to the saloon-at-sunrise of Matt Dennis ("I Bought You Violets for Your Furs"). He was responsive both to the sense and to the poetry of lyrics. His uncanny sureness of phrasing forced a concentration on those words. But for all his success with classics, his alienation from contemporary popular music nagged at Sinatra, and he blamed his 1971 professional retirement on that. "Music was changing," he said. "There wasn't enough material around." As chance would have it, several years later he found a hit in Stephen Sondheim's beautiful new "Send in the Clowns."

Sinatra grew restless in retirement. When he resumed performing in 1974, however, it was not as an elder statesman, or even as the dean of entertainers. It was as star of stars. In 1978 he strolled on stage at the London Palladium to sing the golden classics he'd made his own: from

OPPOSITE, ABOVE LEFT:

Myron Cohen was a cloak-and-suiter in New York's garment industry before he became a professional raconteur. He upheld the anecdotal tradition of the vaudeville monologists and worked steadily for decades doing Jewish dialect jokes long after they'd gone out of fashion.

OPPOSITE, ABOVE RIGHT:

Broadway star Joel Grey doing Jimmy Durante at the Sands Hotel in Atlantic City. Grey was an actor who could work "in one," and he was also that modern rarity, the song-and-dance man. Certainly, entertaining was in his blood, for his father was the Yiddish comic Mickey Katz.

OPPOSITE, BELOW LEFT:

Comedians are not always instinctively funny; some work harder at it than others. Buddy Hackett was among the most naturally funny stand-ups of his era. Late in his career he leaned heavily on raunchy, "blue" material, perhaps out of boredom. Yet his impishness made almost any routine acceptable. Audiences do not complain when they are laughing.

OPPOSITE, BELOW RIGHT:

Shirley MacLaine was a Broadway singer and dancer before she went into the movies, and so when actresses began to turn to nightclub work she was among the best prepared.

Cole Porter's "At Long Last Love" to Richard Rodgers's "The Lady Is a Tramp"—and more Rodgers ("My Funny Valentine")—and yet more Rodgers ("It Never Entered My Mind"). The same year he sold out eight consecutive shows at the Radio City Music Hall in New York. There may have been gaudier stars from moment (Bob Dylan) to moment (Michael Jackson), but for durable appeal and for his inscription of personal statement upon the sensibility of an entire era, no performer can equal Frank Sinatra. He came to be, at last, the ultimate solo performer.

It is tempting to suppose that he can go on forever, tempting to think that performers like him, because they say so much about our time, our bravery, and our survival, can so endure. But is not the "essential" repeatedly rendered obsolete? And do we not adapt and endure? The solo star symbolizes pluck and endurance, but if he goes under, why we will just have to change with life and get by without him.

Have not the jugglers tossed their last hoops while we watched other acts? Have not the magicians as a final trick made themselves disappear while we remained? The dancers no longer dance and the funnymen are funny only for the cameras. If the singers still sing in our presence, they do so at a vast distance. And so as Frank Sinatra mourns for lost lovers into the dawn of our transistorized and computerized age, it is plain that he is the last of the line. Who will ever sing "That Old Black Magic" again? Or "Night and Day"? Nobody, my friend. We watch this fellow, once so frail and young, now a prosperous man of years. He sings the thoughts and melodies of America's youth. Still bold and arrogant, he reminds us of cocky America. This live entertainer works as personally as our nation did in the time of the handmade, when our fortunes lay in ourselves, in our confidence, in our nerve, and in our ambition.

They were wonderful and brave, the solo performers, and so were we.

At the start, Frank Sinatra's act was his voice and the appearance of being in need of help, physical help. The floppy bow tie was his trademark.

ACKNOWLEDGMENTS

Not the last but the first to thank is the editor of this book, Robert Morton, who has tormented me on two books, now, with his regular and indispensable two cents worth. And while no writer would agree that a picture is worth even a single word, the glamor and excitement of this volume just would not exist without John Crowley's enthusiastic and exhaustive picture research or the stunning book design of Judith Michael. My copy was edited with tactful precision by Ellyn Allison.

As for expert help, there is no nonfiction without libraries, and this book could not have been written without the cooperation of Thor Wood, Chief of the Performing Arts Research Center of the New York Public Library, or of Dorothy Swerdlove, Curator of the Billy Rose Theatre Collection at Lincoln Center, New York, and their helpful staffs.

There are few professors of show business. The experts are the professionals. I am grateful to a number of them for having shared their expertise with me: on the subject of nightclubs, Lee Salomon of the William Morris Agency; and on saloon performers, Lee Guber of Westbury Music Fairs. Shelly Rothman told me about the Catskills resort casinos from the booking end, while Roger Riddle shared stageside with me. I heard about the golden age of burlesque from Morton Minsky, and Beverly Anderson recalled the modern era. What Jerry Wexler didn't tell me about popular music, Stuart Ostrow and Mitch Miller did. Milton Berle talked to me about growing up in vaudeville, and Fred Ebb described the business of writing modern acts for Las Vegas.

Some were willing to read and criticize early versions of this work, particularly a couple of swell Kates—my pal Katharine Hepburn and my dear Kate Carmel. Finally, memories of vaudeville were hardly the least that George Burns provided, but they weren't the most either, for —showman to the heart—he communicated the energy, the endurance, and the survivalism that give personal entertainment meaning. Indeed, Mr. Burns represents what this book is ultimately about—performing as an act of survival—and those to whom it is finally dedicated—all the performers who make the nightly high dive to prove it.

PICTURE CREDITS *Numbers refer to pages.*

Agron, Lawrence/FPG International: 149 above; Aliano, Ron/Neal Peters: 19; AP/Wide World: 105, 155 below right, 169, 178 above, 231 center; Baldridge, Robert: 8; Barr, John/Liaison: 11; Barr, Nancy/Retna Ltd.: 210, 211 above right; Bellissimo, John: 4–5, 7, 184, 202–3, 211 center left, 211 center right; Bensimon/Gamma Liaison: 196 above; The Bettmann Archive: 125 below right, 166, 215; Borsari, Peter C./FPG International: 205 above right; Boston Athenaeum: 116; Bridgeport Public Library Historical Collection: 26 above; Brown Brothers: 23, 34, 43 above right, 47, 52, 53, 57, 62, 65, 73, 76–77, 81 above, 86, 89, 92, 100–101, 120, 129, back jacket center right; Burns/FPG International: 147 center; Caesar's Palace, Courtesy of: 225 above; Campbell, Tom/FPG International: 12–13; CBS: 111, 147 above center, center left, center right, below center; Christopher Collection: 128; Columbia University Rare Book and Manuscript Library, Joseph Urban Collection: 80; Culver Pictures: 16, 21, 22, 23, 25 above, 40, 43 above left, below left, below right, 51, 61 above, 82, 85 below, 95, 114, 119 above left, below left, below right, 121; Dean, Loomis/Life Magazine: 163 left; de'Espinasse, Hank/Image Bank: 225 below left; Dixon, Dean/Photo Fair: 211 above center; Edwardo Jaffe Collection: 125 above right; Elvis Presley Enterprises, Inc., Courtesy of: 243 below; Fishback, Glen/FPG International: 155 above left; FPG International: 56, 60, 64, 75, 91, 98, 102, 103 above, 113, 125 above left, 139, 145, 147 above right, 148, 193 center right, 194, 201 below, 223 above, 225 below right, back jacket center left; Frank Driggs Collection: 44, 55, 63, 71, 136 below, 185, 187, 189 above, 190–191, 192, 193 center left, below left, below right, 207 above, 214, 221, 232, 233, 256, back jacket above center; Freeburg, Andy/Retna Ltd.: 153; Gehr, Herbert/Life Magazine © Time Inc.: 135; Gershoff, Gary/Retna Ltd.: 211 below left; Granger Collection: 107; Gubb, L./Gamma-Liaison: 212–13; Hanley, Dick/FPG International: 193 above left; Hooper, Robert Scott: 130 below right, 147 below left, 149 below, 155 above right, below left,

SONG CREDITS

Excerpts from the following songs are used by permission. All rights are reserved and international copyrights secured.

BIBLIOGRAPHY

Adams, Joey. *Here's to the Friars*. New York: Crown Publishers, Inc., 1976.

Adamson, Joe. *Groucho, Harpo, Chico and Sometimes Zeppo: A Celebration of the Marx Brothers*. New York: Simon and Schuster, Inc., 1983.

Barnes, Ken. *Sinatra and the Great Song Stylists*. London: Ian Allen, Ltd., 1972.

Berger, Phil. *The Last Laugh: The World of the Stand-up Comics*. New York: William Morrow and Co., Inc., 1975.

Burke, Peter. *Popular Culture in Early Modern Europe*. New York: New York University Press, 1978.

Cantor, Eddie. *My Life Is in Your Hands*. New York: Harper and Brothers, 1928.

Collins, Pete. *No People Like Show People*. London: Frederick Muller, Ltd., 1957.

Corio, Ann, and DiMona, Joseph. *This Was Burlesque*. New York: Grosset and Dunlap, Inc., 1968.

Csida, Joseph. *American Entertainment*. New York: Watson-Guptill Publications, Inc., c. 1978.

DiMeglio, John E. *Vaudeville, U.S.A.* Bowling Green, Ohio: Bowling Green State University, Popular Press, 1973.

Douglas-Home, Robin. *Sinatra*. New York: Grosset and Dunlap, Inc., c. 1962.

Farren, Mick, ed., *Elvis Presley in His Own Words*. New York: Quick Fox, Putnam Publishing Group, 1981.

Fisher, John. *Call Them Irreplaceable*. London: Elm Tree Books, 1976.

Freedland, Michael. *Maurice Chevalier*. New York: William Morrow and Co., Inc., 1981.

Frost, Thomas. *The Old Showmen and the Old London Fairs*. London: Chatto and Windus, Ltd., 1874.

Gaver, Jack, and Stanley, Dave. *There's Laughter in the Air*. Sykesville, MD: Greenberg Publishing Co., 1945.

Gilbert, Douglas. *American Vaudeville, Its Life and Times*. New York: McGraw-Hill, Inc., 1940.

Goldman, Albert. *Elvis*. New York: Avon Books, 1982.

Gorham, Maurice. *Showmen and Suckers: An Excursion on the Crazy Fringe of the Entertainment World*. London: P. Marshall, Ltd., 1951.

Haney, Lynn. *Naked at the Feast*. New York: Dodd, Mead and Co., c. 1981.

Harbinson, William Allen. *Elvis Presley: An Illustrated Biography*. London: Michael Joseph, Ltd., 1975.

Irving, Gordon. *Great Scot: The Life Story of Sir Harry Lauder, Legendary Laird of the Music Hall*. London: L. Frewin, Ltd., 1968.

Katkov, Norman. *The Fabulous Fanny: The Story of Fanny Brice*. New York: Alfred A. Knopf, Inc., 1953.

Laurie, Joe, Jr. *Vaudeville: From the Honkey-tonks to the Palace*. New York: Henry Holt, 1953.

————, and Green, Abel. *Show Biz, from Vaude to Video*. New York: Henry Holt, 1951.

Liberace. *Liberace*. New York: Putnam Publishing Group, 1973.

Lichter, Paul. *Elvis in Hollywood*. New York: Simon and Schuster, Inc., c. 1975.

McKechnie, Samuel. *Popular Entertainments through the Ages*. New York: Stokes Publishing Co., 1931.

Marks, E. B., and Liebling, A. J. *They All Sang: From Tony Pastor to Rudy Vallee*. New York: The Viking Press, 1935.

Morley, Sheridan. *Marlene Dietrich*. London: Elm Tree Books, 1976.

Oberfirst, Robert. *Al Jolson: You Ain't Heard Nothin' Yet*. New York: A. S. Barnes, 1982.

Pearl, Ralph. *Las Vegas Is My Beat*. Secaucus, NJ: Lyle Stuart, Inc., 1973.

Richards, Dick. *The Life Story of Danny Kaye*. London: Convoy Publications, 1949.

Samuels, Charles, and Samuels, Louise. *Once Upon a Stage: The Merry World of Vaudeville*. New York: Dodd, Mead and Co., 1974.

Seldes, Gilbert. *The Seven Lively Arts*. New York: A. S. Barnes, 1962.

Shaw, Arnold. *Sinatra: Twentieth-Century Romantic*. New York: Holt, Rinehart and Winston, 1968.

Simon, George T. *The Big Bands*. New York: Macmillan Publishing Co., Inc., 1975.

Singer, Kurt. *The Danny Kaye Saga*. London: Robert Hale, Ltd., 1957.

Smith, Bill. *The Vaudevillians*. New York: Macmillan Publishing Co., Inc., c. 1976.

Smith, Lorna. *Judy with Love: The Story of Miss Show Business*. London: Robert Hale, Ltd., 1975.

Sobel, Bernard. *Pictorial History of Burlesque*. New York: Bonanza Books, 1956.

————. *Pictorial History of Vaudeville*. Secaucus, NJ: Citadel Press, 1961.

Welsford, Enid. *The Fool: His Social and Literary History*. New York: Farrar and Rinehart, 1935.

Wilson, Earl. *Sinatra: An Unauthorized Biography*. New York: Macmillan Publishing Co., Inc., c. 1976.

PAGE ONE:

Phyllis Diller's raucous high spirits and absurdist material helped to distinguish her from the ordinary brash comedienne. "I had a classmate so fat," she'd say, "they used to pull her through the Lincoln Tunnel just to clean it." Being funny—which Diller tremendously was—counted for a lot in her act, but opening doors to fancy and escape counted for more.

PAGES TWO AND THREE:

When Diana Ross left the Supremes, their act had transcended the race music from which it sprang. No longer one among many stereotyped, choreographed black singing groups, the Supremes were playing the top white showrooms in Las Vegas and Miami Beach, slicked up, decked out, and made chic. Ross achieved still greater success as a solo, becoming a dominant force on the concert and arena circuits.

PAGES FOUR AND FIVE:

Michael Jackson started out as a youngster in his brothers' act, the Jackson Five. Like Stevie Wonder, he was a show-business veteran at twenty, knowing no other life but performing. Although he has had stupendous success in records and music videos, he remains a live entertainer in spirit. In fact, what Jackson really is, is a good old-fashioned song-and-dance man.

PAGE SIX:

One of the rare performers who bestride the legitimate theater and solo performance, Liza Minnelli has remained a singer of traditional songs—a "belter"—in a world of synthesized rock music. If the so-called standards of American popular song are to be performed in the future, if the Richard Rodgers–Cole Porter style of music is to endure in any way, there will have to be singers to sing them. No one as yet outclasses Minnelli.

PAGE SEVEN:

Peter Allen's exuberance as a performer tended to overshadow his immense gifts as a composer and lyricist. His songs are often rueful and melancholy toasts to lost innocence. Even in the rollicking "I Go to Rio" there is a suggestion of bruise and regret.

PAGE EIGHT:

Although "mime" was coined to describe the broad entertainment that lightened matters between the acts of Greek tragedies, in later times the term came to refer to a special kind of silent, often serious clowning. Marcel Marceau mastered this dancelike form and made it so perfect a thing that he became an international artist. All others are compared to Marceau, the ultimate mime.

PAGE NINE: PAGE TEN:

Bob Hope   *Barbra Streisand*

PAGE ELEVEN:

Challenging the medium's dehumanizing force, Lily Tomlin brought warmth, sensitivity, and humanity to her televised monologues and monodramas. Hers was an artistry and sophistication rare in those tough and impatient times. Like the great monologist Ruth Draper, Tomlin created story lines and multiple characters with breathtaking ease—and she could do it with the same success alone and alive on a stage.

PAGES TWELVE AND THIRTEEN:

The floor show at the MGM Grand Hotel in Las Vegas

PROJECT DIRECTOR: *Robert Morton*
EDITOR: *Ellyn Childs Allison*
DESIGNER: *Judith Michael*
PHOTO EDITOR: *John K. Crowley*

LIBRARY OF CONGRESS CATALOGING IN PUBLICATION DATA
Gottfried, Martin.
In person.

Bibliography: p. 258
Includes index.
1. Performing arts—United States—History.
2. Performing arts—History. I. Title.
PN2221.G67   1985   790.2'09   85–6031
ISBN 0–8109–1613–4